Approximate wavelength, in nanometers

400   450   500   550   600   650   700

Violet Indigo Blue Green Yellow Orange Red

COLOR PLATE 2
The Visible Spectrum

COLOR PLATE 3
Atmospheric Perspective
Photograph courtesy of NYS Department of Economic Development.

Why Do You Need this New Edition?

If you're wondering why you should buy this new edition of *Sensation and Perception* here are five good reasons!

- The authors worked to maintain the **clarity and coverage** of earlier editions, making the information highly accessible.

- The text has been **completely updated**, with over a thousand references.

- Each chapter reflects **new** contributions of research in the **neuroscience** of perception, including brain-imaging (e.g., fMRI) studies. Many chapters also contain new examples of the impact of experience on brain function (brain plasticity).

- Thirteen chapters contain *In-Depth* sections that **explore research** on a specific topic. The topics of the *In-Depth* sections have been changed entirely or the information has been revised extensively.

- Tightly integrated with the text are new Web-based ancillary materials: summaries and updates of information from the chapter, demonstrations, figures, self-test questions, and glossary.

Sensation and Perception

Sensation and Perception

FIFTH EDITION

Hugh J. Foley
Skidmore College

Margaret W. Matlin
State University of New York at Geneseo

Allyn & Bacon

Boston   Columbus   Indianapolis   New York   San Francisco   Upper Saddle River
Amsterdam   Cape Town   Dubai   London   Madrid   Milan   Munich   Paris   Montreal   Toronto
Delhi   Mexico City   Sao Paulo   Sydney   Hong Kong   Seoul   Singapore   Taipei   Tokyo

Acquisitions Editor: *Susan Hartman*
Editorial Assistant: *Mary Lombard*
Marketing Manager: *Nicole Kunzmann*
Production Supervisor: *Roberta Sherman*
Editorial Production Service: *Publishers' Design and Production Services, Inc.*
Manufacturing Buyer: *JoAnne Sweeney*
Electronic Composition: *Publishers' Design and Production Services, Inc.*
Interior Design: *Denise Hoffman*
Cover Administrator: *Kristina Mose-Libon*

Foley, Hugh James.
    Sensation and perception / Hugh J. Foley, Margaret W. Matlin.—5th ed.
        p. cm.
    Prev ed. entered under: Matlin, Margaret W.
    Includes bibliographical references and index.
    ISBN-13: 978-0-205-57980-8 (alk. paper)
    ISBN-10: 0-205-57980-9 (alk. paper)
    1. Perception. 2. Senses and sensation. I. Matlin, Margaret W. II. Matlin,
Margaret W. Sensation and perception III. Title.
    BF311.M4263 2010
    152.1—dc22

        2009019150

10 9 8 7 6 5 4 3 2 1 Q-TAU 13 12 11 10 09

Allyn & Bacon
is an imprint of

www.pearsonhighered.com

ISBN-10: 0-205-57980-9
ISBN-13: 978-0-205-57980-8

Contents

CHAPTER **7**

Color 189

CHAPTER **8**

Motion 218

CHAPTER 14
Perceptual Development 376

Preface

When we completed the fourth edition of this textbook late in 1996, we weren't certain when we would next find the time to work on a new edition. In fact, it wasn't until a decade later that we began to explore the possibility of producing the textbook you now hold in your hands. However, both Susan Hartman and Michelle Limoges at Pearson/Allyn & Bacon encouraged us to revise the textbook. They remained supportive even though the revisions took longer than anyone anticipated.

Writing any textbook is surely a challenge. On the one hand, we worked hard to write a textbook that reflects our genuine enthusiasm for perception. On the other hand, extraordinarily complex mechanisms underlie the richness of everyone's perceptual experiences. How could we accurately portray such complexity without dampening our readers' enthusiasm? The tension implicit in that question was always at the forefront of our thoughts as we worked on this new edition. We have tried to write a book that is interesting, student oriented, comprehensive, and current, yet requiring no specialized background in physiology, mathematics, or experimental psychology. Not a simple task!

However, any textbook should be viewed as a work-in-progress. Given the opportunity, dedicated authors continually strive for improved clarity in their prose. Furthermore, the research community generates new and exciting work at a pace that seems to increase annually. We have been working for the past couple of years to produce the book you now hold in your hands. In fact, we could work continually on polishing our prose and including the new research that crosses our desks daily. We plan to continue this particular work-in-progress in a sixth edition. It may well be a fun retirement project!

For those of you who are unfamiliar with the earlier editions of this textbook, the next section provides an overview of the organization of the book. Those of you who are familiar with the fourth edition may want to skip to the following section, which covers some of the changes we have introduced in this new edition.

Text Organization and Features

Sensation and Perception is intended as an introduction to these topics for use in courses in perception or in sensation and perception. Although primarily a textbook for undergraduates, graduate students seeking an overview of the discipline of perception may also find the textbook useful.

This fifth edition is organized in four major parts. The first part consists of an introductory chapter and a chapter on the methodologies used to study perception; the second part contains six chapters on vision; the third part contains three chapters on audition; and the final part includes the skin senses, the chemical senses, and perceptual development.

Four major themes are introduced in Chapter 1 and are woven throughout the book to provide readers with a sense of continuity across many diverse topics:

1. Our senses evolved over time to enable us to succeed in responding to our environment, so they share some clear similarities and interact with one another.

2. Our senses are exquisitely adapted to perceive a world containing stimuli that are rich with information and are found in a rich context.

3. The information falling on our sensory receptors is inherently ambiguous, yet we typically construct a sufficiently accurate perception of the world to enable us to interact with the world successfully.

4. Cognitive processes make use of knowledge and expectations derived from experience, and they help shape our perceptions.

This edition also includes the following general features:

- Clear, straightforward writing style with numerous examples to illustrate how the sensory systems and perception operate in everyday experience

- Applications in areas such as art, education, and other professions throughout the text

- Thirteen In-Depth sections focusing on recent research on selected topics and providing details on research methods

- A chapter outline at the beginning of each chapter

- Key terms introduced in boldface italics, with their definition in the same sentence

- A summary at the end of each major section of a chapter to provide frequent opportunities for review

- Review questions, a key term list, and an annotated list of recommended readings at the end of each chapter

- A glossary, at the end of the book and online, containing a definition of every key term introduced in the book and a phonetic pronunciation for terms with potentially ambiguous pronunciations

- Many brief, online demonstrations for students to try by themselves, using minimal equipment

- A website for the textbook to provide context for the demonstrations and updated information

- Hugh Foley's perception webpages that will also serve as an aid to both faculty and students interested in perception: www.skidmore.edu/~hfoley/perception.htm

What's New in This Edition?

We approached this new edition armed with input from a number of sources. Students (our own and those at other institutions) helpfully pointed out areas of the earlier edition that they thought merited revision. Faculty who used the earlier edition were also generous with their advice about potential revisions. A select handful of reviewers also provided detailed feedback on the fourth edition. This input

from our readers was extraordinarily helpful. Thus, we would really appreciate hearing about your reactions to this new edition.

In addition to responding to suggestions prompted by the fourth edition, we updated the research covered in the textbook. Ruth Copans and her colleagues at the Lucy Scribner Library (especially Amy Syrell in Interlibrary Loan) provided a wealth of resources. Increasingly, researchers are making their publications available online, which helped immensely.

Professors and students who used previous editions of this text responded enthusiastically to the clarity of writing, the interest level, and the student-oriented features. We have retained those features in this new edition and have made some additions and changes.

We have been quite happy with the general organization of the book, so we decided to minimize the structural changes in this edition. However, we did reorganize the presentation of material within several chapters.

As we mentioned earlier, much of our focus was on integrating new material into the textbook. For instance, we completely changed six of the In-Depth sections and updated the remaining seven. Each chapter received extensive attention, resulting in several changes:

- In Chapter 2, we added a brief discussion of methods of measuring brain activity (e.g., fMRI).

- Chapter 3 includes more detail about retinal organization. We also describe how visual information flows through important pathways (M, P, and K, as well as the *What* and *Where* pathways).

- Chapter 4 begins with a discussion of prerequisites for vision, including a discussion of the role of higher-order processes. Interesting new case studies (e.g., Michael May) illustrate the impact of restoring visual abilities. The new In-Depth section covers the eye movements involved in reading, allowing us to focus on our colleague Rebecca Johnson's research.

- Portions of Chapter 5 were reconfigured for clarity and cohesion. The new In-Depth section on face perception expands on some of the research discussed in the In-Depth section of Chapter 2.

- We live in a three-dimensional world, and Chapter 6 explores how we encode information about that space. The new In-Depth section focuses on how people navigate through this world.

- In Chapter 7, we first cover the basics of color perception (the stimulus, the anatomy and physiology of color perception). The chapter ends with a new In-Depth section on the impact of color names on color perception. This area is both exciting and controversial.

- Chapter 8 focuses on how people perceive both real and illusory motion. We substantially updated the In-Depth section on the perception of biological motion. We also added more detail about the physiological bases of motion perception, especially regarding self-motion.

- The discussion of the auditory system begins in Chapter 9. We updated material throughout the chapter, including the In-Depth section on inner ear hair cells.

- Within Chapter 10 we updated the information about pitch perception. The In-Depth section now adds dolphin research to the work on owls and bats. In these latter chap-

ters, we make every effort to emphasize the integration of the senses (Theme 1 of the textbook).

- Chapter 11 includes new information about music and speech perception. The streamlined In-Depth section remains focused on interactions between vision and audition.

- Researchers have made great strides in understanding the bases of temperature and pain perception. We introduce the important transient receptor potential (TRP) channels in Chapter 12. We also added some intriguing research on touch illusions (rubber hand/arm illusions).

- Chapter 13 continues to explore recent developments in the physiological bases of taste and smell perception. At the same time, we acknowledge the important cognitive contributions to smell and taste perception. The new In-Depth section focuses on the potential influences of odor on behavior. The chapter was reorganized to emphasize the notion of flavor as combining taste and smell.

- Chapter 14 has a new In-Depth section focusing on how infants perceive shape, which allows us to return once again to face perception. The material in the rest of the chapter has been updated extensively.

Acknowledgments

We would both like to thank a number of people whose contributions to the fifth edition of *Sensation and Perception* have been invaluable. First, Lynda Griffiths was Project Manager for Publisher's Design and Production Services, Inc. The devil is surely in the details, so Lynda's care, intelligence, and professional skills improved the final product substantially. We simply cannot offer sufficient praise for her superb work on our book.

Roberta Sherman was the Production Supervisor at Pearson/Allyn & Bacon. Roberta helped with many phases of production, including help with questions about permissions. Denise Hoffman, Glenview Studios, created an attractive and eye-catching design that works perfectly for our book.

As we mentioned earlier, Michelle Limoges and Susan Hartman were instrumental in approving the new edition. Michelle then suffered through the long revision process with considerable patience. Christina Manfroni and Paige Clunie were exceptionally skillful editorial assistants. Finally, we would like to thank the many Pearson/Allyn & Bacon sales representatives who have given us feedback over the years.

We also want to thank the reviewers who provided numerous useful suggestions for improving both factual and stylistic aspects of the manuscript. For help with this fifth edition, we would like to thank Natalie Ceballos, Texas State University; James L. Spencer, West Virginia State University; Ruth Spinks, University of Iowa; Mark Stellmack, University of Minnesota; Martin van den Berg, California State University, Chico; and Alida Westman, Eastern Michigan University. Reviewers who helped on the previous editions also deserve our continuing appreciation: Douglas Bloomquist, Framingham State College; Tom Bourbon. Steven E. Austin State University; James Craig, Indiana University at Bloomington; Susan E. Dutch, Westfield State College; David Emmerich, State University of New York, Stony Brook; Mark Fineman, Southern Connecticut State University; Phyllis Freeman, State University of New York, New Paltz; W. Lawrence Gulick, University of Delaware; Lawrence Guzy, SUNY Oneonta; Richard H. Haude, University of Akron; Morton Heller, Eastern Illinois University, Larry Hochhaus, Oklahoma State University; David Irwin, Michigan State University; Lester Lefton, University of South Carolina; Gloria Leventhal, William Patterson College; Mary Peterson, University of Arizona; Janet Proctor, Purdue University; Alan Searleman, St. Lawrence University; William Tedford, Southern Methodist University; Dejan Todorovic, Boston University and University of Beogradu, Belgrade, Yugoslavia; Benjamin Wallace, Cleveland State University; Lyn Wickelgren, Metropolitan State College of Denver; and James Windes, Northern Arizona University.

Personal Acknowledgments

As I near the end of my career in academia, it's interesting to reflect on the many influences along the way. My first teachers—Griffin and Wanda Foley—fostered in me a love of reading and learning. They have remained supportive and understanding throughout my education and my academic career. Further along the path, three teachers were instrumental: Julian Granberry, Dave Cross, and Dave Emmerich. These gentlemen instilled in me a love of both research and teaching. I can only hope to inspire a similar appreciation of scholarship and teaching in my own students.

Those students have been major contributors to this text. Students in my perception course at Skidmore College have brought great enthusiasm and energy to the course, which encourages me to do everything I can to teach them well. Moreover, the process of completing the current edition was greatly facilitated by some of those wonderful students—especially Cassie Arnold, Anna Cerio, Danie King, Lawanda Peterson, Sarah Pociask, and Emily Schlemmer. Many colleagues at Skidmore made substantial contributions as well: Rebecca Johnson, Chuck Joseph, Flip Phillips, and Bill Standish.

Finally, I must thank my wife/colleague Mary Ann Foley. What an inspiring teacher and supportive colleague! And what a wonderful person with whom to share one's life! Though she often encourages me to use my words, I could never fully express the depths of my appreciation and affection.

H. J. F.

I would like to acknowledge several professors who inspired my interest in perception. These include Leonard Horowitz, who is responsible for my switching from a major in biology to a major in psychology, Douglas Lawrence, and Eleanor Maccoby of Stanford University. Grateful appreciation is also due to my professors in graduate school who provided me with a very solid background in sensation and perception: Daniel Weintraub, Richard Pew, Irving Pollack, and W. P. Tanner at the University of Michigan.

Additional thanks go to people who supplied useful information and reviewed portions of the book in which they are experts. I particularly thank Nila Aguilar-Markulis, Kathy Barsz, John Foley, Morton Heller, Peter Lennie, Daniel Levin, Arnold H. Matlin, Ray Mayo, George Rebok, Lanna Ruddy, John Sparrow, David Van Dyke, Susan K. Whitbourne, and Melvyn Yessenow.

Once again, I thank my husband, Arnie Matlin. Our family now includes our daughter, Beth Matlin-Heiger, Neil Matlin-Heiger, and their children, Jacob and Joshua Matlin-Heiger, as well as our daughter Sally Matlin and her partner Jay Laefer. I thank all of them for their continuing encouragement, optimism, appreciation, and love!

M. W. M.

CHAPTER 1

Introduction

Off to a very interesting start. What's going on here?

Oops! Okay, now we're on track. As you read this text, you are demonstrating extraordinary sensory and perceptual abilities. Once we oriented the text properly, your eyes are moving along this page at a steady pace, identifying letters and words so fast as to defy explanation. If you're like most people, you tend to take sensation and perception for granted because your senses operate so naturally and automatically. You open your eyes and see text, people, plants, and parrots. You open your mouth, insert a morsel of food, and taste tomatoes, cheesecake, curried goat. What could be simpler? Perception, however, is a complex puzzle that has intrigued philosophers and psychologists for centuries.

One important goal of this book is to teach you about the many subtle processes that underlie perception. Just as the beginning of the first paragraph probably brought you to an abrupt halt, we hope to challenge your assumptions about the simplicity of perception. Think about your experience as you started to read the first paragraph. Why did the unusual orientation of the text make reading so difficult? What does such difficulty tell you about the nature of perception? Throughout these chapters, we hope to present you with similar intriguing perceptual experiences that will help you explore the complexities of perception.

The title of this book is *Sensation and Perception*. Before going any further, we should define these terms. *Sensation* refers to the functioning of our sensory systems. *Perception* involves the interpretation of those sensations, giving them meaning and organization. Psychologists acknowledge a fuzzy boundary between these two terms, although we could reasonably shorten the title to *Perception*. William James (1842–1910) has often been called America's greatest psychologist. James (1890) noted, "Whilst part of what we perceive comes through our senses from the object before us, another part (and it may be the larger part) always comes . . . out of our own head" (Vol. 2, p. 103). James is acknowledging the constructed nature of our perceptual experience. Throughout the text, you'll find examples that support James's contention.

A fuzzy boundary also exists between perception and cognition. *Cognition* involves the acquisition, storage, transformation, and use of information. The boundary between perception and cognition blurs because many theorists believe that perception also involves the acquisition, storage, transformation, and

use of information. For example, learning and memory play important roles in cognition, but they also play important roles in perception. If you reflect on your experience as you read the opening paragraph, you likely encountered difficulty because your past experience did not prepare you to read text in an unusual orientation. You might also imagine that, with additional experience, you could become adept at reading text in an unusual orientation. The more you learn about cognition, the more you'll appreciate the complexities of perception. We certainly encourage you to take a course in cognition if you have not already done so. Several good cognition texts are available, should you be interested in exploring this area (e.g., Matlin, 2009; Solso et al., 2008).

Perception and cognition work together to create the world we experience. To examine how they do so, let's consider an example. Figure 1.1 shows a city scene. As you look at the figure, sensory receptors in your eye encode elements of the scene, leading to a series of neural impulses. Those impulses create activity in your brain that yields a reasonably accurate perception of the real world. Your knowledge of the world lets you perceive structures (e.g., different bricks, windows) on three distinct buildings. How do you know that the heads are larger-than-life sculptures? How do you know which of the buildings is closest to you? Try turning the page upside down, to create an unusual viewing perspective. With little experience viewing buildings in this unusual orientation, does your perception change?

Why should you study sensation and perception? We can think of many reasons, but we'll only mention some of them here. As you read through the text, try to identify other reasons that make this an important area of study. One reason concerns a question of interest to philosophers. We mentioned the challenge of re-creating the qualities of objects, of bringing the outside world to the inside mind. A branch of philosophy called *epistemology* concerns how we acquire knowledge, including knowledge about the properties of objects. One intriguing concern of epistemology is whether we require experience with the world before we can perceive it accurately. Can your 2-month-old niece have accurate knowledge, for instance, about how far away the side of the crib is from her nose, or must she learn about distance through repeated experiences of reaching, grasping, and bumping?

Other philosophical questions are equally intriguing. For instance, you might consider the cen-

▶ **FIGURE 1.1**   A typical street scene to illustrate perceptual principles.

tral role that perception plays in your experience of who and where you are. Think of what your life would be like if you had absolutely *no* perceptual experience. Daniel Dennett's (1978) essay "Where am I?" says a lot about the important role of perceptual experience.

The study of sensation and perception has played a pivotal role in the history of psychology. Thus, in learning about sensation and perception, you will also be learning about some of the early research in psychology. Exploring sensation and perception also provides a background for other areas of psychology. As we've already mentioned, these two areas are closely associated with cognition—a vital topic in psychology since the last half of the twentieth century. Sensation and perception also have important links to many other areas of psychology. In fact, if you have an introductory psychology textbook handy, turn to the table of contents and notice how you might relate each of the major topics to perception.

As you read each chapter of this book, you should be able to envision ways that perceptual top-

ics apply to your daily life. For example, you'll learn why you can more easily detect a faint star if you don't look directly at it (Chapter 3). You'll also learn why you shouldn't expose your fragile auditory system to loud sounds (Chapter 9). If you become a parent, you will benefit from knowing how your child's perceptual abilities develop (Chapter 14). Several chapters (e.g., Chapters 3, 9, 14) will provide a forecast of changes in perceptual abilities that you'll likely encounter as you age.

Perception also applies directly to educational and work settings. For example, reading teachers can apply what psychologists have learned about eye movements (Chapter 4) and letter identification (Chapter 5). Topics in many chapters apply to different health professions. For example, our discussions of most senses describe disorders of those senses. Many health professionals would certainly be interested in pain perception and pain reduction (Chapter 12).

Another reason for reading this book is more personal. You own some exceptional equipment. Your sensory systems (e.g., visual, auditory, etc.) are extremely sensitive and even a bit fragile. Nonetheless, you may know more about how a vacuum cleaner or an automobile works. You'll be living the remainder of your life with your sensory systems, so it should be both interesting and useful to know them more intimately.

Finally, you should study perception because it's fun. Okay, maybe we're a bit biased, but we think that it's fun to study perception. If we do our jobs properly, we will convey to you the pleasure we experience when studying these fascinating topics in perception. In the next section, we'll highlight some of the topics that we're about to explore.

Preview of the Book

Did you ever wonder why anyone would write a textbook? We can assure you that writing a perception text is not the path to fame and fortune. Moreover, it's a difficult and time-consuming process. Why, then, did we write this book? The simplest answer is that we're both teachers who take great pleasure in educating the students in our classrooms. We also like the idea that we may play a role in educating students at other institutions.

We chose to write a perception textbook because we both see the area as central to our discipline. As you read this book, you will probably recognize many of the perceptual issues as common to other areas of psychology. For instance, most of the important "stuff" of perception occurs in a person's mind—so it's not directly accessible. You will likely recognize that problem as central to psychology. However, it's not *all* inside a person's mind. We live in a world of other people, other organisms, and inanimate objects. In order to survive in that world, it's vital that we perceive it accurately. This book is about how our senses enable us to function in that world.

A number of different disciplines are interested in perception. As a result, in order to adequately discuss perception, we'll be considering topics that you might regard as anatomy, physiology, or neuroscience. Those disciplines are crucial for understanding how energy from stimuli in the outside world is conveyed to and processed in the brain. Nonetheless, our focus is certainly psychological.

The chapter you're reading provides a helpful overview of the entire text. By reading this chapter first, you'll have a better sense of how we've chosen to organize topics. It also alerts you to concepts that

recur throughout the book. For example, in the next section we'll discuss major theoretical approaches to sensation and perception. As you read later chapters, you'll see how these approaches drive the research in different areas. To further help you integrate material across chapters, we also provide you with some themes that will weave through the text. Finally, we offer some hints about how to use the book to better learn the material.

The next chapter (Chapter 2) is an important methodological one. The chapter focuses primarily on psychophysics—the study of the relationship between physical stimuli and our psychological reaction to them. It's our first opportunity to clarify the distinction between the physical stimulus and the perception of the stimulus. For example, we'll address why you can notice a 5-pound weight loss more easily for Pat, who weighs 100 pounds, than for Chris, who weighs 200 pounds. The chapter also describes the use of some brain-imaging techniques that are used to better understand perceptual processes.

The next five chapters focus on the visual system. Chapter 3 provides an overview of the visual system, because you need to know the structure of the visual equipment before proceeding to other topics. In that chapter, we examine the anatomy of the eye, discuss how visual information travels to the brain, and explore how the brain processes the visual information. Thus, Chapter 3 focuses largely on anatomy and physiology. As a result of technological advances, researchers are making great strides in understanding how the many different areas of the brain process visual information.

Chapter 4 discusses the prerequisites for vision and several basic abilities of the visual system that enable us to see clearly. Consider the perception of darkness and lightness. You might think that it's a simple process to determine which is darker (the print on this page) or lighter (the margins on the page). However, as you'll learn, it's actually a complex process that's not fully understood. In Chapter 4, we also introduce the important concept called a "constancy," which provides stability to our changing sensory experience.

Chapter 5 considers more complex visual processing, particularly the perception of shapes. Our perception of shape exhibits impressive organization; a door seems to have a shape that sets it apart from the surrounding building. We also recognize patterns; we identify a curved line as part of a tree, not a cat's tail. Three issues discussed include the following: What principles have psychologists identified as important to perceiving shapes? Do we recognize a letter more quickly if it is part of an English word than if it appears by itself? Also, why is it more difficult to identify a person whose face is presented upside down?

In Chapter 6, you'll learn about how we perceive depth and size. Each of our eyes can represent only two dimensions. Nonetheless, we manage to perceive objects as three-dimensional and as residing in three-dimensional space. In essence, this problem is the same one facing an artist who wants to represent the world on a two-dimensional canvas. As a result, you'll find that Chapter 6 addresses many topics that might interest artists. Along with the perception of depth and size, we'll also consider illusions that result in misperceptions of depth and size.

If you've watched *The Wizard of Oz*, you have a sense of the difference between a black-and-white world and a Technicolor world. In Chapter 7, we explore the means by which our visual system translates incoming wavelengths into our perception of color. Even if you have a common color-vision deficiency, you still see a world that is richly colored. However, you'll learn about people who see the world only in terms of blacks, whites, and shades of gray—and would do so even if they lived in Oz.

After you've read Chapter 6, you will have a better understanding of how the visual system encodes three-dimensional space. In Chapter 8, we will discuss theories about how people perceive the movement of objects through that three-dimensional space. We'll also discuss various illusions of motion, such as those seen in a motion picture or a television show.

After devoting six chapters to vision, we then move on to other senses. As you will soon see, however, the senses share many commonalities. In the remaining chapters, you will learn that several principles found in vision are also found in the other senses. Our discussion of hearing in Chapters 9, 10, and 11 parallels the discussion of vision in Chapters 3, 4, and 5. We first discuss the anatomy and physiology of audition, then basic auditory processes, and then more complex auditory processes.

Chapter 9 focuses on the physical apparatus necessary for hearing. We discuss the structures in the ear that process the physical stimulus, as well as the neural sites that are involved in auditory perception. You'll learn that your auditory system is quite fragile—so you should take great care of it.

In Chapter 10, we examine basic aspects of hearing. We consider topics such as pitch and loudness perception, auditory localization, and the perception of sound combinations. Some issues addressed include the following: How does the ear manage to encode sounds as different as a train squeaking to a halt, Placido Domingo singing a Verdi aria, and your uncle snoring? Why do some tone combinations sound pleasant, whereas others are unbearable? How do humans and animals decide that a sound is coming from the left side rather than from another direction?

In Chapter 11, we focus on the perception of two related types of complex auditory stimuli—music and speech. We start with basic aspects of both music (e.g., pitch, timbre) and speech (speech sounds) before discussing the areas of the brain that process these complex auditory stimuli. Because both music and speech are quite complex, you can predict that we'll discuss how cognitive factors affect their perception. Have you ever watched a foreign film in which English has been poorly dubbed, so that the actors' mouth movements don't match the words they generate? If so, you can anticipate our discussion of interactions between vision and audition.

We examine the skin senses in Chapter 12 and the chemical senses in Chapter 13. Even though we devote only a chapter to each of these sets of senses, our approach is similar to that for vision and audition. That is, we describe the sensory apparatus and brain processes before talking about the perceptual processes. In the last chapter of the book (Chapter 14), we discuss the development of perception.

Chapter 12 examines the senses related to the skin. Objects and people in the world touch us, and we touch them back. We also perceive a range of temperatures and pain, and we know the positions of our body parts and whether we are standing upright or tilted. Some of the topics covered are Why were you aware of your wristwatch pressing against your skin when you put it on this morning, although you hadn't noticed it again until now? Why is it important that people feel pain? and Why do you sometimes have difficulty deciding whether water is warm or cold?

Chapter 13 deals with the chemical senses—taste and smell. In reality, however, the chapter examines flavor perception, which involves taste, smell, and other senses. We begin by discussing taste perception, beginning with the sensory receptors and later considering the factors that influence taste perception. We then focus on smell perception (olfaction) from the sensory receptors through factors that influence smell perception. Although you may not consider odors to play a large role in your behavior, they do influence the behavior of some organisms—and they likely influence your behavior as well. You may also be surprised to learn that your olfactory abilities are quite good. You can recognize your own odor and the odors of people who are closely related to you—especially if you're a woman. You could also track a scent like a bloodhound, although you'd look a bit ridiculous with your nose pressed to the ground.

In a way, Chapter 14 is a summary chapter. In order to describe the development of perception, we'll revisit both visual and auditory perception. You will learn that infants are born with rudimentary perceptual abilities—certainly sufficient to allow them to interact with their crucial caregivers. The chapter underscores the importance of experience. Experience enables infants to hone their perceptual skills, which become ever more sophisticated throughout childhood. As people age, however, many factors conspire to diminish their perceptual abilities. Nevertheless, as they grow older, most people are able to adapt to these changes.

Overview of Theoretical Approaches to Sensation and Perception

This section outlines some major approaches to sensation and perception. It provides a background for several theoretical topics that we will discuss more completely in other chapters.

A thorough review of theories of sensation and perception would probably begin with theories of perception proposed by Greek philosophers more than 2,000 years ago; it would also include the early explorations of the physiology of the eye and the physics of light. Our survey will be limited to the more recent past and will examine six approaches: behaviorist, empiricist, Gestalt, Gibsonian, information processing, and computational. Other sources can be consulted for details on the early history of perception (Boring, 1942; Gordon, 2004).

The Behaviorist Approach

Behaviorism emphasizes the objective description of an organism's behavior. From the 1930s to the 1960s,

behaviorism was the dominant psychological approach in the United States. Strict behaviorists were uncomfortable with the areas of perception and cognition. As a result, during the heyday of behaviorism, researchers focused on animal behavior rather than perception or cognition (Mandler, 2007).

The area least influenced by the behaviorists' bias against perception was psychophysics. Psychophysics uses clearly defined methods to assess people's reactions to physical stimuli. This objective, quantitative approach was compatible with behaviorism and therefore survived its reign well. However, you'll note that we have little to say about behaviorism throughout the rest of this text.

The Empiricist Approach

George Berkeley (1685–1753) struggled with a basic problem: How can we perceive objects as having a third dimension, depth, if our eyes register only height and width? He came to the conclusion that "the Judgment we make of the Distance of an *Object*, view'd with both Eyes, is entirely the *Result of Experience*" (Berkeley, 1709/1957, Section XX). Thus, we do not know how to perceive depth when we are born; instead, we must acquire this perceptual ability by learning. Berkeley was one of a group of British philosophers who were influential in developing empiricism. Consistent with the Gestalt approach we'll discuss next, *empiricism* emphasizes that sensory information alone is insufficient for our rich perceptual experiences. Instead, information stored in our brain combines with the sensory input to produce perception (Gordon, 2004).

From the earlier William James quote about the contributions of our minds, you should recognize him as an empiricist. To call attention to the important role of experience, James described the perceptual world of the newborn infant as a "blooming, buzzing confusion." Out of this confusing world, a baby's experience allows him or her to construct a world that is relatively orderly. Developmental psychologists, however, have discovered that babies have better perceptual capacities than James described. Their perceptual worlds are not so orderly as they will become in adulthood, but they are far from random, as we will explore in Chapter 14.

Nonetheless, it's clear that some form of empiricism has dominated modern perceptual research (Gordon, 2004). A relatively recent focus on brain plasticity—the ability of experience to shape brain connections—is certainly consistent with empiricism. Thus, throughout the text we will focus on the important cognitive principles of learning and experience.

The Gestalt Approach

From other psychology courses, you've surely encountered the distinction between explanations that emphasize nature or nurture. Obviously, empiricism stresses nurture. *Nativism*, on the other hand, stresses the importance of natural, innate abilities. The fact that newborn infants have greater perceptual abilities than posited by James and other empiricists might be considered support for nativism.

In the 1900s, a number of German psychologists objected to both the behaviorist and empiricist approaches (Koffka, 1935; Köhler, 1947; Wertheimer, 1923). As Ian Gordon (2004) points out, their philosophical roots were not in the British empiricists, but instead could be traced to Immanuel Kant (1724–1804). These psychologists agreed with empiricists that the sensory input was insufficient to explain perception. However, instead of the role of learning, they emphasized people's innate abilities.

These psychologists often focused on form perception, so we'll discuss their ideas in greater detail in Chapter 5. That focus gave rise to the name attached to their approach. *Gestalt* can be translated as "configuration" or "pattern," and the *Gestalt approach* emphasizes that we perceive objects as well-organized, whole structures rather than as separated, isolated parts (Palmer, 1999). Thus, the shape that we see is more than an accumulation of its individual elements. In that regard, the early-twentieth–century psychologists were disagreeing with another group of psychologists called structuralists. The *structuralists*, much enamored of the success of chemistry, sought to explain perception by a focus on individual elements. From the Gestalt perspective, when you look at Figure 1.2 you don't see a simple combination of eight separate lines, as the structuralists would claim. Instead, the well-organized configuration suggests a table.

Throughout this text, you'll find reverberations of the Gestalt approach. In spite of the dominance of the empiricist approach, the Gestalt approach continues to influence psychological thinking—especially when people consider organizational principles.

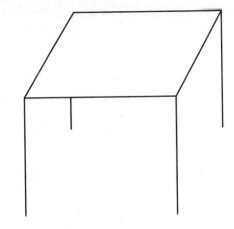

▶ **FIGURE 1.2**   A well-organized configuration: The whole is perceived as different from the accumulation of isolated parts

The Gibsonian Approach

Both the empiricist and Gestalt approaches emphasize **indirect perception**, because they presume that sensory information alone is insufficient. In contrast, **direct perception** argues that sensory information is sufficient; we do not need memories or reasoning processes.

The major proponent of direct perception was James J. Gibson (1904–1979). As Neisser (1981) remarked in an obituary for Gibson, "Gibson begins not with the sense organs or even with organisms but with the environment that is to be perceived" (p. 215). As a result, the *Gibsonian approach* emphasizes that our perceptions are rich and elaborate because the stimuli in our environment are rich with information. That rich information falling on our sensory receptors is adequate to the task of explaining our perceptual experiences. Thus, we do not need to devise elaborate theories to explain the psychological processes that might underlie perception.

How does an organism perceive a three-dimensional world? The empiricists argued that experience is crucial for an organism to properly perceive depth. The Gestaltists argued that we were born with the necessary brain mechanisms for perceiving depth. Along came Gibson, who claimed that both approaches were wrong—all the information we need is in the stimulus itself.

Gibson (1979) also emphasized that our investigation of perception should concentrate on real-world perception. He saw little value in perceptual experiences found only in laboratories, such as looking at a white bar on a black screen in a darkened room while your head movements are minimized because you have been strapped into a head vise.

Although we agree that perceptual information in our world is incredibly rich, we are not strong proponents of the Gibsonian approach. Nevertheless, we provide additional detail about the Gibsonian approach to perception in several chapters.

The Information-Processing Approach

The behaviorist approach was largely supplanted by the cognitive movement, which in its earliest form was called the information-processing approach (Mandler, 2007). In the *information-processing approach*, researchers identify psychological processes and connect these processes together by proposing specific patterns of information flow. For example, one early and influential model proposed that information from our sensory receptors passes through a series of stages: brief sensory storage, short-term memory, and long-term memory (Atkinson & Schiffrin, 1968). After one stage performs its specified operations, the information passes on to the next stage for another kind of processing. Moreover, the connections among the stages may be complex, with later stages affecting the processing at earlier stages.

The information-processing approach differs from the Gibsonian approach because it emphasizes the importance of processing beyond the sensory level. However, unlike the empiricist or Gestalt approaches, the information-processing approach doesn't need to specify whether the additional processes are innate or learned. Nonetheless, because memory plays a vital role in the processing, the information-processing approach is certainly in the empiricist tradition.

With its focus on information and interconnections among processes, the information-processing approach provides some theoretical advantages. Once you start to think of everything as information (e.g., neural firing), it's difficult to label some information as sensation, and other information as perception, cognition, memory, and so on. And once you realize how many different processes contribute to our experiences of the world, it's difficult to give primacy to any one process. Instead, we must realize that these processes are intertwined and interdependent.

If you find that argument compelling, then you can consider the organization of this text a convenient fiction. That is, you may not have completed a course in cognition, but cognitive processes may—at some level—be indistinguishable from perceptual processes. We'll do our best to describe perceptual processing in as simple a fashion as we can. Nevertheless, we'll often alert you to the complexities that we may be glossing over in any description.

It's also convenient to discuss the senses separately, with the organization into chapters we described in the previous section. However, as you'll soon see, we continually emphasize the interconnections among senses. For example, as you read the chapters in this book, pay careful attention to the various brain areas (e.g., amygdala, superior colliculus) that play a role in very different senses.

The Computational Approach

The *computational approach* is similar to Gibson's direct perception approach, because it acknowledges the richness of the visual stimulus. Unlike the direct perception approach, however, and more similar to the indirect perception approaches, the computational approach proposes that perception requires solving problems. The computational approach differs from the information-processing approaches, however, because it attempts to solve perceptual problems with general physical knowledge rather than with specific knowledge about the objects of interest.

David Marr (1982) was an extremely influential researcher in this area before his untimely death. In work that typifies the computational approach, Marr attempted to develop mathematical models through which human vision could be explained. These models were created so that they were consistent with physiological information, and consequently they were not only possible but also plausible. For instance, the change represented by an edge or boundary is very important to the visual system, as you will see in Chapter 4. Marr's computational approach explains how we might perceive edges in a way that is consistent with what we know about the physiology of the visual system (Chapters 3 and 5).

We have reviewed six approaches. Each has had a substantial impact on perceptual research. Throughout this book, we'll draw on the approaches that have influenced the research about perception.

Summary

Overview of Theoretical Approaches to Sensation and Perception

1. The behaviorist approach emphasizes the objective description of behavior. Consequently, behaviorists have not been very interested in the psychological processes underlying perception.

2. Berkeley was an early proponent of empiricism, which proposes that all information is derived from sensory perceptions and experience. Similarly, William James argued that babies' early perceptual experiences are random and disorganized. Thus, experience guided the development of perceptual abilities.

3. The Gestalt approach emphasizes that we perceive objects as well-organized wholes, instead of separate parts. The Gestalt approach proposes that shape perception is inborn and that learning is relatively unimportant.

4. The Gibsonian approach emphasizes that stimuli in the environment are rich with information. Perception is thought to be direct; we do not need to perform calculations and interpretations to perceive.

5. The information-processing approach maintains that information is handled by a series of stages. This approach emphasizes that sensation, perception, and other higher mental processes are interconnected rather than isolated.

6. The computational approach demonstrates mathematical mechanisms that perceptual systems might use to process stimuli. The stimuli are thought to be sufficiently rich that they provide a great deal of information, but higher-level processes involving general physical principles also contribute to perception.

Themes of the Book

Four themes woven throughout this textbook are intended to provide some additional structure for the material and to encourage you to find patterns and relationships among areas that may initially seem unrelated. Incidentally, the themes reflect the eclectic theoretical orientation of this textbook. For example, the second theme is partially based on Gibson's theories, whereas the fourth theme is consistent with the empiricist and information-processing approaches.

1. *Our senses evolved over time to enable us to succeed in responding to our environment, so they share some clear similarities and interact with one another.* Implicit in this theme is the notion that our senses are functional. We live in a physical world and our well-being is very much dependent on our ability to safely navigate that world. Keep in mind that we've evolved in a world that also includes other humans. Because humans are social animals, it's not surprising that our sensory systems seem to be particularly well adapted to humans' specific needs. For instance, our visual system is especially competent in detecting motion by other humans (see Chapter 8). Our hearing apparatus is particularly sensitive to the frequency range of the human voice (see Chapter 10). Newborns arrive with their senses in reasonably good order: They can follow movement, hear distinctions between sounds, and recognize the odors of familiar people (see Chapter 14).

Our different senses (e.g., sight, hearing, smell) have evolved to allow us to detect and interpret different physical stimuli (e.g., light, sound waves, odors). Of course, our sensory systems must differ to enable us to perceive such disparate stimuli. However, in spite of the differences in the nature of the incoming stimuli, each sensory system translates its own unique stimulus information into similar neuronal firing information that is then interpreted by the brain. Different types of stimulus energy are converted into a common form of energy that is processed within the brain. That common neural energy leads to some of the observed similarities among our senses.

Other similarities likely emerge for functional reasons. For example, each sensory system serves to detect change in the world. Such change might involve detecting a stimulus ("Nothing was there before and now I see a dim light") or it might involve detecting a change of state ("That light got brighter"). As you can surely imagine, it is often vital to notice changes in the world ("That car is heading toward me"), so our sensory systems are extremely good at detecting change.

As a corollary, when a stimulus continues unchanged, this stimulus often becomes less important to the senses. For example, it would be inefficient and disadvantageous for us to continually perceive the presence of some stimuli. Just as habits free our minds from concentrating on repetitive tasks, the senses adapt to a stimulus that is presented continuously—its perceived intensity tends to decrease. For instance, the odor in a "fragrant" locker room fortunately seems less overpowering after several minutes. Similarly, you feel the pressure of your watch on your wrist when you first put it on in the morning. However, you no longer notice it a few moments later. In contrast, we exhibit far less adaptation to continuous painful stimuli. As a result, we try to escape from pain or reduce the pain. The lack of adaptation to pain is as useful as the actual adaptation displayed in other senses.

Another reason for commonalities and interactions among the senses is the fact that objects in the world typically affect more than one sense. For example, food cooking on the stove can be simultaneously seen, heard, touched, smelled, and tasted. We don't perceive each aspect of the food as coming through a separate sensory channel but as an integrated whole. Our perceptual systems have evolved to provide us with a unified sense of the world, which means that they must interact with one another.

2. *Our senses are exquisitely adapted to perceive a world containing stimuli that are rich with information and are found in a rich context.* First, our senses function extremely well to capture a wide array of information in the world. As you'll learn in later chapters, our sensory systems are exquisitely sensitive. For instance, in Chapter 3, you'll learn that a single photon of light may cause our photoreceptors to respond. In Chapter 9, you'll learn that sound pressure sufficient to move our eardrum a slight amount—no more than the width of a hydrogen molecule—may produce hearing. Furthermore, our sensory systems have adapted to operate in an impressive range of environments. We can see objects in daylight and, to a degree, in moonlight, even though the bright light reflected off white snow has many billion times more energy than the light from the moon! This example also illustrates that we can perceive a very wide range of stimuli (e.g., from dim moonlight to bright sunlight).

Second, note that this theme acknowledges the Gibsonian adage that the world is filled with useful information. For example, compare the surface texture of the rug or flooring surrounding your feet with the surface texture several yards away. The texture becomes denser as the distance increases, which is useful information when you want to judge the dis-

tance of an object resting on the surface. Now take your book and move it from left to right, then toward you and away from you. Notice that it systematically covers up part of the background and uncovers another part as you move it. You perceive this textbook in a rich context, which includes the texture of the floor, the source of light, and the shadows it creates. This context provides us with a great deal of information about the book's appearance.

Our sensory systems are sensitive and flexible enough to provide very good "bottom-up" processing, a concept we discuss in more detail in Chapter 5. In brief, ***bottom-up processing*** (or ***data-driven processing***) explains how the sensory receptors register the information-rich stimuli. But are the data so rich that they do not require additional processing? Contrary to Gibson, we believe that the information needs to flow from this "bottom" level upward to the higher, more cognitive levels in order for us to perceive the world accurately.

3. *The information falling on our sensory receptors is inherently ambiguous, yet we typically construct a sufficiently accurate perception of the world to enable us to interact with the world successfully.* Consistent with the second theme, stimuli in the outside world *are* rich with information, yet when that information falls on our senses, it is ambiguous. Think, for example, of your rich visual experience of a three-dimensional world. Once you learn that your receptor sites are only two-dimensional, you realize that your sensory system must be dealing with impoverished information compared to the external world. Nonetheless, we ultimately construct the rich perceptual world we live in from such ambiguous information (Hoffman, 1998; Purves & Lotto, 2003). How we construct this world is, of course, the central question of research in perception, and this question motivates the research we will describe throughout this book.

Most of the time, our perceptions are sufficiently accurate to enable us to interact successfully with the world. However, as you'll see throughout the text, we can occasionally be led astray by particular stimuli. Throughout the chapters we will provide illustrations of illusory perceptions—inaccurate perceptions that help us understand how the senses function. For example, look at Figure 1.3. Do the two lines appear to be equal in length, or is one longer than the other? If you measure the two lines, you'll learn that they are equal in length. Why, then, does AC seem longer than AB? We can surely learn a lot

▶ **F I G U R E 1 . 3**   Are the two lines (AB and AC) equal in length or is one line longer than the other? If your visual system is ordinarily so accurate, why is it misled by this drawing? (From Gardner, 1988)

about the senses by examining instances in which our perceptions differ from reality. Nonetheless, keep in mind that such aberrant perceptions are the exception rather than the rule.

4. *Cognitive processes make use of knowledge and expectations derived from experience, and they help shape our perceptions.* Perception involves more than the combination of data from the sensory receptors. As the empiricists emphasized, sensory information is supplemented and transformed by higher, more cognitive processes. The bottom-up, or data-driven, approach can be contrasted with **top-down processing** (or **conceptually driven processing**), which emphasizes the importance of observers' concepts in shaping perception. According to this view, observers have accumulated ideas about how the world is organized. On a Nevada ranch, for example, that four-legged creature on the horizon is more likely to be a horse than a zebra. We will perceive that creature as a horse unless the "data" provide us with very clear information about stripes. You may *hear* your friend mutter as you leave a test, "How did you like the exam?" although the data in that stimulus were really, "Howja like thuzamm?" Once again, your knowledge and

expectations, combined with the context, allowed you to interpret some potentially ambiguous data.

If you keep in mind the inherent ambiguity of the information that arrives at our senses, you realize that something must happen to disambiguate the information. Our knowledge and expectations aid us in "making sense" of such ambiguities. Humans are active and inquiring (i.e., hypothesis-testing) organisms who are typically not satisfied with uncertainties. If you are groping for your bathrobe in a dark room and you're not certain whether you grabbed a shirt by mistake, you actively explore the fabric until you find a button, a familiar feel to the material, or a belt. If you can't read the bumper sticker on the car in front of you, you creep forward until you can. If you can't hear the operator on the telephone, you ask for the message to be repeated. Thus, our concepts about the world help to clarify many ambiguities, and they actively guide us to clarify many other ambiguities.

It is pointless to argue, incidentally, about which approach is correct, the bottom-up or the top-down. Clearly, both processes are necessary to explain how we manage to perceive so quickly and so accurately. We could not function in the world had we not evolved some means of taking in the very rich stimuli that surround us, so bottom-up processing is essential. At the same time, as we'll point out, the information that arrives at our senses is ambiguous. Top-down processes enable us to make a high-probability match between the sensory input and external stimuli, resulting in a reasonably accurate representation of the world.

How to Use This Book

In an effort to help you understand, learn, and remember the material, we've included a number of features in this book. This section tells you how to use these features most effectively.

Each chapter begins with an outline. Inspect the outline before you read a new chapter, and pay particular attention to the structure of the topic. For example, notice the three major sections in Chapter 2 ("Research Methods"): "Measuring Responses to Low-Intensity Stimuli," "Measuring Responses to More Intense Stimuli," and "Measuring Brain Activity Due to Perceptual Stimuli." Subsections and "In-Depth" sections are also included in these outlines to give you a sense of the material in the chapter.

We will often illustrate applications of the perceptual topics we discuss. However, you should always be thinking of potential applications of the topics we cover. Concrete material is typically more memorable than abstract material, so work to make the concepts as "real" as you can.

Along those same lines, you should work to relate the topics to your own experience. Psychologists concerned with human memory have demonstrated that we recall material better if we ask ourselves whether it applies to us (Rogers et al., 1977). Therefore, take advantage of your personal experience! Don't read the chapters passively, but continually try to examine how the information applies to your own perceptual processing.

Throughout each chapter, you'll see callouts for informal experiments labeled www Demonstrations. For these demonstrations, you'll need access to a computer with an Internet connection. Some demonstrations will require equipment no more exotic than flashlights, paper and pencils, and glasses of sugar water. Other demonstrations will take place entirely on the computer. These demonstrations should help

make the material more concrete and easy to relate to your own experiences.

Chapters 2 to 14 each have an "In-Depth" section, which examines recent research on a selected topic relevant to the chapter. These sections focus on a topic that interests us—and we hope will interest you as well.

Throughout each chapter, key terms are introduced in boldface (e.g., *empiricism*), and their definition appears in the same sentence. These terms also appear in the list of "Key Terms" at the end of each chapter in the order of their occurrence. The glossary at the end of the book contains definitions of all the key terms. Thus, if you are uncertain about the meaning of a word, you should check the glossary. The glossary definitions include a phonetic pronunciation for potentially ambiguous terms. These pronunciations are intended not to insult your intelligence but to aid you in learning. Furthermore, you can ask a question in class more easily when you know that the superior colliculus is a "kole-lick-you-luss" and not a "kole-like-you-loos."

You will notice that an unusual feature of this book is a summary at the end of each of the major sections in a chapter rather than at the end of the entire chapter. We chose to include frequent small summaries rather than a single lengthy summary for two reasons: (1) you can review the material more often and (2) you can master small segments before you move on to unfamiliar material. You can take advantage of this feature by testing yourself when you reach the end of a section. Read the summary and notice which items you didn't remember. Test yourself once more, rechecking your accuracy. Some students report that they prefer to read only one section at a time rather than the whole chapter. Then, when they begin a study session in the middle of a chapter, they reread the previous section summaries before reading the new material.

Each chapter also includes review questions. Some review questions are fairly straightforward—asking you to recall important information from the chapter. Other review questions may ask you to apply your knowledge to a practical problem or to integrate material from several parts of the chapter or even across chapters.

The final feature of each chapter is a list of recommended readings. In general, these books, chapters, and articles can help you learn more about topics covered within the chapter. For example, they would help if you want to write a paper on a particular topic or if the area is personally interesting. These resources are often ones that we've used in writing sections of the chapter.

Review Questions

1. What are sensation and perception, and why have they been particularly difficult to differentiate? Return to Figure 1.1 on page 3. Turn the page upside down. How might this new orientation help you to distinguish between sensation and perception?

2. How do sensation and perception differ from cognition? How might sensation and perception be related to cognition? The information-processing approach emphasizes the interrelationship among sensation, perception, and cognition. Use the example of reading text to point out how the boundaries among the concepts must be fuzzy rather than precise.

3. This introduction emphasized that sensation and perception have applications to numerous professions. Contemplate the profession you would like to enter and inspect the preview of the book, considering how some of the topics might be relevant to your future career.

4. Imagine yourself eating a piece of pizza. Review the preview of the book and illustrate how some aspects of the mundane act of eating pizza can be related to each chapter. Would you think that visual perception would have an impact on the taste of the pizza?

5. Use one or two sentences to describe each of the major approaches to perception. Explain briefly how each of these approaches would account for your perception of the picture in Figure 1.1. Why might a photograph be a particularly difficult stimulus from a Gibsonian perspective? (*Hint*: Compare the richness of the stimulus of the actual buildings to the richness of a photo of the buildings.) Can you imagine what Gibson might have to say about such stimuli?

6. How much would each of the theoretical approaches emphasize learning in connection with perception? (In at least one approach, it may be difficult to determine.)

7. Which of the theoretical approaches most closely fits your current ideas about sensation and perception? Which of them seems the least plausible to you?

8. Review the first theme of the book, which focuses on the similarities among the sensory processes. Think about different kinds of adaptation you have noticed. Have you experienced any other kinds of similarities among the processes?

9. Review the last three themes of the book. Now describe how each theme explains why you are able to read this question at a fairly rapid rate.

10. To help you prepare to read this book more effectively, look at Chapter 2 and plan how you can apply the features discussed in the "How to Use This Book" section when you read about research methods in perception.

Key Terms

sensation, p. 2
perception, p. 2
cognition, p. 2
epistemology, p. 2
behaviorism, p. 6
empiricism, p. 6
nativism, p. 7

Gestalt, p. 7
Gestalt approach, p. 7
structuralists, p. 7
indirect perception, p. 7
direct perception, p. 7
Gibsonian approach, p. 7

information-processing
    approach, p. 8
computational approach,
    p. 8
bottom-up processing,
    p. 10

data-driven processing,
    p. 10
top-down processing, p. 11
conceptually driven
    processing, p. 11

Recommended Readings

Benjamin, L. T., Jr. (2008). *A history of psychology: Original sources and contemporary research* (3rd ed.). Malden, MA: Blackwell.

To supplement Mandler's book (see column 2)—especially for the early influences on psychological thinking—you might consider this text. Benjamin provides an excellent resource that combines original source material with secondary sources.

Boring, E. G. (1942). *Sensation and perception in the history of experimental psychology*. New York: Appleton-Century-Crofts.

This classic book provides a good introduction to empiricism and Gestalt psychology, as well as to earlier approaches to perception.

Gordon, I. E. (2004). *Theories of visual perception* (3rd ed.). New York: Psychology Press.

Gordon provides helpful chapters on Gestalt theories, empiricism, direct perception, and computational approaches. Egon Brunswik is a favorite of ours, so we were pleased to see a chapter devoted to his contributions. Be sure to read the endnotes for each chapter.

Mandler, G. (2007). *A history of modern experimental psychology: From James and Wundt to cognitive science*. Cambridge, MA: MIT Press.

After a career filled with many important contributions to cognitive psychology, Mandler "retired" in 1994. May our retirements be as productive! With this text, Mandler has written a brief history of psychology that helps provide a context for contemporary psychology.

CHAPTER 2

Research Methods

HOW BRIGHT is the light where you are reading this book? How loud are the sounds around you? (Is there music playing? Are people talking?) Over the course of hundreds of years, scientists and technicians have developed very accurate instruments for quantifying the physical properties of such stimuli. For example, you could walk into a camera shop today and buy a photometer to measure the brightness of a light or go to an electronics store and buy a sound-level meter to measure the loudness of a sound.

Psychologists, however, are less interested in the physical properties of the stimuli around you. They are more interested in your psychological experience of those stimuli. How can we possibly measure your inner experience of brightness or loudness? This task is especially challenging because perception is a private activity. To experience the difficulties involved in this enterprise, stop reading for a moment and try to think of some ways to tell a friend about how bright a light appears to you or how loud a sound seems.

Given the complexity of the problem, you might be tempted, initially, to think that we could just measure the physical properties of stimuli and be done with it. Can't we simply equate the physical stimulus with the psychological experience of the stimulus? A few examples should convince you that such an approach couldn't work.

Have you ever started your car and discovered that you've left the radio on? What seemed a perfectly reasonable loudness when you were listening to your music over the background of road noise is now extremely loud, so you quickly turn it down. (Similarly, an alarm-radio sounds louder when it goes off in the morning than it did when you set it the night before.) Notice that the energy coming from the radio doesn't change; the volume knob remains in the same position. However, your perception of loudness does change. In other words, two identical physical stimuli can produce different perceptions.

Furthermore, two different physical stimuli can produce identical perceptions. For example, one brand of pea soup may contain more salt than another; these two *physical* stimuli are different. But you might be unable to detect any difference in saltiness, thereby indicating that the two brands are *psychologically* identical.

These examples should convince you that the relationship between the physical properties of stimuli and a person's psychological experience of those stimuli is complex. The same physical stimulus might produce very different perceptions, or different physical stimuli might produce the same perception. The study of the relationship between properties of physical stimuli and psychological reactions to those properties is called *psychophysics*. Gustav Theodor Fechner (1801–1887) coined this term more than 100 years ago.

According to legend, Fechner awoke on the morning of October 22, 1850, with the basic ideas that gave birth to psychophysics; today, psychophysicists celebrate that date annually as Fechner's Day (Boring, 1961; Rosenzweig, 1987). Fechner outlined several basic methods to investigate the psychological experience of physical stimuli, and they have remained essentially unchanged to this day. In fact, one could argue that Fechner's ideas marked the beginning of an experimental approach to psychology, because he was the first person to espouse a rigorous systematic approach to the study of psychological experience. Others, such as Hermann Ebbinghaus, were influenced by Fechner's approach, and they applied it to human memory and other areas of psychology beyond perception.

Figure 2.1 illustrates the relationship between a physical dimension and perceptions of stimuli along that dimension. It also indicates the complexity of the problems confronting a psychophysicist. At the bottom of the figure is the physical dimension. A major advantage in psychophysical research is that the physical dimension can be easily quantified.

The impact of the physical stimulus on the observer is labeled "subjective experience" (Figure 2.1b). This dimension is largely unobservable to the outside world. What we mean by subjective experience is the person's perceptual experience and the brain-cell activity produced by the stimulus. Fechner was actually most interested in studying the two components that we have lumped together as subjective experience, characterized as the mind–body relationship (the relationship between perceptual experience and brain activity).

Although we can measure the physical stimulus with great precision (illustrated by a single point along the dimension), its effect on the observer is not so simple. In Figure 2.1, the physical stimulus causes a range of subjective experience. This is intended to illustrate that many factors (such as inner "noise," wandering attention, differing contexts, etc.) can lead the same stimulus to be perceived differently on different occasions. This variation produces a distribution of assorted levels of subjective experience over

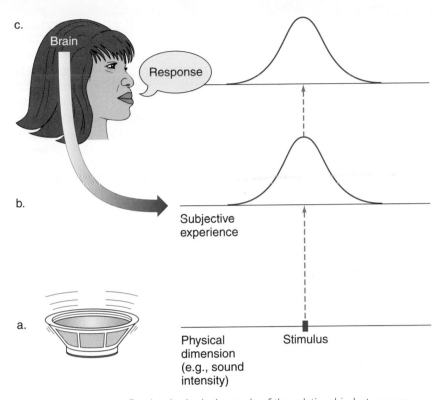

▶ **FIGURE 2.1**   Psychophysics is the study of the relationship between a physical stimulus and our psychological reaction to it. The physical dimension (a) is easily measured. However, the psychological reaction or subjective experience (b) is unique to each individual and can't be universally quantified like the physical dimension. The only way to find out about b is to have a person report what he or she is experiencing (c). Notice that there is not a one-to-one relationship among these dimensions. The bell-shaped distributions for b and c suggest that on different occasions the same stimulus can produce different subjective experiences and different responses. For instance, in the car radio example in the text, the same physical stimulus (sound energy) can seem louder on one occasion than another.

time. (Remember the car radio anecdote.) So, one of the first problems confronting the psychophysicist is that the relationship between physical energy and subjective experience is not one-to-one, but one-to-many. Psychophysicists presume that many contextual factors may lead a person to respond differently on different occasions to the identical level of subjective experience (e.g., Marks & Gescheider, 2002; Poulton, 1989). However, the problems don't stop there.

The subjective dimension portrayed in Figure 2.1 is largely unobservable and hypothetical. Because the perceptual experience is essentially private, the only way an outsider can get any idea of the inner experience of another person is to have that person engage in some behavior. Thus, the final dimension illustrated in Figure 2.1 is the response dimension. From

Fechner's era to now, researchers have been devising methods of measuring these private perceptions by having people engage in behaviors that allow the researcher to derive numbers from the behaviors.

The purpose of this chapter is to explore some of these measurement techniques and the nature of the relationship between physical stimuli and psychological responses. If you're like most people, you are unlikely to find the material in this chapter wildly exciting. As Suzanne McKee (1993) points out, "As any American undergraduate will attest, perception is entertaining and stimulating, while psychophysics is boring and incomprehensible. Who cares about four methods for measuring something you can't see?" But she goes on to say that "in all honesty, I love psychophysics."

Now we can't guarantee that you'll come to love psychophysics, but we'll try to make your excursion through it as painless as possible. We do think that it's a trip you should take. (And we can assure you that you will find much of the rest of the material throughout the book to be very "entertaining and stimulating.")

Why are we so interested in psychophysics? One answer is that psychophysics is important as a self-sufficient area of inquiry. If you are concerned about how the mind works, then you should be curious about how the mind processes physical stimuli from the environment.

Psychophysics is also an essential tool for studying sensation and perception. For example, if you have ever had your hearing tested, the test involved one of the psychophysical methods. Some areas of sensation and perception may initially seem to be unrelated to psychophysics, until someone points out a connection. For instance, in Chapter 4, we will discuss visual acuity, the ability to see fine details. In essence, an acuity test is a detection task from psychophysics. To tell the difference between a *P* and an *R* on an eye chart on your doctor's wall, you need to decide whether you detect an extra little bar in the lower right-hand corner of the letter.

In addition to being used in a wide range of perceptual studies, psychophysical techniques have been adapted for use in many areas beyond perception (Crano & Brewer, 2001). For example, cognitive psychologists have used psychophysical techniques to study memory (e.g., Rotello et al., 2004; Wixted & Stretch, 2004). Forensic researchers have applied psychophysical methods to several areas, including the reliability of eyewitness testimony (Clark, 2005; Phillips et al., 2001). Plant pathologists have used psychophysics to assess people's abilities to determine the extent of disease severity in plants (Nutter & Esker, 2006). Finally, the medical field has applied the methods in a number of ways, including the detection of breast abnormalities in mammograms (Bochud et al., 2004). Whether researchers are exploring theoretical or applied questions, they often find that psychophysical methods are quite useful.

In summary, then, psychophysical methods are important because they serve as the basis for much of the research presented throughout this book. Furthermore, these methods allow us to learn about areas of psychology beyond sensation and perception, including practical applications to problems in everyday life.

Let's now turn our attention to these psychophysical techniques.

The discussion is divided into two sections. In the first section, we will describe how people respond to low-intensity stimuli that are difficult to detect. We will discuss the methodologies of both classical psychophysics and some newer methods. The second section examines how people respond to more intense stimuli, which are easily detectable. We will look at the classical psychophysical methods for measuring discrimination, as well as the nature of the relationship between physical intensity and psychological response.

Measuring Responses to Low-Intensity Stimuli

You are standing on the subway platform, gazing down the dark tunnel to your right. Is that a faint light that you see, signaling the arrival of your train? Do you hear a distant rumble, assuring you that the Lexington Avenue Express is on its way? These are questions involving detection. In *detection* studies, we provide low-intensity stimuli and notice whether people report them.

Classical Psychophysical Measurement of Detection

One application of Fechner's psychophysical methods has been in the measurement of absolute thresholds (Kubovy et al., 2003; Rose, 2000; Schiffman, 2003). Much as the threshold of a house marks the transition from being outside the house to being inside the house, people thought of an ***absolute threshold*** as an abrupt change from not being able to detect a stimulus to just being able to do so. You may also see the absolute threshold referred to as the *absolute limen*, from the Latin term for threshold (and the root of "subliminal"). This approach is illustrated in the results displayed in Figure 2.2.[1]

---

[1]Note that the horizontal axis presents the intensity of the physical stimulus (lower intensities to the left and higher intensities to the right) and the vertical axis presents the perceptual response (0% reports of seeing the stimulus to the bottom and 100% reports of seeing the stimulus to the top). So the graph itself represents the essential psychophysical relationship between physical stimuli and perceptions of them.

Imagine an experiment in which 70 trials are presented, with each of 7 intensity levels presented to a person 10 times, but in a random order. (You will soon come to recognize this study as using the method of constant stimuli.) On each trial, the person is told to respond "Yes" when he or she can see the stimulus and "No" when he or she can't see the stimulus. Thus, that person might respond "No" whenever the stimulus intensity is 1, 2, 3, or 4 (and therefore says "Yes" 0% of the time). However, at a stimulus intensity of 5 or above, the person consistently reports "Yes" (and therefore says "Yes" 100% of the time). Therefore, this person's threshold lies somewhere between an intensity of 4 and 5. For simplicity, we would call it 4.5.

When people started to do actual detection experiments, however, their results did not look at all like those shown in Figure 2.2. Instead, they looked much more like those displayed in Figure 2.3. Notice that the observer shows a gradual increase in the percentage of "Yes" responses. On 2 of the 10 trials on which a stimulus of intensity 3 was presented, this person responded "Yes." (Thus, 20% on the vertical axis corresponds to a 3 on the horizontal axis.) On the remaining 8 trials, this observer reported that she could not see the stimulus. The threshold must lie somewhere between a stimulus intensity of 2 (never say "Yes") and 7 (always say "Yes"), but where? Psychophysicists typically define the absolute threshold as the smallest intensity required for the stimulus to be reported 50% of the time. The threshold for the person represented in Figure 2.3 would be at a stimulus intensity of 5.

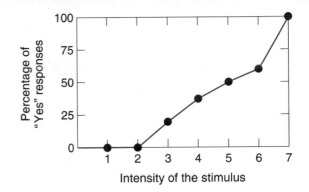

▶ **FIGURE 2.3**   Results of a typical threshold study, showing a gradual change. The threshold is the point at which 50% of the stimuli are reported as being present (50% "Yes" responses). In this case, the threshold would be 5.

Why does the same stimulus sometimes produce different responses? If you remember the car radio example, such results should make sense. Remember, the same physical stimulus can produce one subjective experience on one occasion and a different subjective experience on another (the distribution of subjective experience in Figure 2.1b). So, if the stimulus produces a relatively large subjective experience, the observer would probably respond "Yes." On occasions when the same stimulus produces a relatively small subjective experience, the observer would respond "No." Beyond that, as illustrated by Figure 2.1c, the same subjective intensity can yield a range of responses. Of course, the larger the amount of physical energy in the stimulus, the higher the level of subjective intensity, and the greater the probability of a "Yes" response.

Table 2.1 (page 20) provides some illustrations of absolute thresholds in humans. These thresholds are only meant to give you a feeling for the amazing sensitivity of our senses. The research has not actually been done with bees' wings or candle flames over long distances at night.

In his classic text, *The Elements of Psychophysics*, Fechner (1860) described three different methods that can be used to determine absolute thresholds: the method of limits, the method of adjustment, and the method of constant stimuli. We will describe each of them in turn.

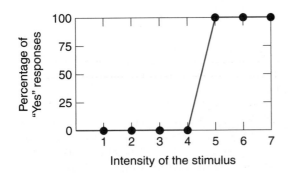

▶ **FIGURE 2.2**   Incorrect conception of a threshold, showing abrupt change. The threshold clearly falls between 4 and 5 because a person shifts from reporting no stimulus (0% "Yes" responses) to reporting the presence of the stimulus (100% "Yes" responses).

METHOD OF LIMITS   Before reading any further, try
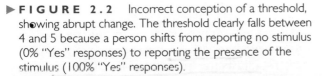 Demonstration 2.1, which is an example of how

▶ **TABLE 2.1**   Some Approximate Detection
Threshold Values

Sense Modality	Detection Threshold
Light	A candle flame seen at 30 miles on a dark clear night
Sound	The tick of a watch under quiet conditions at 20 feet
Taste	One teaspoon of sugar in 2 gallons of water
Smell	One drop of perfume diffused into the entire volume of a three-room apartment
Touch	The wing of a bee falling on your cheek from a distance of 1 centimeter

Source: Adapted from Galanter (1962).

the method of limits can be used to measure a detection threshold. In the ***method of limits***, you might begin with a stimulus that is clearly noticeable and then present increasingly weaker stimuli until the observer reports, "No, I can't detect it." This sequence is referred to as a ***descending series*** of trials. Next, you might begin with a stimulus that is clearly below threshold and then present increasingly stronger stimuli until the observer reports, "Yes, I can detect it." This sequence would be an ***ascending series*** of trials. In a typical psychophysical experiment using the method of limits, the observer would be presented with several alternating ascending and descending series.

When using the method of limits, we need to use both ascending and descending series because we often obtain a different value for the threshold, depending on which series is used. This difference in thresholds has some practical applications. For example, suppose that someone is playing a radio in the room in which you are studying. You could turn down the volume, using a descending series, until you think that the intensity is appropriate. However, you may discover that the final sound intensity is lower if you first turn down the volume until it cannot be heard and gradually make it louder, using an ascending series.

These two sets of series also correct for two other kinds of tendencies. Some people make ***errors of***

habituation; they operate on the principle that "the stimulus is likely to be the same as last time, so I'll keep giving the same answer." Thus, they tend to keep saying "No" on ascending series and to keep saying "Yes" on descending series for some time after it is appropriate to change their response pattern. Other people make ***errors of anticipation***; they operate on the opposite principle, that "the stimulus is likely to be different from last time, so I'll change my answer." As a result, they "jump the gun." On ascending series, they claim that they can detect the stimulus when in fact they can't. On descending series, they claim that they can no longer detect the stimulus when in fact they still can.

How can we correct for errors of habituation and errors of anticipation? If we assume that a person who makes errors of habituation is just as likely to make them on ascending series as on descending series, the errors will cancel each other out. The threshold we obtain will be too high on ascending series, but it will be too low on descending series. If the two are averaged, therefore, we should end up with an accurate threshold. The same kind of cancellation of errors will work for errors of anticipation.

One other human factor can contaminate the method of limits and produce an inaccurate threshold, unless it is controlled. Suppose that every ascending series in www Demonstration 2.1 started with Cup 1. Tasters might notice on the first series that the sugar is detectable by Cup 4. If every series began with that same stimulus, then tasters might simply say "Yes" when they reach the fourth cup, without even paying attention to the taste. If we are inconsistent about the starting point for each series, however, participants in a study using the method of limits cannot get away with simply counting trials. Thus, the ascending series sometimes begins with Cup 1 and sometimes with Cup 2, and the descending series could begin with Cup 9 or Cup 10.

www Demonstration 2.1 shows only eight series of trials. A formal psychophysics experiment would be more likely to have dozens of series. The method of limits is an appropriate name because a series of trials stops when the observer reaches a limit and changes the responses either from "Yes" to "No" or from "No" to "Yes."

METHOD OF ADJUSTMENT   In the ***method of adjustment***, the observer—rather than the experimenter—adjusts the intensity of the stimulus. Typically, the observer makes adjustments that are continuous (e.g., by adjusting a knob) rather than discrete (e.g., by tasting separate solutions containing different amounts of a substance).

This method can be used to obtain a threshold very quickly, and so it may be used to locate an approximate threshold. However, many observers tend to be sloppy when they use this method, leading to great variation from one observer to the next. Consequently, psychophysicists use it less than other methods. Notice, though, that you often use the method of adjustment in everyday life, such as when you adjust the knob on your radio so that the sound is barely audible.

METHOD OF CONSTANT STIMULI   In the ***method of constant stimuli***, the stimuli are presented in random order, as in www Demonstration 2.2. The experimenter usually selects between five and nine stimuli, such that the weakest stimulus is clearly below threshold and the strongest stimulus is clearly above threshold. (As you can imagine, these values must be chosen after pretesting with a speedy method such as the method of adjustment.) Notice that the name *constant stimuli* is appropriate because researchers select a constant set of stimuli before the testing begins, and they present these stimuli a constant number of times during testing.

In www Demonstration 2.2, each of the solutions is presented five times. In contrast, in a formal psychophysics experiment, each stimulus would be presented more often (Gescheider, 1985). The method of constant stimuli is extremely time consuming, particularly because the stimuli must be pretested. However, this method is preferred when psychophysicists want to obtain a careful measurement of a threshold, because it eliminates some biases found in the other two methods.

How do experimenters decide which method to use? The method of constant stimuli provides the most reliable data, and it is relatively free of biases. However, a disadvantage is that the experimenter needs to pretest the stimuli at near-threshold levels. The method of adjustment produces errors and is typically used only for stimuli that are continuously adjustable. Nonetheless, it may be useful for pretesting the stimuli that will be used with the method of constant stimuli. The method of limits requires less planning than the method of constant stimuli and may be the choice of an experimenter who wants fairly reliable thresholds without too much investment of time.

Although our discussion has been oriented toward thresholds, some psychophysicists speak of measuring ***sensitivity***. The technical use of the term closely parallels the common use of sensitivity. When you describe people as highly sensitive, you typically mean that they are capable of detecting minor (usually emotional) changes in those around them, or that they have a low threshold for detecting change. Insensitive people have such high thresholds that a major earthquake is necessary for them to detect a change.

In other words, sensitivity is inversely related to thresholds. When you have a low threshold for a stimulus, that means that only a low intensity of that stimulus is required for you to say, "I perceive it." In other words, you are sensitive to that stimulus. Thus, the *lower* the threshold, the *higher* the sensitivity. Conversely, the *higher* the threshold, the *lower* the sensitivity. For example, when you have been out in the bright sunshine and first enter a dark room, you have a high threshold for perceiving a dim light; your sensitivity is low. After you have been in the dark room for 20 minutes, however, you have a low threshold for perceiving a dim light; your sensitivity is high. Because the terms *threshold* and *sensitivity* are potentially confusing, you should inspect graphs of psychophysical functions carefully to see whether large numbers reflect a high threshold or a high sensitivity.

The original versions of these classical psychophysical methods presented a stimulus on every trial. However, psychophysicists were perplexed by the fact that the same stimulus would be detected on some trials and not on others. Thinking that the observers might be using some sort of guessing strategy, researchers began to insert "catch trials"—trials on which no stimulus at all was presented. They found that people would often report the presence of a stimulus on catch trials. These results could not easily be explained within the framework of threshold theory. However, many years later signal detection theory was developed to explain why observers reported a stimulus on a catch trial. Although Fechner's psychophysics differs from signal detection theory, signal detection theory actually shares a great deal of theoretical underpinnings with Fechner's psychophysics (Link, 1994).

Signal Detection Theory

The three classical methods of psychophysics that we have examined have a common goal: locating a threshold. The implication is that a certain stimulus intensity can be determined that constitutes a borderline between detectable stimuli and those that cannot be detected. Signal detection theory, on the other hand, criticizes the very notion of a fixed threshold.

Signal detection theory (SDT) argues that the thresholds obtained by classical psychophysical methods are composites of two separate processes: (1) the observer's sensitivity to the stimulus and (2) the observer's decision-making strategy or criterion (Green & Swets, 1966; Macmillan & Creelman, 2005). Using SDT, researchers can separate sensitivity from criterion by examining the observer's responses to trials containing a *signal* (where a weak physical stimulus is present) and trials containing only *noise* (where no physical stimulus is present, only background noise). Consistent with one of the themes of this book, signal detection theory emphasizes the importance of top-down processing. Thus, the physical stimulus alone is not sufficient to determine perception—mental factors are also critical.

To clarify how these two processes function, let's consider an anecdotal example. Suppose that your cell phone is in your pocket and it's set to vibrate for an incoming call. Under normal circumstances—with no incoming call—how likely are you to incorrectly report that your phone is vibrating? Pretty unlikely, right? Now suppose that you take a ride on a roller coaster. Because of the vibrations caused by the ride, you may mistakenly think that the phone is vibrating, or else you may miss an incoming call because you can't detect the vibration. The difference between these two situations is one of sensitivity. In the first instance, the signal (phone vibrating) would be superimposed on a very low level of noise (little additional vibration, etc.), so you would be unlikely to miss the phone's vibration. Nor would you report that it was vibrating when it was not. In the second instance, however, the noise level is considerably higher. Thus, you are more likely to report feeling a nonexistent vibration or to actually miss feeling the vibrating phone. So the signal-to-noise (S/N) ratio is much lower when you are on the roller coaster. (If you have purchased a stereo system, you are probably already somewhat familiar with this notion. Receivers often report sensitivity in terms of the S/N ratio, with higher numbers indicating increased sensitivity.)

Now, let's suppose that you've just been interviewed for an important job, and the person who interviewed you told you to expect a call sometime between 3:30 and 5:00 on a particular afternoon. The one thing you *don't* want to do is to miss that phone call. Under these circumstances, you might mistakenly think that you feel your phone vibrating as you go about your business in your room. You would be even more likely to think that you felt the phone vibrating if you happened to be riding a roller coaster during that time period. Compared to the earlier examples, what has changed in this situation to make you much more likely to report feeling the phone vibrating? Your sensitivity hasn't changed, because the signal-to-noise ratio is equally high (working in your room) or equally low (riding a roller coaster). Your expectations, however, have changed substantially. In the earlier examples, you had no real expectations that the phone would ring, and not much was riding on the possibility that you might miss a phone call. However, when you expect a phone call, you shift your *criterion*, or your willingness to say that you detect a stimulus.

We will now examine a typical SDT experiment to illustrate how you might measure an observer's sensitivity and criterion, using a methodology that is not much different from the version used by classical psychophysicists. Not only will you learn some specifics about SDT, but also you will see why such experiments call into question the very notion of a threshold.

DESIGN OF A SIGNAL DETECTION EXPERIMENT
Let's discuss a hypothetical experiment in which an observer is asked to listen for a weak tone. (Although this experiment involves hearing, SDT can be applied equally well to all the senses.) Out of 100 trials, we will randomly select 50 noise trials on which no tone is presented (normal background noise only). (Note that these trials are the equivalent of catch trials in classical psychophysical experiments.) On the remaining 50 trials, a *very weak* tone is presented, essentially added to the noise. We refer to these trials as *signal + noise* trials. (The + is read as "plus.") In trying to conceptualize this experiment, you should realize that the perceived difference between the two types of trials must be very small. In other words, if observers could always tell that a tone was present on a trial, we could not obtain a good estimate of their detection abilities. Each trial, then, represents a difficult decision for the observer.

Table 2.2 illustrates four possible outcomes that can occur on each trial of this experiment. What

▶ **T A B L E 2 . 2**   Four Possible Outcomes of a Signal Detection Trial

		What Did the Observer Respond?	
		"Yes, I hear it"	"No, I don't hear it"
Was the signal present or absent?	Present	Hit (correct)	Miss (mistake)
	Absent	False alarm (mistake)	Correct rejection (correct)

should happen on the noise-only trials? A perfectly accurate observer would always respond "No," to indicate that no stimulus is present. This would be a _correct rejection_. What happens occasionally, however, is that the observer incorrectly responds "Yes," which is a _**false alarm**_. When a stimulus is actually present (a signal superimposed on background noise), a perfect observer would always respond "Yes," which we call a _**hit**_. In reality, however, the observer occasionally will respond "No," which we call a _**miss.**_

In analyzing the data from our experiment, we will determine the proportion of trials on which each of these four outcomes was obtained. Notice, however, that a complementary relationship exists between hits and misses, and between correct rejections and false alarms. Thus, in our hypothetical experiment, on the 50 noise trials an observer who gets 40 correct rejections (proportion = .80) must also get 10 false alarms (.20). On the 50 signal + noise trials an observer who gets 45 hits (.90) will get 5 misses (.10). Researchers can therefore analyze the results of a signal detection experiment by ignoring correct rejections and misses and looking only at hits and false alarms.[2]

RESULTS OF A SIGNAL DETECTION EXPERIMENT
We can now examine the results of our hypothetical experiment for a single observer, expressed as a proportion of hits and false alarms obtained during the 100 trials of the experiment. First, let's consider the noise trials (illustrated in Figure 2.4a), which are the source of our false alarm data. The horizontal axis represents the subjective intensity that the observer is

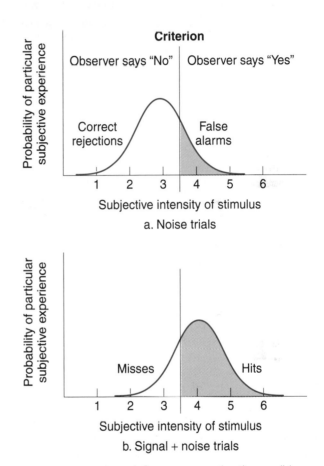

▶ **F I G U R E   2 . 4**   A figure representing the possible outcomes of a signal detection experiment. The observer establishes a subjective intensity as a criterion for reporting the presence of a stimulus. When a stimulus produces a subjective intensity that exceeds the criterion, the observer says that a stimulus is present ("Yes"). Figure 2.4a illustrates trials on which only noise (no actual signal) is present. The observer reports either hearing a signal (false alarm—shaded area) or not (correct rejection—unshaded area). Figure 2.4b illustrates trials on which a signal is presented in addition to the noise, which increases the subjective intensity and shifts the distribution to the right. The observer reports either hearing the signal (hit—shaded area) or not (miss—unshaded area).

---

[2]Those of you who have had a statistics course should also note the similarity between Table 2.2 and the hypothesis testing table showing Type I errors (saying that a difference exists, when in actuality there is no difference) and Type II errors (saying that no difference exists, when in fact there is a difference). Thus, a Type I error is essentially a false alarm, and a Type II error is a miss.

experiencing on any given trial, measured in arbitrary units. The vertical axis represents the probability of a particular subjective intensity arising for the observer. From looking at Figure 2.4a, then, we could determine that on most noise trials, our observer would experience a subjective intensity of 3 (high point of the distribution). On other trials, however, the subjective intensity could go lower than 1 or higher than 5, but the probability of these subjective intensities arising is fairly low (low points of the distribution).

What produces the probability distribution of subjective intensities shown in the figure? After all, no tone is presented on noise trials. As we will see in later chapters, brain cells are always firing—even in the absence of stimulation. We refer to this spontaneous firing as *maintained activity*. So, we could think of the distribution as arising from differing levels of brain-cell activity in the parts of the brain that deal with audition. On some noise trials, this activity is so low that the subjective intensity on that trial is very low (around 1). On other trials, this activity is quite high, leading to a high subjective intensity (near 5). However, the brain-cell activity is rarely at either extreme, and for most trials the subjective intensity is centered around a score of 3.

Next, let's examine the signal + noise trials (Figure 2.4b), from which we derive the proportion of hits. Even though the signal + noise distribution is shown separately from the noise distribution, you should realize that the horizontal and vertical axes are identical. In other words, the subjective intensity units shown on the horizontal axis are the same in Figures 2.4a and 2.4b. The probability distribution illustrated in the signal + noise figure is essentially the same as that for noise trials, with the important exception that the distribution is shifted to the right, in the direction of greater subjective intensity. In fact, you could think of the addition of the tone energy on a signal + noise trial as adding a constant amount of subjective intensity to each of the points in the noise-only distribution. You should also note the similarity in representation and interpretation between Figure 2.1 and Figure 2.4b.

Because the subjective intensity units on the horizontal axes of Figures 2.4a and 2.4b are identical, we can actually place the noise distribution and the signal + noise distribution on the same horizontal axis, as is done in Figure 2.5. Even though the two distributions are being shown on the same horizontal axis, don't lose sight of the fact that they represent

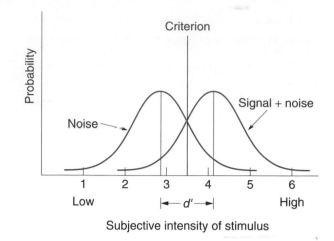

▶ **FIGURE 2.5** A graph representing the results of a signal detection experiment. The graph contains data from two different types of trials: noise only and signal + noise. Notice that this graph is the same as the one in Figure 2.4, but with the two distributions shown on the same horizontal axis.

responses to two distinctly different types of trials in the SDT experiment.

DISTINGUISHING BETWEEN SENSITIVITY AND CRITERION   Remember, one of the benefits of SDT is that we can determine both the observer's criterion and sensitivity. We will use *d'* (or d-prime) as an index of sensitivity, although researchers have developed other measures of sensitivity (Verde et al., 2006). How can we determine both criterion and sensitivity from our data? Figure 2.5 helps illustrate the origin of the measure of sensitivity (*d'*), which is basically the distance between the peaks of the two distributions. With increasing amounts of energy in the tone, the signal + noise distribution will move farther to the right of the noise distribution. If the energy in the tone is minuscule, the noise and the signal + noise distributions would be almost identical.

Figures 2.4 and 2.5 also show the observer's criterion as a vertical line passing through the horizontal axis. You can think of the criterion as representing the observer's decision that if a particular trial produces a subjective intensity greater than the criterion, the observer will respond "Yes." If the subjective intensity on a trial falls below the criterion, the observer will respond "No." Looking at the noise distribution, you can see that the area of the distribution to the right of the criterion represents the proportion of false alarms for this observer (saying "Yes" when no tone was present). The area of the noise distribution to the left of the criterion represents correct rejections (correctly reporting that no tone was present). In the signal + noise distribution, the area to the right of the criterion represents the proportion of hits (saying "Yes" when a tone was present). Furthermore, the area to the left of the criterion represents the proportion of misses (saying "No" when a tone was present). Notice that the single line implies that an observer has a fixed criterion, which remains constant throughout the experiment.

Experimenters use an observer's proportion of hits and false alarms to determine criterion and sensitivity (d'). The procedure is actually fairly simple, but computation of d' requires some background in statistics.[3] We will try to provide you with an intuitive understanding of the process without reference to statistics. To do so, consider five hypothetical participants in our experiment (Aaron, Beth, Chris, Diane, and Eric), whose data are displayed in Table 2.3.

First of all, notice that Aaron and Diane obtained the identical proportion of hits (.50), but they did so with different proportions of false alarms (.16 for Aaron and .31 for Diane). Also, notice that Beth and Diane got an equal proportion of false alarms (.31), as did Chris and Eric (.40). However, in both cases their proportions of hits differed. When observers obtain similar proportions of hits—yet their proportions of false alarms are not similar—we can conclude that their sensitivities (measured by d') differ. A compari-

son of Figures 2.6a and 2.6b illustrates why this must be the case.

Let's look at Figure 2.6a first, where the noise and the signal + noise distributions are separated by a certain amount ($d' = 1.0$). If observers with this sensitivity, such as Aaron, establish a criterion by which they obtain .50 hits, their false alarm rate is fixed at .16. The only way to obtain the same hit rate coupled with a higher false alarm rate of .31 (as Diane did) is for the observer to be less sensitive. That would imply a d' less than 1.0, which means that the two distributions are closer together, as illustrated in Figure 2.6b. On the other hand, with the same sensitivity as Aaron—but with less conservative criteria—Beth and Chris obtain greater proportions of hits and false alarms. Be sure that you can look at Figure 2.6a and identify the

▶ **TABLE 2.3**   Outcome of Hypothetical SDT Experiment

Participant	p (Hit)	p (False alarm)
Aaron	.50	.16
Beth	.69	.31
Chris	.77	.40
Diane	.50	.31
Eric	.60	.40

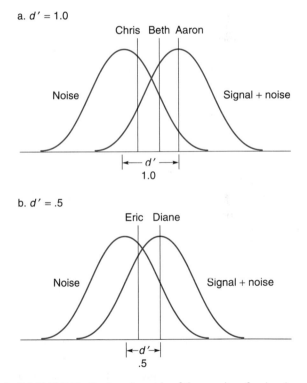

a. $d' = 1.0$

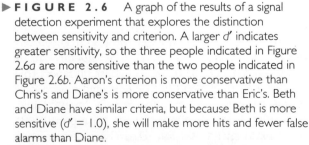

b. $d' = .5$

▶ **FIGURE 2.6**   A graph of the results of a signal detection experiment that explores the distinction between sensitivity and criterion. A larger d' indicates greater sensitivity, so the three people indicated in Figure 2.6a are more sensitive than the two people indicated in Figure 2.6b. Aaron's criterion is more conservative than Chris's and Diane's is more conservative than Eric's. Beth and Diane have similar criteria, but because Beth is more sensitive ($d' = 1.0$), she will make more hits and fewer false alarms than Diane.

---

[3]Assuming that the noise and signal + noise distributions are normal allows one to make use of the properties of the normal curve. Thus, one could determine the distance in standard deviation units from the mean of the noise distribution to the criterion line, and from the criterion line to the mean of the signal + noise distribution. The separation between the peaks of the two distributions, d', is just the sum of the two distances.

portions of the two distributions that indicate hits and false alarms.

How can we be sure that Aaron, Beth, and Chris all have the same sensitivity? The two distributions in Figure 2.6a are identical in shape but fixed at a specific distance from one another. Therefore, when an observer decides on a criterion, the position of the criterion will determine a particular combination of proportion of hits and false alarms. Knowing what proportion of hits and false alarms an observer obtained, we could determine the specific sensitivity that must have produced the two proportions. The specific proportions of hits and false alarms produced by Aaron, Beth, and Chris are each consistent with an equivalent sensitivity ($d' = 1.0$), but with differing criteria. Try www Demonstration 2.3 to illustrate this principle for yourself.

Beth and Diane obtained identical proportions of false alarms (.31). Chris and Eric also obtained identical proportions of false alarms (.40). However, Beth and Chris obtained a larger proportion of hits than their counterparts. How can two people achieve identical proportions of false alarms but different proportions of hits? Such discrepancies can be found only with differences in sensitivity. It should be clear to you that Diane and Eric are less sensitive than Beth and Chris. As you can see in Figure 2.6b, the proportion of hits and false alarms obtained by Diane and Eric are consistent with a signal + noise distribution that is much closer to the noise distribution. Why might Diane and Eric have lower sensitivity than Aaron, Beth, and Chris? This could happen for any of a number of reasons, including some hearing loss resulting from attending loud concerts or playing music too loud through headphones. You should also see that Diane is more conservative than Eric, with a criterion farther to the right, and fewer hits and false alarms.

FACTORS THAT INFLUENCE CRITERIA   As seen in our example, people may come to an SDT experiment with differing criteria. Presumably, observers' past histories incline some to have more conservative criteria ("I won't say that I hear the tone unless I'm absolutely certain") and some to have more liberal criteria ("Maybe the tone was there, so I guess I'll report that I heard it"). Is it possible to encourage a person to change his or her criterion for an experiment? Given the earlier anecdote about waiting for a phone call, you should anticipate that researchers can manipulate a person's criterion during an experiment. We will discuss two ways in which researchers have manipulated criteria.

One important determinant of the criterion is the *payoff*, the rewards and punishments associated with a particular response. From the beginning of SDT, researchers have assumed that observers can be persuaded to adjust their criteria to earn more money (Macmillan & Creelman, 2005). For example, suppose we say that we will pay you 50¢ every time you correctly report seeing a light (hit) and that you will pay us 10¢ every time you incorrectly report seeing a light (false positive). Given the monetary incentives, you should adopt a more liberal criterion and say "Yes, I see it" if there were any chance at all that the light was present.

Contrast this pattern of responding with your behavior if we tell you that we will pay you 50¢ every time you correctly report that you *didn't* see a light that was not presented (correct rejection) and you will pay us 10¢ every time you fail to report seeing a light that was presented (miss). Wouldn't you shift your criterion dramatically so that you would say "Yes, I see it" only if you were absolutely certain that the light had been presented? Notice that the criterion is determined by your strategy in making decisions, rather than your sensitivity, which has remained unchanged.

A second factor that will likely affect the criterion is the probability that the signal will occur (Macmillan & Creelman, 2005). Unfortunately, it is quite tedious to conduct studies to assess the impact of signal probability. Moreover, varying the probability of the signal has an impact on a person's sensitivity *and* criterion.

RECEIVER   OPERATING   CHARACTERISTIC CURVES   The data from signal detection experiments are often depicted in a *receiver operating characteristic curve* (*ROC curve*), which shows the relationship between the probability of a hit and the probability of a false alarm (Macmillan & Creelman, 2005; Wickens, 2001). Figure 2.7 shows a typical ROC curve. Notice that the vertical axis indicates the probability of a hit and the horizontal axis indicates the probability of a false alarm. How is the ROC curve determined? Imagine two distributions separated by a particular d' (e.g., the d' illustrated in Figure 2.5). Suppose you take the criterion line and place it to the far left of the two distributions. Next you determine the proportion of hits (about 1.0) and the proportion of false alarms (also about 1.0). Then you could plot

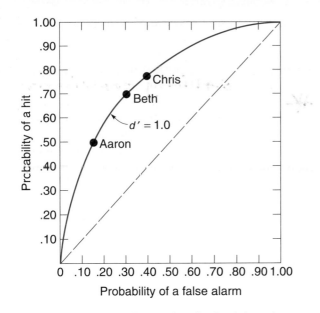

▶ **FIGURE 2.7** The results of a signal detection experiment can be shown using a receiver operating characteristic (ROC) curve, which plots the probability of a false alarm against the probability of a hit. Because Aaron, Beth, and Chris all have the same sensitivity, they fall along the same line. However, because Aaron is the most conservative, he falls to the left of the ROC curve (fewer hits and fewer false alarms). Chris is more liberal than Aaron, so Chris has a larger proportion of hits—accompanied by an increase in the proportion of false alarms.

one of the points on the ROC curve. By moving the criterion a bit to the right, plotting the new proportions of hits and false alarms, and then repeating the process, you would eventually produce the entire curve. Data from observers with that particular d' must fall at some point along the curve.

For any given ROC curve, the sensitivity is constant; that is, the tone does not increase or decrease in intensity, and the observer does not change in perceptual ability. The observer's *criterion* changes within an ROC curve, however, usually due to some of the reasons we have just discussed. Each point along a given ROC curve represents a different criterion. Figure 2.7 shows an ROC curve for $d' = 1.0$. This ROC curve is consistent with the results shown in Table 2.4 and also with the sensitivity of Aaron, Beth, and Chris (Figure 2.6a), whose criteria are plotted on the graph. In the SDT experiment, the probability that Aaron obtained a hit was .50 (proportion of signal + noise trials on which he responded "Yes") and his probability of a false alarm was .16. The intersection of these

two probabilities determines the location of Aaron's point on the ROC curve.

The left-hand portion of any ROC curve represents a strict (conservative) criterion in which the observer is very likely to say "No, I don't hear it" and is very unlikely to say "Yes, I hear it." In contrast, the right-hand portion of any ROC curve represents a liberal criterion in which the observer is very unlikely to say "No, I don't hear it" and is very likely to say "Yes, I hear it." The criterion becomes increasingly liberal as the curve moves from left to right (just the opposite of the situation in politics). Thus, Aaron is a more conservative observer than Chris.

Suppose the signal detection experiment is repeated with a more intense tone (or a more sensitive observer). In this case, the resulting ROC curve might resemble Curve A in Figure 2.8. For comparison's sake, Curve B is taken from Figure 2.7. Curve C represents either a weaker tone or a less sensitive observer. In fact, the results from Diane and Eric (Figure 2.6b) would fall along Curve C. When d' is 0, the observer is forced to simply guess; hits and false alarms occur equally often. In fact, when d' is 0, the ROC curve is a straight line. Compare the four ROC curves. Notice that for any given false alarm rate, the curves differ

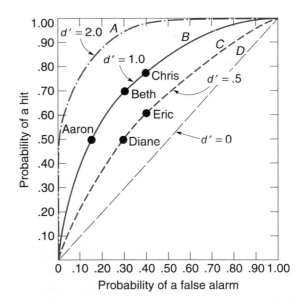

▶ **FIGURE 2.8** Four ROC curves. (A straight line is one type of curve, so the "curve" for a d' of 0 is a straight line.) Notice that at any point along one line, sensitivity is the same, but the criterion changes. (The left portion of each curve represents conservative criteria and the right portion represents liberal criteria.) Also notice that as the curves move up and to the left, sensitivity is increasing.

enormously with respect to the probability of a hit. For example, when the probability of a false alarm is .20, Curve A has a very high hit rate (.88), Curve B has a medium hit rate (.53), Curve C has a low hit rate (.32), and Curve D has only as many hits as false alarms (.20).

Psychologists calculate the proportion of hits and false alarms obtained in an experiment from which they can then calculate d'. Clearly, the graphical comparison of hits and false alarms is useful, because the single graph allows the researcher to examine an observer's criterion *and* sensitivity simultaneously. Try [www] Demonstration 2.4 to make certain that you know how to plot and interpret an ROC curve.

What kind of observer is best with respect to sensitivity and criterion? Clearly, it is best to have a large d' (noise and signal + noise curves as far apart as possible). With a large d', the ratio between the hit rate and the false alarm rate is large. Often, however, the

magnitude of the d' is not under our control. Some people are simply more sensitive than other people; they see better, hear better, and so forth. The only practical way to increase d' is to increase the intensity of the signal. *Explaining Experiment*

Given a particular sensitivity, is it better to set your criterion high or low? This question has no easy answer because you must consider the payoff—the relative advantages and disadvantages—of each outcome. The advantage of a low, or liberal, criterion is a high hit rate, which is good. The high hit rate, however, will be coupled with a high false alarm rate, which is bad. You can lower the false alarm rate by setting a higher, or more conservative, criterion. Now, however, your hit rate will decrease. It may be helpful to think of various situations (e.g., detecting a tumor in an X-ray, detecting a whiff of smoke in a building, detecting an incoming plane on radar) and decide whether a low or a high criterion would be preferable.

IN-DEPTH

Forensics, Faces, and False Alarms: Applied Signal Detection Theory

So far, we've been discussing signal detection theory in the context of simple perceptual stimuli, such as low-intensity sounds and lights. However, we can use signal detection theory to study more complex stimuli that have forensic applications, such as jury decisions (Arkes & Mellers, 2002), face recognition (Macmillan & Creelman, 2005; O'Toole et al., 2000), and lie detection. Unfortunately, the evidence suggests that juries don't appear to be particularly sensitive (low d') in making their decisions (Arkes & Mellers, 2002). Even though only a small percentage of arrests lead to a sentence resulting from a jury trial, it is alarming that juries aren't particularly sensitive. Other forensic applications, such as eyewitness identification and lie detection, are also problematic.

Because we are social animals, it's very important for humans to be able to recognize faces and to "read" facial expressions. Thus, you won't be surprised to learn in subsequent chapters that psychologists are quite interested in facial stimuli. Much theoretical research focuses on the ability to recognize faces, but research on forensic applications is crucial. Whether

or not a trial is involved, it's quite clear that our judicial system relies heavily on information gleaned from faces. Face recognition is often important, as an eyewitness identifies a suspect as the perpetrator of a crime. Investigators also rely on a number of cues, some of them facial, to gain a sense of whether or not a person is lying.

Eyewitness Testimony

Can you apply what you know about signal detection theory to a situation in which you have witnessed a crime? Suppose that you were asked to pick the criminal out of a simultaneous lineup of six potential perpetrators, in which Person #4 is the actual criminal. (Note that in a realistic scenario, you wouldn't really know whether or not the actual criminal is present in the lineup.) If you identify Person #4 as the perpetrator, you have made a hit. If you say that Person #4 is *not* the perpetrator, you have made a miss. If Person #2 looked so much like your mental image of the perpetrator that you picked that person out of the lineup, you have made a false alarm. Finally, if you say that Person #2 is not the perpetrator, then you have made a correct rejection.

Again, let's focus on hits and false alarms. What will determine the probability of making a hit or a false alarm? As before, both your sensitivity and your criterion will determine those probabilities. The other faces in the lineup are drawn from the noise distribution (faces of people who did not commit the crime). Some of them look like your mental image of the criminal (the upper end of the noise distribution), and others look very different from your mental image of the criminal (the lower end of the noise distribution). The face of the actual criminal can also exhibit variability, due to a number of possible changes (hairstyle, glasses, etc.)

The question of sensitivity is a complex one. You'd like to think that you have a very clear image of the person you witnessed committing the crime, so that you could readily identify that person. However, a variety of factors may have affected your memory of the person's face. Moreover, there are ways to manipulate sensitivity in a lineup. Suppose you are certain that the person who committed the crime was at least six feet tall with blond hair. If you're presented with a lineup in which the other five people are short and have dark hair, you might well be inclined to choose the only person in the lineup fitting your description. You might be even more inclined to make that choice if you believe that the actual criminal *must* be in the lineup. That is, your selection is a relative one ("That one looks most like the one I saw commit the crime") from among the people in the lineup. Unfortunately, biased lineups occur with some regularity, and research has shown that they influence an eyewitness's selection of a member of the lineup (Wells et al., 2006; Wells & Olson, 2003).

According to signal detection theory, when the person exceeds your criterion for similarity to your mental image of the criminal, you make a decision ("That person's the criminal!"). At the same time, the other people in the lineup should fall below your criterion. As you know, however, your criterion may vary. For instance, knowing that the person you identified may be incarcerated for a long time could lead you to establish a very conservative criterion. On the other hand, you may be willing to adopt a more liberal criterion if you believe that the police would not have you look at a lineup unless the criminal is among those in the lineup.

As will become increasingly clear in later chapters when we compare our visual sense with other senses, people tend to rely heavily on visual input in making sense of the world. Even the most skeptical people are inclined to believe what they see. In courtroom dramas and most likely in actual courtrooms, an eyewitness to a crime is considered crucial, whereas other evidence is referred to as circumstantial—often with disdain. Given our reliance on visual input, and the importance of faces as stimuli in our environment, wouldn't you think that people would be able to make eyewitness identifications with great accuracy?

You may be surprised to learn that, in fact, witnesses are not particularly good at identifying perpetrators of crimes. With the increasing use of DNA evidence, over 200 people who had been convicted of crimes have been exonerated (Wells et al., 2006; Wells & Olson, 2003). Most of those wrongly convicted people had been identified by at least one eyewitness. To illustrate the fallibility of eyewitness testimony, consider the case of Father Pagano (see Figure 2.9a). He was mistakenly charged with the crimes committed by another man (see Figure 2.9b), based on the testimony of *seven* witnesses. The instructions to the eyewitnesses were probably flawed in this instance. However, you might question how a person could confuse these two men. How similar do they look to you? Clearly, a false alarm in eyewitness testimony is a very serious mistake that can result in the arrest of an innocent person such as Father Pagano. And it's increasingly clear that such mistaken identifications occur routinely.

▶ **FIGURE 2.9** On the left (a) is Father Pagano, who was identified as a thief by seven witnesses. On the right (b) is the actual criminal, who ultimately confessed to the crimes of which Father Pagano stood accused. Do you think you could confuse these two people? (Source: Bettman/CORBIS.)

Obviously, researchers who are interested in the factors that influence eyewitness identification cannot use any actual criminal situations. Instead, they often try to develop a controlled laboratory or field study that resembles the situations in which people serve as eyewitnesses. Such studies are almost always pale reflections of criminal situations, often using photographs or videos of "criminals" and then testing to see how well participants could later pick out the originally presented people from a set containing those people and several distractor people.

First, imagine yourself in the position of a person in such a study. Then imagine yourself as an eyewitness to an actual crime. How would your experiences differ? A number of distinctions should come readily to mind: (1) If you observed an actual crime, you probably would have experienced a great deal of emotion as you observed the crime (fear, anger, etc.). (2) Some emotion is also likely when you select the perpetrator from a lineup or an array of photographs. After all, your decision might help put a person in prison. (3) In witnessing a crime, you are observing a real person, rather than a two-dimensional image. You can certainly think of several other differences. Nonetheless, it should be clear to you that failures in eyewitness identification are a significant real-world problem. In spite of the artificiality of the experimental setting, we can learn some valuable lessons from experiments about factors that influence eyewitness testimony (Lindsay et al., 2007; Toglia et al., 2006). Increasingly, these research findings are affecting the judicial system (Technical Working Group for Eyewitness Evidence, 2003; Wells et al., 2000).

detection

Experiments that use the signal detection approach have an important advantage: Computing d' allows researchers to determine the observers' ability to accurately distinguish between faces they've seen before (the "perpetrators") and new faces ("innocent people"). If d' is near 0, then an eyewitness is unable to reliably identify a perpetrator. As d' increases, people become more capable of distinguishing between the guilty and the innocent faces. Keep in mind, however, that a large d' might not be desirable. A large d' would emerge if the lineup is biased, with the new faces looking nothing like the alleged perpetrator's face. We'll now take a look at some studies that have used a signal detection approach and see what they tell us about eyewitness identification.

A valuable place to begin is a review of facial identification studies provided by Peter Shapiro and Steven Penrod (1986). They looked at over 100 studies on eyewitness identification to see how a variety of factors might influence sensitivity and the criterion. For a range of independent variables (e.g., participants tested on face memory immediately versus at some later point, short versus long amount of time to study the face stimuli, and no training versus training in facial recognition), the criterion is little affected by the variable, but d' often is. Interestingly, over the range of factors summarized by Shapiro and Penrod, the average d' is rarely above .80 for the experimental group that performs better. Such low values of d' indicate that eyewitness identification is a difficult task.

We've already considered how procedural factors influence eyewitness identifications. When using a simultaneous lineup procedure (or a simultaneous photo-array), eyewitnesses may well use a form of relative judgment that selects the person who most looks like the mental image they have of the criminal (McQuiston-Surrett et al., 2006). How might one combat such a bias? One approach that has garnered a lot of attention is to switch to a sequential presentation of the people (or pictures). That way, eyewitnesses are comparing each face with their mental image of the criminal and not with other faces in the lineup or photo-array. However, more research is needed before researchers could claim that sequential lineups are superior to simultaneous lineups (McQuiston-Surrett et al., 2006).

Christian Meissner and his colleagues (2005) have made an important contribution that addresses the issue. They conducted studies that investigated the impact of sequential and simultaneous photo-arrays along with other factors (number of exposures to the target face, use of more versus less conservative instructions, and number of foils present in the photo-array). Throughout their studies, people were equally sensitive whether looking at sequential or simultaneous displays. However, people consistently adopted a more conservative criterion when looking at sequential displays.

Another factor that influences eyewitness identification is the race of the eyewitness and the suspected criminal. There is accumulating evidence that people are better able to identify the face of a person of their own race, called the *own-race bias* (Meissner & Brigham, 2001). To assess the development of this bias, Kathy Pezdek and her colleagues (2003) tested children in kindergarten and third grade, as well as young adults. Half of the participants in each group were White and half were Black. Participants watched a video of two men (one White and one Black). One day later, they were shown a video of a six-person lineup for each man. The researchers found that, overall, the adults were a bit more sensitive than the children. However, across all three age groups, eyewitnesses exhibit higher sensitivity to own-race faces.

Although more research is needed, it's clear that eyewitness identification is a difficult task, with most research reporting less-than-perfect sensitivity. The more we know about the processes involved in eyewitness identification (such as the own-race bias), the better able we will be to make procedural changes to help minimize the number of mistaken identifications that occur.

Lie Detection

Can you tell if someone is lying? You have no doubt encountered someone who has lied to you. You may have even told a lie or two. Most people tell little lies when the truthful alternative might cause someone harm or embarrassment. But suspects in the judicial system likely tell more serious lies related to their criminal activity. And it would be useful if we could detect when criminal suspects are lying.

Physiological lie detection is sufficiently problematic that it is not admissible in a courtroom. Later in this chapter, we'll talk about more promising technologies, such as fMRI, that may be able to provide more reliable means of detecting lies (Mohamed et al., 2006). However, it would be interesting to know if people could detect lies just by "reading" the faces of people making claims that may be true or false.

Once again, you should be able to fit this issue into a signal detection framework. Thus, the person is either telling the truth or telling a lie. The observer

reports that the person told the truth or told a lie. In the context of lie detection, a hit occurs when the observer correctly says that the person was lying, and he or she was actually lying. A false alarm occurs when the observer says that the person was lying, and he or she was actually telling the truth. Note the implications of false alarms in this context—investigators doubting the word of an innocent person. As always, both the sensitivity of the observer and that person's criterion will have an impact on performance.

Earlier research indicated that Secret Service agents were better at detecting lies than other groups of law-enforcement officers (Ekman & O'Sullivan, 1991). Subsequently, Paul Ekman and his colleagues (1999) asked law-enforcement groups (federal officers and judges, sheriffs, etc.) and psychologists (clinical and nonclinical) to watch ten videotapes on which half the people were telling the truth and half were lying. The law-enforcement groups and the clinical psychologists performed fairly well, with d' scores around 1.0. Academic psychologists, however, did not fare so well, with $d' = .38$ (Macmillan & Creelman, 2005). The law-enforcement groups and the clinical psychologists adopted more liberal criteria, so they were more inclined to think that a person was lying. The academic psychologists adopted a more conservative criterion. Note that with d' of around 1.0, there will be quite a few errors (both misses and false alarms) among the most proficient "lie detectors." Even though the academic psychologists performed poorly on this task, you should not be tempted to lie to your professor. After all, the data suggest that your professor may not be predisposed to think that a student is lying. And increased experience with lying students may well lead to a more liberal criterion!

Meissner and Kassin (2002) also conducted research on the ability of law enforcement officers to detect lies in comparison to trained and naïve students. They found no difference in sensitivity among the three groups. However, consistent with the findings of Ekman and his colleagues (1999), the law-enforcement officers adopted more liberal criteria, leading them to correctly say that some liars were lying (hits) but also leading them to incorrectly say that some honest people were lying (false alarms).

Two-Alternative Forced Choice Procedure

In a signal detection experiment, an observer is asked to respond to each of a series of trials, with each trial either a noise or a signal + noise trial. Observers' criteria determine, in part, how they will respond on each trial—either "Yes" or "No."

Is it possible to minimize the impact of an observer's criterion? One approach that attempts to do so is the two-alternative forced choice procedure (Macmillan & Creelman, 2005). In the **two-alternative forced choice procedure** (**2AFC**), a trial consists of two presentations—one that contains the target stimulus and one that does not. The observer's task is to indicate which of the two presentations is the target. Because one of the two presentations really does contain the target, the effects of expectations and criteria are minimized.

As you might well imagine, the 2AFC task is easier than the signal detection task. In an SDT experiment, for example, four trials in a row might be noise trials. Thus, on any particular trial the observer isn't aided by knowing what occurred on the previous trial. In a 2AFC procedure, however, the observer is presented with a pair of stimuli. To use SDT terminology, the observer *knows* that one of the stimuli is noise and the other is signal + noise. So the observer can compare the two stimuli and report that the "stronger" one contains the signal. If neither stimulus appears stronger, she or he will be reduced to guessing, and the hit rate (naming the presentation that correctly contains the target stimulus) will be at the chance level, or .50. As the target becomes more easily perceived, the hit rate will approach 1.0.

Researchers can adapt the 2AFC procedure to include more than two presentations on each trial (i.e., 3AFC, 4AFC, etc.). Further, the 2AFC procedure can be combined with adaptive procedures, in which the level of the stimulus used is varied on the basis of the observer's earlier responses (Macmillan & Creelman, 2005). For instance, researchers could continually reduce the stimulus level, as long as the observer was correctly indicating the presentation containing the target. When the observer makes an error, the level of the stimulus would be raised on the next trial.

Review Fir Quizzes/Exams

Section Summary

Measuring Responses to Low-Intensity Stimuli

1. Psychophysics is the study of the relationship between physical stimuli and the psychological reactions to them.

2. The classical psychophysics methods measure absolute thresholds, the smallest amount of energy required for the stimulus to be reported 50% of the time. The transition between nondetection and detection is gradual rather than abrupt.

3. The method of limits involves presenting systematically increasing or decreasing amounts of a stimulus. It provides a fairly reliable threshold without too much time investment.

4. The method of limits can use both ascending and descending series to correct for errors of habituation and errors of anticipation. The series do not begin with the same starting point every time; this precaution guards against observers' merely counting trials before reporting detection.

5. The method of adjustment involves the observer's adjusting the intensity of the stimulus until it is barely detectable. It provides a threshold very rapidly, but errors are more likely than with the other two methods.

6. The method of constant stimuli involves presenting near-threshold stimuli in random order. It provides a highly accurate threshold, but it is time consuming and requires that the researcher already have a good idea of where the threshold lies.

7. Signal detection theory disputes the very notion of a threshold, because classical psychophysical techniques hopelessly entangle two factors—sensitivity and criterion. Sensitivity depends on stimulus intensity and the sensitivity of the observer. The criterion, which measures willingness to report the stimulus, depends on factors such as probability of stimulus occurrence and payoff (rewards and punishments).

8. The outcome of a signal detection trial can be a hit, a correct rejection, a false alarm, or a miss. The probability of each of these four outcomes depends on the sensitivity measure, d', and the observer's criterion.

9. Signal detection theory can also be represented in terms of probability distributions for trials in which signal + noise occurred and for trials in which only noise occurred.

10. An observer who is very sensitive would produce a large d', but that person's criterion also influences responses. The criterion is determined by several factors, including payoffs for particular responses.

11. ROC curves can be used to plot the proportion of hits and false alarms. Each separate ROC curve represents a different d'.

12. Signal detection theory has been used in research on eyewitness identification and lie detection. Research suggests that eyewitness identification is not particularly accurate, but it is worse under some condition (e.g., identifying suspects whose race differs from that of the eyewitness). Due to experience, some people are better at detecting lies. However, those people may also adopt more liberal criteria.

13. The two-alternative forced choice procedure (2AFC) is often used because it minimizes the influence of the observer's criterion.

Measuring Responses to More Intense Stimuli

So far, the discussion of psychophysics has focused on how people respond to low-intensity stimuli such as dim lights and weak tones. In this section, we turn our attention to the measurement of stimuli that can be detected quite easily. These more intense stimuli figure prominently in everyday experience. We usually have no trouble detecting the vinegar in the hot-and-sour soup at a Chinese restaurant. Instead, the question is whether the Pink Pearl Restaurant uses more vinegar than the Chinese Bowl Restaurant and, if so, is that difference undetectable, just barely noticeable, or very clearly noticeable? In this section we will examine the classical psychophysical measurement of discrimination of stimuli that are above threshold (suprathreshold). We will also look at the more modern approach to psychophysics introduced by S. S. Stevens (1906–1973), in which psychophysicists look at the relationship between the physical magnitude of a stimulus and the observer's estimation of that magnitude.

Classical Psychophysical Measurement of Discrimination

In *discrimination* studies, researchers use a variation of one of the classical psychophysical methods to determine the smallest amount that a stimulus must change to be perceived as different. In such studies, researchers present a *standard stimulus* that remains constant over trials, whereas a *comparison stimulus* varies on each trial. In one type of study, the comparison stimulus changes according to a specified schedule, and the experimenter records how much change is necessary before the observer notices that the comparison stimulus is different from the standard stimulus. For example, to determine a person's ability to discriminate line length, you might present a standard stimulus of a 5-inch line on each trial. The comparison stimulus might be presented at the same time, but in a different location, or it might be presented sequentially, before or after the standard stimulus. The researcher would present some comparison stimuli that were very similar to the standard stimulus (e.g., 5.05 inches) and some comparison stimuli that were less similar (e.g., 5.25 inches). The respondent might simply say "Same" or "Different" in response to each pair of lengths. The actual presentation procedure would vary according to the psychophysical method used, as we will describe later on.

Observers' discrimination ability is measured by a ***difference threshold*** (or *difference limen*), defined as the smallest change in a stimulus that is required to produce a noticeable difference 50% of the time. The term *difference threshold* can be used in defining another important term. A difference threshold is the amount of change in a physical stimulus required to produce a ***just noticeable difference (jnd)*** in the psychological sensation. For example, suppose that the comparison stimulus has to be increased to 5.15 inches to produce a just noticeable change in line length. Then the difference threshold of .15 inch would correspond to one *jnd*. Notice that the term *difference threshold* refers to the physical stimulus, whereas the term *jnd* refers to the psychological reaction. Sensation vs. Perception

The phrase *just noticeable difference*, or its abbreviation, *jnd*, can be useful in daily life. If you add some salt to a soup you're cooking, but the soup doesn't taste different, you could say that the additional salt didn't produce a *jnd*. Or you might find that on a cold winter's night, you need to raise the thermostat by 5 degrees to produce a *jnd* in warmth.

Instead of asking people to report whether or not two stimuli are different, another type of discrimination study asks people to compare the standard and comparison stimuli and forces them to report "Less than" or "Greater than." That is, even if the two stimuli appear to be identical, the observer must use one of those two responses. With this change in procedure comes a new way of determining the difference threshold. For instance, in our line-length example, with a standard length of 5 inches, one might present comparison stimuli that varied from 4.75 inches to 5.25 inches. Hypothetical results of such a study might be like those displayed in Figure 2.10.

In this type of study, we can look at the percentage of "Greater than" responses as a function of the length of the comparison stimulus. In looking at the figure, it should make sense that saying "Greater than" 50% of the time doesn't indicate an ability to discriminate, but instead an inability to discriminate between the standard and comparison stimuli. In other words, the observer is saying, "This line length doesn't really look greater than the standard line length." Instead, the 50% point indicates the **point of**

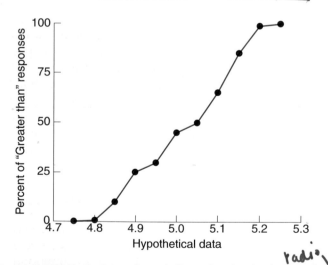

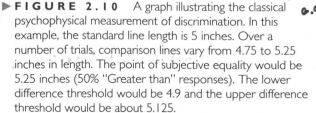

► **FIGURE 2.10** A graph illustrating the classical psychophysical measurement of discrimination. In this example, the standard line length is 5 inches. Over a number of trials, comparison lines vary from 4.75 to 5.25 inches in length. The point of subjective equality would be 5.25 inches (50% "Greater than" responses). The lower difference threshold would be 4.9 and the upper difference threshold would be about 5.125.

subjective equality, which is the value of the comparison stimulus that the observer considers equal to the value of the standard stimulus.

What, then, would make sense as the difference threshold? In this case, researchers use the value of the comparison stimulus that is reported as "Greater than" 75% of the time as the upper difference threshold. The value of the comparison stimulus that is reported as "Greater than" 25% of the time is called the lower difference threshold.

In some cases, the participant is allowed to use an "Equal to" response, which again alters the way in which the difference threshold is determined. Now, let's see how each of the classical psychophysical methods for measuring absolute thresholds can be adapted to measure discrimination. We will describe these methods briefly; more complete descriptions are available elsewhere (Baird & Noma, 1978; Gescheider, 1997).

In the **method of limits for measuring discrimination,** the standard stimulus remains the same, and the comparison stimulus is presented in alternating ascending and descending series. For example, suppose you want to examine the discrimination of pitch. Specifically, you want to determine how much change you can make in a comparison stimulus before the observer notices that it is different from a 1000-Hz standard stimulus. On some ascending series of trials, you could begin with a tone clearly perceived as lower in pitch (e.g., 950 Hz) and present comparison stimuli that increase in frequency. On some descending series of trials, the comparison stimuli might decrease from 1050 Hz. Your observer must judge whether the comparison stimulus is a higher frequency, a lower frequency, or the same frequency as the standard stimulus. Over the various ascending and descending trials, the researcher would take the average of the frequencies that represent the transition from "Lower than" to "Equal to" and from "Equal to" to "Higher than." These values would represent the lower and upper difference thresholds.

In the **method of adjustment for measuring discrimination,** you might determine the point of subjective equality by asking the observer to adjust the comparison stimulus until it seems to match the standard stimulus. The comparison stimulus is set at the beginning of a trial to a level either above or below the standard stimulus. The observer is asked to make this adjustment many times. Consequently, we have a large number of selections of comparison stimuli that the observer believes are equivalent to the standard stimulus. To determine the upper difference threshold, you might ask the observer to adjust the comparison until it is just barely higher than the standard stimulus.

In the *method of constant stimuli for measuring discrimination*, the experimenter presents the comparison stimuli in random order and might ask the observer to judge whether each comparison stimulus is greater than or less than the standard stimulus. In a study of tone discrimination, for example, comparison tones of 1020, 1015, 1010, 1005, 1000, 995, 990, 985, and 980 Hz might be presented in a random order 10 times each for comparison with the 1000-Hz standard stimulus. The frequency corresponding to 25% "Greater than" responses would be the lower difference threshold and the frequency corresponding to 75% "Greater than" responses would be the upper difference threshold.

Thus, each of the three classical psychophysical techniques can be used to measure discrimination as well as detection. The advantages and disadvantages of each method were discussed earlier, and remain basically the same when applied to discrimination studies.

Relationship between Physical Stimuli and Psychological Reactions

Suppose you add 1 ml of vinegar to one glass of water and 2 ml of vinegar to a second glass of water. Does the second solution taste twice as sour? Similarly, does a room that has four candles burning seem four times as bright as a room with only one candle? In this section, we will discuss the relationship between the intensity of the physical stimulus and the magnitude of the observer's reaction. For example, what is the relationship between the amount of vinegar in a solution and how sour the solution seems? Also, what is the relationship between the intensity of the light in a room and how bright the light seems? This is a crucial problem for psychophysicists, and we will discuss the conclusions reached by three prominent researchers.

WEBER'S LAW In the early 1800s, Ernst Weber examined the relationship between physical stimuli and psychological reactions by focusing on the just noticeable difference. He uncovered the important principle that the increase in stimulus intensity needed to produce a *jnd* varied in a consistent fashion across different levels of stimulation. The general principle is that, at low levels of intensity, less additional intensity is needed to produce a *jnd* than is needed at high levels of intensity. Note that this principle highlights the importance of relativity and context in determining perceptual experience.

More formally, *Weber's law* states that when I represents stimulus intensity,

$$\Delta I / I = k$$

Weber Fraction

Verbally, Weber's law states that if we take the change in intensity (Δ, or delta, is the Greek letter used to symbolize change) and divide it by the original intensity, we obtain a constant number (k). The constant, k, is called the **Weber fraction**. Smaller fractions indicate better discrimination abilities, because less change is needed to produce a *jnd*.

For a variety of reasons, you'll typically find a range of different Weber fractions reported for the same physical stimuli. For instance, you might find the Weber fraction for perceiving brightness differences as small as $1/60$ and as large as $1/7$. Note, also, that Weber fractions differ across species. Horses are much less sensitive to brightness differences than humans, with a Weber fraction of $1/2.5$ (Geisbauer et al., 2004).

To provide a better understanding of Weber fractions, consider the following example. For our purposes, we'll treat the Weber fraction for brightness as $1/14$ (Schiffman, 2003). Suppose that you are in a room lit with 14 candles. How many additional candles will you need to light before you can detect that the room is brighter? With a Weber fraction of $1/14$, you would need to light only one more candle in order to produce a *jnd*. Now suppose that 28 candles are lit in a room. Can you discriminate between the brightness in that room and a room in which 29 candles are lit? After all, we have added the same one candle to make the room brighter. However, Weber found that the important determinant of observers' psychological reaction was not the *absolute* size of the change (e.g., 1 candle). Instead, the important determinant was the *relative* size of the change. Specifically, we require 1 additional candle for *each* 14 candles if we want to notice a difference. If the standard stimulus is 14 candles, we notice the difference when 1 candle is added. If the standard stimulus is 28 candles, we require 30 candles in the comparison stimulus to notice a difference.

It should come as no surprise that you are better able to discriminate changes in some types of stimuli than others. For example, most people are better able to detect changes in line length, heaviness of weights, and levels of electric shock than they are able to detect changes in saltiness, brightness of lights, or loudness of sounds (Schiffman, 2003). Furthermore, you now know that you are exhibiting a smaller Weber fraction when you are better able to discriminate such changes. Keep these discrimination abilities in mind when we discuss the contributions of Fechner and Stevens.

Weber's law is nearly two centuries old. How well does it predict the results of psychophysical studies? Research has demonstrated that Weber's law holds true for a variety of psychophysical judgments (Schiffman, 2003). However, it is more successful in the middle ranges than in predicting discrimination ability for high-intensity or low-intensity stimuli.

Perhaps more important than its predictive ability are the general principles embodied in Weber's law. First, for a variety of reasons, humans are not uniformly sensitive to all physical stimuli. Second, different species are differentially sensitive to the same physical stimuli. And most important of all, relative changes in perceptual experience are more helpful than absolute changes in understanding the functioning of our perceptual systems.

FECHNER'S LAW Gustav Fechner used Weber's law to derive a scale that related the size of the physical stimulus to the size of the observer's psychological reaction. He assumed that *jnd*'s were equal, and he plotted these psychological units as a function of the physical units that gave rise to them. From Weber's law, you should be able to figure out that *jnd*'s from the upper end of the scale actually require larger increases in physical stimulation compared to *jnd*'s from the lower end of the scale. (Remember, $\Delta I / I$ is constant, so as I increases, ΔI must also increase.) The relationship, therefore, is not linear, but curvilinear. According to *Fechner's law*, the relationship is logarithmic (Schiffman, 2003). The formula

$$S = k \log I$$

claims that the magnitude of the sensation (*S*) is equal to a constant (*k*) multiplied by the logarithm of the intensity of the physical stimulus (*I*). In other words, Fechner's law states that the psychological

magnitude is proportional to the logarithm of stimulus intensity.

As you may recall, the common **logarithm** of a number equals the exponent, or power, to which 10 must be raised to equal that number. It is important to know that a logarithmic transformation shrinks large numbers more than small numbers. In other words, as I grows larger, S grows larger; however, S does not grow as rapidly as I. For example, suppose that k has a value of 1. If the intensity of the stimulus is 100 units, then $S = 2$ (because the logarithm of 100 is 2; $10^2 = 100$). Now, if we double the intensity of the stimulus to 200 units, then $S = 2.3$ (because the logarithm of 200 is 2.3; $10^{2.3} = 200$).

Notice that a doubling of the intensity of the physical stimulus does *not* lead to a doubling of the psychological response. As I grows from 100 to 200, S grows only from 2 to 2.3. Once again, the correspondence between physical stimuli and psychological reactions is not one-to-one. Incidentally, Fechner's law is reasonably accurate in many situations, but—like Weber's law, on which it is based—it is inaccurate in others.

STEVENS'S POWER LAW Research by S. S. Stevens (1962, 1986) provides an alternative view of the relationship between stimulus intensity and psychological reaction. In general, psychophysicists find Stevens's power law more accurate than Fechner's law. According to *Stevens's power law*,

$$S = kI^n$$

Verbally, Stevens's power law says that the magnitude of the sensation (*S*) is equal to a constant (*k*) multiplied by the intensity (*I*) of the stimulus, which has been raised to the nth power.[4]

The size of the exponent has a major effect on the nature of the relationship between the intensity of the stimulus and the magnitude of the psychological reaction. If the exponent is exactly 1, a linear (straight-line) relationship exists between the intensity of the stimulus and the magnitude of the psychological reaction. The graph of this relationship is a straight line, such that an increase in the intensity of

---

[4]As you may remember, the power to which a number is raised indicates the number of times that a number should be multiplied by itself. For example, 10^3 equals $10 \times 10 \times 10$. Furthermore, powers less than 1 involve taking the root of the number. For example, $9^{.5}$ or $9^{1/2}$ means that you must take the square root of 9, which is 3.

the stimulus is accompanied by a regular and consistent increase in the magnitude of the psychological reaction. When the exponent is greater than 1, increases in the intensity of the stimulus lead to increasingly larger psychological reactions; the graph of this relationship curves upward. The steepness of the curve is determined by the size of the exponent. Finally, if the exponent is less than 1, increases in the intensity of the stimulus are accompanied by increasingly smaller psychological reactions. In fact, with exponents less than 1, the power law relationship is very similar in shape to the relationship depicted by Fechner's law.

Figure 2.11 illustrates three curves, one for each kind of relationship. Notice that when people are making judgments about the apparent length of a line, the correspondence is generally one-to-one—as the magnitude of the line grows, so does an observer's impression of length. When people are supplying their responses to electric shock, with each modest increase in stimulus magnitude, they perceive that the magnitude of the shock is growing rapidly. With a fairly small increase in the physical intensity of electric shock, people judge the increase in intensity to be extremely large. For brightness, though, beyond the lowest magnitudes, the experimenter must increase the stimulus by tremendous proportions before the observer shows even a modest increase in psychological reaction.

Electric shock has a large exponent, although it may not actually be as large as 3.5 (Baird, 1997), and brightness has a small exponent. Researchers studying other physical dimensions have found power function exponents that typically fall between these two extremes. However, the value of the exponent is influenced by a number of methodological factors. Therefore, it provides only a rough estimate of the relationship between a physical stimulus magnitude and the psychological response it elicits.

A technique that Stevens frequently used to obtain judgments is called magnitude estimation. In the ***magnitude estimation*** technique, the observers are asked simply to give numbers to match (estimate) their impression of psychological magnitude. People

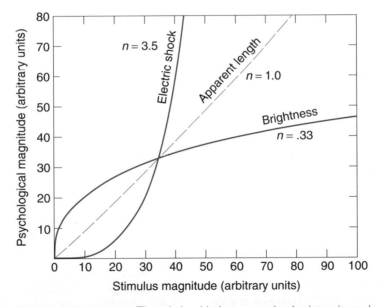

▶**FIGURE 2.11**   The relationship between stimulus intensity and magnitude of psychological response based on Stevens's power law ($S = kI^n$ where n is the value of the exponent). When n is 1, a linear relationship exists (apparent length). When the exponent is greater than 1, the psychological reaction is increasing more rapidly than the stimulus magnitude (electric shock). If the exponent is less than 1, the psychological response is increasing less rapidly than the stimulus magnitude (brightness) (From Stevens, 1961, in Rosenblith, 1961)

are remarkably adept at making such judgments. Usually, only a small number of observations are taken from each observer, and the data of a number of different observers are averaged. www Demonstration 2.5 will give you a feeling for the experience of a participant in a magnitude estimation study.

Stevens also used a *cross-modality matching* procedure. In this method, observers are asked to judge one stimulus modality (loudness of a sound) by using another modality (brightness of a light). At first, this method seems somewhat bizarre ("You want me to turn up this light so it is as bright as the sound is loud?"). Again, however, people take naturally to such an experimental task. Try it yourself. First turn the volume on your radio to a normal listening level. Next, tune your radio to a position that is between stations. The noise you hear is similar to the white noise often used in psychophysical experiments. Now draw a line so that your impression of the length of the line matches your impression of the loudness of the noise. Then adjust the volume to other positions and drawing new lines to represent these different loudness levels. Although you might not feel confident in your judgments, there will be a reasonably consistent relationship between the lengths of the lines you have drawn and the loudness levels to which they were matched.

When the method of cross-modality matching is used, observers are actually telling the researcher about their perception of two modalities simultaneously. In other words, you were setting the sensation magnitude *(S)* for loudness equal to the *S* for line length, which equates two power functions (Gescheider, 1997). In fact, the cross-modality matching relationship is readily described by a power function, and the exponent of this function is a ratio of the exponents of the two modalities. Although the power function is only an approximation of the relationship between the physical stimulus and perception, its common occurrence indicates that it is a reasonable approximation (Krueger, 1991; Schiffman, 2003).

In this section, we have examined the relationship between the intensity of physical stimuli and the magnitude of psychological reactions. If we assume that our perceptual systems map intensity onto the *same* psychological dimension of magnitude, then the characteristic power function exponents make sense (Baird, 1997; Teghtsoonian, 1973). As we will see in later chapters, people can perceive a tremendous range of loudness and brightness. To map these

ranges onto a common magnitude dimension, our system would need to compress the range (yielding exponents less than 1). However, we can undergo only a modest range of electric shock intensity before doing harm to our bodies. To map this rather small range of stimulation onto a common magnitude dimension, our system would need to expand the range (yielding an exponent greater than 1). As you read the next chapter, keep in mind the small exponent for perceived brightness as you consider the wide range of light energy to which you are sensitive.

★ Review for Quizzes/Tests

Section Summary

Measuring Responses to More Intense Stimuli

1. Discrimination studies examine how much to change a stimulus in order for it to be perceived as just noticeably different.

2. Discrimination studies ask people to compare a standard stimulus with a comparison stimulus. These studies typically calculate the just noticeable difference.

3. In the method of limits for measuring discrimination, the comparison stimulus is systematically increased or decreased.

4. In the method of adjustment for measuring discrimination, the observer adjusts the comparison stimulus.

5. In the method of constant stimuli for measuring discrimination, comparison stimuli are presented in random order.

6. Three researchers—Weber, Fechner, and Stevens—have been primarily responsible for formulating equations to describe the relationship between physical stimuli and psychological reactions.

7. Ernst Weber found that observers require larger changes in the stimulus to notice a difference when they are discriminating between intense, rather than weak, stimuli.

8. Gustav Fechner proposed that, as stimulus intensity increases, the magnitude of the psychological response increases, but not as dramatically. Fechner's law states that the magnitude of the psychological response is

related to the logarithm of the intensity of the physical stimulus.

9. Using magnitude estimation and cross-modality matching techniques, S. S. Stevens proposed that the magnitude of the psychological response is related to the intensity of the stimulus, raised to a certain power, *n*. In general, Stevens's predictions are more accurate than Fechner's.

Measuring Brain Activity Due to Perceptual Stimuli

All of the methods we've discussed so far have been used for many decades to measure responses to perceptual stimuli. However, they all require an overt response from the observer. That response is assumed to be a reliable report of some inner state (a perceptual experience) as illustrated in Figure 2.1. For a variety of reasons, many researchers are interested in studying perceptual experience without relying on such responses.

As you'll see throughout this text, researchers have employed a number of different approaches to studying the impact of perceptual stimuli on brain activity. We will briefly review some of these approaches here. In later chapters we'll say a bit more about them in the context of specific research. We'll first focus on a method for studying the function of individual neurons and then move on to methods that look at the activity of groups of neurons.

Studying Individual Neurons

Suppose that you wanted to measure the activity of each neuron in the brain. With over 100 billion neurons in the human brain, you'd be facing a daunting challenge. Even if you restricted your research to a particular area of the brain (e.g., visual cortex), you'd still be quite busy for a long time. Nonetheless, many researchers take this approach to studying perception.

In a text devoted to perception, we cannot hope to fully describe neural functioning. Pinel (2006), for example, has written an introductory text that describes neural functioning more completely. From a very simplistic perspective, however, we can describe neural activity as a rate of firing. Neurons are typically at a negative resting state (–70 millivolts).

When stimulated, they generate an ***action potential***—changing from a negative to a positive state (+40 millivolts) and then returning to the negative state. Neurons fire (i.e., generate action potentials) all the time, regardless of input. However, with some types of input, neurons fire more rapidly (excitation). With other types of input, neurons fire less rapidly (inhibition). Researchers study the stimuli that cause neurons to change their rate of firing (either an increase or decrease).

As you'll see in the next chapter, David Hubel and Torsten Wiesel (2005) are prominent researchers who made great use of a technique called single-cell recording. ***Single-cell recording*** is a technique in which an extremely small ***microelectrode*** (about 0.01 mm in diameter) is used to measure the activity of a single neuron. This technique involves inserting the microelectrode into the brain of a living organism, so its use is restricted to nonhuman animals. Researchers study a variety of different animals, including primates such as the macaque monkey.

In a typical study, researchers immobilize the animal and then insert the microelectrode into an area of its brain. (They later learn about the exact placement of the microelectrode by studying brain slices obtained postmortem.) Researchers then present stimuli of interest (e.g., visual, auditory, and tactile stimuli). The process is quite painstaking, because many of the stimuli will elicit no response. The patient researcher will eventually be rewarded with a change in firing rate. Such a change in firing rate clearly indicates that the neuron is connected to a receptor that encodes some aspect of the stimulus. In future chapters, you'll learn details about how single-cell recording has been used to study particular sensory systems.

Studying Massed Brain Activity

Rather than focusing on the activity of an individual neuron, some researchers study the combined activity of many neurons. These researchers take a number of different approaches, but their methods are noninvasive, so they can be used with humans.

Some approaches focus on the summed electrical activity of the neurons. For example, some researchers use ***electroencephalography (EEG)*** to study the massed activity of many neurons by attaching electrodes to the scalp. EEG data are waves, often with a distinctive pattern. Thus, this method is similar to single-cell recording in that researchers present stimuli and look for changes in the wave pattern. Of course, the waves are quite different, because the waves seen in EEG are not individual action potentials. The big difference, however, is that one cannot attribute the wave to a specific neuron, nor to a particular location in the brain. Researchers use other methods when they are interested in locating the specific area of brain activity.

Throughout this book, you'll read about a number of newer methods that enable researchers to map the brain's activity. As is often the case, advances in technology led to these methodological advances. In spite of their great promise, some researchers question interpretations of results from these methods (Schermer, 2008; Weisberg et al., 2008).

Two approaches to brain mapping that will appear throughout the text are positron emission tomography and functional magnetic resonance imaging. *Positron emission tomography (PET) involves injecting a radioactive chemical into the bloodstream.* Once that chemical is in the brain, a computer-generated image illustrates brain activity. Thus, researchers can present varying stimuli and watch changes in brain activity that follow. *Functional magnetic resonance imaging (fMRI) has become quite prevalent in perceptual research.* Although it is a noninvasive technique, generating the necessary magnetic field requires a participant to remain quite still within a noisy tube.

One of the major advantages of fMRI is the relative precision of its maps (accurate to within a few millimeters). As with PET scans, researchers present stimuli and observe changes in the activity of the participant's brain. With such methods, of course, we're able to learn about many areas of the brain that might be involved in processing a particular stimulus.

#Review Quizzes/ Tests

Section Summary

Measuring Brain Activity Due to Perceptual Stimuli

1. Changes in the rate at which neurons generate action potentials (excitation or inhibition) are crucial neural signals. Researchers use single-cell recording to study the activity of individual neurons.

2. Electroencephalography (EEG) allows a researcher to study the massed activity of many neurons. However, it's difficult to determine the specific location of the activity.

3. Two noninvasive methods for mapping brain activity are positron emission tomography (PET) and functional magnetic resonance imaging (fMRI).

Review Questions → *TEST REVIEW!*

1. Describe how psychophysics might be relevant if you wanted to examine low-intensity stimuli in each of the following areas: vision, hearing, touch, pain, smell, and taste. In each case, briefly describe how you would use the method of limits (or an appropriate modification), the method of adjustment, and the method of constant stimuli to measure a detection threshold.

2. Why do we need both ascending trials and descending trials in the method of limits? Why don't we need to worry about the two kinds of trials in the method of constant stimuli? Similarly, why do we need to vary the stimulus

with which we begin using the methods of limits, and why is this precaution unnecessary when using the method of constant stimuli?

3. Describe the advantages and disadvantages of each of the three classical psychophysics methods, illustrating each method with an example from vision.

4. Suppose you are standing near an electric coffee urn, waiting for the red light to turn on to indicate that the coffee is ready. Apply signal detection theory to the situation, describing aspects of sensitivity and criterion. Now describe the four possible outcomes in this situation with

respect to the occurrence of the signal and your response.

5. The following questions apply to ROC curves:

   a. If d' is large, is the probability of a hit larger or smaller than if d' is small?

   b. What does d' measure?

   c. Suppose that Tuan has a d' of 0.5 and Ramón has a d' of 1.5. If they have the same hit rate, which of them has the higher false alarm rate?

   d. How is a particular point on an ROC curve related to the location of the criterion line in the probability distributions in Figure 2.5?

6. Why might signal detection theory be useful for research on eyewitness testimony? What would be the likely effect on d' of creating a lineup of people who were very similar in appearance? Suppose that the typical d' for eyewitness identification is 1.0. What would be the impact on hits and false alarms if you set a very conservative criterion?

7. Describe how you could use each of the three classical psychophysics methods to measure color discrimination. Then discuss how psychophysics might be relevant if you wanted to examine high-intensity stimuli in each of the areas mentioned in Question 1 (in addition color discrimination). Mention both discrimination studies and studies concerning the relationship between physical stimuli and psychological responses.

8. Which is heavier, a pound of iron or a pound of feathers? Younger children might pause before answering, and might even answer incorrectly. Why? They are probably thinking which would *feel* heavier, rather than which would *be* heavier. How would you determine the Weber fraction for the weight of iron and for feathers? What would it mean if they were different?

9. The section on the relationship between physical stimuli and psychological reactions ended with a statement that a change in the physical stimulus is typically translated into either a magnified or a diminished change in the psychological reaction. Discuss this statement with reference to Fechner and Stevens.

10. If you wanted to learn about perception in humans, what role might the psychophysical methods play? What role might physiological methods (e.g., EEG, fMRI) play? Do you think that it is essential to fully understand brain function to develop an adequate theory of perception? Why or why not?

Key Terms → Study Vocab!

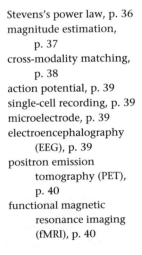

Recommended Readings

Baird, J. C. (1997). *Sensation and judgment: Complementarity theory of psychophysics*. Mahwah, NJ: Erlbaum.

Baird has made many important contributions to the field of psychophysics. In this volume, he summarizes and integrates research in a number of different areas, providing a nice snapshot of the field.

Gescheider, G. A. (1997). *Psychophysics: The fundamentals* (3rd ed.). Mahwah, NJ: Erlbaum.

Although intended for an advanced-level course, this textbook is generally clear. A positive feature is that each chapter is accompanied by psychophysics problems to be solved by the student; the answers are in the back of the book.

Macmillan, N. A., & Creelman, C. D. (2005). *Detection theory: A user's guide* (2nd ed.). Mahwah, NJ: Erlbaum.

Although we've provided a brief introduction to the topic of signal detection theory, you would really benefit from working through this book if you want to become proficient in the use of the theory. Macmillan and Creelman do a good job of covering a range of applications of signal detection theory, offering the reader a number of exercises to insure mastery of the material.

Stevens, S. S. (1986). *Psychophysics: Introduction to its perceptual, neural, and social prospects*. New Brunswick: Transaction.

Published after Stevens's death, this book is a readable summary of his theories and research. However, other books provide better coverage of additional topics, such as signal detection theory.

The Visual System

THE VISUAL SYSTEM is comprised of the eyes and many areas of the brain that are important for processing visual information. This system enables us to make use of some of the electromagnetic energy in the world around us by converting it into neural energy. *Transduction* is the process of converting one form of energy into another, so all the senses serve as transducers. After describing the electromagnetic energy of the visual stimulus, we will focus on the eye, which contains a structure where the transduction takes place. We will then describe how the resulting neural energy is processed in various areas of the brain.

Visual Stimulus

We would not be able to see the world around us without light—but what is light? You may be aware of the controversy about whether light is a particle (a photon) or a wave, but for our purposes we will consider light a kind of electromagnetic radiation. *Electromagnetic radiation* refers to all forms of waves produced by electrically charged particles. As Figure 3.1 illustrates, the visible light that humans see occu-

pies only a small portion of the electromagnetic radiation spectrum. Some of the light that reaches our eyes comes directly from a light source, such as the sun, a lightbulb, a computer screen, or a candle. Such light sources typically emit radiation over a wide portion of the spectrum. Other light reaches our eyes indirectly, after light from a source is reflected off a surface, such as paper, fabric, or skin. Such surfaces tend to reflect selected portions of the spectrum, while absorbing others, a topic that we will explore in the chapter on color perception (Chapter 7).

We can describe light in terms of its *wavelength*, which is the distance the light travels during one cycle. In Figure 3.2, you can see that the wavelength is the distance between two peaks of the wave. The light wave in Figure 3.2a has a longer wavelength than the one in Figure 3.2b.

Wavelength is typically measured in nanometers. A *nanometer* (nm) equals 1 billionth of a meter (10^{-9} m). The shortest wavelengths that we can see are represented by violet, which has a wavelength of about 400 nm. The longest wavelengths are represented by red, which has a wavelength of about 700 nm. Color Plate 1, inside the front cover of this book, illustrates the spectrum between violet and red. In summary, then, *light* is the portion of the electromag-

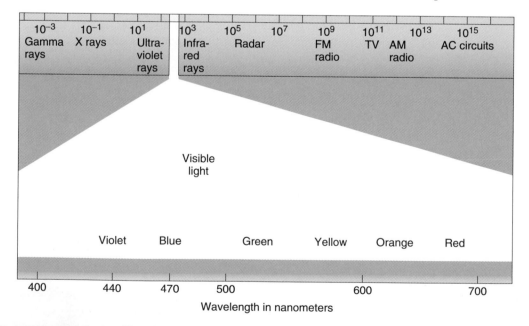

▶**FIGURE 3.1**   The electromagnetic radiation spectrum, a continuum of all forms of waves produced by electrically charged particles. Notice the tiny area between 400 and 700 nm (expanded in the lower part of the figure and also seen in Color Plate 2 inside the front of this text). This is the visible light spectrum, the only part that humans can see.

a. Example of long wavelength

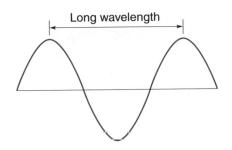

b. Example of short wavelength

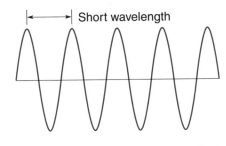

▶ **FIGURE 3.2** Examples of light waves varying in wavelength. *Wavelength* refers to the distance a wave travels during one cycle (of the distance between two peaks).

netic radiation spectrum made up of waves that range from about 400 to about 700 nm.

Although humans are sensitive to this range, other organisms can perceive longer and shorter wavelengths. For example, pit vipers (e.g., rattlesnakes) and boa constrictors have sensory organs that are sensitive to infrared rays, which have longer wavelengths. These animals can form surprisingly detailed heat-sensitive images of their potential prey (Ebert & Westhoff, 2006; Schwarzschild, 2006). Other animals (e.g., some ants, bats, bees, birds, and rodents) are sensitive to ultraviolet rays, whose wavelengths are too short for humans to see (Winter et al., 2003). Thus, even though female birds of some species look drab and indistinguishable to humans, they probably look quite different to the male birds of that species (Goldsmith, 2006).

So far we have focused on the length of light waves. As we will discuss further in the chapter on color vision (Chapter 7), the length of light waves is related to the hue of a visual stimulus. *Hue* refers to the observer's psychological reaction of color pro-

duced, in part, by the wavelengths in the light. Light waves have two other important characteristics, purity and amplitude. *Purity* refers to the extent that the light is composed of a single wavelength versus a mixture of wavelengths. It is related to the perceived saturation of a visual stimulus—for example, a bright red versus a dull, muddy red. Finally, *amplitude*, the height of the light wave, is related to the brightness of a visual stimulus. Figure 3.3 shows how light waves can differ in the height of their peaks. The wave in Figure 3.3*a* has greater amplitude than that in Figure 3.3*b*; its peaks are higher. Light waves that have greater amplitude are typically perceived as brighter.

You may have noticed that we mentioned three *pairs* of attributes: (1) wavelength and hue, (2) purity and saturation, and (3) amplitude and brightness. The first member of each pair describes a characteristic of the physical stimulus, whereas the second member describes a related perceptual experience, a psychological reaction. Keep in mind that the relationship is not fixed. For example, under certain conditions the same wavelength may be perceived as different hues. Under other conditions, different wavelengths may be perceived as the same hue.

a. Example of a bright-looking light, with light waves of a greater amplitude

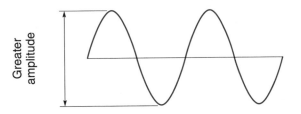

b. Example of a dim-looking light, with light waves of a smaller amplitude

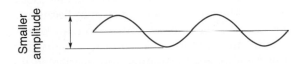

▶ **FIGURE 3.3** Examples of light waves varying in amplitude. You can think of amplitude as the amount of light energy present in the stimulus.

Visual Stimulus

1. Light is part of the electromagnetic spectrum; wavelengths for light (measured in nanometers) range between about 400 nm (typically seen as violet) and 700 nm (typically seen as red). Other organisms are sensitive to different portions of the electromagnetic spectrum, but these wavelengths are either too short or too long for the human visual system.

2. Light can also be described in terms of its purity and its amplitude, as well as its wavelength.

3. Wavelength, purity, and amplitude describe physical stimuli, whereas hue, saturation, and brightness describe perceptions.

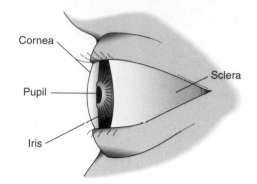

▶ **FIGURE 3.4**   An external view of the eye. The cornea is a clear membrane that bends incoming light rays so that they fall on the photoreceptors at the back of the eyeball. The iris expands and contracts to change the size of the pupil, through which the light passes.

Structure and Function of the Eye

Although the human eye is only about the size of a jumbo olive, it performs impressive tasks. We will now examine the various parts of the eye and the role they play in processing the visual stimulus.

Cornea, Sclera, and Anterior Chamber

The eyeball is a slightly flattened sphere with a diameter of roughly 24 mm. The white external membrane, called the *sclera*, is filled with fluids that serve to maintain the spherical shape of the eye. Muscles that allow us to move our eyes are attached to the exterior of the sclera (Oyster, 1999).

At the front of the eyeball is the *cornea*, a clear membrane that joins with the sclera and bulges out slightly. If you look at someone's eye from the side, you can see both the cornea and the sclera (as illustrated in Figure 3.4). The sclera and cornea are made up of the same collagen fibers, so why do they look so different? The sclera is not transparent because the fibers are thicker and are interwoven to provide strength. In contrast, the cornea is transparent because the fibers are thinner and distributed uniformly (Oyster, 1999).

The incoming light from the visual stimulus must be brought into focus on the retina, which runs along the rear surface of the eyeball. The cornea begins this process; two-thirds or more of the bending of incoming light energy takes place at the cornea.

When the cornea is misshapen, producing an *astigmatism*, a person will experience a blurring of some of the incoming light. An external lens can correct an astigmatism. However, pediatricians have become increasingly sensitive about detecting astigmatisms early. Abnormal neural development can occur due to astigmatism, especially if the problem goes undetected. Although later use of an external corrective lens can address the optical problem, early detection and correction minimize the complications of neural abnormalities (Harvey et al., 2007, 2008).

Other problems with the cornea occur because of its location at the front of the eye. The cornea can be damaged accidentally—through trauma, abrasion, or the introduction of foreign particles into the eye (Asbury & Sanitato, 1992). In addition, many diseases can affect the cornea (Biswell, 2004). If sufficiently damaged, the cornea may be surgically replaced. Unlike many other transplant operations, corneal transplants have a high success rate. Corneas lack blood vessels, which helps make them transparent and also reduces the risk of tissue rejection (Biswell, 2004; Oyster, 1999).

If the cornea lacks blood vessels, how does it receive nourishment? Many parts of the body are nourished by blood vessels—but blood vessels in the cornea would block the incoming light. Instead, the cells in the cornea receive nutrients and oxygen from the *aqueous humor* (humor means fluid), a very clear watery liquid that resembles the cerebrospinal fluid surrounding the brain. Blood plasma is transformed into aqueous humor through several stages of filtration (Oyster, 1999). This fluid flows through the pupil into the *anterior chamber* immediately behind the cornea.

The aqueous humor is continually being recycled, but with a greater rate of replacement during the day. However, the route by which the aqueous humor leaves the anterior chamber can become blocked. This blockage can lead to a buildup of pressure within the eye, which can eventually damage the sensitive nerve cells in the optic disc at the back of the eyeball, a condition referred to as *glaucoma*.

About 3 million Americans have glaucoma, and about 100,000 of them become blind as a result. The disease is stealthy, with early stages characterized by gradual loss of peripheral vision. As a result, without frequent eye exams, people wouldn't even realize that they had the disorder. The best early-detection tests assess elevated levels of pressure using *tonometry* (Chang, 2004; Oyster, 1999). In one such test, the cornea is anesthetized and an instrument presses against the cornea to get a measure of the internal pressure.

If glaucoma is detected in time, the outlook is usually good, because special drugs can be prescribed to reduce the pressure inside the eye (Riordan-Eva, 2004). However, if the increased pressure is not detected in time, surgery is necessary to allow the aqueous humor to drain (Oyster, 1999; Riordan-Eva, 2004).

Iris and Pupil

Most organisms must function under a wide range of lighting conditions. For example, light intensity can be as much as 40 billion times greater during the day than at night (Rodieck, 1998). How does the visual system deal with the wide range of lighting conditions under which it operates? Some of the answer lies in the photoreceptors of the retina, which we will discuss shortly. And some of the answer lies in the iris and pupil.

The *iris* is a ring of pigmented muscles located at the back of the anterior chamber (see Figure 3.5, page 48). The *pupil* is actually just an opening in the middle of the iris through which light information passes. The iris has two kinds of muscles, one to make it *constrict*, or close (making the pupil smaller), and one to make it *dilate*, or open (making the pupil larger).

When the lights are bright, the iris reflexively closes up; when the lights are dim, it opens. Clearly, the dilated pupil is effective for letting in as much light as possible when little light is available. Try www Demonstration 3.1 to illustrate this process.

However, what happens in bright sunlight? Is it possible to have too much of a good thing? Apparently so! You will not see clearly when excess light is scattered through the eyeball. If you've ever been out on a bright beach without sunglasses, you've probably tried squinting or shielding your eyes with your hand so that you can see more clearly. Thus, the eye needs to minimize the amount of light bouncing around in the eyeball.

The opaque sclera helps because it ensures that most light enters only through the transparent cornea. The relative opacity of the iris is also helpful in restricting the incoming light, with darker eye color (e.g., brown) more effective in this regard than lighter eye color (e.g., blue). The distinctive eye color of the iris is due to a combination of pigmentation (melanin), texture, and blood vessels in the outer layer of the iris. Moreover, the back of the eyeball in humans is actually dark, so it serves to absorb some excess light.

You might then reason that the primary advantage of the constricted pupil is to minimize the amount of light entering the eye. However, in bright sunlight the pupil lets in a lot of light, even when fully constricted. Instead, the primary advantage of a small pupil is to take advantage of the bright light to provide an increased distance over which objects will be in sharp focus. If you know something about cameras, you'll recognize this principle as depth of field, which is controlled by the aperture of the camera.

As you know, nocturnal animals, such as the cat, see better than humans in low levels of light. But how does the cat get around so well during daylight hours? Cats and other creatures can limit the amount of bright light that enters their eyes by making their pupil size much smaller than humans. Although not nocturnal, the harbor seal has adapted to searching for food in dark murky water and to caring for its young on the land in bright sunlight (Renouf, 1989). When underwater, the harbor seal's pupil is wide open. When out of the water in bright sunlight, however, the pupil is a narrow vertical slit. In fact, a specific kind of astigmatism—one that aligns with the slit pupil—may well help improve the seal's vision in bright light (Hanke et al., 2006). However, a slit pupil

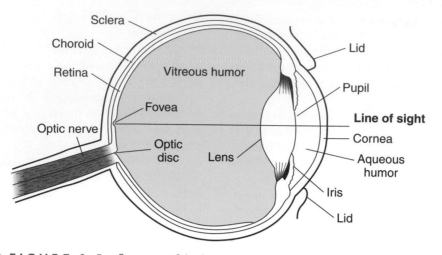

▶**FIGURE 3.5** Structure of the human eye. The cornea and the lens serve to focus the incoming light on the retina, particularly the fovea. As seen in Figure 3.4, the pupil is a hole in the center of the iris, which typically gives people's eyes their distinctive color.

isn't crucial for minimizing pupil size (Land, 2006). Instead, what seems crucial is that the slit pupil allows light to enter across a wider area of the cornea and lens, rather than just the center. As a result, the animal sees more clearly under both dim and bright light conditions.

Why does the pupil look black? Why can't you look into the pupil and see the eye's internal structure? To illustrate the problem, place a small object on a table and then stand a roll of paper towels over the object. Now, try to see the object by looking down through the tube in the middle of the roll. This task is difficult for a couple of reasons. First, most of the light that enters the tube is absorbed. Second, as you peer into the tube, you will be blocking the source of light. On the other hand, if you stand to the side, you cannot see the bottom of the tube. A real Catch-22! A similar problem faces us as we attempt to look into another person's eye.

Ophthalmologists—doctors specializing in eye diseases—and other physicians use a special tool called an **ophthalmoscope** to look inside the eye (Chang, 2004). The ophthalmoscope is equipped with a special mirror and lens so that the light from a person's eye *can* be reflected back to the observer. Instead of the black pupil we ordinarily see, the physician can see structures inside the eye. Actually, you often do see the inside of the eye when you use a flash to take a photograph of a person's face. You can't see details,

but the flash illuminates the blood vessels in the back of the eye, causing red pupils in some photographs.

Lens

The **lens** is a transparent structure located directly behind the pupil. The very core of the lens (nucleus) is formed during gestation, with other layers of the core added later. The nucleus is harder than the outer layers, which contain elongated fibers arranged like the layers of an onion (Oyster, 1999). We noted earlier that the cornea bends light rays as they enter the eye. When functioning properly, the lens completes the task of bringing light waves into focus on the photoreceptors that line the rear of the eye (Harper & Shock, 2004).

In order to see nearby objects clearly, the lens becomes thicker through a process called **accommodation** (Glasser, 2006). Hermann von Helmholtz, a nineteenth-century German physiologist, was the first to describe the mechanism by which it does so. (Remember his name; it will recur throughout this text.)

The **ciliary muscle** surrounds the lens and is attached to it by means of tiny fibers called **zonules** (see Figure 3.6). When you are looking at a distant object (20 feet away or more), the ciliary muscle relaxes, which causes the muscle to expand and pull on the zonules. In this unaccommodated state, the

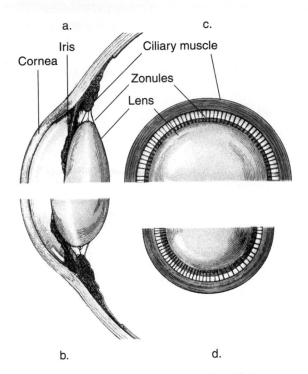

a.

Cornea
Iris

c.

Ciliary muscle

Zonules

Lens

b.   d.

▶ **FIGURE 3.6** Detailed cross-section of the front of the eye, showing changes in lens shape with accommodation. Parts *a* and *b* show the lens from the side, and parts *c* and *d* show the lens from the front. In parts *a* and *c*, the ciliary muscle is relaxed. When the ciliary muscle relaxes, it also expands, pulling on the zonules and flattening the lens (unaccommodated—for viewing distant objects). In parts *b* and *d*, the ciliary muscle is contracted. When contracted, the ciliary muscle does not pull the zonules as much, and the lens becomes thicker (accommodated—for viewing nearby objects). (Adapted from Koretz & Handelman, 1988. Reprinted by permission, Carol Donner.)

lens is pulled out to its flattest shape, so the incoming light is bent the least (see Figure 3.6*a*). When you are looking at an object that is nearer, the ciliary muscle contracts. This contraction relaxes the zonules and causes the lens to become thicker (see Figure 3.6*b*). In this accommodated state, the lens will bend light the most, which is essential for bringing nearby objects into focus (Koretz & Handelman, 1988). Thus, through changes in the shape of the lens, objects can be sharply focused on the retina, regardless of the distance of the objects.

As we grow older, however, the lens loses its ability to accommodate. Around the age of 45, most people find it difficult to focus on nearby objects. This difficulty in accommodation is called *presbyopia*,

caused by the thickening of the lens that happens naturally as we age (Glasser et al., 2001; Kasthurirangan & Glasser, 2006). Because it becomes less elastic, we can no longer accommodate as well. Thus, nearby objects are harder to see, leading people with presbyopia to read by holding a book at arm's length. To correct for this deficit, most people have to wear either reading glasses or bifocals, if their vision needed correction prior to the onset of presbyopia.

It is crucial that the lens be clear so that light can pass through it. A *cataract* is a cloudy lens, which can happen as a result of injury, disease, or ultraviolet light (Harper & Shock, 2004). You really need special equipment to detect a cataract in someone else—unless the disease is fairly advanced. In its advanced stages, the lens will appear to be a milky white color. Luckily, cataracts can be detected with an ophthalmoscope, even in the early stages. Cataracts account for at least half of the blindness in the world (Whitcher, 2004). They are particularly prevalent in elderly people, occurring in more than half of Americans over the age of 65 (Harper & Shock, 2004). When cataracts develop, the clouded lens can be surgically removed. A substitute lens, called an *intraocular lens*, is typically implanted after the surgeon removes the defective lens (Harper & Shock, 2004; Oyster, 1999).

The various structures we have discussed so far, from the cornea through the lens, serve to bring images into focus on the eye's photoreceptors. The actual transduction of light energy takes place in the retina, and we now turn our attention to this crucial component of the visual system.

Retina

The *retina* contains light receptors (or *photoreceptors*), called cones and rods, and different kinds of nerve cells, which we will discuss in greater detail shortly. This extremely important part of the eye is thinner than a page in this book. The retina is comprised of many layers, with the photoreceptors located in a layer near the back of the eye. (Note that, with this arrangement, the light must pass through many layers of the retina before reaching the photoreceptors, but the layers are quite transparent.) The photoreceptors absorb light rays and transduce them into information that can be transmitted by the *neurons*, or nerve cells.

Locate the portion of the retina called the fovea in Figure 3.5. The *fovea* is a region smaller than the period at the end of this sentence. Because the photoreceptors are most densely packed within the fovea, this portion of the retina produces clearest vision. In fact, as you are reading this paragraph, your eyes are jumping along the page to register new words on your fovea. All the words on the page may appear to be clear and readable. However, if you focus on a single word on the page, words more than 3 cm away will be blurry and difficult to read. Those words are reaching areas of the retina outside the fovea, where the vision is substantially less clear. Try www Demonstration 3.2 to illustrate this point.

Humans have a single fovea located in the center of each retina, but we should not assume that this arrangement is common. Many mammals lack foveas entirely, while some birds have two foveas in each eye (Bennett & Théry, 2007; Coimbra et al., 2006).

Figure 3.7 shows a sketch of a cross-section of the retina in the area of the fovea. Notice that the upper layers of cells are much thinner in the central region (fovea). This arrangement allows the incoming light to pass through the layers much more readily to reach the region of the retina so critical for clear vision.

Now return to Figure 3.5 and notice the area of the retina labeled "optic disc." At the *optic disc* the optic nerve leaves the eye. The *optic nerve* is the bundle of neurons that carries information away from the retina. The optic disc has no photoreceptors, so you cannot see anything that falls on this part of the retina. The optic disc therefore creates a *blind spot*.

We will have more to say about the blind spot in Chapter 4. Try www Demonstration 3.3 to illustrate the presence of a blind spot.

Posterior Chamber

The *posterior chamber* lies between the retina and the lens (see Figure 3.5). This compartment contains *vitreous humor*, a jellylike substance that helps maintain the shape of the eyeball and supplies some nutrients to the retina (Oyster, 1999). The pressure from the vitreous humor keeps the eyeball almost spherical, in spite of external pressures. Some solid matter, called *floaters*, may be suspended within the vitreous humor. You may actually be able to see floaters drift across your own eyes, especially as you look at uniform bright white surfaces. Floaters become increasingly common as people age.

Figure 3.5 also shows the choroid, which is on the back of the eye just inside the sclera. The *choroid* is a web of many small arteries and veins behind the retina. The choroid provides nutrients and oxygen for the retina in front of it. In addition, because it is dark in color, the choroid absorbs extra light that the photoreceptors did not absorb. As you may recall, acuity in bright light is improved by eliminating the stray light that would bounce around the interior of the eye. The blood vessels in the choroid cause the red-eye sometimes seen in flash photographs.

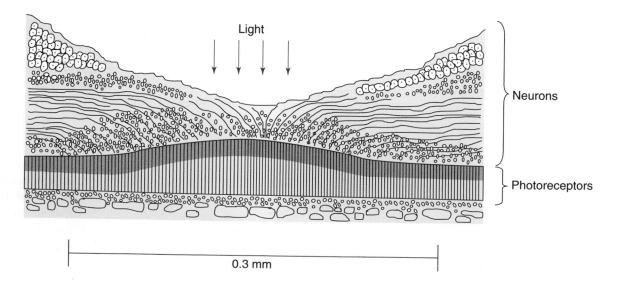

Light

Neurons

Photoreceptors

0.3 mm

▶ **FIGURE 3.7** Cross-section through the fovea. Notice that the layer of neurons is much thinner in the middle of the fovea, facilitating the passage of light rays to the photoreceptors in this region so important for vision.

In nocturnal animals, such as the cat, the choroid is replaced by a reflective surface—the *tapetum*—so that the organism has a greater chance of detecting small amounts of light (Land & Nilsson, 2002). You may have noted that in some flash photographs of cats, their eyes will appear to glow. That glow is actually the flash reflected off the tapetum. As you would imagine, the tapetum actually works against seeing clearly in bright light.

Section Summary

Structure and Function of the Eye

1. Parts of the eye visible from the outside are the sclera, the cornea, the iris, and the pupil.

2. The cornea, a clear membrane in front of the iris, bends light rays to bring them into focus on the retina. A misshapen cornea results in astigmatism.

3. The shape of the lens changes to bring both near and distant objects into better focus through a process called accommodation. A cataract is a cloudy lens.

4. The eye has two chambers, each filled with a different material. The anterior chamber contains aqueous humor, and the posterior chamber contains vitreous humor. Both materials supply nutrients, and the vitreous humor helps maintain the eyeball's shape.

5. The choroid layer contains arteries and veins, and it absorbs extra light.

6. The retina absorbs light rays and changes the electromagnetic information into information that can be transmitted by the neurons. The retina contains the fovea, where vision is sharpest, and the optic disc, where the absence of light receptors creates a blind spot.

Structure and Function of the Retina

Because the retina is extremely important in vision, we will consider the kinds of cells in the retina in some detail. Figure 3.8 (page 52) shows six general kinds of cells. We're going to simplify the reality of

the retina, because over 50 kinds of cells have been identified (Masland, 2001a, 2001b; Rodieck, 1998).

Cones and rods are the two kinds of photoreceptors that transduce the light information into neural information. *Cones* provide our perception of color under well-lit conditions. *Rods* allow us to see under dimly lit conditions, but the same wavelengths that yield color perception in cones yield only black-and-white perception when these wavelengths fall on rods. The information from the cones and rods is transmitted through the other cells toward the visual area of the brain. This information passes through the *bipolar cells* to the next level in the chain, the ganglion cells. *Ganglion cells* take the information from the bipolar cells and bring it toward the brain.

You can think of the chain of interconnections from the photoreceptors to the bipolar cells to the ganglion cells as a vertical chain. However, information also travels horizontally across the retina through horizontal cells and amacrine cells. We will have more to say about these horizontal interconnections later in this chapter and in Chapters 4 and 5. For now, you should understand that various types of *horizontal cells* communicate with bipolar cells and other horizontal cells. Various types of *amacrine cells* communicate with bipolar cells, ganglion cells, and other amacrine cells. Clearly, such horizontal connections serve to process the visual signal as it passes from the photoreceptors to the ganglion cells.

As you peruse Figure 3.8, you'll notice that, as we'd mentioned previously, the light must pass through layers of cells to reach the photoreceptors. Keep in mind, however, that these retinal layers are quite thin and transparent. We will now examine some of these cells in greater detail, beginning with the photoreceptors. Then we will consider several kinds of cells that permit both vertical and lateral communication at the retinal level.

Photoreceptors

The rods and cones transduce light energy by means of chemical substances called *photopigments*. The photopigments are located in the horizontal disc-like structures within the photoreceptors (see the top portions of the photoreceptors in Figure 3.8). Rods and cones contain between about 1,000 and 2,000 of these discs (Fain, 2003). Each disc may contain as many as 3 billion photopigment molecules (Soderquist, 2002).

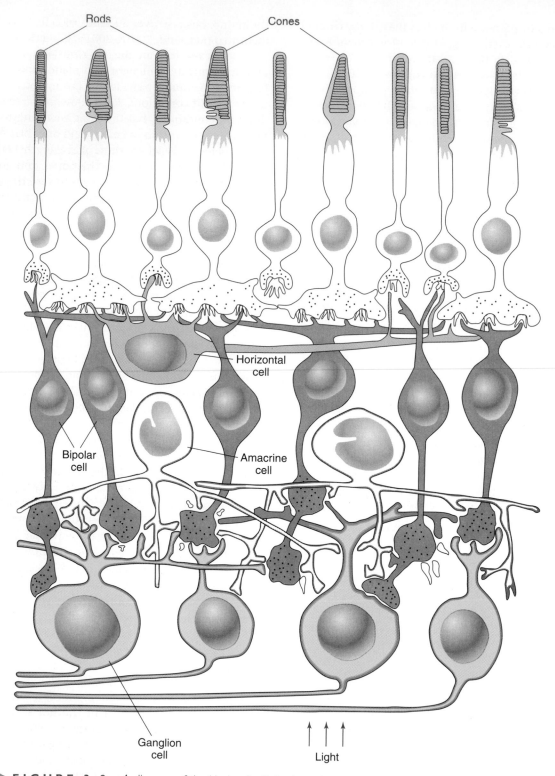

Rods

Cones

Horizontal cell

Bipolar cell

Amacrine cell

Ganglion cell

Light

▶ **FIGURE 3.8** A diagram of the kinds of cells in the retina. Notice the intricate connections among these cells, and that incoming light must pass through the layers of ganglion, bipolar, amacrine, and horizontal cells before reaching the rods and cones. (*Source:* Adapted from J. E. Dowling & B. B. Boycott, "Organization of the Primate Retina: Electron Microscopy," *Proceedings of the Royal Society of London,* Series B, 166, 80–111.)

The photopigments have two components, a large protein called *opsin* and an organic molecule called *retinal* (Oyster, 1999; Soderquist, 2002). The retinal component is the same for all photopigments. Because retinal is derived from vitamin A, depletion of this important vitamin has an adverse effect on vision—especially night vision. Although retinal is found in all photopigments, the exact form of opsin varies from one photopigment to the next. As a result, the photopigments are differentially sensitive to light energy (Cornish et al., 2004).

Although each photopigment absorbs a range of light energy, it absorbs more light in one portion of the electromagnetic spectrum than in any other portion. As seen in Figure 3.9, rods absorb more light in the region of 496 nm. (Keep in mind that this wavelength would typically give rise to a greenish hue when viewed by cones. However, when viewed by rods, it appears to be a shade of gray.) The three photopigments found in the cone systems are each particularly responsive to one wavelength: S-cones with a peak near 420 nm, M-cones with a peak near 530 nm, and L-cones with a peak near 560 nm. (The significance of the three cone photopigments will be apparent when we discuss theories of color perception in Chapter 7.)

Like other higher primates, most humans have four kinds of photopigments, one for rods and three for cones. Some species, such as birds, may have more than three different cone systems (Bennett & Théry, 2007; Goldsmith, 2006). Although very atypical, a small percentage of people have four cone systems (Jameson et al., 2001; J. Neitz et al., 1993; M. Neitz & J. Neitz, 1998). In Chapter 7, we'll discuss another atypical situation: Some humans actually have two cone systems. Other species, such as some nocturnal primates and marine mammals, typically have only two cone systems (Jacobs, 2003). And although it's extremely rare for humans to have no cones and only rods, in some species that is typical (Hirt & Wagner, 2005). Many scientists are working to compile the genetic information that gives rise to the wide variety of opsins that underlie these different cone systems.

How, exactly, do the cones and rods perform their transduction function? How do they convert light energy into a form of energy that can be transmitted through the visual system?

When you are in a completely darkened room, the two components of each photopigment are stable, resulting in a negative resting current (roughly –35 millivolts) called the *dark current* (Fain, 2003). However, when light hits a photopigment molecule, the molecule becomes unstable, and a rapid cascade of changes take place (Frishman, 2001; Rodieck, 1998).

For example, consider *rhodopsin*, which is the photopigment found in rods. The process involved in breaking down rhodopsin and other photopigments has been investigated in great detail (e.g., Palczewski et al., 2006). After light hits rhodopsin, retinal and opsin are separated and retinal is transformed. The process begins with the activation of a G-protein, which initiates several rapid intermediate steps (Oyster, 1999; Rodieck, 1998). ("G-protein" is short for *guanine nucleotide-binding protein*—one of a family of important chemical messengers. G-proteins play a major role in taste and smell perception, so they will reappear in Chapter 13.)

Ultimately, the breakdown of photopigments results in a graded response in the photoreceptor called *hyperpolarization* (Fain, 2003; Frishman, 2001). *Hyperpolarization* is the change in the electrical potential of the photoreceptor from its negative resting state to a more negative state. In other words, the negative sign of the voltage ("polarization") becomes even more negative (*hyper* means "extra"). This change in electrical potential tells the interconnected nerve cells that light energy has struck the photoreceptor. First, light produces hyperpolarization in photoreceptors. Activity in the photoreceptors then produces hyperpolarization in the connected bipolar cells and horizontal cells.

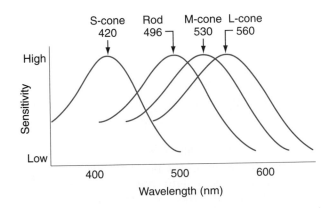

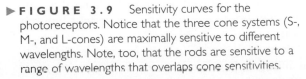

▶ **FIGURE 3.9**   Sensitivity curves for the photoreceptors. Notice that the three cone systems (S-, M-, and L-cones) are maximally sensitive to different wavelengths. Note, too, that the rods are sensitive to a range of wavelengths that overlaps cone sensitivities.

Hyperpolarization is an unusual response to stimulation. Most neurons respond to stimulation by a graded response from a negative state to a more positive state—a process called *depolarization*. However, exposing a photoreceptor to light hyperpolarizes the receptor to a negative potential (–70 millivolts) similar to the resting state of most neurons (Pinel, 2006). So, you could think of the hyperpolarization of photoreceptors as an unusual response, or you could think of the "normal" state of photoreceptors as being bathed in light. When "stimulated" by darkness, the potential of the photoreceptor becomes more positive, as with most neurons.

In order to respond to further stimulation, a photoreceptor must regenerate its photopigments. In rods, for example, vitamin A and other substances work to regenerate rhodopsin from retinal and opsin. Under brightly lit conditions, rods cannot regenerate rhodopsin at a sufficiently rapid rate. Thus, in daylight we are using only our cones to see. The cones also need to regenerate their photopigments. However, cones are able to continue functioning while some of their photopigments are regenerating (up to a rate of a million photons per second). It appears that cones would continue functioning right up to the point that the light was sufficiently bright to burn them (Rodieck, 1998).

Part of the photoreceptor itself also regenerates periodically. Recall the disc-like structures in the outer portions of the photoreceptors illustrated in Figure 3.8. Researchers have discovered that new discs are formed at the base of the stack, and the stack moves away from the base. Early in the morning, the rods cast off a batch of discs at the outer part of the stack, a process known as *disc shedding*. A similar process occurs for cones, except that cones shed their discs in the early evening and may not shed discs on a daily basis (Oyster, 1999). In both cases, the photoreceptor renews itself after the period during which it is likely to have been active.

The Duplex Retina

We've already discussed evidence that rods and cones are quite different. They differ in their photopigments, which has an impact on the wavelength to which they're most sensitive, as well as in their resulting color experience (black and white in rods versus color in cones). They also differ in terms of the timing of their disc shedding. In fact, more than a century ago, the different characteristics of the two kinds of

photoreceptors in humans led researchers to propose *duplex theory* (or *duplicity theory*). We will now examine these two types of photoreceptors in greater detail. Table 3.1 provides an overview of some of the differences we will be discussing.

Shape and distribution differences. As you saw in Figure 3.10, the photoreceptors have different shapes. Cones are typically tapered toward their tips, and rods are relatively blunt-tipped photoreceptors.

In humans, each eye has approximately 100 million rods and "only" about 5 million cones. As you see in Figure 3.11, the cones are most densely concentrated in the center of the retina, near the fovea. The very center of the fovea contains about 7,000 cones and no rods, but there are both cones and rods in the periphery of the fovea (Curcio et al., 1990; Oyster, 1999). In contrast, rods are found nearly everywhere *except* the center of the fovea. The highest concentration of rods is in a circular region with a radius of about 7 mm from the center of the fovea. Notice that the rod density in this region is about the same as the cone density in the fovea. Given that rods are used in poorly lit conditions and that no rods are found in the center of the fovea, then vision may be poor for small objects registered on the fovea at night. Astronomers have learned to use "averted vision," or looking just to the side of the astral object they want to see. You can learn this technique for yourself by trying www Demonstration 3.4.

Not only are the rods distributed differently from the cones, but also the three cone types are differentially distributed. For instance, S-cones are rare, so the M- and L-cones make up the bulk of the cones in the retina, but particularly in the fovea (Rodieck, 1998). Moreover, there are substantial individual differences in the percentage of M- and L-cones in people's foveas. Some people have roughly equal numbers of M- and L-cones, whereas others have substantially more L-cones (Hofer et al., 2005).

Sensitivity and acuity differences. As you may recall from our discussion of the pupil, we live in a world in which the range of light intensities we encounter is huge. Apparently, the two very different types of photoreceptors evolved because people need to survive under both very dim and very bright lighting conditions.

When talking about light energy, *sensitivity* is our ability to detect small amounts of light. Rods are exquisitely sensitive because rhodopsin readily breaks

▶ **TABLE 3.1**   Comparison of Cones and Rods

Characteristic	Cones Photopic (color)	Rods Scotopic (black & white)
Shape	Tapered tip	Blunt tip
Number	5 million	100 million
Distribution	Throughout retina, but concentrated in the fovea	None in the center of the fovea, but concentrated around the fovea
Lighting conditions required for best functioning	Well lit	Dimly lit
Relative number of receptors for each ganglion cell (convergence)	Few	Many
Acuity	Excellent	Poor
Sensitivity	Poor	Excellent
Disc shedding	Evening	Morning
Photopigment	Three types	Rhodopsin
Dark adaptation	Rapid, with high threshold	Slow, with low threshold

down when stimulated by light energy. In fact, researchers have known for many decades that rods are able to respond to a single photon of light (Hecht et al., 1942). Thus, the rods allow us to see in dimly lit conditions. However, the trade-off is that the rods provide us with only black-and-white, or **achromatic**, vision. We call vision that uses rods **scotopic vision**, from the Greek stem *skot*, which means "darkness" and *opia*, which means "eye."

As the light intensity increases (i.e., the rate of photons falling on the retina), the rods become saturated and ineffective. The cones, which produce only a weak response under dim conditions, now come into play. With bright light, cones are particularly

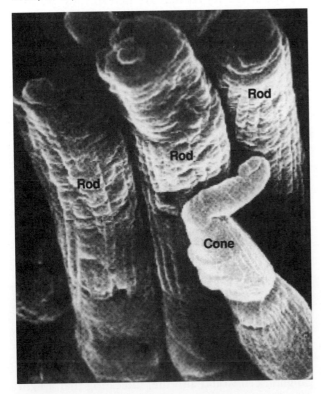

▶ **FIGURE 3.10**   An electron microscopic view of rods and cones. (Photo courtesy of Dr. Frank Werblin)

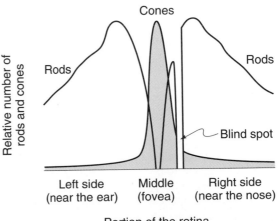

▶ **FIGURE 3.11**   The distribution of rods and cones in the retina of the left eye. Cones are concentrated in the fovea and rods in the area outside the fovea. Notice that no photoreceptors are in the blind spot, which is produced by the optic disc where the optic nerve leaves the eye.

effective—and they allow us to see in color! We call vision that uses cones *photopic vision*, from the Greek stem *phot*, which means "light."

There is a range of light intensity in which both rods and cones may be active. That is, there is just enough light to cause cones to fire, but not so much light as to cause the rods to be completely inactive. Vision that uses both rods and cones is called *mesopic vision*, from the Greek stem *meso*, which means "middle."

Figure 3.12 illustrates the sensitivity differences between rod (scotopic) and cone (photopic) vision. To simplify matters, we'll consider the three types of

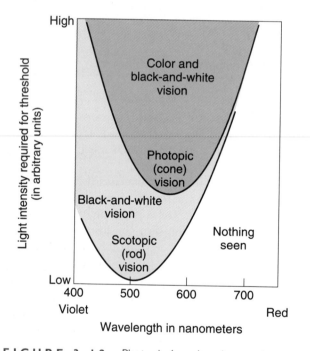

FIGURE 3.12 Photopic (cone) and scotopic (rod) threshold curves. The photopic curve represents the average sensitivity of the three cone systems. Notice that rods are much more sensitive (i.e., have a lower threshold) than cones. In the area above the photopic curve, we can see stimuli as colored as well as black and white. Stimuli that fall between the scotopic and photopic curves can be seen, but would appear to be black, white, or gray (regardless of wavelength). Stimuli below the scotopic curve would not be seen at all. Thus, a stimulus at 600 nm could not be seen until its intensity was increased to the point that it crossed the scotopic line. However, even though a wavelength of 600 nm could produce a sensation of orange, it would appear only as a shade of gray until its intensity was higher than the photopic curve. (Adapted from Chapanis, 1949)

cones together in this figure. Remember, even though the rods are maximally sensitive to a portion of the spectrum that we would ordinarily associate with a color, the rods provide us with only black-and-white vision.

Because a rod produces a stronger response to a dim light stimulus than a cone would, rods are more sensitive than cones. However, the way that these photoreceptors connect to the ganglion cells causes the rods to be even more sensitive. As you know, each eye has roughly 105 million photoreceptors. All of the information from those photoreceptors is transmitted away from the retina through approximately 1 million ganglion cells. As a consequence, there is a funneling of information, with many photoreceptors "sharing" each ganglion cell. As it turns out, however, the sharing is unequal. Greater pooling of information, or *convergence*, is found for rods than cones. A cone in the fovea might connect to a single ganglion cell. Toward the edge of the retina, which is rich with rods, a large number of rods might connect to a single ganglion cell.

Convergence provides greater sensitivity in regions of the retina that are rich in rods, because convergence allows them to pool information. The light energy falling on one specific rod may be insufficient to cause the rod to fire. However, other interconnected rods may fire, with the cumulative effect sufficient to stimulate the ganglion cell to which they are all connected. In contrast, suppose that an equally weak light falls on a cone, which may be the only receptor "assigned" to a particular ganglion cell. This light will probably not be sufficient to stimulate the ganglion cell.

The amount of convergence of information also has an impact on *acuity*, the precision with which you can see fine details. When you want to see fine details of a picture, for example, you would like the information from each receptor on the retina to keep its information separate from the information picked up by neighboring receptors. If you pooled the information from a group of receptors, acuity would be reduced. Suppose, for example, that a design consisting of narrow black-and-white stripes is falling on an area in which 100 receptor cells share a single ganglion cell. As long as the white stripes produced sufficient energy to cause enough rods to fire, the ganglion cell would also fire, indicating that a light stimulus was present. But note that a checkerboard pattern or a square that was half black and half white would also cause the ganglion cell to fire. In other words, the firing of that particular ganglion cell would signal the presence of a stimulus, but would not be particularly helpful in providing details about the stimulus.

So cones and rods differ in their contributions to acuity and sensitivity. Cones provide us with greater acuity and rods provide us with greater sensitivity, partly because of differences in convergence. With greater convergence comes greater sensitivity, but at the expense of acuity. With lesser convergence comes lesser sensitivity, but greater acuity.

Dark-adaptation differences.   Not only are the cones and rods differentially sensitive to light, but they also differ in the speed with which they adapt to changes in illumination. Let's explore how cones and rods differ in their adaptation. In the context of light energy, *adaptation* is a change in sensitivity to a particular light intensity (Lamb, 1990). *Dark adaptation* is an increase in sensitivity as the eyes remain in the dark. *Light adaptation* is a decline in sensitivity as the eyes remain in the light. The two kinds of adaptation can be remembered in terms of the *present* lighting conditions, either dark or light.

Our species evolved in a world in which the transition from light to dark took place slowly. However, as a result of technological innovation, we can greatly speed up the transition from light to dark (or vice versa) at the flick of a switch. If you've gone to a matinee after the movie has already begun, you've probably noticed that dark adaptation is not an instantaneous process. Entering the darkened theater from the bright sunlight leaves you temporarily blinded, and only after you've been in the theater for a while can you determine the wide range of behaviors in which your fellow moviegoers are engaging.

Many laboratory studies have been conducted to investigate dark adaptation. In a typical study, the observer is first exposed to an intense light, called the *adaptation stimulus*, for several minutes. Then the observer is placed in total darkness, and the threshold for detecting a small spot of light is measured; this spot of light is called the *test stimulus*. The threshold may be measured using an ascending series of light intensities, as we discussed in Chapter 2. The experimenter records the intensity at which the observer reports seeing the test stimulus—the threshold. The experimenter then repeatedly measures the threshold after different time periods until the observer experi-

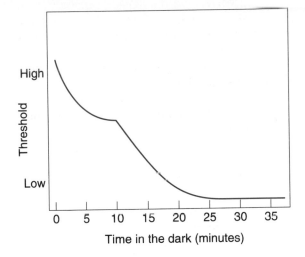

FIGURE 3.13   A dark adaptation curve, showing the relationship between time in the dark and the intensity of light that can be detected (threshold). Keep in mind that a low threshold is indicative of high sensitivity. Notice the kink in the curve at about 10 minutes of dark adaptation, which is clarified in Figure 3.14.

ences complete dark adaptation. The curve shown in Figure 3.13 schematically illustrates the typical adaptation curve for one eye. Try www Demonstration 3.5 to illustrate dark adaptation for yourself.

In Figure 3.13, notice the portion of the curve for a few minutes after the light has been turned off. Note that the light must be relatively intense for a person to detect it. After about 30 minutes, however, dark adaptation is nearly complete; sensitivity is high and threshold is low (i.e., an observer can detect a low-intensity light). In fact, the eye is now about 100,000 times as sensitive as it was in the bright light. A *dark adaptation curve* such as the one in Figure 3.13 shows the relationship between time in the dark and threshold, or the intensity of light that an observer can barely detect.

Why are we talking about dark adaptation in the context of cones and rods? In a typical dark adaptation experiment (Figure 3.13), researchers shine the test stimulus on a part of the retina where it might fall on both cones and rods. Notice the kink in the curve that occurs after about 5 to 10 minutes in the dark. The first part of the curve represents the activity of cones, and the second part represents the activity of rods.

How were researchers able to map the differential dark adaptation of cones and rods? First of all, let's consider the cones. If you wanted to look at the dark adaptation of cones, what could you do? Right, go to the one place on the retina where only cones are found—the very center of the fovea! If you used a really small test stimulus, and ensured that it fell only on the center of the fovea, you would obtain results such as those illustrated in Figure 3.14*a*. Alternatively, you could use a light stimulus (e.g., one near 700 nm) that would excite cones but not rods. Notice that the threshold drops quickly during the first few minutes. Sensitivity levels off at this point, however, and the threshold remains relatively high.

Testing dark adaptation for rods is a bit more difficult. Ideally, you could locate and test a person who has only rods in her or his retina (a ***monochromat***). It is extremely rare for a person to be a monochromat, but that person is truly colorblind! Rather than search for a monochromat, you could minimize the presence of cones by shining the test stimulus only on the periphery of the retina—about 20° out from the fovea—where many rods but few cones are found. In either case, you would obtain a dark adaptation curve similar to the one shown in Figure 3.14*b*. The threshold remains relatively high for about 5 minutes, then decreases sharply, and later levels out at a very low threshold.

Dark adaptation is usually complete after about 30 minutes, but a number of factors influence its rate

(Norton & Corliss, 2002). These factors include the size and shape of the test stimulus and whether it is exposed continuously or in a flashing on-and-off pattern. Other factors include the size of the pupil and the intensity, color, and duration of the adaptation stimulus. For example, an intense adaptation stimulus may prolong the dark adaptation process to 40 minutes (Hood & Finkelstein, 1986; Lamb & Pugh, 2004, 2006).

So the process of dark adaptation actually involves two stages. In the early stage, cones adapt rapidly to the change in lighting conditions. However, because the cones are not as sensitive as rods, we would not be able to detect weak light stimuli. The rods also begin adapting to the change in lighting conditions, but they are slower to adapt than cones. Luckily, they are more sensitive, so we are able to function in relatively low levels of illumination. Remember that rods provide us with noncolored or achromatic vision, rather than color vision. You may have heard the saying, "In the night, all cats are gray." To humans, a marmalade-colored cat indeed looks orange in daylight, when cones can function. At night, after dark adaptation, only the rods are functional, and that cat appears gray.

If you look again at Figure 3.12, you'll notice that the rods are relatively insensitive to long-wavelength

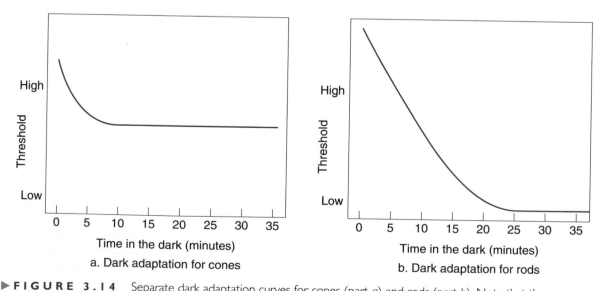

a. Dark adaptation for cones

b. Dark adaptation for rods

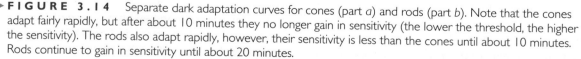

▶**FIGURE 3.14**   Separate dark adaptation curves for cones (part *a*) and rods (part *b*). Note that the cones adapt fairly rapidly, but after about 10 minutes they no longer gain in sensitivity (the lower the threshold, the higher the sensitivity). The rods also adapt rapidly, however, their sensitivity is less than the cones until about 10 minutes. Rods continue to gain in sensitivity until about 20 minutes.

light (the red end of the spectrum). As we mentioned, you could make use of this fact in testing cone dark adaptation. This insensitivity also has very practical implications. If your eyes are dark-adapted and you wish them to remain so, you might turn on a red light. For example, an amateur astronomer could orient herself by looking at a star map under red light. The red light would provide sufficient stimulation for the cones, but it would not affect the rods. Thus, she would maintain her dark adaptation. Then, her rods would be maximally sensitive when looking through her telescope for dim celestial bodies.

How does the eye become more sensitive to light as time passes in darkness? Researchers do not yet know the complete answer to this question. However, let's consider several factors. First of all, as we have mentioned, when you move from an intense light into darkness, your pupil dilates, or widens. When the pupil of the human eye is fully dilated, it is about 16 times larger than when the pupil is at its smallest. The human eye can increase its sensitivity somewhat, then, by letting in more light. (For the sake of comparison, you should notice that a cat's pupil changes much more dramatically. In intense light, the cat's pupils are tiny slits; at night, the cat's pupils are over 100 times larger.) Changes in pupil size increase the eye's sensitivity to light in a limited way. However, the dark-adapted eye is about 100,000 times more sensitive than the light-adapted eye. Pupil dilation is thus only a small part of the story.

A crucial second factor that permits the eyes to be more sensitive in the dark is that dark-adapted eyes have a higher concentration of rhodopsin. As we've mentioned, rhodopsin is broken down in the presence of intense lights. When the lights are turned off, the level of rhodopsin rises again. The concentration of pigment available in the photoreceptor is the major determinant of the level of dark adaptation (Lamb & Pugh, 2006; Pugh, 1988).

The brain also contributes to sensitivity. It is wired to respond to relative lightness—that is, the lightness of one object in comparison to those around it. Therefore, the absolute level of response to a dim stimulus is likely to be less crucial than the relative response. Apparently, the way the brain is wired adds to the sensitivity of the dark-adapted eye. Beyond that, circadian rhythms that arise in the brain or the retina itself may lead some species to become more sensitive to light at night (Barlow, 1990; Barlow & Kaplan, 1993). A *circadian rhythm* (from the Latin

circa meaning "about" and *dies* meaning "day") is roughly a 24-hour cycle of physiological changes that influences many behaviors, including sleeping and eating. Synthesis of the hormone melatonin in the retina exhibits a circadian rhythm and is important in both dark and light adaptation (Tosini, 2000). It may aid dark adaptation by enhancing rod sensitivity (Wiechmann et al., 2003).

Our discussion of dark adaptation has highlighted important differences between cones and rods. Cones adapt more rapidly than rods, but they are ultimately far less sensitive. Rods adapt more slowly than cones, but they provide us with better vision under dimly lit conditions such as those you find in a movie theater. Later, when you leave a matinee on a brightly lit day, you initially find the daylight to be extremely bright. However, through light adaptation, you quickly adapt to the sunlight. We'll now consider this process, which also serves to illustrate differences between cones and rods.

Light adaptation differences.   Dark adaptation takes about 30 minutes. In contrast, light adaptation takes about 1 minute (Hood & Finkelstein, 1986). During light adaptation, the pupils reflexively become smaller, allowing less light to enter the eyes. Shortly after the change from dark to bright light, the rods become bleached (i.e., the rhodopsin is broken down) and no longer function. However, there's now enough light for the cones to become fully functional. Just as the processes underlying dark adaptation are complex, so too are the processes that underlie light adaptation (Shapley et al., 1993).

As we mentioned earlier, we are less sensitive to light when we are light-adapted. However, at the levels of illumination typically present during the day, we do not need to be light sensitive. Instead, we would rather see clearly, and the cones allow us to do so.

Vertical Connections: Bipolar and Ganglion Cells

As you can see in Figure 3.9, photoreceptors pass their information to bipolar cells, which connect to ganglion cells. Our retina contains many different types of bipolar cells and ganglion cells, but we'll focus on just a few of each. In general, keep in mind that, although researchers have identified a wealth of cells, they don't yet know how all of them function. Still, it is reasonable to presume that dramatically different shapes lead to different functions.

Let's first focus on the connections to cones. Each M- and L-cone typically connects to two *midget bipolar cells*. One is an "on" midget bipolar cell, which responds to an increase in photoreceptor activity (i.e., an increase in light). The other is an "off" midget bipolar cell, which responds to a decrease in photoreceptor activity. Clearly, this arrangement indicates that our system is designed to respond to changes in light intensity. Each of these midget bipolar cells typically connects to a *midget ganglion cell*.

The situation is just a bit different for the S-cones. S-cones are connected to "off" midget bipolar cells that are just like the "off" midget bipolar cells that connect to M- and L-cones. However, these S-cones also connect to "on" bipolar cells that have diffuse dendrites, so their connections are more complex. These bipolar cells provide for convergence of information from a number of different S-cones. The bipolar cells pass their information to *small bistratified ganglion cells*. These ganglion cells seem to serve the function of comparing S-cone input with input from M- and L-cones (Rodieck, 1998).

Other convergence of information in the visual system arises with a class of bipolar cells called "diffuse" because they have a tree-like cluster of dendrites connected to many photoreceptors. *Diffuse cone bipolar cells* connect to up to 10 cones, and appear to pass their information along to *parasol ganglion cells*. With their widely spread dendrites, these ganglion cells look a bit like a parasol with the fabric stripped away.

The bipolar cells for rods (*rod bipolar cells*) are also diffuse, with their dendrites making connections with up to 50 rods. These bipolar cells appear to pass their information to amacrine cells, with the information ultimately passed along to the same ganglion cells that receive input from cones (Masland, 2001a; Oyster, 1999). The sharing of such ganglion cells should make sense to you. First, it is more efficient to make use of the ganglion cells for both rods and cones. Second, except under mesopic conditions (when both rods and cones might be active), cones send information to the ganglion cells when the rods are inactive and vice versa.

Some ganglion cells actually contain a photopigment (melanopsin) and serve as photoreceptors themselves (Barinaga, 2002; Berson, 2003; Rollag et al.,

2003; Wong et al., 2005). Apparently, these ganglion cells play an important role in controlling pupil size and circadian rhythm.

When properly stimulated, a ganglion cell generates an action potential. As we noted in Chapter 2, an action potential is a swift change in the potential of a nerve from a negative resting state (usually around −70 millivolts) to a positive state (usually around +40 millivolts). Unlike the hyperpolarization that takes place in the photoreceptors, note that this process is depolarization (a change in polarity). After the cells generate an action potential, they take a break, called a *refractory period*. During this refractory period, the cells return to their resting potential.

In the absence of a visual stimulus, the ganglion cell fires at a relatively low rate, referred to as spontaneous or *maintained activity* (Rodieck, 1998). Some activity occurs in neurons, then, even when the cell is receiving no stimulation. The information from the bipolar cells can result in excitation or inhibition of the ganglion cell. *Excitation* occurs when the incoming information leads to an increased firing rate in the ganglion cell. *Inhibition* occurs when the incoming information leads to a decrease in the firing rate of the ganglion cell.

We provided a brief overview of single-cell recording in Chapter 2. We'll now describe how single-cell recording can be used to study ganglion cells (and most of the neural functioning we are about to discuss). Researchers operate on an experimental animal, such as a monkey or a cat, to place a microelectrode in an exact location in the visual system. To study ganglion cells, for example, the microelectrode can be placed within the optic nerve after it leaves the eye. Small spots of light are then presented on a screen in front of the animal (whose head movements are restrained). The researcher then records the ganglion cell's responses to these stimuli. The portion of the retina that, when stimulated, produces a change in the activity of the ganglion cell is called the ganglion cell's *receptive field*.

What does the receptive field of a ganglion cell look like? In mammals, these receptive fields are roughly circular (Pinel, 2006). They generally come in one of two varieties: (1) on-center, off-surround, or (2) off-center, on-surround. The surrounds of these receptive fields are often referred to as *antagonistic surrounds* because they respond to light in a fashion opposite to (antagonistic to) that of the center. For example, if a ganglion cell has an on-center, off-surround receptive field, shining a light in the center of the receptive field will produce a burst of electrical activity in the ganglion cell. That is, the cell will show activation. However, if light shines in the surrounding, outer portion of its receptive field, the ganglion cell will show inhibition. If no light reaches any portion of the receptive field, the ganglion cell will fire spontaneously at a low rate, as mentioned earlier.

Furthermore, if light shines on the entire receptive field, the activation in the center will be only slightly greater than the inhibition in the surround. The result will be a low rate of firing—only slightly higher than when no light is present. So you see why the size of the light stimulus used is crucial. Too large a stimulus could cover the entire receptive field, and the researcher could easily miss the change in firing rate. Figure 3.15 (page 62) illustrates how an on-center, off-surround ganglion cell would respond in these four situations.

The second type of receptive field responds in exactly the opposite fashion. This receptive field has an off-center and an on-surround arrangement. Ganglion cells with this type of receptive field fire more often if the surround receives light and less often if the center receives light. Spend a moment figuring out how these cells would react to the four stimulus situations illustrated in Figure 3.15 (page 62).

From this brief overview, you might think that using single-cell recording to determine receptive fields is an easy process. We are glossing over several details, which actually make the process fairly arduous. Keep in mind that the microelectrode is recording from a ganglion cell that might be connected to *any* area of the retina. So the researchers must move their stimulus around over the whole field of vision until they find just the right location. Not only is the location crucial, but the size, shape, and direction of movement of the stimulus might also be crucial for some cells. The process is a painstaking one, and discovering the receptive field for a particular cell can take several hours. David Hubel, who is well known for research on the visual system, likens the process to mowing a lawn with nail scissors (Hubel, 1990). (Apparently he has some experience in these matters. Not only has he done an enormous amount of single-cell recording but he also did mow his lawn using scissors when he was a graduate student.)

We will have more to say about bipolar and ganglion cells when we begin to discuss the pathways leading from the retina to the visual cortex. For now, we will turn our attention to the horizontal connections in the retina.

Lateral Connections: Horizontal and Amacrine Cells

As you'll discover, visual input is processed in a very complex fashion within the brain. However, it's also true that a lot of processing takes place within the retina. Much of that processing is due to the lateral connections provided by the horizontal and amacrine cells. Researchers have identified two types of horizontal cells and over 30 types of amacrine cells. However, with so many different types of lateral connections, they do not yet fully understand the exact nature of the processing (Masland, 2001a).

The two types of horizontal cells differ in terms of the types of cells to which they connect (Oyster, 1999; Rodieck, 1998). However, all horizontal cells are crucial for creating the antagonistic surrounds in the receptive fields we discussed earlier. Because they seem to highlight spatial differences in light intensity, they are also essential for producing lateral inhibition, a topic that we will discuss further in the next chapter.

Given the large number of amacrine cells, you should envision that they serve a wide variety of roles in the processing of visual information. In general, amacrine cells receive input from bipolar cells and other amacrine cells while sending input to bipolar cells, other amacrine cells, and ganglion cells (Rodieck, 1998). We'll now look at just a few types of amacrine cells and their functions.

We previously mentioned the fact that rod bipolar cells ultimately pass their information to the same ganglion cells that receive information from cones. In fact, they do so by means of a class of amacrine cells (called AII) that pass the information from rod bipolar cells to cone bipolar cells (Masland, 2001a; Rodieck, 1998).

Researchers have known for a while that some ganglion cells are sensitive to movement of an image on the retina (Masland & Raviola, 2000). Apparently, much of this sensitivity is due to amacrine cells. For instance, the starburst amacrine cell (so named because of its widely branching dendrites) is directionally sensitive, as well as sensitive to changes in light intensity (Masland, 2005).

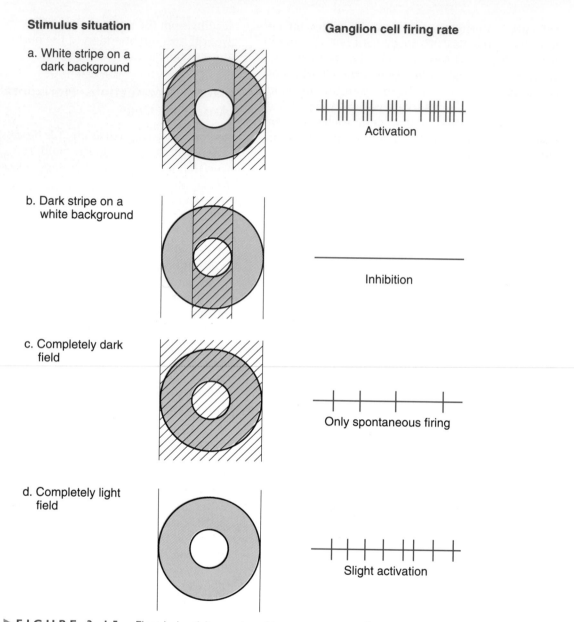

Stimulus situation

Ganglion cell firing rate

a. White stripe on a dark background

Activation

b. Dark stripe on a white background

Inhibition

c. Completely dark field

Only spontaneous firing

d. Completely light field

Slight activation

▶**FIGURE 3.15** Electrical activity produced by an on-center, off-surround ganglion cell in response to four stimulus situations. Stimulation of the receptive field on the retina can lead to excitation of the ganglion cell when the on-center is primarily stimulated (*a*), or inhibition of the ganglion cell when the off-surround is primarily stimulated (*b*). When no light falls on the receptive field (*c*), the ganglion cell fires irregularly (spontaneous firing). When light completely covers the receptive field (*d*), the ganglion cell is slightly activated.

Because our eyes are constantly in motion, it's important to detect movement on the retina that is not due to the global motion of the eye. Another type of amacrine cell, called polyaxonal (because of its numerous widely spread out axons), appears to be essential to making this discrimination in the retina (Ölveczky et al., 2003). When we discuss motion perception in Chapter 8, you'll learn that a lot of motion perception must take place beyond the retina. However, it appears that these polyaxonal amacrine cells play an important role by working to suppress ganglion cell firing that is due to movement of the eye itself.

Amacrine cells seem to play an important role in modulating the activity of ganglion cells. In many cases, these amacrine cells have quite wide fields, with their dendrites and axons covering a relatively wide area. In other cases, amacrine cells have relatively narrow fields. Amacrine cells also differ in terms of the neurotransmitters they release. One of the fertile areas of vision research is in determining how this wide variety of amacrine cells contributes to visual processing.

6. Cones and rods also differ in their reaction to a change from dimly lit to brightly lit conditions (light adaptation). Cones adapt rapidly, allowing us to see clearly. Rods rapidly become bleached and are not functional under brightly lit conditions.

7. Ganglion-cell electrical activity is studied by inserting a microelectrode near a ganglion cell, using single-cell recording techniques. The receptive fields of ganglion cells are either on-center, off-surround or off-center, on-surround.

8. Amacrine cells and horizontal cells provide lateral connections within the retina to influence the activity of the cells providing vertical connections (i.e., the photoreceptors, bipolar cells, and ganglion cells).

Section Summary

Structure and Function of the Retina

1. Cells in the retina include the photoreceptors, bipolar cells, ganglion cells, horizontal cells, and amacrine cells.

2. Light energy breaks down the photopigments found in rods and cones. This process causes the photoreceptor to become hyperpolarized, which is the neural signal that initiates the sensory experience of vision.

3. Cones allow color vision in well-lit, or photopic, conditions. They are located throughout the retina but concentrated in the fovea, where cones typically connect to ganglion cells in a one-to-one fashion. As a result, acuity in cones is excellent but sensitivity is poor.

4. Rods allow black-and-white vision in dimly lit, or scotopic, conditions. Rods are concentrated in the part of the retina outside the fovea, and many rods share each ganglion cell. As a result, acuity in the rod region is poor but sensitivity is excellent.

5. Cones and rods differ in their reaction to a change from brightly lit to dimly lit conditions (dark adaptation). Cones adapt rapidly but are relatively insensitive. Rods adapt more slowly but allow us to see in very dimly lit conditions. The eyes require about 30 minutes to completely adapt to the dark.

Pathways from the Retina to the Visual Cortex

Before exploring the details of the visual processing that takes place in the brain, we'll first lay out a basic map of the primary route we'll explore. Let's begin, however, with a few caveats!

What do you think is the purpose of all the processing of visual information that takes place in the retina and beyond? You may be thinking that the purpose of the visual system is to construct an accurate representation of the outside world somewhere inside your brain—some mega-pixel screen showing the scene you're viewing. One problem with such a perspective is that you then need to posit some entity inside your brain (a homunculus, or "little person") to view the screen. That seems unlikely! Instead, it makes more sense to think of the brain as an information-gathering device that receives its essential information from the senses. Experience interacting with the world allows the brain to construct a "world" based on the information it receives (e.g., Zeki, 2001), which is consistent with Theme 3 of this text.

As complicated as it may seem as you read through the following descriptions, we are actually presenting you with a simplified depiction of visual processing in the brain. As a result, you may be inclined to think of visual processing as a stream of information flowing like a river to the ocean. That is certainly not the case, because many areas of the brain are interconnected with one another in a complex fashion. Thus, the visual information doesn't flow directly from the eye through the brain. Think, instead, of your river branching off, turning upstream and joining a lake and then reconnecting with itself further upstream!

We're simplifying the story in another fashion. Researchers often use species other than humans (e.g., macaque monkeys) to explore visual processing in the brain. More recent work—often using fMRI—has identified human analogs of areas originally studied in other species (Orban et al., 2004; Sereno & Tootell, 2005; Tootell & Hadjikhani, 2001; Van Essen et al., 2001). Thus, when we describe different areas of the brain that process visual information, we're using an amalgam of research on humans and other species.

Even as we focus on one area of the brain or another, we ask that you keep in mind the interconnected nature of brain areas. As you'll soon realize, areas that are not directly responsible for visual information nonetheless play important roles in our visual experience. For example, you would find it difficult to read the emotional expressions on people's faces if your visual system didn't connect to areas of the brain that process emotional information. In essence, we're concerned that you not lose sight of the forest when focusing on a particular tree. We'll discuss a number of different areas of the brain, each of which plays an important role in the processing of visual information. However, if you keep in mind that perceptual experience emerges from the cumulative activity of many brain areas, you'll come to consider the role of each area as a small piece of the beautiful mosaic we call perception.

Information Flow from Retina to Visual Cortex

In our discussion of the retina, you learned that the ganglion cells leave the eye through the optic nerve. The optic nerve is almost as big around as your little finger. Figure 3.16 shows a view looking down on the brain; the optic nerve and other structures in the visual pathway are labeled. As you know, the information traveling along the optic nerve has already undergone extensive processing within the retina. Interconnections between neurons in the retina and elsewhere help in processing information. The processing takes place at a *synapse*, the space between two neurons, over which information is transmitted.

Neurons can be very long, so you shouldn't think of a synapse as a means of keeping neurons short.

In looking at Figure 3.16, keep in mind that the first synapse of the ganglion cells in the optic nerve occurs in either of two structures, each found on both sides of the midbrain: the superior colliculus and the lateral geniculate nucleus. Each *superior colliculus* is located below the thalamus in the mesencephalon. Each *lateral geniculate nucleus (LGN)* is located within the thalamus. Thus, once visual information has left the eye, the first opportunity for further processing occurs in these two locations. The next synapse is found in the back of the cerebral cortex, in an area called the *visual cortex*.

We'll have more to say about these structures as we trace the flow of information from the eye to the visual cortex and beyond.

OPTIC CHIASM   Most of the ganglion cells in the optic nerve terminate in the LGN. However, before they do, half of the ganglion cells cross over to the other side of the brain. In Figure 3.16, notice the *optic chiasm*, where the two optic nerves come together and cross over. The name *optic chiasm* makes sense because *optic* means "having to do with the eye" and *chiasm* (pronounced "kie-as-em") is based on the Greek letter *X (chi)*; the shape of the *X* corresponds to the crossover in the optic chiasm. No synapses are found in the optic chiasm; it is merely the location where the portions of each optic nerve cross over to the other side of the brain.

The ganglion cells from the left half of the left eye do not cross over at the optic chiasm. Instead, they continue back to the left LGN. Likewise, the ganglion cells from the right half of the right eye remain on the right side of the brain. However, the ganglion cells from the right half of the left eye cross over to the right side at the optic chiasm. The ganglion cells from the left half of the right eye cross over to the left side of the brain.

The visual system actually provides two kinds of crossovers. The first occurs before the image is formed on the retina. Suppose you are looking at a series of numbers from 1 to 8. Because of the optics of the eye, the external image is reversed and upside down on the retina, so the numbers are reversed and upside down on the retina in Figure 3.17 (page 66). As you look at the world, something on the left-hand side (*left visual field*) is registered on the *right*-hand side of each retina. In contrast, something on the right-hand

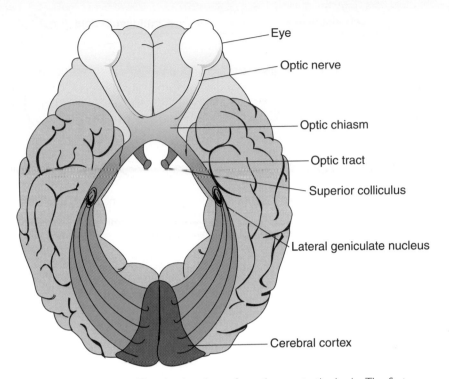

Eye

Optic nerve

Optic chiasm

Optic tract

Superior colliculus

Lateral geniculate nucleus

Cerebral cortex

▶ **F I G U R E 3 . 1 6** The visual pathway from the eye to the brain. The first synapse of the majority of the ganglion cells in the optic nerve is at the lateral geniculate nucleus. The next synapse in the visual pathway occurs in the occipital lobe of the cerebral cortex.

side (***right visual field***) is registered on the *left*-hand side of each retina.

Due to the crossover of cells in the optic nerve, information from the left visual field (the numbers 1, 2, 3, and 4) of both eyes is carried to the LGN and the visual cortex on the right of the brain. Right visual field information (5, 6, 7, and 8) is carried to the left LGN and left visual cortex. Because this is potentially confusing, study Figure 3.17 (page 66) carefully.

Why does this complex crossing pattern exist? As we will see in Chapter 6, small differences in the images formed on the two retinas help humans to see the world as three-dimensional. The crossover that takes place at the optic chiasm brings the crucial information from each retina to the same region of the visual cortex. Look straight ahead and notice some object in the left visual field. Although this object is being registered on both the right and left retinas, information from both sources will end up on the right side of the visual cortex, where the information can be combined.

In Figure 3.16, notice that the bundle of ganglion cells is called the **optic tract** after it crosses the optic chiasm. Groupings of ganglion cells are first called the *optic nerve*. Then, after passing through the optic chiasm, the cells are regrouped and called the *optic tract*. Keep in mind, however, that in the absence of a synapse, the information from the retina remains intact and untransformed. So the change in name reflects the fact that the optic tract contains information from half of each eye. However, those two sources of information are kept separate until later in the visual system. The optic tract fibers travel to two areas. Some of the fibers go to the superior colliculus, but most go to the LGN.

THREE PARALLEL VISUAL PATHWAYS   We're now ready to discuss three important visual pathways through which information flows from the eyes to the LGN and into the visual cortex. The three visual pathways have their origins in the retina, so let's start there.

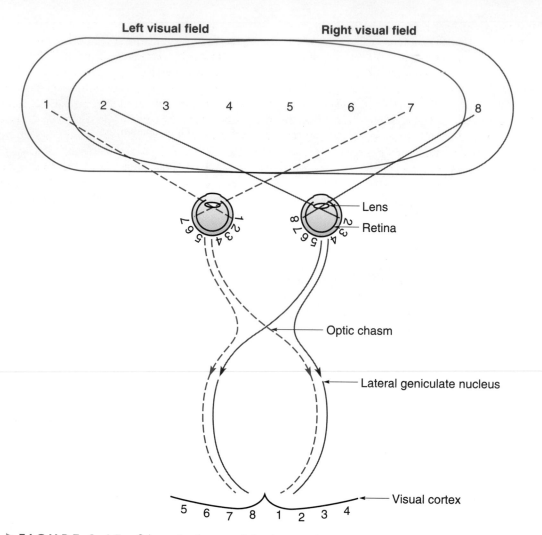

Left visual field   **Right visual field**

1   2   3   4   5   6   7   8

Lens
Retina

Optic chasm

Lateral geniculate nucleus

Visual cortex

5   6   7   8   1   2   3   4

▶**FIGURE 3.17**   Schematic diagram of visual processing, showing two kinds of crossings, one at the retina and the other at the optic chiasm. The optics of the eye cause information from the right visual field to fall on the left side of the retina. The crossings at the optic chiasm ensure that information from the same side of each eye reaches the same brain hemisphere for processing (i.e., information from the left side of each eye goes to the left hemisphere, and likewise with the right).

We'll call the first pathway the **P pathway**, which is a shortened version of *parvocellular pathway* (in Latin *parvus* means "small"). The name derives from the fact that this pathway originates in the midget bipolar and midget ganglion cells that typically receive input from single cones. Because cones are concentrated in the fovea, midget ganglion cells are also concentrated in the fovea. Midget ganglion cells are the most common ganglion cells, representing about 70% of all ganglion cells. When stimulated,

these ganglion cells produce a sustained response, but they are relatively slow to respond to stimulation. Given the input from cones and the midget ganglion cells, you should predict that the P pathway is predominantly responsible for carrying information about the color and detail of stimuli, but this pathway is not particularly sensitive.

We'll call the second pathway the **M pathway**, which is a shortened version of *magnocellular pathway* (in Latin *magnus* means "large"). This pathway begins with diffuse bipolar cells, which feed parasol ganglion cells. Parasol ganglion cells are relatively uncommon, making up about 10% of all ganglion cells. These cells conduct information at a relatively fast rate. The parasol ganglion cells respond with quick bursts of action potentials when they are stimulated. Because they receive input from many photoreceptors, parasol ganglion cells have larger receptive fields and cannot provide us with the level of detail provided by the midget cells. Because the parasol ganglion cells receive input from different types of cones, they are insensitive to color information. Given the convergence that takes place, the parasol ganglion cells are relatively sensitive to light. As a result, the M pathway is involved in the perception of illumination differences and moderate or rapid movement.

We'll call the third pathway the **K pathway**. Input to this pathway comes from the S-cone "on" bipolar cells that feed information to the small bistratified ganglion cells. These ganglion cells serve to compare input to S-cones with input to M- and L-cones (Rodieck, 1998), so they play some role in color perception but are not as sensitive as the midget ganglion cells. Because of the convergence that takes place in these cells, they do not provide the acuity of midget ganglion cells. However, because their convergence is less than parasol ganglion cells, they are not particularly sensitive to light.

Table 3.2 summarizes the characteristics of the ganglion cells and the three pathways. We will now trace these three pathways into the LGN and beyond.

LATERAL GENICULATE NUCLEUS   Jargon shock may have reached an advanced state when you first encountered the term *lateral geniculate nucleus*, but the name makes sense. *Lateral* means "on the side," and one LGN is found on each side of the thalamus. *Geniculate* means "bent like a knee," and this description is also accurate (see Figure 3.18 on page 68). *Nucleus* means "little nut." So a lateral geniculate nucleus looks like a little nut that is bent like a knee, located on the side of the brain.

The ganglion cells of the P, M, and K systems have their first synapse at the LGN. From the LGN, the three pathways continue to the visual cortex. Because the ganglion cells entering the LGN have passed through the optic chiasm, input to the LGN comes from both eyes. However, input from the two eyes is kept separate in the LGN in a layered, or laminated, fashion. Although it's not immediately obvious from Figure 3.18, because only six layers are labeled, there are actually twelve layers to the LGN. Layers 1 and 2 receive M pathway input and Layers 3 through 6 receive P pathway input. Then, below each layer there is a less easily detected layer (like dust on the floor) that receives input from the K pathway,

▶ **T A B L E   3 . 2**   Characteristics of Ganglion Cells That Initiate the three Pathways

	Type of Ganglion Cell		
Characteristic	**Midget**	**Parasol**	**Small Bistratified**
Pathway	P (Parvocellular)	M (Magnocellular)	K (Koniocellular)
Nature of receptive field	Center-surround	Center-surround	Center-surround
Cell body size	Small	Large	Small
Dendrite field size	Small	Large	Large
Percent of ganglion cells	70%	10%	10%
Bipolar cell input	Midget	Diffuse	S-cone "on" bipolar
Speed of conduction	Slow	Fast	Very slow
Sensitivity to details (acuity)	High	Low	Low
Sensitivity to light	Low	High	Low
Sensitivity to wavelength	Yes	No	Yes
LGN connection	Top (dorsal) 4 layers	Bottom (ventral) 2 layers	Sublayers below the 6 P and M layers

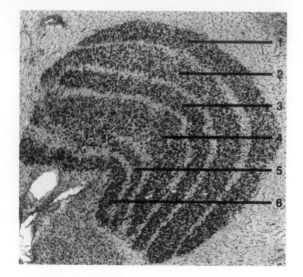

▶**FIGURE 3.18**   The lateral geniculate nucleus. Note the six layers that keep separate the P and M pathways from the two eyes. (Photo courtesy of Dr. Joseph G. Malpeli and Dr. Frank H. Baker)

which is a shortened version of *koniocellular pathway* (in Greek *konio* means "dust"). Layers 1, 4, and 6—as well as the K layers beneath them—receive input from the eye on the opposite side of the head from the LGN. Layers 2, 3, and 5, as well as the K layers beneath them, receive input from the eye on the same side of the head as the LGN.

We've just seen that the P, M, and K pathways are arranged in layers within the LGN. Furthermore, the cells also have a particular order within each layer. The order is called **retinotopic** because the location of cells in the LGN has an approximately maplike correspondence to the location of cells on the retina. Thus, cells near one another in the LGN receive information from photoreceptors near one another on the retina. This retinotopic organization also characterizes the visual cortex.

The LGN cells receive their input from ganglion cells, and so they function much like retinal ganglion cells. In other words, LGN cells have circular receptive fields, with on- or off-centers and antagonistic surrounds (Xu et al., 2002). However, the LGN is not a simple relay station on the way to the visual cortex (Pasternak et al., 2003). Input to the LGN comes not only from the retina but also from other parts of the brain. In fact, up to 90% of the synapses in the LGN are nonretinal (Kaplan et al., 1993). The inputs from other areas of the brain are crucial to the LGN, enabling it to function as a gate or a filter.

Much of the research into the functioning of the M and P pathways came from studies in which lesions were made to layers of the LGN. Unfortunately, many of these studies were done before the K pathway had been identified, so it may well be that the lesions affected the K pathway as well.

The rest of the pathway from the LGN to the visual cortex is relatively straightforward, with no other crossovers or synapses. However, before discussing the visual cortex, we'll briefly turn our attention to the superior colliculus.

SUPERIOR COLLICULUS   Two superior colliculi are found in the visual system, one for each optic tract. Most of the ganglion cells go to the LGN, but a small percentage goes directly to the superior colliculi. The nature of these ganglion cells is not completely known, but they all appear to have large dendritic fields, and some may be from the K pathway (Boothe, 2002; May, 2006).

There are a number of similarities between the superior colliculus and the LGN. For instance, the right visual field information goes to the left superior colliculus and left visual field information goes to the right superior colliculus. The superior colliculus also has multiple layers and its cells exhibit retinotopic organization. However, unlike the LGN, there are connections among the layers within the superior colliculus (May, 2006). Like the LGN, the superior colliculus receives input from the visual cortex, which serves to modulate its activity. The pathway of visual processing continues from the superior colliculus to the K layers of the LGN and through the thalamus to the secondary visual cortex.

As we've just seen, the superior colliculus receives input from the visual ganglion cells and the visual cortex. However, both the auditory system and the skin senses (e.g., touch) also send information to the superior colliculus. This nonvisual information is arranged to coincide spatially with the organization of the visual input. For example, at the beginning of this chapter we discussed infrared-sensitive snakes. As it happens, the information from their infrared-detecting pit goes to the superior colliculus. This information is also arranged to coincide with the visual input. Thus, the superior colliculus works toward integration of information from various senses (Stein & Meredith, 1993), which is consistent with Theme 1 of the text. In addition, the superior colliculus plays some role in controlling eye movements, such as the ones we'll discuss in Chapter 4.

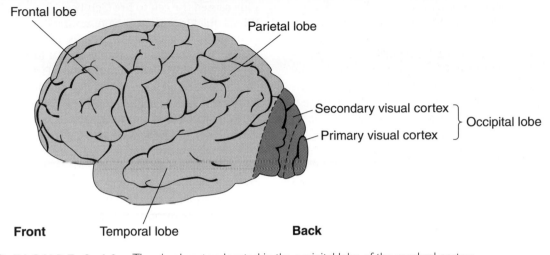

Frontal lobe

Parietal lobe

Secondary visual cortex

Primary visual cortex

Occipital lobe

Front   Temporal lobe   **Back**

▶ **FIGURE 3.19**   The visual cortex, located in the occipital lobe of the cerebral cortex.

Visual Cortex

Figure 3.19 shows a side view of the brain, with areas that are important for visual perception labeled. If you place your hand on the back of your head, just above your neck, the visual cortex will be immediately in front of your hand.

The cerebral cortex consists of many other parts—in addition to the visual cortex—and it is vital for human functions. In animals other than mammals, the cerebral cortex is either extremely tiny or nonexistent. In some primates such as monkeys and chimpanzees, the cerebral cortex is important. However, in humans the cortex is essential.

The entire cerebral cortex is only about 2 mm thick. In other words, the cover on your textbook is thicker than the covering on your brain! This covering is elaborately folded. If we could spread it out, the total area would be about 1,400 cm², about the size of the screen on a 21-inch (53 cm) television. As Hubel and Wiesel (1979) note, the folding probably occurs because this extensive structure has to be packed into a box the size of a human skull.

The visual cortex is subdivided into the primary and secondary visual cortex (see Figure 3.19). Neurons from the lateral geniculate nuclei terminate in the **primary visual cortex** (V1), which is also referred to as **Area 17** of the visual cortex or the **striate cortex**. *Striate* means "striped": a microscopic investigation of

this area of the cortex reveals pale stripes. As early as 1776, Francesco Gennari suggested that anatomical differences in this area of the cortex might lead to differences in function (Glickstein, 1988). The importance of this area for vision was firmly established by the mid-1800s.

As illustrated in Figure 3.21 (page 71), the outer layer next to the skull is layer 1, and the innermost layer is layer 6. (You may also see these layers labeled with Roman numerals I through VI, but the trend seems to be away from such a labeling system.) In this numbering system, the cells from the LGN terminate in the region at the bottom of layer 4, which is called *layer 4C*. All those neuronal messages traced from the photoreceptors in the retina, through the bipolar cells, through the ganglion cells, and through the LGN ultimately pass through layer 4C of the primary visual cortex.

The retinotopic organization of the LGN is maintained in layer 4C of the visual cortex. Do not take this retinotopic arrangement too literally, however. When you look at a picture of the Mona Lisa, for instance, a perfect picture-like representation of her (complete with smile) is *not* found in your visual cortex.

Many factors cause the cortical representation to differ from the original image. For example, about half the neurons in the visual cortex receive information from the fovea, which is an extremely small area of the retina. Thus, a relatively large area of the visual cortex encodes the relatively small part of a picture that is registered on the fovea. The overrepresentation of information from the fovea with respect to the cortex is called **cortical magnification**. Furthermore, your perception of the Mona Lisa is actually a composite of several fixations of your fovea on different parts of the picture. Thus, areas of the brain that store information from each fixation play an important role in your perception.

As was true in the LGN, the inputs from the P, M, and K pathways are kept separate in layer 4C of the cortex. Moreover, the cells in layer 4C have the same kind of center-surround receptive fields as ganglion and LGN cells. Other neurons in the visual cortex have very different receptive fields, as we will explore in the next section.

NEURONS IN THE VISUAL CORTEX   Our understanding of the visual cortex can be attributed to a number of diligent researchers. As we noted, two of the most prominent researchers are David Hubel and Torsten Wiesel (2005). They first began reporting their research in the late 1950s and shared the 1981 Nobel Prize in physiology with Roger Sperry. Hubel and Wiesel initially used the single-cell recording technique to determine the characteristics of cells in the visual cortex. Their findings were particularly exciting to psychologists because they suggested a way in which the visual system could analyze the parts of a pattern.

Hubel and Wiesel (1965, 1979, 2005) isolated two kinds of neurons, each with response patterns different from the center-surround patterns found at earlier stages of visual processing. Their names are impressively straightforward: simple and complex cortical cells.

Simple cells.   **Simple cells** are found in layer 4B of the primary visual cortex, and they receive input from layer 4C neurons directly underneath. Neurons in the earlier stages of visual processing have roughly circular receptive fields, but the simple cells respond most vigorously to lines and to edges (Pinel, 2006). As is often the case in research, this finding was made serendipitously. Hubel and Wiesel were investigating a cell in the striate cortex by presenting all sorts of stimuli that had been found to elicit responses from optic nerve cells in the cat. The striate cortex cell remained unresponsive. Then Hubel and Wiesel inserted a new glass slide into their stimulus-presentation device, and the inadvertently cast shadow of the slide caused the cell to fire (Schiller, 1986). Hubel and Wiesel quickly switched to presenting lines to the cat's visual field and found that cells in layer 4B were extremely responsive to these straight lines.

These cells are fairly selective. First of all, the light must fall on a particular part of the visual field. Diffuse illumination of that area will not work, although the cells might give a sputter of activity to small spots of light. Also, the lines must be in the correct orientation for the cells to respond *enthusiastically*. The most effective line orientation depends on which cell you are examining. Furthermore, these cells are so picky that a change of about 15° may cause them to stop responding. For example, a cell that would respond optimally to the small (hour) hand of a clock that reads 12:00 would stop responding if that hand advanced a mere 15° to its position at 12:30!

Figure 3.20*a* illustrates the electrical activity that might be generated if this cell were to respond to several different orientations of a line. Notice that the cell produces only a low level of spontaneous firing if the line is horizontal. The cell produces somewhat more firing if the line is close to vertical. But a maximum firing rate occurs only when the line is perfectly vertical. These firing rates can be used to construct a graph illustrating the relationship between the angular orientation of the line and the cell's response rate; this graph is known as an **orientation tuning curve**, and it is illustrated in Figure 3.20*b*. Similar tuning curves can be constructed for other cells, and these cells might be optimally responsive to other orientations such as diagonal or horizontal lines.

Complex cells.   **Complex cells** are usually found in layers 2, 3, 5, and 6 of the cortex (but not in layer 4, where simple cells are found). Complex cells respond best to moving stimuli (Pinel, 2006). We saw that simple cells respond best to lines registered in a specific portion of the retina. In contrast, complex cells respond to a larger receptive field. Some complex cells respond with particularly vigorous bursts of electrical activity when a line moves in a particular direction— for example, when a vertical line moves to the left (but not to the right). Other complex cells respond to movement in both directions. Simple cells are monocular, but many complex cells respond to stimulation of either or both eyes. In fact, complex cells that receive input from both eyes contribute to depth perception (Read, 2005).

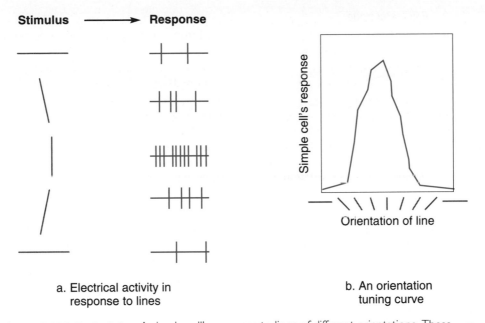

a. Electrical activity in
response to lines

b. An orientation
tuning curve

▶ **FIGURE 3.20**   A simple cell's response to lines of different orientations. These cells are very selective. Notice that maximum firing occurs when the stimulus is vertical and activity drops significantly when the stimulus is rotated just a few degrees (*a*). This selectivity is apparent in the orientation tuning curve shown in part *b*. The peak response of this simple cell occurs when the line is oriented vertically.

Some simple cortical cells and some complex cortical cells are referred to as end-stopped cells. ***End-stopped cells*** will respond most vigorously if the stimulus ends within the cell's receptive field (Frishman, 2001). A line or edge that extends beyond the receptive field of an end-stopped cell would produce less firing. Therefore, these cells are particularly useful for detecting corners and other boundaries.

A consistent trend emerges in moving toward higher levels in the visual processing system; cells become more selective. Photoreceptors respond when the light reaches them. Ganglion cells and LGN cells respond more strongly if stimulation of the center of the receptive field contrasts with the surrounding area. Simple cells require lines or edges, and complex cells require moving lines or edges. End-stopped cells require that the lines end within their receptive fields.

Hubel and Wiesel and their coauthors, as well as other research groups, have conducted more recent research that provides additional details about the structure of the visual cortex. In particular, their explorations have revealed that the primary visual cortex is arranged in a series of columns.

CORTICAL ARCHITECTURE   When Hubel and Wiesel were exploring the properties of individual cells, they became intrigued with a feature that they refer to as "architecture" (Hubel, 1982). When researchers lower a microelectrode through layers of the cortex, they find that all the cells have the highest response rate to a line of one orientation. This vertical series of cells responding to stimuli with a particular orientation is referred to as a ***column*** (Pinel, 2006). Figure 3.21 (page 72) illustrates how inserting a microelectrode perpendicular to the surface of the cortex would pass through a large number of cells. All of these cells might produce the highest response rate when a line was presented in the visual field at a 45° angle. Hubel and Wiesel inserted the microelectrode through the 2-mm thickness of one point in the primary visual cortex. Next, they tested the animal and recorded the orientation the cells in that column preferred. Then they moved on to a new location only a fraction of a millimeter away and tested again.

Hubel and Wiesel discovered that by moving the microelectrode as little as 0.05 mm—literally a

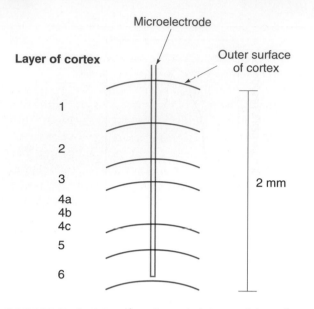

Layer of cortex

Microelectrode

Outer surface
of cortex

1

2

3

4a
4b
4c

5

6

2 mm

▶ **FIGURE 3.21**   If an electrode is inserted through
the visual cortex, all the cells through which it passes
respond maximally to a line of one particular orientation.
This vertical series of cells is called a *column*.

hairbreadth—from its previous location, they found
a column of cells that no longer responded so enthusiastically to a line of the previously tested orientation. Instead, the preferred orientation had shifted
to a line that had rotated by about 10°. For example,
suppose that the cells in the previously tested column had produced the highest response rate to a
line at a 45° angle. Hubel and Wiesel found that the
cells in the column 0.05 mm away would be likely to
produce the highest response rate to a line at a 55°
angle.

Hubel and Wiesel repeatedly moved the microelectrode a distance of 1 mm along the cortex. They
encountered a series of columns in which the preferred stimulus had changed from a perfectly horizontal line to a vertical line and completed the cycle
by returning to a perfectly horizontal line. Figure
3.22 illustrates these results schematically. (Because
layer 4C has cells with center-surround preferences
rather than orientation preferences, that layer shows
a blank space.) Because 18 to 20 adjacent columns
are required to complete a full cycle of stimulus-

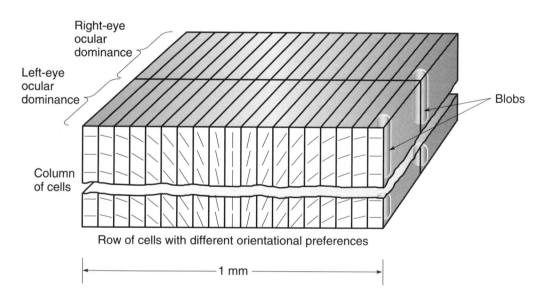

Right-eye
ocular
dominance

Left-eye
ocular
dominance

Column
of cells

Blobs

Row of cells with different orientational preferences

1 mm

▶ **FIGURE 3.22**   Schematic diagram of a hypercolumn. Note that the hypercolumn includes
cells from all layers of the cortex (I through VI), cells with all orientation preferences, and cells with
both right- and left-eye ocular dominance. The break in the middle of the figure indicates layer IVc,
where the cells are not sensitive to orientation. Interspersed within the hypercolumns are blobs,
which convey information about color. As indicated in the figure, any vertical column contains cells
sensitive to only one orientation. However, as you insert the microelectrode at different horizontal
locations, the orientation of the receptive field changes in a systematic fashion.

orientation preferences, Hubel and Wiesel called this sequence of columns a *hypercolumn*.

Notice that Figure 3.22 is a three-dimensional diagram. The third dimension is labeled "right-eye ocular dominance" and "left-eye ocular dominance." Cells in the cortex receive information from both eyes, but they usually have a higher response rate to one eye, a tendency called *ocular dominance*. The clump of cells nearer to the viewer would be more responsive to stimuli from the left eye. The next clump of cells would be more responsive to stimuli from the right eye.

It might be tempting to believe that all the columns are similar, as long as they share a given preference for stimulus orientation and a given ocular dominance. Within each set, however, each column corresponds to a particular location in the visual field. Thus, within every tiny patch in V1 of your visual cortex—a patch no bigger than 1 mm^2 and 2 mm deep—your visual system encodes a variety of stimulus-orientation preferences, two kinds of ocular dominance (right-eye and left-eye), and a variety of locations. We do not yet fully understand the roles played by all these parts of the visual cortex. However, you should be struck by way this exquisite organization supports our visual perception, which is consistent with Themes 1 and 2.

Later research in V1 uncovered patches of neurons that were *not* sensitive to orientation. These neurons, seen in Figure 3.22, were referred to by the delightfully straightforward name "blobs." (Actually, their full name is "cytochrome oxidase blobs," but "blobs" will suffice.) The *blobs* supplement the spatial orientation information found in the hypercolumns by providing color information (Pinel, 2006). Given the color information in blobs, you should realize that the P system provides the input to the blobs, as does the K system (Boothe, 2002).

The blobs within a column are not joined, and the space between blobs is filled with cells called *interblobs*. Interblobs are more like other cells in the column, because they are sensitive to orientation, but not to wavelength. The interblobs also receive their input from the P pathway.

In the end, of course, we perceive a world of colored objects moving in depth. The neurons in V1 clearly play essential roles in providing us with our rich perceptual experience. However, the processing of the visual information acquired in the retina continues beyond V1, and we'll now turn our attention to those areas.

IN-DEPTH

Beyond the Primary Visual Cortex

Early research on cortical processing in vision concentrated on the primary visual cortex (V1). Although many researchers continue to focus on V1, other researchers are exploring the functioning of areas beyond the primary visual cortex. As Figure 3.19 illustrated, other regions at the back of the brain are also concerned with vision. Collectively, these regions are called the *secondary visual cortex* (as opposed to the primary visual cortex) or the *extrastriate cortex* (where *extra-* means "beyond," as in "extraterrestrial"). As you can see in Figure 3.23 (page 74), several visual areas are located in front of the primary visual cortex. Each of these areas plays an important role in visual processing. However, these areas are not the end of the story, because they pass information to other areas of the brain.

As we discuss these areas beyond V1, keep in mind the trend in receptive fields that we've already observed as we moved from ganglion cells to V1. You should expect that the cells in these later areas will best respond to increasingly specific kinds of input. It also makes sense to think of the interconnections of cells in earlier areas of visual processing that give rise to the specificity of the receptive fields found in later areas. Not only do the receptive fields become more specific, but they are also typically increasingly larger (Bullier, 2002).

In all, more than 30 different regions of the brain are involved in processing visual information (Frishman, 2001). A map of all these areas and their interconnections looks a bit like a plate of spaghetti and meatballs (see Van Essen et al., 1992)! In this section of the chapter, we will briefly explore the contributions of some of these areas that extend beyond V1.

In so doing, we will continue to explore the visual pathways that we've been discussing, but par-

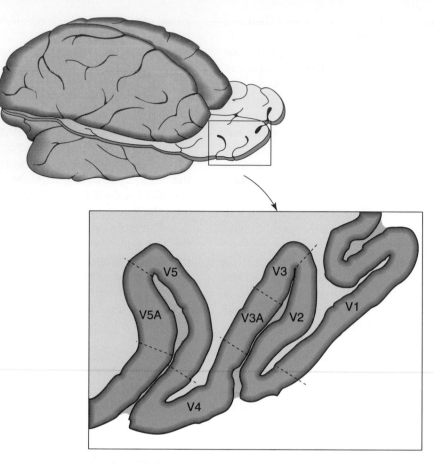

▶ **FIGURE 3.23**   Area V1 (primary visual cortex) and Areas V2 through V5 (secondary visual cortex). (From Zeki, 1993)

ticularly the P and M pathways. We'll have less to say about the K pathway in the visual cortex for a few reasons. One reason is that the research on the K pathway is fairly recent. Another reason is that the K pathway is both complex (with distinct classes of cells) and difficult to isolate and study, with P, M, and K input intermingled in V1 (Sincich & Horton, 2005). For instance, both the P and K pathways send information into the blobs of V1. Nonetheless, there may be parallel pathways of information through the brain, including a distinct K pathway (Hendry & Reid, 2000).

The P pathway feeds into the **What pathway** (the color-and-form pathway). It is also called the *ventral* (lower) pathway because it flows into the lower temporal areas we're about to discuss. The K pathway may also feed into the *What* pathway (Boothe, 2002; Bullier, 2002). As the name implies, this pathway seems to be important for object perception.

Information from the M pathway feeds into the **Where pathway** (the motion pathway). It is also called the *dorsal* (upper) pathway because it flows into the parietal lobe (above the temporal lobe). The cells in the parietal area are directionally sensitive, and they also encode location information (Boothe, 2002; Pasternak et al., 2003).

Because both pathways pass through V2 and V3, we'll first discuss these two areas. As you see in Figure 3.23, V2 is adjacent to V1. Although other areas (e.g., LGN) provide input to V2, most input is from V1. As is true of V1, V2 contains cells that are sensitive to orientation and direction. Moreover, V2 also exhibits retinotopic organization and cortical magnification. Information within V2 appears to be organized in a series of stripes (dark thin and thick stripes as well as pale stripes). Unlike V1, most cells in V2 exhibit binocular disparity, so they must combine input from both eyes (Pasternak et al., 2003).

Area V2 then sends signals back to V1, as well as to V3, V4, and V5.

Area V3 is right next to V2 and receives input directly from V1 as well as V2. Cells in this area are similar to V2 cells in that they are sensitive to both orientation and direction. However, V2 cells seem to be more sensitive to contrast and are often color sensitive (Pasternak et al., 2003). Information flows from V3 into V4 and V5 (as well as other areas of the *Where* pathway). We'll first explore the *Where* pathway and then turn our attention to the *What* pathway.

The *Where* Pathway

Area V5.   Researchers interested in the *Where* pathway have focused much of their attention on Area V5, also called *MT* (middle temporal area). Areas V1, V2, V3, and V4 provide input to V5. Thus, the directionally sensitive complex cells of V1 provide strong direct input to V5. Keep in mind that most information from V2, V3, and V4 originated in V1, but these areas process the information from V1 before it arrives at V5. There is also direct input to V5 from the K pathway (from the LGN) and from information originating in the superior colliculus (Born & Bradley, 2005).

Both the retinotopic organization and the emphasis on foveal information that is found in other areas of the visual cortex are also found in V5. Furthermore, V5 is also organized in columns that are sensitive to direction (rather than sensitive to orientation). Input from both eyes must be available in V5, because many of the cells in this area are sensitive to binocular disparity (Born & Bradley, 2005).

Since V5 was first identified in the early 1970s, researchers have thought that this area played a substantial role in motion perception (e.g., Zeki, 1993). More recent evidence suggests that much of motion perception actually takes place in V1. The role of V5 seems to be to integrate and combine the information coming from V1 about an object's motion. V5 may also help to discriminate object motion from background motion. More recent evidence suggests that V5 plays a role in determining the structure of objects in motion (Born & Bradley, 2005).

Damage to V5 may result in a condition called **akinetopsia**, in which motion perception is disrupted (Zeki, 1993). Researchers have extensively studied a woman known by her initials, L. M., who has this disorder as a result of bilateral damage to V5 (Rizzo et al., 1995; Zihl et al., 1983; Zihl et al., 1991).

Fast-moving targets as well as moving targets seen against visually noisy backgrounds seem to particularly confuse L. M. Her perceptual experience of motion is often described as a series of separate still photos, which makes living in a world of moving objects (such as cars) a real challenge!

Researchers can also temporarily disrupt processing in human brain areas by focusing a powerful magnet on specific brain areas (transcranial magnetic stimulation). Disrupting V5 activity affects motion perception and acting on moving targets (e.g., catching a thrown ball) (Beckers & Homberg, 1992; Schenk et al., 2005). Inducing lesions to V5 in other species also affects aspects of motion perception, including making visual noise more disruptive to motion perception (Pasternak et al., 2003). Thus, the convergence of many types of research makes it clear that V5 plays a vital role in the processing of motion (Grill-Spector & Malach, 2004). We'll explore motion perception in more detail in Chapter 8.

Areas beyond V5.   *Where* pathway information flows from V5 toward a number of different areas of the parietal cortex. On its way, the information flows through Area MST (medial superior temporal), which contains neurons that have very large receptive fields. This area may well be crucial to the perception of **optic flow**, which we can think of as the passing of images over your retina as a result of your movement through the world (Pasternak et al., 2003). Optic flow is crucial to the theories of James J. Gibson, so we'll return to this concept in Chapter 8. Area MST is also involved in eye movements (both voluntary and involuntary).

Other areas in the *Where* pathway are involved in motion perception or the integration of motion information with other perceptual information. We'll return to a discussion of these areas in Chapter 8. For now, however, we'll wander along the *What* pathway for a while.

The *What* Pathway

Area V4.   Just as our discussion of the *Where* pathway focused first on Area V5, here we'll first focus our attention on Area V4. V4 receives input directly from V1, V2 (particularly from the thin and pale stripe areas), and V3. Moreover, as we noted earlier, V4 connects with V5, which provides at least one means of communication between the *Where* and *What* pathways. V4 sends information to the inferotemporal cortex.

The cells in V4 share many properties with V1 neurons. That is, they are sensitive to orientation and motion. However, most neurons in V4 exhibit binocular disparity, which would be useful in identifying three-dimensional objects. Area V4 does appear to play an important role in processing complex shape and texture information (Pasternak et al., 2003). Its role in color perception is more controversial, with some of the controversy centered on the placement of the boundaries of V4 (Grill-Spector & Malach, 2004).

Evidence from people with damage to the V4 area suggests that this area plays a role in color perception. Such damage results in a disorder called ***cerebral achromatopsia*** (Bouvier & Engel, 2006; Heywood & Kentridge, 2003; Zeki, 1993). If the damage is bilateral (affecting both brain hemispheres), people with this disorder experience the world as though they were looking at a black-and-white television! If the damage is unilateral, such people cannot see color in one visual field.

However, the evidence that V4 is *the* color center remains unclear. First of all, when such lesions occur naturally, they are rarely so neatly located, so multiple areas are likely to be affected. Second, it is rare for people to suffer damage solely to their color vision. Thus, other deficits (such as spatial vision) are usually found along with the color deficits. Finally, there are cases in which damage to this area does not result in a total loss of color perception.

In contrast, it is clear that there is a stream of color-coded information that flows in the P pathway from cones to LGN to V1 (e.g., Lennie & Movshon, 2005). That information continues to flow through the *What* pathway, although there may not be a site specific to color perception (Grill-Spector & Malach, 2004). Both color and form information play important roles in our perception of objects, for which other areas of the *What* pathway are particularly responsible.

The inferotemporal cortex.   The ***inferotemporal cortex (IT)*** (or inferior temporal cortex) is located on the lower part (*inferior*) of the side (*temporal*) of the cortex and is considered the end of the *What* pathway. As Figure 3.18 shows, the temporal lobe occupies the lower part of the brain in front of the occipital lobe. IT receives input from V2 and V3 as well as V4. As you should now expect, a number of other areas of the brain also send information to IT, including areas of the *Where* pathway.

In general, given its input, IT shares some similarities with neurons in V1, V2, V3, and V4. Although the receptive fields found in IT are larger, these IT cells respond to the same simple features of stimuli, such as orientation, length, and wavelength. However, what distinguishes this area is that some of these IT cells are sensitive to very complex patterns (Pasternak et al., 2003). Moreover, it appears that learning may well shape the nature of the receptive fields.

Of course, at the very beginning of research in this area, no one had a clue as to the complex nature of these receptive fields. Thompson (1985) provides a particularly vivid account of early research in this area of the cortex. Charles Gross and his colleagues were using the single-cell recording technique to map the receptive field of a cell in the IT. They presented the usual visual stimuli, including spots of light, bars, and other stimuli, to one monkey. The neurons responded weakly to these stimuli, but they did not provide any enthusiastic bursts of electrical activity. The researchers had been studying a particular cell for an extended time, but the response had been so minimal that they decided to move on to another cell.

One whimsical experimenter bade that cell a symbolic farewell by waving goodbye. The cell immediately began to respond rapidly to the moving hand. Serendipity had struck once again! As you can imagine, the researchers did *not* proceed to the next cell. Instead, they began cutting out hand-shaped stimuli and waving them in front of the monkey's eyes. Their inquiry demonstrated that the stimulus that produced the most vigorous response from the cell was an upright hand shaped like a monkey's paw.

Researchers have found that neurons in IT that are sensitive to objects as specific as the body parts discovered by Gross and his colleagues, as well as chairs, buildings, tools, and words (Grill-Spector & Malach, 2004). Moreover, these cells are arranged in a columnar fashion, as seen in Figure 3.24. Many theories of object perception hypothesize that we piece together unique features or components of complex objects in the process of recognizing them. We will discuss object perception in greater detail in Chapter 5.

Such specificity of response led researchers to speculate jokingly about a "grandmother cell." A grandmother cell would be one that responds most rapidly to a *very* specific stimulus—as specific as your grandmother's face (Gross, 2002). Clearly, a number

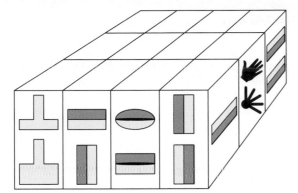

▶ **FIGURE 3.24** Columnar organization found in inferior temporal cortex. Note the features to which cells in the columns are sensitive. (From Stryker 1992)

of different areas of the brain exhibit activity when you see a specific stimulus such as your grandmother. Nonetheless, research indicates that some neurons have very specific receptive fields, and they fire very selectively to a particular object or face (Gaschler, 2006; Quiroga et al., 2008; Quiroga et al., 2005). Faces appear to be a very special class of objects, which is consistent with the presence of a specific area of the temporal lobe (part of the fusiform gyrus called the *Fusiform Face Area,* or FFA) for processing faces (e.g., Kanwisher, 2003).

Other areas of the brain are also involved in visual perception. For instance, the IT is connected to the limbic system, which is important for emotion. Although we would not ordinarily think of the limbic system as having a function in face perception, it appears to play an important role. For example, one woman suffered damage to a structure in her limbic system (the amygdala), which rendered her incapable of feeling fear (Allman & Brothers, 1994). Not only could she not feel fear but she also could not perceive fear on the faces of others! Clearly, visual perception is a complex process that involves a wide array of brain structures.

The pathway from the primary visual cortex to the IT is vital for object perception. As you might expect, disruption of the information in this pathway leads to problems in the perception of objects. However, by this point you should have reached a level of healthy skepticism that all of object perception takes place in IT! In the final part of this section, we will turn our attention to problems in object and face per-

ception that emerge as a result of damage to parts of this pathway.

Agnosia.   Damage to IT often results in some form of agnosia (from the Greek *a gnosis* "no knowledge"). In ***visual object agnosia,*** a person with intact basic visual abilities cannot identify an object or a picture of an object (e.g., Farah, 2004). However, people with agnosia *understand* what a pencil, an umbrella, or a pair of glasses looks like, because they can draw pictures of such objects from memory (see Figure 3.25). Moreover, they can copy, match, and draw objects after very brief presentations, which shows that they can see clearly. However, when they see pictures of objects, people with agnosia simply cannot identify them.

For instance, S. M. is a man with visual agnosia who has been studied extensively (e.g., Behrmann & Kimchi, 2003a; Behrmann et al., 2005; Behrmann et al., 2006). He has damage to his right inferotemporal cortex as a result of an automobile accident in 1994. With corrective lenses, S. M. has normal visual acuity. He also has no difficulty with simple visual judgments, such as judging the length of lines. When S.M. looks at simple pictures of objects that most people can readily identify, he misidentifies about one-third of the pictures. For instance, he might mistakenly call an acorn a coconut, or an octopus a spider. His disorder has been labeled *integrative agnosia* because S. M. has difficulty "putting together" the pieces of a picture to arrive at a sense of the whole (Behrmann & Kimchi, 2003b; Behrmann et al., 2006).

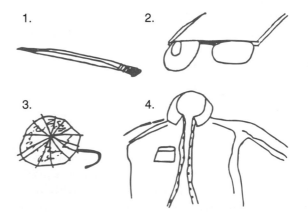

▶ **FIGURE 3.25** Drawings made by a person with agnosia (a pencil, a pair of glasses, an umbrella, and a shirt). After drawing these objects from memory, the person would be unable to identify the objects depicted. (From Jankowiak et al., 1992)

There are actually several different types of agnosia, which may well indicate damage to different areas of the brain. In some cases, people have difficulty identifying both objects and human faces. However, some people have no difficulty identifying faces, but they cannot identify objects (Moscovitch et al., 1997). We'll now discuss a disorder in which people may be able to identify objects, but not faces.

Prosopagnosia.   People with *prosopagnosia* are incapable of identifying faces (Duchaine & Yovel, 2008; Harris & Aguirre, 2007). Thus, a man with prosopagnosia could look at the very familiar face of his wife and not recognize her. In fact, he could not identify his own face. An early report of prosopagnosia concerned a gentleman in a club who was annoyed by another man who kept staring at him. Such rude behavior was actually produced by a mirror—the gentleman was seeing his own reflection!

As is true for people with visual object agnosia, people with prosopagnosia can see all the parts of a face clearly. However, faces are full of details, making them extremely complex objects. One possible interpretation of prosopagnosia is that this disorder is not specific to faces; instead, it is simply a type of visual agnosia for very complex objects. It's also possible that the problem comes from distinguishing among individual examples of a class. Thus, people with prosopagnosia would be able to distinguish a face from a nonface. However, they would not be able to distinguish among examples of the class of faces or other categories of complex objects such as types of cars or animals.

Although the debate rages on, accumulating evidence supports the notion that prosopagnosia is specific to faces. There appears to be a very small area of IT referred to as the *fusiform face area (FFA)* that is crucial for face perception (Kanwisher, 2006). Damage to FFA results in acquired prosopagnosia (Kanwisher & Yovel, 2006). One interesting piece of evidence for the specificity of this disorder comes from a sheep farmer with prosopagnosia. He is capable of recognizing and naming his sheep by seeing their faces, but he cannot recognize human faces (McNeil & Warrington, 1993)!

It's also possible to be born with prosopagnosia. Researchers refer to this disorder as *congenital* or *developmental prosopagnosia* (Behrmann & Avidan, 2005; Duchaine & Yovel, 2008). The specific neural site of this variety of prosopagnosia is not as clear as it appears to be in acquired prosopagnosia. Nonetheless, there appears to be a genetic component because many members of the same family exhibit difficulty in identifying faces (De Haan, 1999; Duchaine & Nakayama, 2006). As you might imagine, regardless of the type of prosopagnosia, being unable to identify faces leads to difficult social interactions (Duchaine & Nakayama, 2005).

Concluding Remarks about the Visual System

The majority of this chapter has emphasized a bottom-up, or data-driven, approach to perception. Data gathered from the receptors are passed up to higher levels in the visual processing system. Theme 2 of this book emphasizes that human sensory systems are well adapted to gather the rich information available in the world. Consistent with this theme, this chapter has emphasized that our visual systems are impressively designed to pass information through increasingly sophisticated kinds of processing.

It should also be clear that our visual system has evolved to allow us to function in a world that is filled with a wide range of electromagnetic energy with varying levels of that energy. Humans have adapted to perceive only a segment of that electromagnetic energy, but we function quite well in that realm. Moreover, you've already seen hints of the ways that the information from various senses comes together in the brain (e.g., in the superior colliculus and the *Where* pathway). These points are entirely consistent with Theme 1.

We have not yet explored Theme 4—that cognitive processes help shape our perceptions. This prior knowledge is relevant in the higher areas of visual processing—especially in IT. Recent research focuses on the important connections between memory areas and visual areas of the brain (e.g., Bar et al., 2006;

Fenske et al., 2006). Throughout this book, we will highlight the importance of top-down, or conceptually driven, processes. Our discussion of the role of the higher levels of visual processing, such as IT, illustrates the origins of such top-down processes.

In this chapter, we have focused on the specialization of function within the visual system. Our discussion should lead you to pose an important question. If our visual system is made up of so many independently functioning areas, how do we arrive at the unitary perception of the world that we all share? Some people refer to this issue of unitary perception as the binding problem. The binding problem refers to joining smaller pieces of our visual experience, such as how we add together color, shape, and motion information (Blaser et al., 2005). It can also refer to the broader question of how we arrive at our overall integrated perceptual experience. We certainly don't have an answer to this question. However, the answer may lie in the common firing rhythm of neurons in different locations of the cortex (but see Palanca & DeAngelis, 2005; Thiele & Stoner, 2003). The ultimate answer to the broader question will be important not only for visual perception but also for the very nature of consciousness (Logothetis, 1999; Revonsuo, 1999; Zeki, 2001).

Section Summary

Pathways from the Retina to the Visual Cortex

1. The visual system has two kinds of crossovers: (a) visual material is reversed by the lens onto the retina and (b) at the optic chiasm, half of the fibers in each optic nerve cross over. As a result of these crossovers, everything from the left side of the visual field ends up on the right-hand side of the head, and everything from the right side of the visual field ends up on the left-hand side of the head.

2. The optic nerve is called the optic tract beyond the optic chiasm. The optic track travels to the superior colliculus, which is important in the detection of movement, and to the lateral geniculate nucleus, which is an important way station for processing visual input.

3. The lateral geniculate nucleus is organized into layers that keep separate the information from the two eyes; cells in the LGN function like ganglion cells.

4. The visual cortex, which is responsible for higher levels of visual processing, is divided into the primary visual cortex (also called Area 17, striate cortex, and V1) and the secondary visual cortex (also called the extrastriate cortex).

5. Neuronal messages from the lateral geniculate nucleus arrive in layer 4C of V1, which has a retinotopic arrangement.

6. Outside of layer 4C, the primary visual cortex has two basic kinds of neurons: simple cortical cells (responding to lines and edges) and complex cortical cells (responding to movement). Some of both types of cells are end-stopped, which means that they respond most to lines that end within their receptive fields.

7. Neurons in V1 are arranged in columns. Neurons within each column respond best to a line of one particular orientation. Cells in an adjacent column have the highest response rate to a line whose orientation has shifted by only about 10°.

8. A hypercolumn is a series of columns that covers a full cycle of stimulus-orientation preferences. Cells in the cortex are arranged according to ocular dominance and location, as well as stimulus-orientation preference.

9. Located within a hypercolumn are regions of cells that are not orientation sensitive. These regions are called blobs, and they are important for color perception. Between blobs is a region of neurons called interblob cells.

10. Three visual pathways (P, M, and K) originate in the retina with different gaglion cells (midget, parasol, and small bistratified). Each pathway has different characteristics and functions.

11. The secondary visual cortex receives information from the primary visual cortex. Within the secondary visual cortex are two important pathways: the *Where* pathway and the *What* pathway.

12. The *Where* pathway is important for spatial location; it runs from the primary visual cortex through the secondary visual cortex to the parietal lobe. The *What* pathway is important for

object recognition; it runs from the primary visual cortex through the secondary visual cortex to the temporal lobe.

13. People with agnosia have basic visual abilities but cannot recognize objects. Thus, they can

see all the detail in a picture and draw a clear picture of the object they are looking at. However, they cannot recognize the object depicted in their own drawing. People with prosopagnosia have a specific agnosia for faces.

Review Questions

1. The beginning of the chapter discussed the visual stimulus. List the three pairs of attributes that are concerned with light, specifying which member of the pair concerns the physical stimulus and which concerns the psychological reaction. What psychological reaction do we have to (a) short wavelengths, (b) long wavelengths, (c) low-amplitude wavelengths, and (d) high-amplitude wavelengths?

2. Discuss the portion of the electromagnetic radiation spectrum that humans can see. Describe differences among species with respect to the part of the spectrum to which they are sensitive and the nature of the photoreceptors.

3. Review the location and the function of the following: sclera, iris, pupil, cornea, and lens. Describe how light is focused on the retina.

4. What is the fovea, and where is it? How is the distribution of cones and rods relevant to a discussion of the fovea? Compare acuity in the fovea and nonfovea regions of the retina. Then compare sensitivity in these two regions, noting how the issue of convergence is relevant.

5. Rods and cones differ in a number of ways. List as many differences as you can. Compare the process of dark and light adaptation for cones and rods. Try to think of practical applications of both processes (devising brightness and color spectrum of lights along highways, preserving dark adaptation for drivers, etc.).

6. Ganglion cells in the retina were discussed in some detail. Can you describe the differences among the various types of ganglion cells? Ganglion cells are similar in the shape of their receptive fields. How does the shape of their receptive fields differ from cells later in the visual pathway?

7. The arrangement of the neurons in the lateral geniculate nucleus and in layer 4C of the visual cortex was described as retinotopic. Discuss this term in relation to those two areas.

8. What is the function of neurons in the remaining layers of V1, above and below layer 4C? How could such simple and complex cortical cells arise from the input found in layer 4C? How do end-stopped cells differ? How do the blobs differ?

9. Damage to particular areas of the visual pathway often helps researchers understand the function of a particular area. Describe the impact of damage to the following areas: the P pathway, the M pathway, the K pathway, all three pathways (P, M, and K), the ganglion cells going to the superior colliculus, V1, V4, V5, the pathway from V1 to the parietal lobe, or the pathway from V1 to IT.

10. Try to imagine and then describe the perceptual experience of a person with agnosia or prosopagnosia. Why would such people be capable of seeing the detailed information in objects or faces? What does agnosia or prosopagnosia tell us about the organization of our visual systems?

Key Terms

transduction, p. 44
electromagnetic radiation,
  p. 44

wavelength, p. 44
nanometer, p. 44
light, p. 44

hue, p. 45
purity, p. 45
amplitude, p. 45

sclera, p. 46
cornea, p. 46
astigmatism, p. 46

Recommended Readings

Hubel, D. H., & Wiesel, T. N. (2005). *Brain and visual perception: The story of a 25-year collaboration.* New York: Oxford.

Two influential and prolific Nobel-prize winners provide us with a compendium of their papers and lectures along with biographical information. Although the book simplifies accessing their work by collecting a lot of it in one place, it's a real joy to listen to these prominent researchers discuss their lives.

Oyster, C. W. (1999). *The human eye: Structure and function.* Sunderland, MA: Sinauer.

Oyster has written a very extensive text that provides detailed information about the parts of the eye, including extensive coverage of the retina. Because of its emphasis on structure, the book contains a large number of useful black-and-white illustrations.

Pinel, J. P. J. (2008). *Biopsychology* (7th ed.). Boston: Allyn & Bacon.

This text is extremely well written and contains excellent illustrations. The chapters on the visual system

and the mechanisms of perception are particularly relevant.

Riordan-Eva, P., & Whitcher, J. P. (Eds.). (2007). *Vaughn & Asbury's general ophthalmology* (17th ed.). New York: McGraw-Hill Medical.

Most ophthalmology textbooks require an extensive medical background. In contrast, this book is clearly written and well organized, but with a decidedly clinical orientation. Thus, for example, the chapter on the lens will tell you more about what can go wrong with the lens than it will tell you about how the lens works.

Rodieck, R. W. (1998). *The first steps in seeing.* Sunderland, MA: Sinauer.

Although you'll find some overlap with both the Oyster text, Rodieck (1937–2003) produced a text that is beautifully illustrated and rich with detail. See, for example, his notes regarding the distinction between describing light as photons at particular frequencies versus light as having wavelengths.

CHAPTER 4

Basic Visual Functions

CHAPTER 4

IN CHAPTER 3, we provided a basic introduction to the anatomy and physiology of visual perception. Although you might have found the discussion to be extremely detailed, trust us when we tell you that we covered only the essential principles. Surely, you must have come away with the sense that our visual system is extremely complex. In this chapter, we begin to address why this complexity is necessary, as we explore the ways in which our visual system attempts to interpret some simple aspects of visual stimuli.

Let's start with a seemingly simple question: What do we need in order to see the world around us? Obviously, we need visual stimulation (energy from a small segment of the electromagnetic spectrum) brought into focus on our receptors (retinas) by our cornea/lens system. So far, the process may seem much like that in a camera, which also uses a set of lenses to bring light into focus on film or the light sensor in a digital camera. Soon, however, we will provide many examples that illustrate the sharp differences between the human visual system and a camera.

In this chapter, we first highlight some very basic visual processes that indicate major differences between our visual system and even the most sophisticated cameras. Next, we will examine the way we perceive the lightness of surfaces and the processes that give rise to clear vision. Finally, we will briefly survey the types of eye movements that keep objects in clear focus.

Prerequisites for Normal Vision

You should recognize that we are discussing normal vision and not the visual experience that one might have in dreams or hallucinations. As we discussed in Chapter 3, normal vision requires sufficient light energy from the range of electromagnetic radiation to which a person's eyes are sensitive. However, what we mean by "sufficient" is not constant—more light energy is necessary when a person's eyes are light adapted.

Basically, the cornea and lens bring the light energy into focus on the retina, where the photoreceptors transduce the light energy into neural energy. The neural impulses are then further processed as they move through the visual pathway. In the last chapter, we discussed an array of problems in the eye and brain that affect our ability to process visual stimuli. Here, however, we will posit an intact visual system. As you will now see, visual perception depends on several other factors that we have not yet addressed.

We will first examine some prerequisites for vision beyond light energy and a receptor system—specifically, the need for edges and change. Next, consistent with Theme 4 of this text, we will show that visual perception is an extremely active process, with central processes and experience crucial for visual perception.

Edges Are Important

An *edge*, or *contour*, may be thought of as a location in space where a sudden change in color, brightness, or lightness occurs (Hesse & Georgeson, 2005; Regan, 2000). The distinction between these last two characteristics, brightness and lightness, may not be that obvious, but it is very important (Gilchrist, 2006). *Brightness* refers to the perceived intensity of light energy (i.e., perceived luminance). Thus, the light energy falling on the retina can vary in brightness, whether it comes from a light source or surface reflecting light energy. However, a light source does not have lightness. Instead, *lightness* refers to the perceived reflectance of surfaces, from dark to light. For example, a deep red would be dark and a pale pink would be light. Thus, even objects reflecting wavelengths that people would perceive as colors may be thought of as *achromatic* (noncolored), much like seeing the objects as they would appear on a black-and-white television screen. Surfaces appear to have lightness as an inherent property, depending on the proportion of light they reflect. We will discuss lightness perception later in this chapter, and color perception in Chapter 7.

If you look around for a moment, you will notice many edges. In fact, each letter on the page—even a simple letter, such as *I*—contains many edges. Note that for the vertical portion of the letter there is a left edge (from white to black) and a right edge (from black to white). Similarly, there are edges you can identify in the small horizontal parts at the top and bottom of the letter.

To illustrate the importance of edges, consider a scene without edges. Such a scene is called a *Ganzfeld* (German for "whole field"). If you were looking at a uniform red field, that's what you'd see initially. After 10 or 15 minutes, however, your experience would have changed radically, and you would be seeing a uniform gray field! Regardless of the color of the field, after a period of time you would perceive the same uniform gray field. Try www Demonstration 4.1 to see how a primitive Ganzfeld works. You will demonstrate to yourself a central visual principle: Without edges, we could not see! Even though light energy is falling on a fully functional receptor system, a person would see nothing unless the stimulus has edges. However, you would be sensitive to gross changes in basic perceptual experience, such as how bright the Ganzfeld is. If you change the amount of light in the Ganzfeld very slowly, people cannot detect the change. Nonetheless, after very slowly making *many* indetectable increases (or decreases) in luminance, people can reliably report that the Ganzfeld has gotten brighter (or darker) (Gilchrist, 2006).

In our everyday experience, edges are everywhere, which is why we rarely have an experience similar to the Ganzfeld. However, people who have been trapped outdoors in a severe snowstorm do report a similar experience. As you might imagine, such whiteout conditions are quite disorienting.

LATERAL INHIBITION   Given the importance of edges, you should not be at all surprised to learn that our visual system is equipped to highlight edges. This process is called **lateral inhibition**, where *lateral* means "sideways": Whenever a light reaches one point on the retina, it inhibits the neural activity for nearby points. The more intense the light source, the greater the inhibition of nearby points.

Lateral inhibition was studied initially in the compound eye of Limulus, the horseshoe crab (Hartline et al., 1956). In the Limulus, each photoreceptor registers light independently and is attached to its own "private" neural cell. (In contrast, recall from Chapter 3 that the human retina is arranged so that several photoreceptors often "share" each neuron.) Because each photoreceptor in the Limulus's eye is relatively large, researchers can stimulate a single photoreceptor without stimulating adjacent photoreceptors. Researchers can also select the neural cell corresponding to that photoreceptor, and they can record the electrical activity from that neural cell.

Figure 4.1 illustrates a prototypical study of lateral inhibition. Hartline and his colleagues presented light to a photoreceptor at Point 1. The recording of the electrical activity at the corresponding neural cell is illustrated in Figure 4.1a. As you can see, the electrical activity is strong. Then these researchers presented simultaneous lights to photoreceptors at Points 1 and 2, as illustrated in Figure 4.1b. Notice that the electrical activity from the neural cell corresponding to Point 1 shows a clear *decrease*. When the researchers increased the intensity of the light at Point 2, the electrical activity from the critical neural cell decreased even further, as illustrated in Figure 4.1c.

Thus, the electrical activity of a Limulus photoreceptor depends not only on that photoreceptor's level of stimulation but also on the level of stimulation of nearby photoreceptors. The more these neighboring photoreceptors are stimulated, the lower the electrical activity of the neural cell. In other words, lateral inhibition is present. The mechanism for lateral inhibition in the Limulus is the lateral plexus, a primitive net that connects the photoreceptors and allows them to influence each other's electrical activity.

The human retina is much more complex than the visual system of the Limulus. Nonetheless, the system of lateral connections within the retina operates in a somewhat similar fashion. In Chapter 3, we discussed the horizontal cells, which serve the same function as the lateral plexus in Limulus.

Lateral inhibition might seem like an inefficient process. After all, what purpose could be served by inhibiting the firing of adjacent receptors? Although it's not immediately obvious, lateral inhibition serves to enhance our perception of edges, and edges are crucial for perception. Figure 4.2 (page 86) illustrates a simple model of how lateral inhibition might serve to highlight edges.

As Figure 4.2a shows, the physical stimulus is an edge produced by a change from lower- to higher-intensity light, as measured by an instrument such as a photometer. Let's say that the light source would produce 40 units of activity in photoreceptors on the dark side of the edge and 100 units of activity in photoreceptors on the light side (Figure 4.2b).

Suppose that the horizontal cells transmit inhibition from each receptor to its neighbor and that this inhibition equals 10% of the "sender's" activity. Thus, a receptor that produces 40 units of activity transmits 4 units of inhibition to each of its neighbors, and a receptor that produces 100 units of activity transmits 10 units of inhibition to each of its neighbors. Figure 4.2c shows how much inhibition each receptor receives from each of its two neighbors. (We will not

a. Light presented only at Point 1

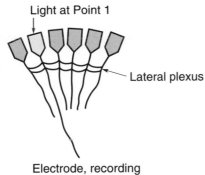

Light at Point 1

Lateral plexus

Electrode, recording
electrical activity

Electrical activity
from cell at Point 1

b. Light presented at Point 1 and Point 2

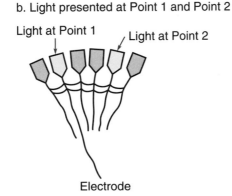

Light at Point 1   Light at Point 2

Electrode

Electrical activity
from cell at Point 1

c. Light presented at Point 1 and
   intense light presented at Point 2

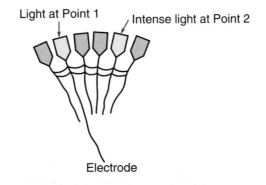

Light at Point 1   Intense light at Point 2

Electrode

Electrical activity
from cell at Point 1

▶ **FIGURE 4.1**   Illustration of a lateral inhibition study using the compound eye of the horseshoe crab (Limulus). In Figure 4.1*a*, the light presented to the photoreceptor at Point 1 causes an increase in electrical activity of that photoreceptor. In Figure 4.1*b*, even though the photoreceptor at Point 1 receives the same stimulation, it fires less because of the inhibition sent over the lateral plexus from Point 2, where another light is stimulating that photoreceptor. As illustrated in Figure 4.1*c*, increasing the intensity of the light at Point 2 further inhibits the firing of the photoreceptor at Point 1.

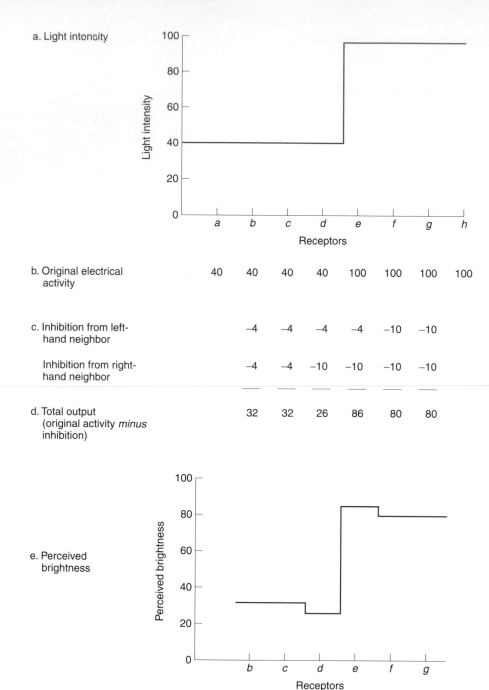

a. Light intensity

b. Original electrical activity

a	b	c	d	e	f	g	h
40	40	40	40	100	100	100	100

c. Inhibition from left-hand neighbor

	−4	−4	−4	−4	−10	−10

Inhibition from right-hand neighbor

	−4	−4	−10	−10	−10	−10

d. Total output (original activity *minus* inhibition)

32	32	26	86	80	80

e. Perceived brightness

▶ **FIGURE 4.2** Schematic diagram of the way in which lateral inhibition can serve to highlight edges. The change in light intensity is abrupt between receptors *d* and *e* (part *a*). Part *b* shows hypothetical graded response activity of the receptors from 40 (for receptors *a* through *d*) to 100 arbitrary units (for receptors *e* through *h*). Because of the inhibitory lateral connections between receptors, firing in neighboring receptors is reduced by 10% of the original activity (part *c*). (The graded responses and inhibitory percentage are arbitrarily chosen numbers to illustrate the point.) The net effect of the lateral inhibition is illustrated numerically (part *d*) and graphically (part *e*). Without lateral inhibition, the change in graded responses would be a step function like that seen in the physical stimulus (part *a*). With lateral inhibition, however, the change in graded response is more abrupt at the transition point (between receptors *d* and *e*) than between other points away from the transition.

discuss receptors *a* and *h* because, for simplicity, the activity of their outside neighbors is not illustrated.) The numbers in Figure 4.2*d* show the total output after subtracting the inhibition. A graph of the total output appears in Figure 4.2*e*.

Thus, our visual system improves on the information arriving at the retina by exaggerating the contrast between the dark and light sides. Objects in our world are typically defined by reasonably clear boundaries or edges. Consistent with Theme 2 of the book, our visual system is adapted to detect those edges. Moreover, our visual system enhances the incoming edge information through lateral inhibition.

LATERAL INHIBITION AND MACH BANDS   Not only does lateral inhibition enhance edges, but it also produces a perceptual phenomenon known as Mach bands. Ernst Mach, an Austrian physicist and philosopher, first described these bands in 1865. In a ***Mach band***, people perceive bright and dark bands within a single stripe, even when the physical distribution of light does not vary (Ratliff, 1984). You can illustrate Mach bands for yourself in www Demonstration 4.2.

Mach bands are a byproduct of lateral inhibition in which the physical contrast that already exists is exaggerated still further. When there is a dark-to-light edge, lateral inhibition serves to sharpen the edge by making the darker side just a bit darker and the lighter side just a bit lighter. That same process creates Mach bands—the borders to the sides of edges seen in www Demonstration 4.2. Keep in mind the distinction between physical stimuli and perceptions of those stimuli. Mach bands do not exist in the physical world, so a photometer would never detect their presence. Instead, Mach bands are perceptual phenomena, with no real counterpart in the physical world.

Change Is Important

In order to see, we need sufficient light energy falling on our receptors, and at least one edge must be present. Is that all that we need? Actually, another component is crucial to visual perception, and that is *change over time*. Even if all the other conditions are present, we would be unable to see without such change. An edge represents a change over space, so the overall importance of change for perceptual experience should be clear to you.

To ensure that change occurs, the human visual system is constantly producing change by means of

involuntary eye movements—spontaneous, unconscious, and unavoidable minor movements and tremors made by our eyes when we look out at the world (Engbert & Kliegl, 2004; Martinez-Conde et al., 2004; Martinez-Conde et al., 2006). Our eyes exhibit three of these involuntary eye movements: (1) a constant very small tremor (2) a slow drift, and (3) a fast-jerking motion called a ***microsaccade***. As you might reasonably infer, a microsaccade is a very small saccade, which is an eye movement we'll discuss at the end of this chapter.

The tremor takes place over a *very* small distance—about one cone. A drift takes place over a greater distance—equivalent to about a dozen cones. The eye executes a rapid (about 25 ms) microsaccade—presumably to shift the image back on the retina after a drift. However, microsaccades can occur over greater distances than drifts. These involuntary eye movements serve to sweep edges back and forth over the photoreceptors, creating constant change. Figure 4.3 illustrates the sorts of motion typically produced. Notice that the direction, curvature, and length of these movements are random. So, even if you try to hold your gaze steady on a single point in the visual field, involuntary eye movements guarantee that change will still be present.

As you look out at the world, you are typically unaware of these involuntary eye movements. Apparently, your lack of awareness is partly due to the richness of the typical visual experience. That is, if the *whole* visual field jumps up a bit, then down, then left,

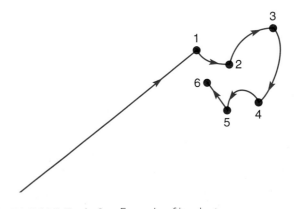

▶ **FIGURE 4.3**   Example of involuntary eye movements. Numbered dots show the order of eye fixations. The time interval between dots is about 0.2 second. The distance between dots 1 and 2 is about 4 cones. The direction of involuntary eye movements is random.

your visual system would refuse to treat those retinal changes as due to real movement. However, in an impoverished visual environment, you can actually detect these involuntary eye movements. To experience your own involuntary eye movements, try www Demonstration 4.3.

Early astronomers were among the first to notice the effects of involuntary eye movements (Hochberg, 1971). The stars appeared to move around as the astronomers viewed them. A visual field of scattered points of light is sufficiently impoverished that these astronomers perceived their own involuntary eye movements as small tremors in the stars. Think of this experience in the context of Theme 3. Even when we keep our eyes fixed, involuntary eye movements cause edges to move on our retina. However, the signal sent to our brains might also be due to real movement in the world, rather than due to movement of our eyes. In some circumstances, such as impoverished viewing conditions, we perceive those retinal changes as due to movement in the world. In other circumstances, such as a rich visual context, we perceive those same retinal changes as not being due to movement in the world. Instead, our visual world seems stable. In Chapter 8, we'll explore the role of these involuntary eye movements and the general problem of perceiving motion due to retinal changes.

How might we illustrate that change is important for vision? One approach is to eliminate the changes that are due to involuntary eye movements. But how can we do this? Researchers have developed many means of creating a **stabilized retinal image**, where an image always falls on exactly the same retinal location (Martinez-Conde et al., 2004). Older approaches actually used a form of contact lens mounted directly on the cornea. With technological advances, stabilization is now accomplished by means of a computer-controlled display coupled to an eye-movement detector. When eye movement is detected, the computer shifts the image so that it remains in the same location on the retina. With this approach, involuntary eye movements continue, but the image remains in the same position on the retina.

Another (more dangerous) approach is to stop involuntary eye movements by injecting someone with a muscle paralyzer. John Stevens (see Stevens et al., 1976) underwent such paralysis, except for one arm that he used to signal the researchers about what he was experiencing (including a signal that meant "Stop the experiment and get me out of here!"). The

near-total paralysis required the use of an artificial respirator—indicating the extremes to which some researchers will go to collect data. This approach stabilizes the entire visual field because the eye no longer moves at all.

Keep in mind that sufficient light is falling on an intact receptor system—and that edges are present. So, what happens when those edges are stabilized on the retina? If *none* of the edges moves on the retina, as in the case of paralysis, then one cannot see anything! That complete lack of change produces a situation similar to the Ganzfeld, and temporary blindness results. If you stabilize the image of an object on the retina, gradually the borders of the image fade, and then the entire object disappears. But what do you see in place of the object that is stabilized?

A study by Krauskopf (1963) will give you a sense of what happens when you stabilize an image. He presented a green ring with a red disc inside it and stabilized the red inner disc. Because the outer ring was not stabilized, people continued to see the green ring. What happened to the red disc? It was stabilized, so it disappeared (as expected). But did people see a green ring with a hole in it? No, they just saw a solid green disc—in spite of the fact that the photoreceptors for the inner part of the disc were still receiving red light. Keep this result in mind when we discuss color perception (Chapter 7).

Krauskopf's results further highlight the importance of edges. One way to interpret his results is that the visual system is very efficient. It looks at points of change (edges) and then "fills in" the areas between edges with the color found on that side of the edge. Can you see why this process is more efficient than determining the color of every unique point in a scene? If you've ever used the *fill* function in typical computer paint programs, you'll understand why this process is efficient. Because the only edge seen by the people in Krauskopf's study appeared between the green outer disc and the surround, they unconsciously "filled in" the entire disc with green.

Such filling-in or completion processes don't require a stabilized retinal image. You experience such completion processes routinely—at your blind spot. In fact, the filling-in that takes place at the blind spot is so effective that the blind spot wasn't even discovered until the seventeenth century (Albright & Stoner, 2002). In www Demonstration 3.3, you experienced some very elementary filling-in at the blind spot. When you moved your eyes so that the black dot was registered on your blind spot, it disappeared. After all, it was surrounded by white, so your visual system filled in the black spot with white. Suppose that you close one eye and move the other eye over the page so that the blind spot is centered over text. Now, you will notice that the blind spot is not at all obvious, and you do not see a hole in the page of print. In this case, your visual system has filled in the area of the blind spot with "letters" just like those that are registered on your retina surrounding the blind spot. Of course, you cannot actually read those filled-in letters. In fact, you might have difficulty reading actual letters that far from your fovea.

The complexity of the information you fill in at the blind spot is quite intriguing (Ramachandran, 2003; Ramachandran & Gregory, 1991). Try www Demonstration 4.4 to illustrate the complexity to yourself. Notice that you fill in the blind spot quite differently, depending on how you've interpreted the context surrounding the blind spot.

So far, we've looked at completion processes that occur due to stabilized retinal images and at the blind spot. Another example of completion processes is found in people with *scotomas* (blindness due to damage to the visual system). Pinel (2006) points out the interesting case of a scotoma experienced by the eminent psychologist Karl Lashley. Lashley (1941) had a scotoma that affected vision near his fovea. He described a situation in which his scotoma actually obliterated the head of a friend. As Figure 4.4 (page 90) shows, Lashley did not see a hole in his visual field; instead, the area affected by the scotoma was filled in with the surrounding information. As is true for the blind spot, the visual system is capable of filling in an area with very complicated patterns.

The processes by which we fill in information at the blind spot or scotomas (whether natural or artificial) are of great interest to researchers (e.g., Albright & Stoner, 2002; Pessoa & De Weerd, 2003). Some behavioral studies suggest that the filling-in takes place at early stages of visual processing (i.e., primary visual cortex). However, evidence from fMRI studies shows little evidence for filling-in processes in primary visual cortex, suggesting that filling-in takes place at later stages in visual processing (Awater et al., 2005; Cornelissen et al., 2006; Mendola et al., 2006; Zur & Ullman, 2003).

Researchers have discovered good evidence for the role of edge information in determining lightness (e.g., Becker & Anstis, 2004), although not everyone is convinced (e.g., Gilchrist, 2006). Nonetheless, it's quite clear that edges are important sources of information for our visual system. Moreover, the position of the edges on the retina must change over time, which our involuntary eye movements ensure will be the case. Finally, the importance of the rich context in which stimuli occur is evident in the filling-in processes that occur at the blind spot and in scotomas. Whether those completion processes emerge due to lower- or higher-level processes is a lingering question. However, it's clear that higher-level processes play an important role in perception.

Higher-Level Processes and Experience Are Important

As Richard Gregory (1997) notes, some authorities "see perception as passive acceptance of what is out there, as a window facing the world" (p. 2). If you reflect on your own perceptual experience, you might also think of perception as passive. After all, you seem to look out and effortlessly perceive all the richness of the world that surrounds you. However, researchers emphasize the "organic machinery that hums continuously below the threshold of visual consciousness" (Brown & Thurmond, 1993, p. 200). These unconscious processes are essential for what we perceive—perception is a very active experience-based process (Hoffman, 1998; Purves & Lotto, 2003). Of course, this perspective is entirely consistent with Theme 4. We will have more to say about these processes in later chapters. For now, let's explore the important role of experience.

Imagine a person who was born blind and had lived that way for many years. What would that person see if you could restore her or his sight? The seventeenth-century philosopher William Molyneux first posed a variant of this question. With the advent of modern medicine, we actually have some evidence with which to address the question.

Three cases of restored vision provide us with important insights into the role of experience. Richard Gregory and Jean Wallace (Gregory, 1974) reported on their studies of S. B. About 20 years later, Oliver Sacks (1995) reported on the experiences of a man he called Virgil. More recently, Ione Fine and her colleagues (2003) reported on the remarkable case of Michael May (see also Kurson, 2007). What's common across all three cases is that these men lost their

a. Lashley's scotoma

b. What Lashley saw

▶ **FIGURE 4.4** Illustration of the effects of Lashley's scotoma. The left side of the figure (a) shows the position of Lashley's scotoma as he looked at his friend. The right side of the figure (b) shows what Lashley actually saw. Notice that the completion processes filled in the area occupied by the friend's head with the pattern of the wallpaper behind the friend. (*Source:* J. P. J. Pinel, *Biopsychology,* 6th ed. (Boston: Allyn & Bacon), 2006.)

sight at an early age and then had their vision restored after many years of blindness.

Striking similarities emerge in reviewing all three cases. Basic visual abilities (color perception, acuity, etc.) developed fairly quickly after the operations, although some acuity impairments remained. However, some more complex visual tasks, such as face perception, presented a far greater challenge to these men. In the end, both S. B. and Virgil were transformed from competent blind people into tentative and confused sighted people.

Michael May appears to have adapted better than S. B. or Virgil to the restoration of his vision. It may be, in part, that he seems to treat vision as "icing on the cake" rather than an essential perceptual ability. And although Michael May has difficulties with object and face perception (*What* pathway, see page 74), he does much better with motion perception (*Where* pathway, see page 74). Even so, visual motion perception can be confusing to him. For example, Michael May had adapted remarkably to the loss of his vision, even learning to ski (with a companion to direct him). However, he reported that after his operation he would often close his eyes when skiing because of the confusing flow of visual information.

Cases of restored vision certainly provide evidence for the importance of experience. First of all, these three men had no visual experience over many years. Therefore, all three men had to *learn* to see once their vision was restored. Second, the lack of visual experience over many years almost certainly influenced the organization of the visual cortex. That is, after the onset of blindness, these men had virtually no input going from their eyes to visual cortex. In the absence of such input, the brain tends to reorganize itself (Baker et al., 2005; Baseler et al., 2002; Kaas, 2000; Merzenich et al., 1984). Such "rewiring" due to the nature of one's experience after the onset of blindness may well make it difficult to restore visual abilities fully. It certainly argues that an extended period of experience may be essential for subsequent cortical reorganization.

If a person with restored sight experienced many subsequent years of visual input, would you expect improvement in cortical processing of visual information? For example, would you expect that Michael May would become increasingly adept over time at using visual information? At least one case provides hopeful information (Ostrovsky et al., 2006). S. R. D. was born with congenital cataracts, which were removed when she was age 12. In part because no intraocular lens was implanted, her visual acuity is poor. S. B., Virgil, and Michael May were assessed for visual abilities immediately after vision was restored and thereafter. In contrast, S. R. D. was not examined until 20 years after her surgery. Thus, no one tracked the development of her visual abilities. However, when she was examined, S. R. D. exhibited impressive visual abilities. For instance, she had little difficulty with tasks (e.g., face perception, determining gender from facial information) that prove to be quite difficult for people right after having their vision restored.

Another way to examine the role of experience in visual perception is to alter the visual input in people with normal vision. As you know, the optics of the eye create an image on the retina that is upside down and reversed, in relation to the object in the world. In the late 1800s, George M. Stratton wore lenses that inverted the image on the retina. Stratton experienced all sorts of difficulties initially. However, after experience with the inverted input, he began to adapt. Many studies have examined adaptation to rearranged visual input, and they have all emphasized the importance of interacting with objects in the environment (e.g., Held, 1965, 1980). We will have more to say about this research in Chapter 14.

In this section, we have attempted to convince you that a person's visual perception is the result of much more than light energy falling on photoreceptors. Vision is a very active process that requires edges, change, higher-level processes, and experience (Hoffman, 1998; Peterson et al., 2007; Purves & Lotto, 2003). We will now turn our attention to a very basic visual process—determining which parts of the visual field are lighter and darker.

Section Summary

Prerequisites for Normal Vision

1. In order to see, we require a physical stimulus and an intact visual system (as discussed in Chapter 3).
2. A Ganzfeld is a uniform visual stimulus that lacks edges. People who look at a Ganzfeld long enough report seeing a uniform gray field, regardless of the color of the light entering the eyes. Edges are therefore extremely important for our visual system.
3. Lateral inhibition, due to the lateral connections among photoreceptors, serves to enhance edges and to produce Mach bands.
4. Research on stabilized retinal images shows that edges are important and that the visual system requires changes in the position of the edges on the retina. Even when we try to hold our gaze steady, these changes are brought about through involuntary eye movements.
5. The surrounding context is vitally important for the filling-in or completion processes that occur at the blind spot (or in people with scotomas).
6. Vision is an active process involving higher-level processes.
7. Case studies of both restored vision and adaptation to rearranged visual input show us that experience is vital for visual perception.

Perceiving Light Energy

As we discussed in Chapter 3, light energy falls on retinal receptors and is transduced into neural energy. We know that neurons fire at a greater rate when more light falls on the photoreceptors. You might then think that we have a simple explanation for lightness perception: When more light energy falls on photoreceptors, we perceive that area as lighter; and when less light energy falls on photoreceptors, we perceive that area as darker. We could refer to this explanation as the *photometric approach*—lightness perception as analogous to measurement by an instrument such as a photometer. However, this simplistic notion of the relationship between light energy and perceived lightness is far from accurate, as you will see shortly. Instead, your perception of the lightness of a stimulus is determined by the rich context in which the stimulus occurs—consistent with Theme 2.

Light Energy and Lightness Perception

This section emphasizes the distinction between the physical stimuli falling on our receptors and our psychological reactions to them. We can measure many aspects of a light wave, including its amplitude or intensity. Our psychological reaction to the level of energy might be considered lightness, with greater light energy leading to a perception of greater lightness. Lightness, as we mentioned earlier, refers to our perception of the achromatic characteristics of a surface (whites, grays, and blacks).

The physical property of objects that corresponds most closely to lightness is not amplitude of light energy. Instead, it is the percentage of light reflected by a surface. This property is referred to as *albedo*. As it turns out, surfaces reflect a constant proportion of the light energy falling on the surface. Thus, an object with a high albedo (such as the moon or white paper) reflects a large percentage of the light energy that falls on it. When the moon or the paper is in shadow, it will still reflect the same large percentage of the light falling on its surface, but there is less light to reflect, so it will reflect less light. On the other hand, an object with a low albedo (such as the print on this page or a dark suit) reflects a small percentage of the light energy that falls on it.

You might then assume that our visual systems assess the albedo of a surface to determine its lightness. But unfortunately, our visual systems cannot directly assess a surface's albedo. To illustrate this point, consider the albedo of the print and paper in this book. The black print on the paper may reflect only 3% of the light falling on it, whereas the white paper may reflect 90% of the light falling on it, as illustrated in Figure 4.5.

Although it may not be immediately obvious to you, under different lighting conditions, the black print can sometimes reflect more light energy than the white page! As illustrated in the figure, suppose you are reading this book on a sunny day, when the illumination is 1,000 units (in some unspecified light measurement system). If the black print has an albedo of 3%, the letters will reflect 3% of the 1,000 units, or 30 units. Now suppose that you move indoors so that you are looking at the white page in a dimly lit setting, where the illumination is 10 units. If the page has an albedo of 90%, it will reflect 90% of 10 units, or 9 units. Thus, your eye actually receives more light energy (30 units) from the black print under bright conditions than it does from the white page under dim conditions (9 units).

This example illustrates that the light energy on the photoreceptors is not sufficient for determining our perception of lightness. That's because the same amount of light could come from a surface with low albedo under bright light and a surface with high

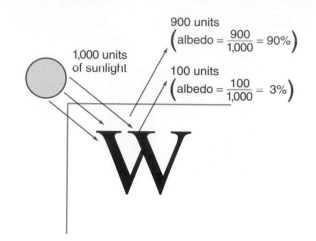

▶ **FIGURE 4.5** Illustration of the physical stimuli involved in lightness perception. The black letter *W* has an albedo of 3% and therefore reflects only 30 of the hypothetical 1,000 units of light produced by the sun. The white paper on which the letter is printed has an albedo of 90% and therefore reflects 900 units of light. Lightness constancy is apparent when the page is moved indoors under 10 units of light produced by a lamp. Under the reduced-intensity light, the black letter would reflect 0.3 unit and the white page would reflect 9 units of light. The white page reflects a smaller amount of light energy into the eye indoors than the black letter outdoors (30 units of light compared to 100 units of light). Nonetheless, we readily see the page as white and the letter as black under both lighting conditions. The absolute amount of light energy cannot be the sole determinant of lightness perception!

albedo under dim light. The example also illustrates that we cannot assess the albedo of a surface, knowing only the amount of light energy falling on the photoreceptors. If you see an isolated gray surface, you cannot know if it's gray paper under moderate lighting, white paper under dim lighting, or black paper under very bright lighting.

At this point, you should protest, "But I *can* tell that it is white paper, regardless of the amount of light falling on it!" And you're absolutely correct, although you should now have the suspicion that your assessment is not a simple process. Consider Figure 4.6, which was developed by Ted Adelson. The array should make perfect sense to you (as it does to your visual system). That is, you're looking at a checkerboard pattern with a cylinder sitting on it and a light source coming from the right. When you look at the two squares labeled *A* and *B*, they do not appear to be

Edward H. Adelson

▶ **FIGURE 4.6**   Ted Adelson produced this clever demonstration. Compare the areas marked *A* and *B*. Which area is darker? You may be surprised to learn that the two areas are equally dark. To convince yourself, cover up the rest of the figure, so that only the two areas are visible. Seen in isolation, it's easy to determine that the two areas are equal in lightness. Why don't they appear equally light when seen in the complete context?

important principle before talking about a variety of explanations for lightness perception.

Lightness Constancy

As you routinely experience, the perceived lightness of an object remains the same despite changes in illumination; we refer to this phenomenon as *lightness constancy*. Lightness constancy provides us with our first example of a constancy—a concept considered throughout the textbook. A *constancy* is a tendency for qualities of objects to stay the same despite changes in the way we view the objects. This is certainly an important tendency! Try to imagine a visual system that allowed qualities of objects to change whenever you changed the viewing conditions. A piece of paper might appear to be white under some lighting conditions, gray under other conditions, and black under still other conditions. Living in this world with such a visual system would certainly be a challenge.

We need to have some vocabulary to refer to objects "out there," as opposed to the objects as they are registered on the retina. The term *distal stimulus* refers to the objects "out there" in the world, such as a page of print. The term *proximal stimulus* refers to the representation of objects in contact with a sense organ. You can remember which term is which by thinking of distal as "in the distance," because for visual stimuli the distal stimulus makes no contact with the retina. In general, then, a constancy occurs when our perception of the distal stimulus remains roughly the same in spite of changes in the proximal stimulus.

Researchers have studied constancies for several qualities of objects, including lightness, size, shape, and color. You should note that one implication of a constancy is that the same proximal stimulus could result from a number of different distal stimuli. For example, a white stimulus under one lighting condition might lead to the identical retinal stimulation as a black stimulus under a brighter lighting condition. The ambiguity of the proximal stimulus, as well as our visual system's ability to resolve the ambiguity, is consistent with Theme 3.

In subsequent chapters, we will address other constancies, but for now, we will explore lightness constancy. Try www Demonstration 4.5 to see that objects appear to be equally light under different illuminations.

identical in lightness. Nonetheless, they are! But they do not appear to be equally light—nor should they. It makes perfect sense for a white square in shadow to reflect less light than a white square directly in the light. In fact, as illustrated here, the white square in shadow (Square *B*) may reflect the same amount of light as a black square directly in the light (Square *A*). It should be increasingly clear to you that lightness perception is not determined solely by the absolute amount of light energy falling on the retina.

Before we talk about some explanations that people have proposed for our ability to perceive the lightness of surfaces, we need to discuss an important perceptual principle. If you open your book and look at it under a variety of different lighting conditions, you should note that the page remains white and the print remains black. In fact, people can continue to make these discriminations even when the amount of light falling on the page is very low (Arend, 1994). Knowing what you now know about the ambiguity of the light energy falling on your photoreceptors, the fact that the perceived lightness of a surface doesn't change under different levels of light should be perplexing to you. We will now turn our attention to this

As you should expect, lightness perception and lightness constancy are closely intertwined. That is, a good explanation for how we perceive lightness would also explain how a surface appears to be the same lightness regardless of changes in illumination. At this point, you should have a sense that the albedo of the surface on which the light is falling is important. The amount of light reflected into the eye is also important. However, you also know that neither of these types of information is sufficient to create lightness constancy, nor to explain lightness perception. What, then, determines lightness?

Explanations for Lightness Perception

Hermann von Helmholtz (1866), the nineteenth-century German physiologist we first mentioned in Chapter 3, proposed an early theory of lightness perception. Helmholtz proposed that we make an unconscious inference about the level of illumination when we perceive the lightness of a surface. In other words, the print on this page stays black outdoors because we are sensitive to the fact that the sunlight is very bright. The page remains white indoors because we are sensitive to the fact that the indoor light is much less intense. Can you see that Helmholtz's approach helps to explain both lightness perception and lightness constancy?

Helmholtz's theory is quite logical. For instance, think about the scenario we described in Figure 4.5. If you could tell that there were 1,000 units of incident light, you could then tell that an object was reflecting a large percentage of that light (high albedo) or little of that light (low albedo). Unfortunately for Helmholtz's theory, there is a great deal of ambiguity in the information falling on our retinas. How, then, can we assess the level of illumination, if not by way of the information reflected off surfaces into our eyes? In the end, research suggests that people cannot effectively determine the level of illumination in a setting (Rutherford & Brainard, 2002). Moreover, people are not particularly sensitive to surfaces that are illuminated in a fashion inconsistent with the ambient light (Cavanagh, 2005; Ostrovsky et al., 2005). As you'll see in later chapters, Helmholtz had a gift for identifying major issues in perception, but his explanations were often modified by subsequent research.

Instead of the unconscious inference proposed by Helmholtz, many theories of lightness perception have at their heart the notion of contrast (Gilchrist,

2006). One such contrast approach was developed by Hans Wallach (1948). According to Wallach's *ratio principle*, the important factor that determines an object's lightness is the brightness of that object in comparison to the brightness of other objects in the scene. Thus, this page looks white because—under a wide range of illumination levels—it reflects substantially more light energy than the print does.

Wallach's ratio principle grew out of a study in which observers looked at two discs, each surrounded by a ring. As illustrated in Figure 4.7, Wallach set the intensity levels of the standard disc and ring, as well as the ring around the variable disc. He instructed the observer to adjust the intensity of the variable (second) disc so that it matched the intensity of the standard disc. Wallach found that the observer's match was influenced by the intensity of the ring surrounding the variable disc. Basically, the results showed that the observer varied the disc's intensity so that the ratio between the variable disc and ring was the same as the ratio between the standard disc and ring. Keep in mind that the observer was trying to make the two

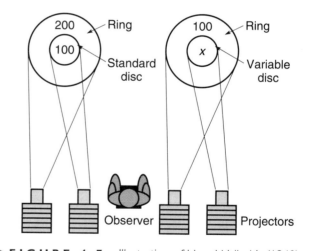

▶ **FIGURE 4.7** Illustration of Hans Wallach's (1948) study underlying the ratio principle. Observers looked at a standard ring and disc and adjusted the lightness of the variable disc so that it matched the lightness of the standard disc. Wallach controlled the lightness of the standard ring and disc as well as the ring around the variables disc. The results showed that the observers set the lightness of the variable disc so that the ratio of the right-hand ring to the variable disc was the same as the ratio between the left-hand ring and the standard disc. In this case, the ratio for the standard is 2:1, so the observer would set the variable disc to 50.

discs appear to be equal in lightness (e.g., the same shade of gray).

According to the ratio principle of lightness perception, observers pay attention to the relative intensity of the stimuli, rather than the absolute intensity. An object may reflect very little light energy. However, it will appear to be light (e.g., light gray or even white) as long as it is lighter than other objects in the scene. The objects do not need to be next to each other, because we appear to integrate information about the light reflected off many objects in the scene (e.g., Arend, 1994).

Lightness constancy occurs because the relative intensity of an object remains the same, even when illumination varies. Thus, the ratio of light reflected off the white page to the light reflected off the print remains about 30:1, regardless of viewing conditions. Your white shirt therefore looks light in the moonlight because it is the lightest object in sight. Your dark shoes look dark in the noonday sun because they are the darkest objects in sight.

Research suggests that the ratio principle holds over an extremely wide range of illumination. For example, Alan Jacobsen and Alan Gilchrist (1988) varied the reflected light energy over a range of 1,000,000:1. They found that observers' responses were consistent with the ratio principle.

Nonetheless, there are critics of the ratio principle and of contrast theories in general. One problem with such relational approaches is that it's difficult to understand how they might lead us to perceive a surface as a specific achromatic color, such as white. That is, the ratio principle does a great job of predicting why one surface will appear to be lighter or darker, but when we look at the world we don't see lighter and darker—we see whites and blacks! Imagine, for example, that you're looking at four surfaces, with each one-third as light as the next. Given the ratio principle, it's quite clear which surfaces you'll see as lighter or darker, but the ratio principle can't tell us whether we would actually label *any* of the surfaces as white or black.

To circumvent that problem, some researchers have proposed the introduction of anchors (Bressan, 2006; Gilchrist, 2006; Gilchrist et al., 1999; Logvinenko, 2002). For example, if you considered the lightest surface in the array as white, that would allow you to assign specific achromatic colors to the surfaces in the array. In fact, there is evidence that when people can see only two achromatic colors (gray and

black), they will usually see the gray surface as white and the black surface as gray (Li & Gilchrist, 1999). A visual scene may involve a variety of illuminations (sunlight here, bright incandescent light there, shadow there). Therefore, our visual system must first organize the scene before determining the anchors needed to allow us to interpret the lightness of the surfaces in the scene. In the next section, we'll discuss the importance of organizing the scene before determining lightness.

Another approach to understanding lightness perception emphasizes the importance of experience (Purves & Lotto, 2003; Purves et al., 2004). To a degree, this approach follows in the tradition of Egon Brunswik's (1903–1955) probabilistic functionalism. According to this empirical theory, an individual's experience in interacting with the environment over time (or one's species' experience over eons) provides that individual with expectations (probabilities) of what's "out there." Thus, if two objects differ in lightness and that difference is important in navigating the world, then people should perceive the objects as differing in lightness. Presumably, if the differences had no practical significance, then one might not perceive any differences in the lightness of the objects. Given the contentious world of psychological research, you should not be the least bit surprised to learn that this approach has its detractors as well. Nonetheless, the consistency of this empirical approach with Themes 3 and 4 of the text is appealing.

Perceptual Organization Precedes Lightness Perception

You might think that lightness perception is a very primitive perceptual ability. However, the evidence suggests that you must organize the visual scene before you can perceive the lightness of objects in the scene (Agostini & Proffitt, 1993; Gilchrist, 1977, 1980, 2006). In other words, you must first decide which objects go together before you can determine their lightness. The situation is complicated by the fact that lightness itself might serve as an organizational cue (Rock et al., 1992). We will have more to say about these organizational principles in Chapter 5.

As you know, the context within which stimuli are perceived is very important (Theme 2). One classic example of the role of context is simultaneous lightness contrast (see Figure 4.8, page 96). Although the small gray square in the center of the white square

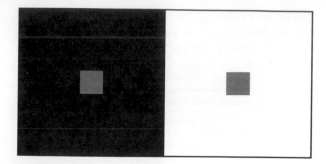

▶ **FIGURE 4.8**   Simultaneous lightness contrast.
Compare the two inner squares. Do they differ in lightness?
Because of the context, the inner gray square will likely
appear to be darker when seen against a lighter
background. The inner gray square will likely appear to be
lighter when seen against a darker background.

is actually the same lightness as the one in the center
of the black square, it should appear to be darker.

Simultaneous lightness contrast may seem simple to you. That is, you might extract the simple rule
that surfaces appear darker against a light background
and lighter against a dark background. In fact, you
may even be inclined to invoke lateral inhibition to
explain the effect. Oh, were it only so simple! To give
you a sense of the organizational capabilities of our
visual system, look at Figure 4.9, which is a variant of
a figure developed by Paola Bressan (2001).

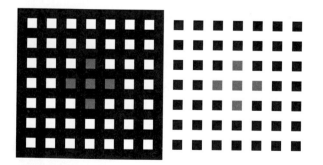

▶ **FIGURE 4.9**   Based on simultaneous lightness
contrast (Figure 4.8), you might expect that the small gray
squares seen against a light background would appear to
be darker than those seen against a dark background.
However, as Paola Bressan discovered, your visual system
organizes the scene first. Thus, instead of comparing the
small gray squares against the immediate background, you
compare all the little squares. In the context of small white
squares, the gray squares appear to be darker. In the
context of small black squares, the gray squares appear to
be lighter.

Note that the gray squares seen against the light
background are *lighter* than the identical gray squares
seen against the dark background. How did that happen? It appears that our visual system first organizes
the scene and decides that it's looking at an array of
squares against (and in front of) two different backgrounds. On the left, most of the squares are black,
but five squares in the middle are gray. Given that
organization, the apparent lightness of those gray
squares is determined by their mates, which are all
black. So, even though the gray squares are seen right
next to a white surface, our visual system actually
determines their lightness in comparison to the other
squares, which happen to be black. In comparison to
those black companion squares, the gray squares seem
lighter. The same sort of comparison goes on with the
squares on the right, but in this setting the gray
squares seem darker in comparison to their fellow
white squares.

Objects can also be grouped together because
they appear to be at the same depth from the observer,
which would typically place them in the same illumination. The lightness of objects appears to be determined in comparison to other objects at the same
depth (coplanar). For example, experiments by Gilchrist have shown that lightness judgments depend
on the relative intensity of objects perceived to be the
same distance from the viewer (Gilchrist, 1977, 2006).
In contrast, the relative intensity of objects merely
next to each other in the retinal image (but perceived
to be at different distances from the viewer) is less
important. In other words, viewers must make depth
perception judgments before they make lightness
judgments.

Another way to illustrate the importance of first
determining depth before lightness is to consider surfaces that are covered by a transparent surface. Think,
for example, of how the world looks to you when
you're wearing sunglasses. You can tell that there's
some clear-colored surface between you and the
world, but even though everything is darker, you
don't have any difficulty in determining the relative
lightness of an object (Gilchrist, 2005). Barton Anderson and his colleagues are interested in the perceived
lightness of objects behind transparent surfaces
(Anderson et al., 2006; Anderson & Winawer, 2005;
Singh & Anderson, 2006).

In one compelling demonstration of the impact
of organization, consider the "moons" in Figure 4.10.
In both cases, your visual system seems to organize

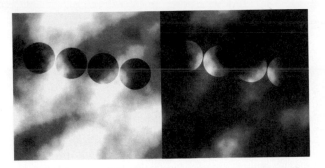

FIGURE 4.10 Barton Anderson developed this example of the role of context. Though they appear to differ in lightness, the moons in the figure on the left are identical to the moons on the right. (*Source: Reprinted by permission from Macmillan Publishers Ltd: Nature, 434, 79–83, copyright © 2005.*)

the scene into layers, with the moons in one layer behind wispy clouds. However, the clouds on the left seem to be light (white and light gray) and the clouds on the right seem to be dark (black and light gray). But what about the two sets of moons? Even though the moons on the left appear to be black and the moons on the right appear to be white, they are actually identical!

How can stimuli with identical lightness be perceived so differently? Notice, for example, that the left sides of the moons on the far left of each display are black. However, for the display on the left, your visual system interprets that black as due to the intrinsic lightness of the moon in back of light clouds. For the display on the right, you interpret the identical information as due to an inherently white moon in the back covered by very dark clouds. Different organizations lead to radically different perceptions of lightness.

Some organizations of the scene can take place entirely within your mind. Ernst Mach, of Mach band fame, developed an illustration of the role of organization on lightness perception. Try www Demonstration 4.6 to experience Mach's book for yourself. What's important for our purposes is that the apparent lightness of the two sides of Mach's book change once you've managed to change the perceived depth relationships. In spite of the fact that the identical light energy is reaching your retina, your perception shifts. Thus, the perceived depth of the two sides of the "book" is crucial for your perception of lightness.

Lightness judgments therefore involve more than simple contrast of adjacent retinal stimulation. Note how far we have come from Wallach's "simple"

ratio principle! All of these examples illustrate not only the importance of organizing the scene before perceiving lightness but also the complexities of lightness perception. We'll now explore other examples that illustrate how sophisticated a complete theory of lightness perception must be.

Further Complexities in Lightness Perception

The preceding section should have convinced you that perceiving lightness is a complex process. That is, you need to first organize a scene before you can determine the lightness of a surface in the scene. To do so, you certainly need to know where that surface is located in space, and you also seem to perceive the lightness of the surface relative to "similar" surfaces that may not even be next to the surface in question.

Other factors come into play as we consider lightness perception. As we've already noted, in the context of Helmholtz's approach, perceiving the illumination of a scene would be helpful. As you look around, you are likely to observe a variety of illuminations. That is, some parts of the room may be bathed in sunlight, other parts may be lit by an incandescent lamp, and still other parts may be in shadow. In spite of the differences in illumination, you will still be able to assess the lightness of the surfaces under the different illuminations. Doing so, of course, requires that you determine the nature of the illumination in parts of the scene. What would happen, however, if you misjudged the illumination?

Gelb (1929) conducted a classic study of lightness perception in which he fooled the visual system about the nature of illumination present. Observers sat in a dark room and looked at a disc made of black velvet. From a hidden projector, Gelb projected a bright beam of light that fell precisely on the black velvet disc, as seen in Figure 4.11 (page 98). The observers reported that they saw a *white* disc! Do Gelb's results make sense to you? Because the observers could not detect the presence of the hidden light source, they could only assume that illumination was constant throughout the room. The illuminated black disc was reflecting much more light than any other objects in the room, so the observers were forced to infer that it must have a very high albedo.

Then Gelb placed a little slip of white paper in front of the disc, so that the light was shining on the piece of white paper as well as the black disc. Presto!

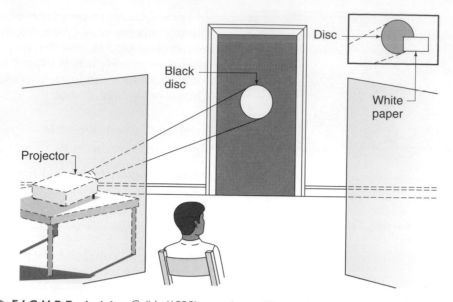

Disc

Black
disc

White
paper

Projector

▶**FIGURE 4.11**   Gelb's (1929) experiment. The projector was hidden from the observer's view so that the observer would assume that there was no additional illumination in the room. The light from the projector fell only on the rotating velvet disc, which then appeared to be white to the observer. When a piece of white paper was placed in the path of the light from the hidden projector, the observer saw the disk as black and the paper as white. In spite of this experience, when the piece of white paper was removed, the observer again saw the disc as white.

Observers suddenly reported that the disc was black. Once the white piece of paper was also placed in the light from the hidden projector, the proportion of light reflected from the black disc became small in comparison to that reflected from the white paper. Now that the observers knew that the disc was truly black, they would certainly remain convinced that it was black, wouldn't they? Actually, Gelb found that when he removed the slip of white paper, people again reported seeing a white disc. Gelb's study is a convincing demonstration of the point we made earlier—people do not perceive albedo directly. If they did, the hidden light would not have fooled them.

Even without sneaky illumination, lightness perception can be tricky. Look, for instance, at Figure 4.12 (Adelson, 2000). In the snake illusion, the eight gray diamonds are identical in lightness. In fact, the four diamonds on the right do appear to be of similar lightness, which should surprise you a bit given the different backgrounds. The two diamonds on the top of the left side definitely appear to be lighter and the two diamonds on the bottom of the left side appear to be darker. The effect likely depends on how you organize

the scene, as discussed in the previous section. It may even depend on perceived depth and transparency. Nonetheless, given that the surrounding surfaces are identical in lightness, it's interesting that the perceived lightness of the diamonds is so very different.

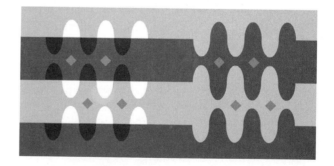

▶**FIGURE 4.12**   Do the eight diamonds appear to vary in lightness? As you might expect, the eight diamonds are identical. Your perception of lightness depends on how you organize the scene. (*Source:* E. H. Adelson, "Lightness Perception and Lightness Illusions," in M. S. Gazzaniga (Ed.), *The New Cognitive Neurosciences* (Cambridge, MA: MIT Press, 2000.)

Another factor that has an impact on lightness perception is a smooth lightness transition (or gradient), rather than an abrupt edge between surfaces. Purves and Lotto (2003) have created a powerful illustration of the Craik–O'Brien–Cornsweet effect, as seen in Figure 4.13. The top half of the object appears to be dark and the bottom half of that object appears to be light. Surely you couldn't be confused about the lightness of those two surfaces! Now place one finger over the junction between the top and bottom of the figure and watch what happens to the lightness of the two surfaces. The two surfaces now appear to be equal in lightness! So, it's the gradient information at the junction of the two surfaces that yields the apparent lightness difference.

Given all these complexities and errors in lightness judgment, how can we explain lightness percep-tion and constancy? Unfortunately, no current theory can fully explain how we perceive lightness. However, we can determine the strengths and weaknesses of various approaches as they encounter particularly difficult situations. Moreover, there is a clear sense that researchers are making progress (Gilchrist, 2006). Thus, we know that context is critical for perceiving lightness, but it's not necessarily the immediately surrounding context that is important. And we know that lightness is driven by relative rather than absolute information about light energy, but we also know that some anchors are necessary.

Now that you have a better idea of various factors that influence the perception of simple achromatic light, we will turn our attention to other basic visual processes. In our discussion of the visual system in Chapter 3, you saw that the fovea was crucial for seeing detail in the visual stimulus. We will first review the notion of acuity raised in Chapter 3, as well as factors that influence acuity. We will then discuss the ways people maintain acuity as an object moves around them.

▶ **FIGURE 4.13**   Does the upper part of this object appear to be darker than the bottom part? Given the shadows, where is the light source located? To determine the actual lightness of the parts of the object, place your finger over the intersection of the two parts. Are the two parts now equally light? (From Purves & Lotto, 2003. Image by R. Beau Lotto at www.lottolab.org.)

Section Summary

Perceiving Light Energy

1. Objects vary in their albedo, or percentage of light reflected. Lightness constancy occurs when low-albedo objects are seen as dark under widely varying illuminations, and high-albedo objects are seen as light under widely varying illuminations.

2. Many explanations of lightness perception have been proposed. For example, according to Wallach's ratio principle, perceived lightness is determined by the relative amounts of reflected light from surfaces in the scene. Objects in the visual field that reflect relatively little light are seen as dark, and objects that reflect relatively large amounts of light are seen as light. Some explanations couple the ratio principle with anchors (e.g., the lightest surface is white).

3. Perceptual organization is very important for lightness perception. Perceived lightness emerges by comparing the reflectances of objects that are grouped together (even if they

Acuity

If you are one of the many people who have less-than-perfect vision, then you already know the importance of visual acuity. Simply removing your glasses or contact lenses is all it takes to demonstrate the problems that emerge when the world can't be brought into focus on your retina.

Visual acuity is the ability to see fine details in a scene. Thus, acuity is concerned with our ability to make discriminations between stimuli in space. One can actually measure many different types of acuity (Smith & Atchison, 1997). For example, one type of acuity measures the ability to discriminate two black dots—placed close to each other on a white background—as two separate objects rather than one blurred object. Such acuity allows us to notice, for example, that a friend has a rash—rather than a mild sunburn—before the friend comes close.

Visual angle is an important concept for assessing acuity, as well as many other topics we'll address in subsequent chapters. *Visual angle* means the size of the angle formed by extending two lines from your eye to the outside edges of a target. Visual angle is a useful measure because it is not dependent on a spe-

cific distance. Thus, even though the sun is much larger than the moon, because the moon is closer, the two celestial objects have roughly the same visual angle (0.5° or 30 minutes). As seen in Figure 4.14, if an object with a diameter of about 2.4 cm (e.g., a quarter) is held at arm's length (70 cm), it will subtend a visual angle of 2°. A target with half that diameter (1.2 cm) at half the distance (35 cm) would also subtend a visual angle of 2°.

Thus, knowing that a person with good acuity is able to detect two black dots if they are separated by one minute of visual angle (one-sixtieth of a degree) means that it doesn't matter if the dots are 2 feet or 20 feet away. It's just that at 2 feet the dots would be closer to one another and at 20 feet they would be farther apart (and larger), to maintain the constant one minute of visual angle.

You should also remember that in Chapter 3 we described the fovea as having a visual angle of 5°. Furthermore, the rod-free part at the center of the fovea, which also has the greatest concentration of cones, has a visual angle of 2°. That information should now make more sense to you. For instance, holding a quarter at arm's length (70 cm) would give you a sense of the portion of your visual field that can fall on the portion of the fovea providing greatest acuity. Furthermore, at a distance of 70 cm, an object larger in diameter than a couple of quarters put together could not all fall within the fovea.

Measuring Acuity

Acuity can be measured in many different ways. The most common means for measuring acuity is the Snellen eye chart, devised by Hermann Snellen (1834–1908), a Dutch oculist, in 1862. The Snellen

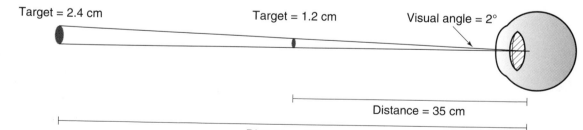

Target = 2.4 cm Target = 1.2 cm Visual angle = 2°

Distance = 35 cm

Distance = 70 cm

▶**FIGURE 4.14** An illustration of visual angle. The two target circles have the same 2° visual angle. Thus, they will cast identical images on the retina. However, the more distant target (70 cm) is larger than the nearer target (35 cm). Without information about distance, the visual system couldn't accurately estimate the size of the two objects.

eye chart is a standard screening test in many doctors' offices. As Figure 4.15 will remind you, the eye chart has rows of letters ranging from large to small. The observer is instructed to say the names of the letters in a particular row. The tester notes the row with the smallest letters that the observer can name correctly using one eye or the other.

Acuity on the Snellen chart is typically measured by comparing your performance with the performance of a normal observer. Suppose that you stand 20 feet from the chart. If you can read the letters that a person with normal sight can read at 20 feet, then you have 20/20 vision. If you have poor acuity, however, you would have to stand closer to read the letters. If you need to stand 20 feet from the chart to see the letters clearly that a normal person could see at 40 feet, then you would have 20/40 vision. The World Health Organization categorizes people as "blind" if they have 20/400 vision (or worse) after correction (Whitcher, 2004). In the United States, 20/200 vision (or worse) in the better eye after correction is typically used as the definition for blindness. With that definition, a blind person would need to stand 20 feet from the chart to read the letters that a person with normal vision could read at 200 feet.

The Snellen eye chart has some problems, though. One problem, of course, is that a person needs to know the names of the target letters in order to take the test. To address a variety of concerns, people have developed other acuity measures. One such test (Lea test) uses pictures of common objects to test visual acuity in young children. Other tests don't require identification of a stimulus, but they assess acuity by asking the person being tested to indicate the orientation of the stimulus. The tester may use rings of varying sizes with small gaps in different places (Landolt rings) or the letter *E* in one of four orientations. In all cases, the person being tested merely has to point to indicate the position of the gap or the direction in which the *E* is oriented (Chang, 2004). In its defense, however, the Snellen chart has practical significance. In real life, adults need to identify letters at a distance, and the Snellen chart does measure letter identification.

Characteristics of the Eye That Affect Acuity

Two characteristics of the eye play important roles in determining acuity. In Chapter 3, we discussed how

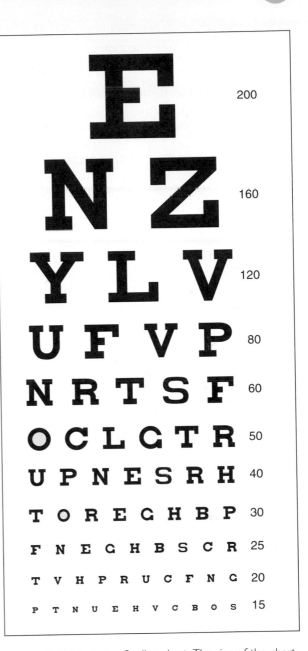

► **FIGURE 4.15** Snellen chart. The size of the chart is reduced in this figure. On a full-sized chart, someone with 20/20 vision would be able to recognize letters in the next-to-last line at a distance of 20 feet. On this substantially reduced chart, someone with 20/20 vision should be able to read the last line at about 30 inches (roughly arm's length). If you can only read the line labeled 30, then you have 20/30 vision. (You would have to be at 20 feet to read what a person with normal vision could read at 30 feet.)

the distribution of cones in the retina has an influence on acuity. Because the cones in the fovea are connected to ganglion cells in a one-to-one fashion, they provide the greatest acuity. We'll first revisit the contribution of cone distribution to acuity and then turn our attention to factors that affect the focusing of the image on the retina.

IMPACT OF CONE DISTRIBUTION Try [www] Demonstration 4.7 to illustrate the effect of cone distribution on acuity. You can see the letters in [www] Demonstration 4.7 most clearly when they are registered on the rod-free portion of the fovea, which occupies approximately 2° in the center of the eye. This area is so small that if you are holding your book roughly 18 inches away from you, only about ten letters of the text will fall on that portion of the fovea. Just a short distance from the center, acuity drops off rapidly. Look at Figure 4.16, which illustrates the relative acuity at various points on the retina. As the figure illustrates, 10° away from the center of the fovea, the relative visual acuity drops to about 30% of the acuity found at the center of the fovea. Notice the relative acuity for different parts of your eye as you look at this sentence in your book. The letters you are looking at right now are clear and sharp, but the letters on either side are blurry.

You may recall the explanation for the tremendous increase in acuity at the center of the fovea. Look back at Figure 3.11, which shows the distribution of cones across the retina. Clearly, this figure is similar to Figure 4.16. Acuity is excellent at the center of the fovea, where cones are abundant and connected to ganglion cells in a one-to-one fashion. Acuity is poor in the periphery, where cones are few and far between and more receptors are connected to each ganglion cell.

FOCUSING THE IMAGE ON THE RETINA   As we discussed in Chapter 3, the cornea first bends light entering the eye, then the lens bends it still further. The cornea bends the light rays by a constant amount, but the shape of the lens changes according to the distance of an object from the retina. When looking at distant objects, the lens is relatively thin. However, when looking at nearby objects, you reflexively increase the power of the lens by making it thicker—a process called *accommodation*. Along with accommodation, looking at nearby objects leads to constriction of your pupils (for greater depth of field)

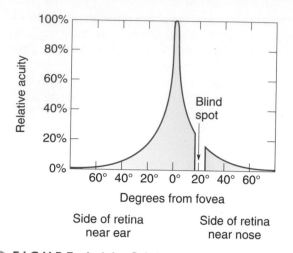

▶ **FIGURE 4.16**   Relative visual acuity as a function of position on the retina. As discussed in Chapter 3, greatest acuity occurs at the fovea (set to 100%), and it declines to either side of the fovea. Because of the absence of receptors at the blind spot (about 20° to one side of the fovea), there is no acuity.

and eye movements to focus the object on both foveas (Glasser, 2006).

The signals that produce accommodation are a blurred retinal image and indications (such as eye movements) that the object is nearby. However, suppose that your lens could not accommodate (as in presbyopia or in the case of a person whose lenses have been removed—such as S. R. D., mentioned on page 90). You'd be able to see relatively distant objects, given the optical power of your cornea. However, a problem would arise if you wanted to look at a nearby object. The image of the object would be blurred on the retina because the light rays from that object would be focused on a point behind the retina rather than on the retina itself. However, people without a flexible lens could do nothing to increase acuity. If you are relatively young, however, your lens is still flexible. Thus, your lens changes shape to bring light rays from nearby objects into focus on the retina, as we'll discuss in the next section.

Normal focusing.   Let us first consider focusing in eyes with normal accommodation ability. Imagine a lit candle on a dark night, which would radiate light in all directions. If the candle is far away, the light rays actually reaching your eye are roughly parallel. (Only a very small segment of the radiating rays would actually reach your eye.) When the candle is close, how-

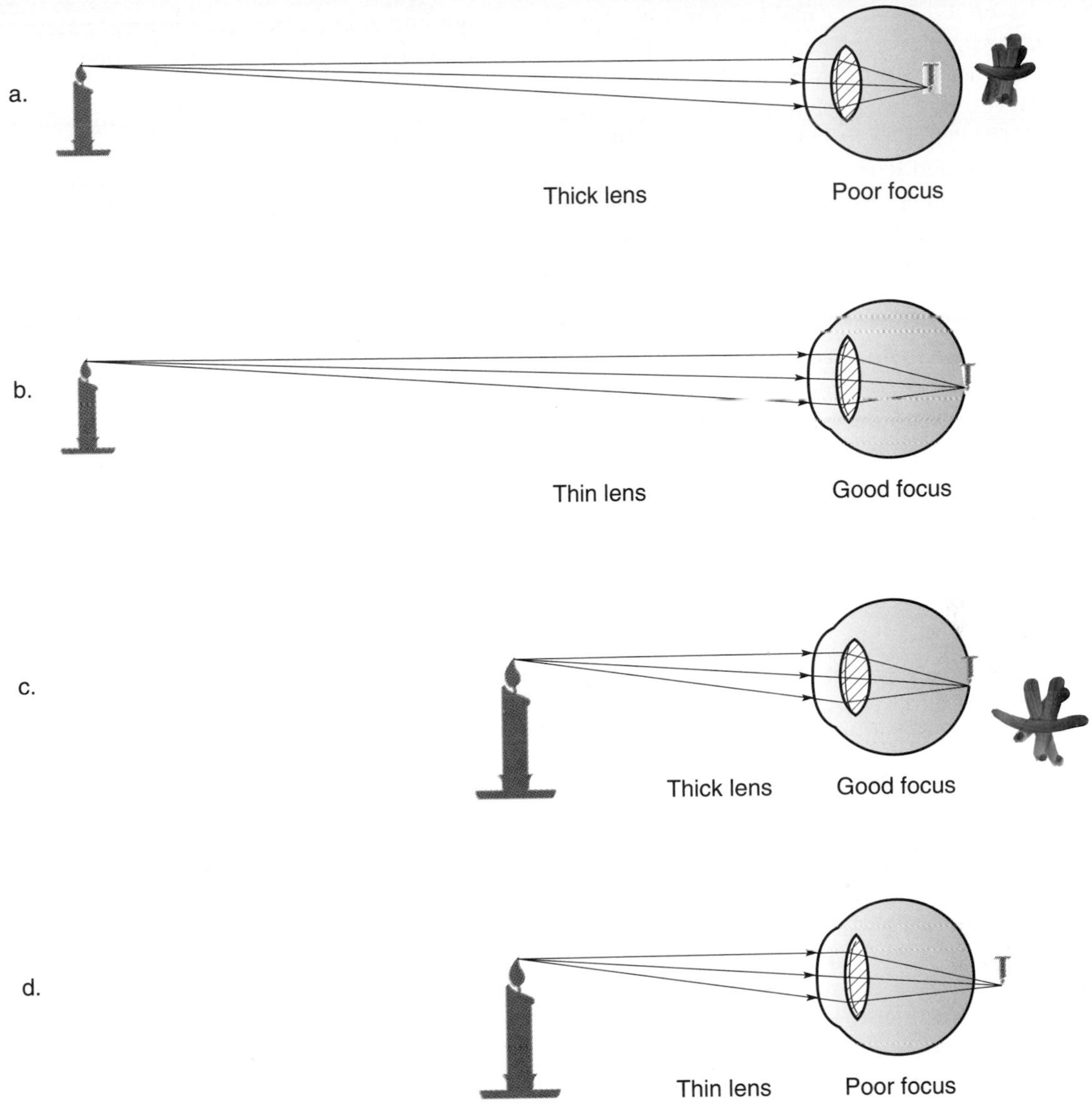

a.

Thick lens   Poor focus

b.

Thin lens   Good focus

c.

Thick lens   Good focus

d.

Thin lens   Poor focus

▶ **FIGURE 4.17** Illustration of accommodation. For distant objects, if the lens is thick it will bend the incoming light too much, causing the image to be in focus ahead of the retina rather than on the retina (4.17a). As a result, the image will be blurred when the light reaches the retina. To produce good acuity, the lens must be relatively thin for looking at distant objects (4.17b). For close objects, if the lens is thick it will bend the incoming light sufficiently to bring the image into focus on the retina (4.17c). If the lens is thin, however, the image will be brought into focus behind the retina, leading to a blurred image on the retina (4.17d).

ever, a larger segment of radiating rays would reach your eye. As a result, the rays would be more divergent (i.e., not parallel).

Look at Figure 4.17. Let's concentrate on the very tip of the flame. Consider two situations in which the candle is far away. Suppose that you had been looking at a nearby object, so that your lens was accommodated. If you then shift to look at the tip of the far-away flame, the thick lens (4.17a) would bend the rays, causing them to gather in focus at a point in front of the retina. The fuzzy image on your retina would be a signal that you needed to adjust the thickness of the lens. By making the lens thinner (4.17*b*), the light rays are bent just the right amount so that they gather in focus right at the retina.

Now consider two situations in which the candle is near. If the light rays from the tip of the flame enter an accommodated lens (4.17*c*), the thick lens bends them substantially, enough so that they gather in focus at the retina. If your lens had not been accommodated (4.17*d*), however, the thin lens would not bend the light rays sufficiently to bring them into focus on the retina. If light could pass through the retina, the rays would focus at a point behind the retina. The fuzzy image on the retina would be a signal to accommodate the lens. Now try www Demonstration 4.8, which illustrates accommodation.

The *ciliary muscle*, a tiny muscle attached to the lens, causes the lens to accommodate. When this muscle contracts, the lens becomes thicker, enabling you to see nearby objects. When this muscle relaxes, the lens becomes thinner, enabling you to see distant objects. For young adults, adjustment to changes in viewing distance through accommodation takes about 0.4 second.

Notice that accommodation involves a muscle inside the eye. The involuntary eye movements talked about earlier in the chapter, as well as the eye movements discussed in the next section, involve muscles outside the eye.

A normal eye can bring into focus a point far away. The farthest point that you can see clearly is referred to as the *far point*. Nearby objects can be kept in focus until they are just a few centimeters away from the eye, but then the curvature of the lens has reached its limits. Try bringing your finger close to your eye to determine the limits of accommodation. The closest point at which you can see your finger clearly is referred to as the *near point*.

Focusing problems.   We have been discussing the capabilities of the normal eye. Unfortunately, the shapes of many people's eyeballs and lenses do not allow them to bring an image into clear focus on the retina. Vision for a dot at a certain distance may therefore be blurred rather than crisp. People who are *myopic*, or *nearsighted*, can see objects nearby but cannot see those objects clearly if they are far away. Myopes cannot focus on a point far away; in fact, they may not be able to see clearly any object farther than a meter away. Relative to people with normal vision, myopes have closer far points and closer near points. The increased ability to see objects near one's nose

does not compensate for the loss of ability to see distant objects clearly, so most myopes choose to wear corrective lenses.

Nearsighted people typically have eyeballs longer than normal, although myopia can arise from other causes. Figure 4.18 shows the situation in which the eye is too long. Notice that, without correction, the image of distant objects is focused in front of the retina for nearsighted people—even with the lens as thin as possible. For nearby objects, however, myopic people can see clearly. Look at Figure 4.17*d* and you'll see why. If the lens were thin in a normal eye, a nearby object would be brought into focus behind the eye. Because of the elongated eyeball of myopic people, nearby objects can be brought into focus with the lens made thin. (Imagine that the eyeball in Figure 4.17*d* were somewhat longer.) So people with normal vision accommodate to look at a nearby object through a thick lens. In contrast, myopes look at a nearby object through a thin lens. Remember, then, that *nearsighted* (myopic) people can see things *nearby*, and images of distant objects are focused in *front* of the retina.

Nearsightedness can be corrected by wearing corrective lenses, as illustrated in Figure 4.18. Notice how this corrective lens makes the light rays diverge more, so that after passing through the lens of the eye, the rays end up exactly on the retina. The vision of a myopic person, when corrected, resembles the vision of a person with normal vision. Incidentally, the corrective lens is intended to correct vision for distant objects, but vision for nearby objects is also affected. Nearsighted people wearing corrective lenses cannot focus on objects as close to their eyes as they could without corrective lenses. If you are nearsighted and wear glasses or contact lenses, see how close you can bring your finger to your eye and still keep it in focus (your near point), both with and without corrective lenses.

Why is myopia a problem for so many people (over 30% of Americans)? One cause of myopia is genetic predisposition (e.g., Hammond et al., 2004). In addition to the hereditary component, several lines of research suggest that myopia is due to experience (Chen et al., 2003; Schwartz, 2004). For instance, the time spent doing close work, such as reading, is correlated with degree of myopia. However, correlation is not necessarily causation, so that evidence alone is not compelling. It would be unethical to study the impact of near work experimentally with humans. Therefore, researchers have turned to animals such as monkeys, tree shrews, and chickens to study this

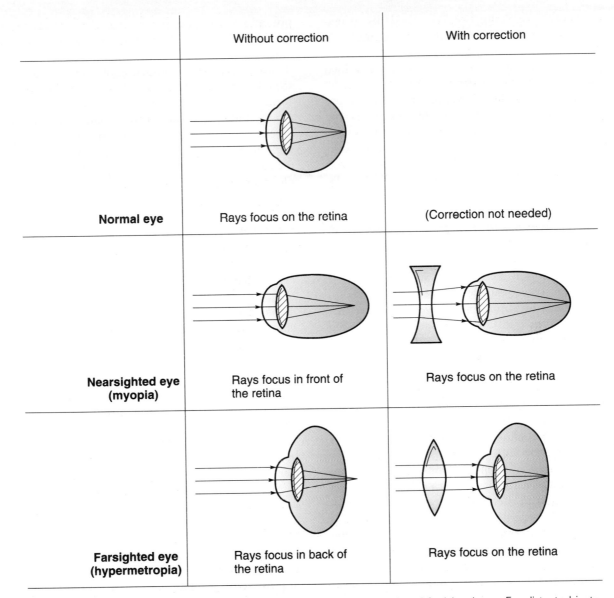

	Without correction	With correction
Normal eye	Rays focus on the retina	(Correction not needed)
Nearsighted eye (myopia)	Rays focus in front of the retina	Rays focus on the retina
Farsighted eye (hypermetropia)	Rays focus in back of the retina	Rays focus on the retina

▶ **FIGURE 4.18** Comparison of visual abilities of normal, nearsighted, and farsighted eyes. For distant objects, the normal eye makes the lens thin, bringing the image into focus on the retina. The nearsighted eye, on the other hand, cannot focus on distant objects. If the lens were to be made thicker, it would just bend the light to a greater extent, causing the image to focus even farther in front of the retina. Instead, an external lens must be placed between the object and the eye. By using the external lens, light can now be brought into focus on the retina. A different problem confronts the farsighted eye. Now the image is brought into focus in back of the retina. The farsighted eye can bring the object into focus by thickening the lens, enabling it to focus on distant objects (hence the term *farsighted*). For nearby objects, however, the farsighted eye would be unable to thicken the lens sufficiently to bring the objects into focus, so a corrective external lens is necessary. Corrective external lenses allow both nearsighted and farsighted people to use their internal lenses to accommodate in a fashion similar to that used by people with normal vision.

issue. For example, Young (1981) pursued this intriguing correlation by studying the development of myopia in monkeys. Instead of inducing myopia in monkeys by teaching them to read, Young provided them with extensive experience with close objects by raising them in conditions where nothing was more than 20 inches from their eyes. After three years, the monkeys had become myopic. Other researchers have induced myopia by having other animals wear external lenses (e.g., chicken goggles) for extended periods of time. Presumably, the strain on the various ocular muscles from doing close-up work is a contributing factor in myopia.

People who are *hypermetropic*, or *farsighted*, can see objects far away, but they cannot see nearby objects clearly. Their farsightedness typically emerges due to eyeballs that are shorter than normal. People with normal vision would look at distant objects with their lens as thin as possible. However, if hypermetropes looked at a distant object through a similar thin lens, the object would be out of focus on the retina. As Figure 4.18 shows, if the light rays could go through the eye, they would come into focus behind the eye. The hypermetrope can bring the object into focus, however, by further bending the light rays with a thickened lens. Although a person with normal vision and a hypermetrope can see distant objects clearly, the person with normal vision is using a thin lens and the hypermetrope is using a thick lens. People with normal vision can shift to looking at nearby objects by making their lens thicker, but hypermetropes already have their lens thickened, so they cannot thicken it further to see nearby objects. With the use of an external corrective lens, hypermetropes (and myopes) are able to accommodate to nearby and distant objects in a fashion similar to that of people with normal vision.

Characteristics of the Stimulus That Affect Acuity

A number of different stimulus factors affect acuity. As you can tell from the Snellen chart, one obvious factor is the size of the stimulus. It is very difficult to see extremely small stimuli, especially at a distance. Of course, this factor also allows us to ignore the fact that a color comic strip or a television image is actually comprised of many very small dots.

Another stimulus factor that affects acuity is contrast. That is, if you could imagine the Snellen chart printed on dark gray paper rather than white paper (or the letters printed in light gray on white paper), you would recognize the importance of contrast (Brabyn et al., 2001; Brabyn et al., 2007). The same stimulus that would be visible under high contrast conditions would be much more difficult to see clearly under very low contrast conditions. Unfortunately, graphic artists often fail to acknowledge the importance of contrast. Check the posters announcing events at your college. You'll probably find examples such as black print on a dark red background or yellow print on an orange background.

If you have ever struggled to read a map in the car at night, you know one additional stimulus characteristic that influences acuity: luminance, or the amount of light that enters the eye (MacLeod et al., 1990). That map would be perfectly legible in the daytime, but you will not find the street you are pursuing if you have to rely on occasional light from dim street lamps. Riggs (1971) notes that in starlight (luminance of about 0.0003 cd/m^2), we can see the white pages of a book but not the writing on them. In moonlight (luminance of about 0.03 cd/m^2), we can notice separate letters but cannot read the text. (In other words, if you have the romantic notion of reading poetry by moonlight, take a flashlight!)

Obviously, many of these acuity problems arise because, under low light conditions, we must rely on rods to see. Because of the greater convergence of rods to ganglion cells, acuity will always be low with rod vision. Cone vision becomes effective above 3 cd/m^2, and we feel comfortable reading at a luminance level of about 30 cd/m^2. Acuity increases with increases in luminance up to roughly 80 cd/m^2, after which further increases in luminance lead only to small improvements in acuity (Ricci et al., 1998). To provide optimal conditions for testing visual acuity, the World Health Organization recommends luminance conditions between 80 and 160 cd/m^2.

To illustrate the influence of luminance on acuity, identify a few different levels of luminance that you encounter in a typical day, ranging from very bright (e.g., outside in the intense sunlight at noon) to very dim (e.g., your room at night, with no lights on but with some light coming in the window). In each of these conditions, turn to the Snellen eye chart in Figure 4.15, prop the book up, and move about 10 feet away. On which line can you successfully identify all the letters accurately? Does your acuity decrease as the luminance decreases?

Section Summary

Acuity

1. Visual acuity is the ability to see fine details.

2. The Snellen chart measures acuity by asking observers to identify a target letter.

3. Acuity is influenced by several factors, including the person's ability to focus an image, the position of the image on the retina, and the lighting conditions under which the object is viewed.

4. Accommodation is the process whereby the ciliary muscles contract, increasing the power of the lens by making it thicker. Without accommodation, the light rays from a nearby object would be focused on a point behind the retina rather than on the retina.

5. People who are nearsighted (myopic) and cannot see distant objects typically have eyeballs longer than normal; the image of a distant object is focused in front of the retina.

6. People who are farsighted (hypermetropic) and cannot see nearby objects typically have eyeballs shorter than normal; the image of a distant object would be focused behind the retina if light could pass through the retina.

7. The size of a stimulus and the contrast of a stimulus with its background both have an impact on acuity. Low levels of illumination also cause acuity to decline.

Eye Movements

As we've already discussed, your eyes are constantly in motion due to very small involuntary eye movements. In this section, we're going to talk about other types of eye movements. As you know from Chapter 3, we see most clearly when we focus the image of an object on our foveas. The greatest acuity occurs in the rod-free area of the fovea, which has a visual angle of 2°. Therefore, to see the world clearly, you really need to move your eyes! (Remember, a visual angle of 2° is about the size of a quarter at arm's length.)

Basically, then, both accommodation and eye movements are important for acuity. In this section, we're going to discuss two basic types of eye movements, but both types of movement provide us with acuity. Hold your book at arm's length and look at the print. Your lens will be relatively thin and the alignment of the line of sight in your two eyes will form an acute angle. As you read the book at that distance, your eyes will have to move over the page, but the angle between the lines of sight for the two eyes remains constant as your eyes move. *Version movements* is the term used for eye movements in which the angle between the lines of sight remains relatively constant and the eyes move in the same direction.

Now slowly bring the textbook closer to you until you can just barely read the text. (In doing so, you will have determined your near point.) What happened to your lens and to your eyes? Your lens will have accommodated in order to focus the nearby text on your fovea. As we'll discuss in the next section, your eyes have made a vergence movement, because the lines of sight of your two eyes now form a wider angle. If you now read at this close distance, the necessary eye movements will be version movements, because that wider angle won't change. We'll first discuss the vergence eye movements that result in changes in the angle between two lines of sight, and then we'll explore version movements in some detail.

Vergence Movements

Vergence movements is the term used for eye movements in which the angle between the lines of sight changes and becomes smaller or larger, as when you focus on your book and move it closer or farther away. More specifically, in order to look at nearby objects your eyes *converge*, with the line of sight for each eye moving toward your nose. When looking at distant objects, your eyes *diverge*, with the line of sight for each eye moving away from your nose. (*Convergence* and *divergence* are the nouns corresponding to those verbs; they refer to the act of moving together or moving apart. Notice that you can remember the general term *vergence* because it is a part of those two words.)

The purpose of vergence movements is to allow both eyes to focus on the same target—which is crucial for maintaining acuity. Try www Demonstration 4.9, which shows how you would have double vision if you did not focus both eyes on the object of interest.

Vergence movements are relatively slow; their velocities rarely exceed 10° per second (Hallett, 1986).

The average vergence movement takes about 1 second, a relatively long time in comparison to other eye movements. Vergence movements are also slower than accommodation (which uses muscles inside the eye), even though your visual system uses both operations when you shift your fixation between far objects and near ones.

Hoffmann and Sebald (2007) found that convergence is influenced by illusory distance. With proper lighting, a concave facial mask will appear to be convex. If you want to see the nose clearly, your eyes should converge on its actual location in space.

Nonetheless, people's eyes converge on the apparent (closer) location of the nose. It's as though our visual system is willing to tolerate a slightly less clear image in order to see a face in its normal (convex) state.

In Chapter 6, we will talk about vergence movements in connection with distance perception. Under some circumstances, we may use the degree of convergence as one cue to the distance of an object. When both eyes are looking straight ahead, we are focusing on a more distant object. When our eyes are rotated inward, we are focusing on a nearer object.

IN-DEPTH

Version Movements

Have you ever had the sense that someone was watching you from a distance? Or have you had a conversation in which the other person *never* looked at you? Because we are social animals, human beings are quite sensitive to the direction of one another's gaze. For a number of reasons, psychologists are also quite interested in studying how we direct our gaze. As you know, in order to see clearly, we must move our eyes to focus on objects in the world that interest us. Thus, watching a person's eye movements is a way to learn about that person's interests. Psychologists who study infants have developed methods that make use of this fact. Because infants can't tell us directly what interests them, researchers watch infants' eyes to determine which objects capture their interest (e.g., Fantz, 1961). In Chapter 14, you'll learn more about how researchers use this technique to study perception in infants.

In some cases, researchers can learn a lot just by observing the direction of a person's gaze. However, to record the small and rapid eye movements we're about to consider, researchers need much more sophisticated equipment (Henderson, 2006). Early versions of eye-tracking equipment were large and cumbersome, restricting research to laboratory settings. Some modern equipment is actually portable, allowing researchers to study eye movements in natural settings. Using such sophisticated eye-tracking equipment has produced a wealth of information

about two important kinds of version movement: pursuit movements and saccades.

Pursuit Movements

When a bird flies back and forth across your visual field, you may track it to keep it on your fovea. In so doing, you are engaging in ***pursuit movements***. You would not ordinarily engage in pursuit movements when looking at a static scene, so motion in the field is usually required to initiate pursuit movements.

Pursuit movements have several important characteristics. They are relatively slow, with velocity typically ranging between 30° and 100° per second. A second attribute of pursuit movements is that they are smooth. In fact, they are often called *smooth pursuit movements* to emphasize this important characteristic.

People often distinguish between pursuit movements and saccadic movements. However, they are probably more similar than different (Burke & Barnes, 2006; Krauzlis, 2004, 2005). For instance, both eye movements involve a similar network of brain sites, including the cerebellum, the superior colliculus, area V5 (MT), and the frontal eye field (Carpenter, 2005; Ilg et al., 2005; Krauzlis, 2005; Robinson & Fuchs, 2001). In essence, our visual system is faced with the problem of controlling eye movements to ensure that the fovea registers objects of interest. Doing so may require pursuit movements, saccadic movements, or a combination of the two.

Saccadic Movements

When you look out at the world, you see a fairly wide visual field—and it seems that you see all of it clearly. However, only the part falling on the fovea is actually seen clearly. Some of the apparent clarity comes about because your eyes make a series of jerky movements. **Saccadic movement** is the term used to refer to these rapid movements from one fixation point to the next. These movements are necessary to bring the fovea into position over the objects of interest. You don't see during the **saccade**, in which the eye moves from one location to the next. Instead, you see during the **fixation pause**—the pause between saccades. Next, you knit together a clear composite view of a larger portion of the visual field based on several different fixations. Thus, memory is involved. Note how you are largely unaware of any of these processes!

Characteristics. Saccadic movement has some important attributes. First, saccades are probably the most frequent kind of eye movement. You make about 3 saccades each second of your waking life, so while you're awake, they occur more often than resting heartbeats (Carpenter, 2000; Findlay & Gilchrist, 2003). Second, saccades are jerky, rather than smooth. Third, saccades are rapid—much faster than the "leisurely" eye movements made in smooth pursuit or in vergence movement. The most rapid saccades are estimated to have a peak velocity greater than 600° per second. Fourth, the same brain sites that control pursuit movements also control saccades (Carpenter, 2005; Girard & Berthoz, 2005; Krauzlis, 2005; Robinson & Fuchs, 2001). Finally, the eye muscles do not tire substantially, in spite of all the saccades generated throughout the day.

Let's look at the timing of the phases in saccadic movements. To plan a saccade requires about 0.20 second (200 milliseconds). For example, if participants in a study are instructed that they must execute a saccade each time they see a specified signal, a delay of about 0.20 second occurs after the signal before the eye begins to move. This delay is longer than the time required for the saccade itself, which ranges from 0.02 to 0.10 second, depending on the distance the eyes move. Because of the speed of the saccade, the infor-

mation on the retina would be blurred during the saccade. To avoid this problem, the visual system ignores the input by means of **saccadic suppression** (Findlay & Gilchrist, 2003). Although we suppress the blur of information caused by the saccade, we can perceive some motion that may take place during saccades (Castet et al., 2002; Castet & Masson, 2000). The final stage of a saccade is the fixation pause, which lasts about 0.20 second before the eye begins another cycle. Information across the various saccades is linked together via a process called **transsaccadic integration**.

To appreciate eye movements more thoroughly, imagine your life if your eyes were "glued" in a stable position in your head. Such is the case of A. I., who had a congenital problem with the muscles controlling her eye movements (Land et al., 2002). In essence, A. I. must generate saccade-like motions using her whole head. Her "saccades" are fewer and slower, and they last longer than actual saccades. Nonetheless, using head movements, A. I. has learned to navigate her world quite effectively.

Of course, it is much more efficient to generate saccades normally. And we make use of those saccades for a wide variety of purposes. We'll briefly discuss the role of saccades in perceiving the world around us, completing simple tasks in that world, and reading.

Real-world scenes.   The problem is obvious. We need to navigate a large three-dimensional world, but we can see clearly only the very small portion of the world that is imaged on our foveas. How do we determine where to look first? Where should we next direct our gaze? And how many fixations do we need in order to figure out "what's out there"? For the most part, researchers address these questions by studying eye movements in people looking at pictures of real-world scenes. Using portable eye-tracking equipment, researchers are also studying eye movements as people move about the world engaged in everyday activities.

Eye movements in real-world scenes are basically those we've just discussed. That is, you fixate on some target in the visual field and then make a very fast saccade to another fixation target elsewhere in the display. And remember, you see virtually nothing during the saccade itself. Thus, anything you see happens during a fixation. So, within one second you might well fixate three (or even four) times with saccades between each fixation. Depending on the scene, you may well engage in fixations that are quite long (up to one second), though most tend to be in the range of .20 to .30 second.

Let's think about your very first fixation. Do you think it's made randomly? Not at all! Some researchers suggest that our first fixation is made based on low-level information, such as a concentration of edges, without any awareness of actual objects (e.g., Henderson & Ferreira, 2004a). That's certainly an intelligent rule, because we wouldn't learn much by looking at an area of blank space. But we probably do even better than that. Mark Becker and his colleagues (2007) conducted a couple of clever experiments showing that our first fixation is drawn to unusual information in the display. People first fixate on a point in the center of a blank screen, and then the researcher presents a picture. The picture might contain a scene with nothing amiss, or it might contain something unusual as a result of orientation (e.g., an upside-down face in a family portrait) or color (e.g., a green hand on a person). When seeing the unusual picture, people tend to fixate first on the upside-down face or the green hand. These results indicate that people must have understood enough of the scene to direct their very first fixation toward an object that was strange!

Given these results, you shouldn't be surprised that we learn a lot about a visual scene on that very first fixation. In fact, results from a number of different experimental paradigms attest to our ability to extract the gist of a scene (e.g., seashore, urban scene, etc.) with a single fixation (Oliva, 2005; Oliva & Torralba, 2006; Underwood, 2005).

What, then, drives the saccades to subsequent fixations? Again, low-level perceptual information (e.g., detecting that space is filled or empty) must play a role, allowing us to ignore empty space. But we're also drawn to change in the display, so we fixate on blank areas that used to contain an object, or we fixate on objects that suddenly appear (Brockmole & Henderson, 2005; Henderson & Ferreira, 2004a). Consistent with Theme 4, cognitive information also plays a role in directing saccades. That is, if we're trying to learn about one aspect of the scene (e.g., "What is the economic background of this family?"), our saccades and fixations are quite different than if we're trying to learn about a different aspect of the scene (e.g., "How old are the people in this scene?").

Everyday activities. Several research teams are doing interesting work investigating how we move our eyes during visually guided actions. They have studied eye movements while people engage in a variety of activities such as playing sports, driving a car, and making a sandwich or making tea (Findlay & Gilchrist, 2003; Hayhoe & Ballard, 2005; Land et al., 1999; Shinoda et al., 2001). These studies differ from the type of study we discussed in the previous section. In these studies, people are actively engaged with objects in the world, rather than simply looking at real-world scenes. Thus, the eye movements serve to guide actions, and these eye movements occur prior to actions.

When engaged in relatively simple and well-rehearsed activities such as making tea or making a peanut-butter-and-jelly sandwich, your eye movements can be classified into some basic categories (Findlay & Gilchrist, 2003; Land & Hayhoe, 2001). You direct your gaze to *locate* objects you'll need for your task (e.g., tea kettle, bread). Depending on the location of the objects of interest, some of these saccades can be quite large. Once located, you look at an object to *direct* movement toward that object. You look to *guide* one object (e.g., kettle lid, knife) toward another object (e.g., kettle, jelly jar). And, finally, you look to *check* on some condition (e.g., is the water boiling, is the bread covered with jelly). Some of the fixations made while completing these tasks are also relatively long (e.g., looking to see if the water is boiling).

This kind of work clearly complements the work done by researchers studying eye movements while looking at static pictures displayed on a monitor. As is often the case, a major distinction between the two approaches is the trade-off between an experimenter's control over the experimental environment and the extent to which the situation is realistic (external validity). Researchers can tightly control the contents of a static picture. However, once researchers allow people to move freely about their environments, they lose some control. We'll now turn our attention to eye movement research on reading. This research will often use static displays of text, but that is typical of the text we ordinarily read. Thus, studies of eye movements in reading are attractive because they may be highly controlled and yet are fairly realistic.

Reading.   You are unlikely to be aware of the saccades that occur as you read this text. In fact, you may think that your eye movements are quite smooth as you read, even though you are making a series of fixations and saccades (Rayner, 1998; Rayner & Liversedge, 2004; Rayner et al., 2005; Reichle & Laurent, 2006). As is true when looking at natural scenes, the duration of each fixation is variable (.05 to .5 second or more), depending on factors such as the nature of the passage being read and the nature of the word itself. As always, the saccades take very little time to complete (.02 to .05 second), and they typically move your eyes 6 to 9 letters to the right. (If you were reading Hebrew text, saccades would typically move your eyes to the left.) However, some saccades can move your eyes forward only 1 letter, while others can move your eyes forward as many as 20 letters (Rayner et al., 2005). Other saccades, called *regressive saccades,* actually move your eyes backwards to produce fixations on words that you want to study again (Inhoff et al., 2005; Vitu, 2005). And, of course, when you reach the end of a line of text, your eyes move to the beginning of the next line of text.

As you might expect from earlier discussions of eye movements, saccades in reading are not random. Even when the information doesn't fall on our foveas, our visual system makes use of retinal input from outside our foveas to direct the saccade. Just as your eyes don't move to empty spaces as you look out at the real world, saccades don't often move your eyes to a space between words. But the spaces are important because they mark boundaries between words, so your visual system can decide where next to fixate. In fact, some words (e.g., short ones, especially articles such as *the*) are skipped over altogether (Findlay & Gilchrist, 2003). And when you do fixate on a word, your eyes usually land just to the left of the center of the word.

In fixating on a single letter, we actually perceive a range of letters and spaces to the left (about 4 positions) and to the right (about 15 positions) of the fixated letter. This region is referred to as the **perceptual span** (Rayner & Liversedge, 2004). Of course, some of the positions to the right are outside the fovea, so we couldn't actually fully read those upcoming words. However, we can get a helpful preview of what's next.

Rebecca Johnson and her colleagues (2007) conducted a series of experiments that illustrate how specific that information might be. You may have received an email claiming that researchers at Cambridge University had learned that people are capable of reading text, even though letters in the words are jumbled. If not, try out www Demonstration 4.10. Not only is the email a hoax (no one at Cambridge was doing such research) but its claims are not entirely accurate (Grainger & Whitney, 2004; Rayner et al., 2006). However, it is true that some changes in the letters of an upcoming word have a larger negative impact than other changes.

Johnson and her coauthors had people silently read a number of passages on a computer screen. In each passage a target word would either be untransformed, have two internal letters transposed, have two final letters transposed, have two internal letters replaced with different letters, or have the final two letters replaced with different letters. As the reader's eyes moved to the target word, the computer replaced whatever had been present with the actual target word.

For example, consider the following sentence: *Christopher's tiny fleas performed flawlessly in the miniature circus.* With *fleas* as the target, that word would be unchanged for some people, but for other readers, it might appear as *flaes* (internal transposition), *flesa* (final transposition), *fluos* (internal substitution), or *fleve* (final substitution). Keep in mind that no matter what string might have been present initially, once the reader's eyes moved to the target word, the computer replaced it with the actual word.

If we get little explicit information from the letters to the right of the perceptual span, then none of the replacements for *fleas* should make a difference in the time to process *fleas* when our eyes get to the target word. However, people spent more time fixating on *fleas* when it had previously contained substituted letters than when it was intact or when it contained transposed letters. Thus, reading is indeed disrupted when the upcoming word contains a couple of letters that are "wrong." Furthermore, reading is also disrupted when the upcoming word contains the correct letters, but when two letters are transposed. Note that in all cases, the first couple of letters (*fl*) were the same and were correct. However, you can read the word more effectively if you get a preview of *fleas* compared to a preview of *flesa*, which helps you more than a preview of *fleve*.

As you might expect, good readers make better use of their eye movements than do poor readers, with longer saccades, fewer regressive saccades, and shorter fixations. At the extreme is a person with pure alexia, who must read by fixating on each separate letter of a word (Rayner & Johnson, 2005).

Even with this brief overview of eye movements in reading, you probably have a sense of the complexities involved. However, as an accomplished reader, you likely have no sense of the complexity of the process as you read. In Chapter 3, you got a sense of the complexities that underlie the basic processes of vision. In future chapters, you'll acquire even more evidence of the complex processes that researchers explore in an effort to explain perceptual processes that seem so simple to the human perceiver. In fact, much of the attraction of the study of perception is the exploration of these "hidden" processes.

At this point you might be scratching your head and wondering how it is that, when you look out at the world, it isn't bouncing all over the place! After all, your eyes are traveling in a series of tiny involuntary movements as well as the vergence and version movements we've just discussed. And we haven't even considered the impact of the movement of your body. Nonetheless, consistent with Theme 3, you should note that you *do* perceive a stable world in spite of all the retinal information that might signal that the world is in motion. Moreover, it should be increasingly clear to you that we can learn a great deal about what people are thinking or doing by watching how they move their eyes.

Section Summary

Eye Movements

1. Vergence movements occur when the angle between the lines of sight changes. The eyes converge to look at nearby objects and diverge to look at distant objects. Vergence movements are slower than version movements.

2. Version movements of the eyes occur when the angle between the lines of sight remains constant; version movements include pursuit movements and saccadic movements.

3. Our visual system uses pursuit movements to track moving targets; these movements are slow and smooth, and they attempt to match the speed of a target.

4. Saccadic movements are the rapid movements of the eye from one fixation point to the next. They are frequent, jerky, rapid, and ballistic. Saccadic movements do not produce substantial fatigue.

5. When looking at a real-world scene, we don't fixate on empty spaces, which suggests that simple elements of the scene drive fixations. However, we do fixate on anomalies in the scene, which suggests that we have some basic understanding of the scene. Moreover, saccades and fixations vary depending on what we are trying to learn about a scene.

6. We engage in a series of saccades and fixations as we move about the world and perform various tasks, such as playing sports, driving, making tea, and reading. The size of the saccades and the duration of the fixations are dependent on a number of factors, including many cognitive factors.

7. Good readers make better use of eye movements than poor readers, gaining a sense of upcoming words as they're reading.

Review Questions

1. What are the prerequisites for vision, and how do they illustrate clear differences between our visual system and the functioning of an automatic camera?

2. Review the connection between lateral inhibition and Mach bands. Then try to integrate the information on lateral inhibition with information from Chapter 3 on receptive fields. How might receptive fields give rise to lateral inhibition?

3. A frog does not have involuntary eye movements. Discuss the implications of this deficit for the frog's visual perception. What would you predict would happen if a frog's head were immobilized?

4. Discuss theoretical approaches to lightness constancy. What role does albedo play in determining lightness constancy? Describe several instances in which constancy appears to fail, and indicate how each of these instances might be addressed by one of the theories of lightness constancy.

5. Many of your friends may think of perception as a passive process. Using information from different sections of this chapter, construct an argument for the active nature of perception.

6. Think about all the characteristics of the visual system and of a stimulus that could influence acuity. Combining all these factors, describe a situation in which acuity would be the best possible. Then describe a situation in which acuity would be the worst possible.

7. What are the four kinds of eye movements discussed in this chapter? What is their function? Identify the kind of eye movement(s) represented in each of these situations: (a) You watch a bird fly away from you in a diagonal direction, so that its flight is also from right to left. (b) You are staring into someone's pupils, but your eyes move slightly. (c) You are carefully examining a painting in art class.

8. In Chapter 3, we discussed many of the structures that are important for visual perception. Draw on that information to discuss various topics from this chapter. Here are some questions you might try to answer: (a) How does your knowledge of the retina, particularly the fovea, help you to understand saccades? (b) What area of the visual cortex would process information important to directing pursuit movements? (c) What visual pathway would be important for lightness perception?

9. Describe the accommodation process that takes place in normal eyes when viewing a *nearby* object, and then summarize how this focusing is abnormal in nearsightedness and farsightedness. How can each of these disorders be corrected?

10. Contrast the focusing performed by the eye muscles during accommodation with the other eye movements mentioned in this chapter. Be certain to mention location of the muscles and speed of the movement.

Key Terms

edge, p. 83
contour, p. 83
brightness, p. 83
lightness, p. 83
achromatic, p. 83
Ganzfeld, p. 83
lateral inhibition, p. 84
Mach band, p. 87

involuntary eye
   movements, p. 87
microsaccade, p. 87
stabilized retinal image,
   p. 88
scotomas, p. 89
albedo, p. 92
lightness constancy, p. 93

constancy, p. 93
distal stimulus, p. 93
proximal stimulus, p. 93
ratio principle, p. 94
visual acuity, p. 100
visual angle, p. 100
accommodation, p. 101
ciliary muscle, p. 104

far point, p. 104
near point, p. 104
myopic, p. 104
nearsighted, p. 104
hypermetropic, p. 106
farsighted, p. 106
version movements,
   p. 107

Recommended Readings

Findlay, J. M., & Gilchrist, I. D. (2003). *Active vision: The psychology of looking and seeing*. New York: Oxford.

In an early chapter, this book provides a good overview of eye-movement characteristics. Later chapters discuss eye movements during search, reading, and looking at natural scenes. You'd be hard-pressed to find a better brief introduction to this fascinating area.

Gilchrist, A. (2006). *Seeing black and white*. New York: Oxford.

Gilchrist provides both a historical survey of explanations for lightness perception and a critical analysis of the explanations. Gilchrist's career has been devoted to explaining lightness perception, and although a complete explanation remains elusive, this text provides a clear statement of his perspective on the field.

Henderson, J. M., & Ferreira, F. (Eds.). (2004). *The interface of language, vision, and action: Eye movements and the visual world*. New York: Psychology Press.

In this edited text, you'll find excellent chapters on topics we discussed in this chapter, including reading and perceiving natural scenes. However, you should also enjoy the other chapters on visual search, language comprehension, and other topics.

Pessoa, L., & De Weerd, P. (Eds.). (2003). *Filling-in: From perceptual completion to cortical reorganization*. New York: Oxford.

Because this is an edited volume, you'll find some chapters more interesting and accessible than others. You should certainly enjoy reading the foreword by V. S. Ramachandran.

Visual Pattern Perception

CHAPTER 5

IN THE TWO preceding chapters, we examined some basic aspects of the visual system. In Chapter 3, we studied the mechanisms that transduce light energy into the energy required by our neural processing apparatus. In Chapter 4, we outlined some of the prerequisites for vision, with an emphasis on the importance of edges and change. Although you may not be consciously aware of edges, you certainly can notice them when we call your attention to them. For instance, as you look at this textbook, you can readily perceive the letters on the page as patterns of edges. Your book's cover forms edges against a background that is itself filled with edge information. Edges abound, yet you do not see edges—you see objects! You see letters, books, faces, tables, chairs, and walls. Of course, most of these objects are three-dimensional. To simplify our discussion of shape perception, we'll defer most of the discussion of how we perceive the depth of such objects until the next chapter.

These objects have their distinctive shapes or forms, so you might think that we could define the terms *shape* and *form* with little difficulty. Unfortunately, a precise definition is extremely problematic (Peterson, 2001). For our purposes, we can simply consider **shape** or **form** to be an area set off from the rest of what we see because it has one or more edges. Thus, the shape of your book is determined by a particular arrangement of edges.

Look at a simple object, such as a coffee mug, and view it from different angles. Assuming that the rim of the mug is circular, you should note that it forms a circular image on your retina only when viewed from directly above. From most perspectives, the rim forms an elliptical image on your retina. Nevertheless, the rim of a cup seems to stay circular. You should recognize such stability in your perception of an object's shape as a constancy.

We introduced the notion of a constancy in Chapter 4. Remember that a perceptual constancy occurs when we perceive a distal stimulus as remaining roughly unchanged in spite of changes in the proximal (retinal) stimulus. **Shape constancy** means that an object appears to stay the same shape despite changes in its retinal image. Of course, we would find it most difficult to move through a world in which objects appeared to change shape as our point of view changed.

How, then, are we able to recognize objects when seen from novel perspectives? That is one of many challenges facing researchers who seek to understand object perception and recognition. We will first examine several attempts to unravel the mysteries inherent in object perception. Next, we will turn our attention to illustrations of the complexities involved in shape perception—illustrations that often pose challenges to the approaches we've discussed.

Approaches to Shape and Pattern Perception

How does your visual system determine that particular edges go together to form an object, such as your book? Any approach to shape perception must uncover the processes that enable you to integrate the edges of an object, such as your book, to arrive at the perception of that object. As we explained in Chapter 4, a number of processes (including depth perception) contribute to lightness perception. Similarly, you should expect that a number of processes underlie the perception of shape. Some of these processes may occur sequentially, with the output of one process providing the input to another process. Other processes may occur simultaneously, in parallel.

In Chapter 1, we described some processes as bottom-up processes (data-driven) and other processes as top-down (conceptually driven) processes. The very earliest stages of visual experience, which analyze data from the sensory receptors, must involve **bottom-up (data-driven) processing**. The data arrive and set into motion the process of recognizing various shapes. You should recognize that this process echoes Theme 2 of this text, which emphasizes the importance of the stimulus and the sensory systems.

Top-down (conceptually driven) processing emphasizes the importance of the observers' concepts in determining perception. In top-down processing, observers have expectations and concepts about how the world is organized. They believe that certain objects are likely to be found in certain situations. These expectations and concepts set into motion the process of recognizing various shapes. Thus, perception is a construction that is influenced by prior knowledge, expectations, and intentions (Peterson, 2007). In fact, consistent with Theme 4, such cognitive factors may influence the very earliest processing of incoming stimuli.

We will now examine several approaches to shape perception. As you read about each approach, try to identify whether it emphasizes a bottom-up or top-down process. Of course, you'd do well to assume that when you perceive a shape, you're using both processes.

Spatial Frequency Analysis Approach

Instead of focusing on edges, the *spatial frequency analysis approach* focuses on luminance changes as a cue to shape (Regan, 2000). According to this approach, the visual system breaks down the stimulus into a series of lighter and darker stripes (Palmer, 1999). You may well be scratching your head as you try to figure out what these patterns of stripes (called *sinusoidal gratings*) have to do with shape perception. Were it not for the contributions of the French mathematician Jean Baptiste Joseph Fourier (1768–1830), it would be impossible to see these patterns as the potential building blocks of shape perception.

FOURIER ANALYSIS   Fourier made several mathematical contributions that form the basis of spatial frequency analysis. Although we will focus on visual stimuli, his work can also be applied to the analysis of sound waves, as you will see in Chapters 9 and 10. *Fourier analysis* involves analyzing a stimulus into its component sine waves (Palmer, 1999). If you have taken a trigonometry course, you may recall that a *sine wave* is a smooth wave pattern resembling the light waves discussed in Chapter 3. As you can see in Figure 5.1*a*, the wave pattern is repeated at regular intervals, fluctuating from high intensity to low intensity and back. Figure 5.1*a* shows a single sine wave and how it corresponds to a stimulus that is a blurry set of stripes. This sine wave corresponds to a narrow horizontal segment taken from Figure 5.1*b*. Figure 5.1*b* shows a sinusoidal grating, a set of blurry stripes that alternate between dark and light. (The dark stripes represent the low-intensity areas of the sine curve; the light stripes represent the high-intensity areas.)

Fourier proved that a wave of any complexity could be analyzed into many component sine wave gratings (Regan, 2000). So let's consider the kind of sine waves that might be the components for a horizontal strip taken from a set of stripes. Suppose that we add together a series of sine waves, a process known as *Fourier synthesis*. (We perform a Fourier *analysis* to analyze a stimulus into its component sine waves; we perform a Fourier *synthesis* for the reverse process of combining sine waves to represent the pattern in the stimulus.) We could select a series of sine waves that have 1, 3, 5, and 7 cycles within the same

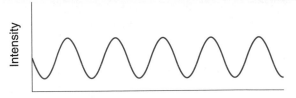

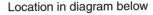

a. Sine wave

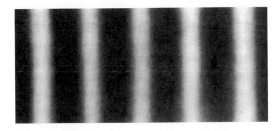

b. Sinusoidal grating

▶ **FIGURE 5.1**   A sine wave *(a)* and its corresponding sinusoidal grating *(b)*. Notice that the darker stripes in the grating correspond to the low points on the sine wave. The lighter stripes in the grating correspond to the high points on the sine wave.

horizontal distance, as shown in Figure 5.2 (page 118). If we add these waves together, this Fourier synthesis results in the figure at the bottom of the diagram. You'll notice that it is similar to the square wave shown in Figure 5.3*a*. As seen in Figure 5.3*b*, a square wave corresponds to a series of regularly repeating dark and light stripes that have crisp, not blurry, edges. In order to achieve the square wave seen in Figure 5.3, we would have to add together many more than the five sine waves seen in Figure 5.2.

SPATIAL FREQUENCY   How can we describe a sinusoidal grating so that it is most useful in relation to visual processes? The grating in Figure 5.1*b* has a spatial frequency of about 2 cycles per inch. However, this system of measurement will not be useful when we want to discuss visual processes. If that pattern is presented 4 inches from your nose, the stripes are relatively broad; at a distance of 4 feet, the stripes are relatively narrow. Because of this ambiguity, spatial frequency is typically measured in terms of the number of cycles in each degree of visual angle.

As we discussed in Chapter 4, *visual angle* means the size of the angle formed by extending two lines from your eye to the outside edges of the target. The

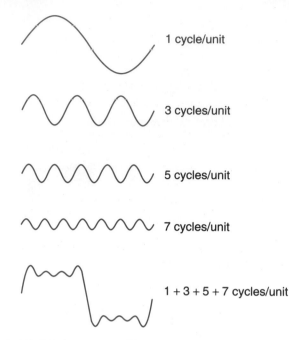

▶ **FIGURE 5.2** The complex wave produced by adding four sine waves resembles a square wave. Fourier analysis would involve going from the complex wave to the four constituent sine waves. Fourier synthesis would involve adding the four sine waves to produce the complex wave.

a. Square wave

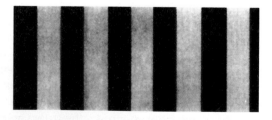

b. Intensity distribution for a square wave

▶ **FIGURE 5.3** A square wave (a) and its corresponding intensity distribution (b). Compare this figure to Figure 5.1, particularly noting that the smooth transitions from lighter to darker areas in Figure 5.1 are replaced by more abrupt transitions in this figure.

visual angle is measured in degrees, minutes, and seconds. A circle has 360 degrees (symbolized °). However, because your eyes cannot see in back of your head or even straight above your head, visual angles are always much smaller than 360°. Just as an hour is divided into minutes and seconds, a degree in space is divided into minutes and seconds. Each degree has 60 minutes (symbolized '), and each minute has 60 seconds (symbolized ").

The size of the visual angle depends on the size of the target and the distance of the target from the eye. Larger targets at the same distance would create larger visual angles. The size of the visual angle also depends on the distance of the target from the eye. As you move the target away from you, it occupies an increasingly smaller visual angle.

Look again at Figure 5.1 and hold this book 14 inches (35 cm) from your eyes. Figure 5.1 shows a 1-cycle grating at that distance. In other words, one complete cycle, including a dark and a light phase, is found within 1 degree of visual angle. Incidentally, if you move the book to a distance of 28 inches (twice as far away), you will achieve a 2-cycle grating. You could also create a 2-cycle grating by making twice as many stripes in the same horizontal distance of Figure 5.1, and then viewing the figure from 14 inches.

CONTRAST SENSITIVITY FUNCTIONS The patterns you have seen so far are comprised of high-contrast stripes of black and white. Alternating black and *gray* stripes would reduce the contrast. The contrast between the two kinds of stripes can be decreased to the point that an observer cannot distinguish between the pattern of alternating stripes and a uniform gray patch. For example, a researcher might take the 1-cycle grating shown in Figure 5.1 and gradually lower the contrast until the observer reports, "I can't distinguish that figure from the gray patch." (You should recognize this psychophysical technique as the method of limits.) This procedure could be repeated with a variety of gratings, perhaps representing spatial frequencies between 0.1 cycle and 50 cycles/degree.

Figure 5.4 shows a typical ***contrast sensitivity function***, a diagram that illustrates the relationship between spatial frequency and sensitivity. Notice that the y-axis is labeled "Sensitivity." As you'll recall from Chapter 2, high sensitivity corresponds to low threshold. The sensitivity is highest for gratings with spatial frequencies of 4 to 5 cycles/degree (Palmer, 1999).

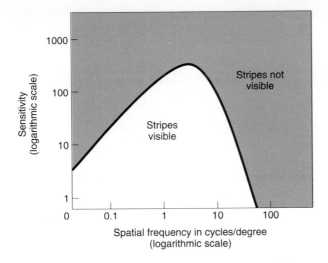

►FIGURE 5.4   The solid line represents a typical contrast sensitivity function for an adult human. Most adults are maximally sensitive to a spatial frequency of about 5 cycles/degree, which is roughly the high point of the function. The stripes in high spatial frequency stimuli, such as those above 100 cycles/degree, are not visible to most adults.

Thus, observers are particularly skilled at discriminating between this particular grating and a gray patch. In fact, observers can still perceive the grating when the contrast between the black and gray stripes is quite low. Spatial frequencies of 1 cycle/degree or less and spatial frequencies of 10 cycles/degree or more require much higher contrast between the two kinds of stripes. The visual system simply does not process those gratings as well. Incidentally, if you want to know just what the "ideal" grating that you can see so well looks like, turn back to Figure 5.1, prop up your book, and back up about 7 feet (2.1 m).

Fergus Campbell and John Robson (1964, 1968) were early proponents of the importance of spatial frequency information. They proposed that our visual system has several sets of neurons, each of which responds best to a particular spatial frequency. These neurons, located in area V1 of the visual cortex, are sensitive to particular spatial frequencies due to the size of their receptive fields (Wandell, 1995). The sensitivity of these neurons to particular spatial frequencies creates multiple **spatial frequency channels**. These multiple analyzers can explain most of the research on pattern perception, particularly for near-threshold stimuli.

How do the differences in receptive field size give rise to neurons tuned to particular spatial frequencies? As you will recall, in Chapter 3, we discussed tuning curves, which demonstrate that simple cells in the visual cortex respond better to some orientations than to others. Similarly, tuning curves can be derived for particular spatial frequencies.

For example, let's consider a particular cell that has an on-center, off-surround arrangement, as shown in Figure 5.5a (page 120). If a sinusoidal grating is presented so that the white portion stimulates the center and the gray portion stimulates the surround, the cell will respond at a high rate. However, if the sinusoidal grating shows wide stripes (i.e., low spatial frequency), the strong excitation of the center is canceled by the strong inhibition of the surround; this situation is shown in Figure 5.5b. Finally, if the sinusoidal grating shows narrow stripes (i.e., high spatial frequency), the moderate excitation of the center is canceled by the moderate inhibition of the surround; this situation is shown in Figure 5.5c.

Naturally, however, we manage to perceive sinusoidal gratings that have either higher or lower spatial frequencies than the one in Figure 5.5a. For example, one set of neurons with wide receptive fields might respond best to a spatial frequency of 0.5 cycle/degree. Another set of neurons might respond best to 1 cycle/degree, and other sets to frequencies such as 6, 10, and so on. As seen in Figure 5.4, the ideal combined frequency is 4 to 5 cycles/degree, based on the contrast sensitivity functions of all the component neurons that make up the visual system.

An illustration of spatial frequency analysis.   It is quite useful to think of visual perception in terms of spatial frequency, whether considering the stimulus or the visual system. Stimuli in the world may be characterized in terms of their high spatial frequency information (i.e., detail), as well as their low spatial frequency information (i.e., broad patterns of lightness and darkness). Moreover, cells in our visual system vary in the size of their receptive fields, which gives rise to channels that are sensitive to different spatial frequencies. As a result, most approaches to shape perception acknowledge the contribution of spatial frequency analysis.

A great deal of research supports the contribution of spatial frequency analysis to visual perception (Schwartz, 2004). However, you may have a difficult time visualizing some of the studies. Fortunately,

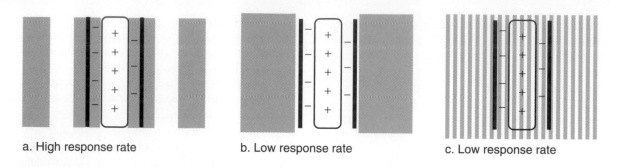

a. High response rate   b. Low response rate   c. Low response rate

▶ **FIGURE 5.5**   An illustration of how three different spatial frequencies would affect an on-center, off-surround simple cortical cell. The spatial frequency in part *a* would produce the highest response rate because the high intensity of the stimulus falls on all of the on-center (and only a little of the off-surround). The spatial frequency in part *b* also stimulates the on-center. However, the inhibition caused by stimulating the off-surround would result in a reduced rate of firing. In part *c*, the spatial frequency is so high that again both the on-center and the off-surround would be stimulated, resulting in a lower firing rate.

Phillipe Schyns and Aude Oliva (1999) developed hybrid images that provide a vivid illustration of the functioning of your spatial frequency channels. These images are constructed by combining low and high spatial frequency information in a single image. As a result, your perception will differ depending on the distance at which you view the hybrid image.

Look at the hybrid image in Figure 5.6 (Oliva et al., 2006). When your textbook is near you, you will see a bicycle, with accompanying shadows. However,

▶ **FIGURE 5.6**   This hybrid image illustrates the role of low and high spatial frequency information. What do you see when you look at the figure right now? Next, prop up your book and step far away from the figure. Now, what do you see? The shift from bicycle to motorcycle is due to changes in the spatial frequency information. (From Oliva et al., 2006)

when seen from a distance, you'll see a motorcycle! When seen from nearby, the motorcycle information is low frequency, so your visual system focuses on the high-frequency information in the bicycle. When you are sufficiently far away from the picture, however, the bicycle information has too high a frequency for your visual system (refer to the upper end of the graph in Figure 5.4). At that distance, the motorcycle information is now at a spatial frequency that makes it visible.

Spatial frequency analysis is quite useful as a way to understand the processing of visual stimuli. At the same time, you probably anticipate that shape perception involves more than just spatial frequency analysis. We'll now turn our attention to another influential approach to shape perception.

Gestalt Approach

We provided a brief introduction to Gestalt psychology in Chapter 1. The three psychologists most closely associated with the classical Gestalt approach—and whose work forms the basis for most of this section—are Max Wertheimer (1923), Kurt Koffka (1935), and Wolfgang Köhler (1947). According to the **Gestalt approach**, we perceive objects as well-organized "wholes" rather than separated, isolated parts. Such an emphasis epitomizes a **holistic orientation** to perceptual processing. Thus, the perceptual whole that we experience is not simply the sum of its parts (Palmer, 2002). www Demonstration 5.1 illustrates the principle that we process more than isolated features.

The holistic Gestalt approach is distinctly different from a more analytical orientation, such as spatial frequency analysis. An ***analytical orientation*** emphasizes the importance of the components that combine to form our perceptual experiences. However, you should think of these two general orientations as complementary, because perception relies on both holistic and analytic processes.

Gestalt psychologists investigated three areas that we will consider here: the laws of grouping, the "goodness" of figures (known as the law of Prägnanz), and figure-ground relationships. We will see that many of their ideas are still considered central to understanding shape perception, because they provide a means for organizing the edges extracted in the early stages of visual processing.

LAWS OF GROUPING   Max Wertheimer (1923) was the first to describe the Gestalt laws of grouping. You'll see these laws illustrated in 🔵www Demonstration 5.2, as well as in Figure 5.7 (page 122). Five major ***laws of grouping*** describe why certain elements seem to go together:

1. The ***law of proximity*** states that elements near each other tend to be seen as a unit.

2. The ***law of similarity*** states that elements similar to each other tend to be seen as a unit.

3. The ***law of good continuation*** states that elements arranged in either a straight line or a smooth curve tend to be seen as a unit.

4. The ***law of closure*** states that, when a figure has a gap, we tend to see it as a closed, complete figure.

5. The ***law of common fate*** states that, when elements move in the same direction, we tend to see them as a unit.

LAW OF PRÄGNANZ   Kurt Koffka described the ***law of Prägnanz***: "Of several geometrically possible organizations the one will actually occur which possesses the best, simplest and most stable shape" (Koffka, 1935, p. 138). For instance, the law of Prägnanz predicts that some geometric figures (e.g., perfect circles and squares) are "better" than others (e.g., ellipses and rectangles).

Figure 5.8 (page 123) shows a design that could be interpreted in at least two ways. It could represent three squares, two of which have small squares cut

out of the lower right corner, or it could represent three squares overlapping each other. The law of Prägnanz predicts that you will see three overlapping squares. In doing so, you are also exhibiting a closure process (one of the laws of grouping). You likely view each square as complete, but the corners of two are hidden. We'll return to this notion when we discuss completion processes.

You may think of Prägnanz as a general principle that underlies the Gestalt laws of organization. That is, the laws work to produce a good or simple figure. Ironically, it isn't simple to define *simplicity* or *complexity* (Donderi, 2006). Thus, although the law of Prägnanz has intuitive appeal, it is notoriously difficult to define (Cutting, 2007).

FIGURE-GROUND RELATIONSHIP   In the section on the laws of grouping, we saw that people organize elements of an array according to certain rules. In the section on the law of Prägnanz, we saw that people tend to organize forms to produce a simple interpretation, such as three overlapping squares. Organization is not random; we perceive patterns in the world around us. Parts of a design are also organized with respect to figure and ground. When two areas share a common boundary, the ***figure*** is the distinct shape with clearly defined edges. The ***ground*** is what is left over, forming the background. Look, for example, at your textbook (the figure) lying on your desk (the ground). The notion of the figure-ground relationship is one of the most important contributions of Gestalt psychologists. 🔵www Demonstration 5.3 illustrates the separation of figure from ground, including the apparent depth relationships.

Edgar Rubin (1915–1958), a Danish psychologist, was one of the first to try to clarify what constitutes the figure, as opposed to the ground. For example, he noted that the figure is closer to the viewer than the ground and has a distinct shape. Rubin was also responsible for a famous reversible (or multistable) figure. ***Ambiguous figure-ground relationships*** are situations in which the figure and the ground reverse from time to time, the figure becoming the ground and then becoming the figure again. These reversals often arise spontaneously, although you can also force the reversals to occur. Figure 5.9 (page 123) shows Rubin's vase-faces reversible figure. Even though the distal stimulus never changes, you can see either a white vase or two outlined faces. Can you understand why this demonstration was so important

○　○　○　○　○　○
○　○　○　○　○　○
○　○　○　○　○　○
○　○　○　○　○　○
○　○　○　○　○　○
○　○　○　○　○　○

a.　**The law of proximity.** You will see this arrangement as a set of columns—not a set of rows. Items that are near each other are grouped together. Now notice the typing in this book. You see rows of letters rather than columns because a letter is closer to the letters to the right and left than it is to the letters above and below.

+　+　+　+　+　+　+

○　○　○　○　○　○　○

+　+　+　+　+　+　+

○　○　○　○　○　○　○

+　+　+　+　+　+　+

○　○　○　○　○　○　○

b.　**The law of similarity.** You will see this arrangement as a set of rows rather than columns. Items that are similar to each other are grouped together. Now look at the two words at the end of this sentence that are in **boldface type.** Notice how these two words in heavier print cling together in a group, whereas the words in regular, lighter print form their own separate groups.

c.　**The law of good continuation.** You will see a zigzag line with a curved line running through it, so that each line continues in the same direction it was going prior to intersection. Notice that you do not see the figure as being composed of the two elements below:

Look out the window at the branches of a tree, and focus on two branches that form a cross. You clearly perceive two straight lines, rather than two right angles touching each other.

d.　**The law of closure.** You will see a circle here, even though it is not perfectly closed. A complete figure is simply more tempting than a curved line! Now close this book and put your finger across one edge, focusing on the shape of the outline of your book. You should still see your book as complete, but with a finger in front of it.

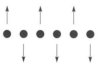

e.　**The law of common fate.** If dots 1, 3, and 5 suddenly move up and dots 2, 4, and 6—at the same time—suddenly move down, the dots moving in the same direction will be perceived as belonging together. The next time you look at automobile traffic on a moderately busy street, notice how clearly the cars moving in one direction form one group and the cars moving in the opposite direction form another group.

▶**FIGURE 5.7**　An illustration of five of the Gestalt laws of grouping.

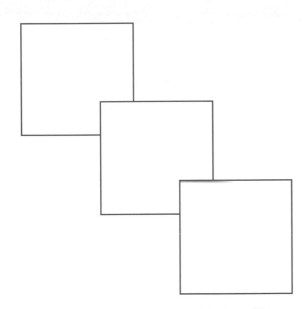

▶ **F I G U R E   5 . 8**   An illustration of the law of Prägnanz, which predicts that you will see this figure as three overlapping squares because that is the simplest interpretation of the figure.

▶ **F I G U R E   5 . 9**   The vase-faces figure illustrates the potential ambiguity of figure-ground relationships. You can see the white vase against a dark background or you can see the black faces against a white ground. Notice how difficult it is to see both the faces and vase simultaneously.

to the Gestalt psychologists? Your ultimate perception should not change if the elements of the stimulus define the shape. Clearly, shape perception is not entirely defined by the parts of the stimulus.

The Dutch artist M. C. Escher (1898–1972) enjoyed playing perceptual tricks on his viewers. You will find several examples of ambiguous figure-ground relationships in Escher's work. In *Circle Limit IV*, for example, light-colored angels and dark-colored devils take turns becoming figure and ground.

It's sometimes helpful not to stand out against the background. That, of course, is the principle underlying camouflage. Many organisms have evolved natural camouflage that makes it more difficult to detect them against their normal background. In fact, some camouflaged figures may not be distinguished from the ground until they move (Regan, 2000).

EXPLORING GESTALT PRINCIPLES   The Gestalt approach continues to influence psychological research, especially in the perception of objects. In this section, we'll briefly review some research that explores Gestalt organizing principles and even extends them. We'll also discuss research that attempts to understand the processes by which we separate figure and ground.

As we mentioned earlier, closely related to the Gestalt principle of closure is the notion that people complete the missing contours of an incomplete image (i.e., the two occluded squares in Figure 5.8). This process, called **amodal completion**, may also occur quite early in the perception of objects. Many researchers are interested in the nature of these processes (e.g., Albert, 2007; de Wit et al., 2006; Lee & Vecera, 2005). For example, Mary Ann Foley and her colleagues (2002, 2007) presented people with a series of complete and incomplete pictures of familiar objects (Figure 5.10, page 124). Pictures are often made incomplete by covering them with another object, such as a black rectangle. When later asked whether they had seen the original pictures as complete or incomplete, people often mistakenly claim that they had seen the incomplete pictures as complete. People only rarely claim that they had seen a complete picture as incomplete. These results indicate the strength of amodal completion processes.

Although the Gestalt psychologists espoused many principles of perceptual organization, researchers have proposed new principles. For example, Stephen Palmer (2003a) has proposed a principle of organization called **common region**. According to the principle of common region, we tend to group together stimuli that appear to occur within the same region. For instance, looking at a map of the United States,

Complete   Incomplete

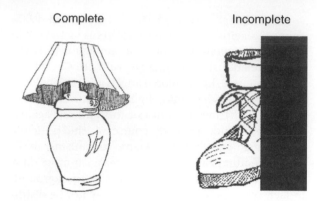

▶ **FIGURE 5.10** Examples of stimuli from studies of amodal completion. People first see a series of drawings of complete and incomplete objects, such these. At a later test, people mistakenly report that the incomplete pictures had been seen as complete. Such results likely emerge because people complete the incomplete objects in their "mind's eye." (From Foley et al., 2007)

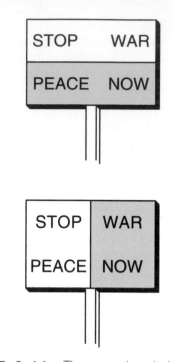

▶ **FIGURE 5.11** These two placards demonstrate the importance of common region. By changing the regions that are common to two of the four words, the message of these two placards is changed dramatically. (*Source:* Reprinted from *Cognitive Psychology,* 24, 3, Stephen E. Palmer. "Common Region: A New Principle of Perceptual Grouping," p. 12, copyright © 1992, with permission from Elsevier.)

would you group Pittsburgh, PA, with Harrisburg, PA, or with Columbus, OH? Although Pittsburgh is actually closer to Columbus, people tend to group it with Harrisburg—another city within the bounds of Pennsylvania. As you can see in Figure 5.11, in spite of identical arrangements of the words on the two placards, the message is changed radically by changing the regions that bound the words. Do you get the impression that far too many people are adhering to the message of the lower placard?

Another principle is **uniform connectedness**, in which we organize input as a single unit when we perceive a connected region of uniform visual properties, such as lightness, color, and so on (Palmer, 2003b). Figure 5.12 illustrates the operation of uniform connectedness. Notice how easily this principle overrides the laws of proximity and similarity. Palmer and Irvin Rock (1922–1995) have argued that uniform connectedness arises very early in the organization of a visual scene. Uniform connectedness clearly plays a role in shape perception, but other organizing principles may be equally important (Kimchi, 2003b; Peterson, 2001).

Researchers remain quite interested in the processes underlying figure-ground organization. At one level, it may seem perfectly logical that, in order to recognize an object, we must first distinguish it as a figure against a background (Palmer, 2002). However, Mary Peterson and her colleagues argue that some form of object recognition must *precede* figure-ground organization (Peterson, 2003; Peterson &

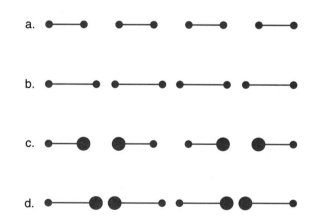

▶ **FIGURE 5.12** Four patterns, that illustrate the principle of uniform connectedness. In each of the four patterns, the lines create a pattern connecting each set of two dots. Notice that the connection is able to override the Gestalt grouping laws of proximity (in *b*), similarity (in *c*), and even proximity and similarity together (in *d*). (From Palmer & Rock, 1994)

Grant, 2003). Peterson has conducted a number of studies that support the important role of memory and experience in the early stages of shape perception (e.g., Peterson & Enns, 2005). Of course, Peterson's position is entirely consistent with Theme 4.

First, look for a while at Figure 5.13a and then look for a while at Figure 5.13b. Did you continue to see the symmetrical black area in the middle of the two figures as figure? If you are like most people, you will find it easier to see the black area as figure in Figure 5.13a than in Figure 5.13b. Why? Presumably because you notice that the white space in Figure 5.13b could be seen as two half-silhouettes of standing women. The "trick" is that the two stimuli are identical, except that one is the other turned upside down. Because the two stimuli are identical, except for orientation, you should see the black area as figure with equal ease in both cases. Peterson and her colleagues argue that people have more difficulty seeing the inner black area of Figure 5.13b as figure. Therefore, they must perceive the objects (the white silhouettes) prior to organizing the stimulus into figure and ground.

As you can tell, the questions that stimulated the Gestalt psychologists continue to generate research.

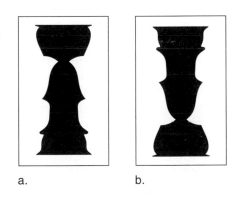

a.   b.

▶ **FIGURE 5.13** Two patterns used by Peterson and her colleagues to illustrate the precedence of object perception over figure-ground organization. Figure 5.13a is simply Figure 5.13b upside down. You should find it fairly easy to see the middle black area in Figure 5.13a as figure. However, because you can more easily see the white area in Figure 5.13b as two white silhouettes of women, you should find it more difficult to perceive the black middle area as figure, compared to Figure 5.12a. (*Source:* M. A. Peterson, E. M. Harvey, & H. J. Weidenbacher, "Shape Recognition Contributions to Figure-Ground Reversal: Which Route Counts?" *Journal of Experimental Psychology: Human Perception and Performance, 17* (1991): 1075–1089.)

We will now turn our attention to the computational approach. Note that both spatial frequency analysis and Gestalt organizational principles are important to this approach.

Computational Approach

The *computational approach* tries to formally define the visual processes necessary to represent the world. A computational theorist is often interested in developing programs that can take in the sort of information falling on the human retina and process the information to yield representations of the world. Although even the simplest organisms seem to accomplish this task quite easily, computational theorists find it difficult to program artificial systems to accomplish the task (Bruce et al., 2003).

Much of the work emphasizing the computational approach has focused on the early stages of visual processing, or what might be referred to as low-level scene analysis. However, these theorists explicitly acknowledge the operation of higher-level processes (Gordon, 2004). For instance, recognizing an object as a house requires that we know what a house is (Ullman, 1996). Thus, a computational approach must incorporate such specific knowledge. At the same time, computational theorists emphasize the role of general knowledge about physical principles, rather than specific information about the world.

DAVID MARR'S CONTRIBUTIONS David Marr (1945–1980) had a tremendous influence on the development of computational vision. In fact, his ideas have been so influential that we'll focus on them in this section. Of course, computational theorists have made many advances in the decades since Marr's early death (Bruce et al., 2003). Nonetheless, as we describe Marr's contributions, you will gain a general sense of the computational approach.

Marr analyzed the perceptual process into three different levels: the computational theory, representation and algorithm, and the hardware implementation (Gordon, 2004). The computational theory is relatively abstract and most closely related to the perceptual problem facing your visual system. One such problem might be, Why do we see the world as unchanging, in spite of retinal changes?

Nature might solve the same problem in potentially different ways (algorithms) using different hardware. The distinction between algorithms and hardware roughly resembles the distinction between software and computer. To solve the problem of writing a paper, you might choose one of several different word-processing programs. Versions of the chosen program might have been implemented for totally different brands of computers, so you next choose the hardware to solve your problem. You should note that the actual program, or code, used to invoke the algorithms of the word processor could differ substantially.

When researchers explore the neuroanatomy and neurophysiology of vision, they are primarily investigating hardware implementation. Although we must ultimately understand the hardware, Marr was not confident that studying the hardware of vision would help us understand visual processes. He likened that approach to studying feathers to learn about bird flight. Instead, Marr argued that we should study aerodynamics, which would lead us to better understand bird flight—as well as the anatomy of bird wings. Likewise, if we learn about the principles necessary to solve the problem of edge detection, we would have a better understanding of the nature of the algorithms *and* hardware involved in vision.

FROM EDGES TO SHAPE PERCEPTION   In Chapter 4, we discussed the importance of edge detection. The computational approach also emphasizes the importance of edge detection for early stages of visual perception. Marr (1982) offered the notion of a zero-crossing as the starting point in edge detection. A *zero-crossing* is the point at which a function changes from positive to negative; this zero-crossing occurs when there is an intensity change in the visual field. Mathematically, a particular filter—called a *Mexican-hat filter*—can detect a zero-crossing (Gordon, 2004). Figure 5.14 shows a cross section through the center of the function. You will see the origin of the filter's name when you look at the three-dimensional representation in Figure 5.15*b*.

What happens when we pass an image through this filter? In part, it depends on the size of the filter used. In Figure 5.15, the original picture *(a)* was analyzed by both a wide and a narrow Mexican-hat filter to produce the two pictures seen in *(c)* and *(d)*, respectively. Notice that in both cases, edges and blobs are extracted from the original image, with the narrower filter producing greater detail.

If you recall the receptive fields we discussed in Chapter 3, you should see the close connection between the Mexican-hat filter and the "hardware"

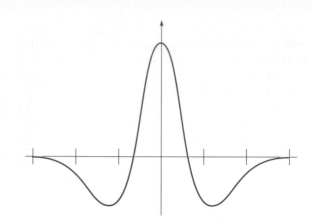

▶ **FIGURE 5.14**   A cross-section through the center of a Mexican-hat filter. The *x*-axis represents area and the *y*-axis represents intensity.

that appears to produce the filter. A ganglion cell's on-center off-surround receptive field is much like the Mexican-hat filter shown in Figure 5.15 seen from overhead. In other words, the horizontal interconnections among our photoreceptors produce receptive fields that can function as edge-producing filters.

The computational approach certainly relies on the spatial frequency approach. Recalling the information in the earlier section, you should see that the width of the receptive field (filter) would determine the spatial frequency to which the neuron is most sensitive (Bruce et al., 2003). Narrower filters would be more sensitive to higher spatial frequencies. Presumably, the visual cortex receives zero-crossing "maps" of input from the multiple spatial frequency analyzers and combines them into a representation of the original image.

According to Marr (1982), the information from the filters leads to the primal sketch. The raw *primal sketch* is like "a map specifying the precise positions of the edge segments, together with the specifications at each point along them of the local orientation and of the type and extent of the intensity change" (Marr, 1982, p. 71). Organizing principles, such as the Gestalt principles discussed previously, operate on the elements of the raw primal sketch to group the elements together and produce the full primal sketch.

These organizing principles become apparent when you look at the pattern in Figure 5.16 (page 128), designed by José Marroquin. Notice how your visual system continually reorganizes the elements in the figure. Your system seems to be trying to organize

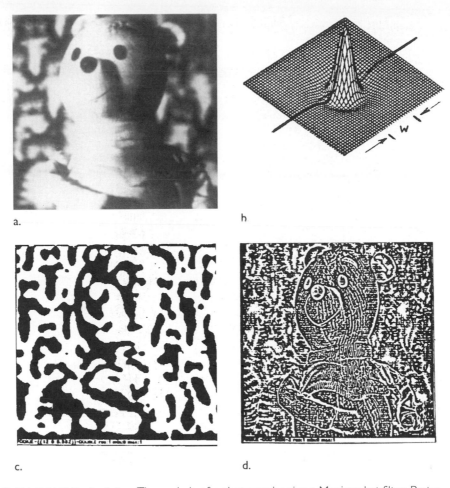

a.

h

c.

d.

▶ **FIGURE 5.15** The analysis of a photograph using a Mexican-hat filter. Part *a* shows the original photograph. Part *b* captures the three-dimensionality of the Mexican-hat filter, with the dark line through the center yielding Figure 5.14. Analyzing the picture in part a with a wide filter (the width, *W*, in part *b* is large) yields part *c*. Analyzing the picture with a narrow filter (*W* in part *b* is small) yields part *d*. (From Richards et al., 1988)

the display into "objects" that may even appear to be defined by *virtual lines*—lines that aren't really there! These virtual lines play an important role in computational theories. These virtual lines may be the precursors of the illusory contours we'll discuss shortly.

How can we extract three-dimensional (3-D) information from two-dimensional (2-D) retinal input? This is a topic we will explore in great detail in Chapter 6. Take a moment now to look up from your textbook and notice the rich sense of depth that you experience, even though your retinas register only two dimensions. One step in the process of extracting three dimensions will likely be the determination of figure and ground, for which some computational

theorists have already developed algorithms (Peterson & Skow, 2008).

Marr proposes that we achieve a three-dimensional representation in two stages. The first stage, called the *2.5-D sketch*, is a representation of the visible surfaces in the visual field from the viewer's perspective. The sketch is labeled 2.5-D to indicate that it does not fully capture all of the 3-D information, nor is it completely two-dimensional. The 2.5-D sketch is built up from the full primal sketch along with information derived from motion, as well as the differences between the images on the two retinas (Bruce et al., 2003). Because it is viewpoint-dependent, the 2.5-D sketch wouldn't be effective for recog-

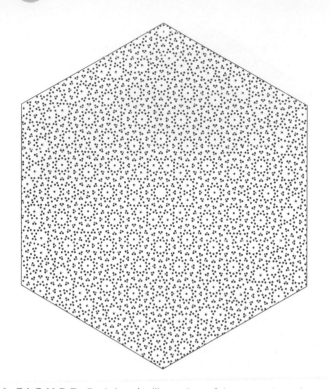

▶ **FIGURE 5.16** An illustration of the operation of organizing principles in the visual system. As you stare at this figure, you will see many different shapes. Most of the shapes will be circles of different size, but you should also see squares and rectangles. Notice that an element of the figure is part of one shape, and at other times that same element is part of another shape. (*Source:* J. L. Marroquin, Master's Thesis, MIT, 1976, as seen in Marr, 1982.)

nizing an object if you looked at it from a novel perspective.

Prior to recognizing an object, Marr proposed that we transform the 2.5-D sketch into a representation that is object-centered. This object-centered ***3-D sketch*** represents depth more accurately than the 2.5-D sketch. Moreover, the representation is no longer viewpoint-dependent. Therefore, you could recognize the object from many different perspectives. Contrary to Marr's perspective, some theorists argue that the viewpoint-dependent representation remains crucial for object recognition (Peissig & Tarr, 2007). In other words, there must be *some* computational cost involved in viewing an object from a novel perspective. Consequently, a theory of object perception must be viewpoint-dependent (Biederman, 2007).

Marr's approach to object perception might be labeled a structural-description model (Tarr & Vuong, 2002). You might be able to imagine how a person could construct a 3-D sketch by mentally combining various malleable cylinders. Think of each cylinder as though it were made of clay. You could then compress the entire cylinder, making it thinner. You might also compress only one end, turning the cylinder into a cone.

Suppose that you had a bunch of cylinders of various sizes. As you can see in Figure 5.17, combining these cylinders in various ways allows for a fairly flexible representation of objects. Construction of objects from such cylinders is useful because it allows

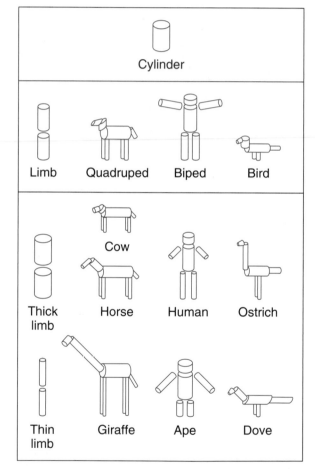

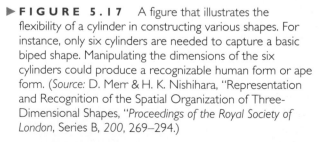

▶ **FIGURE 5.17** A figure that illustrates the flexibility of a cylinder in constructing various shapes. For instance, only six cylinders are needed to capture a basic biped shape. Manipulating the dimensions of the six cylinders could produce a recognizable human form or ape form. (*Source:* D. Merr & H. K. Nishihara, "Representation and Recognition of the Spatial Organization of Three-Dimensional Shapes, "*Proceedings of the Royal Society of London*, Series B, *200*, 269–294.)

us to predict the parts of the objects that would be visible from a particular perspective and the parts that would be hidden. In order to create such representations, people must be able to mentally attach the cones or cylinders to one another at different positions and different angles. Put the six cones together one way and you have a roughly human form. Shorten the two leg cylinders and lengthen the two arm cylinders and you now have a roughly simian form. Change the orientation and size of the six cylinders and you now have an ostrich.

A similar structural-description model is Irving Biederman's *recognition-by-components approach* (Palmer, 2003b). The components that lead to recognition are basic shapes called *geons* (short for *geometric icons*). Biederman proposed that one might construct a vast array of objects from a relatively small number of geons. You should recognize that these geons are quite similar to Marr's cylinders. However, in Biederman's model, geons allow the extraction of three-dimensional information from the primal sketch, which is purely two-dimensional (Bruce et al., 2003; Peterson, 2001). The recognition-by-components approach also acknowledges the contribution of top-down processes to object recognition. Accumulating evidence from a variety of sources supports the explanatory value of this approach to object recognition (Biederman, 2007).

Recognition may not require that all of the component geons be processed, however. For instance, in Figure 5.18 you can recognize a stylized penguin com-

posed of just a few geons as easily as you can recognize a more completely drawn penguin—a fact that eases the task of a cartoonist.

SOURCES OF SHAPE INFORMATION   As we emphasize in Theme 2, natural stimuli are rich sources of information. Part of the task confronting a computational theorist is to identify the types of information in natural stimuli that might be used to derive an object's shape. Computational theorists have identified a number of different aspects of stimuli that aid in the perception of shape, such as motion, shading, texture, and color (Regan, 2000). These theorists tend to identify the aspect of the stimulus that gives rise to shape information as "shape-from-_____," where the blank is filled in with the crucial aspect of the stimulus. We will now review some of these sources of information about shape.

Shape-from-motion indicates that we gain a good deal of information about an object's 3-D shape when it is in motion (Giaschi, 2006; Regan, 2000). As we will discuss in Chapter 6, when you look at the shadow of a 3-D object projected onto a 2-D surface, you have no sense at all that the object has any depth. However, as Hans Wallach (1953) noted long ago, when the object is placed into motion, so that the 2-D shadow moves, the object immediately appears to be three-dimensional. You will also see the power of motion in providing a sense of shape when we discuss biological motion in Chapter 8.

Because the image cast on our retinas is 2-D, computational theorists have developed algorithms that derive 3-D shape from moving 2-D images (Regan, 2000). Neurophysiological research also supports our ability to extract shape from motion (Hou et al., 2006; Peuskens et al., 2004). It's interesting to note that this cue to shape may become less effective as we age (Blake et al., 2008; Norman et al., 2008).

Computational theorists have determined that the way light falls on an object provides important cues about 3-D shape; these cues are called *shape-from-shading* and *shape-from-highlights* (Khang et al., 2007; Norman et al., 2004). Look around you and notice that the curvature common to many objects—like faces—tends to create some areas that receive less light than other areas. Notice how an overhead light creates shading under a person's nose and chin. These shadows attached to the object provide important information about the shape of the object. As is true of shape-from-motion, neurophysiological evidence supports shape-from-shading (Georgieva et al., 2008).

▶**FIGURE 5.18**   A penguin is distinguishable in either drawing, even though the drawing on the left contains only a few geons. In order to recognize shapes, we need not analyze all of the constituent geons. (*Source:* Reprinted from *Computer Vision, Graphics, and Image Processing,* Irving Biederman, "Human Image Understanding: Recent Research and a Theory," copyright © 1985, with permission from Elsevier.)

We will have more to say about the role of shadows in depth perception in Chapter 6.

Notice also that shiny surfaces, such as a billiard ball or some people's foreheads, may also reflect the light source more directly. Such highlights are also important cues to an object's shape (Fleming et al., 2004). As a result, computer graphics make great use of this cue in providing a vivid sense of depth and lighting.

Computational theorists have identified other aspects of the stimulus that give rise to shape information. Many of these cues are effective for the perception of three-dimensional shape, so we'll return to them in the next chapter. For now, however, we will turn our attention to other approaches to shape and pattern perception.

Feature-Integration Approach

The previous approaches to shape perception have made little specific mention of the role of attention. Attention is a word with varied meanings. We define **attention** as the focusing or concentration of mental activity. Anne Triesman and her colleagues developed the **feature-integration approach** in which attention—especially spatial attention—plays a vital role. According to Treisman (2006b), we organize a scene into perceptual units called *object files* with specific locations. Because an object may change or move through a scene, we must continuously update these object files. Object files are the means through which we bind the various features of objects, such as their color, shape, or orientation.

Such features are automatically encoded in the first stage in this model. **Preattentive processing** involves the automatic registration of features, using parallel processing across the visual field. A **parallel process** is one that allows us to process many targets simultaneously. Thus, we encode different types of features and locations of objects in parallel (M. E. Wheeler & Treisman, 2002).

The binding of features is due to **focused attention**, which is the "glue" that binds the separate features into a unitary object. Unlike preattentive processing, focused attention requires serial processing. A **serial process** requires us to process the targets one at a time.

What led Treisman to propose this combination of parallel and serial processes? We'll briefly review some studies that illustrate feature integration. In one study, Treisman and Gelade (1980) proposed that, if isolated features are processed automatically in preattentive processing, then a target should be located rapidly if it differs from its neighboring, irrelevant items. It should seem to "pop out" of the display automatically. In a series of studies, Treisman and Gelade discovered that if a target feature differed from the irrelevant items with respect to a simple feature such as orientation or color or curvature, observers could detect the target just as fast when it appeared in an array of 30 items as when it appeared in an array of 3 items.

In other research, Treisman and Souther (1985) found that people use preattentive processing when a simple feature is *present* in a target, but they must use focused processing when that same feature is *absent* from the target. Figure 5.19 shows displays similar to the ones people examined in Treisman and Souther's study. In Figure 5.19a, people searched for a circle with a line; in Figure 5.19b, they searched for a circle without a line. As you can see, the circle with a line "pops out" in the upper display, but you must inspect the display in Figure 5.19b more closely to determine that it contains the target.

If you process all the features of an object separately, then it's possible that they won't always be bound together properly. For example, if you're distracted or your attention is overloaded, you might combine the features inappropriately. An **illusory conjunction** arises when the circumstances prevent us from looking at an object with focused attention, leading us to inappropriately bind features as we perceive the object (Treisman, 2006a). Most experiments that create illusory conjunctions use very brief exposures. For example, in such a display, you may perceive a green E as red because a nearby O actually is red.

The organization of the stimuli in the array also plays a role in illusory conjunctions. Thus, people are especially likely to produce illusory conjunctions between objects that are grouped by proximity, similarity, or good continuation—basic Gestalt principles. Esterman and his colleagues (2004) found that the category of a stimulus also affects illusory conjunctions. Thus, in a rapidly presented array (e.g., 37E), if the number 7 is in red and the 3 and the E are in black, you're more likely to mistakenly perceive the 3 as red than the E. Similarly, features of letters are more likely to be affected by nearby letters.

Conflicting results have led researchers to modify some aspects of the feature-integration approach.

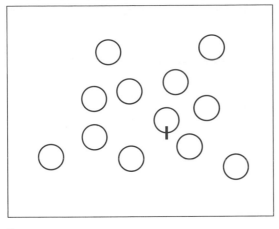

a.

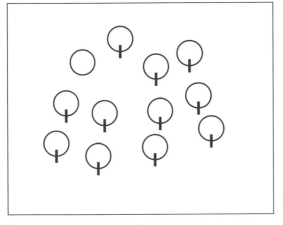

b.

▶ **FIGURE 5.19** Do you find the different stimuli more easily in part *a* or in part *b*? Why? (*Source:* A. M. Treisman & J. Souther, "Search Asymmetry: A Diagnostic for Preattentive Processing of Separable Features," *Journal of Experimental Psychology: General, 114* (1985): 285–310.)

Nonetheless, it continues to provide an important framework for understanding the role that attention plays in the process of shape perception. Researchers are particularly interested in the binding problem, including the brain areas that are involved in the binding of features (Esterman et al., 2007; Robertson, 2003).

Prototype-Matching Approach

So far, we have examined four approaches to shape and pattern perception: spatial frequency analysis, the Gestalt approach, the computational approach,

and the feature-integration approach. According to another perspective, the ***prototype-matching approach***, we store abstract, idealized patterns in memory. When we see a particular object, we compare it with a ***prototype***, or an ideal figure. If the object matches the prototype, we recognize the pattern. If it does not match, we compare it with other prototypes until we find a match. For example, you have likely developed a prototype for a bird. This prototype represents an organism of a certain size (probably small), certain features (e.g., a beak, wings, and feathers), and certain abilities (e.g., can fly). This prototype does not need to specify a particular color of feathers or a particular shape of the beak—after all, a prototype is abstract. When you see a bird, you recognize it because the organism you're watching matches the prototype.

The prototype-matching view is flexible. The prototype is a general pattern, not a specific one with every feature well defined. We can, for example, recognize a penguin as a bird. Moreover, we can recognize a letter even when it is distorted. Consider the letter M, for example. Look at the assorted M's in Figure 5.20. You recognize those letters as M's even though they are all different. You can also recognize an M in various orientations like M and *M* and in various sizes like M and M.

You might wonder where prototypes come from. A good deal of research suggests that we may extract prototypes from repeated exposures to different examples (e.g., Love et al., 2004; Smith et al., 2008). Thus, once you know that all the letters in Figure 5.20 are M's, you can extract the essential characteristics

▶ **FIGURE 5.20** The fact that you can readily recognize all of these stimuli as M's is an indication of the flexibility of your visual system. Does this flexibility seem consistent with the template-matching approach?

that determine M-ness. Your prototype might be something like "roughly vertical stroke up, stroke down and right, stroke up and right, stroke down." If you know about the work of the developmental psychologist Jean Piaget, you might also relate the formation of prototypes to his concept of assimilation.

Do not confuse the prototype-matching view with another approach—template matching (Palmer, 2003b). According to the ***template-matching approach***, we have many templates, or specific patterns, stored in memory (Rolls & Deco, 2002). When we see a letter, for example, we determine whether it matches one of the templates. If it matches, we recognize the letter. If it does not fit the template, we search for another template. In a way, the template is like a lock, and a letter is like a key. As you know, a key may be only a tiny bit different from the appropriate shape, yet that difference is sufficient to prevent the key from opening the lock.

However, consider the problem of perceiving an object from different distances. When nearby, the object would produce a relatively large retinal image. When far away, the object would produce a relatively small retinal image. To address this issue, some theorists add a scaling component to the template, allowing the template itself to vary in size.

The idea of each pattern fitting into an appropriate template is quite consistent with what we know about complex receptive fields found in the visual cortex. Thus, it might work well for relatively simple shapes (e.g., squares, triangles, letters, hand-shaped stimuli). However, the template-matching approach may strike you as inefficient—especially for more complex objects. We would need literally millions of templates to be able to recognize all the objects in the world. At the same time, the finding that some neurons may encode specific objects (Gaschler, 2006; Quiroga et al., 2008) makes the notion of templates more feasible. It's certainly true that humans are capable of storing great quantities of visual information (Brady et al., 2008). This information-storage capacity would support the development of both prototypes and templates.

Both the prototype- and template-matching approaches are useful because they emphasize the distinction between your perceptual experience and the mental representation to which it must be compared in order for us to recognize an object. Any approach to object recognition must at some point hypothesize some form of comparison.

Section Summary

Approaches to Shape and Pattern Perception

1. A shape or form is determined by particular arrangements of edges. We perceive shapes by a combination of bottom-up and top-down processes.

2. The spatial frequency analysis approach proposes that Fourier analysis can be used to break a complex scene into its component sine waves, each corresponding to a different sinusoidal grating. People have multiple spatial frequency channels, each with a different ideal frequency determined by the receptive fields of its neurons. Overall, however, people are most sensitive to gratings with spatial frequencies of 4 to 5 cycles/degree.

3. The Gestalt approach emphasizes that we see objects as well-organized "wholes" rather than separate parts. The perception of objects arises through the organization of elements according to the laws of grouping, which include the laws of proximity, similarity, good continuation, closure, and common fate.

4. The law of Prägnanz refers to our tendency to perceive figures as good, simple, and stable. Thus, some figures are "better" than others and are easier to encode into memory than poor figures.

5. In figure-ground relationships, the figure has a definite shape with clearly defined contours, in contrast to the ground, or background. The figure also seems closer and more dominant. In ambiguous figure-ground relationships, the figure and the ground reverse from time to time.

6. The principle of uniform connectedness, whereby similar areas of the visual field are linked together, appears to operate at very early stages of visual perception. Some researchers think that figure-ground relationships are determined fairly early in visual perception, but other researchers argue that some form of object perception actually precedes figure-ground organization.

7. According to the computational approach, we build up our perception of shapes through a

series of processes. The circular receptive fields of our visual system serve as Mexican-hat filters that extract edge information. Edge information is then combined into a primal sketch. The primal sketch, combined with other information, produces the 2.5-D sketch. The completed representation, the 3-D sketch, emerges from the combination of the 2.5-D sketch with other information.

8. A number of factors aid in our perception of shape, including shape from motion, shape from shading, and shape from highlights.

9. The feature-integration approach emphasizes the importance of attention. This approach proposes that shape perception emerges from two processes—one parallel (preattentive processing) and one serial (focused attention).

10. The prototype-matching approach proposes that people recognize an object by comparing its perceptual image with an ideal figure or prototype stored in memory.

Influence of Context on Shape and Pattern Perception

Context plays an important role in many areas of psychology. For example, consider the difference between yelling "Fire!" in a theater and yelling "Fire!" on a shooting range (Capaldi & Proctor, 1994). On some occasions, context is crucial! We believe that context plays a very important role in perception generally, but particularly in shape perception.

You can think of context in at least two ways. First, you can think of context as the stimuli that surround a target stimulus, because they are likely to affect your perception of the target stimulus. Thus, when looking at Figure 5.21, you will read the same stimulus as B in the top array and as 13 in the bottom array. Second, you can think of context as existing in the mind of the perceiver. Have you noticed how your own experience, your mood, or your state of arousal can influence your perception of events? Top-down processing emphasizes the role of the perceiver's knowledge in creating a context within which stimuli are interpreted. Thus, an expert computer programmer will perceive flaws in code to which a neophyte would be oblivious.

BRONZE
B60428

▶ **FIGURE 5.21** An illustration of the role of context in object perception. Note that the initial parts of the two lines are identical, but will be perceived as a *B* in the top line and as *13* in the bottom line. Note, also, that the same symbol is perceived as an *o* in the top line and as a *zero* in the bottom line.

Obviously, these two types of context are interrelated. If you know what kind of scene you are examining, you can rely on important information about the kinds of objects you are likely to find in that scene. For example, if you are looking at a scene we could call "Psychology Building on a Tuesday Morning," you know that you are more likely to find your perception professor there than, say, Meryl Streep or William Shakespeare. The contextual stimuli evoke a set of mental expectations, which, in turn, provide a context that aids you in identifying the people you see in that context.

In this section, we will review some of the ways in which context influences perception. We'll first look at the perception of letters in the context of words. Next, we'll focus on the perception of objects within visual scenes. Finally, we will examine how context can give rise to illusory contours and can lead us to misperceive stimuli.

Perceiving Letters in the Context of Words

Throughout our existence on this earth, humans have seen a variety of salient shapes, such as other human beings, animals, trees, mountains, and so on. From an evolutionary perspective, written language is of relatively recent vintage. However, the shapes of letters in written language have become quite central to our lives. Keep in mind that not only are written languages relatively recent human inventions but they are also almost as varied as their spoken counterparts.

Nonetheless, most humans learn to read at least one of these written languages.

As you read through this book, you are constantly processing the unique shapes of letters and extracting meaning from them. The processes by which you do so represent an area of intense research, some of which we reviewed in Chapter 4. Many researchers study how we might encode individual letters in isolation (Grainger et al., 2008). Other researchers focus on the perception of letters in context, which is the focus of this section. This research is particularly important to our contention that context plays a major role in perception (Theme 2). It also illustrates the important contribution of top-down processes (Theme 4).

We are primarily interested in the word-superiority effect. According to the **word-superiority effect**, we perceive letters better when they appear in words than when they appear in strings of unrelated letters. For example, the letter *R* is easier to perceive when it appears in the word *TIGER* than when it appears in the nonword *GIETR*. Cattell (1886) first demonstrated the word-superiority effect, also known as the **word-apprehension effect**, more than 100 years ago. He presented a series of letters for 10 milliseconds and asked observers to report as many letters as they could. When he presented random letters, the observers usually reported only about four or five individual letters. However, if he presented English words, the observers usually reported three or four complete words—that is, several times as many letters as in the random-letter condition.

The word-superiority effect was generally ignored for many decades, until Gerald Reicher (1969) and Daniel Wheeler (1970) revived interest in the phenomenon. In what is often referred to as the *Reicher-Wheeler task*, observers first see a stimulus, such as a four-letter word (e.g., *WORK*), a pronounceable pseudoword (e.g., *GORK*), or a four-letter nonword that is both meaningless and unpronounceable (e.g., *ORWK*). Each stimulus is presented very briefly (e.g., 50 milliseconds). Immediately afterward, a visual mask covers the four letters. At the same time, off to one side, two letters appear. These letters appear in one of four letter positions, and the observers are asked to report which of the two letters had actually appeared in the stimulus.

For example, the word *WORK* might be followed by the display

Observers specify whether they had seen a *D* or a *K* in the fourth position of the earlier stimulus. Notice that both letters form an acceptable English word. Thus, an observer could not use a strategy of guessing the letter that would complete an English word. Furthermore, this experiment eliminated an accusation that could have been applied to Cattell's study: Perhaps observers can *perceive* the letters equally well in words and in isolation, but they *remember* the words better and therefore report more items. The Reicher-Wheeler task does not rely on observers' memories, however, because they simply chose between two alternatives. Therefore, this task examines whether the word-superiority effect would persist, even when two important advantages for words (guessing and memory) had been eliminated. Many studies using the Reicher-Wheeler task provide strong support for the word superiority effect (Grainger et al., 2003; Laszlo & Federmeier, 2007).

Perceiving Objects in the Context of Scenes

Just as some researchers focus on the perception of letters in isolation, other researchers focus on the perception of objects in isolation. For example, computational theories emphasize that shape perception may occur without recourse to knowledge about the context within which they appear. Thus, your visual system can "construct" an object-centered 3-D shape by binding cones, cylinders, or geons with orientation information. Other researchers emphasize the importance of context for object perception. For example, Julian Hochberg takes a more strongly top-down approach, in which mental structures or schemas are important for the perception of objects (Peterson et al., 2007). In this section, we will selectively review some work that investigates the importance of context for object recognition.

Stephen Palmer conducted a number of studies that illustrate the role of context in object perception (Palmer, 1999, 2003b). For example, Palmer studied object recognition within a natural scene. You know that you are likely to find bread in a kitchen, a mailbox in a front yard, and a drum in a band. Palmer showed his observers scenes such as the one on the left in Figure 5.22. Then he *very briefly* showed them

▶ **FIGURE 5.22** Context scene and target objects used in Palmer's experiment. People are more accurate in recognizing briefly presented objects (such as the bread in part *a*) when seen in the appropriate context. (*Source:* S. E. Palmer, "Visual Perception and World Knowledge: Notes on a Model of Sensory-Cognitive Interaction," in D. A. Norman & D. E. Rumelhart (Eds.), *Explorations of Cognition* (San Francisco: Freeman).)

figures such as the ones you see in 5.22*a*, *b*, and *c*. In some cases, the figure was appropriate for the scene, such as the bread in (*a*). In other cases, it was inappropriate, but its shape was similar to that of an appropriate figure, such as the mailbox in (*b*). In still other cases, the figure was inappropriate, and the shape was different from the appropriate figure, such as the drum-shaped item in (*c*). In a final condition, observers did not see any contextual scene; they were asked to identify the figure without any context. In each condition they were asked to name the object and to rate their confidence that their identification had been correct.

When the figure was appropriate for the scene, such as a loaf of bread in a kitchen, the observers were 84% accurate in their identification. They were substantially less accurate when they had no contextual scene. However, they were even less accurate when the figure was inappropriate for the scene, such as the mailbox or the drum in the kitchen. Of course, with longer presentations, people could accurately identify objects, even when they appeared in an unusual setting.

Another approach to studying the impact of context on object perception is to study the time to find an object in a scene. Using this approach, some researchers have found results that support the impact of context on visual search for objects, but others have not (Hollingworth & Henderson, 1998).

However, it is becoming increasingly clear that the nature of a scene affects how we process the objects within that scene (Becker et al., 2007; Brockmole & Henderson, 2008). The research shows that we direct our eyes toward an unusual stimulus in the scene. These findings demonstrate that we are aware of the nature of the scene (Greene & Oliva, 2008).

Helene Intraub and her colleagues have taken a different approach to show that people make use of context in perceiving a scene (Intraub, 2007). To get a sense of Intraub's early research, we want you to do a bit of drawing. You need not be a great artist—a rough sketch should suffice. Look quickly at Figure 5.23, then try to replicate the illustration as accurately as you can without looking back at the figure. (So that you're not tempted to look at the picture again, you may want to close your textbook.)

When people see a tightly framed picture of an object, such as a person's head or a basketball, they later remember seeing more of the scene than was actually present in the picture. Intraub refers to this tendency to report seeing more of the scene than was present as

▶ **FIGURE 5.23** After briefly looking at this picture, close your book and sketch a drawing of the picture on a piece of scrap paper.

boundary extension. Compare your drawing to Figure 5.23. Did you exhibit boundary extension?

Earlier in the chapter, we discussed the amodal completion of incomplete objects and the Gestalt closure principle. Boundary extension is similar, in that it goes beyond the actual information present in the original stimulus. However, boundary extension is different because it goes beyond completing an object to adding information that likely surrounds an object.

Why would we "perceive" more of a scene than we actually saw? To explain boundary extension, Intraub invokes a very top-down interpretation. She thinks that people activate a mental representation (schema) based on the information in the original picture. However, the activated representation contains elements not actually in the original picture. As a result, when people later attempt to replicate the picture, they draw on their schemas in addition to the actual picture.

Boundary extension actually makes a good deal of sense. Keep in mind that when you look at the world, the only portion of a scene that you see clearly falls on the fovea. In that sense, with any given fixation, you are seeing the equivalent of a close-cropped photograph. Boundary extension may well result from an anticipatory eye movement to a portion of the scene that will contain useful information (Intraub et al., 2006). Your knowledge of what's likely present in the unseen portion of the scene guides your visual processes. In that sense, Intraub's work fits neatly with other work on the influence of top-down processes on eye movements.

The research we've reviewed in this section illustrates the importance of top-down processes in object perception. Of course, such results are entirely consistent with Theme 4. Context can certainly influence the perception of objects. This influence is especially evident in the role that context plays in leading us to perceive objects that are not actually present.

Illusory Contours

An *illusion* is an incorrect perception. In an illusion, what we see does not correspond to the true qualities of an object. Illusions are interesting phenomena, but they are particularly important for what they can tell us about perceptual processes. For example, many illusions remind us that the proximal stimulus is often ambiguous (Theme 3). We will now examine some illusory stimuli that are problematic for many theories of shape perception.

Sometimes we can see a shape against a background, even when no concrete contour or edge separates the shape from the background. An *illusory contour* (also called a *subjective contour*) is an edge that we see, even though it is not physically present. In other words, context alone is sufficient to give rise to the perception of edges or contours. Gaetano Kanizsa (1976) conducted research on subjective contours, producing the figure now known as the *Kanizsa triangle* (Figure 5.24). You should see a white triangle against a background of three dark circles and an outline triangle. Each side of the white triangle appears to be a continuous line, even though no line is actually present. (Remember Marr's virtual lines?) Imagine the problems that these apparent edges present for any theoretical approach to shape perception.

Not only are you seeing a white triangle that isn't actually there, but you're also seeing the triangle as lighter than the white background. Of course, the Kanizsa triangle and its background must be equal in actual lightness. The perceived lightness of the triangle may have to do with lateral inhibition, but a complete explanation eludes researchers (Hoffman, 1998). As Donald Hoffman points out, not all illusory figures exhibit an illusory lightness. Moreover, it's possible to produce an apparent change in lightness without creating an illusory figure. As seen in Figure 5.25, both

▶ **FIGURE 5.24** An example of illusory contours producing a triangle, often called a *Kanizsa triangle*.

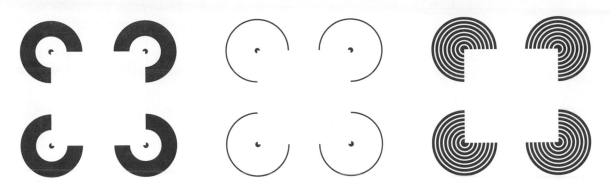

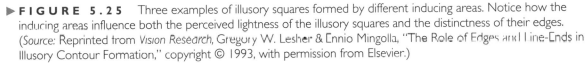

▶**FIGURE 5.25**   Three examples of illusory squares formed by different inducing areas. Notice how the inducing areas influence both the perceived lightness of the illusory squares and the distinctness of their edges. (*Source:* Reprinted from *Vision Research,* Gregory W. Lesher & Ennio Mingolla, "The Role of Edges and Line-Ends in Illusory Contour Formation," copyright © 1993, with permission from Elsevier.)

the distinctness of the edge and the lightness of the illusory figure are diminished when the inducing figures are thinner, or have fewer lines (Lesher & Mingolla, 1993).

Why do we see subjective contours? Explanations range from the physiological to the more cognitive, with some emphasizing both. From Hoffman's (1998) perspective, *every* line is constructed from discrete neural input, so a subjective line is not all that different from a real line. Such an approach is potentially integrative, placing research on subjective contours in the realm of research on edge perception. It also acknowledges both the underlying physiology and the cognitive processes involved in shape perception. From this perspective, illusory contours arise due to the filling-in processes that occur in many areas of vision (Grossberg, 2003).

Hoffman's position is entirely consistent with the findings that cells in V1 respond to both illusory contours and real lines (Maertens & Pollmann, 2005). Accumulating research shows that V1, V2, and other brain areas process illusory contours (Montaser-Kouhsari et al., 2007; Seghier & Vuilleumier, 2006). Although a good deal of evidence supports such low-level explanations of illusory contours, other researchers hypothesize the need for higher-level processes (e.g., Gillam & Nakayama, 2002).

Some researchers use Gestalt principles to explain illusory contours. From the principle of Prägnanz, they argue that we create subjective contours because we see simple, familiar figures in preference to meaningless, disorganized parts. Notice that in Figure 5.24 we could see three circles with wedges sliced out, alternating with three V-shaped lines.

However, this interpretation of the picture is unnecessarily complicated. Instead, we use depth cues (described in detail in Chapter 6) to sort out the picture, placing a simple white triangle in front of the background. This interpretation "explains" why we see peculiar gaps in the three circles—the triangle is merely hiding portions of them. Some researchers combine neural explanations with Gestalt principles to better explain illusory contours (Qiu & von der Heydt, 2005; von der Heydt, 2003).

A cognitive perspective views perception as hypothesis testing and problem solving. From that perspective, illusory contours arise because the visual system tries to solve the problem of what is figure and what is ground. Thus, we use top-down processing, consistent with Theme 4 of the book, to make sense of an otherwise puzzling and disorderly jumble. In that sense, the cognitive approach is quite similar to the Gestalt approach. When you look at Figure 5.26 (page 138), such cognitive processes seem important in producing the contours of the illusory objects that appear to be supporting the people (Bonaiuto et al., 1991).

Needless to say, illusory contours present a real problem to the various approaches to shape perception. As a result, illusory contours represent a rich research area for the foreseeable future.

Distortions of Shape Due to Context

Context can often help us arrive at an accurate representation of an object in the world. However, context can also mislead us, as we saw in the previous section. Context can also produce distorted shapes. For

a.

b.

▶ **FIGURE 5.26** An example of illusory figures that emerge from the positioning of human figures. (From Bonaiuto et al., 1991)

instance, Figure 5.27 shows two examples of the twisted-cord illusion, produced by designs that involve a twisted black and white cord. Notice how the context leads us to misperceive the orientation and shape of the figures.

If you look at Figure 5.28 (page 140), you will see other examples of illusions in which the orientation of the lines or the shape of the geometric figures is distorted by the context. For instance, as you can determine with a ruler, the lines in Figure 5.28*a* are parallel to each other, even though they appear to bulge outward in the middle. In contrast, the parallel lines in Figure 5.28*b* appear to be closer to each other in the middle. Parts (*c*) and (*d*) show a circle and a square that are distorted by the surrounding lines. Keep Figure 5.28*d* in mind when we discuss the Ponzo illusion in Chapter 6.

Section Summary

Influence of Context on Shape and Pattern Perception

1. Research has supported the importance of context in determining pattern recognition. Context can be helpful, but it can also be misleading.

2. We perceive letters better when they appear in words than when they appear in strings of unrelated letters—the word-superiority effect. Cattell first demonstrated the effect in 1886. Researchers using the Reicher-Wheeler task continue to affirm the word-superiority effect.

3. The computational approach tries to explain object perception based on information in the stimulus itself. However, a good deal of research shows that the context, or scene, within which we view an object is important. For example, we perceive an object more rapidly when it appears in an appropriate context.

4. In illusory-contour figures, we see contours even though no edge appears between the shape and the background. Researchers have proposed several explanations for the illusory contours, some with a more physiological, bottom-up orientation and others with a more top-down orientation.

5. Although context usually aids shape perception, both illusory contours and other illusions—such as the twisted cord illusions—demonstrate that context can occasionally lead to misperceptions.

Selected Topics in Shape and Pattern Perception

The Role of Time in Shape Perception

Shape perception does not occur instantaneously but requires a brief amount of time. As a result, you can likely tell that an object is present before you can determine exactly what that object might be (Mack et al., 2008). Your perception of a visual scene must emerge over time. Recall that the foveal region of the retina produces high visual acuity. However, the fovea can take in only a very small portion of the visual field. Nonetheless, your whole visual field probably seems rich in detail. As Julian Hochberg pointed out long ago, this illusion of clarity over the

a.

b.

▶**FIGURE 5.27**   Twisted cord illusions. Are the vertical parts of the letters in LIFE parallel to one another? Do you see a spiral in part *b*? Use a ruler to convince yourself that the letters in part a are not in unusual orientations. Trace the "spiral" in part *b* to convince yourself that the spiral is actually a series of concentric circles.

whole visual field is the result of a series of fixations (Enns & Austen, 2007; Hayhoe, 2007). Thus, your perception of most objects is not based on a single retinal image. Instead, your visual system integrates many separate fixations to produce the resulting "image."

Another way to illustrate the fact that shape processing takes time is a phenomenon called backward masking (Breitmeyer, 2007). In ***backward masking***, it's more difficult to "see" a briefly presented stimulus if it is followed by an overlapping second stimulus. Notice that the second figure masks the first figure and that masking therefore works in a backward fashion.

Werner (1935) was among the first to demonstrate backward masking. He very briefly presented a black square, as in Figure 5.29*a* (page 140). Then that square disappeared and was quickly replaced by the square-outline shape in Figure 5.29*b*. Werner constructed the outline shape so that the square fit neatly inside its inner boundary. He presented the black square very briefly, then a gray surface for about 0.15 second, then the square-outline shape.

With this sequence, observers failed to see the first square.

Werner did not find forward masking, the tendency for the first figure to mask a second figure. When he presented the square-outline shape (Figure 5.29*b*) and then the black square (Figure 5.28*a*, page 140), observers perceived both figures. In visual perception, backward masking is easier to produce than forward masking.

Researchers have demonstrated masking by using other figures in addition to ones in which an inner contour of one shape matches the outer contour of another (e.g., Francis & Cho, 2008). The important attribute of masking is that, when another stimulus interferes with the formation of a contour, observers will not see the shape.

The research on backward masking demonstrates the importance of time factors in perception. Other shapes presented immediately afterward will influence shape perception. Specifically, if another shape is presented too soon after the original one, you won't perceive the original shape's contour.

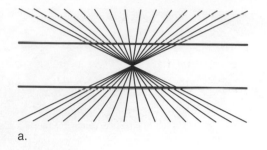

a.

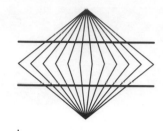

b.

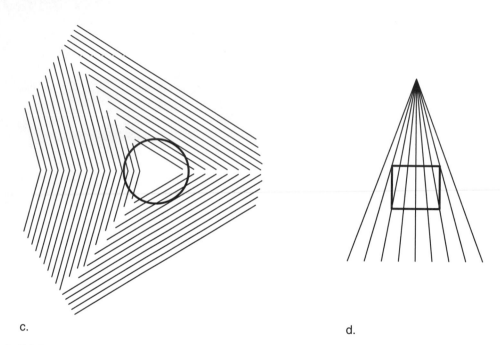

c.

d.

▶ **FIGURE 5.28** Four examples of shape distortions produced by context. Ordinarily, context is helpful to perception, as seen in Figure 5.21. In these figures, however, the context distorts the two parallel lines seen in parts *a* and *b* and the circle and square seen in parts *c* and *d*, respectively.

a.

b.

▶ **FIGURE 5.29** Shapes used in a masking study. If the black square in part *a* is presented briefly and followed rapidly by the black square outline in part *b*, people will not report seeing the original black square.

Ambiguous Figures

Rubin's vase/faces illusion (Figure 5.9) is an example of an ambiguous figure. (You might see such figures referred to as *multistable images*.) The crucial point is that the stimulus never changes, but our perception of the stimulus does change. Imagine the difficulty of developing a theory of shape perception that can predict the perception of different stimuli from the same image. Figure 5.30 is the classic illustration of an ambiguous figure. Do you see the elderly woman or the young woman? Can you switch to the other perception?

As Hoffman (1998) points out, you're a master at constructing the parts of a shape. For instance, notice that, when the ambiguous figures in Figure 5.31 reverse, the dots become attached to different parts of the figure. Thus, when viewing the Schroeder staircase (Figure 5.31a) as stairs seen from above, the dots are both attached to the second stair up. However, when viewing the same stimulus as if from a basement looking up at the stairs from below, one dot is attached to one stair and the other dot is attached to the stair above. Similarly, the three dots in Figure 5.31b could all decorate one single cube or—when the design reverses—three adjacent cubes.

Ambiguous stimuli such as these are particularly compelling. How can a single stimulus lead to two such radically different interpretations? Why should the visual system shift from one interpretation to the other? The answers to such questions require that researchers learn much more about the processes involved in shape perception. However, the fact that the same stimulus can yield such different perceptions suggests that factors beyond the stimulus alone contribute to perceptual experience.

▶ **FIGURE 5.30**   A figure that can be seen in two different ways without inversion. When you first look at this image, do you see the elderly woman or the young woman?

Effects of Unusual Stimulus Orientations

The importance of experience, emphasized in Theme 4 of this text, becomes evident when we view the

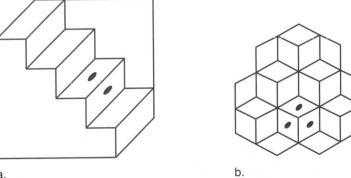

a.   b.

▶ **FIGURE 5.31**   Two ambiguous figures. You can perceive the Schroeder staircase in part *a* as seen from above or below. In part *b*, you might see six cubes or seven cubes. (If you have difficulty seeing seven cubes, it might help to turn the page upside down.) In both figures, notice how the spots become attached to different parts of the figure when you switch perceptions. (*Source*: Reprinted from *Cognition, 18*, 1–3, D. D. Hoffman & W. A. Richards, "Part of Recognition," p. 32, copyright © 1984, with permission from Elsevier.)

world from an unusual orientation. Because we have little experience with objects in the unusual orientation, our perceptions are disrupted. To create such novel orientations, you need look no further than the simple mirror (Gregory, 1996). Even though you may use mirrors frequently, you will make a variety of errors regarding the nature of the mirror image (Bertamini et al., 2003; Hecht et al., 2005; Lawson et al., 2007). For example, people are often confused about what someone (e.g., a person in a painting portrayed as looking into a mirror) can actually see in a mirror. Although you can easily read this text, hold the text up to a mirror and try to read the mirror-reflected words. Not a simple task! Another way to convince yourself of the novelty of a mirror image is to try to trace a complex object while looking only at its mirror image.

As we mentioned at the beginning of this chapter, our visual systems are masterful at perceiving objects from a variety of perspectives. At the same time, we're more likely to see objects from some perspectives than others. As a result, it may be more difficult to recognize an object when it's not seen from a typical perspective. What is the object in Figure

¡amazing!

is

Perceqtion

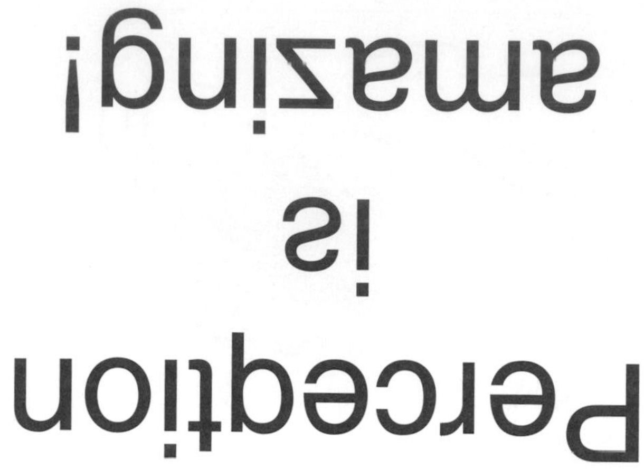

▶ **FIGURE 5.33** Can you read this text, even though it is upside down? Turn the book until the text is in its normal orientation. Do you notice any problems? Why were they less apparent in the unusual orientation?

5.32? (If you can't figure it out, keep reading, or check out the web pages for clarification.)

Consider another unusual orientation, such as inversion (180° rotation). We are accustomed to seeing text in one particular orientation. As illustrated at the very beginning of this textbook, you find it more difficult to read inverted text. As Figure 5.33 illustrates, we are less able to detect disparities in text that is inverted. Keep this effect in mind when we examine inversion of faces.

The impact of inverting an image is not restricted to the difficulty of noting discrepancies. In fact, with some shapes, an inversion yields a totally different interpretation or meaning. For example, one hallmark of a normal person is the ability to distinguish between fantasy and reality. Do you see fantasy or reality in Figure 5.34? What do you see when you invert the figure?

As we will see in Chapter 6, inversions can even lead to a reversal of depth information. Look at Figure 5.35 and determine if the dotted lines fall on the peaks of the figure or in the valleys. Now invert the figure and determine where the dotted lines fall.

Note that in each of the figures, the physical stimulus remains unchanged except for its orientation. In other words, the image falling on our retinas is identical, yet we find it difficult to detect discrepancies in one orientation that are readily

▶ **FIGURE 5.32** We are able to recognize objects from a variety of different perspectives. However, some perspectives are more challenging than others. What is this object?

apparent in another (Figure 5.33). In other situations, we see only one of two possible forms when viewing the figure from one particular orientation (Figure 5.34).

Keep the notion of unusual orientations in mind as you read the final section of this chapter on face perception. Although faces are quite important shapes, they pose a challenge to our visual system—especially when we see them from unusual perspectives.

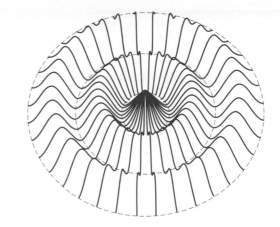

▶ **FIGURE 5.35**   Another example of the effects of changes in orientation on perception of a stimulus. The dotted lines are in the valleys of the sine function in this orientation. What happens when you invert your textbook? (*Source:* Reprinted from *Cognition,* 18, 1–3, D. D. Hoffman & W. A. Richards, "Part of Recognition," p. 32, copyright © 1984, with permission from Elsevier.)

▶ **FIGURE 5.34**   Orientation can lead us to see the same stimulus in completely different ways. Can you distinguish between fantasy and reality? Do you still see "fantasy" when you turn your book upside down?

IN-DEPTH

Face Perception

As you know, humans are social creatures, which is why we find the human face to be a very important shape. In earlier chapters, we addressed aspects of face perception, exploring eyewitness identification (Chapter 2) and prosopagnosia (Chapter 3). You may want to review those face-perception topics before reading the material in this section. The sheer volume of research on face perception prevents us from providing more than a sampling of research. We'll focus on face recognition, the impact of inverting faces, facial attractiveness, and the neural processing of faces.

Face Recognition

Earlier in the chapter, we focused on the perception of the shapes of objects. The basic question in object recognition often differs from that in face recognition. That is, researchers wonder how people can recognize an object, such as the water bottle shown in Figure 5.32. They are typically interested in how we

identify the class of objects from which the target object is drawn. How do we recognize a chair? A book? When studying face recognition, the focus shifts to the identification of specific members of the class of objects we call "faces." Researchers are less interested in our ability to say, "That's a face." Instead, they are interested in our ability to say, "That's my perception professor's face."

However, it's possible to equate the questions we ask of faces and other objects. Can you identify a picture of your best friend's face from among a group of other pictures of faces? Can you identify a picture of your house from among a group of other pictures of houses? Consider the complexity of such recognition processes. After all, human faces are basically the same. They are all roughly oval in shape, with the same features (e.g., mouth, eyes, nose, ears) in roughly the same locations. Given that basic similarity, how are you able to identify people based on their faces? Houses may present a similar challenge (especially in some neighborhoods). That is, within a box-

IN-DEPTH continued

like shape, one finds similar features (e.g., doors, windows, roof) in similar locations. One major research question is whether or not the processes that underlie visual object recognition generally also apply to face recognition.

When we recognize objects, whether faces or houses, do we rely more on the component features or on the arrangement of those features? Processes that focus on the arrangement of features are called *holistic* or *configural*. It's certainly the case that holistic processes play a role in object perception (Kimchi, 2003a; Kimchi et al., 2005). However, holistic processes are even more central for adult face perception (Schiltz & Rossion, 2006; Tanaka & Farah, 2003). That is, even though people certainly perceive the features of a face, it's the configuration of those features that is crucial for face recognition (Bartlett et al., 2003).

One way to illustrate the holistic processing of faces is to blur the features, as seen in Figure 5.36. You should be able to recognize the faces—even though the images are quite small and blurred. You're able to do so because the configuration information remains (Sinha et al., 2006). Although younger children may focus on features, by about four years of age children

process faces holistically (de Heering et al., 2007; Pellicano et al., 2006).

Inverted Faces

Earlier in the chapter, we noted that people often find it more difficult to identify objects in some orientations. The same is true for faces. For example, it's more difficult to identify faces seen in profile, compared to a frontal view (McKone, 2008). However, faces are particularly difficult to process when seen in an inverted, or upside-down, orientation (Robbins & McKone, 2003).

As we noted, holistic processing is particularly important for faces, and inverting faces disrupts that processing (Mondloch & Maurer, 2008; Rossion, 2008). However, researchers do not completely agree about *how* the inversion disrupts face processing (Goffaux & Rossion, 2007; Sekuler et al., 2004; Sekunova & Barton, 2008). One brain area that is important for face perception (the fusiform face area) appears to be the site of the inversion effect (Yovel & Kanwisher, 2005).

Peter Thompson (1980) demonstrated that people are insensitive to major changes in the features within inverted faces. As seen in Figure 5.37, Thompson inverted two pictures of former British Prime Min-

▶ **FIGURE 5.36** An illustration of holistic processing of faces. Even though these pictures of the faces of famous personalities are small and blurred, you can likely identify them. (In alphabetical order: Hillary Clinton, Angelina Jolie, Jay Leno, Barack Obama, Arnold Schwarzenegger, Oprah Winfrey.)

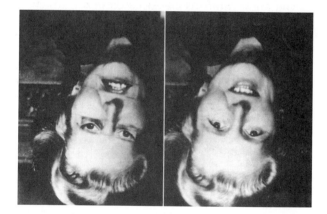

▶ **FIGURE 5.37** Do these two faces look different to you? Inverting faces disrupts holistic processing, which makes it more difficult to detect differences in facial features. In the left picture of Margaret Thatcher, her eyes and mouth are upright—even though the rest of her face is inverted. Although you will see little difference between the two faces in this unusual orientation, turning your book over will lead you to see the two pictures as distinctly different. (From Thompson, 1980)

ister Margaret Thatcher's face. However, for the picture on the left, her eyes and mouth have been kept in the upright position. When we view the inverted pictures, we see little or no difference between the two pictures. However, when we turn the book over to view the two pictures in the normal, upright orientation, the pictures are decidedly different. Many researchers now refer to such inverted faces as *Thatcherized* (Carbon et al., 2007; Wade, 2008).

Facial Attractiveness

What leads some faces to be more attractive than other faces? Surely you can identify faces that strike you as attractive. Would your choices be similar to those of other people? Although you might think that it's impossible to quantify beauty, researchers are learning quite a bit about what makes a face beautiful.

One factor that may underlie facial attractiveness is symmetry (Jones et al., 2007; Little et al., 2007). Symmetry is certainly an important characteristic of objects in the world for humans and other species (Lehrer, 1999; Little et al., 2008; Sasaki et al., 2005). Thus, it makes sense that symmetry may be a component of beauty. Of course, the asymmetry in faces is usually fairly minor. That is, the eyes are evenly spaced to either side of the nose, the mouth is centered under the nose, and so on. Do minor departures from symmetry, such as a crooked nose, lead you to perceive a face as less attractive?

Another factor that may underlie facial attractiveness is averageness. You may readily accept that facial symmetry is attractive, but wouldn't an average face be, well, *average*? In this case, average is a mathematical term. To create an average face, researchers first collect a number of faces and then create a composite face that is a mathematical average of the individual faces. For example, Figure 5.38 shows two faces that are each the average of 20 individual faces. Do you find these faces attractive? Try [www] Demonstration 5.4 to experience the impact of averaging on perceived attractiveness.

Given our earlier discussion of prototypes, it may help you to think of an average face as a prototype based on many examples. From that perspective, you might think that attractiveness must emerge as a result of experience. That is, over the course of your life, you see many faces that contribute to a prototypical face, which you then use as a model of attractive-

▶ **FIGURE 5.38** A sophisticated morphing algorithm (Tiddeman et al., 2001) generated these two "average" faces from 20 individual faces. (Images courtesy of faceresearch.org.)

ness. However, even very young infants prefer to look at attractive faces (Hoss & Langlois, 2003; Quinn et al., 2008). Thus, humans seem predisposed to see some faces as attractive.

To the extent that attractive faces are near a mathematical average of many faces, they should be similar to one another. However, unattractive faces are not near any average, so they may not be similar to one another. That is, unattractive faces may differ from the attractive average in many different ways. To test this hypothesis, Timothy Potter and his colleagues (2007) first accumulated photographs of attractive and unattractive faces. People rated pairs of faces on a 7-point similarity scale. As expected, people judged the attractive faces as quite similar to one another, but they judged the unattractive faces as far less similar to one another.

The averaging process also makes the face more symmetrical. However, it's possible to examine the separate contributions of averageness and symmetry. Some researchers argue that symmetry is important, independent of the averaging process (e.g., Rhodes et al., 2007; Rhodes et al., 1999). Others argue that symmetry makes little contribution to attractiveness (e.g., Bronstad et al., 2008).

Attractiveness is an important area of face research because its roots are likely found in evolutionary processes. That is, people choose to mate with people they find attractive. Both symmetry and averageness may be useful because they signal important information about genetic fitness (Rhodes, 2006). Findings that a person's hormonal state influences perceived attractiveness lend further support to the biological importance of attractiveness (Jones et al., 2008; Welling et al., 2008).

The Neural Processing of Faces

When a face is registered on the retina, the information will flow through the usual channels (LGN, primary visual cortex, secondary visual cortex). As we noted in Chapter 3, the fusiform face area (FFA) on the fusiform gyrus in the temporal lobe is crucial for processing faces (Tsao & Livingstone, 2008). The FFA doesn't respond to facial features in isolation, so it is processing the face holistically (Schiltz & Rossion, 2006). However, the FFA does respond to other objects, so it may not be specific to faces. Some researchers contend that the FFA processes objects

for which we have a great deal of experience, which would certainly include faces (Gauthier & Bukach, 2007; Tarr & Gauthier, 2000). Other researchers argue for the specialized processing of face information (McKone et al., 2007; Robbins & McKone, 2007).

Faces may well be a very special class of objects, with brain areas specialized for face perception. However, you should keep in mind that many areas of the brain process facial information (O'Toole, 2004). For example, we've already mentioned the role of the limbic system in coding the emotional aspects of faces. Thus, the amygdala plays an important role in face perception (Adolphs, 2007; Taylor et al., 2008). The notion that multiple brain areas process perceptual information is a theme that will recur in future chapters.

Section Summary

Selected Topics in Shape and Pattern Perception

1. Shape perception is typically built up over time, based on the integration of images that are the end products of several saccades.

2. Masking is an example of a more general phenomenon in which one stimulus interferes with the processing of a second stimulus. In backward masking, a later figure can mask an earlier figure. Visual backward masking is easier to demonstrate than forward masking.

3. The role of learning in shape perception becomes apparent when we view familiar objects, such as faces or letters, from unusual perspectives.

4. Ambiguous figures illustrate the operation of higher-level processes, because a single stimulus can give rise to totally different perceptions.

5. Because humans are social animals, faces are important stimuli. Faces are processed holistically, so we are quite good at recognizing faces—even when they are blurred. However, inverting faces disrupts the holistic processing.

6. Faces are attractive if they are symmetrical and if they are consistent with a prototype extracted from averaging together a number of different faces.

7. Some researchers argue that faces are processed in a special fashion (e.g., in the FFA), but other researchers argue that faces are processed in a fashion similar to other objects with which we have a great deal of experience.

Review Questions

1. Describe bottom-up (data-driven) processing as if you were talking to a student studying introductory psychology. Use your own words in this description, and use examples from the material in this chapter. Which approaches to shape perception seem most dependent on bottom-up processes? What role do these processes play in the particular approaches?

2. Throughout this book, we emphasize the importance of top-down (conceptually driven) processing. What *is* top-down processing? Which approaches to shape perception seem most dependent on this kind of processing?

3. In Chapter 3, we examined the anatomical and physiological bases for visual perception—essentially the hardware of vision. Evaluate each of the approaches to shape perception in terms of the extent to which it is consistent with our knowledge of the anatomy and physiology of vision.

4. Theme 2 of this book emphasizes the importance of the rich context within which we perceive objects. Use several examples from this chapter to support the importance of context in shape perception.

5. You are driving along a country road. Next to a farmhouse you see a crude hand-lettered sign, "EGGS FOR SALE." Describe how the following approaches account for your recognition of letters in that sign: the spatial frequency analysis approach, template-matching approach, prototype-matching approach, computational approach, and feature-integration approach. Do you think you would find it more difficult to read the sign if you saw it in front of an urban apartment?

6. Think of yourself as you are reading this book. How does the word-superiority effect facilitate reading? How does context facilitate reading? How are saccades involved in reading?

7. Draw an example of a figure with a subjective contour. How would you explain the subjective contour in your drawing? What problems do subjective contours pose for the various approaches to shape perception?

8. Why are ambiguous (multistable) images so important for Gestalt psychologists? Why are these images problematic for approaches to shape perception? In your daily life, you likely see very few shapes that are ambiguous. Why are most shapes *not* ambiguous?

9. We're quite good at perceiving faces, and we can recognize hundreds of faces. At the same time, as we discussed in Chapter 2, people are not particularly reliable eyewitnesses. How might you reconcile our prowess at face perception and recognition with our inability to identify perpetrators of crimes?

10. Given all that you've learned up to this point, provide your own description of the processes involved in shape perception. Start with a distal stimulus in an unusual orientation, such as a person swinging upside down on some monkey bars. Because of the swinging, that person's face will not fall on one spot on your retina. What approaches do you think would be most useful to you in explaining how you come to recognize the person?

Key Terms

Recommended Readings

Hoffman, D. D. (1998). *Visual intelligence: How we create what we see.* New York: Norton.

Hoffman's book is clearly written, extremely intriguing, and thought provoking. He addresses a number of issues in shape perception, as well as color and motion perception. As you might infer from the title, Hoffman emphasizes top-down processes in perception. He developed a number of motion demonstrations to accompany the text, which he makes available on his webpages: www .cogsci.uci.edu/personnel/hoffman/vi6.html.

Peterson, M. A., Gillam, B., & Sedgwick, H. A. (Eds.). (2007). *In the mind's eye: Julian Hochberg on the perception of pictures, films and the world.* New York: Oxford.

Julian Hochberg has had a tremendous impact on our understanding of perceptual processes. This volume contains many of Hochberg's important papers, as well as a new chapter he wrote specifically for this book. In addition, his students and many admirers contribute chapters that further illustrate the range of Hochberg's influence.

Peterson, M. A., & Rhodes, G. (Eds.). (2003). *Perception of faces, objects, and scenes: Analytic and holistic processes.* New York: Oxford.

Virtually all the chapters in this compendium are relevant to the current chapter. Some of the authors (e.g., Kimchi, Peterson, Tarr) address object perception, and other authors (e.g., Bartlett et al., Tanaka and Farah, McKone et al.) address face perception. Researchers are increasingly interested in the perception of scenes, a topic addressed in a couple of chapters.

Regan, D. (2000). *Human perception of objects: Early visual processing of spatial form defined by luminance, color, texture, motion, and binocular disparity.* Sunderland, MA: Sinauer.

As the title indicates, Regan provides a detailed description of how we might obtain shape from a variety of sources (luminance, etc.). This text and the Bruce et al. (2003) text recommended in Chapter 8 both exemplify the computational approach to shape perception. If you'd like to delve more deeply into Fourier analysis, you should consult one of the appendices.

CHAPTER 6

Distance and Size Perception

BEFORE BEGINNING this chapter, let's review the areas of visual perception we've explored. First, we looked at the biological underpinnings of vision. Next, we examined some basic visual processes, such as edge detection and lightness perception. We then looked at more complex visual processes, such as how people organize edges into shapes and how patterns emerge in looking at the world.

We hope that you no longer take your visual perceptions for granted. Even the simple detection of edges should now seem to you an extraordinarily complicated process. Human visual abilities should strike you as nothing less than minor miracles.

One of those miracles is our ability to see the world as three-dimensional. As James Todd (2004) notes, "Were it not for our own perceptual experiences, it would be tempting to conclude that the visual perception of 3D shape is a mathematical impossibility" (p. 115). In spite of the complexities involved, our visual system has evolved to provide a vivid sense of depth, based on retinal input that is itself two-dimensional. The retina in each eye can encode information directly only in a two-dimensional fashion (up-down and left-right), yet we see some three-dimensional objects as near us and other objects as far away. We alluded to the importance of depth information when we discussed lightness perception in Chapter 4 and figure-ground distinctions in Chapter 5. Therefore, you should realize that the processes are strongly interrelated, even though we've explored them separately.

In the first part of this chapter, we will explore some of the processes that must underlie the miracle of depth perception. If you are like us, however, your sense of wonder will be further increased, rather than diminished, by learning about how the visual system works to provide a sense of depth.

Closely tied to the perception of depth, as you will soon see, is the perception of the size of objects. Because of this close relationship, after discussing depth perception, we will turn to the perception of size. Our discussion of size perception will also enable us to explore another important constancy—size constancy.

Finally, in keeping with Theme 3 of this text, we will note the ambiguities of the stimuli that fall on your retinas. One byproduct of these ambiguities is that our remarkably capable visual system can sometimes be led astray. Some of the most fascinating visual illusions involve the processes that underlie depth and size perception, so we will examine several of those illusions. As we mentioned in Chapter 5, the illusions are intrinsically interesting, but their major importance lies in what the illusions tell us about how the visual system must be functioning.

We will begin our discussion by addressing the principles that give rise to the perception of depth or distance. Like most of your other perceptual experience, depth perception seems automatic—even unavoidable. Because of the immediacy of your experience of depth, you seldom think about the processes that might underlie this perceptual experience.

Before you begin reading the next section, take a few minutes to look around you as if you were seeing for the first time. Note the vivid impression of depth that emerges and try to determine how you are able to see in depth. How can you tell which of two buildings or people is nearer to you? How can you catch a ball thrown at you, or judge the distance (or size) of a bird in flight? Join the psychologists who take a more analytic approach to the perception of depth, and you may discover many of the principles for yourself before we describe them to you.

Perceiving a Three-Dimensional World

How many cues to depth did you identify? We will now begin a systematic investigation of the major cues to depth or distance. First, however, let's be a bit more specific about what we mean by distance perception.

Distance perception (or ***depth perception***) refers to your ability to perceive the distance relationships within the visual scene. We can think of three different types of distance or depth relationships. First, ***egocentric distance*** refers to the distance of an object from you, the observer. (You can remember the word *egocentric* because it literally means "self-centered.") When you estimate how far you are from the car in front of you, you are judging egocentric distance. Second, ***relative distance*** refers to how far two objects are from each other. Because this distance doesn't directly involve the observer, it is also called ***allocentric distance*** (*allo-* means "other"). When you decide that the library is closer to the dining hall than it is to the gym, you are judging relative distance. Finally, as we mentioned in the last chapter, you perceive objects as three-dimensional. In addition to height and width, objects have depth or thickness. Thus, you see your textbook as a solid object, with the open pages closer to you than the parts of the cover you can see. Of course, all three situations involve distance or depth perception, with many of the same principles underlying your perceptual experience.

We'll begin our discussion of distance perception by examining the retinal sources of information about an object's distance. Figure 6.1 provides an overview of the retinal cues to depth we will describe. A *cue* is a factor that enables you to make a decision automatically and spontaneously.

Although you would typically use two eyes to perceive most of these cues to depth, you could perceive them equally well with only one eye. Because they require only one eye to be effective, these are *monocular cues*. As you thought about sources of your rich experience of depth, you may well have identified several monocular cues to depth. Many of these monocular cues are also effective when looking at a two-dimensional representation of a three-dimensional world, such as realistic paintings or photographs. Other monocular cues to depth arise when stimuli move within a scene.

We'll next consider the contribution of our two eyes to depth perception. When you look at a nearby object, the image on your left retina differs from that on your right retina. This *binocular cue* only works because of the disparity between the images on your left and right retinas.

We'll also mention a couple of weaker cues to depth based on information from eye muscles. Finally, we'll discuss several theoretical approaches to distance perception. As you learned in Chapter 5, researchers approach shape perception in a number of different ways. We'll look at two approaches to depth perception before revisiting the computational approach as it applies to depth perception.

Monocular Cues to Depth

Most of our sources of information about distance are monocular. Lest you think of these monocular factors as "second-class citizens," keep in mind that we all rely solely on monocular cues when judging the distance of objects that are far away. To illustrate the effectiveness of monocular cues to depth, consider professional athletes who have competed successfully even though they had vision in only one eye. In spite of relying totally on monocular cues, athletes such as Wesley Walker (football) and Eddie Shannon (basketball) have been quite successful.

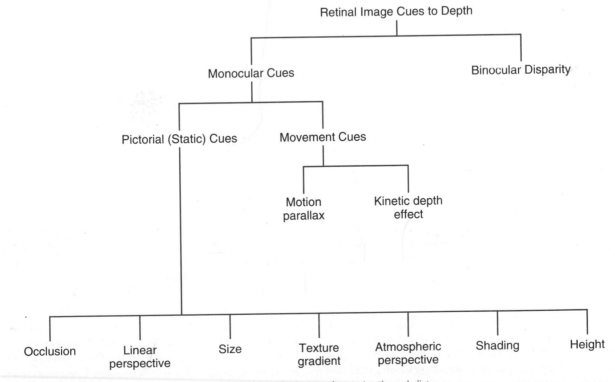

▶ **FIGURE 6.1**   A classification scheme for retinal cues about depth and distance.

Before exploring monocular depth cues that require motion, we'll focus on monocular cues found in static scenes. Keep in mind that even though we discuss these cues separately, they most certainly work together to provide your sense of depth. Moreover, the context of the scene within which the cues occur also has an impact on your sense of egocentric distance (Lappin et al., 2006).

PICTORIAL DEPTH CUES   Artists interested in portraying the world realistically face a practical problem: How can they portray three-dimensional space on a two-dimensional canvas? In a sense, that's the same problem facing our visual system. How might it construct a three-dimensional world from a two-dimensional retina? To do so, our visual system uses a set of cues that are called *pictorial cues*, or static cues, because they do not move. Artists have learned to use these cues to represent distance in a picture.

Occlusion.   Also called *interposition* or *overlap*, *occlusion* means that one object partly covers another. When interposition occurs, we judge the partly covered object to be farther away than the object that is completely visible. For example, your textbook looks closer to you than the desk that it partly covers. As we noted in Chapter 5, you may mentally complete the covered object (amodal completion). Occlusion is one of the most important monocular cues.

Although we discuss these depth cues separately, keep in mind that they likely combine to yield a sense of depth. For example, although occlusion may be a static cue, it gives rise to a sense of depth in moving displays (Gray et al., 2008). Furthermore, occlusion plays an important role in conjunction with the binocular cue of disparity (Pianta & Gillam, 2003; Sachtler & Gillam, 2007).

Linear perspective.   *Linear perspective* is a strategy used by artists to represent a three-dimensional world on a two-dimensional surface. Look at Figure 6.2 for one example of linear perspective. In order to accurately draw the two parallel railroad tracks, an artist would have to draw the two tracks so that they meet at a vanishing point on the horizon. Of course, the true distance between the railroad tracks remains constant. However, this distance occupies an increasingly smaller part of the retina as we see portions that are closer to the horizon.

Linear perspective is closely related to the next two cues. For example, nearby objects are typically larger than more distant objects. Similarly, as a result of linear perspective, the nearby objects on the ground would be larger and more detailed than distant objects on the ground. As many researchers have noted, information on the ground is very important to distance perception. Linear perspective is one type of surface information that is important for judging distance (Cook et al., 2008; Wu et al., 2007).

Size cues.   *Size cues* refer to the influence of an object's size on distance estimates. One kind of size cue comes from familiar objects. The *familiar size* of an object can be a helpful cue because objects are often found in standardized sizes. For example, you know how big most books are—including this textbook. In keeping with linear perspective, if a book occupies a tiny space on your retina, you judge it to be far away.

Familiar size may well be an effective cue for relative distance (Howard, 2002). However, other cues to distance are likely more effective. Moreover, relying on familiar size may occasionally lead us astray, as many researchers have noted. For example, even if you aren't familiar with Adirondack chairs, a chair is a familiar object with a typical size. Thus, were you to see the chair in Figure 6.3a (page 154), you would likely think it was relatively nearby. However, when you look at Figure 6.3b, you recognize that the chair is quite large. The chair's unusual size would lead you to misperceive its distance.

Of course, many objects don't come in a standard size, and other objects are completely novel. Would the *relative size* of a novel object—the object's size relative to other objects—be a helpful cue in telling us which of two objects is closer? Consistent with Theme 3, the size of the retinal image is an ambiguous cue. A large retinal image may be due to a distant large object *or* a nearby small object. Thus, as we'll discuss later in this chapter, perceived distance is quite important when judging the size of an object. With unfamiliar objects you're in a bit of a Catch-22. Knowing their size might help you to judge their distance. However, you need to know their distance in order to judge their size.

Consider a classic study by William Ittelson and Franklin Kilpatrick (1951). They asked people to judge the distance of two balloons. The two balloons were actually the same distance away, but the room was dark, so distance cues were missing. The researchers changed the size of the balloons by inflating them

▶ **FIGURE 6.2** A photograph illustrating several cues. Changes in texture gradient are evident when you look at the rocks closer to you (larger and more distinct) compared to the rocks farther away (smaller and less distinct). Linear perspective is evident in the vanishing point to which the parallel railroad tracks recede. The ties are clearly below the tracks because the tracks cover the ties (occlusion). Objects lower in the visual field appear to be closer, and objects nearer the horizon appear to be farther away (height cues). Knowing that the railroad ties are the same size helps us to see the ties that produce a smaller retinal image as farther away (size cues). (Photo by Ron Pretzer)

with bellows. People reported that the larger balloon appeared to be closer. As a balloon was inflated, it seemed to zoom forward in space. As the air was let out, the balloon seemed to zoom backward. Of course, this situation is unusual, because you would typically see distance cues. However, when distance cues are unavailable, you would perceive a novel object as closer if it produced a larger retinal image.

Texture gradient. *Texture gradient* refers to the fact that when you view surfaces at a slant, the texture of surfaces becomes denser as the distance increases. Pay attention to the ground around you, and you'll see texture gradients. Can you see why this cue is related to linear perspective? The units that make up the texture (e.g., floor tiles or stones) are the same size throughout the scene, yet they look smaller and closer together in the distance than in the foreground. You can see an example of a texture gradient in the rocks in Figure 6.2. The nearby rocks surrounding the tracks

appear to be larger and more detailed. In the distance, the rocks appear to be smaller and less detailed.

James J. Gibson (1950) was among the first psychologists to emphasize the role of texture gradients in distance perception. We'll examine Gibson's approach to distance perception a bit later in the chapter. As Gibson noted, the texture gradients provide a scale by which we can measure objects. Thus, a nearby object that hides three texture units is the same size as a distant object that also hides three texture units—whether the texture units are floor tiles, strands of rug yarn, or pebbles.

Texture gradients are such powerful cues to depth that even simple schematic representations are sufficient to produce a clear sense of depth. For example, all three parts of Figure 6.4 (page 155) clearly illustrate the same complex three-dimensional shape. Notice that Figure 6.4*a* contains shading information in addition to the texture gradient information. Although parts *b* and *c* of the figure contain *only*

▶ **FIGURE 6.3**   Known size may be an effective cue to depth. However, when you encounter an object whose size is unusual, your depth perception may be distorted. If you perceive the Adirondack chair in part *a* to be normal in size, you may perceive it to be relatively nearby. However, when another object of familiar size is introduced (part *b*), you can see that the chair is actually much larger than normal.

texture gradient information, the shape of the object is readily apparent. Thus, the depiction of this extremely complex object appears to be taking place at a fairly global level of analysis, because the actual texture used seems to be relatively unimportant.

Atmospheric perspective.   *Atmospheric perspective*, or aerial perspective, refers to the observation that distant objects often look blurry and bluish, in contrast to nearby objects. This effect arises because the air between you and the distant objects is not perfectly clear. In that sense, atmospheric perspective is a type of occlusion. When you ordinarily think of occlusion, a tree may cover part of a dog that is farther away from the viewer. In atmospheric perspective, the objects that are performing this "covering" are tiny particles in the air. These accumulated particles partially obscure your view of a distant object.

Furthermore, the particles in the air slightly change the light reflected from objects, so that they appear bluish. Thus, compared to nearby objects, distant objects appear to be blurrier and bluer. Color Plate 3, inside the front cover, is an illustration of atmospheric perspective. Notice that the distant mountains are softly blurred and faintly blue. If you

look at realistic paintings of hills, you will see that they are also blue. Painters have used this distance cue for centuries. For instance, Leonardo da Vinci (1452–1519) discussed adding blue when painting distant objects.

Shading.   *Shading* is a cue provided by the pattern of light and shadows. An object may cast shadows onto other objects, or it may have shadows attached to its surface. As we mentioned in Chapter 5, shading helps define the shape of objects, because it provides information about parts of an object that stick out or cave inward and also about flat or curved parts (Koenderink & van Doorn, 2003).

You are accustomed to being upright and seeing shadows produced by overhead lighting (Gerardin et al., 2007). Perhaps as a result, you interpret shadows as though the light source is above your head—even when you invert your head (Howard, 2002). Look at Figure 6.5 and note how the shading in the figure creates apparent depth, with some dimples concave (pushed in) and some convex (pushed out). Now, instead of inverting the book, turn your head upside down and look at the figure again. Note that doing so reverses the apparent depth of the dimples.

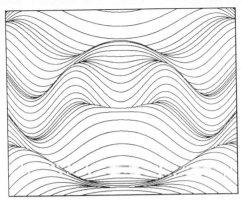

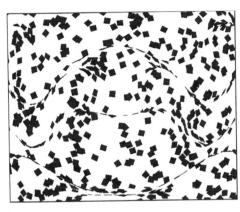

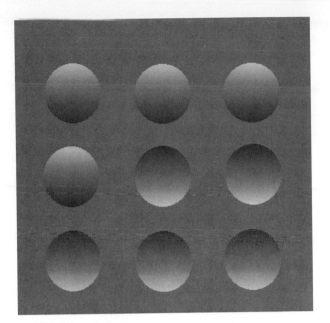

▶ **FIGURE 6.5**　The impact of shading on depth perception. Do some of the dimples appear to be concave? Are others convex? Leave your book in the same position, but invert your head as you look at the figure. Do the dimples changes in apparent depth?

▶ **FIGURE 6.4**　A complex three-dimensional figure represented in two dimensions. In part *a*, the shape is represented by both contour lines and some shading. In part *b*, the same shape is represented by a texture gradient. In part *c*, a different texture is used, and shading information is minimized. Notice the effectiveness of texture gradients in capturing the object's shape—even without shading information. (From Todd & Akerstrom, 1987; Todd & Reichel, 1990)

You can experience a similar effect of shadows in Figure 6.6 (page 156). When the picture is in the proper orientation, you see what appears to be a lake nestled in a volcano. Now, either turn the picture upside down, or invert your head as you look at the picture. The dark shadowy area no longer makes sense as a convex shape. The shadowy area is now a concave shape from which a new, tiny volcano pops out, topped by a lake at its crest. Compare this result with the effects of inversion on shape perception discussed in Chapter 5.

The position of a light source has an impact on shape and depth perception (Koenderink et al., 2006). At Halloween, or when telling ghost stories, you may have placed a flashlight under your face to distort it. As you can see in Figure 6.7 (page 157), illuminating an object from different directions will create shadows that change your perception of the image. Regardless of the differences in the three images of the crumpled paper, note the apparent depth that is due to shading.

As we noted in Chapter 5, shadows and other lighting information (highlights) help you see the depth of objects—especially when they're in motion (Norman, Todd et al., 2004). Just as we interpret

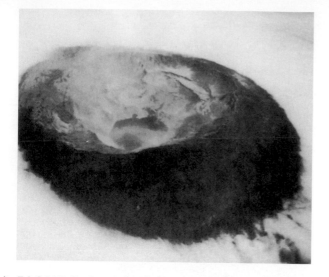

▶ **FIGURE 6.6** Look at this picture and decide which surface is closer to you. Now, turn your book upside-down and decide which surface appears closer to you. (Reprinted with permission from the cover of *Science, 169,* July 31, 1970. Copyright 1970 American Association for the Advancement of Science)

shadowy regions as farther from a light source, we interpret highlighted areas as closer to the light. As long as the surface is glossy (e.g., chrome, a polished apple), it will produce such highlights, which are powerful cues to depth (Fleming et al., 2004). When shading and highlights are absent, it's much more difficult to determine depth relations (Liu & Todd, 2004).

Height cues.   *Height cues,* or elevation cues, refer to the observation that objects *near* the horizon appear

to be farther away from us than objects *far* from the horizon. This statement may seem initially confusing, so look at Figure 6.8. Because the line represents the horizon, we interpret the triangles as resting on the ground. Notice that triangle *b* is nearer the horizon, so we interpret it as being farther away from us than triangle *a*. The same closeness-to-the-horizon rule applies to the clouds. Cloud *b* is nearer the horizon, so we interpret it as being farther away from us than cloud *a*. Verify that this relationship holds true in "real life" by looking out a nearby window. Notice that objects near the horizon are far away, whereas objects far from the horizon (either at the top or bottom of your visual field) are nearby.

Awareness of the height cue is literally as old as the ancient Greeks. In fact, the first description of height cues can be traced to Euclid, a mathematician living in Greece about 300 BC. Euclid is better known for developing the principles of geometry that you probably studied in high school.

Before we move on to other monocular sources of distance information, let's review the pictorial cues. These factors are occlusion, linear perspective, size (familiar and relative), texture gradient, atmospheric perspective, shading, and height. Occlusion is perhaps the most basic of the pictorial cues. The next three factors are related to each other. Because of linear perspective, the same fixed distance or area creates a larger retinal image when closer and a smaller retinal image when distant. As a result, the separation between parallel train tracks decreases with increasing distance, objects appear to be smaller with increasing distance, and texture elements become smaller and lose detail with increasing distance. Atmospheric perspective and shading are both factors that involve lighting. Finally, height cues involve the placement of

▶ **FIGURE 6.7** Three different pictures of the same sheet of crumpled paper. The left picture is illuminated from the left, the center picture is illuminated from the bottom, and the right picture is illuminated from the right. Note how the differences in direction of lighting change the images. Nonetheless, each image illustrates depth from shading.

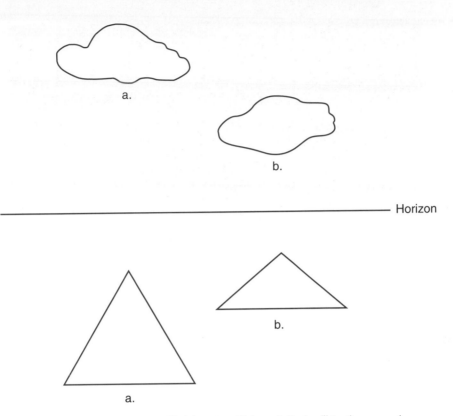

a.

b.

Horizon

b.

a.

▶ **FIGURE 6.8**   Depiction of height cues. Objects "attached" to the ground are farther away when higher in the visual field. Objects "attached" to the sky are farther away when lower in the visual field.

objects in the visual field. This observation brings us full circle to the first of the pictorial cues, occlusion, which also involves placement in the visual field.

As you look around the three-dimensional world you inhabit, you should now be able to identify many of these monocular cues. What makes them pictorial depth cues is the fact that they also work to effectively portray depth on a two-dimensional surface. To illustrate that point, try www Demonstration 6.1. Next, we'll consider how artists make use of these pictorial depth cues.

PICTORIAL DEPTH CUES ON TWO-DIMENSIONAL SURFACES   You should have found www Demonstration 6.1 informative. Even if you aren't a great artist, you were probably able to provide a reasonable representation of three-dimensional space on a two-dimensional piece of paper. As you have surely noticed, accomplished artists can use the monocular cues so effectively that the sense of depth in their art is compelling.

However, the pictorial depth cues were not readily apparent to ancient artists. As a result, you can easily find examples of art that attempt to portray a three-dimensional world accurately, but fail miserably. You'll also find modern painters who are not concerned about the accurate representation of distance. Consider American folk artists. Figure 6.9 (page 158) is a painting by Helen Fabi Smagorinsky, a twentieth-century painter from upstate New York. The painting shows impressive vitality and activity, but Smagorinsky made no attempt to accurately portray depth. For example, Smagorinsky chooses not to fully use the following cues: size (notice that the people in the background are the same size as those in the foreground), texture gradient, linear perspective, and atmospheric perspective. She did use shading to some extent. However, notice that occlusion and height are clear distance cues.

Artists intent on accurately depicting a three-dimensional world on a two-dimensional surface have learned to make use of the pictorial depth cues.

▶ **FIGURE 6.9** *Genesee Country* (1981) by Helen Fabi Smagorinsky. Identify the depth cues that are present and the depth cues that are absent. How powerful an impression of depth does the painting produce?

Renaissance artists studied depth cues to help them portray distance on a flat canvas. For example, in 1423, Filippo Brunelleschi (1377–1446) used a special apparatus to allow him to introduce linear perspective into his drawings (Goldstein, 2001). Some Renaissance artists, such as Leonardo da Vinci, used pictorial depth cues extensively in their paintings.

Later artists became quite proficient with pictorial depth cues. Consider the portrait in Figure 6.10 by the French painter Marie-Denise Villers (1774–1821). This portrait uses a number of cues: size (the distant people are small), linear perspective (the lines on the distant building converge), shading (depth information can be seen in the woman's dress), interposition (her left arm covers part of the window and part of her body), and height cues (the distant couple is higher on the page than the woman).

Some pictures are so effective that they hardly seem two-dimensional. ***Trompe l'oeil*** is French for "fool the eye," and such art fools the eye by creating a vivid impression of depth on a two-dimensional surface. Figure 6.11 (page 160) shows a mural created by John Pugh (*Study with Sphere and Water*). As you can

see, even though the surface is two-dimensional, Pugh uses the pictorial cues very effectively.

Of course, even the most effective pictures actually *are* two-dimensional. As a result, other depth cues that we'll soon discuss work against seeing the picture as three-dimensional (Goldstein, 2001). You can enhance the sense of depth by viewing the picture monocularly through a reduction screen, so that your visual field is limited to the picture.

Portraying a three-dimensional world on a two-dimensional surface actually leads to some anomalies. For instance, take another look at Figure 1.3 on page 11. You'll note the use of linear perspective and other pictorial depth cues. If you were to actually see such a three-dimensional scene, the distance from A to C would be greater than the distance from A to B. However, if you measure the lines in the two-dimensional picture, you'll note that the two lines are equal.

Figure 6.12 (page 160) illustrates a room that appears to use pictorial depth cues effectively. However, those cues lead to other problems, some of which we'll discuss at the end of the chapter. For example, did you notice that the distance across the

▶ **FIGURE 6.10**   *Young Woman Drawing* by Marie-Denise Villers
(1774–1821). Can you spot the several cues that give rise to the perception of
depth in viewing this painting? Close one eye and look at the painting again
through your cupped hand so that you see little or nothing of the surrounding
page. Does the painting take on a greater depth? Why? (*Source:* The Metropolitan
Museum of Art, Mr. and Mrs. Isaac D. Fletcher Collection, Bequest of Isaac D.
Fletcher, 1917 (17.120.204). Image © The Metropolitan Museum of Art.)

front of the rug is actually the same as the distance
across the back wall of the room? Get out your ruler
and check! Of course, in a real three-dimensional
room, the width of the carpet would *have* to be less
than the width of the room.

Clearly, there's something tricky about representing a three-dimensional world on a two-dimensional surface. Some artists choose to focus on that
trickery and create two-dimensional representations

of objects that would be impossible to construct in a
three-dimensional world. One of the earliest artists to
do so was William Hogarth (1697–1764) in his picture *False Perspective*. Such impossible figures are common in the works of Maurits C. Escher (1898–1972),
the Dutch artist we mentioned in Chapter 5. For
example, Figure 6.13 (page 160) is an impossible
figure. Did the figure strike you as impossible when
you first saw it? If you restrict your vision to small

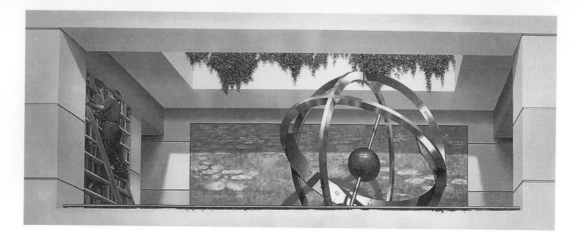

▶ **FIGURE 6.11** *Study with Sphere and Water* (1999) by John Pugh. This *trompe l'oeil* mural is located at the University of North Florida in Jacksonville, FL. Note the vivid sense of depth due to the masterful use of pictorial cues. You can see other examples of Pugh's work at his website: www.illusion-art.com/.

portions of the figure, each portion could be readily produced in a three-dimensional world. It's only when you consider the figure as a whole that its impossibility becomes apparent.

Of course, describing a figure as impossible represents a challenge to some people. In response to

that challenge, people such as Jerry Andrus, Shigeo Fukuda, and Walter Wick have constructed three-dimensional versions of impossible figures. It's actually possible to do so, but the three-dimensional figure must be viewed from a single unique vantage point. For example, Andrew Lipson creates whimsical Lego versions of Escher's impossible figures. You can find a link to Andrew's site on the webpage for this chapter.

▶ **FIGURE 6.12** An illusory room that shows how seeing a two-dimensional illustration as representing three-dimensional space might give rise to illusions. Which is longer: the front of the carpet or the wall at the back of the room? Two other illusions are also present in the drawing. Get out your ruler; you can't trust your eyes! (From Gillam, 1998. Image courtesy of Barbara Gillam)

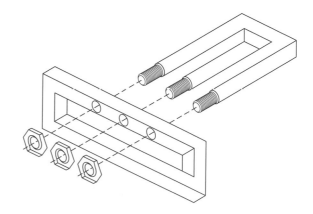

▶ **FIGURE 6.13** The three-pronged, one-slot widget, the frame, and the nuts are all impossible figures. As a simple two-dimensional line drawing, this figure is unremarkable. However, when we view it as a two-dimensional representation of three-dimensional objects, we see the difficulty of constructing such objects from this "blueprint." (From Gardner, 1988)

MONOCULAR DEPTH CUES INVOLVING MOTION The pictorial depth cues we've been discussing are effective for stationary scenes. However, most of your visual experience involves moving objects or moving retinas, as you turn your head and move your body past objects. Such motion is an important cue for shape perception (Chapter 5) and depth perception. That observation highlights the point that your perceptual experiences are interrelated. Thus, even though we're discussing depth perception in this chapter, you learned in Chapter 4 that lightness perception depends on depth.

We'll defer a more detailed discussion of motion perception to Chapter 8. For the purposes of this chapter, it's probably sufficient to note that your movement through the world creates important information about the relative depth of objects. Similarly, even though you might be stationary, the movement of objects in the world around you provides a sense of depth. Of course, a static picture cannot represent this information, so motion cues are definitely not pictorial. In fact, if you move as you look at a painting that uses pictorial cues, you'll find that it's more difficult to have a vivid sense of depth.

Motion parallax. ***Motion parallax*** refers to the fact that, as you move your head, objects at different distances appear to move in different directions and at different speeds (Ono & Wade, 2005). *Parallax* means a change in position, so motion parallax is a change in the position of an object that is caused by your motion. At minimum, you could think of snapshots of the world taken at two different times (and positions) as you move your head. In that sense, motion parallax is similar to binocular disparity, which we discuss in the next section (Gillam, 2007). Binocular disparity depends on two simultaneous images from different locations (your two eyes). Motion parallax depends on at least two sequential images from different locations (caused by your motion). As you'll learn, in both cases, the focal point plays a vital role in your perceptual experience. Try www Demonstration 6.2 to gain a sense of how motion parallax provides a sense of depth.

Motion parallax is a good source of both shape and distance information (Nawrot et al., 2008). However, its effectiveness also depends on the pursuit eye movements we discussed in Chapter 4 (Mitsudo & Ono, 2007; Nawrot & Joyce, 2006). Consistent with Theme 3, the retinal changes due to motion parallax

would be similar for near or distant objects. Thus, pursuit eye movements help disambiguate the depth information.

Even though motion parallax is a powerful depth cue, you may never have noticed how much information these head movements provide. Go to a window and focus on a part of the window frame. Hold your hand in front of your eyes. Now move your head to the left and notice that your hand seems to move in the opposite direction, to the right. In contrast, objects you can see out the window, which are farther away than the window frame on which you are focusing, appear to move to the left. Thus, they seem to move in the same direction as your head.

Notice that the direction in which objects appear to move is related to the fixation point, the part of the scene registered on your fovea. Objects closer to you than the fixation point seem to move in a direction opposite to your own movement. In contrast, objects farther away than the fixation point seem to move in the same direction as your own movement. Have you ever noticed that when you're driving at night, the moon seems to follow you? Like other distant objects, the moon often seems to move in the same direction as your own movement.

Kinetic depth effect. The motion of a three-dimensional object provides cues to its structure, hence the general term *structure-from-motion* (sometimes abbreviated as *SfM*). One such cue is called the ***kinetic depth effect***, in which a figure that looks flat when stationary appears to have depth once it moves. Try www Demonstration 6.3 to illustrate the kinetic depth effect with a rotating figure. The kinetic depth effect was first demonstrated with the shadows of rotating objects, and it has been explored in many other studies. In one well-known set of experiments, Wallach and O'Connell (1953) found that the two-dimensional projection of wire figures, for example, looked flat when the objects were stationary but looked three-dimensional when they rotated. Similarly, a transparent sphere with dots on its surface looks solid when rotated (Hoffman, 1998).

Notice that most other depth cues are missing in the kinetic depth effect. For example, cues such as interposition, shading, and texture gradient are absent. Nonetheless, once the figure moves, you notice that some parts move faster than others and that they also move in different directions. This kind of movement forces you to conclude that the object casting the shadow must be three-dimensional. Once the movement stops, however, the object can be interpreted as two-dimensional.

We've now discussed many monocular retinal cues to depth. However, as we mentioned earlier, just because we've discussed them separately doesn't mean that they function separately. For instance, the motion cues to depth are quite important, but especially in combination with the pictorial cues we've discussed (Ni et al., 2005; Tozawa & Oyama, 2006). Motion cues to depth also combine with the binocular cue we'll soon discuss (Cao & Schiller, 2002; Ichikawa et al., 2003). The importance of multiple cues becomes apparent when we consider changes that accompany aging, a topic we'll explore in Chapter 14. For example, as people age, they continue to make good use of multiple cues to depth, but the motion cues become less effective (Blake et al., 2008; Norman et al., 2008; Norman, Clayton et al., 2004).

MOVIES The modern motion picture originated in the 1800s, when several people developed devices that produced the illusion of movement. Although stationary pictures are limited to the pictorial cues, moving pictures can take advantage of the monocular depth cues that involve motion. As a result, motion pictures typically exhibit rich depth.

For example, the camera can duplicate your head movements to create motion parallax. A tracking shot, a special film technique in which the camera moves sideways along a track, effectively mimics motion parallax. Figure 6.14 illustrates three representative shots from a series of frames that could be taken as the camera moves sideways. If the camera is focused on the man, the child in front of him seems to move to the left as the camera moves to the right. On the other hand, the pictures on the wall seem to move to the right as the camera moves to the right.

Motion pictures can also mimic motion in depth as seen by a stationary observer. Even though the camera does not move, a motion picture sequence can use the kinetic depth effect to provide a sense of depth. If you haven't already done so, watch the opening credits of the movie *The Matrix Reloaded* (Herbert et al., 2005). The increasing use of computer graphics in movies allows many opportunities to create a rich sense of depth due to the motion of objects on the screen.

Although they are not common, you are probably aware of 3-D movies (Zone, 2007). The full experience of depth in these movies requires sending a slightly different image to your left and right eye—usually accomplished with some kind of glasses. In the next section, we will explore the binocular cue that produces the sense of depth in 3-D movies.

Binocular Disparity

We have discussed several monocular cues to depth, as well as their application in creating the sense of three-dimensionality from two-dimensional representations. Because they are monocular cues, a person who is blind in one eye or who has lost one contact lens can perceive depth using these factors almost as well as a person with binocular vision. However, a person with input from only one eye would be missing a crucial cue to the depth of nearby objects. In

▶ **FIGURE 6.14** Example of a tracking shot used in moviemaking. Notice how the changing interposition cues provide a sense of the relative depth of the child, man, and pictures as the camera moves from left to right.

this section, we will describe how the slightly different images in the two eyes give rise to depth.

BINOCULAR DISPARITY AND STEREOPSIS   Your eyes are roughly 2.5 inches apart, certainly not a tremendous distance. Nevertheless, this distance guarantees that your two eyes will have slightly different views of the world whenever nearby objects are at different distances. *Binocular disparity* refers to the different information that is registered on the two eyes.

You can illustrate binocular disparity by holding your left thumb about 6 inches from your eyes and to the left. Hold your right thumb about 2 feet directly ahead of you. Focus on your right thumb. Keep your head stable, close your left eye, and open your right eye. What happens to your right thumb? Does it appear to stay in the same position? Now close your right eye and open your left eye. Does your left thumb appear to jump back and forth? Your right thumb is creating no disparity, but your left thumb is creating disparity. Binocular disparity is important because it provides the information needed to judge depth binocularly, an ability known as *stereopsis* (Schor, 2003).

Let's examine the concept of binocular disparity in more detail and introduce a concept called the horopter. Figure 6.15 (page 164) shows a schematic example of two different disparity situations. In both cases, the eyes are focused on an object at point F. Using a focal point at location F, an imaginary curved line called the *horopter* can be drawn to represent all the points that are equally distant from the observer. For example, position your thumbs as you did earlier. Imagine a curved line passing through your right thumb and continuing on either side—but always 2 feet away from your eyes; this curve is the horopter. Objects on the horopter and near the horopter, in an area called *Panum's area*, can be fused into a single image. Outside of Panum's area, objects will typically produce double images. When looking at your right thumb, your left thumb appears as two thumbs.

In Figure 6.15a, an object at point A would be the same distance from the observer as the focal object, F. As you can see in the figure, the focal object will create images that fall at the same relative location on each retina (labeled f and f' for the left and right eyes, respectively). Because the object at point A is equidistant from the observer (i.e., on the horopter), its image will also fall at the same relative location on each retina. However, because the object

at point A is to the right of the focal object, its image will fall to the left of the focal object on each retina. For objects at both A and F, no disparity is found on either retina. As a consequence, the objects would appear (accurately) to be equidistant.

What about the object at point B in Figure 6.15a? As you can see, the object at B is in front of the horopter. Therefore, its image will fall at different locations on the two retinas (labeled b and b'). Objects in front of the horopter create *crossed disparity* because the image crosses to the outside of the focal point on each retina. Notice that b is to the left of f, but b' is to the right of f'. Thus, crossed disparity is a cue that objects are near us (relative to the focal object).

In Figure 6.15b you see a different situation illustrated. Here, an object is located at point C, which is beyond the horopter. Notice that disparity still arises—the images of this object will fall at different locations on the two retinas (labeled c and c'). However, in this case, the image in both eyes falls to the inside of the focal object. Objects behind the horopter create *uncrossed disparity*, which is a cue that objects are far from us (relative to the focal object).

Binocular disparity is primarily effective for perceiving depth in nearby objects. Research typically shows that people perform more accurately in judging the distance of nearby objects when they use binocular information rather than just monocular information (e.g., Roumes et al., 2001). Whether they judge distance monocularly or binocularly, people misperceive distant objects as being nearer than they really are. In at least one study, people were more accurate when making monocular judgments of distance (Foley et al., 2004).

Thus, binocular disparity and monocular cues give rise to a sense of depth. However, the cues may not give an accurate sense of egocentric distance. For example, even when the scene provides many depth cues (e.g., binocular disparity, texture, and motion), people do not judge depth accurately (Todd & Norman, 2003). As John Foley and his colleagues (2004) note, "Our space perception system is not very elegantly designed, nor is it very accurate, but it is good enough to keep most of us alive most of the time" (p. 154). Hardly a ringing endorsement, but it is entirely consistent with Theme 3.

Even though binocular disparity may not provide an accurate sense of egocentric distances, it certainly provides a vivid sense of depth. Moreover, as

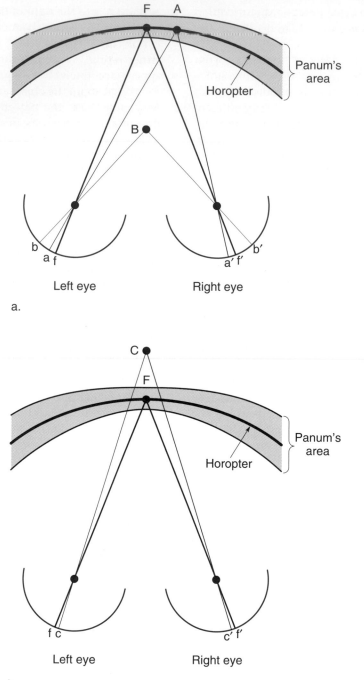

we mentioned earlier, we don't use depth cues in isolation. For example, disparity works in conjunction with shading and occlusion to give rise to a sense of depth (Anderson, 2003; Zhang et al., 2007). In the next section, we'll provide illustrations of ways in which researchers have explored binocular disparity as a depth cue.

USING BINOCULAR DISPARITY TO CREATE DEPTH IN PICTURES Charles Wheatstone (1802–1875) invented the stereoscope—an instrument that has contributed greatly to our knowledge about depth perception. A *stereoscope* is a piece of equipment that presents two photographs of a scene taken from slightly different viewpoints. Typically, these viewpoints are separated to the same extent as human eyes (about 2.5 inches).

A *stereoscopic picture* consists of two pictures, one for the right eye and one for the left eye. When the two pictures are seen at the same time in the stereoscope, they combine to make a three-dimensional scene. Notice how the stereoscopic pictures in www Demonstration 6.4 are slightly different. When each eye looks at the appropriate view and you manage to fuse the two images, you should have a vivid sense of depth. Stereoscopes became popular in the nineteenth century, and you might have used a modern version of the stereoscope, called a *Viewmaster*.

Stereoscopes also have a number of practical uses. For instance, aerial surveys and the space program (the Mars Rover) use stereoscopic pictures to give a more accurate depiction of depth. In these cases, the two cameras used to make the pictures are typically mounted quite far apart to emphasize the apparent depth of ground surfaces. Visual displays with stereoscopic capabilities have a variety of applications (Post & Task, 2006). For example, the medical field is a fertile area for such displays—especially for robotic surgery (e.g., Bhadri et al., 2007; Bhayani & Andriole, 2005; Vasilyev et al., 2008).

Astronauts used a technique for photographing moonscapes stereoscopically—one that you can use to create your own stereoscopic pictures. They shifted all their weight onto one foot and took one picture of a scene, then they shifted all their weight to the other foot and took another picture of the same scene. Shifting their weight actually had the effect of displacing the pictures by just the right amount. Using the two pictures produced by this technique, you should be able to create your own stereoscopic pictures that you could then view in a stereoscope.

One problem with using stereoscopic pictures to study stereopsis is that they often incorporate pictorial depth cues, in addition to binocular disparity. Thus, you could not know for sure that the sense of depth emerged solely from the binocular information. To counteract this problem, Béla Julesz (1928–2003) developed random-dot stereograms (e.g., Julesz, 2006). In Figure 6.16*a* (page 166), neither of the images makes any "sense" when viewed alone—no picture emerges. No pictorial distance cues are present in the random-dot stereogram. Thus, only stereopsis can explain the apparent depth that emerges when the two images are fused. Because of this fact, random-dot stereograms have become the favored tool of researchers interested in stereopsis.

Initially, you might find it difficult to fuse the random-dot stereograms. Evidence suggests that people become increasingly adept over time at fusing random-dot stereograms (O'Toole & Kersten, 1992). Don't give up; the ultimate perception of depth will be quite rewarding—and fusing the images will be easier the next time!

Closely related to random-dot stereograms is a class of illusory depth experiences. When presented with a repetitive pattern—such as a repeating wallpaper pattern, or rows of tiny dots on ceiling or floor tiles—people often report that part of the pattern seems to pop out toward them. This phenomenon can be traced to a mismatching in the two retinas of repeating elements in the pattern (Ninio, 2007).

Essentially, the sense of depth that emerges from such stimuli arises because the visual system devises an inappropriate solution to the correspondence problem (Goutcher & Mamassian, 2005). The *correspondence problem* is the difficulty our visual system can face in linking the input from the two retinas. Ordinarily, the input from the two retinas is so distinctive that the solution to the correspondence problem is relatively simple. Thus, as you look at your textbook with first your left eye and then your right eye, you should get the sense that the two images are fairly similar. The upper left corner of the book in the left-eye image would combine naturally with the same corner in the right-eye image, even though the location of the corner may not be identical on both retinas.

When you look at a repetitive pattern, such as that found in some floor and ceiling tiles, you should recognize that your visual system faces a more serious correspondence problem. Which pattern of three little dark spots in the left-eye image should combine with a pattern of similar dark spots in the right-eye

a.

b.

▶**FIGURE 6.16**   An example of Julesz's random-dot stereograms. The two fields in part *a* are identical random displays of dots except for the central area. As seen part *b*, a square section is displaced in the two views. In the left view, the "square" begins in the fifth column. In the right view, the "square" begins in the fourth column. (The square is labeled with As and Bs instead of 1s and 0s to make it stand out from the rest of the figure, but think of the As as black dots and the Bs as white dots.) The shift in the two patterns represents the binocular disparity that would arise if a square were floating above a random dot background. When viewed stereoscopically, as in 𝗪𝗪𝗪 Demonstration 6.4, a perception of depth will emerge. Because no monocular depth cues are present, the sense of depth must come solely through binocular disparity. The square might not appear immediately, but continue to look at the patterns and it should eventually emerge. (From Julesz, 2006)

image? If your visual system links the "wrong" portions of the two images, you may perceive depth that is not present in the stimulus. In fact, your visual system may switch among possible solutions to the correspondence problem (Goutcher & Mamassian, 2006).

A related phenomenon is the autostereogram, as seen in Figure 6.17. An **autostereogram** is a single image that contains binocular depth information when viewed appropriately (Tyler & Clarke, 1990). The popular *Magic Eye* books are filled with these

images. Your visual system can solve the correspondence problem of the autostereogram in at least two ways. One solution gives rise to a flat random pattern, which you will see if you just glance at the figure. In another solution, you seem to be looking through the page, as though into a window. When you are able to take this perspective, the parts that are linked together differ from those that you linked when you saw the autostereogram as a flat figure.

Autostereograms are more difficult to perceive than random-dot stereograms. In fact, some people

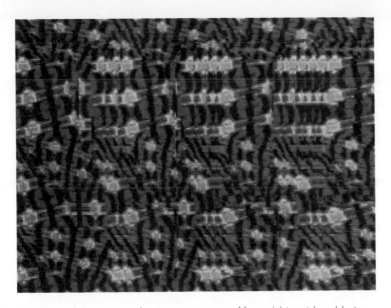

▶ **FIGURE 6.17**   An autostereogram. You might not be able to see this image as three-dimensional initially. Try bringing your nose right up to the page and then slowly moving your head back from the page while keeping your eyes looking straight ahead. In other words, try *not* to bring the page into focus. The simple image should eventually emerge. (Hint: It's the Greek letter Ψ.)

find it almost impossible to see depth in autostereograms. It's often the case that people who have difficulty seeing depth in autostereograms also have difficulty seeing depth due to binocular disparity (Wilmer & Backus, 2008).

BINOCULAR RIVALRY   The different images presented to the two eyes are typically fused into a single image containing depth information, leading Julesz (2006) to refer to the percept as *cyclopean*. (Remember the one-eyed Cyclops monster from Greek mythology?) If the images presented to the two eyes are too different, however, they cannot be fused into a single percept. When the images cannot be fused, a situation called **binocular rivalry** exists. Typically, your visual system perceives the image from one eye, and it suppresses portions of the image from the other eye. As an indication of the role of top-down processes, if you've initially seen or imagined one of the two possibilities, that's the one you're likely to see first (Pearson et al., 2008). Then, after a few seconds, the suppressed image becomes more salient, and you now perceive the image from the suppressed eye (Paffen et al., 2008). It's interesting to note that the suppression actually increases with aging (Norman et al., 2007).

Binocular perception ultimately involves both rivalry and stereopsis (Blake, 2003). Objects that are located far from the object of focus will fall on such different areas of the two retinas that they cannot be fused. Because objects that fall outside Panum's area cannot be fused, rivalry is a common aspect of binocular perception. However, when images can't be fused, you are consciously aware of input from only one eye. What happens to the suppressed input? That question is interesting because it provides a linkage between binocular rivalry and consciousness (Mitchell et al., 2004).

Binocular rivalry even has practical uses—detecting counterfeit money. Using a stereoscope, a real dollar bill can be presented to one eye, and a dollar bill suspected of being counterfeit can be presented to the other eye. Even the tiniest difference in detail between the two bills can be detected immediately. Thus, our visual system is acutely sensitive to differences in binocular input.

Eye Muscle Cues to Depth

Two other potential cues to depth aren't based on retinal information. Instead, they're based on input from the muscles that control the shape of the lens or the position of two eyes. Although these cues may provide some information about depth, they appear to be far less useful than the cues we've been discussing.

Accommodation, as you recall from earlier chapters in this book, is the change in the shape of the lens in your eye as you focus on objects at different distances. When you look at distant objects, the lens is relatively thin. When you look at nearby objects, the lens is relatively thick. Eye muscles that control lens shape therefore respond differently to objects at different distances. However, accommodation is a rather weak cue to distance, even when the distance is fewer than 10 feet (Howard, 2002).

As you may recall from Chapter 4, *convergence* means that the eyes converge, or move inward together, to look at nearby objects. Demonstrate convergence for yourself by looking at a distant object on the horizon and then shifting your focus to the tip of your finger placed on the end of your nose. When you are looking at an object that is about 10 feet away, your eyes are not converged—neither of your eyes is rotated inward. Furthermore, the position of your eyes does not change as you change your fixation from an object 10 feet away to one 10 miles away. In contrast, the degree of convergence does change impressively when you change your fixation from an object 10 feet away to one 10 inches away. Convergence may provide useful information for objects within an arm's reach (Viguier et al., 2001). However, for other near distances, convergence alone doesn't lead to accurate depth perception (Howard, 2002; Logvinenko et al., 2001).

Approaches to Distance Perception

We can identify three major theoretical approaches to distance perception: the Gibsonian position, the empiricist position, and the computational approach. As you will see, the emphases of these three theories are different. The Gibsonian position stresses the richness of environmental input, which corresponds to Theme 2 of this book. The empiricist position stresses the contribution of memory and cognitive processes, which corresponds to Theme 4. The computational approach, as we have discussed previously, grew out of attempts to develop programs that would enable machines to perceive the world in depth (Marr, 1982; Pizlo, 2008). Essentially, the computational approach asks what "knowledge" and what "perceptual abili-

ties" are required to enable a computing machine to extract depth from a rich environment. Let's examine these three approaches in more detail.

THE DIRECT PERCEPTION APPROACH   According to James J. Gibson, the visual stimulus that reaches the retina is rich and full of information. James Cutting (2007) summarizes the *direct perception* (or *Gibsonian*) *approach*, "For Gibson, information was present in the environment and needed only to be picked up" (p. 499). Gibson argued that the stimulus contains sufficient information to allow for correct perception. According to Gibson, visual information does not involve internal representations or mental processes (Greeno, 1994; Nakagama et al., 2006).

Gibson (1979) argued that most traditional cues—such as occlusion, linear perspective, size, and atmospheric perspective—are not relevant for depth perception in real-world scenes. He arrived at this conclusion after inspecting research on student pilots: Tests based on the cues for depth did not predict their success or failure. Therefore, Gibson suspected that many monocular cues did not provide adequate information about distance.

In his early writing, Gibson (1950) emphasized the importance of texture gradients as a source of information about distance. As discussed earlier, texture gradients provide a scale whereby we can measure objects' distances from us. Gibson's emphasis on texture gradients is part of his more general ground theory. According to *ground theory*, distance perception depends on information provided by surfaces in the environment. The ground, floors, and building walls are all examples of surfaces that provide information. In the real world, these surfaces help us know the distance of objects. As you look out your window, the objects you see do not float in air. Instead, the ground serves as their background, so distance can be seen directly (Gibson, 1979). More recent work continues to confirm the importance of ground information for distance perception (Bian et al., 2006; He et al., 2004; Wu et al., 2004). Other surfaces, such as ceilings, may also provide useful information about depth (Thompson et al., 2007).

As we noted earlier, either observers or objects are likely to be moving. Gibson's later work (e.g., Gibson, 1966) pointed out the importance of motion for depth perception. As a result, Gibson had little interest in the perceptual experience of organisms forced to perceive the world in a completely stationary fashion.

Gibson proposed that motion parallax is part of a more general motion pattern that he calls motion perspective. ***Motion perspective*** refers to the continuous change in the way objects look as you move about in the world. As you directly approach a point straight ahead, objects on all sides seem to move away from that point. For example, as you walk between the rows of books in the library, staring straight ahead, you should have the sense of motion perspective illustrated in Figure 6.18. In Chapter 8, we'll have more to say about how such optic flow of surrounding objects provides rich spatial information (Warren, 2008).

Gibson emphasized the concept of ***affordances***, or actions that a person could perform with objects (Heft, 2003; Jones, 2003). Even though Gibson emphasized the richness of the environment, experience is necessary to learn many affordances of an object. Thus, a large tree might be climbable, huggable, or a perfect back support, but it would not be throwable or easily leapt over. Some objects, such as

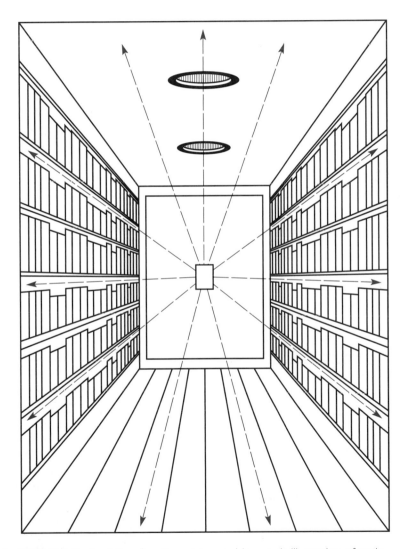

▶**FIGURE 6.18**   An attempt to provide a static illustration of optic flow. If you pay attention to the relative motion of objects as you walk along, you'll get a better idea of the notion of optic flow. As you focus on an object ahead of you and move toward it, notice that objects nearer to you flow past rapidly, whereas objects near the point of fixation move little, if at all.

a sheet of paper, have a wealth of affordances (Cutting, 1993). When you are writing, paper might be a means of conveying perfectly lucid prose. All too often, however, the affordance is compactibility, prior to throwing the wadded paper toward the circular file!

As we have seen, a sheet of paper can also contain a picture that portrays a rich sense of depth. In some natural, evolutionary sense, pictures or photographs are surely novel items. Nonetheless, Gibson tried to explain how we *could* perceive depth in pictures, which he called *indirect perception*. In fact, Gibson's attempts to explain how we perceive depth in pictures may well have contributed to the development of his broader theories (Cutting, 1993). One weakness in his approach is that he tried to explain pictorial depth without recourse to the pictorial depth cues.

Gibson's impact on perceptual thinking is substantial. Nonetheless, as Zygmunt Pizlo (2008) points out, "Gibson was engaged in wishful thinking. He grossly underestimated the difficulty of reconstructing 3D visual space" (p. 80). We agree with Gibson that the depth information in the environment is quite rich (Theme 2). At the same time, as the Gestalt psychologists argued, our perceptions often differ from the stimuli. The illusions we'll discuss at the end of this chapter illustrate that our perceptions of distance are occasionally inaccurate (Purves & Lotto, 2003). In other cases, we may perceive more in a stimulus than is actually present (Proffitt, 2006b; Stefanucci et al., 2008). For example, if you're afraid of heights, you will likely judge a height to be greater than someone who is not afraid of heights. This connection between emotion and perception will reappear later in the text.

We'll now discuss the empiricist position on depth perception, which emphasizes how we enrich the visual stimulus with associations and expectations. This view proposes that perception involves cognitive processes as well as learning.

THE EMPIRICIST APPROACH As discussed in Chapter 1, *empiricism* is a philosophical approach stating that all information is derived from sensory perceptions and experiences. For example, we are not born knowing how to perceive distance; we must acquire this skill by learning.

In 1709, Bishop George Berkeley outlined the empiricist position in an essay entitled *An Essay Towards a New Theory of Vision*. Basically, the problem that Berkeley tackled was this: The stimulus registered on the retina has only two dimensions: height and width. Nonetheless, we also see depth or distance. How can we judge how far away an object is if "we cannot sense distance in and of itself" (Berkeley, 1709/1957, p. 13)? We do have retinal size information—the amount of space an object occupies on the retina—but distance cannot be registered on the retina in an equivalent way. Still, we do perceive depth, so how does this perception emerge?

Berkeley proposed that we come to perceive distance by learning and experience. Specifically, we learn to associate various cues for distance with kinesthetic information about distance. ***Kinesthetic information*** is nonvisual information that includes all the muscular information we receive as we interact with objects. For example, we receive muscular information as we walk toward a distant object. In fact, perceived distance is greater when people walk toward it wearing a heavy backpack (Proffitt et al., 2003). Thus, we perceive distance indirectly because we link up kinesthetic information with various kinds of visual distance cues (e.g., monocular depth cues). Notice that kinesthetic information is primary in Berkeley's theory, and vision is secondary.

According to the empiricist tradition, then, the retinal image alone is *not* sufficient for depth perception—it is limited to two dimensions. Only with the enhancement of retinal information through experience can we come to see the world in depth. The important role of experience is entirely consistent with Theme 4 of this book.

Julian Hochberg has added to the depth-perception theories developed by the empiricists (Peterson et al., 2007). His approach emphasizes the perceiver's active role in interpreting the visual world. Hochberg argues that we constantly interact with objects around us. As a consequence, we develop certain expectations. When we encounter a new scene, we perceive what we expect to perceive. That is, we construct the most reasonable interpretation of the evidence before us, and this interpretation is what we actually see.

Many modern-day perceptual theorists who have borrowed from the empiricist tradition prefer to call their approach a ***constructivist theory***. According to the constructivist theory, the perceiver has an internal constructive (problem-solving) process that transforms the incoming stimulus into the perception. Basically, constructivist theory proposes that the stimulus is often ambiguous, consistent with Theme 3.

The perceiver's task is to solve the problem: What arrangement of objects in the environment is most likely to produce the stimulus registered on my retina? As we discussed in Chapter 5, some theorists suggest that people "solve" illusory contour figures such as Figure 5.24 by reasoning that the most probable explanation is that a white triangle is covering the background figures. Similarly, constructivist theory proposes that people use their experience with objects at different distances to solve problems about depth perception.

In summary, the empiricist position—in both its original and modern forms—emphasizes that the visual stimulus on the retina does not provide adequate depth information (Theme 3). Thus, as Richard Gregory suggests, perception is a kind of hypothesis testing (Gordon, 2004). Our visual system learns to combine other information with retinal cues to determine depth information.

THE COMPUTATIONAL APPROACH We began discussing the computational approach in the context of edge and shape perception (Chapter 5). The goal of the *computational approach* is to develop a set of rules and procedures that could give rise to the perception of complex stimuli. The computational approach shares many characteristics of the constructivist approach and the direct perception approach. Thus, the computational approach states that knowledge is crucial for perception. However, that knowledge is more general than the constructivist approach might posit. For instance, Marr (1982) used the research of Warrington and Taylor (1978) to show that humans can perceive an object without specific knowledge of that object's name or function. Thus, according to a computational approach, we should be able to perceive a pen on top of a desk without using any specific knowledge we might have about the likelihood that a small cylindrical object on top of a desk might be a pen.

The computational approach makes use of general knowledge (e.g., laws of physics and geometry) in analyzing a complex scene into separate objects and shapes—rather than specific knowledge. Unlike the direct perception approach, then, the computational approach recognizes the importance of prior knowledge for perception. Furthermore, researchers with the computational orientation are not content simply to identify factors that might give rise to depth perception. Computational researchers also mimic those

factors in programs to see if computers could then extract depth information from visual input.

Like the direct perception approach, the computational approach recognizes the richness of the visual input. However, the computational approach does not state that perception is direct. Instead, it proposes that several perceptual modules operate simultaneously during low-level processing of input. A *module* is a distinct processor that has a limited function, performs its function rapidly, has a specific neural architecture, and is not accessible to central processes (Fodor, 1983; Marr, 1982).

As we have discussed earlier, the computational approach attempts to develop computer algorithms that are capable of processing visual input. The actual computations involved are too complicated to describe in an introductory-level perception textbook. Instead, it's far easier to describe the modules that are likely involved in depth perception. Thus, computational theorists attempt to develop algorithms that produce three-dimensional shape from motion, shading, texture, and binocular disparity information (Pizlo, 2008). A computational theorist would argue that depth perception arises from the combination of input from such different processing modules (Sedgwick, 2001).

Overall, then, you should not think of the computational approach as being vastly different from the direct perception or constructivist approaches in terms of the factors that are important for depth perception. Instead, the computational approach differs in terms of the extent to which it invokes mental operations (more than the direct perception approach allows) and the extent to which it assumes specific knowledge (less than the constructivist approach might allow).

Perceiving Three-Dimensional Objects

To simplify the discussion of shape in Chapter 5, we treated objects largely as two-dimensional. Of course, in doing so, we were ignoring the reality that most objects in the world are three-dimensional (Tyler, 2006). We want to briefly elaborate on our discussion of shape perception, now that you've read about depth perception.

Most of the depth cues that we've discussed are important for perceiving the three-dimensionality of objects as well as egocentric distance. For example, you may perceive an object as three-dimensional because of cues such as lighting (highlights and shadows), texture information, motion, and binocular disparity (Todd, 2004). However, other researchers (e.g., Pizlo, 2008; Purves & Lotto, 2003) focus on processes that enable you to make sense of the ambiguous retinal image. They conceive of depth perception as determining the likelihood that a particular three-dimensional object gave rise to the two-dimensional retinal image.

Whatever the processes actually involved, it's quite clear that you perceive three-dimensional objects. Moreover, your experience leads you to perceive objects as three-dimensional and convex, which is consistent with Theme 4. As a result, when you see a concave object, you may misperceive it as convex. Look at the two pictures in Figure 6.19. You are likely to perceive both of them as convex faces, which is the sort of face you're used to seeing. However, the face on the left is concave (note the forehead letters). Even though it's unusual to see objects lit from below, you likely perceive the concave mask as both convex and lit from below.

The hollow-face illusion is not limited to faces; we tend to see other concave objects (e.g., jello molds)

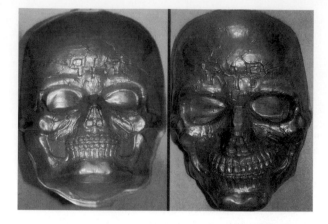

▶ **FIGURE 6.19**   Pictures of the same Halloween mask. One picture is taken from the outside of the mask (convex) and one is taken from the inside of the mask (concave). Nonetheless, you are likely to see both masks as convex. (The concave mask is on the left. Where does the illumination appear to originate?)

as convex. We are likely to do so for a number of reasons, including our proclivity to see objects as convex and our greater familiarity with specific convex objects, such as faces (Hill & Johnston, 2007).

IN-DEPTH

Where Am I?: Navigating a Three-Dimensional World

You've already seen ample evidence that perception is an active process. You don't passively take in the retinal input; rather, you actively process it. However, there's another way to think of perception as active—perception is purposeful. You perceive objects in order to grasp them or avoid them. You perceive space in order to move through it successfully. In other words, you perceive in order to act (Proffitt, 2006a). For example, the distance to an unreachable object will seem smaller if you have a tool (e.g., a broom) to aid you in reaching the object (Witt & Proffitt, 2008; Witt et al., 2005).

You live in a three-dimensional world, and in order to move through that world successfully you need to mentally represent that space. We've described many cues and theoretical approaches to depth perception. Some of the cues (e.g., kinetic depth) may be more helpful in perceiving three-

dimensional objects than spatial layouts (Cutting & Vishton, 1995). Whatever cues may most effectively signal depth, or whatever approach may best explain how we perceive depth, we must ultimately generate a fairly accurate sense of the space around us.

Wayfinding and Cognitive Maps

Interest in mental representations of space likely begins with Edward Tolman (1886–1959). He published an influential paper arguing for the existence of such mental representations, called *cognitive maps* (Tolman, 1948). Do you have a cognitive map that would allow you to locate your authors in upstate New York? Do you have a cognitive map that would allow you to locate your current position relative to salient buildings on campus? It's clear that memory plays an important role in navigating the three-dimensional world. However, the metaphor of an internal map may not be the best way to characterize how humans navigate the world (Wang & Spelke, 2002).

Given our emphasis on the distinction between the perceptual world and the physical world, we certainly recognize that the correspondence between the two is never exact. Instead, our perceptual systems have evolved to provide us with a sense of space that is not totally accurate, but it's accurate enough to allow us to navigate the world successfully (Theme 3). In fact, people who are visually impaired share the same navigational problem. However, they also develop a sense of spatial organization, but it is based on nonvisual cues (cf. Rieser et al., 2008).

People's internal sense of space is certainly less accurate than the external maps or GPS systems they rely on for navigation. As we noted earlier, various factors beyond depth cues influence your perception of distance. For example, distance seems greater if you're wearing a heavy backpack or climbing a steep hill (Proffitt et al., 2003; Stefanucci et al., 2005).

It should come as no surprise that cognitive factors affect your spatial sense. As a result, you would perceive distances as greater when walking through a picturesque village compared to a busy city (Crompton & Brown, 2006). You might also find that outdated information may still affect your estimation of distances. Claus-Christian Carbon and Helmut Leder (2005) asked people to judge the distances between various German cities. Even though East and West Germany were reunited in 1990, years later people judged distances as though the Iron Curtain still separated the country. For example, people tended to overestimate the distances between cities that were located in the former West Germany (e.g., Hannover) and former East Germany (e.g., Magdeburg), compared to roughly equidistant cities that were both located within the same former country (e.g., Erfurt and Magdeburg).

Locating Objects in Space

Walter Gogel (1918–2006) referred to the perceptual experience of space as *phenomenal geometry* (e.g., Gogel, 1993). To accurately locate objects in the environment, you need information about the egocentric distance of the object, the direction of the object relative to the observer, and whether or not the observer or object is in motion.

In this chapter, we've focused almost exclusively on how people determine egocentric distance. For the most part, you can think of wayfinding as an individual navigating through a world of nonmoving objects (e.g., buildings, streets, tables, chairs). Here, we'll explore studies that illustrate how we locate objects that are moving through space. As you might expect, both bottom-up and top-down processes work to help us perceive the location of moving objects (Whitney, 2006). We'll have more to say about motion perception in Chapter 8.

Many sports require an athlete to locate and connect with (e.g., catch, kick, hit) a moving object in space. Now that you're thinking about space perception, these tasks should strike you as quite complex. Nonetheless, even people who aren't gifted athletes can perform such tasks. How do they do so?

Let's consider a stationary observer, such as the batter in baseball or softball. With only a very small amount of information collected in a fraction of a second as the ball is first released, the batter has to determine when and where to swing the bat (Bahill, 2005). Seeing the rotation of the ball—detectable due to the spinning seams—helps the batter determine its speed and likely direction. Interestingly, the better hitters actually perceive the ball as larger (Witt & Proffitt, 2005). Golfers also misperceive size. In fact, better golfers actually perceive the hole as larger (Witt et al., 2008). Although this effect is psychological, it is certainly correlated with performance. We'll have more to say about size perception later in the chapter.

Although it may seem to be an impossible task, we know that people can hit a moving ball with a bat. So, let's consider a fly ball. How does a fielder catch the ball? Now not only is the ball moving, but the fielder is also moving. That's about as complicated as it gets! As a result, fielders use a variety of strategies to catch the ball (Gray & Sieffert, 2005). For example, they might attempt to cut off the ball in flight or they might try to beat the ball to a position and wait for it.

It's difficult to determine the path of the ball—especially when we're moving. Apparently, fielders use visual angles to determine the geometric properties of the trajectory of the fly ball (Shaffer & McBeath, 2002; Shaffer et al., 2003). The same principles of determining the linear trajectory seem to guide the catching of Frisbees, whether by humans or dogs (Shaffer et al., 2004; Shaffer et al., 2008). It's interesting that fielders may not have a precise sense of the path of the ball, but they are still able to catch it

(Shaffer & McBeath, 2005). Consistent with what we said earlier about distance perception, our perceptions may not be completely accurate, but they do allow us to interact with the world.

Deficits in Space Perception

We can learn a great deal about perceptual functioning from people whose perceptual experience is unusual. To give you an example of spatial problems that some people experience, we'll briefly explore unilateral neglect and problems in spatial orientation.

Try to imagine that you could experience only half of the world. That's the spatial experience of a person with unilateral neglect (Robertson, 2004). People with this disorder might eat only the food on one side of their plates, or fail to read words on one side of a page (Humphreys & Riddoch, 2001). Damage to the parietal lobe of the brain often results in unilateral neglect. It's as though the left half of space disappears for a person with damage to the right parietal lobe.

For other people, all of space is present, but locations are misperceived. Knowing that food is about 100 yards away would do you little good if you had no

idea of which direction you should set out in, to get the food. Imagine how difficult your life would be if you confused direction, so that the food appeared to be 100 yards to your left when it was actually 100 yards to your right!

A. H. has a localization deficit of this sort (McCloskey, 2004; McCloskey et al., 1995). When an object is to her left, she will often reach out to her right to grab the object! In her daily life, A. H. is able to correct herself, because she can see that her hand is getting farther away from the object. Because she could compensate, A. H. was an undergraduate before anyone studied her disorder. However, several tests show that the localization deficit is a real one, particularly for stationary objects.

At the same time, A. H. has no difficulty localizing with her other senses. She also has no difficulty with other visual tasks, such as identifying objects. When we discussed illusory conjunctions in Chapter 5, we mentioned that shape information was processed separately from location information. Thus, A. H.'s deficit seems to be specific to the visual localization mechanisms, which is a spatial deficit quite different from unilateral neglect.

Physiological Bases for Depth Perception

As we'll note throughout the text, a particular perceptual experience typically involves more than one area of the brain. That's certainly true of our experience of three-dimensional space (Morgan, 2003). For example, as we noted in Chapter 3, the superior colliculus provides a spatial map combining visual input with other sensory input. The superior colliculus plays a vital role in directing eye movements, so in that sense it plays a role in depth perception.

Monocular depth cues don't require input from both eyes. However, some of them do require motion. Thus, areas of the brain that process motion are important for depth perception. We'll defer a discussion of neural processing of motion to Chapter 8. Binocular disparity does require input from both eyes (as does binocular rivalry), so that information can emerge only in cells that combine input from the two eyes. However, we've already discussed how our perception of depth arises from many types of cues—

both monocular and binocular. Thus, many different areas of the brain contribute to our ultimate experience of depth (Orban et al., 2006).

All visual depth information begins at the retina and flows through the three visual pathways (M, P, and K). The M pathway seems to convey motion cues for depth (e.g., motion parallax) and the P pathway seems to carry information that is important for binocular disparity (Schiller et al., 2007). Although the P pathway is likely crucial for binocular disparity information, remember that input from each eye is kept separate until the primary visual cortex (V1).

Researchers have found cells in V1 that are sensitive to binocular disparity (Cumming & DeAngelis, 2001; Durand et al., 2007; Trotter et al., 2004). These *disparity-selective cells* actually respond to different types of disparity in input from the two eyes. Some cells respond to horizontal disparities, some respond to vertical disparities, and some respond to phase differences between the two eyes. Horizontal disparities are most important for depth perception, but vertical disparities may help locate objects in space (Read & Cumming, 2004, 2006). Phase disparities may contribute to solving the correspondence problem (Read & Cumming, 2007). However, as Jenny Read (2005) points out, even though these V1 cells are important for depth perception, stereopsis must occur at higher cortical areas.

One area crucial for depth perception is surely MT (also called V5). As we noted in Chapter 3, this cortical area also has disparity-sensitive cells (Born & Bradley, 2005). MT may also be the site where other cues to depth combine with binocular disparity information. For instance, MT appears to combine linear perspective information and disparity information (Welchman et al., 2005). Motion parallax and eye-movement cues also appear to combine with disparity cues in MT to provide depth information (Nadler et al., 2008).

You also need spatial memory to successfully navigate through space. MT doesn't appear to be the area responsible for spatial memory (Campana et al., 2006). Instead, the hippocampus plays an important role in representing space (Moser et al., 2008). For example, the hippocampus has cells (place cells) that respond strongly to specific spatial locations (Best et al., 2001; Postma et al., 2004). However, the hippocampus is a complex part of the brain. For example, the hippocampus plays a role in memories for objects as well as spatial memory (Broadbent et al., 2004). Moreover, damage to the hippocampus doesn't seem to disrupt some spatial memories (Rosenbaum et al., 2005; Shrager et al., 2007; Shrager et al., 2008). As a result, researchers have yet to determine the exact role of the hippocampus in space perception.

Section Summary

Distance Perception

1. Of the monocular depth cues, seven pictorial cues do not require movement.
   a. Occlusion means that we judge a partly covered object to be farther away than the object that covers it; it is a primary source of distance information.
   b. Linear perspective, by which parallel lines appear to meet in the distance, is an important pictorial cue.
   c. Size (either familiar or relative) is a depth cue that is related to linear perspective.
   d. Texture gradient, or the increase in surface density at greater distances, is also related to linear perspective. Gibson made use of texture gradients in his approach.
   e. Atmospheric perspective means that distant objects often look blurry and blue.
   f. Shading conveys depth information, because the lighting is not uniform across a surface and because objects far from a light source are more shadowy.
   g. Height cues tell us that objects near the horizon are farther away from the observer.
2. Artists can make use of the pictorial depth cues to create a very realistic representation of a three-dimensional world on a two-dimensional surface.
3. Two monocular depth cues involve movement—either of the observer or of objects around the observer.
   a. Motion parallax means that as you move your head sideways, objects at different distances seem to move in different directions.
   b. Because of the kinetic depth effect, the two-dimensional projection of an object seems to have depth when the object rotates.
4. In addition to the pictorial cues, movies can make use of motion cues to depth.
5. In binocular disparity, the two eyes present two slightly different points of view; this is an important source of information about the distance of nearby objects. Stereopsis is the sense of depth that emerges from binocular disparity cues.
6. Binocular disparity can be represented in stereograms, random-dot stereograms, and autostereograms.
7. Two less useful depth cues come from eye muscles. Accommodation of the lens may provide some weak depth information. Convergence is a binocular cue in which the eyes move together to look at a nearby object. Convergence might sometimes be a helpful source of depth information, at least for objects within an arm's reach.
8. Gibson's direct theory of depth perception argues that the visual stimulus is rich with information; texture gradients and motion perspective are particularly important.

9. The empiricist position on depth perception states that we perceive distance by associating various cues for distance with kinesthetic information; the visual stimulus itself is inadequate. Modern variations of empiricism, including constructivist theory, emphasize the importance of our expectations and problem-solving abilities in determining what we perceive.

10. The computational approach blends aspects of constructivist theory and Gibson's direct perception theory. Researchers in this interdisciplinary field have developed mathematical models that can be used by computers to perceive depth and distance.

11. Through the various depth cues, people are able to represent the three-dimensional world in which we live. This spatial representation allows them to navigate the world successfully.

12. Using visual angle information about the trajectory of a moving object, people can track the object and catch it.

13. People with unilateral neglect or directional deficits illustrate the fragility of our space perception mechanisms. Damage to our brains (e.g., parietal lobe) may cause a portion of space to disappear.

14. Many areas of the brain process spatial information. The M pathway carries motion information, and the P pathway carries information for binocular disparity. The primary visual cortex (V1) has cells that process disparity information, but MT (V5) seems to integrate various types of depth information.

15. The hippocampus is important for memory, including spatial memory. Place cells respond to particular locations.

Size Perception

You perceive the world so effortlessly that you might have been inclined to think that perception is simple. Of course, one insidious purpose of this book is to convince you that even the simplest perception is the result of complex processes. You look out at the world and see that one building is far away, whereas another building is close. You are typically unaware of any computations involved in judging those distances, yet now we've told you about many factors that affect distance perception.

Likewise, you look out at the world and see some objects as large and others as small. The perception seems immediate and effortless, yet from the other topics we have discussed, you should expect the underlying processes to be fairly complex. We will first explore the factors that influence size perception, and then we will turn our attention to another important constancy—size constancy.

Factors Influencing Size Perception

As we stated earlier in this chapter, the perception of distance and the perception of size are interrelated. In the preceding section, for example, you saw that the known size of various objects could serve as a cue to the distance of those objects. To simplify matters, we will first examine factors influencing the perception of the size of objects that are equidistant from us. Next, we will examine how the perceived distance of an object is important in determining its perceived size.

DETERMINING THE SIZE OF OBJECTS AT THE SAME DISTANCE FROM THE OBSERVER When two objects are the same distance from you, how do you determine which of the two is larger? If you could know, for instance, that two circles were the same distance from you, the solution is simple—the circle with the larger visual angle is larger. Of course, size perception is not that simple. It's not always easy to determine the distance of an object, and you're often judging the size of objects with very different shapes.

A number of investigators have determined that an object's shape influences perception of its size. Anne Anastasi (1908–2001) conducted some early research in this area. Anastasi (1936) demonstrated that a square or a circle appears to be smaller than a star or diamond of equal area. In general, more elongated objects appear to be larger than equal-size objects that are more compact.

However, shape is not the only characteristic of the stimulus that affects its perceived size. Consistent with Theme 2, the context in which the stimulus is viewed is also crucial. For example, an object viewed against a large background will appear smaller than an object of equal size viewed against a small background. Similarly, as seen in Figure 6.20, surrounding objects affect perceived size. For example, the two inner circles in part *a* (the Ebbinghaus illusion) are identical in size. Nonetheless, the larger surrounding circles make the circle on the left appear smaller. As you might expect from Anastasi's work, the shapes of the stimuli affect the illusion, as do other factors (Roberts et al., 2005; Rose & Bressan, 2002). People from other cultures (such as the Himba of Namibia) experience the illusion, but in some cases to a lesser extent than people from English-speaking cultures (de Fockert et al., 2007).

You can also see the effect of context in the second illusion. There is the tested element (e.g., the circles in part *b*, which are equal) and the inducing elements (e.g., the arrows in part *b*). You would have no difficulty judging the two circles to be equal if they were presented to you without the inducing elements. The inducing elements provide the context that produces the misperception. Note the similarity between these context effects on size perception and Wallach's

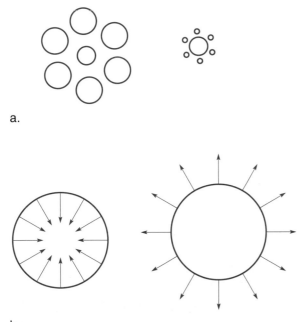

a.

b.

▶ **F I G U R E   6 . 2 0**   A couple of examples of area illusions created by context. The two inner circles in part *a* are equal (the Ebbinghaus illusion). The two circles in part *b* are equal.

ratio principle of lightness perception (discussed in Chapter 4).

DETERMINING THE SIZE OF OBJECTS AT VARYING DISTANCES FROM THE OBSERVER

The shape of an object, the context within which the object is viewed, and other factors all influence size perception. In addition to all these factors, the perceived distance between an object and the viewer will also influence size perception. The egocentric distance between the viewer and an object is crucial for determining the perceived size of the object. Thus, perceived distance and perceived size are inextricably linked.

Look again at Figure 4.14 on page 101. Notice that two very different distal objects can cast the same proximal image. Thus, an object could be twice as large as another object but twice as far away. The two objects, therefore, would have the same visual angle and their images would cover the same area of the retina. Consistent with Theme 3, the retinal image alone is ambiguous. If we were unable to determine that the objects were at different distances, we would have a difficult time deciding that their sizes differed.

We can illustrate the relationship between size and distance by exploring Emmert's law, named after the man who discovered it in 1881. First, try www Demonstration 6.5 to experience the principles underlying Emmert's law. You'll notice that this demonstration uses a negative afterimage. Staring at the circle in www Demonstration 6.5 leads to adaptation; as you look away from the black circle, a white circle appears. However, the perceived size of the circle depends on the background against which it is viewed. *Emmert's law* states that an afterimage projected on a more distant surface appears bigger than the same afterimage projected on a nearby surface (Howard, 2002). In terms of an equation, Emmert's law can be stated as

$$\text{Perceived size} = K \, (\text{Retinal image size} \times \text{Perceived distance})$$

This equation, in which K represents a constant, says that an object's perceived size is a function of both the size of the retinal image and the perceived distance of the object. Notice how this equation explains www Demonstration 6.5. The afterimage has a constant retinal image size (and K is a constant), so both those values remain the same under all viewing conditions. However, when you look from a nearby surface to a faraway surface, both perceived size and perceived distance change. Specifically, an increase in the perceived distance (when you look off at the farther surface) means that the perceived size must increase as well. As a consequence, perceived size is larger on the farther surface, at least up to about a yard away (Lou, 2007). Perceiving the afterimage on surfaces farther away than one yard has little impact on perceived size.

Although Emmert's law deals with afterimages, it reveals the crucial relationship between perceived size and apparent distance. Changes in the size of the retinal image (the proximal stimulus) that are accompanied by corresponding changes in the perceived distance of the object (the distal stimulus) would lead us to perceive the object as having constant size. It's interesting to note that V1 seems to encode the apparent size of objects, rather than retinal size (Murray et al., 2006; Sterzer & Rees, 2006). We now direct our attention to this important constancy.

Size Constancy

Size constancy means that an object seems to stay the same size despite changes in the size of the object's retinal image. Notice, then, that the proximal (retinal) size of the object can shrink and expand, depending on how far away it is, yet the distal size of the object stays the same. Try www Demonstration 6.6 to help you notice how the visual angle and retinal size change as an object moves away from your eye. As you learned in Chapter 4, visual angle means the size of the arc that an object forms on the retina. Retinal size refers to the amount of space the object occupies on the retina. Visual angle and retinal size are closely related terms.

Think about how size constancy operates in the real world. As your professor steps forward to make a particularly important point, he or she does not expand magically before your eyes (although the retinal image does). As a car drives away from you, you don't see it shrink to matchbox size. The next time you get up from reading this book, notice how objects seem to stay the same size as you move away from them. Obviously, size constancy plays an important adaptive role.

You might argue that you have size constancy because you know the size of your professor or a car. Yes, familiarity may help to preserve size constancy

(Wagner, 2006), but size constancy operates for unfamiliar objects as well, as long as distance information is present. Thus, a random shape cut out of white paper would seem to stay roughly the same size as you changed your distance from that unusual shape. That said, familiar size and other cognitive factors could well influence your perception of size, consistent with Theme 4.

DISTANCE INFORMATION AND SIZE CONSTANCY In everyday life you have substantial information about distance that can tell you how far away an object is. Theoretically, you could combine knowledge about an object's distance and knowledge about its retinal size to determine how big an object "really" is—that is, its distal size.

A classic experiment demonstrated the importance of distance information in determining size constancy (Holway & Boring, 1941). As Figure 6.21 shows, observers were seated so that they could look down either of two darkened hallways. Down the right-hand hallway, a standard stimulus could be placed at any distance from 10 to 120 feet. The standard stimulus was a circle whose size could be systematically varied to produce a visual angle of 1° regardless of its distance from the observer. (Consequently, the circle was 12 times as large at the 120-foot distance as at the 10-foot distance.) Down the left-hand hallway, 10 feet away, was a comparison circle, which observers were instructed to adjust until it matched the size of a particular test stimulus.

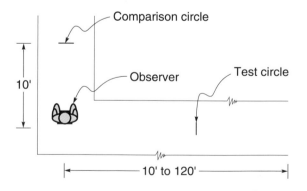

▶ **F I G U R E   6 . 2 1**   Setup for the Holway and Boring experiment (looking down on the hallways). The observer would view the test circle at varying distances so that the visual angle was constant. The observer viewed the test circle under four different conditions and adjusted the comparison circle so that it appeared to be equally large.

This study had four experimental conditions:

1. Normal, binocular viewing with all distance information present

2. Monocular viewing with all other distance information present

3. Monocular viewing through a peephole, which removed the distance information available from motion parallax (the head-movement factor)

4. Monocular viewing through a peephole with drapes along the hallway, which removed almost all distance information.

Notice, then, that the amount of distance information available to observers differed in the four conditions.

Figure 6.22 shows the observers' performance in the four conditions. First look at the two dashed lines, placed on the figure as guidelines. The top dashed line represents how people would perform if they had perfect size constancy and the object seemed to stay exactly the same size, no matter how distant it was. The lower dashed line represents how people would perform if they had absolutely no (zero) size constancy—if in judging its true size, they considered only retinal size and not the distance of the object.

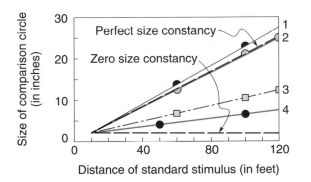

▶ **F I G U R E   6 . 2 2**   Results of four viewing conditions in the Holway and Boring experiment. The horizontal dashed line indicates no size constancy. Because the visual angle was constant, if the observers could not take distance into account, the test circle should always appear to be equally large. The oblique dashed line indicates perfect size constancy. As the viewing conditions changed from 1 to 4, the observers received increasingly restricted distance cues. In the presence of distance cues, the observers exhibited size constancy. In the absence of distance cues, the observers lost size constancy.

Now notice how people performed in the four conditions. When people had a lot of distance information, whether binocular or monocular (viewing conditions 1 and 2), they exhibited size constancy. In the monocular/peephole condition (3) and in the monocular/peephole/drapes condition (4), people did not exhibit constancy; they provided estimates that were too small for distant objects. Without information about distance, people do not show much size constancy.

EXPLANATIONS FOR SIZE CONSTANCY   Researchers have proposed several explanations for size constancy. We already mentioned that familiar size may be helpful. If you know how big a pencil is, you can guess its size even when the distance varies. Of course, as Figure 6.3 illustrates, familiar size can occasionally lead us astray.

A common explanation of size constancy is the size-distance invariance hypothesis. This explanation applies to both familiar and unfamiliar objects. According to the *size-distance invariance hypothesis*, a viewer calculates an object's perceived size by combining an object's retinal size and its perceived distance. Note the similarity between this hypothesis and Emmert's law. Notice another prediction that can be derived from Emmert's law. If two objects have the same retinal size, the object that appears to be farther away will be perceived as larger. This classic theory was originally proposed by Helmholtz (1866), the empiricist whose name recurs throughout the textbook. Do not take this principle too literally, however. You don't take out a pocket calculator to figure the objective size. In fact, you probably are seldom aware of this process.

Gibson provides another explanation of size constancy based on the relationships in a scene. According to Gibson's direct perception explanation, mentioned earlier, we can directly perceive the environment from the information in the stimulus (Gibson, 1959). For example, people notice the size of an object by comparing it to the texture of the surrounding area. As you saw earlier in this chapter, Gibson emphasized texture in distance perception; texture is equally important in his theory of size constancy. Try ⟨www⟩ Demonstration 6.7 to illustrate the importance of texture in size constancy.

We have mentioned that Gibson's emphasis on the information available in the stimulus provides support for Theme 2 of this textbook. At the same time, Gibson may have underestimated the difficulty of extracting that information from the retinal images (Howe & Purves, 2005a; Pizlo, 2008).

An important Gibsonian concept, particularly relevant to the constancies, is invariants. *Invariants* are aspects of perception that persist over time and space and are left unchanged by certain kinds of transformations. For example, in **www** Demonstration 6.7, the relationship between the two sheets of paper and the texture units surrounding them may provide sufficient information to establish size constancy. Regardless of distance, the same piece of paper consistently covers an invariant number of texture units. Thus, we can tell that its size must remain invariant. In spite of the intuitive appeal of the notion of invariants, it may not have the explanatory power that Gibson intended (Pizlo, 2008).

Mark Wagner (2006) has extended a theory of size constancy that he developed with Jack Baird. Their *transformation theory* involves two stages. The first stage is the creation of the proximal stimulus on the retina, which is a strictly physical process. The second stage is psychological, translating the retinal image into a spatial perception. It's in the second stage that there is room for error, for instance in perceiving the visual angle of the stimulus.

Our discussion of distance perception concluded that explanations from both the empiricist and the Gibsonian traditions are probably valid. By extension, the computational approach also captures many elements of distance perception. We can assess distance relatively accurately because we can take advantage of a wide variety of information sources about distance. Similarly, we will conclude the discussion of size constancy by noting that several factors are probably responsible for our remarkable accuracy in preserving size constancy: Objects seem to stay the same size because of familiarity, the size-distance invariance hypothesis, the relative size of other objects, and the texture of the surrounding areas.

Section Summary

Size Perception

1. The egocentric distance of the object is important in the accurate perception of an object's size. Several other factors also influence the perceived size of an object, including its shape and the surrounding context.

2. Emmert's law illustrates the crucial relationship between size perception and distance. Although the law was formulated on the basis of afterimages, it is useful for explaining how size perception generally depends on distance perception.

3. The classic experiment by Holway and Boring points out the importance of distance information for the accurate perception of size. In the absence of distance information, people judge size based on visual angle.

4. Size constancy arises when the distal size of an object remains constant in spite of proximal changes. Several theories have been proposed to explain size constancy, including the size-distance invariance hypothesis, Gibson's direct perception explanation, and the two-stage transformation theory.

Illusions of Distance and Size

In our discussion of distance and size perception, we have focused on the many factors that provide adequate information about the world around us. As we saw with the perception of shape, our perceptions are not always veridical. We would probably not survive for long if the majority of our perceptions were illusory, so part of the charm of illusions is their rarity. For the psychologist, however, illusions are important because they provide clues to the functioning of the visual system. Just as we can learn a great deal about normal perception by studying people with perceptual abnormalities, we also learn a great deal from studying illusions. Illusions of distance and size are particularly intriguing, as you will soon see.

Ambiguous Depth or Distance Information

People—particularly in our culture—have a tendency to perceive two-dimensional drawings as representing three-dimensional space. Such a tendency may give rise to many illusions, such as those we will examine at the end of this chapter. Some two-dimensional drawings resemble the ambiguous figures discussed in Chapter 5 and can be seen as either two-dimensional or as three-dimensional. The Necker cube, seen in Figure 6.23, is probably the best known of these fig-

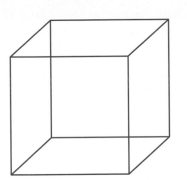

▶**FIGURE 6.23** The Necker cube. This ambiguous figure was first described in 1832 by the chemist Louis Albert Necker.

ures. You will most likely perceive the Necker cube as representing a three-dimensional object, but you can also see it as two-dimensional. As with the ambiguous figures in Chapter 5, as you look at the Necker cube, you should see it change orientations spontaneously—all the while remaining three-dimensional.

Another example of such an ambiguous figure is quite old. Figure 6.24 is a rendering of a hexagon from

the floor of Arena Chapel, built in Padua, Italy, in 1306. The entire floor is filled with this hexagonal pattern! Notice how you can perceive the figure as a flat white six-pointed star on a shaded background. You can also see the pattern as three cubes in depth. In fact, you can see three cubes in two different ways. As with the Necker cube, you should find yourself spontaneously seeing first one set of three cubes and then another set of three cubes.

Illusions Involving Line Length or Distance

Figure 6.25 shows one of the most famous illusions, the Müller-Lyer illusion, first demonstrated in the late 1800s. In the ***Müller-Lyer illusion***, the two horizontal lines are actually the same length. Nonetheless, the line with the wings pointing outward looks about 10% longer than the line with the wings pointing inward (Howe & Purves, 2005a). Thus, if the wings-inward figure were 10 inches long, the wings-outward figure would have to be about 9 inches long for people to consider their lengths equal.

Researchers have conducted hundreds of studies to investigate this illusion (Howe & Purves, 2005b). In so doing, psychologists have tried many variations of the figure, including those in Figure 6.26 (page 182). Impressively, the illusion remains strong in all these variations. In fact, the Müller-Lyer illusion is so powerful that Alex the Gray parrot was susceptible to it (Pepperberg et al., 2008).

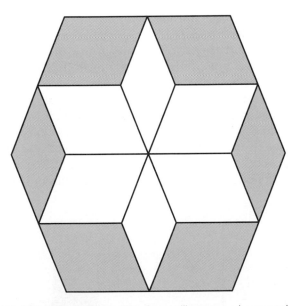

▶**FIGURE 6.24** This figures illustrates a hexagonal section of the floor of Arena Chapel in Padua, Italy. The chapel was constructed in 1306. Note that you can perceive the figure as purely two-dimensional and also as a two-dimensional representation of three-dimensional space.

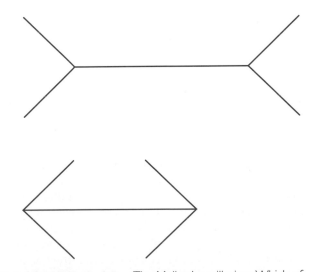

▶**FIGURE 6.25** The Muller-Lyer illusion. Which of the two horizontal lines is longer?

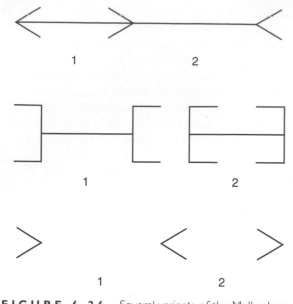

▶ **FIGURE 6.26**   Several variants of the Muller-Lyer illusion. In each case, segment 1 is equal to segment 2.

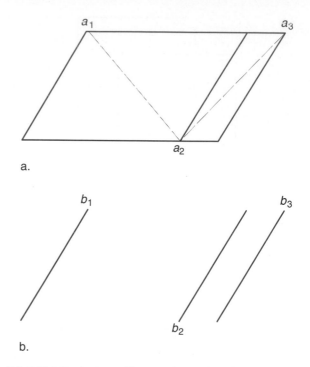

▶ **FIGURE 6.27**   Two versions of the Sander parallelogram. The distances a_1a_2, a_2a_3, b_1b_2, and b_2b_3 are all equal.

Another line-length illusion is the ***Sander parallelogram***, presented in two versions in Figure 6.27. The distance a_1a_2 (or b_1b_2) is equal to the distance a_2a_3 (or b_2b_3). Nonetheless, the distance a_1a_2 looks much longer than the distance a_2a_3. If you can ignore the inducing parallelogram, you might be able to see the figure $a_1a_2a_3$ as an upside-down isosceles triangle. If you can do that, then you can convince yourself that the line lengths are equal—even without a ruler. However, you'll probably need a ruler to demonstrate that the two distances in Figure 6.27b are equal.

Figure 6.28 shows a line-length illusion called the ***horizontal-vertical illusion***, which is similar to the top hat illusion. You probably find it difficult to believe that the horizontal and vertical lines are equal in length. Generally speaking, people perceive vertical lines as longer than horizontal lines.

The horizontal-vertical illusion isn't restricted to lines on a page. People often overestimate the height of vertical objects such as parking meters, lampposts, and buildings. Thus, a standing tree looks taller than the same tree after being chopped down. One of the most famous architectural examples of this illusion is the Gateway Arch in St. Louis (Figure 6.29). Only by measuring can you convince yourself that the height and the width are equal. In reality, both height and width are 630 feet.

The ***Ponzo illusion*** is shown in Figure 6.30. Notice how the figure in part *a* creates the impression of linear perspective, even though it is drawn with only a few lines. In part *b*, additional distance cues convince you that the distant bar must be larger because it has the same retinal size as the closer figure. We can call the figure in part *a* an illusion. Is the figure in part *b* an illusion? The field depicted in part *b* certainly has depth, so size constancy should lead the upper bar to appear larger. As you can see, the boundary between "inaccurate" perception in illusions and

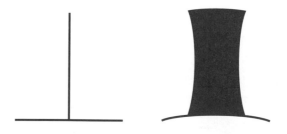

▶ **FIGURE 6.28**   The horizontal-vertical illusion and a variant called the top-hat illusion. The horizontal and vertical lines are equal.

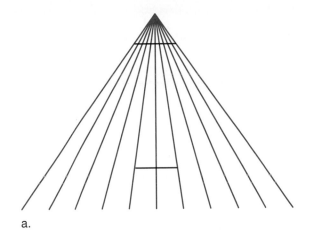

a.

▶ **FIGURE 6.29**   Gateway Arch in St. Louis, Missouri—another example of the horizontal-vertical illusion. (Photo courtesy of St. Louis Regional Commerce & Growth Association)

b.

"accurate" perception in size constancy is extremely fuzzy. Suppose the observer interprets certain cues in a line drawing to be depth cues, although no instructions specified to do so. In this case, judging two equal figures unequal in objective length is called an *illusion*. When more depth cues are present, judging two equal figures unequal in objective length is called *size constancy*. Indeed, the distinction between illusions and size constancy does sound arbitrary!

Explanations for Line-Length and Distance Illusions

As you might expect at this point, researchers have proposed many different explanations for distance illusions. However, there is currently no consensus about the bases of these illusions (Day, 2006; Howe &

▶ **FIGURE 6.30**   Ponzo illusion. The two horizontal lines in part *a* are actually the same length. The two bars in part *b* are also the same length. The depth cues in both illustrations lead us to see the upper line or bar as farther away. How might the distance information explain the illusion? Notice in part *b* the power of texture gradients. In the photo, can you point out the dip in the field (just above the upper bat?) (Photo by Ron Pretzer)

Purves, 2005a). It seems safe to say that there may well be different explanations for some distance illusions.

One psychological explanation for illusions involves misapplied constancy. According to the *misapplied constancy explanation*, observers interpret certain cues in the illusion as cues for maintaining size constancy. Therefore, they make length judgments on the basis of size constancy, and a line that looks farther away will be judged longer (Ramachandran & Rogers-Ramachandran, 2008). This explanation is particularly relevant for the Ponzo illusion. Look again at Figure 6.30a and notice how the top line does indeed look farther away. Invoking this explanation, we would conclude that the top line must be longer because it appears to be more distant.

Many of the illusions we have been discussing can be explained by interpreting the illusory figure as representing three-dimensional space in two dimensions, as a picture does (Gillam, 1998). Barbara Gillam produced an effective demonstration of how this explanation might work in Figure 6.12. When you first look at the picture, you see nothing at all unusual. However, the room is filled with illusions! As we noted earlier, the length of the front of the carpet is exactly equal to the length of the back wall. If you trace over the edges involved, you will find that each looks like half of the Müller-Lyer illusion with one part of the wing removed. The two dogs are equal in size, although the apparent depth should make the rear dog appear to be larger (as in the Ponzo illusion). Finally, the length from the front to the back of the carpet is equal to the length of the back of the carpet (horizontal-vertical illusion).

The misapplied constancy explanation argues that people are sensitive to distance cues in illusions because they have had experience with pictorial depth cues such as converging lines (linear perspective). Even though the Ponzo illusion is a two-dimensional display, people use their experience to interpret the converging lines as signaling depth. According to this view, then, *experience* is a crucial factor, which is consistent with Theme 4 of this book. Thus, visual illusions support the active role of the mind in interpreting the potentially ambiguous retinal images. Unfortunately, misapplied constancy cannot explain a number of visual illusions.

The misapplied constancy approach *might* explain some illusions, such as the Ponzo illusion. However, other approaches may be equally effective in explaining these illusions. One explanation, which we might call the *incorrect comparison explanation*,

states that observers' perceptions are influenced by parts of the figures that are not being judged (Rock, 1997). For instance, people's attention may be more easily drawn to the oblique lines when looking at the upper horizontal line in the Ponzo illusion. The oblique lines may be too far away from the lower line to have any influence over its perceived length. Thus, the upper horizontal line would be perceived as longer, regardless of perspective cues (Pressey & Epp, 1992).

In the Müller-Lyer illusion, people's attention may be drawn to the ends of the figures, which would make the arrows-out version appear to be longer. Thus, observers cannot separate the lines from the wings in this illusion. Experimental evidence supports this explanation. For example, the magnitude of the Müller-Lyer illusion is greatly reduced when the wings are a different color from the lines, so that the wings would be less likely to enter into the comparison.

The *eye-movement explanation*, a somewhat more physiological approach, states that illusions can be explained by differences in actual eye movements or in preparations for eye movements. There is some evidence that eye movements are consistent with the Müller-Lyer illusion, but it's not clear that they would explain other geometrical illusions (Knox & Bruno, 2007). Strongly physiological explanations of illusions are likely to become more prevalent with the increasing influence of neuroscience on perceptual research (Hayashi et al., 2007; Qiu et al., 2008; Read & Cumming, 2005).

It remains unlikely that any of the approaches we have discussed can fully explain all the line-length illusions. For example, William Prinzmetal and his colleagues have proposed a tilt-constancy explanation for illusions such as the Ponzo illusion (Prinzmetal & Beck, 2001; Prinzmetal et al., 2001). They argue that cues about tilt may help explain the Ponzo illusion. They find that the effect of the Ponzo illusion is actually increased when observers are tilted (about 30°). At the same time, the Müller-Lyer illusion is unaffected by tilt. Each illusion probably depends on at least one of these explanations, as well as other factors that no one has yet developed.

Illusions Involving Area

Earlier in the chapter, you saw some illusions of area (Figure 6.20). Unlike the illusions of distance, area illusions involve two dimensions. The book you are holding in your hands right now presents you with an area illusion. What proportion of the book page is taken up by margins? Did you guess that about one-third of the page was margin? If you guessed a smaller proportion, you fell victim to the *margin illusion*. People typically underestimate the area of the margins on a page.

THE AMES ROOM   Another classic size illusion is the Ames room, named for its creator, Adelbert Ames (1952). The *Ames room* is an unusually shaped room that causes distortions in apparent size because it is perceived as a normally shaped room. Looking through a peephole into an Ames room, such as the one at the Exploratorium in San Francisco, you would see a scene like that in Figure 6.31a. Can you believe that the two girls are the same size?

The Ames room is actually hexahedral in form. Thus, the rear wall is not at all rectangular—the right corner is both much closer and shorter than the left corner. As Figure 6.31b illustrates, the rear wall actually slants away from the viewer. However, when viewed monocularly, it appears to be a normal cube-shaped room. Because of the clever construction of the Ames room, all of the cues present at the retina are consistent with a normally shaped room (Day, 1993).

As a result, we perceive the room to have a normal cubic shape. Once we do so, the illusory size experiences are inevitable.

THE MOON ILLUSION   If you enjoy moonlit walks, you've probably noticed that the full moon appears to vary in size. Due to the *moon illusion*, observers generally report that the moon at the horizon may look as much as 50% bigger than the moon at the zenith, or highest position (Ross & Plug, 2002). (A similar illusion is found with the sun, but you should never look directly at the sun.) Given that both the visual angle and distance of the moon remain unchanged, why should the apparent size of the moon change? This question has intrigued scientists since the origins of scientific thought.

Helen Ross and Cornelis Plug (2002) have reviewed numerous attempts to explain the moon illusion. Physical explanations (e.g., the atmosphere enlarges the horizon moon) can be ruled out by comparing photographs of horizon and zenith moons. The remaining explanations are likely to be cognitive, which is consistent with Theme 4 (Westheimer, 2008). For the moon's apparent size to change, you need to misperceive the distance, the visual angle, or both.

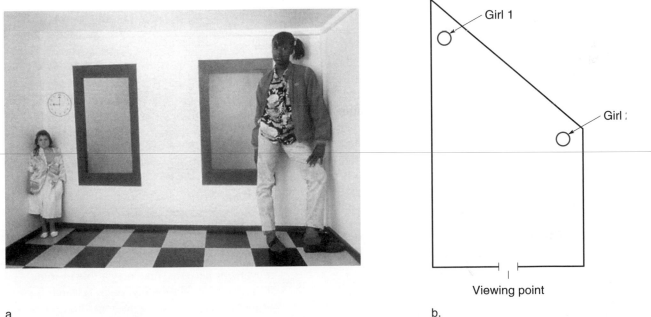

a   b.

▶ **FIGURE 6.31**   The Ames room. The girls are actually the same size! Because of the unique construction of the room (see part b), Girl 1 is much farther away from the viewer. Our experience with symmetrical rooms and the construction of the room conspire to deliver an illusory experience. (*Source:* © 1990, The Exploratorium photograph by Susan Schwactzenberg.)

One major source of distance misperception may be context (Ross & Plug, 2002). The zenith moon is isolated in the sky, with only distant stars surrounding it. As a result, it may not appear to be that distant. In contrast, the horizon moon is seen behind distant trees, buildings, and mountains. Due to those contextual cues, people perceive the horizon moon as more distant than the zenith moon (Kaufman et al., 2007). (Notice that this explanation is similar to Emmert's law, which says that an afterimage will be smaller if you shift your gaze from a distant to a nearby background.) Figure 6.32 illustrates why the zenith moon would appear smaller.

So far, so good, right? However, it's not that simple. When asked to judge which moon appears to be closer, the horizon or zenith moon, observers typically report that the horizon moon is closer! How could the horizon moon be larger because it was both farther away than the zenith moon *and* closer than the zenith moon? One possible explanation is that the visual system unconsciously computes the registered distance to the moon and then derives the perceived size of the moon. When people are later asked to make a conscious judgment of the distance of the moon, they use a simple rule—larger objects are closer.

Ross and Plug (2002) label this explanation the *further-larger-nearer theory*. Even if you find such an explanation to be unsatisfactory, it does seem likely that visible-terrain effects account for a good portion of the moon illusion.

Why is it so difficult to explain the moon illusion? First of all, keep in mind that people tend to underestimate even relatively nearby distances. Great terrestrial distances pose a greater problem, leading

people to misjudge the size of large terrestrial objects at great distances (Higashiyama & Shimono, 1994). Imagine how much more difficult it is to judge the egocentric distance to celestial objects, which people have never really experienced. As a result, it's no surprise that people significantly underestimate the size of the moon, even at the horizon. None of us looks up at the moon and accurately sees its diameter as equal to the length of the United States!

As intriguing as the moon illusion is, its scientific value lies in what it may tell us about the perception of size. Ultimately, the moon illusion must be understood in the context of a more general theory of size and distance perception (Ross & Plug, 2002). To try to explain the moon illusion without a fully developed theory of size perception might well be lunacy.

Section Summary

Illusions of Distance and Size

1. The line-length and distance illusions include the Müller-Lyer illusion (and its many variants), the Sander parallelogram, the horizontal-vertical illusion, and the Ponzo illusion.

2. A popular psychological explanation for some illusions is the misapplied constancy explanation, in which cues in the illusion are interpreted as cues for maintaining size constancy. Research has demonstrated that experience with depth cues enhances these illusions, a finding that supports the misapplied constancy explanation. However, this explanation cannot explain all the illusions.

3. The incorrect comparison explanation proposes that illusions occur when observers base their judgments on the incorrect parts of the figures. Thus, when judging the horizontal lines in the Ponzo or Müller-Lyer illusions, people's judgments are influenced by the inducing elements in the illusions.

4. More physiological explanations, such as eye-movement patterns, may play a role in some illusory effects. Ultimately, brain research is likely to address many issues regarding the perception of illusions.

5. Two important area illusions are the Ames room and the moon illusion, in which the hori-

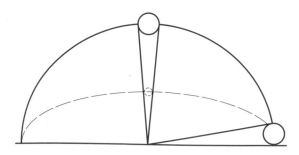

▶ **FIGURE 6.32** Effect of apparent distance of the moon on judgments of moon size. Context effects lead the horizon moon to appear to be more distant, so people perceive it as larger. Because the zenith moon appears to be closer, people perceive it as smaller.

zon moon looks as much as 50% bigger than the zenith moon.

6. A number of factors likely contribute to the moon illusion. A major factor is contextual, with the horizon moon appearing to be farther away because of the objects between the observer and the moon. However, estimating the size of the moon is an extremely complex judgment. Thus, only with a more complete theory of size perception will researchers be able to explain the moon illusion.

Review Questions

1. Even before reading this chapter, you probably could list several distance cues, such as familiar size. Other depth cues may not have been so obvious. Describe each of these cues, and point out their importance in theories about distance perception.

2. Many of the distance cues we discussed are "relative" cues to distance because they do not seem capable of enabling us to measure distances exactly. Nonetheless, people are relatively good at estimating nearby distances. Try to explain which cues, if any, might give rise to absolute, rather than relative, distance perception. Then, try to figure out how the depth cues might work to provide us with absolute information about nearby distances.

3. Artists interested in realistic portrayals of depth must solve the same problem facing the visual system—they must create a perception of three-dimensionality on a two-dimensional surface. *Trompe l'oeil* art is particularly effective in this regard. Is *trompe l'oeil* art illusory? How many of the illusions discussed in this chapter seem to arise from the same principles used to represent depth pictorially?

4. Describe the binocular cues to depth. Why are random-dot stereograms and autostereograms important? Given all that you now know about the cues to depth, how important are the binocular cues relative to the monocular cues? (Think of the spatial circumstances under which binocular cues are useful.)

5. Summarize the direct perception approach, the empiricist approach, and the computational approach with regard to distance perception. In what ways is the computational approach similar and dissimilar to the other two approaches?

Which approach seems best able to explain your experience of depth? Why?

6. How accurate is your representation of space? Close your eyes and try to reach out and grasp nearby objects or point to more distant objects in the room, estimating their egocentric distance in feet. You should find that you are fairly accurate. What factors give rise to your sense of space? Do you agree with Berkeley that your sense of space emerged from experience, or do you think that space perception is innate? What evidence would you use to support your claim?

7. One tactic suggested to people trying to lose weight is to put their food on a small plate. What factor in size perception suggests that a person might think that more food was on the plate? What other factors might be used to bias size perceptions?

8. Why are constancies important, particularly size constancy? To answer this question, imagine trying to move around in our world if constancies did not exist. Try to describe a specific, concrete experience (e.g., catching a ball).

9. What mechanisms seem to be important in maintaining size constancy? How is Emmert's law useful in understanding size constancy? If distance cues were unavailable but other cues were present, do you think that size constancy could be maintained? Why is the size of the moon not constant?

10. Anastasi found that a parallelogram appears to be larger than a square of equal area. Examine the theories provided to account for visual illusions to see if you can find one that might give rise to the misperceived area of parallelograms. (Hint: Look at the top of the Necker cube in

Figure 6.23.) Which explanations of visual illusions seem best able to deal with each of the illusions in this chapter? Pay particular attention to the area illusions.

Key Terms

distance perception, p. 150
depth perception, p. 150
egocentric distance, p. 150
relative distance, p. 150
allocentric distance, p. 150
cue, p. 151
monocular cues, p. 151
binocular cue, p. 151
pictorial cues, p. 152
occlusion, p. 152
linear perspective, p. 152
size cues, p. 152
familiar size, p. 152
relative size, p. 152
texture gradient, p. 153
atmospheric perspective, p. 154
shading, p. 154
height cues, p. 156

trompe l'oeil, p. 158
motion parallax, p. 161
kinetic depth effect, p. 161
binocular disparity, p. 163
stereopsis, p. 163
horopter, p. 163
Panum's area, p. 163
crossed disparity, p. 163
uncrossed disparity, p. 163
stereoscope, p. 165
stereoscopic picture, p. 165
correspondence problem, p. 165
autostereogram, p. 166
binocular rivalry, p. 167
accommodation, p. 168
convergence, p. 168
direct perception (Gibsonian) approach, p. 168

ground theory, p. 168
motion perspective, p. 169
affordances, p. 169
empiricism, p. 170
kinesthetic information, p. 170
constructivist theory, p. 170
computational approach, p. 171
module, p. 171
disparity-selective cells, p. 174
Emmert's law, p. 177
size constancy, p. 178
size-distance invariance hypothesis, p. 179
invariants, p. 180

transformation theory, p. 180
Müller-Lyer illusion, p. 181
Sander parallelogram, p. 182
horizontal-vertical illusion, p. 182
Ponzo illusion, p. 182
misapplied constancy explanation, p. 184
incorrect comparison explanation, p. 184
eye-movement explanation, p. 184
margin illusion, p. 185
Ames room, p. 185
moon illusion, p. 185

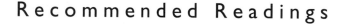

Recommended Readings

Julesz, B. (2006). *Foundations of cyclopean perception*. Cambridge, MA: MIT.

This very influential book was first published in 1971, but had been out of print for many years. Lovingly reproduced by Thomas Papathomas and Flip Phillips, the new version ensures that this resource will remain available to future students interested in stereopsis. In the book, you'll find many random-dot stereograms that accompany Julesz's thinking about binocular disparity.

Morgan, M. (2003). *The space between our ears: How the brain represents visual space*. New York: Oxford.

Morgan wrote this text to inform a general reader about depth perception. As a result, you'll find that his prose is both engaging and scholarly—a triumph of near effortless learning. Morgan does tend to meander a bit, but the side-trips are always interesting.

Pizlo, Z. (2008). *3D shape: Its unique place in visual perception*. Cambridge, MA: MIT.

Pizlo reviews and criticizes the contributions of many approaches to three-dimensional shape perception (e.g., empiricism, direct perception, computational). He then proposes a different approach that begins with figure-ground organization. His approach doesn't target depth cues, but instead focuses on the nature and operation of constraints on the possible three-dimensional objects that gave rise to the two-dimensional retinal image.

Robertson, L. C. (2004). *Space, objects, minds, and brains*. New York: Psychology Press.

If you're interested in a book that explores research on the role of the brain in encoding spatial information, then this is the book for you. Robertson provides a well-organized overview of the neuroscience and neuropsychology of space perception. Her coverage of unilateral neglect is particularly interesting.

Ross, H. E., & Plug, C. (2002). *The mystery of the moon illusion: Exploring size perception*. New York: Oxford.

If you'd like to learn more about the moon illusion, this is the book to read. Ross and Plug have long been engaged in the study of the moon illusion, which makes this book quite authoritative. The book summarizes and evaluates many approaches researchers have taken to understanding the moon illusion (and size perception).

Color

IN THE WIZARD OF OZ, Dorothy and Toto have a number of clues indicating that they're not in Kansas anymore. Leaving aside all the strange creatures, Oz is a world of vivid colors! Stop for a minute and consider how different your world would be without color. At one level, it wouldn't be too bad. You'd certainly appreciate watching a movie such as *The Wizard of Oz* on a black-and-white television. (We know it might be difficult to imagine, but not too long ago the typical television showed only black-and-white images!) However, it's certainly true that color adds richness to your perception of the world.

Christine Ladd-Franklin (1847–1930) was an early advocate of the position that seeing in color provides a number of adaptive advantages. Creatures with a single type of photoreceptor could distinguish lightness but couldn't distinguish colors (Verdon & Adams, 2002). The world they see might be like that displayed on a black-and-white television screen. That would likely suffice to avoid a predator approaching across a plain, but it might make it difficult to detect a camouflaged predator stealthily approaching through some bushes. A plant-eating monochromat would certainly find it more difficult to distinguish among potential food sources.

As we'll discuss in the context of color-vision deficiencies, two different types of photoreceptors would confer *some* color vision. In fact, most mammals have only two types of photoreceptors. Besides humans, some other species have evolved to make use of three types of photoreceptors (Arrese et al., 2006; Davies et al., 2007). As a result, these species would be able to discriminate among a wide range of wavelengths. Such color vision would enable these creatures to better detect fruits or distinguish among varieties of green leaves (Gegenfurtner & Kiper, 2003; Sumner & Mollon, 2003). In fact, color may aid in a variety of detection tasks (Kingdom & Kasrai, 2006).

In addition to its evolutionary consequences, color perception plays important roles in our everyday lives. As a result, the perception of color has been a consistently popular topic for researchers. In this chapter, we'll first focus on the physical aspects of color and color mixing. We'll next review and expand on material about the visual system introduced earlier in the text, along with a discussion of theories of color perception. We'll also look at individual differences in color vision before discussing various color phenomena.

Nature of Color

An object's *color*, as we typically use the term, has several components. Three terms are used to describe our perception: *hue, saturation,* and *lightness*. As we discussed in Chapters 3 and 4, a physical dimension generally determines each of these qualities. As indicated in Chapter 4, the intensity of the light source determines much of your experience of **brightness**. As illustrated in Table 7.1, wavelength primarily determines an object's hue, purity basically determines saturation, and the amount of light reflected basically determines lightness.

Let us first examine **hue**, which is the psychological reaction to wavelengths ranging from about 400 nm (seen as the hue *violet*) to about 700 nm (seen as the hue *red*). Hue is a perception; out in the world, we find only light of many different wavelengths and no hues at all. Thus, red (or any other hue) is in your head.

One person who understood that distinction was the famous British scientist Sir Isaac Newton (1643–1727). Newton completed his undergraduate career at Trinity College, Cambridge, in the summer of 1665. To avoid the plague, Newton returned to his home in a rural area of Lincolnshire County. Apparently, he put his time at home to good use, developing theories of calculus and gravity in addition to his work on the nature of light.

At that time, prisms were novelty items sold at fairs, so people were well aware of the spectrum revealed by the prism (Mollon, 2003). However, they thought that white light was basic and that the prism itself produced the spectrum seen in Color Plate 2 inside the front cover. One of Newton's many contributions was the demonstration that white light really consists of a combination of wavelengths that were refracted more (with a hue of violet) or less (with

▶ **TABLE 7.1**   General Relations among Physical and Perceptual Properties of Color

Physical Term	Perceptual Term
Wavelength	Hue
Purity	Saturation
Reflectance	Lightness
Intensity	Brightness

a hue of red) by the prism. Moreover, these wavelengths were basic, because passing these separated wavelengths through other prisms had no effect on the hue. Newton also demonstrated that all the separate wavelengths could be combined to produce white light.

From an intuitive perspective, sunlight doesn't seem to be comprised of many different wavelengths. Nonetheless, as you can see in Figure 7.1, sunlight contains some portion of every wavelength from the visible spectrum. Notice, incidentally, that the light from a standard incandescent light bulb also contains all different wavelengths, but a greater proportion comes from the longer wavelengths.

Another observation that doesn't match our intuitions is the fact that objects *look as if* they are colored, but they are really reflecting light from selected portions of the spectrum. Your jeans may look blue—and blueness seems to be a quality as inseparable from those jeans as their pockets. Nevertheless, the jeans are blue because their surface is absorbing most of the long and medium wavelengths (from the red, orange, yellow, and green portions of the spectrum) and reflecting to your eyes primarily the light from the blue portion of the spectrum. Similarly, your white

shirt is reflecting light to your eyes from the entire spectrum, and your black shoes are reflecting almost no light. So the colors we perceive are partially determined by the nature of the light falling on the surface (the illumination) and the nature of the absorption and reflectance of the surface on which the light is falling.

In his 1704 treatise, Newton also proposed a common way to organize colors—the color wheel. As illustrated in Figure 7.2, a *color wheel* is a circle with all the different wavelengths arranged around the edge. The hues that people perceive to be similar are located near one another. Thus, yellow is near red and also near green. However, red and green, which seem quite different, are separated on the color wheel.

Next, notice the dotted line at the top of the color wheel. This part of the circle represents *nonspectral hues* that cannot be described in terms of a single wavelength from a part of a spectrum. Instead, combining other hues produces these hues. Purple is a combination of blue and red. Similarly, studies show that, when asked to choose one hue as the best example of red, people choose a red that contains a little touch of blue.

Notice also that some colors are not on the circle. Brown and pink aren't there, let alone the more exotic colors such as silver and gold. In fact, you see on the wheel only a small proportion of the crayons you can

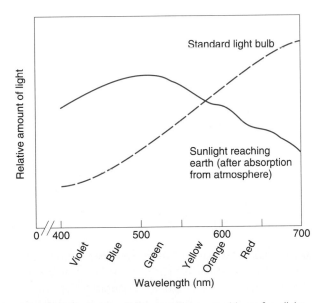

▶ **FIGURE 7.1**   Wavelength composition of sunlight and light from a light bulb. Both contain all wavelengths of light. However, compared to sunlight, the standard bulb has less energy among the shorter wavelengths and more energy among the longer wavelengths.

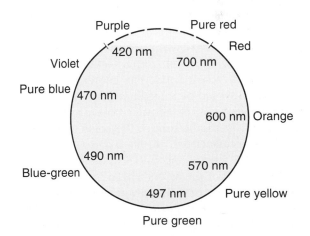

▶ **FIGURE 7.2**   The color wheel, a method of organizing all the wavelengths of the visible light spectrum. The layout places colors that seem similar (like red and orange) near each other and colors that seem opposite (like red and green) across from each other.

buy in the extra-fancy, super-duper collection. Where is burnt sienna or carnation pink or periwinkle or mauve? The outside of the color wheel represents only the **monochromatic colors**—those that could be produced by a single wavelength—plus the nonspectral hues necessary to complete the circle.

In addition to hue, our experience of color is determined by lightness and saturation. Remember from Chapter 4 that objects vary in the amount of light they reflect from their surfaces. Regardless of the intensity of the light shining on an object, we tend to perceive its lightness as constant. Thus, *lightness* is the apparent reflectance of a color; lightness describes our psychological reaction to the physical characteristic, reflectance. Objects run the gamut from very dark (black) to very light (white), with other shades of reflectance in between.

Hue, lightness, *and* saturation cannot easily be represented on a single color wheel. Instead, we require a three-dimensional representation of color, as seen in Figure 7.3, which is a picture of a color solid. A **color solid** or **color spindle** represents the hue, saturation, and lightness of all colors. Color Plate 4, inside the back cover, shows one example of a color solid.

The axis along the center of the color solid represents the **achromatic colors** discussed in Chapter 4 (white, grays, and black). You might think of the color solid as a series of color wheels stacked one on top of the other. If you were to take a horizontal section through the color solid at any point, you would see the color wheel associated with a particular lightness. You could think of Newton's color wheel as the circle formed by taking the horizontal section through the middle of the color solid. The center of Newton's color wheel would be a medium gray. At the top of the color solid are the lighter colors associated with light grays. At the bottom of the color solid are the darker colors associated with dark grays.

Figure 7.4 represents one possible section of the color solid. All of the colors within this cross section are equal in lightness. However, the colors vary in purity. The physical **purity** of a stimulus is determined by the amount of achromatic light added to the monochromatic light. Colors high in purity and with no achromatic light added are arranged around the edge of the circle. As we move toward the middle of the circle, we see the colors low in purity and with increasing amounts of achromatic light added. The center of the circle represents a shade of gray, an

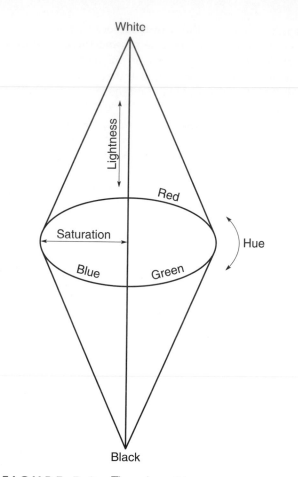

▶ **FIGURE 7.3**   The color solid, a way to represent all visible wavelengths in terms of hue, saturation, and lightness. Compare this figure to Color Plate 4 inside the back cover.

evenly balanced mixture of light waves, with no single wavelength dominant.

Notice that as we move inward from blue to white, we move from a true, deep blue to more "washed out" shades of blue, such as sky blue and baby blue. As we have discussed, the physical characteristic is customarily referred to as *purity*. The *apparent* purity of a color, however, is called **saturation**. Purity is a term from physics, and saturation describes a psychological reaction. Thus, we say that baby blue looks highly unsaturated because we are discussing our psychological reaction. Furthermore, the achromatic colors (grays, black, and white) are all unsaturated.

You may wonder why the color solid is pointed at both ends rather than cylindrical. The answer is that some combinations of saturation and lightness are

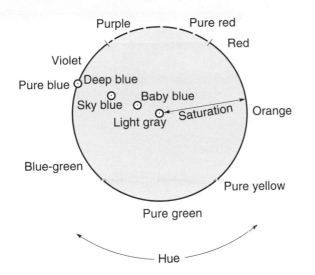

Purple   Pure red

Red

Violet

Pure blue Deep blue

Sky blue   Baby blue

Light gray   Saturation   Orange

Blue-green

Pure yellow

Pure green

— Hue —

▶ **FIGURE 7.4**   The color wheel plus saturation, the psychological reaction to the amount of white light added to a hue. A saturated blue lying on the edge of the wheel (i.e., no white light added) is perceived as a deep hue; an unsaturated blue close to the center (a lot of white light added) is perceived as a much lighter hue (e.g., baby blue).

impossible. For example, you cannot have a very dark or light color that is highly saturated. As you approach the ends of the color solid, the achromatic light becomes so strong that it overwhelms the monochromatic lights. You might often mistake a dark navy blue sweater for black because the reflectance is so low that the blue in the sweater is harder to detect. In summary, high saturation is possible only with intermediate levels of lightness, neither too dark nor too light.

Section Summary

Nature of Color

1. Color is a psychological reaction to wavelengths in the range of approximately 400 nm to 700 nm. Thus, color exists only in the mind of the perceiver. Hue is the psychological response to the length of light waves.

2. Sir Isaac Newton made a number of important contributions to our understanding of color. He developed a color wheel, which represents monochromatic wavelengths along the edge of a color wheel. The color wheel also shows nonspectral hues such as purple and pure red.

3. The apparent purity of a color is referred to as saturation. On a color wheel, the hues near the center of a circle are less saturated and hues near the edge are more saturated.

4. A color solid represents hue, saturation, and lightness (which corresponds to the physical term, reflectance). Lightness is represented along the vertical dimension. Horizontal slices through the color solid are the equivalent of color wheels. The solid is shaped so that the broadest portion occurs at medium lightness.

Color Mixing

What happens when we mix colors? We can actually mix colors in two different ways. The *subtractive mixture* method means that we mix dyes or pigments, or we place two or more colored filters together and shine a light source through them. The *additive mixture* method means that we add together beams of light from different parts of the spectrum. Subtractive mixtures involve only a single light source, whereas additive mixtures combine colors from separate light sources. We will discuss both types of color mixing because they have had a real impact on the development of theories of color perception. However, keep in mind that the same color perception principles are the basis of both subtractive and additive color mixing.

Subtractive Mixtures

Suppose that we were to ask you the color that would result from mixing blue and yellow. If you respond "Green," then you are already familiar with subtractive color mixing. Subtractive mixtures, as we said before, involve mixing pigments or placing colored filters together. They are called *subtractive* because when a beam of white light passes through filters or falls on pigments, parts of the spectrum are absorbed or subtracted. As Figure 7.5 shows (page 194), blue paint absorbs the yellow, orange, and red (the long wavelengths) from the white light. Only the light from the violet, blue, and green portions of the spectrum passes on to your eyes. However, yellow paint absorbs violet and blue (the short wavelengths). Consequently, when you mix blue and yellow paints, only the medium wavelengths are *not* absorbed by either of the paints, so you see a green.

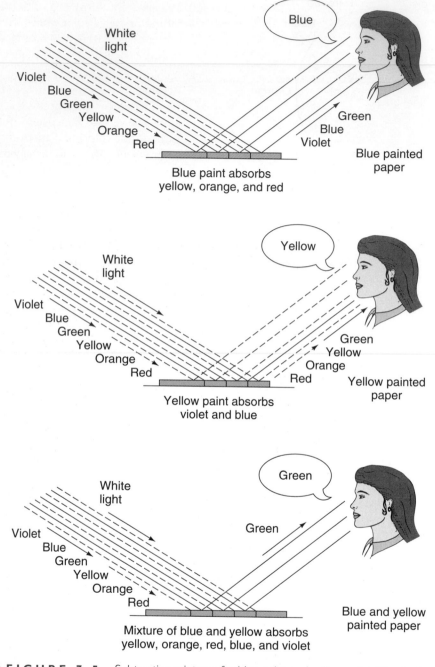

▶ **FIGURE 7.5** Subtractive mixtures for blue paint and yellow paint. The final perception, green, results from the only wavelengths not absorbed by the blue or yellow paints. In other words, the subtraction takes place at the level of paints. (From Lindsay & Norman, 1977)

Remember that we are dealing with subtractive mixtures whenever we mix dyes or pigments. Artists work with subtractive mixtures when they mix pigments on a palette or when they put one color on top of another on the canvas. If you are repainting a room, you will also need to worry about subtractive mixtures, because yellow painted over blue may turn out a sickly green. Anyone who works with colored filters would also be concerned about subtractive mixtures. For example, a window display that uses various colors of cellophane might unintentionally reveal a new color if two colors overlap.

How can people tell what kinds of colors will result from the subtractive mixture technique? Unfortunately, predicting exactly what wavelengths a particular pigment will absorb is quite difficult. If we do not know exactly what wavelengths the individual pigments will absorb, we cannot accurately predict the results of the combination of pigments. Rather than rely on trial and error, artists have developed a variety of systems for determining the colors on their palette (e.g., Sidaway, 2002; Wilcox, 2002). Whether they are working in oils, acrylics, watercolors, or digital graphics, it's especially helpful for novice artists to know which colors work well together.

Additive Mixtures

Keep in mind that with an additive mixture of colors, we are combining colored lights and not pigments. Thus, as you watch your television, all the colors you see come from combining various intensities of three different light sources. Unlike subtractive color mixing, in additive mixing, the wavelength of each light source actually reaches the photoreceptors. After examining how the color wheel can be used to make rough predictions of additive color mixtures, we will look at instances in which you've probably experienced additive color mixtures. Finally, we will look at the important concept of metameric matching—a topic to which we will return later in the chapter.

PREDICTING ADDITIVE MIXTURES USING THE COLOR WHEEL   Let's return to the color wheel. Look at Figure 7.2 and notice that the wavelengths are not evenly arranged around the periphery of the wheel. The portion of the spectrum from about 420 nm to about 500 nm clearly has more than its fair share of the wheel. This unequal distribution is neces-

sary to place complementary hues on exactly opposite sides of the color wheel. *Complementary hues* are those whose additive mixtures make an achromatic color. Notice, then, that when we add together equally intense lights of two highly saturated complementary hues, the result is a shade of gray. You should have a better sense of why such hues are complementary after we discuss color vision theories.

Figure 7.6 shows how an additive mixture would work if you mixed lights of the two complementary hues blue and yellow. Incidentally, these two hues were at the center of an early controversy. Newton was convinced that one could produce white light only by combining many different hues, but others argued that combining blue and yellow lights would suffice to produce white (Mollon, 2003).

Additive mixing of equal amounts of complementary hues produces an achromatic color. What color do you see in an additive mixture of unequal amounts of other colors? In general, you will produce a color between the two colors and lower in saturation. Here is how you can predict the results:

1. In Figure 7.2, locate the two colors on the color circle and connect them with a line.

2. Place a dot along the line to represent the relative amount of each light in the combination.

3. Draw a second line from the center of the circle so that it passes through the dot and ends at the edge of the circle.

4. The point at which that line ends on the circle tells you the name of the color; the distance of the dot from the center tells you its saturation.

These predictions will be only rough approximations, and more accurate predictions require using a "color wheel" that is decidedly noncircular (Valberg, 2005). In 1931, the International Commission on Illumination (CIE) produced the two-dimensional representation of color space seen in Color Plate 7. We have clearly come a long way from the color wheel and the color solid!

We should point out that an additive mixture cannot be highly saturated. Whenever we combine two colors additively, any point along the line connecting those two colors in a color circle cannot lie on the edge of the circle. Instead, it lies in the less saturated region. If the two colors are similar, the additive combination can still be fairly saturated. If the two

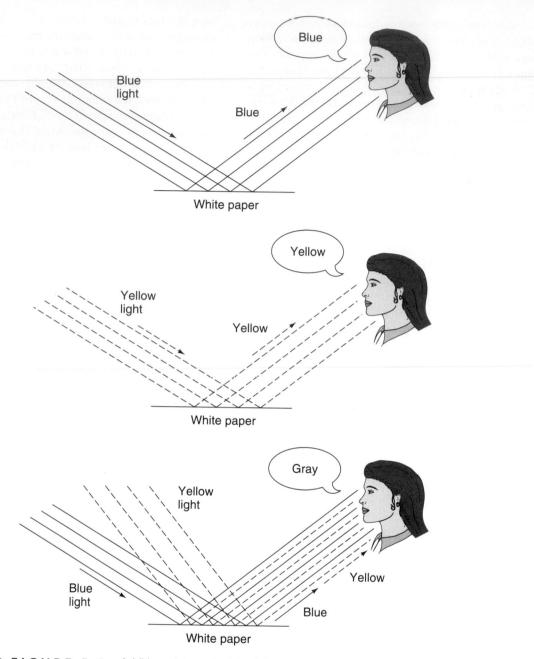

▶**FIGURE 7.6** Additive mixtures for blue light and yellow light. The final perception, gray, results from both the blue and yellow lights reaching the photoreceptors. In other words, the addition takes place at the photoreceptors. (From Lindsay & Norman, 1977)

colors are complementary, however, and if the mixture uses equal quantities of both, the result is an extremely unsaturated mixture. Try www Demonstration 7.1 to illustrate additive mixtures and clarify the issue of saturation.

When we mix blue and yellow in a subtractive mixture, we produce a green. However, when we mix blue and yellow in an additive mixture, we produce gray. Thus, the two mixture techniques produce different results. The point at which the mixing occurs will help you keep the two techniques separate. In subtractive color mixing, the combination of pigments takes place *before* the light stimulus reaches the eye. In additive color mixing, the combination of the light sources occurs *after* the light stimulus reaches the eye. Try [www] Demonstration 7.2 to illustrate the two techniques.

EVERYDAY EXAMPLES OF ADDITIVE MIXTURES

In our everyday lives, we do not often see mixed beams of lights of different colors. A more common way to produce additive mixtures is to place very small patches of color next to one another. For example, color televisions typically produce their range of colors by using red, green, and blue dots. From a typical viewing distance, these dots are too small and closely spaced to be discriminated with normal vision. Your eyes blend them together in what appear to be solid colors of assorted hues. Try [www] Demonstration 7.3 to convince yourself that, when you watch television, you are really watching spots in front of your eyes.

Artists can also produce additive mixtures with their paints. With a technique called **pointillism**, discrete dots of pigments are applied to a canvas. Using this method, an artist can create the perception of colors that aren't found on the artist's palette. Viewed from a distance, the points blend together, but when viewed closely, the separable points become apparent. Another technique, called **divisionism**, is based on the interactive effects of larger patches of colors. We will discuss such effects, called *simultaneous color contrast*, later in this chapter.

Georges Seurat (1859–1891), for example, didn't mix a large number of subtle shades on his palette. In fact, a reconstruction of the palette for his best-known painting contained only about a dozen colors. Some of these pigments were probably mixed in a subtractive fashion, including desaturating the pigments by mixing them with white paint (Lanthony, 1997). Yet, from this small number of pigments, Seurat was able to produce the wide range of colors seen in *Un Dimanche après-midi à l'Île de la Grande-Jatte (Sunday Afternoon on the Island of the Grand Jatte)*. Color Plate 5 on the inside back cover shows this painting, with some unavoidable loss of accuracy in the process. The painting is probably the best exemplar of the Neo-Impressionist movement, illustrating both the pointillist and the divisionist techniques. In the accompanying detail of the painting, you can see the small dots of pigment used in pointillism. Note that you see none of the individual dots when viewing the entire picture from an appropriate distance.

We have been discussing mixtures of two colors. When equal parts of *three* colors are mixed together, the color can be predicted by connecting the three dots representing each color and then calculating the center point of that triangle. When the mixture is unequal, the resulting color shifts toward the color that contributes the largest portion, as you might expect.

ADDITIVE MIXTURES AND METAMERIC MATCHING

Early color theorists were greatly influenced by a type of additive color mixing referred to as *metameric matching*. **Metamers** are pairs of lights that look exactly the same but are composed of physically different stimuli. Imagine two patches of color. The patch on the left is blue-green with medium saturation, and it comes from a single light source. The patch on the right is created by mixing equal parts of highly saturated violet and green, as represented by the black dot in [www] Demonstration 7.1. Our eyes could not distinguish between these two metamers, even though they are physically different.

In a **metameric matching** experiment, an observer is presented with a target color (consisting of a single wavelength of light) and asked to match it by mixing together lights of different wavelengths. An observer with normal color vision can make a metameric match for each color of the spectrum by mixing the correct amount of three different colored lights. Most often, the three colored lights are red (650 nm), green (530 nm), and blue (460 nm). A person with normal color vision would not be able to make a match if given only two different colored lights to mix. This observation led early color theorists to argue that human beings are equipped with three types of color receptors. In the next section, we'll further describe metameric matching to illustrate the logic behind their position.

Section Summary

Color Mixing

1. The subtractive mixture method means that we mix pigments or we place colored filters together. Parts of the spectrum are subtracted or absorbed by the filters. Predicting the color of

the resulting mixture is difficult because the patterns of absorption may be complex.

2. The additive mixture method means that we add together beams of different colored lights. We can predict the color of the resulting mixture by using the color wheel. Outside the laboratory, additive mixtures can be accomplished by color television and an artistic technique called pointillism.

3. The additive mixture method can produce metamers, which are pairs of lights that look identical but are physically different.

Anatomy and Physiology of Color Vision

In Chapter 3, we talked about the structures that provide color vision, from photoreceptors to areas of the brain. As you'll recall, the typical human retina contains three different cone systems—each maximally sensitive to different wavelengths of light. We refer to these three kinds of cones as *S (short wavelength)*, *M (medium wavelength)*, and *L (long wavelength)*, based on the wavelengths to which they are most sensitive. Figure 7.7 illustrates the sensitivity of these three sys-

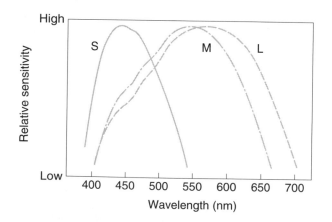

▶ **FIGURE 7.7** Absorption curves for the three cone pigments. Although the three systems overlap considerably, each is maximally sensitive to a different wavelength. Note that the curves in this graph are more accurate than the somewhat stylized curves shown in Figure 3.9. (Adapted from Gegenfurtner & Kiper, 2003)

tems. Notice that the M- and L-curves overlap considerably. In other words, these curves do not differ much in their *spectral sensitivity*, or the region of the spectrum in which they absorb light. Finally, notice that the M- and L-curves absorb some amount from nearly the entire visible spectrum, and the S-curve absorbs from almost half the visible spectrum.

Color information is then conveyed via the P pathway to visual centers in your brain. In this section, we'll expand a bit on that discussion. In doing so, we'll review two very influential color vision theories: trichromatic theory and opponent-process theory. In resolving the controversy between these two theories, researchers arrived at a better understanding of color vision. Have no fear—other controversies remain!

In this section, we will first consider how color is coded by the photoreceptors in the retina. Then we will see how your brain processes this information from the receptors.

The Cone Mosaic and Trichromatic Theory

As you learned in Chapter 3, humans typically have three different cone systems. We now have sophisticated technologies that enable us to determine many details about the cones. However, hundreds of years before the advent of those technologies, some scientists proposed that humans have three kinds of color receptors, each differentially sensitive to light from a particular portion of the spectrum. This *trichromatic theory* of color vision was based on logic and careful observation, including metameric matching research mentioned earlier.

The founders of trichromatic theory include Sir Isaac Newton in the 1600s (whose work with prisms we mentioned earlier) and three researchers in the 1800s. These were James Clerk Maxwell, a Scottish physicist who conducted research on electromagnetic radiation; Thomas Young, an English physician who also achieved fame by translating the Rosetta stone; and—no surprise—our old friend Hermann von Helmholtz. You might see the trichromatic theory referred to as the Young-Helmholtz theory.

TRICHROMATIC THEORY AND METAMERIC MATCHING   It's impressive that these early theorists were able to anticipate later research that has confirmed the three different cone systems. They knew that people with normal color vision needed to add three different lights in order to match a target color (metameric matching). They also knew about color vision deficiencies, which they correctly thought could emerge as the result of problems with one of the three cone systems. We'll say more about such color vision deficiencies later in the chapter. For now, let's explore how metameric matching supports trichromatic theory.

By working with Figure 7.7, you are now in a position to better understand the reason that metameric matching works as it does. Remember, an observer typically adjusts three primary wavelengths of 650 nm (red), 530 nm (green), and 460 nm (blue). What impact would each of these lights have on the retina? By drawing a vertical line through 650 nm on the horizontal axis of Figure 7.7, you can see that 650-nm light would lead to a low amount of absorption (and firing) in the L-cone system, very little in the M-cone system, and virtually none in the S-cone system. The 530-nm light would lead to a fairly large amount of absorption (and firing) in the L-cone system, a slightly higher amount in the M-cone system, and a small amount in the S-cone system. What about the 460 nm light? Would you agree that it should produce a small amount of activity in the L-cone system, a bit more in the M-cone system, and a large amount in the S-cone system?

You should now have a good sense of how color information is encoded at the retinal level by means of relative absorption and firing of the three cone systems. Let's consider a metameric matching study in greater detail. Suppose that you present a target color of 580 nm (yellow) to an observer. This target should produce a large amount of absorption in both the L- and M-cone systems (with slightly more in the L-cone than in the M-cone system) and virtually none in the S-cone system. The observer would be able to produce a fairly close match by mixing large quantities of the 530-nm and 650-nm lights, resulting in a yellow light with a slight bluish tinge. Why? If you add together the absorption patterns for the 530-nm and 650-nm lights discussed above, you'll be able to make a fairly good prediction of the result: high absorption in both the L-cone and M-cone systems, but slightly higher for the L-cone system (just what we want), and a small amount of absorption in the S-cone system (which is not present in the target, so we don't want it). To obtain a perfect match, the third primary (460 nm)

must be introduced. However, adding it to the existing mixture would further increase the unwanted activity in the S-cone system. Instead, the observer would have to add a small amount of the final primary to the yellow target! It turns out that, in metameric matching experiments, the observer often has to add small amounts of one of the primaries to the original target.

MORE EVIDENCE FOR TRICHROMATIC THEORY

With the advent of sophisticated technology, researchers began to produce physiological evidence in support of three kinds of color receptors. For example, William Rushton (1901–1980) found that humans definitely have at least two kinds of cones. Rushton (1958) projected a beam of light into the eyes of human observers and compared the composition of ingoing and returning light. These comparisons unveiled the M- and L-cone systems. However, Rushton found no evidence for the proposed S-cone system.

Soon thereafter, researchers used other techniques to uncover the S-cones. They were difficult to detect because they represent only 5 to 10% of the cones in the retina (Solomon & Lennie, 2007). More recently, David Williams and his colleagues have used high-resolution adaptive-optics imaging to map the distribution of the three cone systems in people (Hofer et al., 2005; Putnam et al., 2005). It's now clear that the S-cones are distributed in a fairly regular pattern throughout the retina. On the other hand, the M- and L-cones are distributed in a more random pattern in most people. Together, the M- and L-cones comprise over 90% of the cones in most people's retinas. However, the proportion of M- and L-cones varies across individuals with normal color vision. In some people, the proportions are roughly equivalent. In other people, L-cones greatly outnumber M-cones.

Thus far, we've been considering people with normal color vision. Early on, Arthur König (1856–1901) correctly predicted that color vision deficiencies were linked to problems with one of the three cone systems (Pokorny, 2004). Thus, when we consider people with such color vision deficiencies, the variability in the cone systems is greater still. What is the source of all the variability in the cone systems across people with normal and abnormal color vision? It's all in your genes!

Details about the nature of these photopigments and their genetic coding have been identified by

Jeremy Nathans and his colleagues (1989; 1986). You may remember from Chapter 3 that the rods contain rhodopsin, which breaks down into retinal and opsin when light reaches the rods. Similarly, the cones contain retinal and a specific opsin that is most sensitive to a particular wavelength (Nathans, 1999; Solomon & Lennie, 2007). Different genes determine the nature of the opsin found in S-, M-, and L-cones (Sharpe et al., 1999). The opsin for M- and L-cones is encoded on the X chromosome, which has implications for individual differences in color vision, as we'll discuss later.

It's quite clear that most humans are trichromats, albeit with some variability in the exact nature of the distribution of the three cone systems. It's equally clear that trichromacy is relatively rare in the animal kingdom (Rowe, 2002). As we noted at the beginning of this chapter, some primates and other species evolved trichromatic color vision (Arrese et al., 2002; Jacobs & Rowe, 2004). However, it's much more common for species with color vision to be dichromats. With a little help from humans, they might become trichromats. For example, Gerald Jacobs, Jeremy Nathans, and their colleagues (2007) were able to add a third cone system to mice. These genetically engineered trichromatic mice exhibited a greater sensitivity to the color spectrum than is true of regular dichromatic mice.

Trichromacy may be the norm in humans, but even small changes in the form of the opsin are sufficient to change the wavelengths to which the cone is sensitive. As a result of these modest genetic differences, some women have four different types of cones (Jameson et al., 2001). We'll say a bit more about the impact of four-cone systems later in the chapter.

Even with the evidence that some people have retinas containing more than three cone systems, the input from the cones appears to be combined into three independent channels. These three opponent channels are the topic of the next section.

Opponent-Process Theory

In spite of the logic of the Young-Helmholtz trichromatic theory, not everyone found the theory compelling. One skeptic was Ewald Hering (1834–1918), a German physiologist. Certain observations about color perception puzzled Hering. For example, he had noticed that it was easy to report seeing color mixtures such as bluish green or yellowish red, but other color mixtures—such as greenish red or yellowish blue—were impossible. (Try for a moment to picture either of these mixtures.)

Instead of three color receptors, Hering argued that there were three *pairs* of color receptors. Each color in these pairs was opposite the other, which is why they couldn't be mixed. Hering proposed three opponent pairs: red-green, yellow-blue, and white-black.

Negative afterimages also provided evidence for these opponent pairs. The term **negative afterimage** makes sense because the *image* appears *after* the original image. Further, the color of the afterimage is the opposite (or negative) of the opponent pair. You've surely experienced a negative afterimage. For example, place Color Plate 6 (inside back cover) under a bright light and stare at it for a while. If you then look at a plain sheet of paper, you should experience a negative afterimage. Thus, red is the afterimage of green, blue is the afterimage of yellow, and so on.

Hering proposed that the visual system uses opponent processes to perceive color. In its most general form, the **opponent-process theory** specifies that cells respond to stimulation by an increase in activity when one color is present and by a decrease in activity when another color is present. For example, the activity rate might increase for a given cell when green is present and decrease when red is present. In other words, each cell shows activation to some parts of the spectrum and inhibition to other parts. Hering incorrectly proposed that these opponent processes occurred at the receptor level rather than higher levels in the nervous system. Thus, the *original* version of opponent-process theory was incompatible with trichromatic theory.

Hering's theory did not receive a wide following until Hurvich and Jameson (1957) wrote an article called "An Opponent-Process Theory of Color Vision." The purpose of their psychophysical studies was to determine the amount of light of one color that would be necessary to cancel all perception of the opponent color (Knoblauch, 2002). For example, they showed a red light and measured the amount of green light that had to be added for observers to report that the light no longer looked red. (Remember from our discussion of additive color mixing that the right amounts of carefully chosen samples of red and green will make a neutral color, one that is neither red nor green, because red and green are complementary colors.) This procedure was repeated with different shades of red and with various shades of green, yellow, and blue.

Hurvich and Jameson therefore made an important contribution to color research by developing a technique that allows us to measure opponent-response functions directly. As we will now explore in some detail, horizontal connections among the three cone systems in the retina initiate opponent processes (Lennie, 2000). In essence, then, trichromatic theorists and opponent-process theorists were both correct. Trichromatic theorists correctly identified the receptors involved in color perception. Opponent-process theorists correctly identified the organization of color information beyond the receptors.

Color Coding beyond the Photoreceptors

Much of what we are about to discuss makes reference to information introduced in Chapter 3. You might find it beneficial to review the material on the visual pathways (pages 63–75) before reading this section. Given its importance for color perception, much of the discussion in this section will deal with the P pathway. The topics that we are about to explore will reinforce and extend the information introduced in Chapter 3.

OPPONENT PROCESSES IN THE RETINA AND LGN   At this point you know that normal color perception requires input from at least three cone systems. At the same time, you also know that two opponent pairs (red-green and yellow-blue) encode colors. How does our visual system obtain the four opponent colors from three types of cone?

First, let's address the origins of the opponent processes. You may want to refer to Chapter 3, where you learned that cones have a circular receptive field, with a center and an antagonistic surround. Actually, each cone would activate the center of two different receptive fields, because it is typically connected to both an excitatory (+) and an inhibitory (–) midget bipolar cell. The antagonistic surround is due to horizontal connections that send opposing input from the surrounding cones to the bipolar cell. Thus, the antagonistic surround to the excitatory bipolar cell would provide inhibition. The antagonistic surround to the inhibitory bipolar cells would provide excitation.

Next, let's consider how this generic notion of receptive fields yields the opponent processes. As seen in Figure 7.8 (page 202), there are actually six different opponent mechanisms (Valberg, 2005). Although it's not quite accurate to do so, it may help you to think of the four mechanisms based on M- and L-cones as green-red. M-cones would receive opposing input from nearby S- and L-cones. However, given the scarcity of S-cones, effectively M-cones would receive opposing input only from L-cones. Thus, one type of receptive field would have +M center and –L surround. What happens if a medium-wavelength light falls on this whole receptive field? Firing would increase (excitation) because the center is excited by medium-wavelength light and the surround isn't sensitive to medium-wavelength light. Thus, the +M/–L receptive field signals the presence of medium-wavelength (e.g., green) light. What happens if a long-wavelength light (e.g., red) falls on this receptive field? Firing would decrease (inhibition) because the center isn't sensitive to long-wavelength light, but the surround sends inhibitory input when stimulated by long-wavelength light. Finally, work out how this receptive field would respond to short-wavelength light. Look at Figure 7.8 and map out how the –M/+L receptive field would respond to various wavelengths of light. Can you see why we might refer to cells with these receptive fields as green-red?

You should also be able to work out the functioning of the receptive fields with L-cone centers. As was true for the receptive fields with M-cone centers, L-cones effectively would receive opposing input only from M-cones. Thus, one type of receptive field would have +L center and –M surround and the other type of receptive field would have –L center and +M surround.

Finally, let's consider the two other opponent mechanisms, which signal blue-yellow. S-cones would receive opposing input from both M- and L-cones. This configuration would produce two different types of receptive fields: +S center with –ML surround and –S center with +ML surround. However, receptive fields may be a bit messier for S-cones, with the M-cones in the surround not always antagonistic to the –S center (Solomon & Lennie, 2007).

What happens when white (achromatic) light falls on cells with these receptive fields? As seen in the final column of Figure 7.8, the three excitatory-center opponent mechanisms would operate as on-center off-surround receptive fields. The three inhibitory-center opponent mechanisms would operate as off-center on-surround receptive fields. Thus, these opponent mechanisms encode more than color information (Lennie & Movshon, 2005). In addition to color, the ganglion

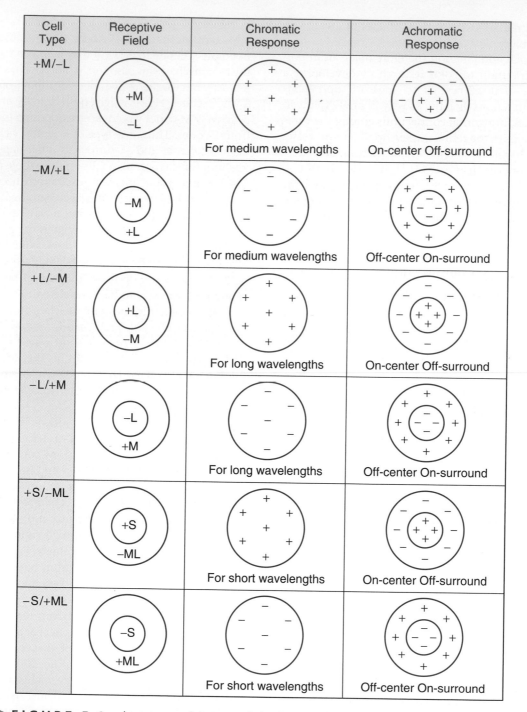

Cell Type	Receptive Field	Chromatic Response	Achromatic Response

+M/–L — +M / –L — For medium wavelengths — On-center Off-surround

–M/+L — –M / +L — For medium wavelengths — Off-center On-surround

+L/–M — +L / –M — For long wavelengths — On-center Off-surround

–L/+M — –L / +M — For long wavelengths — Off-center On-surround

+S/–ML — +S / –ML — For short wavelengths — On-center Off-surround

–S/+ML — –S / +ML — For short wavelengths — Off-center On-surround

▶ **FIGURE 7.8** A summary of six types of circular receptive fields. Each receptive field has a center and an antagonistic surround. Note that we might label the first four receptive fields as green-red because of their chromatic response. Thus, a medium-wavelength light (e.g., green) would increase firing in a cell with a +M/–L receptive field. A long-wavelength light (e.g., red) would decrease firing in a cell with a +M/–L receptive field. We might label the final two receptive fields as blue-yellow because of their chromatic response. With achromatic light (e.g., white), these receptive fields function as on-center off-surround or off-center on-surround receptive fields.

cells that convey information from the retina must also encode luminance information, spatial information, motion information, and so on.

The M- and L-cones ultimately stimulate the ganglion cells that initiate the P pathway. As we noted in Chapter 3, that information flows through the lateral geniculate nucleus (LGN) to the visual cortex (Gegenfurtner, 2003). S-cone information also flows through the LGN (K pathway) to the visual cortex.

COLOR CODING IN THE CORTEX   After the LGN, color information enters the primary visual cortex (V1) and then goes to other areas of visual cortex (e.g., V2, V3, V4). At one time, researchers thought that V1 had little to do with color perception. Increasingly, however, researchers have come to recognize the important role of V1 in color perception (Hurlbert, 2003; Solomon & Lennie, 2007). For example, researchers have found cells with double-opponent receptive fields in V1 (Gegenfurtner & Kiper, 2003). The center of the receptive fields of these cells is excited by L-cone input and inhibited by M-cone input. The surround, on the other hand, is inhibited by L-cone input and excited by M-cone input. Such cells would play a vital role in color constancy (Hurlbert, 2003).

In Chapter 3, we introduced you to the P, M, and K pathways. Neurons in the P pathway convey information about color and shape. At some point, however, your visual system needs to differentiate information such as color, shape, and motion. Researchers are now examining these processes, typically studying macaque monkeys. According to this research, there are cells in V1 and V2 that receive input from both eyes, and these cells are color sensitive. Thus, there may well be some binocular cells in V1 that signal color and other binocular cells in V1 that signal depth (Peirce et al., 2008).

As you'll see in other chapters, researchers often look for a brain center for a particular type of perception (e.g., music, speech). In a similar fashion, some researchers argued that V4 was the "color center." In fact, as you'll see in the next section, damage to an area in humans that corresponds to V4 leads to a loss of color vision. However, other deficits accompany that damage, so V4 serves many more functions than color perception. Furthermore, the percentage of color-tuned cells in V4 may be no higher than that found in other areas of visual cortex (Gegenfurtner & Kiper, 2003). Numerous areas of the brain are

involved in all perceptual processes, and so it's unlikely that there is a single "center" for any type of perception.

Section Summary

Anatomy and Physiology of Color Vision

1. Trichromatic theory was developed in the mid-1800s, and it is sometimes referred to as the Young-Helmholtz theory. Trichromatic theory proposes that the retina contains three different types of receptors. More recent evidence has confirmed the existence of—and genetic basis for—the three cone systems.

2. Hering developed the opponent-process theory at the end of the 1800s. According to current theory, opponent processes operate at levels beyond the receptors. Green and red work in opposition, as do blue and yellow and black and white.

3. Cones send information to ganglion cells and LGN cells that have circular receptive fields with centers that are either excitatory (+) or inhibitory (−) for particular wavelengths (i.e., short, medium, or long). In addition, the receptive fields have antagonistic surrounds formed by inhibitory input from surrounding cones. As a result, these cells have receptive fields that may be thought of as green-red or blue-yellow.

4. Many areas of the visual cortex (e.g., V1, V2, V3, V4) are involved in color perception. Before V1, individual neurons convey different types of information (e.g., color, shape, motion). However, within the visual cortex, different types of information may be processed in different areas. Nonetheless, it's unlikely that the visual cortex has a single color center.

Individual Differences in Color Vision

In earlier chapters, we've described a number of ways in which people might differ in their visual experience. Because color vision is linked to genes, people vary quite a bit in their color experience. This section will focus on individual differences in color vision that are due to biological differences. In later sections, you'll learn that experience can also lead to differences in color perception.

Color-Vision Deficiencies

Some people cannot tell the difference between two colors that differ in hue. We often refer to those people as being "colorblind," but that term is much too strong. As you will see, only a few people are totally unable to discriminate colors. We will use the term *color-vision deficiencies* instead. People with **color-vision deficiencies** have difficulty discriminating different colors.

About 8% of males have some form of red-green color vision deficiency, in contrast to about 0.4% of females (Birch, 2001). In other words, if you have 250 males and 250 females in a room, approximately 20 males and 1 female will have some trouble discriminating colors. Such color vision deficiencies are linked to the X chromosome. Because males have only one X chromosome, they are more vulnerable to such deficiencies.

We need to discuss color vision deficiencies for two reasons. First, the problem is fairly common. You may be color deficient yourself, and you probably have friends who are color deficient. Second, color deficiencies have important implications for color theories, a topic discussed in the preceding section. In this section, we'll consider how people diagnose color-vision deficiencies, and then we'll explore some causes of such deficiencies.

DIAGNOSING COLOR DEFICIENCIES How might you determine that someone has difficulty distinguishing particular colors? Color-vision researchers have developed many different ways of diagnosing red-green color deficiency. One approach is to ask people to identify an object (such as a number) that is presented as a configuration of different colors against a background of other colors. You may well have encountered the **Ishihara Test**, in which the observer tries to detect a number hidden in a pattern of different colored circles (Dain, 2004). Color Plate 6 (on inside back cover) provides an example of the Ishihara Test. To test children and others who don't know letters or numbers, clinicians can use a subset of items from the 38-plate Ishihara Test or other tests (Birch, 2001).

Another approach is to ask people to match colors. The anomaloscope is a device based on the prin-

ciple of metameric matching, discussed earlier. The person being tested attempts to match the yellow half of a circle by mixing the amount of red and green in the other half of the circle. People with color vision deficiencies make mistakes in a predictable and diagnostic fashion.

A final approach we'll discuss involves arranging colors. The Farnsworth-Munsell tests are examples of this type of color vision test. If you were taking a test of this type, you'd see a bunch of movable colored disks and a tray, with a colored disk anchored at each end. Your task would be to place the movable disks in order from one anchor color to the other. The ordering of the movable disks allows the clinician to detect problems with any of the three cone systems.

RETINAL COLOR-VISION DEFICIENCIES Some kinds of color vision are listed in Table 7.2. If you have normal color vision, you are a normal trichromat. A **normal trichromat** requires three colors, such as red, blue, and green, to match all the other colors of the spectrum. The word *trichromat* consists of two parts: *tri*, which means "three," and *chroma*, which means "color."

Researchers can often learn a great deal about the functioning of perceptual systems by studying people with abnormal abilities. Early color theorists were influenced not only by evidence from metameric matching experiments, but also by information about abnormal color vision. A very early and influential report came from John Dalton (1798/1948), who studied his own color deficiency using ribbons, flowers, and other objects as stimuli. Dalton found that his brother saw colors in a similar fashion, as did several male members of other families. Such observations led theorists to suggest that color deficiencies were consistent with an abnormality in one of the three cone systems, and that such abnormalities were genetically linked. Subsequent research has confirmed both hypotheses (Sharpe et al., 1999).

A person with the most common form of color deficiency is an **anomalous trichromat**. An anomalous trichromat has all three cone systems, but one of the systems has an abnormal absorption spectrum. As Table 7.2 shows, the cone system that is abnormal determines the three different types of anomalous trichromats (Birch, 2001). Depending on the nature of the abnormality, an anomalous trichromat might experience either a mild impairment or a more severe impairment in color perception. About 6% of males

▶ **TABLE 7.2**   Kinds of Color Vision, Normal and Deficient

Classification	Cone System Affected	Description
Normal Trichromat	None	Normal color vision
Anomalous Trichromat		
Protanomalous	L-cones	Insensitive to red-green
Deuteranomalous	M-cones	Insensitive to red-green
Tritanomalous	S-cones	Insensitive to blue-yellow
Dichromat		
Protanope	L-cones	Insensitive to red-green
Deuteranope	M-cones	Insensitive to red-green
Tritanope	S-cones	Insensitive to blue-yellow
Monochromat	All	No color vision

are anomalous trichromats, most of whom have an abnormality in the M-cones (Smith & Pokorny, 2003).

In contrast, a *dichromat* (*di* means "two") is a person who has only two of the three cone systems. As a result, a dichromat requires only two primary colors to match all the colors he or she can see. If you look at Figure 7.7 and imagine that one of the three curves is missing, you will see why the dichromat needs only two colors to match any target color. As is true of the many species that are normally dichromats, human dichromats can see colors. However, dichromats have difficulty making some color discriminations that are easy for trichromats. Obviously, this is a more severe color deficiency than that experienced by an anomalous trichromat. Luckily, dichromats are relatively rare (2% of males).

Loss of one of the three cone systems produces each of the three types of dichromats. Protanopes and deuteranopes are the most common dichromats, with each occurring in about 1% of males. Their perception of the world is similar, and both are referred to as being "red-green colorblind" because they are likely to confuse red and green. *Protanopes* have no L-cones, and *deuteranopes* have no M-cones. It may be that these dichromats have the typical number of cones in their retinas (Carlson, 2007). That certainly seems to be that case for protanopes, who have the typical number of S-cones, but an increased number of M-cones. However, it may be that deuteranopes have the regular complement of S-cones *and* L-cones, so that the cones that would have been M-cones are absent. Thus, deuteranopes may have fewer cones than normal (Carroll et al., 2004).

You may know some protanopes and deuteranopes. The third kind of dichromat is rare. Only about one person in 5,000 to 10,000 of the population is a tritanope (Birch, 2001). *Tritanopes*, who confuse blues and yellows, lack the S-cones. Because this deficiency is not linked to the X chromosome, it occurs equally often (though rarely) in both males and females.

How can we tell what the world looks like to a dichromat? Some evidence comes from a study by Graham and Hsia (1958). They located a woman who, amazingly enough, had normal vision in her right eye but was a deuteranope in her left eye. These researchers presented different hues to each eye and asked the woman to match colors. For example, they showed a red to her color-deficient eye and asked her to adjust the color presented to the normal eye until it seemed to be the same hue. They found that her color-deficient eye saw all the colors between green and violet as blue and she saw all the colors between green and red as yellow.

Don't presume that the situation of the dichromat is extremely bleak. In fact, dichromats may be better than trichromats at detecting rapidly flickering color stimuli (Sharpe et al., 2006). Moreover, aside from the difficulty of discriminating some colors, dichromats have fairly normal visual acuity. Even though it's true that color is extremely useful for detection and discrimination, color vision is not a crucial ability. Most animals survive quite well, even though they do not see the world with the full range of colors perceived by a trichromat. Furthermore, color deficiencies went virtually unnoticed for many centuries, so "colorblind" humans were apparently able to function almost flawlessly in their societies. In fact, most dichromats can learn to use a number of color terms accurately—perhaps based on perceived lightness differences—even though they do not see the colors as a normal trichromat would (Wachtler et al., 2004).

On some occasions, however, dichromats face a real disadvantage. For example, isn't it unfortunate that traffic lights are red and green? Until traffic light configurations became relatively standard (a vertical column of three lights, with red on top), protanopes and deuteranopes driving toward an intersection were playing a dangerous guessing game. Now they simply have to stop when the top light is lit.

The information on color deficiencies fits the color-vision theory discussed earlier. Consistent with the findings at the receptor level, color deficiencies arise from the loss of function in particular cone systems. Consistent with the findings beyond the receptor level, people who cannot see red also have difficulty with green, and people who cannot see blue also have trouble with yellow.

We have discussed trichromats, who make matches based on three colors, and dichromats, who make matches based on two colors. We now turn to the monochromats. A **monochromat** (*mono* means "one") requires only one color to match *all* other colors. Every hue looks similar to this person, so he or she is truly colorblind. Fortunately, this disorder is relatively rare, with an incidence of only about one person 30,000 (Carroll et al., 2008).

We'll focus on rod monochromats, rather than those with a single cone system. As you might expect, a genetic mutation (to a gene named CNGB3) accounts for a great deal of rod monochromacy (Kohl et al., 2005; Sundin et al., 2000). Unfortunately, rod monochromats have other visual problems, including reduced acuity, excessive sensitivity to bright lights (e.g., sunlight), and unsteady eye fixations. It does appear that rod monochromats have no cones in their retinas (Carroll et al., 2008).

BRAIN COLOR-VISION DEFICIENCY: CEREBRAL ACHROMATOPSIA *Cerebral achromatopsia* is the loss of color vision due to damage to the ventromedial occipital cortex, illustrated in Figure 7.9 (Bouvier & Engel, 2006; Heywood & Kentridge, 2003). The loss of the ability to see colors defines the disorder. Many people with achromatopsia have normal form vision, so they see shapes clearly, but everything appears as shades of gray (Zeki, 1993). When damage is localized to one hemisphere, the person with achromatopsia will see half of the visual field in color and the other half in black and white (Heywood & Cowey, 2003).

It's important to note that people with achromatopsia have fully functional cone systems. Thus, input from the cones is necessary, but it's not sufficient for color perception. As we noted earlier, this area of the brain must be important for color vision, but it is not likely *the* color center (Solomon & Lennie, 2007). One reason is that damage to this area of the brain causes visual deficits other than color perception (e.g., Cole et al., 2003; Kentridge et al., 2004).

More than Three Cone Systems

As we noted in Chapter 3, many birds have more than three cone systems (Beason & Loew, 2008; Goldsmith, 2006). As a result, they are able to see ultraviolet light. Some humans, typically women, also have more than three cone systems. However, the effect is not to extend the visible spectrum into the ultraviolet. Instead, people with four cone systems are able to make more precise discriminations among wavelengths in the usual human range (Jameson et al., 2006; Jameson et al., 2001). Although trichromacy may be the norm, there appears to be quite a lot of variability in the nature and distribution of photoreceptors in the human retina.

Aging and Color Perception

In earlier chapters, we noted that aging is often associated with a decrease in visual abilities (Schieber, 2006). We'll return to this topic in Chapter 14. One side effect of aging is that your lens tends to become yellow. The result is much like adding a yellow filter in front of the incoming light (Suzuki et al., 2005). The result is that, as people age, there is a change in

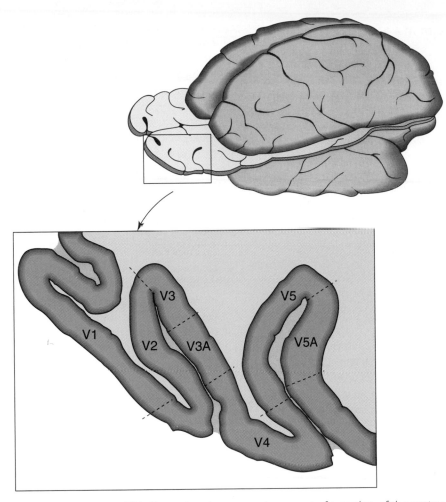

▶ **FIGURE 7.9** This illustration shows an enlargement of a section of the cortex. The upper part of the illustration shows the brain, with a horizontal section removed (and slid backwards). The area from the occipital lobe to be enlarged is indicated with a rectangle. (From Zeki, 1993)

the wavelengths reaching the retina. As we've often noted, the brain adapts as a result of experience. Because brain changes accompany the changes in the lens, there seems to be little change in color appearance among older people (Hardy et al., 2005).

What would happen if you wore a yellow lens for an extended period of time? To assess the impact of such altered visual input, Jay Neitz and his colleagues (2002) had people wear colored lenses for differing portions of each day (4, 8, or 12 hours). Consistent with other research, doing so immediately affected the person's color vision. However, after a few days of wearing the lenses, the shifts

became more pronounced. Moreover, after the people stopped wearing the lenses, their color perception did not return to normal for a couple of weeks. Clearly, perceptual experience causes changes in brain function, which then affects subsequent perception.

Furthermore, older people often develop cataracts, so that corrective surgery may involve replacing the lens with a clear artificial one. Would such a change affect color perception? Data suggest that is definitely the case (Delahunt et al., 2004). Immediately after removal of the cataract, most people show a pronounced shift in color perception.

Section Summary

Individual Differences in Color Vision

1. For a variety of reasons, people may differ markedly in their perception of colors.

2. Researchers have developed a variety of tests to assess individual differences in color vision. These tests involve detecting a colored stimulus against a colored background (e.g., Ishihara Test), matching a color using an anomaloscope, or arranging color chips (e.g., Farnsworth-Munsell tests).

3. Trichromats have normal color vision. They require three colors to match any target color.

4. Anomalous trichromats have an unusual absorption spectrum in one of their three cone systems. As a result, their color matches differ from those of normal trichromats.

5. A dichromat requires only two primary colors to match all other colors, because they are missing one of the three cone systems. Protanopes (missing L) and deuteranopes (missing M) cannot see reds and greens. Tritanopes (missing S) cannot see blues and yellows. These color deficiencies are consistent with color vision theories.

6. Dichromats have normal visual acuity and can even make some color discriminations on the basis of lightness differences.

7. A monochromat requires only one color to match all other colors. These people are truly colorblind.

8. People with cerebral achromatopsia are also truly colorblind, even though they have three completely functional cone systems.

9. Aging affects lens coloration, which has an impact on the wavelengths reaching the retina. Nonetheless, older people exhibit little change in color appearance—possibly due to brain changes.

Color Phenomena

So far, we have been discussing sensory factors in color perception—how color stimuli are processed from the retina to the cortex. However, keep in mind our discussion of lightness perception and lightness constancy in Chapter 4. Just as the perceived lightness of a stimulus isn't solely determined by retinal activity, color is not fully determined by retinal activity. The surrounding context has a tremendous effect on the perceived lightness of a stimulus, and context also influences color perception (MacLeod, 2003b). Moreover, consistent with Theme 4, color perception involves prior knowledge and expectations. Thus, identical levels of activity in S-, M-, and L-cones may lead to different color perceptions, depending on the surrounding context and the person's experience.

In this section, we discuss a variety of color phenomena that illustrate these extra-retinal influences on color perception. These color phenomena make it clear that the color of a stimulus is partly determined by factors other than its wavelength, intensity, and purity. We'll begin by focusing on color constancy, because it shows that perceived color could remain the same in spite of changes in the wavelengths reaching the retina.

Color Constancy

In Chapter 4, we introduced the notion of a constancy. In general, a constancy occurs when your perception of the distal stimulus remains the same, in spite of changes in the proximal stimulus. As we noted, constancies help you perceive a stable world.

In *color constancy*, we tend to use the same color name for an object despite changes in the wavelength of the light illuminating the object. For instance, during the day, objects are viewed under natural light, and then at night they are viewed under artificial light. Still, we assign the same color names to objects under both types of illumination. This is an impressive feat when you look again at Figure 7.1, which illustrates the increased long-wavelength energy present in an incandescent light compared to sunlight.

ASSESSING COLOR CONSTANCY   Let's first consider a demonstration of color constancy developed by Edwin H. Land (1909–1991). He presented three stimuli made up of patches of colors—each illuminated by a very different light source. The illuminations were chosen such that the red patch in one stimulus, the blue patch in the second stimulus, and the green patch in the third stimulus reflected *identical* wavelengths. If our sense of color emerged strictly from the physical information we received, observers should call all three of these patches the same color. Instead, observers showed strong color constancy—correctly identifying each of the three patches. As is true of lightness constancy, our perception of color doesn't depend on the absolute wavelengths reaching our retinas. Instead, color perception depends on reflectance relationships among objects in our field of vision.

In spite of Land's demonstration, when researchers study color constancy in the laboratory, their results may lead them to question the very existence of color constancy (Foster, 2003; Hurlbert, 1999). No one really questions a weak form of color constancy. That is, the *color name* will be constant, regardless of changes in illumination. Instead, they question a stronger form of color constancy, which asserts that an object's *color appearance* remains constant, regardless of changes in illumination. As we'll discuss later in this section, color names are categories that encompass a range of wavelengths. Thus, it's possible that a change in illumination could change an object's color appearance, even though you'd still give it the same color name.

Consider a blue carpet that might look "perfect" under a store's fluorescent illumination. When the carpet is installed in your home, where the illumination is either natural sunlight or incandescent lights, it might look terrible—but you'd still call it blue! Thus, the color name has remained constant, but the color appearance has changed substantially.

Even when assessing color appearance, laboratory studies using a range of methods typically demonstrate reasonably accurate color constancy (Foster, 2008). That is, if perfect color constancy is defined as 1 and complete inconstancy is 0, these studies find color constancy in the range of .70 to .80. In fact, under certain laboratory conditions, color constancy nears perfection (Ling & Hurlbert, 2008).

However, it may be that the laboratory is not the best setting in which to study color constancy. In the tradition of Brunswik and Gibson, one might argue that color constancy evolved in the natural world to create stability. On that basis, the stimuli used in laboratory studies may be too restrictive. Thus, it may be better to study color constancy under natural conditions (MacLeod, 2003a; Shevell & Kingdom, 2008). For a variety of reasons, including the range of colors found in natural scenes and the changes in illumination that occur over time, such studies may hold great promise for studying color constancy (Foster, 2008).

EXPLANATIONS FOR COLOR CONSTANCY   How are we able to maintain color constancy? Helmholtz proposed that, after experiencing the same object under a wide range of illuminations, we make an unconscious inference about how the object would appear under white light. Hering thought that the color remained constant because of memory. In other words, color and other properties of the object had become permanently fixed. Our current theories are much more complex, but they are more accurate in predicting the evidence that has accumulated over the years.

Johannes von Kries (1853–1928) proposed an early theory that is still influential. In 1905, he suggested that the illumination causes adaptive changes in our photoreceptors (chromatic adaptation). These changes then influence our perception of the incoming reflected light (Shevell, 2003a). This theory has intuitive appeal, because the illumination falling on the objects also falls on our eyes, affecting them in proportion to the wavelengths present in the light source. The illumination would provide our visual system with a reference point, which we can use to interpret the incoming reflected light.

A similar theory is Edwin Land's retinex (retina-and-cortex) theory (Valberg, 2005). **Retinex theory** seeks to explain color perception and color constancy based primarily on perception of the pattern of reflectances from the stimuli (Land, 1977). Essentially, the visual system determines the lightest part of the stimulus and then seeks to determine if that part could be "white." If you recall our discussion of lightness perception in Chapter 4, you'll recognize the similarity to anchor theories of lightness perception (Gilchrist, 2006).

Neither von Kries's theory nor retinex theory can fully account for color constancy. Nonetheless, they continue to play a role in more complex theories. Such complex computational theories may be necessary to incorporate the mechanisms that may be at work at different stages of processing. For example, one such mechanism may be the encoding of simultaneous color contrast found in the scene (Hurlbert & Wolf, 2004). The profusion of computational models indicates the extent of interest in the area of color constancy, as well as the inadequacy of any of the proposed models.

One important contributor to color constancy is our early visual experience. Yoichi Sugita (2004) raised monkeys under unusual lighting conditions.

Instead of a broad spectrum of light (e.g., sunlight), the monkeys lived in a room that was illuminated by lights of a single wavelength. Other researchers had raised animals under a single monochromatic light, with little impact on color constancy (Brenner & Cornelissen, 2005). So, what was different about Sugita's study? He randomly changed among four different wavelengths every minute. Thus, for the 12 hours of illumination each day, the monochromatic light in the monkeys' room changed every minute. After a year, the monkeys were shifted to normal lighting conditions. Even though their color perception was relatively normal, these monkeys could not take changing illumination into account. That is, being raised under constantly changing illumination disrupted color constancy. After living under normal lighting conditions for at least nine months, the monkeys still showed no color constancy.

Simultaneous and Successive Color Contrast

Both simultaneous and successive color contrast illustrate the importance of context for color perception. Neither effect is an anomaly; instead, they represent the typical scenario for color perception. That is, objects rarely occur in isolation, so the colors of surrounding objects (in space or time) will affect the object's color (MacLeod, 2003b). Once again, the wavelength(s) of light coming from a stimulus are not sufficient to determine the color perceived.

Try www Demonstration 7.4, which shows simultaneous color contrast. *Simultaneous* means "at the same time," so *simultaneous color contrast* means that the appearance of the color can be changed because another color is present at the same time. Notice in www Demonstration 7.4 that the neutral color gray appears to be slightly yellow when a blue background is present. However, it appears to be slightly blue when a yellow background is present. Consistent with simultaneous lightness contrast (Chapter 4), your perception of color is influenced by its context. This principle is operating in several works of the artist Josef Albers (1888–1976).

In his dissertation and prior published work, Vebjørn Ekroll has investigated simultaneous color contrast (Ekroll, 2005; Ekroll et al., 2004; Ekroll et al., 2002). For example, Ekroll has shown that people perceive colors differently when seen against an achromatic background (i.e., black) compared to a colored background (MacLeod, 2003b). Moreover, people perceive colors differently against uniform surrounding colors (i.e., a plain red field) compared to a variegated surround (i.e., splashes of many different colors). Clearly, context is important for color perception.

www Demonstration 7.5 illustrates successive color contrast. *Successive color contrast* means that the appearance of a color can be changed because of another color presented beforehand. Consistent with negative afterimages, if you stare at a figure of a particular hue, you'll see the complementary hue once that hue is removed. Thus, staring at a brightly lit blue color for a while will lead you to see other colors as somewhat yellow.

Successive color contrast can be traced to chromatic adaptation. *Chromatic adaptation* means that your response to a color is diminished after you view it continuously for a long time. Adaptation is a general phenomenon found in all our sensory systems. Adaptation is yet another example of Theme 1 of this book, that the sensory systems share similarities. In the case of chromatic adaptation, either (or both) of two kinds of mechanisms may be involved. Continuous exposure to a particular color may deplete the photopigments associated with that color, leaving the other photopigment levels relatively high. Or the phenomenon may involve adaptation at the opponent-process level. For example, staring at blue may weaken the blue response, leaving its opponent, yellow, relatively strong. As a consequence, an observer who has been staring at a blue patch will see a yellow afterimage.

Evidence that the effect is not due to photoreceptor adaptation came from Celeste McCullough (1965). People were successively presented with two different stimuli. One stimulus showed alternating black and green vertical stripes. The other stimulus showed alternating black and red horizontal stripes. After repeated exposure to these two stimuli, McCullough presented an array containing both horizontal and vertical black-and-white stripes. People reported that the white horizontal stripes had a greenish tint and the white vertical stripes had a reddish tint. Thus, the successive color contrast was orientation specific. Moreover, the effect could last for days. Both results seem to rule out a retinal explanation. Since it was first reported, researchers have been working to explain the cause of the McCullough Effect.

Subjective Colors

Most of the color phenomena we will discuss involve colored stimuli. In contrast, *subjective colors* are color impressions produced by black-and-white stimuli. Try www Demonstration 7.6 to see how uncolored figures can produce subjective colors. Fechner was the first to notice this phenomenon. Later in the nineteenth century, Charles E. Benham (1894) developed a spinning top that also created these subjective colors. When such a top rotates, people see desaturated colors along the curved lines.

How can we be sure that the colors are really produced within our visual systems? Could it be that the whirling somehow causes white light to break down into its components, much as a prism separates the colors of the spectrum? The question can be answered by taking a color photograph of a spinning Benham's top. If the color can really be traced to different wavelengths in the stimulus, then the color film should register the same color as our visual system. However, the photograph of the spinning top looks gray, rather than colored. The answer lies within the observer, not within the stimulus.

Researchers have suggested a number of theories for such subjective colors. For example, Garrett Kenyon and his colleagues (2004) propose that the antagonistic surrounds of cortical neurons in the P pathway contribute to the effect. These neurons carry information about both color and luminance contrast. Stimulating their model neuron in a fashion similar to Benham's top (dark field followed by dark bar followed by full field illumination) produced a firing pattern similar to presenting a red spot.

Purkinje Shift

Johannes Purkinje (1787–1869), a Czechoslovakian physiologist, was the first to describe this phenomenon in 1825, so it is appropriately named after him. Because of the *Purkinje shift*, our sensitivity to various wavelengths *shifts* toward the shorter wavelengths as we change from photopic (cone) to scotopic (rod) conditions. *Mesopic* conditions exist when the light is sufficiently bright that cones are still functional, but sufficiently dim that rods can also function. As we noted in Chapter 3, the prefix *meso-* means "in the middle," and *mesopic* is in the middle between photopic and scotopic conditions. Try www Demonstration 7.7 to illustrate the Purkinje shift.

Figure 7.10 will help you clarify reasons for the Purkinje shift. Under photopic conditions, two wavelengths (e.g., 480 nm and 600 nm) may appear to be equally light. In other words, your visual system is about equally sensitive to both wavelengths. Now contrast the sensitivity as you approach scotopic conditions. As you can see, rods are more sensitive to shorter wavelengths. Thus, the 480 nm wavelength will now appear to be lighter than the 600 nm wavelength.

Under mesopic conditions, the increased activity of the rods causes the shorter wavelengths to appear to be lighter (Anstis, 2002). In Chapter 3, you learned that the cones are concentrated in your fovea, with rods more prevalent in the periphery (see Figure 3.11). As your visual system becomes dark adapted, can you predict what should happen to the lightness of shorter wavelengths in the center of your visual field? In the periphery? Yes, indeed, to the dark-adapted eye the same blue in the periphery of your visual field will appear lighter than when seen in the center of your visual field.

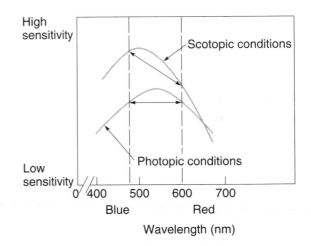

▶ **FIGURE 7.10** Purkinje shift. Under photopic conditions (cones only), blue and red are equally light. Under scotopic conditions (rods only), blue is perceived as lighter than red. However, because only rods are involved, both blue and red would appear as grays. Mesopic conditions occur between these two curves. (Imagine the lower curve lifting up to form the upper curve.) Under mesopic conditions, both the cones and the rods are functional. Thus, under mesopic conditions, the combined input of cones and rods would lead a blue flower to appear lighter than a red flower.

Memory Color

At a very basic level, successive color contrast involves memory. If your visual system had no memory for the initial color, it wouldn't affect perception of a later color. However, memory can influence color perception in another way. Imagine a banana, an apple, and a crown of broccoli. Your memory for the colors of such fruits and vegetables is quite strong (Hurlbert & Ling, 2005). In fact, simply by imagining such colorful objects, you're creating activity in areas of the brain that process color (Rich et al., 2006).

As you'll learn in Chapter 13, violation of those color expectations can affect the flavor of such foods. Your memory for the typical colors of objects also has an influence on your perception of the color of those objects. In *memory color*, an object's usual color influences your perception of that object's actual color.

Thus, an apple may appear to be redder than it actually is.

For example, Hansen and his colleagues (2006) found that people are quite accurate when adjusting a spot of color (e.g., yellow) to make it appear achromatic (e.g., gray). However, if people were adjusting the same color in a banana (instead of a spot), they tended to make the banana a slightly bluish-gray. In other words, their memory for the banana's usual color led them to see the actual gray as yellowish. To get the banana to appear to be gray, they needed to offset the "memory yellow" with a bit of blue. Our knowledge and expectations can often shape our perceptions. Consistent with Theme 4 of this book, top-down processing may influence what we perceive. In the next section, we'll explore the possibility that the names we give colors may influence our perceptions of those colors.

IN-DEPTH

Color Names and Color Perception

In spite of the fact that the visible spectrum is continuous, people tend to organize the wavelengths into categories of colors. Psychologists have studied this common tendency toward *categorization* in many areas beyond color categorization. When we categorize, we treat objects as similar or equivalent. For example, when you categorize food into meats, vegetables, desserts, and so forth, you are treating all the items within one category as similar, despite their variations in appearance. Thus, green beans, okra, potatoes, and eggplant are all classified as vegetables, despite their obvious differences. Similarly, we can discriminate among many wavelengths in the short-wavelength end of the spectrum, yet in English we would call all these colors "blue."

In Spanish, we would call those same colors "azul." Thus, people who speak different languages have different words for the same objects and concepts. However, suppose that two languages don't have equivalent words. For example, speakers of English (or Spanish) would label one wavelength as "blue" (or "azul") and another wavelength as "green" (or "verde"). However, unlike English and Spanish, some languages use the same name for wavelengths that would be called "green" and "blue" in English.

These languages, such as Welsh, are called *"grue" languages*. By using the same label for those two wavelengths, that person is saying that they are members of the same category. Does that also mean that, unlike people who speak English or Spanish, people who speak such a language actually *see* those two wavelengths as the same color?

Two linguists, Edward Sapir (1884–1939) and Benjamin Lee Whorf (1897–1941), were early proponents of the position that language influences cognition and perception, so it is often called the *Sapir-Whorf hypothesis*. In support of the hypothesis, you may have heard the example that the Eskimo language has many more words for snow than does English. Even though everyone might experience the same "continuum" of snow, the qualities of snow are more important to some people's lives, so their languages developed many more categories for snow. That claim is actually an urban legend (e.g., Pullum, 1991). For example, there is no single Eskimo language, nor is the number of snow words as large as some people have claimed. Nonetheless, there is a kernel of truth, because some languages have more terms for snow than English does. The phenomenon serves to illustrate the basic notion that our language might influence our perception. The hypothesis is controversial; the influence of color names on color perception is a frequent battleground.

In this section, we'll first review some research on differences in color names among languages. We'll then explore the evidence that such language differences have an impact on perception of color.

Are Color Categories Universal?

Which came first, the chicken or the egg? Sorry, but we don't have an answer to that question. Nor do we have a firm answer to another perplexing question: Which came first, color categories or color naming? As a starting point, you might assume that humans with normal color vision use the same basic visual apparatus to experience the same wavelengths of light. Based on that logic, you would conclude that the human experience of color is universal, and the color names found in various languages are based on that common experience. People who take a **universalist** position believe that the color categories are common to all people, but that languages developed different names for those categories. That is, all people would categorize the visible spectrum in a consistent fashion, even though the names themselves would differ (e.g., *blue* in English and *azul* in Spanish). What kind of evidence would you seek to support the universalist position?

One place to look would be the color names used in various languages. Early research examined a wide range of languages from largely industrialized societies. Brent Berlin and Paul Kay (1969) reported that people use 11 basic color categories that English speakers would name blue, green, yellow, orange, red, pink, brown, purple, black, white, and gray. Notice that this list includes achromatic colors (white, black, and gray), nonspectral colors (pink, brown, and purple), and spectral colors (blue, green, yellow, orange, and red).

As you might expect, those 11 color categories are not found in all languages. However, languages that don't include the equivalents of all 11 names tend to have particular subsets, which people considered evidence for a universal evolutionary trend in the development of color names. For instance, names for white and black emerge first. Next to emerge are names for the opponent-process colors: red, green, blue, and yellow. Because people in all cultures share the same underlying mechanisms for color perception, you might predict that color categories would be consistent with the mechanisms.

Languages that have only a small number of color terms use those terms to label all of the color space. Thus, a Berinmo speaker from Papua New Guinea would use only five color terms (*nol, wap, mehi, kel,* and *wor*) to label all 330 of the color chips presented by the ethnographer. Wavelengths that you and I might label as blue and green (as well as some purples and browns) would all be called *nol. Wap* would be used to label lighter colors we might call pinks, greens, and yellows. Consider the colors that we would label as red and darker pink (as well as some browns, oranges, and purples); a Berinmo-speaker would call these *mehi. Kel* would be used to label darker wavelengths we would call brown, green, blue, or purple. *Wor* is used to label wavelengths we'd call yellow, pink, and green.

Berinmo should strike you as a "grue" language, in that it doesn't distinguish between green and blue (using *nol* for both). As such, it doesn't seem to fit neatly with the universalist notion that the opponent-process colors should be among the first to be named. Could it be that color names used in various languages don't fit neatly into the color categories that universalists propose? That's the position of a **relativist**, who would argue that color naming is arbitrary.

Other languages (e.g., Himba of Namibia) are similar to Berinmo, which relativists view as support for their position (Davidoff et al., 1999; Roberson et al., 2005). When universalists such as Paul Kay and Terry Regier (2007) examine the same Berinmo color names, they conclude that the data actually support the universalist position. However, their conclusions may well result from the statistical analyses they employ (Dedrick, 2006). Before we examine the potential impact of color names, let's explore evidence from infants who have yet to develop language. If color categories are not arbitrary, but universal, then infants should exhibit behaviors that suggest that some wavelengths are primary (e.g., opponent-process colors) and that others are secondary (e.g., at boundaries between primary colors, nonspectral colors).

In a series of studies, Anna Franklin and her colleagues have explored the nature of infants' color categorization. Consistent with results from earlier researchers, Franklin and her colleagues found that prelinguistic infants do exhibit categorical perception of colors—especially those presented to the right hemisphere (Franklin & Davies, 2004, 2006; Franklin et al., 2008). In Chapter 14, we'll have more to say about the methodologies used in developmental research. For now, let's simply say that infants are relatively slow to discriminate two wavelengths that would both be included within the same color-name category (e.g., two shades of blue). In contrast, they can quickly discriminate wavelengths that occur on different sides of the color boundaries (e.g., blue versus green). Moreover, the infants' discrimination remains unchanged as they age and acquire color names (Franklin et al., 2005). These data are certainly consistent with the universalist position.

The controversy in this area is generating a wealth of research. Some evidence suggests that color categories may be universal, and other evidence that suggests that color names may be arbitrary. As Kay and Regier (2006) point out, the Sapir-Whorf hypothesis plays an important role in the relativist-universalist controversy. Consistent with the Sapir-Whorf hypothesis, a relativist would argue that language affects color perception. Because of their emphasis on common color categories, one would expect a universalist to argue that language does not affect color perception. However, as data supporting the Sapir-Whorf hypothesis accumulate, the situation is becoming complicated. For example, some researchers maintain that color categories are universal, but that language *does* affect color perception (Kay & Regier, 2006). In the next section, we'll examine some relevant research.

Would Renaming a Rose Affect Your Perception of It?

In *Romeo and Juliet*, Shakespeare wrote, "a rose by any other name would smell as sweet." Clearly, Shakespeare wouldn't have been a strong proponent of the Sapir-Whorf hypothesis. In fact, until fairly recently, he would have been in good company. In spite of the intuitive appeal of the Sapir-Whorf hypothesis, supporting data were not compelling. However, the tide may now be turning.

Earlier researchers showed that, regardless of the number of color names in their language, people behaved as though they had similar color categories. Imagine two different pairs of colors. One pair contains two wavelengths we might call "blue" (e.g., a

lighter blue and a darker blue), and the other pair contains one wavelength we'd call "blue" and one we'd call "green." The Sapir-Whorf hypothesis would predict that a person who speaks English would treat the blue-blue pair as more similar than the blue-green pair. It would also predict that a person who speaks a "grue" language would not treat the blue-blue pair as different from the blue-green pair. However, using a variety of measures, researchers found that, regardless of the number of color terms in the language, people made similar distinctions. Thus, one's language appeared to have no impact on one's color perception.

However, using similar procedures, Debi Roberson and her colleagues have demonstrated that language *does* affect color perception (Davidoff et al., 1999; Roberson et al., 2000). For example, both Berinmo and Himba have only five basic color names, which map onto the color space in similar, but not identical, fashions. Using a variety of discrimination and memory tasks, Roberson and her colleagues (2005) found that English speakers exhibited categorical perception that differed from speakers of either Berinmo or Himba. For example, the blue-green distinction was quite salient for English speakers, but not for Berinmo or Himba speakers. On the other hand, distinctions that were salient for Himba speakers (e.g., *dumbu-burou*, basically yellow-green vs. green-blue) were not salient for English or Berinmo speakers.

Some languages make even more color distinctions than English. For example, Russian forces a distinction between lighter blues (*goluboj*) and darker blues (*sinij*) (Paramei, 2007). Jonathan Winawer and his colleagues (2007) found that people who speak English responded in a similar fashion to lighter and darker blues, consistent with other research on categorical perception. If such categories are universal, then Russian speakers should exhibit a similar indifference to such shades of blue. However, that was not the case. Unlike English speakers, Russian speakers were much faster to discriminate between a lighter and a darker blue than they were to discriminate between two darker blues or two lighter blues. In other words, even though the task didn't involve memory, for Russian speakers the *goluboj-sinij* boundary is similar to the blue-green boundary in English.

Increasing evidence supports the notion that language has an impact on perception of color categories (Roberson & Hanley, 2007). Unlike young children, who show a right-hemisphere advantage for color discrimination tasks, adults show a left hemisphere advantage (Drivonikou et al., 2007; Gilbert et al., 2006). Such results are certainly consistent with a language-perception interaction. Researchers using fMRI have demonstrated the impact of language-processing areas on color discrimination tasks (Tan et al., 2008). The pendulum appears to be swinging in favor of the Sapir-Whorf hypothesis!

Where Might the Truth Lie?

Even the most die-hard relativist acknowledges that the visual system plays a vital role in color perception. Moreover, color names are never truly arbitrary. Different languages draw color-name boundaries in different places, but the naming is systematic. No language sprinkles color names randomly throughout color space. At the same time, universalists are increasingly likely to acknowledge the roles of language and culture in the perception of color (Jameson, 2005b).

Earlier in this chapter, we noted that the controversy between trichromatic and opponent-process theorists ultimately evaporated. Although the relativist-universalist controversy may linger, researchers are apparently searching for new ways to reformulate the issues in color names and color perception (Jameson, 2005a; Regier et al., 2007).

Section Summary

Color Phenomena

1. An object appears to be the same color under a wide range of illuminations. This phenomenon—color constancy—is an example of the set of constancies that produce stability in our perception of the world.

2. In simultaneous color contrast, the appearance of a color is changed because of another color present at the same time. For example, a gray looks slightly blue against a yellow background.

3. In successive color contrast, the appearance of a color is changed because of another color presented earlier. For example, white looks slightly blue if you previously looked at yellow. The McCullough Effect suggests that successive color contrast is not likely due to retinal changes.

4. Subjective colors are pastel colors resulting from black-and-white stimuli, such as Benham's top.

5. In the Purkinje shift, the sensitivity of the visual system shifts toward the shorter wavelengths under mesopic conditions.

6. In memory color, our expectations about an object's typical color influence our perception of that object's actual color.

7. In categorization, we treat objects as similar or equivalent. For example, certain colors are all classified as blue, even though they are discriminable.

8. Universalists argue that color names result from color categories that are common to all people. Relativists argue that color names are arbitrary. They also believe that the color terms in a language affect color perception, which is consistent with the Sapir-Whorf hypothesis that language affects cognition and perception.

9. Evidence from Berinmo, Himba, and Russian speakers supports the Sapir-Whorf hypothesis. In addition, some lateralization and brain imaging research supports the connection between language and color perception.

Review Questions

1. Try to think of some evolutionary advantages that color vision afforded our early ancestors. For example, how might a predator benefit from seeing colors? What advantages might come to a herbivore that could see colors? Why might a trichromat be at an adaptive advantage to a dichromat?

2. Each of the following is an example of a color mixture; specify whether it represents a subtractive or an additive mixture: (a) you are winding strands of purple and blue yarn together to knit a sweater; (b) you paint a layer of light green paint over a wall painted dark blue; (c) you mix red food coloring into yellow egg yolks; (d) you cover one flashlight with green cellophane and another with red cellophane and then shine them both on a white sheet of paper. Predict the color of the mixtures in as many of the combinations as possible. What happens when you make an additive mixture of complementary hues?

3. Summarize the trichromatic theory, as developed by Young and Helmholtz, and the original form of the opponent-process theory, as developed by Hering. Why were the two initially incompatible, and how was the controversy resolved?

4. To be sure that you understand the function of the six color opponent-process receptive fields, describe the activity of a ganglion cell with a –M center and a +L surround receptive field. What would happen if you illuminated all the cones contributing to the receptive field with short-wavelength light (i.e., what we'd call "blue")? What would happen if you illuminated all the cones contributing to the receptive field with long-wavelength light (i.e., what we'd call "red")? What would happen if you illuminated all the cones contributing to the receptive field with sunlight (i.e., what we'd call "white")?

5. Imagine that a red light flashes in your left visual field. Trace the processing of that light as far as you can from the retina to areas of the visual cortex.

6. How does a normal trichromat differ from the three types of dichromats in color perception and in acuity? What everyday color discriminations would each type of dichromat find difficult? How would a rod monochromat or a person with cerebral achromatopsia differ in color perception from a normal trichromat?

7. Suppose that someone who didn't know much about color vision asked the following questions about phenomena he or she had noticed. What explanations would you provide? (a) Why does a blue bird look gray when it's far away? (b) Why does a white shirt look a little green when worn with a red vest? (c) Why does the world look slightly yellow after you take off blue-tinted dark glasses? (d) Why does a red stop sign look darker at twilight than a blue car near the stop sign?

8. Throughout the text, you've encountered a number of different constancies. Describe color constancy in terms of the proximal and distal stimuli. Why might color constancy be easier to establish using naturally occurring stimuli under normal viewing conditions?

9. If you were interested in the impact of language on color perception, why would you study infants and people from other cultures? Regarding color names, would you consider yourself a universalist or a relativist? Why? Describe the evidence to support these two approaches.

10. Theme 4 stresses the role of cognitive factors (e.g., top-down processes) in perception. Use as many examples as you can from the chapter to support the premise that color perception involves much more than the wavelengths of light falling on the retina.

Key Terms

Recommended Readings

Birch, J. (2001). *Diagnosis of defective colour vision* (2nd ed.). New York: Elsevier.

This small book provides a very readable overview of color vision deficiencies. You'll learn about the origins of color vision deficiencies and many of the tests designed to detect those deficiencies.

MacLaury, R. E., Paramei, G. V., & Dedrick, D. (Eds.). (2007). *Anthropology of color: Interdisciplinary multilevel modeling.* Philadelphia: John Benjamins.

In the In-Depth section, we explored the issue of color naming and color perception. If you'd like to know more about the topic, this edited volume contains a number of chapters that will be of great interest to you.

Mausfeld, R., & Heyer, D. (Eds.). (2003). *Colour perception: Mind and the physical world.* New York: Oxford.

This book contains 16 chapters on a variety of issues in color perception. Admittedly, some are more accessible than others. The real fun, however, is in reading the commentaries that accompany the chapters. Psychologists are certainly a contentious lot! However, if you throw some philosophers into the mix, the discussions really get interesting.

Shevell, S. K. (Ed.). (2003b). *The science of color* (2nd ed.). New York: Elsevier.

This edited text is beautifully produced, with many full-color illustrations. Prominent color-vision researchers (e.g., Williams, Brainard, Wandell, Smith, and Pokorny) contributed to the eight chapters. Some of the chapters are denser than others, but John Mollon's overview of the history of color vision research is a great starting point. Peter Lennie has a knack for conveying very complex material in a clear fashion, so his chapter about the physiology of color perception is quite helpful.

CHAPTER 8

Motion

TRY TO IMAGINE a situation in which you are not moving and nothing around you is moving. Such a static situation is a rarity. To minimize distractions, you may well have chosen to read this text in a place with minimal activity, such as a study carrel. Nonetheless, you are in motion as you breathe, scan and turn pages, take notes, glance at your watch, and so on. Your daily life is filled with constant activity. Your entertainment involves motion—television, movies, sports, games, dancing, and many other activities. In the classroom, the professor likely walks around the room, people wiggle, and your pen moves across your notebook. In social situations, speaking people approach you, move their mouths and bodies, and depart. On the road, you are in motion as you gauge the movement of vehicles around you, pulling over when you see and hear a fire truck or ambulance approaching you.

As we discussed in Chapter 6, the visual system uses an array of monocular and binocular cues to determine the spatial location of an object. However, objects never remain in the same relative spatial location—either they move or you move. In this chapter, we'll first describe human visual abilities to detect motion of objects in the world as well as our own motion. We'll then consider a very important type of motion—that produced by humans and other animals. Next we'll focus on illusory experiences of motion, all of which will inform our understanding of the perception of real motion. Then we'll discuss theories that have been proposed to explain visual motion perception. Finally, researchers are making great progress in understanding the physiological underpinnings of visual motion perception, so we'll briefly review some of their findings.

Visual Perception of Real Movement

We have often used the term *retinal image* in discussing vision. However, the image of an object rarely remains in one location on the retina. Either the object moves or you move your eyes. In fact, as we discussed in Chapter 4, motion on the retina is crucial for vision. If an image is stabilized on our retina, it will fade away. Moreover, an object's motion enables us to perceive properties of the object, such as its shape and depth.

To convince yourself of the importance of motion perception, imagine that you couldn't perceive continuous motion. Have you ever been in a dark room illuminated by the flashing light of a stroboscope? If the stroboscope fires fairly rapidly, the motion around you appears quite jerky. If the stroboscope fires slowly, you'll perceive the world as a series of still images. Such is the regular daylight viewing experience of L. M., who suffered damage to an area of the brain that is important for motion perception (Heywood & Zihl, 1999). Imagine how difficult it would be to cross the street when an approaching car first appears to be quite distant and then in the next "instant" is quite close.

Even before rapidly moving vehicles became so common, movement in the world might signal danger or opportunity. As a result, seeing or hearing approaching creatures provided clear adaptive advantages (Barrett, 2005; Maier & Ghazanfar, 2007). For example, if an object is coming toward you on a collision course, you may want to avoid it (or catch it). However, if you could tell that the object will miss you, you may not need to take action. Even very young infants can make such discriminations (Kayed & van der Meer, 2007; Schmuckler et al., 2007).

This part of the chapter is concerned with real movement, which involves either movement of the observer or movement of the objects and people being watched by the observer. We first need to discuss factors that affect our ability to perceive movement. Next, we will discuss the challenges for motion perception posed by the fact that we are constantly in motion.

Detecting Motion

How good is the visual system at detecting motion? That question seems deceptively simple. The answer is quite complex—essentially, "It depends." A good deal of research has investigated the perception of motion of a single object. Certainly, the speed of the object has an impact on motion perception. For example, under normal conditions, you cannot detect grass growing, or hour hands on clocks moving, or bread rising. These movements are all too slow. At the other extreme, you cannot detect extremely rapid motion (Palmer, 1999). Thus, you can't see a bullet moving at over 1,000 feet per second.

However, velocity is not the only factor that influences motion detection. The distance an object moves is also important. Generally speaking, to detect the motion of a simple object, the object must move a distance of at least 1 minute of arc (Sekuler et al., 2002). To better understand this measure, think of yourself at the center of a circle, which is comprised of 360°. Now, imagine that the one degree directly ahead of you is divided into 60 minutes. Thus, each minute is 1/21,600 of the entire circle. If you were to hold this book at arm's length, a minute of arc would be about the distance between the two *l*s in "basketball." Clearly, with optimal conditions, we can detect movement over very short distances, such as 2 or 3 minutes of arc (Tayama, 2000). However, even if all conditions are just right, if the object moves less than 1 minute of arc, we won't detect the motion.

You are sensitive to movement over such small distances only if the stimuli fall on your fovea. The periphery of the retina is less sensitive to motion than the fovea. However, you should not infer that the periphery is *in*sensitive to motion. For example, if an object in the periphery is moving, you can see it more easily than if it is stationary. Try [www] Demonstration 8.1 to illustrate this point. Notice how often you tend to pay attention to objects that move in your peripheral vision. For example, when you are driving, you can see a car approaching on the left or a pedestrian moving on your right.

Many other factors influence the perception of the motion of a single object (Sekuler et al., 2002). For example, you can better detect motion under conditions of greater luminance, or if the stimulus is visible for longer durations. The context of the stimulus is also crucial. Thus, it's easier to detect motion if you see the stimulus against a stationary textured background, as opposed to a blank field. It's also easier to detect relative motion than absolute motion. That is, it's easier to determine that an object is in motion when you see it in the context of other objects, which might also be in motion.

To establish the detection of motion in such a context, researchers have developed stimuli that are comprised of arrays of moving dots. These displays are referred to as *random-dot cinematograms*, which should remind you of the random dot stereograms we discussed in Chapter 6. If all the dots move in a random fashion, no coherent motion emerges. However, if only a small percentage (e.g., 5%) of the dots begin to move together, people can detect that common motion amidst the random motion of the other dots.

Thus, to return to the original question, people are quite good at detecting motion—especially relative motion. However, it is more difficult to detect movement of some stimuli, especially under less-than-ideal circumstances. In other words, we would have greater difficulty detecting the motion of an object if it occurred against a plain background in the periphery of our retina under poorly lit conditions.

Movement of the Observer

So far, we have discussed the movement of objects and the impressive ability of the human visual system to detect this movement. However, people are rarely stationary, so the perception of motion in the environment is even more complicated. To appreciate the complexity, think of a volleyball player who is in motion at the same time as she is using pursuit eye movements to follow the path of the moving ball. Not only must she move her body, head, and eyes to keep the rapidly moving ball focused, but she must also keep track of the positions of the net and her nearby teammates, who are also in motion!

Several questions emerge when you consider a person moving and looking out at the world. Why does the world seem to be stationary when we move, even though our movement is producing change on the retina? What information allows people to detect their direction of movement through the environment? How capable are we at determining the motion of objects around us as we move? In this section, we try to answer these questions.

PERCEIVING A STABLE WORLD DESPITE SELF-MOTION Let's consider the fact that the world remains stable in spite of your movement through the world. Consider the fact that, consistent with Theme 3, motion information on your retina is ambiguous (Purves & Lotto, 2003). That is, a variety of different movements in the world could create the same pattern of changes on your retina. Moreover, if you move your head while observing an immobile object, you can also create that same pattern of changes on your retina. How are you able to determine which retinal changes are due to movement in the world and which are due to your own movement?

To solve that problem, you must have a sense of how your body is moving through space. Some information about body movements comes from your vestibular and kinesthetic senses, which we will discuss in Chapter 12. Some information might come from nerves in your muscles that signal what the muscles are doing (an *inflow* of information from muscles to the brain). Of course, you control the movement of your body with signals from the motor area of the brain (an *outflow* of information from the brain to muscles). Charles Sherrington (1857–1952) thought that the inflow of information was most important for the perception of self-motion. Sherrington's primary opponent was our old friend Helmholtz, who argued for the importance of the outflow of information. Helmholtz won this argument, with most evidence supporting the important role of the outflow of information (Munoz, 2006; Wurtz, 2008). Keep these motor signals in mind when we discuss the corollary discharge theory later in this chapter.

PERCEIVING THE DIRECTION OF SELF-MOTION

Think of the complex pattern of movement on your retinas as you drive along a crowded highway. If you are looking at the car directly ahead of you, it remains fairly stable on your retina. Objects in your periphery—such as stationary signs or slowly moving cars—seem to be a blur as you go past them. Researchers refer to this complex pattern of motion on our retinas as an *optic flow field*. Direct perception theorists in the Gibsonian tradition argue that the optic flow field is essential for determining many aspects of self-motion, including the direction of movement (Bruce et al., 2003). Other researchers would describe the optic flow field as necessary, but not sufficient, for determining direction of movement (Loomis et al., 2006; Macuga et al., 2006). However, it's clear that visual information plays a dominant role in determining the direction in which you are moving (Wilkie & Wann, 2005).

Observer motion, combined with the motion of objects in the field of view, creates complex patterns of optical flow on our retinas (Warren, 2008). The wealth of information in these optic flow patterns enables us to determine what is moving—ourselves, objects around us, or both. Consider that we often move in one direction while looking in a different direction. Even under such conditions, the optic flow patterns provide us with a rich source of information to determine our direction of movement accurately.

We are, in fact, quite accurate in judging our own motion and the motion of objects around us. When we walk, we typically do not bump into objects or fall into holes. Runners and swimmers rarely collide as they compete. We can perceive our direction of self-motion with an accuracy of 4° or less (Warren, 2008). (You may want to review Figure 4.14 on page 101 to refresh your memory regarding visual angle.)

PERCEIVING MOVING OBJECTS AROUND US

As we noted earlier, motion perception has many adaptive advantages. Because we are often in motion, it's important that we be able to perceive the location of objects around us, whether or not they are moving. Athletes, such as the volleyball player we mentioned earlier, provide just one example of people who must keep the location of multiple moving objects in mind as they themselves move. Whether or not you're an athlete, you are quite adept at moving through a world filled with motion. Consider, for instance, how you keep track of other cars, pedestrians, and other objects as you drive a car.

Only very recently in our evolutionary history have humans been able to move at speeds achieved when driving automobiles. Nonetheless, most of us are quite capable at maneuvering such vehicles. However, accidents do occur. Consider, for instance, that in a recent year about 30% of automobile accidents involved rear-end collisions (Li & Milgram, 2008). In many of those accidents, the difference in velocity between the two vehicles is relatively small. Thus, when people themselves are in rapid motion, they may misjudge the time to contact another moving vehicle.

Of course, the movement that occurs as we drive an automobile is quite real. However, many researchers study such movement using simulations—typically generated or controlled by a computer. In some cases, researchers choose to simulate motion to gain greater control over the stimulus. In other cases, researchers simulate motion so that people don't injure themselves. Whatever their reasons, it's clear that researchers treat such apparent movement as an appropriate analog of real movement (Krekelberg, 2008). As we'll discuss later, such an assumption appears reasonable, in that we may process apparent motion in a fashion similar to real motion. However, you should keep in mind that results obtained while actually driving a car may differ from results obtained from simulations (e.g., Rock et al., 2006).

A number of different visual cues contribute to our perception of an object's changing location in the environment (Kim & Grocki, 2006). One cue to an approaching object is that it will take up increasingly

▶ **FIGURE 8.1**   An illustration of a looming stimulus. Looming is a cue to time-to-contact. When the car is most distant from the truck, the visual angle of the truck will be smallest. As the car gets closer, the size of the visual angle increases. That is, the area on the truck's image on the retina becomes increasingly large.

large portions of your retina—a process called *looming*. As illustrated in Figure 8.1, if you're driving ever closer to a vehicle in front of you, the visual angle of that vehicle will increase. The rate of expansion allows you to estimate the time to contact, called τ (tau) (Berthoz, 2000).

Looming serves as an important motion cue under a variety of circumstances. As we noted earlier, even very young children are sensitive to looming cues (Schmuckler et al., 2007). For example, they can detect whether or not a looming object is likely to make contact with them. Adults are certainly sensitive to looming cues (Neppi-Mòdona et al., 2004). Obviously, looming cues can play an important role when driving. Imagine that you're driving and the brake lights on the car in front of you aren't functioning. Under those conditions, the looming of the car in front of you should be sufficient to capture your attention and lead you to brake (Terry et al., 2008). However, if you were distracted (e.g., engaged in a cell-phone conversation), you wouldn't respond as effectively.

Of course, ordinarily you would have more than looming information about a car in front of you. Brake lights would typically alert you that the car is decelerating. To help drivers notice that a car is braking, manufacturers now mount an additional single brake light in the rear window of most cars. This innovation illustrates an important real-life application of perceptual research. However, it may well be that changing the color of those lights from red to yellow would provide even greater protection (McIntyre, 2008). Given what you learned about the sensitivity to different wavelengths in earlier chapters, can you understand why yellow lights might be more easily seen? It may also help to create brake lights that appear to expand from the center, thereby mimicking looming. An approaching driver who saw such brake lights at night would slow down more rapidly than when seeing "normal" brake lights (Li & Milgram, 2008).

IN-DEPTH

Perceiving Biological Motion

People are remarkably sensitive to the structured motion created by objects, including people and other animals (Hiris, 2007). In this section, we will discuss *biological motion*, or the pattern of movement of living creatures (Blake & Shiffrar, 2007; Troje, 2008). Of course, biological motion is real movement. However, most of the research on biological motion doesn't actually use images of organisms in motion. As seen in www Demonstration 8.2, researchers often use a display comprised of moving points of light. A *point-light display* involves a minimal number of lights (e.g., 10 to 12) that are

typically assigned to joints (e.g., shoulders, hips, and knees).

You might worry that such displays are only a very weak simulation of actual biological motion. However, point-light displays contain even more information than people need to extract biological motion (Gold et al., 2008). Moreover, research shows that observers can determine a wealth of information from point-light displays: what organisms are being depicted, what they are doing, and even subtle differences among members of the same species. In fact, we can make such judgments with only very brief exposures to the displays, so our performance is particularly impressive.

Determining Biological Motion in Point-Light Displays

Gunnar Johansson (1973, 1975) conducted the first systematic research on biological motion perception. Johansson attached a small light bulb to each of a co-worker's shoulders, elbows, wrists, hips, knees, and ankles. He then filmed the man moving around a dark room. In the resulting point-light display, a viewer sees nothing but the lights moving around in darkness. Researchers have developed several variants of point-light displays over the years (Thornton, 2006).

As you might imagine, a stationary point-light display isn't particularly informative. However, once the lights begin to move, the observer's task is much easier. Johansson (1975) reported that, as soon as the point-light display was animated, observers quickly perceived that the lights were attached to a human being. Researchers have found that observers can easily tell the difference between walking and jogging movements, detect when a person is limping, determine the effort expended in throwing objects, and so forth.

From the evidence presented so far, you should be impressed by people's ability to extract a large amount of meaning from the information present in point-light displays. Because of these abilities, we are better able to detect pedestrians at night when they wear reflectors similar to those worn in point-light displays (Owens et al., 1994).

Not only can people detect the biological motion of other humans but they can also perceive the biological motion of nonhuman animals. In fact, people are very accurate in determining the type of animal (baboon, camel, cat, horse, pig, etc.) moving in a dynamic point-light display, but not in a static display (Blake & Shiffrar, 2007).

Do you think that other animals are able to detect biological motion? Of course, biological motion is ecologically important for the survival of other species, not just for humans. Animals need to recognize the motion of other animals to know which animal is a potential *mate*, which a potential *dinner*, and which a potential *diner*. Therefore, animals should be quite good at deciphering point-light displays of biological motion. For example, cats can reliably discriminate between a dynamic point-light display of a cat walking and a dynamic display that doesn't depict biological motion (Blake, 1993).

The Development of Biological Motion Perception

The perception of biological motion may well be innate. For example, newly hatched chickens with virtually no visual experience prefer the point-light display of a walking hen to other types of motion (Vallortigara et al., 2005). In fact, they prefer the motion of a walking hen to the motion of a walking cat. Unfortunately, they also prefer the motion of a walking cat to nonbiological motion. Thus, the chicks certainly respond to biological motion, but not in a very sophisticated fashion.

What about humans? To address that question, Francesca Simion and her colleagues (2008) showed 2-day-old infants point-light displays of walking hens, inverted point-light displays of the walking hens, and point-light displays of random motion. She chose to use point-light displays of hens because these infants may already have noticed human motion. Even though they had never seen a walking hen, 2-day-old infants prefer to watch biological motion. It seems clear, then, that both chicks and humans are born with the ability to detect biological motion. Interestingly, as growing infants gain more experience viewing human biological motion, they may actually become *less* sensitive to other types of biological motion (Pinto, 2005). We may well be innately prepared to perceive biological motion. However, with experience, we develop greater sophistication in biological motion perception.

Social Information in Point-Light Displays

As we've noted again and again, humans are social animals. Thus, you should predict that we extract a great deal of social information from biological motion. In their review article, Randolph Blake and Maggie Shiffrar (2007) report that point-light displays enable people to determine a person's gender and even sexual orientation at better than chance levels. People can also determine a person's emotional state from a point-light display, especially when it interacts with the point-light display of another person.

Do any of your friends have a distinctive walk? Would you be able to identify a friend on the basis of a point-light display? It turns out that humans are quite good at learning to identify people on the basis of point-light displays (Loula et al., 2005; Troje et al., 2005; Westhoff & Troje, 2007). In fact, after learning to identify a point-light display showing the side view of an individual walking, people can later identify that person when seen from a different orientation (e.g., a frontal view).

Disrupting Biological Motion

So far, we've seen that people are able to extract a great deal of information from point-light displays. However, you might also predict that biological motion may be disrupted in a variety of ways. For example, consider face perception and prosopagnosia. As social creatures, we value face perception, but neural damage can disrupt this face perception. Can biological motion be similarly disrupted? A number of different neural disorders can disrupt the perception of biological motion. Consider one brain area—the superior temporal sulcus (STS)—that plays an important role in the perception of biological motion. Abnormalities in the STS—which may occur in autism—lead to diminished perception of biological motion (Troje, 2008).

It's also possible to disrupt biological motion in people who don't have neural problems. One approach considers the reality that biological motion typically occurs in a motion-filled context—some of which might be biological motion from other organisms. How well can people discriminate biological motion in a point-light display if other motion is present in the display? That is, how well would people perceive biological motion in point-light displays if additional irrelevant lights were added to the display in an effort to mask the biological motion?

A number of researchers have examined the impact of masking biological motion with additional lights. The point-light display (seen in static fashion in the middle frame of Figure 8.2a, but with no outline) moves in place in the center of the screen. A number of static images of the biological motion are illustrated in Figure 8.2b. The point-light display might appear with varying numbers of distractor lights (the left and right frames of Figure 8.2a).

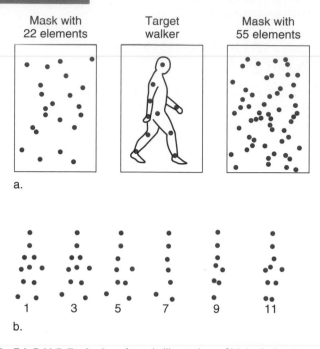

a.

b.

▶ **FIGURE 8.2** A static illustration of biological motion as seen in a point-light display. The outline of the walker, seen in the middle panel of part *a*, is not seen by the observers. A number of studies attempt to mask the biological motion by adding additional points, as seen in the left and right panels of part *a*. Part *b* illustrates movement of dots that would be consistent with a person moving to the right. (From Cutting et al., 1988)

Generally speaking, when the mask behaves in a uniform fashion (all lights stationary or else all lights moving in the same direction), people can easily detect biological motion (Thornton, 2006). For example, Bennett Bertenthal and Jeannine Pinto (1994) showed that 66 masking points of light did not affect people's ability to detect biological motion. However, people have trouble detecting biological motion when the masking lights themselves move in a fashion that might be confused with biological motion (e.g., triads of "noise" lights that move as an arm might move).

Another approach is to scramble the lights that make up the point-light display. Researchers do so by randomly changing the timing or the trajectories of the lights. For example, Eric Hiris and his colleagues (2005) scrambled the point-light display by delaying the movement of lights within the point-light walker by different amounts of time. That is, imagine that the right elbow light doesn't move to the right as it would if the walker were to move to the right. Instead, it moves to the right after a delay. Now, imagine that the movement of *each* of the lights would be delayed. In addition to the amount of delay, Hiris presented the 11 lights of the walker against a background of 88 masking lights. Hiris found that, when the offset time was very brief, people could still detect the biological motion against the moving masking dots. Performance dropped as the offset time increased. However, even when researchers scramble the point-light display, people are often able to determine the direction of movement (Troje, 2008).

Just as it's more difficult to perceive inverted faces, it's also difficult to perceive inverted bodies (Reed et al., 2003). Thus, a final strategy that researchers use to disrupt biological motion is to invert the point-light display. Inversion greatly dis-

rupts the perception of biological motion in upside-down point-light displays (Troje & Westhoff, 2006).

Is Biological Motion Special?

The research we have reviewed is quite persuasive. Humans and other animals seem to have an innate ability to detect biological motion. The range of actions that we can discriminate on the basis of point-light displays is truly amazing. Furthermore, we can perceive biological motion even when it is distorted or presented in the context of a fair amount of visual noise.

Is biological motion somehow special? Perhaps we perceive biological motion in a fashion that differs from our perception of the motion of other objects (Blake & Shiffrar, 2007). However, it may also be that humans are equally adept at perceiving the structured motion of inanimate objects (Hiris, 2007). Future research will help clarify the extent to whether or not our perception of biological motion is special.

This section focused on the perception of real movement. However, introducing the notion of driving simulators and point-light displays muddies the waters a bit. We'll next explore illusory motion. As you read the next section, ask yourself which examples of illusory motion are more similar to—or more different from—real motion.

Section Summary

Visual Perception of Real Movement

1. Objects rarely cast a stationary image on our retinas. As a result, it's essential that we perceive motion. Moreover, motion perception provides a number of adaptive advantages—enabling us to avoid or capture moving objects.

2. Our ability to detect motion is influenced by several factors, including the luminance of the stimuli, the presence of a stationary background, and the region of the retina on which the movement occurs.

3. Although we are typically in motion—creating movement on our retinas—we perceive the world as stable. In order to do so, we must be able to determine which movements on the retina are due to self-motion.

4. As we move, the optic flow field provides us with a great deal of information about movement, including the direction in which we are moving.

5. We are adept at perceiving the motion of objects around us, using visual cues such as looming. Such cues enable us to drive cars successfully. The prevalence of rear-end collisions suggests that we may have difficulty reacting to changes in movement around us—especially when we are distracted.

6. Organisms have evolved to be especially adept at perceiving biological motion. In fact, perception of biological motion is likely innate. Point-light displays allow us to perceive an array of socially important information, such as a stranger's gender and the identity of someone we know.

7. Not only are we quite accurate in our perception of biological motion, but we are also quite adept at perceiving biological motion in the midst of noise. However, inverting biological motion typically disrupts the accuracy of our perception.

Illusory Movement

We began our discussion of motion perception by focusing on the perception of real movement in the world around us. Now we will discuss apparent or illusory movement, just as we have discussed illusory experiences in earlier chapters. In *illusory movement*, observers misperceive an object's motion.

We'll first discuss stroboscopic movement, which will seem virtually indistinguishable from real movement. As you watch television or a movie, you are completely aware that people do not really exist inside the screen, yet you would probably argue that the movements you see are not illusory. When watching cartoons or playing video games—especially those in which the animation is well executed—you have a sense of motion that is compelling. In all these examples, the fact that you are actually seeing a series of rapidly presented "still" pictures is completely lost on your visual system!

Some illusions lead us to misperceive the trajectories of objects that are in motion. For instance, baseball players speak of rising fastballs. However, even though the batter may perceive the oncoming fastball as rising, it's actually an illusion (Bahill, 2005; Bahill & Baldwin, 2004). In this section, we will focus our attention on several factors that lead stationary objects to appear to be moving.

Stroboscopic Movement

Stroboscopic movement is the illusion of movement produced by a rapid pattern of stimulation on different parts of the retina. In a typical demonstration of stroboscopic movement, a light flashes briefly at one location. Less than a tenth of a second later, another light flashes briefly at a different location. Observers usually report that the light seems to move from the first location to the second. Although the path between successive presentations is ambiguous (the path could be a curve, or a curlicue), people tend to perceive the sim-

plest possible path (a straight line) between pairs of presentations. Max Wertheimer, the Gestalt psychologist you read about in Chapter 5, initiated the first serious investigation of this phenomenon.

If the spatial separation and the timing of the two stimuli are just right, stroboscopic movement can be a powerful movement illusion. The timing of the two light flashes must be precise. With some stimulus conditions, for example, an interval of about 60 milliseconds is ideal to produce the perception of an object moving through space. Intriguingly, an interval of about 100 milliseconds in those same conditions may result in the sensation of *phi movement*, in which observers report that they see movement, yet they cannot perceive an actual object moving across the gap. If the interval is longer than about 200 milliseconds, they do not perceive apparent movement—two lights just appear to go on and off.

Flip books as well as motion pictures use stroboscopic movement to give the impression of movement. In essence, a movie film is a series of still pictures presented sequentially, as depicted in Figure 8.3. Have you ever wondered how a series of isolated snapshots can give the impression of movement? Observers perceive movement because the movie projector exposes each frame in the series very quickly, so that the dog's paw in Figure 8.3 exhibits stroboscopic movement from Position 1 to Position 2. You perceive movement from one place to the next, rather than a succession of static views.

Most studies of stroboscopic movement use simple stimuli (points of light, squares, etc.). For example, [www] Demonstration 8.3 provides three examples of stroboscopic movement. Even though no real motion is present, your visual system readily interprets the changing stimuli as moving. A number of factors influence the nature of this illusory movement, including the rate of change and the presence of other objects.

Instead of successive frames showing simple objects, researchers have also used pictures of humans in two different positions. As we saw in the In-Depth section, people seem to be especially sensitive to patterns of motion in other humans. What would happen if people saw two successive frames depicting a human in positions for which the simplest path between the two positions would be impossible?

Figure 8.4 (page 228) illustrates one such example of biological motion. The picture on the left would be shown first, followed by the picture on the

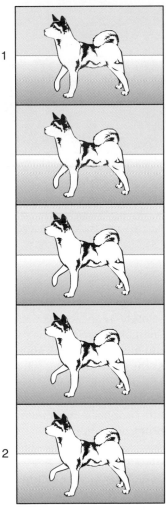

Position 1

Position 2

▶ **FIGURE 8.3** Separate still frames that might comprise a flip book or a motion picture. If each successive picture from Position 1 to Position 2 is presented at the proper rate of speed, the dog's right paw will appear to move. Because the dog's paw is not really in motion, this example illustrates a form of illusory motion referred to as stroboscopic motion.

right. Going between the two frames, the simplest path for the woman's right hand would be directly through her head. Of course, the actual path for her hand would be outward *around* her head. If you saw these two pictures presented rapidly, to produce stroboscopic movement, what would you see the woman's hand doing?

What you perceive depends on the speed with which the two pictures are presented (Shiffrar, 2001). When the presentation times are very rapid, you

would perceive the impossible—the woman's hand would appear to move directly *through* her head! However, at an appropriately longer presentation time, you would perceive the biologically correct pathway (around her head).

Perceiving Motion in Stationary Stimuli

Stroboscopic movement should strike you as quite similar to real movement. For example, both real movement and stroboscopic movement produce similar retinal activity. In this section, we're going to examine situations in which you misperceive stationary objects as moving. Sometimes, the illusion will depend on some kind of movement. Thus, the context in which you perceive the stimulus will lead you to perceive the illusory motion. In other cases, the stimulus itself is all that's required to produce the illusory motion.

AUTOKINESIS *Autokinesis* occurs when a stationary light, seen in total darkness, appears to move. When you tried www Demonstration 4.3, you experienced the autokinetic effect. As you know, your eye muscles continually produce very small movements of your eyeballs. Ordinarily, when those movements occur, you would be looking at the light against a rich context. However, when you see only the light against a uniform dark background, your visual system has no context information. When you look at the light for a long time under those conditions, it will appear to move in a random fashion. As you might expect, adding more lights minimizes or eliminates the autokinetic effect. This movement is clearly illusory. However, the autokinetic effect causes activity in an area of the brain (MT) that processes real movement (Riedel et al., 2005).

INDUCED MOVEMENT Karl Duncker (1903–1940) was a Gestalt psychologist who first studied induced movement. *Induced movement* occurs when a stationary object appears to move in one direction because its contextual frame of reference moves in the opposite direction. Even though your visual system is misperceiving the real movement, it is making a safe bet—objects tend to move against their surround. In a typical study of induced movement, an observer in a dark room views a luminous dot that is surrounded by a luminous rectangular frame (Duncker, 1929; Wallach, 1959). When the rectangular frame moves to the

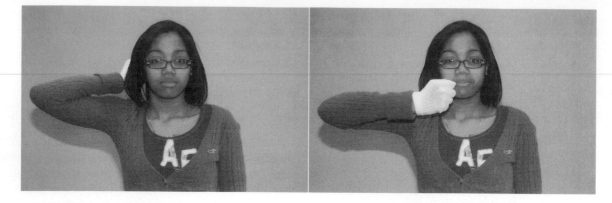

▶ **FIGURE 8.4** Two frames of biological motion. The simplest path between the left and right frame is directly throughout the woman's head. At rapid presentation rates, people will perceive such biologically impossible action. When presentation rates are slowed, people will perceive a more realistic path, with the woman's hand moving around the outside of her head. (From Shiffrar, 1994)

right, the observer perceives the frame as stationary and the dot as moving to the left. The next time the moon is bright and the sky is cloudy, see whether you notice any induced movement. The moon is essentially stationary, yet the clouds are moving in front of it. Consequently, the moon may appear to move in a direction opposite to the clouds' motion.

In addition to lateral induced motion, researchers are interested in other types of induced motion. For example, it's possible to induce rotational motion (Reinhardt-Rutland, 2003). When people see an outer stimulus moving in a circular fashion, they perceive that a stationary inner disc appears to move in the opposite direction. In both lateral and rotational induced motion, the inducing objects are all located the same distance from the observer. However, other research shows that it's possible to induce motion in depth (Harris & German, 2008).

SELF-MOTION ILLUSION Another kind of induced motion arises when the context leads you to believe that you are in motion when you're not. Have you ever been seated on a stationary train awaiting departure when a train on the next tracks begins to move? You are likely to think that it's your train that is moving. The perception that you are moving when you are really stationary—and other objects are moving—is sometimes called the *self-motion illusion* or visually induced self-motion. The illusion was initially described by pioneering researchers with whom you are already quite familiar—Mach (of the Mach bands and Mach book) and Helmholtz.

Your visual system is likely confused because the illusion closely replicates the situation when the train is actually moving. That is, while the train moves, you might be looking ahead of you or reading a book. At the same time, the countryside outside the window is moving rapidly in your peripheral vision. The self-motion illusion mimics that scenario, with peripheral movement that is consistent with self-motion.

PERCEIVING MOTION IN A STATIONARY IMAGE WHEN YOU MOVE The self-motion illusion leads you to perceive that you're in motion when you're not. It's also possible that your own motion can lead you to perceive motion when there is none. A number of artists (e.g., Patrick Hughes, Dick Termes) have produced works that appear to move as the person looking at the piece moves (Papathomas, 2007).

To experience this illusory movement yourself, look at the dot at the center of Figure 8.5, and then move your head toward and away from the textbook. The diamond-shaped objects in the two concentric circles will appear to rotate, even though they are completely stationary. Baingio Pinna and Gavin Brelstaff (2000) introduced this illusion, so you may see it referred to as the *Pinna-Brelstaff illusion*. Two components of the stimulus seem important. First, you are focused on the center of the display, so the objects in apparent motion are in the periphery of your vision. Second, the direction of motion is due to the location of the dark and light surrounds of the objects, which give the objects an apparent depth.

▶ **FIGURE 8.5**   The Pinna-Brelstaff illusion. If you move your head closer to the page and then away from the page, the two objects in the two peripheral concentric circles will appear to move in opposite directions. (*Source:* Reprinted from *Visual Research, 40,* 16, Baingio Pinna & Garvin J. Brelstaff, "A New Visual Illusion of Relative Motion," p. 6, copyright © 2000 with permission)

MOVEMENT AFTEREFFECTS   So far, we've been considering illusions in which simultaneous movement (of our eyes, our heads, or objects around us) leads us to perceive a stationary object as moving. We'll now consider a situation in which prior movement leads us to perceive a stationary object as moving. *Movement aftereffects* occur when you have been looking at a continuous movement and then look at a different surface. The new surface will seem to move in the opposite direction (Snowden & Freeman, 2004).

You might try to demonstrate movement aftereffects if you can visit a waterfall. Stare for several minutes at the waterfall, then turn your gaze toward nearby trees or rocks. These stationary objects will seem to flow in the direction opposite to that of the waterfall. The longer you look at the inducing stimulus (the waterfall), the more powerful the aftereffect. Try 🔲 Demonstration 8.4 to see an example of movement aftereffects.

Movement aftereffects resemble other aftereffects, such as successive color contrast and achromatic afterimages discussed in Chapter 7. One explanation for these phenomena involves some kind of adaptation or fatigue of cells involved in visual processing. However, simple adaptation or fatigue cannot fully explain the color phenomena (e.g., the McCullough effect). In a similar fashion, it's unlikely that we can explain such motion aftereffects with simple, low-level mechanisms. Consistent with Theme 4 of this text, higher-level processes are likely involved.

STATIONARY IMAGES THAT APPEAR TO MOVE
Some artists, particularly those working in the genre of op art, have created stationary stimuli that provide a sense of motion. Akiyoshi Kitaoka is a psychologist and artist whose stationary works often give a sense of motion. For example, as you can see on his webpages, Kitaoka's "Rotating Snakes" provides a compelling sense of motion for most observers. Kitaoka's work is quite popular on the Internet, although often without proper attribution. Thus, you may have already seen some of his work.

Misperceiving Motion Due to Context

Stuart Anstis is responsible for a number of different demonstrations in which the context leads people to misperceive motion. For example, Anstis and Clara Casco (2006) found that people misperceive the motion of small moving objects (e.g., flies) when the background moves. They refer to the effect as the *Flying Bluebottle illusion.* The two flies move in clockwise circles. However, when the background moves in either a clockwise or counterclockwise fashion, we either misperceive the size of the flies' orbits or the direction of their motion.

Anstis (2007) has also investigated the chopstick illusion, in which the motion of two lines ("chopsticks") varies whether or not they are viewed through a window. When seen in the window, the lines appear to move in a clockwise fashion. When seen without the window, both lines appear to move in a counterclockwise fashion. Anstis has also investigated the footsteps illusion, in which two squares (one yellow and one blue) move smoothly back and forth along a horizontal path (Howe et al., 2006). However, when seen against a set of vertical black and white bars, the two squares no longer move smoothly, but appear to stutter-step. None of these descriptions do justice to the powerful illusions, so you should visit Anstis's webpage to experience them for yourself. (The webpages for this text have links to all these motion effects.)

Section Summary

Illusory Movement

1. Stroboscopic movement is produced by sequential presentation of stimuli at different locations on the retina. In order to produce an effective illusion of motion, the distance and timing between the stimuli are crucial.

2. People tend to perceive apparent movement along the most direct path. With sufficiently brief presentations, this tendency leads people to perceive impossible biological movements.

3. Context—or the absence of context—may contribute to illusory movement. For example, when you look at a small stationary light in a dark room, it will appear to move (autokinesis). When the surrounding context moves, you'll misperceive an object as moving (induced movement) or even perceive yourself as moving (self-motion illusion).

4. Movement aftereffects occur after watching continuous movement. Stationary objects will appear to move in a direction opposite to the previously viewed movement.

5. Illusions such as the Flying Bluebottle illusion, the chopsticks illusion, and the footsteps illusion illustrate ways in which context can lead us to misperceive motion.

Theoretical Explanations for Motion Perception

How is it that you perceive motion? You might suggest that you perceive motion whenever the image of an object moves on the retina. That answer is appealing, but it is incomplete. After all, the images of the words on this page are sliding all over your retina as you read, yet the page does not seem to wiggle. In this case, images move on your retina, yet you do not perceive motion. Furthermore, when your eyes follow the flight of a bird in smooth pursuit movement, the image of the bird remains on approximately the same part of your retina. In this case, an image does not move on your retina, yet you perceive motion. Motion perception must involve more than movement of images on the retina.

We have seen that motion perception is a complex process, allowing us to perceive our own movement and that of objects around us. Any adequate theory of motion perception must explain how all this occurs. Two of these theoretical approaches for motion perception should seem familiar to you, as you've seen both the direct perception approach and the computational approach in earlier chapters. First, however, let us discuss an approach that will probably be new to you—corollary discharge theory.

Corollary Discharge Theory

According to *corollary discharge theory*, the visual system compares the movement registered on the retina with any signals the brain might have sent regarding eye movement. Corollary discharge theory specifically tries to explain why we do *not* perceive movement during normal eye movements. The theory can explain why we perceive movement when there is movement on the retina and when there is no movement on the retina. It can also explain why we perceive no movement when there is movement on the retina and also when there is no movement on the retina.

Corollary discharge theory proposes that, when your brain sends a message to your eye muscles, it also sends a copy of this message to a structure in the visual system. This copy is called a corollary discharge; the word *corollary* means "related." In the next section, we'll discuss the brain structures involved in this process. For now, we'll simply employ the *comparison structure* illustrated in Figure 8.6, which shows a schematic representation of the process. Richard Gregory (1997) refers to this portion of the corollary discharge model as the *eye-head system*, because it keeps track of motor signals sent to the eyes and the head.

Images often shift across the retina, whether due to movement in the world or due to movement of our eyes. Gregory refers to this portion as the *image-retina system*. When the comparison structure detects a difference between the input from the image-retina system and the input from the eye-head system, people perceive motion. When the sensory input (image-retina) is consistent with the corollary discharge expectation (eye-head), the information is canceled, and people perceive no motion. We'll attempt to clarify this theory with four examples.

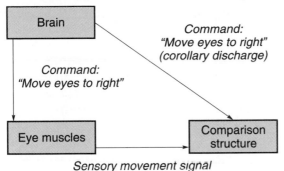

► FIGURE 8.6 A schematic illustration of corollary discharge theory. When the brain sends a signal to move the eyes, a corollary discharge is sent to the comparison structure. Movement on the retina results in a sensory signal, which is also sent to the comparison structure. The observer will perceive no motion if the sensory signal is consistent with the corollary discharge. However, the observer will perceive motion if the sensory signal is not anticipated by the corollary discharge.

FOUR OUTCOMES IN COROLLARY DISCHARGE THEORY   Let's examine four simple outcomes of the interaction of sensory input and corollary discharge, beginning with two cases where the eyes are stationary. First, think of what happens if you are looking straight ahead at a field of stationary objects. You won't produce any corollary discharge, because you aren't telling your eyes to move. Likewise, because your eyes are basically stationary, objects in the visual field remain in the same positions on the retina. With no corollary discharge and no sensory input from the retina, you perceive no movement.

Second, think of the case when your eyes are stationary and a person moves in front of you. Again, the eye-head system receives no command to move, so no corollary discharge is produced. However, the person moving across your field of view causes movement in your image-retina system. With no corollary discharge—but with sensory input from the retina—you *do* perceive movement. In other words, the actual sensory input does not cancel out the corollary discharge expectation. This discrepancy between the actual sensory input and the corollary discharge gives rise to the perception of motion.

In the final two cases, your eyes are moving. Imagine you are in a museum looking at a *stationary* woman, guard, and picture (Figure 8.7*a*). When you

scan the scene by moving your eyes from right to left, you produce a corollary discharge associated with the command to move your eyes. As you scan from right to left, the woman shifts from the left to the right of your visual field. The retinal images of the woman, the guard, and the picture all move in a fashion consistent with the expectations produced by the corollary discharge. Therefore, the sensory input is canceled out and no movement is perceived.

The final example involves moving eyes as well as a moving object. Suppose that the woman now moves from your right to your left, and you track her movement with your eyes (Figure 8.7*b*). In this case, a corollary discharge will be produced as you send the message to your eye muscles to track the woman. Any sensory input from your retina that is consistent with the corollary discharge will be canceled out, resulting in the perception of stationary objects (the guard and the picture). The image of the woman you are tracking, however, continues to fall on the same area of the retina, which is *inconsistent* with the corollary discharge. Thus, she is perceived as moving from right to left.

At some level, of course, it's absolutely crucial that we know about our own movements. As we noted earlier, unless we know whether we are moving or not, it would be difficult to disambiguate the source of motion on the retina. We'll return to corollary discharge when we discuss the physiology of motion perception.

DISRUPTING THE NORMAL COROLLARY DISCHARGE   Corollary discharge theory suggests that you will perceive movement whenever the information from the eye-head system is inconsistent with input from the image-retina system. Sometimes the discrepancy can result in the perception of movement that has not occurred. You can demonstrate this motion perception by placing your finger on the side of your upper eyelid. Keep your eye open and press gently. You are passively moving your eye with your finger, rather than through your brain's normal commands to the eye muscles. Therefore no corollary discharge is produced. A sensory signal *is* sent from the retina, however. The mismatch between the moving retinal image and the lack of corollary discharge results in the perception of movement.

What would happen if you sent a message to move your eyes, but your eyes were paralyzed? John Stevens and his colleagues (1976) actually did such research, as we discussed in Chapter 4. Stevens found

a. Stationary woman and moving observer

b. Moving woman and stationary observer

▶ **F I G U R E 8 . 7** Two illustrations of motion in the world. In part *a*, the observer is in motion from right to left and everything else is stationary. Notice that the relation of the woman to the picture remains constant from Frame 1 to Frame 3. In part *b*, the woman is moving from right to left and everything else (including the observer) is stationary. Notice that the relation of the woman to the picture changes from Frame 1 to Frame 3.

that, if he told his paralyzed eye muscles to move, the whole room appeared to move! In terms of corollary discharge theory, Stevens had created a corollary discharge expectation of movement that was accompanied by *no* sensory input from the retina. The discrepancy between the two pieces of information led to the perception of the movement of the room.

Look again at the explanation of Figure 8.7b. If you tell your eyes to move from right to left, the only objects that should remain stationary on the retina are those that are also moving from the right to the left. Similarly, Stevens told his eyes to move, so the only objects that should have remained stationary on the retina were those that are also moving. However, because his eye muscles were paralyzed, the whole room remained stationary on his retina. The discrep-

ancy between the sensory input (no change) and the corollary discharge (expect change) led to the perception that the room moved.

Direct Perception Approach

James Gibson and others who favor the direct perception approach have argued that the environment is rich with information about movement, a claim consistent with Theme 2 of this textbook. In contrast, corollary discharge theory emphasizes processing in the visual system. Although many theorists have taken positions that differ from the direct perception approach, Gibson's contributions to the study of motion perception were substantial (Blake, 1994). Thus, Gibson's early work anticipated much of the subsequent research on motion perception. In this current section, we will examine five sources of information available from the environment. Gibson would argue that such sources are crucial for the perception of motion.

1. *Optic flow fields.* As we discussed in Chapter 6, motion information (e.g., motion perspective) provides an important cue to depth or distance. When you drive down a road, images of objects flow across your retina at different rates. Such movement on your retina creates an optic flow field, which plays an important role in determining our motion in the world (Warren, 2008). If you look straight ahead, for example, nearby objects on either side of you flow by quickly; objects farther away flow slowly. Parts of the world expand and contract as you move around. The next time you are in a car, look straight ahead at a point on the horizon and notice how everything seems to expand outward from that point. Figure 6.18 on page 169 provides a static image to illustrate such an optic flow field.

2. *Relative movement.* We can tell whether we are moving or whether an object is moving by noticing the object's movement relative to its background. Notice in Figure 8.7a that the woman is always in front of the painting. Because the woman does not move in relation to the painting, you conclude that she is stationary and you—the observer—are moving. The patterns of movement shown in the tracking-shot illustration (Figure 6.14) are also consistent with movement of the observer and no movement of the people in the scene. In Figure 8.7b, the woman is moving in relation to the background. In the first picture, she is to the right of the painting, then she moves in front of the museum guard, and finally she moves in front of the doorway. As the observer, you would conclude that she is moving and you are stationary.

3. *Occlusion and disocclusion.* Consistent with the illustration in Figure 8.7b, moving objects show a systematic covering and uncovering of the background. Pick up your textbook and move it from the right to the left in front of your eyes. Your book systematically covers up the background on the left; this process is called **occlusion**. At the same time it systematically uncovers the background on the right; this process is called **disocclusion**. Occlusion and disocclusion tell us the direction of objects' movement (Gibson, 1979).

Looming objects also show a systematic occlusion and disocclusion pattern. Pick up your textbook again and move it toward you so that it is about to hit your face. Notice how the occlusion occurs to the same extent on both the right and the left side of the book. When the occlusion is equal, we perceive that an object is coming directly toward us. At other times the occlusion is not equal—for instance, when you move your book toward your left ear. In this case, the left side of the background becomes occluded at the same time as the right side becomes disoccluded. You perceive that the object will miss you. If the occlusion is extremely unequal, then the object will miss you by a large distance.

4. *Image size.* In describing looming earlier (Figure 8.1), we noted that the size of the image on your retina increases as you approach objects or they approach you. Have you ever noticed how cartoonists successfully exploit the image-size cue for motion? A character falls off a cliff, and then sees the features on the ground below expand suddenly. We then see the final "splat!"

5. *Binocular cues.* So far, we have been discussing monocular cues. However, when objects are sufficiently close to us, binocular cues become helpful in motion perception (Fernandez & Farell, 2005; Hess et al., 2007). If you watch a ball coming directly at you, for example, the image moves at the same speed on both your right and left retinas. However, if the left retinal image is moving more slowly than the right retinal image, then you perceive that the ball will pass toward your right side. Thus, comparing the speeds of the left and the right retinal images gives you information about the direction of movement.

Computational Approach

The computational approach also acknowledges the richness of the visual stimulus. However, unlike the direct perception approach, the computational approach also holds that perception requires problem solving. Unlike more cognitive approaches, though, the computational approach attempts to solve perceptual problems with general physical knowledge, rather than with specific knowledge about objects in the visual field.

To acknowledge the dynamic nature of retinal information, computational theorists talk about the space-time image on the retina. The first step in the model, then, would be to describe motion detectors that would extract motion from the dynamic image. One early motion detector model is called a Reichardt detector in honor of one of its developers (Krekelberg, 2008). Essentially, changes in retinal stimulation over time and space are encoded by nearby photoreceptors. That is, light first falls on one receptor, and then dark falls on that receptor while light falls on a nearby receptor. The motion detector would interpret such stimulation as motion in a particular direction (consistent with the location of the two receptors on the retina).

Of course, your visual system must interpret the light falling on the two receptors as coming from the same source. This is the *correspondence problem* that the visual system faces as it detects motion—how are elements of the visual field connected over time? The binocular perception of depth must solve the correspondence between stimulation of the two retinas. In order to perceive depth, the image on one retina must be linked to a slightly different image occurring simultaneously on the other retina. The perception of motion may need to solve a similar problem, but it must also determine the correspondence between points on the same retina at different times (Pack & Born, 2008). Look back at Figure 8.7*b* and try to imagine how your visual system would "connect" a dot presented in one frame with a dot in the next frame.

Another computational approach to motion detection sidesteps the correspondence problem entirely. An *energy model* focuses on the changes that take place over space and time (Bruce et al., 2003). For example, consider Figure 8.8, with space on the *x*-axis and time on the *y*-axis. In the graph, motion would appear as a pattern of intensities, with the orientation of the patterns indicating both direction of motion and velocity. Figure 8.8 might represent a white ball moving against a black background. Early in time, the ball is located to the left, and it is moving over time to the right. The result is a white diagonal line in these space-time coordinates. Can you figure out how the graph would differ if the ball were moving more rapidly?

These motion detectors are important for perceiving what computational theorists call *first-order motion*. However, we can also perceive motion that isn't dependent on luminance differences (e.g., a white ball moving against a black background). Imagine a ball that flickers from black to white as it moves against a gray background. On average, there is no luminance difference between the "ball" and its back-

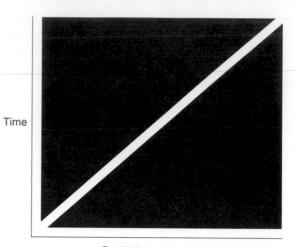

Time

Spatial location on retina

▶ **FIGURE 8.8** An illustration of a relative energy explanation of motion perception. The *x*-axis indicates space and the *y*-axis indicates time. Imagine a white ball moving against a black background. At the earliest time (bottom), the ball is on the left of the retina. Over time, the ball moves to the right. If the ball were moving faster, it would cover the space in less time, so a flatter slope would indicate greater velocity.

ground. Nonetheless, we would still perceive motion. Computational theorists use the term *second-order motion* when referring to motion due to cues other than luminance differences, for example, flicker, contrast, and texture (Bruce et al., 2003). Clearly, at some point in the visual system, we must integrate first-order and second-order motion information.

In this discussion of theoretical explanations of motion perception, we have mentioned corollary discharge theory, the direct perception approach, and the computational approach. These explanations for motion perception have emphasized the richness of the stimulus and the spectacular construction of the human visual processing system (Theme 2).

Experience and higher-level processes (Theme 4) seem to be crucial to corollary discharge theory and to perceiving a stable environment when we move. However, Johansson (1982) argued that cognitive processes play a relatively minor role in motion perception. He asked us to consider the housefly, an organism not known for its impressive cognitive ability. Johansson described how the male and female housefly perform the mating procedure. The female partner circles around in a random path while the male partner follows the same pattern several inches above her. The male housefly's mating movements are far more accurate than those of talented airplane pilots. Certainly our cognitive processes are important in the *interpretation* of motion, but many aspects of motion perception clearly can be accomplished with little thought or memory.

Section Summary

Theoretical Explanations for Motion Perception

1. Corollary discharge theory proposes that the visual system compares the movement registered on the retina (image-retina system) with any signals the brain may have sent about eye movement (eye-head system). We perceive movement when the two systems register discrepant information.

2. The direct perception approach argues that the environment provides information that includes background information, occlusion/disocclusion information, image size, motion parallax, motion perspective, and binocular cues.

3. The computational approach provides mathematical models for the computation of movement. Motion detectors that rely on feature analysis must solve the correspondence problem. Another computational approach—an energy model of motion detection—focuses on the space-time qualities of retinal stimulation.

Physiological Basis of Motion Perception

Theories that are better able to explain behavior are more powerful. It's also important that the theories are realistic, in that they are consistent with what we know about an organism's physiology. In this section, we'll examine the physiological underpinnings of motion perception. Before reading this section, you may want to review the information in Chapter 3.

Processing Motion Information Before V1

As we noted in Chapter 3, motion processing begins in the retina and continues through areas of primary and secondary visual cortex. The retina plays an important early role in motion detection and analysis (Billino et al., 2008). For example, starburst amacrine cells are directionally sensitive, so they may contribute to motion perception (Masland, 2005). The retina is also the source of the M, P, and K pathways. Of these three pathways, the M pathway certainly plays an important role in motion perception (e.g., Chapman et al., 2004; Ray et al., 2005).

However, the M pathway cannot be solely responsible for motion perception. As we know, the M pathway is not particularly sensitive to color information. Nonetheless, people perceive motion when color (and not luminance) is the only cue to motion (Cropper & Wuerger, 2005; Ruppertsberg et al., 2003). It's possible that P pathway information may contribute to motion perception (Nassi et al., 2006). It's also possible that the K pathway plays a role in motion perception (Ruppertsberg et al., 2007).

Many researchers believe that motion perception begins in V1 (Blake et al., 2004). It's certainly the case that researchers have traced the path of motion information through V1 and on to areas of secondary visual cortex. However, some of the motion information may go directly to areas of the secondary visual cortex from LGN without passing through the primary visual cortex (Sincich et al., 2004). Nonetheless, areas of the visual cortex from V1 and beyond are certainly important for motion perception, so we'll consider those areas now.

Processing Motion Information in V1 and Beyond

As we mentioned in Chapter 3, Hubel and Wiesel determined that many cells in V1 are directionally sensitive (Blake et al., 2004). Thus, input to V1 from the LGN is organized to encode basic motion information. Of course, all sorts of visual information (e.g., form, color) flow through V1. The initially separate input from the M, P, and K pathways is combined into two main streams of information flowing from V1 to V2 (Sincich & Horton, 2005). In addition to the flow of information from V1 to V2, information flows in the reverse direction *from* V2 and other areas of the secondary visual cortex *to* V1. Feedback of information to V1 may allow this region of the visual cortex to play an important role in making us aware of motion (Silvanto et al., 2005).

Some of the information from V2 goes to V5 (also called the *middle temporal area*, or *MT*), as seen in Figure 7.9, on page 207. Researchers have focused attention on MT as a central site for motion perception because of the high proportion of motion- and direction-sensitive cells in this area of the cortex. Although MT is surely not the only source of motion information, this region certainly seems central. Area MT also appears to be the site of the motion aftereffect, showing activity when people experience this illusory motion (Snowden & Freeman, 2004).

As we have mentioned in earlier chapters, unfortunate incidents in which people sustain neural damage may lead to important theoretical knowledge. One such disorder is *akinetopsia*—the inability to perceive movement. Earlier in this chapter, we mentioned L. M., a woman with akinetopsia due to lesions to both sides of her occipital cortex (Schenk et al., 2000; Zihl et al., 1983). L. M. lost the ability to detect peripheral movement, and she could not perceive three-dimensional motion. However, she had normal acuity and color vision, and she could detect some linear movement when it occurred near her foveas. Walking across an intersection is dangerous for L. M. because oncoming cars first appear to be far away and then jump very near. Even the simple act of pouring a cup of tea becomes difficult if one cannot perceive motion in depth! Apparently, L. M.'s visual experience is like a series of still photographs, with little sense of transition between the snapshots.

L. M.'s bilateral damage included area MT, but the damage was so widespread that her akinetopsia may not be attributed solely to MT damage (Blake et al., 2004). In fact, people who have sustained damage to nearby brain areas, but no damage to the middle temporal area, also exhibit some deficits in motion perception. Thus, even though MT surely plays a vital role in motion perception, it's also the case that other brain areas must be involved as well.

Thus far, we've been tracing the *Where* (dorsal) path, which we mentioned in Chapter 3. This path is important for motion perception. From MT, that path continues to the medial superior temporal (MST) area. The dorsal portion of MST (MSTd) appears to play an important role in processing optic flow information (Warren, 2008).

Another area that is important for motion perception is the superior temporal sulcus (STS). In general, the STS is important for integrating visual, auditory, and tactile information (Beauchamp et al., 2008). As we mentioned earlier, the STS plays an important role in the perception of biological motion (Beauchamp et al., 2003; Pelphrey & Morris, 2006; Saygin, 2007). In fact, the STS may respond to biological motion from real actors, but not from similar "cartoon" characters (Mar et al., 2007). As important as the STS may be, it's clear that other brain areas must also be involved in perception of biological motion (Grossman, 2006).

Processing Self-Motion Information

In this chapter, we've described at least two ways in which it's important that we know about self-motion: determining how we're actually moving through space and determining how we've told our eyes to move. Researchers have identified two areas of the brain (the medial superior temporal and the ventral intraparietal areas) that play key roles in determining how we ourselves are moving through space (Britten, 2008). Recall that the direct perception theorists emphasize the role of optic flow fields in determining how we're moving through space. Optic flow fields are not the sole source of information about such self-motion, but areas of the brain do produce optic flow signals.

Central to the corollary discharge theory is knowledge about signals sent to control the eye-head system. The theory would remain purely theoretical without evidence for brain mechanisms that process such signals. Many researchers, including Marc Sommer and Robert Wurz (2008a, 2008b), have provided such evidence.

As you may recall from Chapter 3, some of the ganglion cells leaving the eye go to the superior colliculus. (The superior colliculus is shown in Figure 3.16 on page 65.) The superior colliculus plays an important role in integrating information from various senses, as well as in controlling eye movements. The superior colliculus is the likely origin of the corollary discharge information; in other words, it sends a copy of the motor command to move the eyes. The information would next go to the medial dorsal (MD) nucleus of the thalamus and then to the frontal eye field (FEF) of the frontal cortex (Wurtz, 2008).

Consistent with corollary discharge theory, information about impending eye movements would aid us in planning movements and in creating a stable world (Sommer & Wurtz, 2008b). Other creatures would also need information about self-motion in order to disambiguate retinal motion. Although the neural pathways involved may differ from the pathways in humans, corollary discharge is certainly not limited to primates (Crapse & Sommer, 2008; Poulet & Hedwig, 2007).

Section Summary

Physiological Basis of Motion Perception

1. The M pathway plays an important role in motion perception, although the P and K pathways may also contribute.

2. The *Where* pathway is important for motion perception. Input from the M, P, and K pathways to the primary visual cortex (V1) is organized so that many of the cortical cells are directionally sensitive. For a number of reasons, V1 is important for motion perception.

3. The *Where* pathway continues from V1 to V2 to V5 (also called the middle temporal, MT, area). Area MT is important for motion perception, with many directionally sensitive cells. Akinetopsia is the inability to perceive movement, due to damage to the brain around MT.

4. The dorsal portion of the medial superior temporal (MSTd) area is important for perceiving optic flow. The superior temporal sulcus (STS) is important for perceiving biological motion.

5. A system for encoding corollary discharges from eye movements likely begins in the superior colliculus, continuing through the medial dorsal (MD) nucleus of the thalamus to the frontal eye field (FEF) of the frontal cortex.

Review Questions

1. William Shakespeare wrote, "Things in motion sooner catch the eye than what stirs not." How is this comment relevant to your visual system? Compare your peripheral vision and vision in your fovea with respect to motion detection.

2. Imagine that an industrial employee has been instructed to report whether a dial on a piece of equipment moves the slightest amount. Describe how uncertainty and the background behind the dial might be important, and mention why apparent movement might be a problem.

3. Summarize the studies on biological motion discussed in the In-Depth section. What kinds of information about motion can we pick up readily, without seeing an entire organism? Obviously, we most often see a complete organism. Why, then, is research on biological motion so important for theories of perception?

4. Suppose you are playing softball and you are up at bat. How would Gibson's theory explain your perception of motion as the ball is being pitched toward you? Suppose you are pitching and you quickly move your head to determine whether the person on second base is trying to steal third. How might corollary discharge theory account for the stability, despite the motion of images across your retina?

5. Name the kind of apparent movement represented in each of the following situations:

   a. On a dark night, you see a single small light in a neighbor's house, and you know that the neighbor is on vacation. The light appears to move, and you suspect a burglar.

   b. You're surfing the Web and come across a site at which a set of "lights" appear to go off and on in succession, so that the "light" appears to move across your monitor.

   c. In a planetarium, the star show ends with the stars whirling swiftly about in a clockwise direction for several minutes. Out in the darkened lobby a few seconds later, the room around you seems to be whirling in the opposite direction.

   d. On a dark night, you watch a plane fly over a radio tower. For a brief moment the plane seems to be stationary and the tower light seems to move.

6. Compare the perception of real movement with illusory movement—particularly stroboscopic movement. To answer this question, think about the movement seen on a movie screen as compared to movement in the real world. Why might you think that the same movement perception system gives rise to the perception of both types of movement?

7. We tend to think of some brain areas as specialized for one particular sense (e.g., the visual cortex) or a particular perceptual experience (e.g., motion). Of course, given what we know about brain plasticity, the situation is rarely that clear. That said, there are certainly areas of the brain whose role seems to be to integrate information from various senses (e.g., the superior colliculus and the superior temporal sulcus). Why might some brain areas be more focused and other brain areas be more integrative? (Hint: It may help to contrast the benefits of specialization with the need to perceive the world in a unitary fashion.)

8. Think of a situation involving complex movement perception, such as playing tennis. Players are moving as they track a moving opponent and the ball being returned to them over a stationary net. How would each of the theoretical approaches to movement perception deal with this situation? Which approach do you find best able to deal with the complexities of the situation, and why?

9. Many perceptual phenomena require explanations that are more complicated than you might have anticipated. For example, someone unfamiliar with the topic of motion perception might guess that we simply perceive motion whenever our retinas register a change in an object's position. Why would that explanation be inadequate? What other explanations would you add?

10. In this chapter, we focused on motion perception and argued that it is a basic process. One argument that a person might make for the importance of motion perception is the extent to which it plays a role in other perceptual processes. Using information in previous chapters, show how motion plays a role in other perceptual processes such as shape and distance perception.

Key Terms

optic flow field, p. 221
looming, p. 222
biological motion, p. 222
point-light display, p. 222
illusory movement, p. 226
stroboscopic movement,
    p. 226

phi movement, p. 226
autokinesis, p. 227
induced movement, p. 227
self-motion illusion, p. 228
movement aftereffects,
    p. 229

corollary discharge theory,
    p. 230
occlusion, p. 233
disocclusion, p. 233

correspondence problem,
    p. 234
energy model, p. 234
akinetopsia, p. 236

Recommended Readings

Berthoz, A. (2000). *The brain's sense of movement.* Cambridge, MA: Harvard.

    This text was originally published in 1997, and it was moderately updated for the English translation in 2000. Berthoz provides a clear integration of a range of work on motion perception—especially as a multisensory experience. His engaging writing style and clever examples make the text quite readable. (Kudos to the translator: Giselle Weiss.)

Blake, R., Sekuler, R., & Grossman, E. (2004). Motion processing in human visual cortex. In J. H. Kaas & C. E. Collins (Eds.), *The primate visual system* (pp. 311–344). Boca Raton, FL: CRC.

If you're interested in a more detailed overview of the brain areas involved in motion perception, you'll appreciate this chapter. You may want to supplement the information in this chapter with other sources, such as the *Annual Review of Neuroscience* article by Sincich and Horton (2005).

Bruce, V., Green, P. R., & Georgeson, M. A. (2003). *Visual perception: Physiology, psychology and ecology* (4th ed.). New York: Psychology Press.

This text covers a wide array of topics (e.g., object perception, depth perception). However, you'll find several chapters that further explore topics addressed in this chapter. If you're intrigued by the computational approach, you'll appreciate their chapter on the computation of motion. Other relevant chapters address optic flow and biological motion.

Knoblich, G., Thornton, I. M., Grosjean, M., & Shiffrar, M. (Eds.). (2006). *Human body perception from the inside out.* New York: Oxford.

This edited volume contains a number of interesting chapters that investigate perception of the human body. However, for the purposes of this chapter, you'll find the chapters about biological motion to be particularly helpful. For example, Jeannine Pinto provides an informative review of research on infants' perception of biological motion.

CHAPTER 9

The Auditory System

TAKE A MINUTE to appreciate the variety of sounds nearby. You may hear voices and music, rattles, thuds, whines, buzzes, squeaks, roars, and drips. Some sounds are loud and some are soft. Some are high, others are low. Each sound also appears to come from a distinct direction.

Most of us assume that vision is our most important perceptual ability, preferring to navigate the world by means of sight alone rather than hearing alone. However, think of the variety of ways in which hearing is superior to vision in providing us with information about the world. Consider, for example, the advantage of being able to hear sounds before we can see the source of those sounds (e.g., an ambulance's siren, the footsteps of an approaching person). Hearing is also vital to human communication, because it is central in social interactions and in transmitting knowledge. Communication would be possible, but cumbersome, if dependent solely on visual information. (Imagine that you could communicate *only* through text-messages!) And although music may not be as essential to personal survival as Shawn Colvin claims in "I Don't Know Why," music and other forms of entertainment certainly rely on auditory information to enhance our lives.

Chapter 3 introduced the visual stimulus—light—and the structure of the visual system. Now we need to examine the equivalent topics for hearing: the auditory stimulus—sound waves—and the structure of the auditory system. In this chapter, we also consider hearing impairments.

The Auditory Stimulus

Auditory stimuli are caused by displacement of an elastic medium. To understand an elastic medium, think of a rubber band. The rubber band can be stretched, but when the pressure is removed, the rubber band returns to its original shape. The molecules of an elastic medium can be displaced, but they have a tendency to return to their original position. Some examples of elastic media include liquids (such as water), the ground, metals, wood, and—most important for our purposes—air. The vacuum of space cannot transmit sound waves. So, despite any science fiction movies you might have seen, space would always be eerily silent. On earth, elastic media abound. In western movies, you might have seen scouts place an ear to the ground or railroad tracks,

enabling them to detect approaching horses or trains. Car mechanics use a trick for learning about the internal functioning of an engine. They listen at the end of a long piece of wood placed against different parts of the engine. Each of these examples illustrates a major advantage of our auditory sense—we can hear things that are out of sight.

Our most common experience of sound comes from the displacement of air molecules. An object vibrates, and the vibration causes molecules of air to change their positions and collide with each other, producing changes in air pressure. Perhaps the easiest way to visualize these pressure changes is to consider how air molecules respond to a vibrating diaphragm in a loudspeaker. If you remove the cover from a speaker, you can see it move in and out.

The movement of the speaker diaphragm influences the surrounding air molecules. When the diaphragm moves forward, it shoves the surrounding air molecules closer together. The density of the air molecules next to the diaphragm increases. (Imagine people milling around in a room, and consider how the density of people would increase if one wall were to move inward.) When the diaphragm moves backward, the air in front of the speaker becomes less dense as the nearby air molecules move apart. (Now imagine the wall moving outward and consider how few people would be immediately in front of the wall, right after it moved.)

Typically, the vibrations of a speaker diaphragm would be far too fast for you to see all of them. For example, to reproduce the musical note A above middle C, the speaker diaphragm would repeat the cycle of moving forward and backward a total of 440 times in 1 second. In other words, the atmospheric pressure next to the diaphragm could increase and decrease 440 times in the time it takes you to blink your eye. And most young people can hear sounds that arise from even faster pressure changes (as many as 20,000 times per second).

A wave of pressure moves continuously outward from the vibrating diaphragm until it no longer has the energy to move any more air molecules. In Figure 9.1, notice the areas of high atmospheric pressure, represented by the high density of air molecules, and the areas of low atmospheric pressure, represented by the low density of air molecules. (Of course, this diagram is schematic, because air molecules are invisible.) However, each individual air molecule moves very little during this process. Think of the ripples created when you throw a stone into a pond, with the

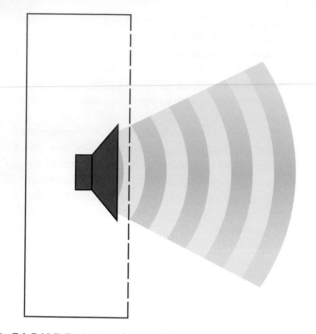

▶ **F I G U R E 9 . 1**   Areas of high and low atmospheric pressure created by a vibrating speaker diaphragm.

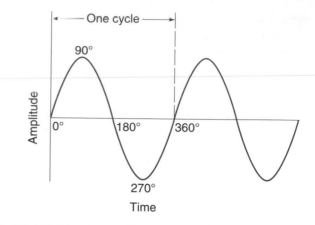

▶ **F I G U R E 9 . 2**   Characteristics of a sound wave. The change from normal atmospheric pressure to above-normal pressure, to below-normal pressure, with a return to normal pressure is referred to as one cycle. Within the cycle, the phase angle of the wave changes from 0° to 360°. The frequency of the sound is determined by the number of cycles completed in 1 second. The amplitude of the sound is determined by the height of the wave.

ripples traveling outward from the source of the disturbance. Each individual water molecule moves very little, but they bunch up to create the crest of a wave and move apart to create the trough of a wave. And, as is true of sound waves, over time the energy dissipates and the waves become smaller until they disappear entirely.

Figure 9.2 represents a *pure tone*, which is a simple sine wave. In the laboratory, simple sine waves are often used as stimuli; in the "real world," pure tones are actually quite rare. Your stereo, for instance, would rarely emit a pure tone. For the sake of simplicity, however, we will focus our discussion on pure tones.

Suppose that your stereo speaker emitted a pure tone. We could measure the atmospheric pressure near the speaker diaphragm, recording the pressure as it increases and decreases before finally returning to its original pressure. The pure sine wave in Figure 9.2 arises from mapping such pressure changes over time. From its resting state, the speaker first pushes out, creating an increase in pressure. The speaker then returns to its resting state, and then goes back behind its original starting point, creating a decrease in pressure. Finally, the speaker returns to the original starting point. The full range of pressure changes—from

normal, to high, to normal, to low, and back to normal—is referred to as a *cycle*. You can see that the shape of the sound wave resembles the sine-wave functions discussed in Chapters 3 and 7 in connection with light waves.

Although a number of factors affect its speed, the sound wave travels outward from your stereo at over 1000 feet per second until it reaches your eardrum. The rapid increase and decrease in atmospheric pressure will cause your eardrum to move backward and forward. These successive air-pressure changes falling on our ears are called *sounds*.

You hear a sound because of tiny disturbances in air pressure. This seems incredible. How can the motion of invisible air molecules possibly be strong enough to cause your eardrum to move? The sensitivity of the system becomes clearer when you realize that the sounds need to displace your eardrum by only a minuscule amount—less than one-tenth of the diameter of the hydrogen atom (Puria & Steele, 2008).

In the next sections, we will describe three physical properties of sound waves: frequency, amplitude, and phase angle. These physical properties are the bases of our perceptual experience of sound, but the linkage between the physical and the perceptual remains complex. Try www Demonstration 9.1 to give yourself an intuitive understanding of these three properties of sound waves.

Frequency

We discussed the visual stimulus in terms of its wavelength. By convention, we describe the sound wave in terms of its frequency. *Frequency* is the number of cycles that a sound wave completes in 1 second. Thus, shorter wavelengths have higher frequencies because more waves can occur in each second. Generally speaking, the wavelengths of auditory stimuli are much greater than the wavelengths of visual stimuli. For example, the A above middle C on the piano has a basic frequency of 440 cycles per second, or 440 Hz. (The abbreviation *Hz* is derived from the name of Heinrich Hertz, a German physicist.) That frequency would translate to a wavelength of about 0.8 meter. By contrast, the longest visible wavelength is about 0.0000008 meter.

Frequency generally corresponds to the psychological experience of pitch, although the correspondence is far from perfect. Thus, the A above middle C sounds higher in pitch than the lowest note on the piano, which has a frequency of about 27 Hz. The sound wave in Figure 9.3a has a higher frequency (the sound source vibrates more frequently) than the one in Figure 9.3b and will typically sound higher in pitch. Try www Demonstration 9.2 to listen to three different pure tones.

What range of frequencies can humans hear? Young adults can typically hear tones that have frequencies as low as 20 Hz and as high as 20,000 Hz (Yost, 2007). Older adults, as we will see in Chapter 14, typically have difficulty hearing tones as high as 20,000 Hz. (You might even have heard of high-frequency ring tones for cell phones that seek to take advantage of this disparity in auditory capabilities—audible to younger people and inaudible to older people.) Most of our auditory experience, however, involves only a small fraction of that 20- to 20,000-Hz range. For example, the typical vocal range is from about 80 Hz (for a bass) to about 1100 Hz (for a soprano).

Within the range of sounds we can hear, which frequencies do we hear best? Using the methodologies discussed in Chapter 2, we could compute *absolute thresholds* (the smallest amount of a stimulus that can be detected 50% of the time) for the human auditory range. Research has determined that humans are most sensitive to frequencies from 1000 to 4000 Hz (Yost, 2007). Intriguingly, the energy of a baby's cries falls within the range of frequencies to which humans are most sensitive.

The frequency of a tone influences discrimination as well as detection. You will recall from Chapter 2 that psychophysical techniques can be used to measure a difference threshold. A *difference threshold* is the smallest change in a stimulus that can produce a difference that is noticeable 50% of the time. Data on difference thresholds can be expressed in terms of Weber fractions, in which the difference threshold is divided by the frequency of the tone. Compared to the sensitivity of other senses, the Weber fraction is particularly remarkable in the intermediate frequency range (from 500 to 2000 Hz). We are so sensitive to changes in frequency in this range that the Weber fraction can be as small as 0.002 (Yost, 2007). In other words, we need to change a tone's frequency by only 0.2% to notice a difference (e.g., a 1000 Hz tone and a 1002 Hz tone). We are less sensitive in judging differences between two very low-frequency tones or two very high-frequency tones. However, it's clear that humans are quite sensitive to small differences in frequency across a wide range of frequencies.

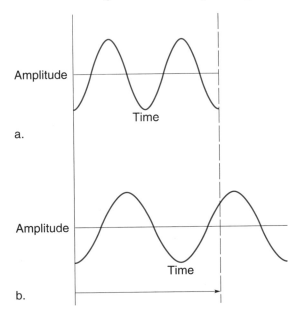

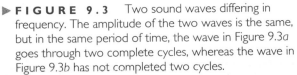

▶ **F I G U R E 9 . 3**   Two sound waves differing in frequency. The amplitude of the two waves is the same, but in the same period of time, the wave in Figure 9.3a goes through two complete cycles, whereas the wave in Figure 9.3b has not completed two cycles.

So far our discussion of frequency has included only pure tones. Most tones we hear in our everyday lives—including those produced by musical instruments and singers—are complex. **Complex tones** are tones that cannot be represented by one simple sine wave. Nonetheless, as you may remember from our discussion of Fourier analysis in Chapter 5, no matter how complex the tone, it can be analyzed into component pure tones. Moreover, these complex tones will each have a basic, or fundamental, frequency. For example, look at the complex tones illustrated in Figure 9.4, each of which represents the combination of several different pure tones. Notice that one com-

bination of pure tones produces a square-shaped wave (Figure 9.4*a*). However, a different combination of pure tones produces a sawtooth wave (Figure 9.4*b*). In both cases, the periodic nature of the wave is evident. We will consider these more complex auditory stimuli in Chapters 10 and 11.

Amplitude

Another aspect of sound waves is their peak *amplitude*—or the maximum pressure change from normal. In general, amplitude corresponds to the psy-

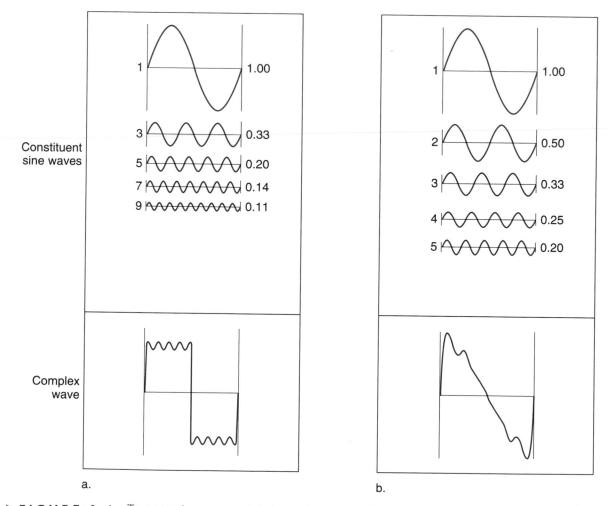

Constituent sine waves

Complex wave

a.

b.

▶**FIGURE 9.4** Two complex waves and their constituent pure sine waves. Using Fourier synthesis, both waves can be created by adding together several sine waves in particular phase relationships. For instance, adding together a pure wave of a particular frequency (arbitrarily 1.0) with a wave having frequencies 3, 5, 7, and 9 times greater creates the complex wave shown in Figure 9.4*a*. Using Fourier analysis, such complex waves can be decomposed into their constituent pure sine waves. (Adapted from Gulick et al., 1989. Used with permission.)

chological experience of loudness. That is, a high-amplitude sound wave moves your eardrum more than a low-amplitude sound wave, and the sound seems louder. Thus, the sound wave in Figure 9.5a has a higher amplitude than the one in Figure 9.5b, and it will usually also sound louder. Try www Demonstration 9.3 to illustrate the impact of different amplitudes on your experience of a particular frequency.

Sound pressure can be measured in terms of a standard force (called a **dyne**) per square centimeter. A 1000-Hz tone can just barely be detected under ideal conditions when produced with about 0.0002 dynes/cm² of pressure. Human beings begin to feel pain if the amplitude is above 2000 dynes/cm². So the range of sound pressure—from detection to pain—is greater than about 10 million to 1. Because these numbers are a bit unwieldy for day-to-day use, researchers developed a logarithmic scale of sound pressures relative to the threshold pressure (0.0002 dynes/cm²). This scale is **sound-pressure level (SPL)**, measured in units called decibels.

A **decibel (dB)** of SPL is computed by using the following equation:

$$\text{Number of decibels} = 20 \log(P_1/P_0)$$

According to this formula for decibels, we multiply 20 times the logarithm of the ratio of P_1 to P_0. In this equation, P_1 is the sound pressure level of the stimulus we want to convert to decibels and P_0 is the reference level of 0.0002 dynes/cm². Thus, a sound pressure level of 2,000 dynes/cm² would become 140 dB. (Divide 2,000 by 0.0002, then take the logarithm of that ratio, and multiply by 20.) At the other extreme, threshold pressure of 0.0002 dynes/cm² would translate into 0 dB. So, instead of dealing with numbers between 0.0002 and 2,000, researchers can deal with values between 0 and 140.

Don't be confused by the logarithmic scale of decibels. For instance, don't think that an SPL of 140 dB is seven times greater than an SPL of 20 dB. In terms of the actual pressures (2,000 and 0.002 dynes/cm²), the higher pressure is a million times greater than the lower pressure! In fact, with every 6 additional dB SPL, the sound pressure *doubles*. Table 9.1 shows some representative decibel levels for sounds that humans can hear. Notice that decibels are standardized so that 0 dB represents the weakest 1000-Hz tone you can hear. Values near 140 dB are painful and can cause permanent hearing loss.

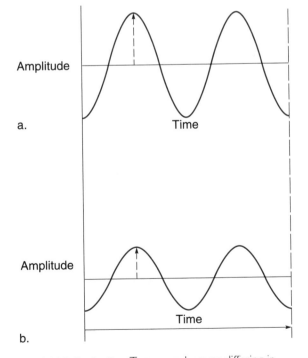

a.

b.

► **FIGURE 9.5** Two sound waves differing in amplitude. The two waves have identical frequencies, but the maximum and minimum amplitudes are greater in the wave in Figure 9.5a compared to the wave in Figure 9.5b.

► **TABLE 9.1** Some Typical Amplitudes of Various Noises, Measured by the Decibel Scale of Sound Pressure

Description	dB	Example
	160	
Intolerable	140	Near jet airplane taking off
	120	Very loud thunder
Very noisy	100	Heavy automobile traffic
Loud	80	Loud music from stereo
Moderate	60	Average conversation
Faint	40	Quiet neighborhood
	20	Soft whisper
Very faint	0	Softest detectable noise

We discussed our impressive ability to discriminate differences in frequency. Humans are also quite good in their ability to discriminate differences in amplitude for pure tones and white noise, though intensity discrimination can be measured in a number of different ways (Moore, 2001; Plack, 2005). The Weber fraction for intensity discrimination is a bit messy, because it's not quite constant. However, it's clear that the Weber fraction for intensity discrimination is larger (typically between 0.2 and 0.5) than that for frequency discrimination. Nonetheless, over a range of pure tones, we can detect differences in amplitude of between 1 and 2 dB, although we're better with noise than pure tones. We can also detect small amplitude differences in complex sounds. For example, you can detect the difference between two complex sounds, each consisting of 21 simple tones of identical frequencies, but with a single tone in one of the complex sounds at a somewhat greater amplitude (Plack, 2005).

Phase Angle

Another way to characterize the sound wave is in terms of the position of the pressure change as it moves through one complete cycle. As seen in Figure 9.2, *phase angle* indicates the angle in degrees at each phase, or position, of the cycle. If you think of sounds moving through air, 0° represents normal air pressure just before the air pressure begins to increase. Normal air pressure is a function of altitude, so it would be lower for higher altitudes, and vice versa. The wave returns to normal pressure at 180°, on its way to less-than-normal pressures. Maximum pressure occurs at 90°, and minimum pressure occurs at 270°.

As we will see in Chapter 10, phase angle is particularly useful in comparing two different sound waves, or the same sound wave at two different times. When you hook up your stereo system, your instructions probably cautioned you to be sure that the speaker wires were hooked up identically to both speakers. If you did not do so, the speakers would be out of phase. Thus, when one speaker was pushing out (0° through 90°), the other speaker would be going in (180° through 270°). As a result, the sound coming from your speakers would not be as rich (or as loud) as it would be if the speakers were in phase (with both speakers going out and in at the same time). In fact, if two waves are identical in frequency and amplitude but perfectly out of phase, they would cancel each other out—producing silence. This principle has been useful in the development of headphones that reduce the amplitude of unwanted low-frequency sounds (Biersdorfer, 2004). Some car manufacturers have also developed anti-noise systems that use wave cancellation to reduce the noise inside cars.

Section Summary

The Auditory Stimulus

1. Sound waves can be described in terms of their frequency and their amplitude. Frequency (measured in Hz) is the number of cycles that a sound wave can complete in 1 second; frequency is an important determinant of pitch. Humans hear pure tones with frequencies between 20 and 20,000 Hz.

2. We detect the presence of tones best in the 1000- to 4000-Hz range. We can discriminate between two very similar tones in the 500- to 2000-Hz range, where the Weber fraction can be as small as 0.002.

3. Pure tones are represented by sine waves. Auditory researchers frequently use pure tones; however, complex tones are more common and represent the combination of a number of different pure tones.

4. Amplitude is the maximum pressure created by sound waves, often measured in decibels; amplitude is an important determinant of loudness. The Weber fraction for intensity discrimination is between 0.2 and 0.5.

5. The phase angle of a sound wave is measured in degrees; it indicates the position of a wave in its cycle.

The Auditory System

In Chapter 3, we discussed how the visual system solved the problem of transducing electromagnetic energy into neural energy. The auditory system must solve a similar problem of transducing sound pressure changes into neural energy. We've briefly reviewed the physical stimuli important to audition, so we now need to look at the transduction process. What happens to sound waves when they reach the ear, and how do the various parts of the ear contribute to the transformation of sound waves into neural information?

The ear has three anatomical regions. Fortunately, their names are refreshingly straightforward: *the outer ear, the middle ear,* and *the inner ear.* As we'll discuss, the outer and middle ear both have an impact on the incoming sound stimulus, but the receptors in the inner ear are responsible for the transduction.

As you read about the sound stimulus, you should have noted many ways in which it differs from the visual stimulus. Thus, you should expect that the transduction process for the sound stimulus is different from the transduction of the visual stimulus. At the same time, and consistent with Theme 1 of this text, you should also expect to find similarities between the auditory and the visual system.

Outer Ear

The most obvious part of the outer ear is what people ordinarily refer to as "the ear." The technical name for this distinctive flap of external tissue is the **pinna**. The pinnae are important because they increase the sound amplitude that will reach the inner ear, especially the sounds between 1500 and 7000 Hz (Yost, 2007). They also help in determining the direction from which a sound is coming. However, our pinnae would be more useful if they were larger and/or movable, as is true for other animals such as cats, dogs, and bats (e.g., Chiu & Moss, 2007).

Figure 9.6 (page 248) shows other structures in the outer ear. Notice the **external auditory canal** that runs inward from the pinna. The external auditory canal is about 0.3 inch in diameter and 1 inch long. This structure helps keep insects and small objects, such as dirt, away from the sensitive eardrum (Yost, 2007). Furthermore, this canal behaves somewhat like a resonant tube, such as an organ pipe, and can amplify some frequencies impressively. Because of the pinna and the external auditory canal, frequencies in the range of 1000 to 6000 Hz are amplified by as much as 20 dB (Plack, 2005; Yost, 2007). (Use the formula for decibels to convince yourself that a 20-dB increase means that the sound-pressure amplitude is roughly tripled.) If you are able to hear the piccolo in a symphony orchestra, partial credit goes to your external auditory canals!

Finally, we come to the **eardrum**, or **tympanic membrane**, which is the boundary between the outer and middle ear. This thin piece of membrane vibrates in response to sound waves, causing movement in the bones of the middle ear. Puncturing the eardrum results in a hearing deficit. Depending on the size and location of the puncture, the deficit can be quite extreme (Martin & Clark, 2005). For this reason, you might have been advised never to stick anything smaller than your elbow in your ear. You should also avoid large and rapid pressure changes (such as those caused by explosions, discharge of firearms, watersport accidents, etc.), which may also rupture the eardrum (e.g., Carson, 2004).

Sound waves travel through the air until they reach the eardrum. Air does not offer much opposition to the flow of sound waves. This resistance to the passage of sound waves is known as **impedance** (Yost, 2007), so air has relatively low impedance. However, the eardrum is more difficult for the air to move, so it has a higher impedance than air. Moreover, as we'll soon discuss, the inner ear is filled with liquid, a medium that also has a higher impedance than air.

You can demonstrate the differences in impedance for air and water by trying www Demonstration 9.4. When the impedances for two media differ, **impedance mismatch** results, and sound waves cannot be readily transmitted from one medium to another. For example, when a sound wave in air reaches a liquid, the wave loses about 30 dB in pressure, or about 99.9% of the power. Most of the sound energy is simply reflected back into the air.

We've already discussed the fact that the outer ear actually amplifies some frequencies due to the resonance of the pinna and external auditory canal. The middle ear also plays a crucial role in overcoming the impedance mismatch between sound waves in the world around us and the waves that must emerge in our inner ears.

Middle Ear

The middle ear is the area on the inner side of the eardrum, occupying a volume of only about 2 cm^3 (0.1 cubic inch). The space in each middle ear is filled with air and a **eustachian tube** (pronounced "you-stay-shun") connects the middle ear to the throat. The eustachian tubes help equalize the air pressure in

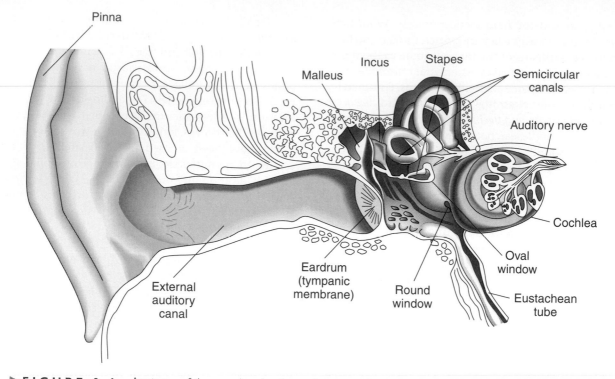

▶**FIGURE 9.6**   Anatomy of the ear, showing the major parts of the outer, middle, and inner ear.

the auditory system. When you swallow, for instance, the eustachian tubes open up and allow air to flow into or out of the middle ear. You've probably heard your ears "pop" when you change altitudes in an airplane or in an elevator in a tall building. The tiny explosion represents the sudden flow of air during a dramatic change in pressure.

Note in Figure 9.6 that the middle ear contains three bones known as the *ossicles*, the smallest bones in the human body. They are individually called the *malleus* (or hammer), the *incus* (or anvil), and the *stapes* (or stirrup), all referring rather poetically to their shapes. The malleus is connected to the eardrum and the stapes is connected to the oval window.

Two aspects of the middle ear help solve the impedance mismatch problem by increasing the efficiency with which sound is transmitted to the inner ear. The first, and more important, process occurs because the eardrum is much larger than the oval window. You can see this relationship in Figure 9.6. In humans, the ratio of the effective size of the eardrum to the size of the base of the stapes may be as high as 17 to 1 (Yost, 2007). This difference in area helps min-

imize the impedance mismatch because moving the larger area (the eardrum) will move the smaller area (the oval window) more efficiently.

The three ossicles also provide an important mechanical advantage. The shape of the eardrum is such that it increases the force produced by the malleus. Moreover, the lever action of the ossicles also increases the force at the stapes.

Because of the size difference of the eardrum and the oval window and the mechanics of ossicle movement, the magnitude of the incoming sound pressure may be increased by a factor of over 30 dB at the stapes (Yost, 2007). This magnification in the middle ear compensates for much of the loss due to the impedance mismatch between air and the fluid-filled inner ear. As emphasized in Theme 2 of this textbook, our perceptual systems are impressive structures that are well suited to accomplish perceptual tasks.

Another example of the elegance of our perceptual systems comes from the two middle-ear muscles, particularly the one attached to the stapes. The ossicles serve to amplify sounds, but what happens when a very loud sound falls on our ears? If the sound were further amplified by the ossicles, it could damage both the delicate structures of the inner ear and the ossicles themselves. The middle-ear muscles in humans contract in a reflexive fashion shortly after either ear is exposed to sounds above 80 dB, resulting in a decrease of as much as 30 dB (Yost, 2007). However, the major benefit of the reflex may be to minimize the masking effect of the low-frequency sounds (Møller, 2006). Without the middle-ear reflex, we would not hear speech as clearly as we do.

Although there is a brief delay (as little as 25 msec) before the muscles respond to a loud sound, they can actually contract in anticipation of some loud sounds. Though you may not realize it, when you speak you're actually generating quite a bit of sound pressure within your head. In anticipation of that sound, the middle ear muscle attached to the stapes contracts before you begin to speak.

Inner Ear

The hardest bone in the human body is found at each side of the head, and within this bone is found a cavity containing the two structures that make up the inner ear. You learned that the pupil in the eye does not really exist as a separate structure, but is simply the area where the iris is retracted. Similarly, the inner ear does not really exist as a freestanding structure, but is just the area where the bone is absent. As seen in Figure 9.6, the semicircular canals and the cochlea make up the inner ear. The inner ear "is an evolutionary triumph of miniaturization, a three-dimensional inertial-guidance system and an acoustical amplifier and frequency analyser compacted into the volume of a child's marble" (Hudspeth, 1989, p. 397). We will wait until Chapter 12 to discuss the semicircular canals, because they deal with our sense of orientation and not with audition. However, the fluid-filled *cochlea*, which contains receptors for auditory stimuli, is crucial for audition. Cochlea means "snail" in Latin, appropriately describing its coiled shape. Because an understanding of the cochlea is crucial to understanding audition, we will now discuss it in some detail.

The stapes is attached directly to the *oval window*, a membrane that covers an opening in the cochlea. When the stapes vibrates, the oval window vibrates, creating pressure changes in the liquid inside the cochlea. Figure 9.7 shows a schematic diagram of

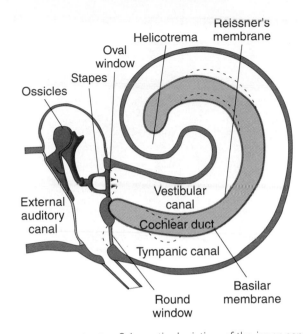

▶ **FIGURE 9.7** Schematic depiction of the inner ear, with the cochlea partially uncoiled. The stapes pushes on the oval window (shown pushed in as a dashed line), displacing the fluid of the vestibular canal. The fluid passes through the helicotrema and into the tympanic canal, causing the round window to move (dashed line) in opposition to the movement of the stapes. The cochlear duct is suspended between the two canals, separated from the vestibular canal by Reissner's membrane and from the tympanic canal by the basilar membrane. The movement of the stapes causes the traveling wave to move along the basilar membrane. The dashed lines along the basilar membrane and Reissner's membrane illustrate the motion.

the cochlea, including the relationship between the stapes and the oval window. If the cochlea were uncoiled, it would be about 1.4 inches long.

Figure 9.7 also shows that the cochlea has three canals running through its entire length. To keep you from being misled by the schematic nature of Figure 9.7, Figure 9.8 shows a cross-section of the cochlea. Figure 9.7, then, shows the relationships among the three canals as if the cochlea were stretched out, whereas Figure 9.8 clarifies the fact that the cochlea is really wrapped around and around itself, like the shell of the snail for which it is named.

The canal into which the stapes pushes is called the *vestibular canal*. At the far end of the vestibular canal is a tiny opening called the *helicotrema*. Here, the fluid can flow through to the second canal, the *tympanic canal*. Notice that the tympanic canal has

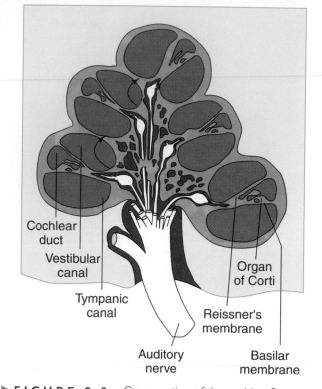

Cochlear
duct

Vestibular
canal

Tympanic
canal

Organ
of Corti

Reissner's
membrane

Auditory
nerve

Basilar
membrane

▶ **FIGURE 9.8** Cross-section of the cochlea. See how the canals wrap around the cochlea. Pay particular attention to the basilar membrane and the organ of Corti as they wind through the cochlea. Note the auditory nerve fibers, and how they reach into the hair cells of the organ of Corti. The actual orientation of the cochlea in the upright head is quite different from that displayed here (see Figure 9.6).

its own membrane-covered opening, the ***round window***. The round window must move in opposition to the oval window, to relieve the pressure on the fluid that fills the vestibular and tympanic canals. If your auditory system didn't have the round window, the stapes would have a difficult time pushing into the oval window.

The ***cochlear duct*** is the smallest of the three canals in the cochlea, and it houses the auditory receptors. The cochlear duct is separated from the vestibular canal by ***Reissner's membrane***, and from the tympanic canal by the ***basilar membrane*** and the bony shelves to which the basilar membrane is attached. Not only is the cochlear duct separate from the other two canals but it also contains a completely different type of fluid.

When the stapes causes the oval window to vibrate, the vibration is transmitted to Reissner's membrane and the basilar membrane, on which the auditory receptors rest. This vibration in turn stimulates the receptors. The basilar membrane is relatively narrow and stiff at its base (near the stapes). As it winds through the cochlea it becomes wider (as the bony shelf to which it is attached gets narrower) and also more flexible. The pattern of vibration within the basilar membrane is referred to as a ***traveling wave***. Have you ever set out with your garden hose to water a distant flowerbed and found that the hose is caught on a rock or curb? If, instead of walking back to the obstruction, you've shaken the end of the hose up and down to free it, you are familiar with a traveling

Stapes end of
basilar membrane

Direction of movement

Helicotrema end of
basilar membrane

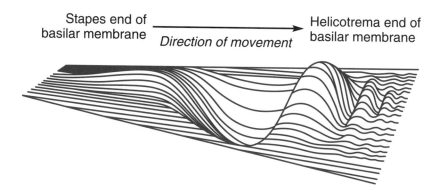

▶ **FIGURE 9.9** Traveling wave moving through the basilar membrane. Notice that the end of the basilar membrane nearer the stapes is narrower than the end near the helicotrema. Also notice how the wave dies down rapidly after peaking.

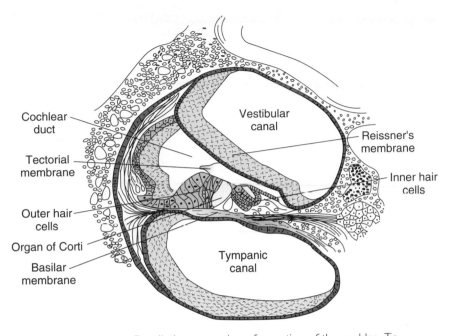

Cochlear duct

Tectorial membrane

Outer hair cells

Organ of Corti

Basilar membrane

Vestibular canal

Reissner's membrane

Inner hair cells

Tympanic canal

▶ **FIGURE 9.10**   Detailed cross-section of a portion of the cochlea. To orient yourself properly, compare this figure to Figure 9.8. Be sure to note the position of the inner and outer hair cells, the basilar membrane, and the tectorial membrane. (Adapted from Bloom & Fawcett, 1975)

wave. As you yank on the hose, a wave travels along the length of the hose, with the wave getting much smaller as it nears the faucet. Figure 9.9 provides a schematic representation of a traveling wave moving along the basilar membrane.

Our understanding of basilar membrane motion and inner ear functioning is the result of the efforts of Georg von Békésy, whose research earned him the Nobel Prize in 1961. Using evidence from mechanical models and cadavers, von Békésy (1960) demonstrated that vibrating the stapes produces a traveling wave along the basilar membrane. We'll have more to say about von Békésy in Chapter 10, but for now it's important to understand that the traveling wave produced by different frequencies peaks at different points along the basilar membrane. Specifically,

higher frequencies peak nearer to the stapes and lower frequencies peak nearer to the helicotrema.

Now let's enter the cochlear duct, which holds several structures crucial to hearing. Figure 9.10 shows an enlargement of the triangular-shaped cochlear duct and the organ of Corti. The ***organ of Corti*** contains the receptors that transduce the pressure energy from a sound wave into the kind of electrical and chemical energy that can be carried through the higher pathways in the auditory system.

The basilar membrane forms the base of the organ of Corti, and the ***tectorial membrane*** rests on top of the organ of Corti. (It may help to remember that <u>b</u>asilar is the <u>b</u>ottom and <u>t</u>ectorial is the <u>t</u>op.) The organ of Corti also includes both kinds of ***hair cells***, some of which are the actual receptors for hearing.

IN-DEPTH

Inner and Outer Hair Cells

The cochlea contains two kinds of hair cells: inner hair cells and outer hair cells. Figure 9.11 (page 252) shows an electron micrograph of these structures, after the

tectorial membrane has been removed. The ***inner hair cells*** are arranged in a single row along the inner side of the organ of Corti, and they are relatively scarce

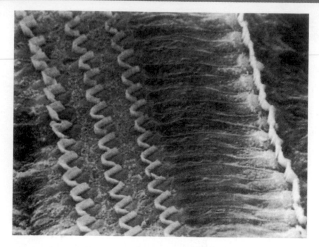

▶ **FIGURE 9.11**   A picture of the inner and outer hair cells, with the tectorial membrane pulled back. The stereocilia of the inner hair cells (single row on the right) and the outer hair cells (three rows on the left) are visible, as is the basilar membrane. (Photo courtesy of Dr. David Lim.)

(about 3,500). Three or four rows of *outer hair cells* are located on the outer side of the organ of Corti, and they are relatively abundant (about 12,000).

Recent research has led to a much greater understanding of the roles played by both types of hair cells. Although the numerical differences between inner and outer hair cells might lead you to compare these cells to the cones and rods of the retina, you'll see that the functions of these two types of hair cells are not analogous to cones and rods. As you will recall, the cones and rods work together to provide us with vision over a wide range of light intensities (cones for higher intensities and rods for lower intensities). There is no equivalent problem in the auditory realm. However, as you'll see, the inner and outer hair cells do work together to provide us with excellent auditory capabilities.

Innervation of the Hair Cells

A large clue to the difference in function between inner and outer hair cells is found in the nature of the innervation of the two types of cells. When discussing the visual system, we focused on neurons that transmit information from a receptor toward the brain areas where the information is processed. In general,

nerve fibers that carry information from a receptor or lower-level brain structure to higher-level brain structures are referred to as *afferent fibers* (from the Latin "to bring toward"). However, you may recall that we also discussed important nerve fibers that carry information downward from higher-level brain structures to lower-level brain structures. These nerves are called *efferent fibers* (from the Latin "to carry away"). You may recall that input from these efferent fibers likely modifies the information flowing through the afferent route.

The *auditory nerve* contains about 30,000 afferent fibers and 500 efferent fibers (Møller, 2006). In the next section, we'll explore the areas of the brain involved in auditory perception, but for now we'll focus on the afferent and efferent fibers in the auditory nerve itself. The crucial difference is that the inner hair cells and the outer hair cells do not share the auditory nerve fibers equally. The relatively scarce inner hair cells have the luxury of "owning" about 90 to 95% of the afferent fibers (Yost, 2007). In contrast, the relatively abundant outer hair cells must share the remaining 5 to 10% of the afferent fibers.

Even though the inner hair cells receive most of the afferent input, they receive none of the efferent input. Instead, even though there are relatively few efferent fibers in the auditory nerve, most of them go to outer hair cells. The remaining efferent fibers actually connect to afferent fibers. Why, then, do so many of the afferent fibers connect to inner hair cells and so few connect to outer hair cells? As you'll soon see, these major anatomical differences are tied to important functional differences.

Anatomy and Physiology of Inner and Outer Hair Cells

The tiny hairs you see extending from the hair cells in Figure 9.11 are called *stereocilia*. In a typical inner hair cell, about 40 stereocilia are formed in the shape of a shallow U. In a typical outer hair cell, about 150 stereocilia are formed in the shape of a V or a W. As you can see in Figure 9.12, each hair cell contains two or more rows of stereocilia, arranged such that the outer row contains longer stereocilia than inner rows. The stereocilia are linked to one another by fine strands called *tip links*. To appreciate how thin these tip links are, keep in mind that the stereocilia

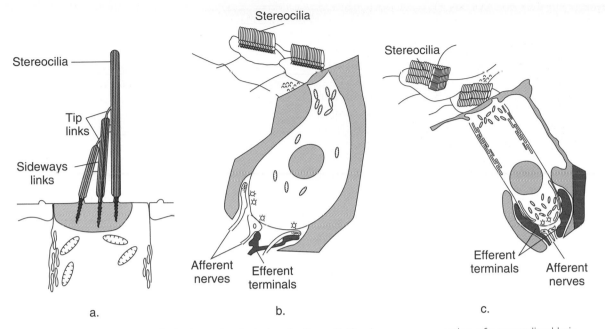

Stereocilia

Stereocilia

Stereocilia

Stereocilia

Tip
links

Sideways
links

Afferent
nerves

Efferent
terminals

Efferent
terminals

Afferent
nerves

a.

b.

c.

▶ **FIGURE 9.12** Detailed schematics for hair cells. Figure 9.12*a* shows a cross-section of a generalized hair cell, with the tip links and sideways links connecting the stereocilia. Figure 9.12*b* shows an inner hair cell; Figure 9.12*c* shows an outer hair cell. (Adapted from Pickles, 1988)

themselves are only about 0.05 micrometers in width (0.000005 centimeters).

Everyone agrees that the transduction of sound information takes place in the hair cells, as a result of stimulation of the stereocilia. If the basilar membrane is displaced just a tiny amount, we can perceive a sound. As you might imagine, then, an even smaller movement of the stereocilia is sufficient to produce a change in the potential of the hair cells. A displacement of 0.3 nm (3/10 of a billionth of a meter) is sufficient to give rise to the perception of sound. According to Dallos (1996), this displacement is the proportional equivalent to the top of the Sears Tower in Chicago moving about 5 cm!

Not only are hair cells exquisitely sensitive to small displacements but they also respond to stimuli that change so rapidly that their motion would not be detectable if they were visual stimuli falling on the retina. What is the source of these abilities? The answer lies in the tip links seen in Figure 9.12. The tip links are mechanical devices, and they initiate the response of the hair cells to basilar membrane displacement (Fettiplace & Ricci, 2006; Furness & Hackney, 2006).

When the stereocilia are displaced toward the outer part of the cochlea, the stereocilia pull on the connecting tip links. Pulling on the tip links allows a greater number of positive ions to flow from the endolymph into the hair cell, depolarizing it. In contrast, when motion displaces the stereocilia toward the inner part of the cochlea, pressure on the tip links is reduced. As a result, the flow of positive ions into the hair cell is closed off, causing the potential of the hair cell to become more negative (hyperpolarized).

In Chapter 3, you learned that the photoreceptors produce graded potentials that ultimately produce action potentials in the bipolar cells and connected neurons. Similarly, the hair cells produce graded potentials that cause action potentials (firing) in afferent bipolar cells of the auditory nerve. When the stereocilia are displaced toward the inner part of the cochlea, the hair cells become hyperpolarized (more negative than their resting potentials). When the stereocilia are displaced toward the outer part of the cochlea, the hair cells become depolarized (less negative than their resting potentials). Hyperpolarization inhibits the firing of the afferent bipolar cells, and depolarization excites the afferent bipolar cells.

The structure of the inner and outer hair cells is actually quite similar. Thus, the outer hair cells can produce graded potential changes (depolarization and hyperpolarization), just like the inner hair cells (He et al., 2006). However, compared to the inner hair cells, the outer hair cells have virtually no afferent connections. For that reason, it's clear that the inner hair cells are responsible for the transduction of incoming sound-pressure changes into neural impulses (Jia et al., 2007; Yost, 2007).

The inner hair cells rest all along the basilar membrane as it winds through the cochlea, with each inner hair cell connected to about 10 afferent neurons. You'll recall that the sound stimulus creates a traveling wave along the basilar membrane, which displaces the inner hair cells. Lower frequency sounds will cause slower vibration of the basilar membrane, with a wave that peaks nearer the helicotrema. Higher frequency sounds will cause faster vibration of the basilar membrane, with a wave that peaks nearer the stapes. Wherever the basilar membrane might be displaced, the peaks and troughs of the wave cause depolarization and hyperpolarization of the inner hair cells, as seen in Figure 9.13. Transduction takes place as the afferent neurons connected to particular inner hair cells fire as a result of the depolarization.

However, can the differential firing of the afferent fibers really explain our ability to make such fine frequency discriminations? We will discuss frequency encoding and pitch perception in greater detail in Chapter 10. For now, though, you should realize that human beings make very fine discriminations among stimuli varying in frequency. (Remember our discussion of the Weber fraction for frequency discrimination at the beginning of this chapter?) We know from von Békésy's research that the traveling wave will peak at different points along the basilar membrane, depending on the frequency of the sound wave. However, in the basilar membranes that von Békéksy studied, the traveling waves are quite similar, even for frequencies that we can easily discriminate. Part of the problem arises because the inner ear is filled with fluid, which dampens movement of the basilar membrane (Brownell, 2006).

If the information in the traveling wave is not sufficient to explain our frequency-discrimination abilities, what might be the source? Thomas Gold (1948, 1989; Gold & Pumphrey, 1948) proposed an early theory in which active fibers in the hair cells produced positive feedback as a sort of cochlear amplifier. Because von Békésy conducted his research on cadavers of many different species, there were *no* active fibers. (The critters were dead!) However, von Békésy's was very influential, and most researchers accepted his theory that the auditory system was linear. As a result, Gold's theory about a nonlinear cochlear amplifier fell on deaf ears, so to speak.

Decades after the notion of a cochlear amplifier was proposed and dismissed, auditory researchers began to argue that our superb frequency-discrimination abilities are partly due to activity of the outer hair cells. As we will discuss in the next section, researchers have found that outer hair cells can elongate and contract, and these movements provide us with our superb frequency-discrimination abilities.

Outer Hair Cell Function

As the basilar membrane vibrates, its motion stimulates both the inner and the outer hair cells. The tectorial membrane further stimulates the outer hair cells. Although it may not be obvious in Figure 9.10, at least the longer stereocilia of the outer hair cells are often embedded in the tectorial membrane. When the basilar membrane moves, it causes the tectorial membrane to pull on the embedded outer hair cells in a shearing motion, which further stimulates the cells.

Given that they have so few afferent connections, what happens when the outer hair cells are stimulated? Unlike the inner hair cells, which move passively along with the basilar membrane, the outer hair cells seem to bounce "up and down like manic kids on a trampoline" (Gutin, 1993, p. 52). This *motility*—the independent elongation and contraction of the cells— is the source of the cochlear amplifier (Brownell, 2006; He et al., 2006; Jia & He, 2005; Yost, 2007). Much like giving a push at just the right time to someone on a swing, the outer hair cells amplify the wave moving along the basilar membrane (Plack, 2005).

What gives outer hair cells such motility? Both types of hair cells contain a number of important proteins such as myosin and actin, which are a significant part of the stereocilia. However, only the outer hair cells contain prestin, a protein found in their lateral walls. Prestin appears to be the crucial piston within the engine that drives outer hair cell motility (Brownell, 2006; Dallos et al., 2006; He et al., 2003; He et al., 2006).

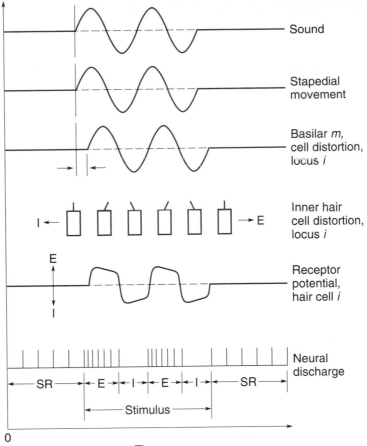

▶ **FIGURE 9.13**   A summary of the auditory transduction process. Moving from left to right in the figure indicates the passage of time. Moving from top to bottom indicates the processes involved. The top of the figure illustrates the changes in the incoming sound stimulus. The sound-pressure changes produce movement in the stapes, which produces movement in the basilar membrane. Basilar membrane motion produces movement of the stereocilia, causing a graded potential response in the hair cells. Depolarization of the hair cells causes increased firing in the connected neurons (E). Hyperpolarization of the hair cells causes decreased firing in the connected neurons (I), relative to the standard rate of firing (SR). (Adapted from Gulick et al., 1989. Used with permission)

The efferent input to outer hair cells must play some role in modifying the response of the outer hair cells. For example, efferent input may well inhibit outer hair cell motility in response to high-intensity sounds, thereby minimizing the risk of damage to the fragile stereocilia (Luebke & Foster, 2002; Luebke et al., 2002; Maison et al., 2002). Efferent connections also enhance the perception of some sounds, while inhibiting other sounds. These connections make it easier to hear sounds in a noisy background (Cooper & Guinan, 2006; Tomchik & Lu, 2006).

One of the reasons that Gold's theory of the cochlear amplifier was not originally accepted is that he also proposed that the feedback would not always be stable, and that the instabilities would actually produce sounds from our ears! This prediction is similar to the totally incorrect notion that the eyes emit light energy (Plack, 2005). You can therefore understand why other researchers were incredulous. Nonetheless, subsequent research has demonstrated that our ears *do* produce sounds.

Otoacoustic Emissions

As strange as it might sound, people actually do emit sounds from their ears. These sounds are referred to as **otoacoustic emissions** (the prefix *oto-* means "related to the ear"). The first person to demonstrate this phenomenon was David Kemp (1978), who presented a click to the ear while a miniature microphone was inserted into the external auditory canal. After a short delay (10 msec), a much weaker echo was recorded. These echoes are known as **evoked otoacoustic emissions**. The search for the source of these evoked acoustic emissions would have been sufficient to occupy auditory researchers for many years. However, shortly after Kemp reported his findings, researchers began reporting that they could record sounds in the external auditory canal *without* presenting a stimulus!

Emissions when no click or tone is presented are called **spontaneous otoacoustic emissions**. These emissions occur in about 50% of people with normal hearing. In some rare cases, spontaneous otoacoustic emissions are loud enough that—without amplification—they can be heard *outside* a person's ear. Surprisingly, the people themselves are totally unaware of the emissions. So the odds are pretty good that at this very moment your ears are emitting a soft sound of which you are totally unaware!

Spontaneous otoacoustic emissions may be produced by instabilities in the feedback system, as predicted by Gold (Yost, 2007). However, they may also be produced by standing waves that arise in the cochlea (Shera, 2003). There are actually a number of different types of evoked otoacoustic emissions, but they all seem to emerge due to the functioning of outer hair cells (Siegel, 2008; Yost, 2007). In fact, if the outer hair cells are not functioning properly, evoked otoacoustic emissions are disrupted (Lonsbury-Martin, 2005; Thornton et al., 2006). As a result, clinicians can now use a test for otoacoustic emissions to determine if the outer hair cells are functioning properly.

This test is particularly useful in infants because it does not require the infants to respond. Nonetheless, these tests are still fairly crude and will likely improve as we learn more about otoacoustic emissions (Shera, 2004).

Cochlear Microphonic

The outer hair cells are also involved in another interesting auditory phenomenon. In 1930, Wever and Bray were recording from the auditory nerve and playing the output through an amplifier and into a speaker. They found that whatever material they played into the ear was faithfully reproduced in their speaker (Wever & Bray, 1930). In other words, if you sang the national anthem into the ear of the auditory nerve from which they were recording, you heard the national anthem through the speaker! The visual equivalent would be passing the output from a microelectrode imbedded in the optic nerve into a television set and seeing on the television screen whatever the eye was looking at.

It turns out that the sounds Wever and Bray were hearing were not summated action potentials from the auditory nerve, as they initially thought. Instead, they were actually hearing graded potentials (depolarization and hyperpolarization), primarily produced by the outer hair cells. These graded potentials, which mimic the waveform falling on the ear, are referred to as the **cochlear microphonic**. The cochlear microphonic replicates not only the frequency characteristics of the wave falling on the ear but also its amplitude over a wide range of pressure (Yost, 2007).

How did researchers learn that the outer hair cells were the primary source of the cochlear microphonic? They could rule out auditory-nerve activity because degeneration of the auditory nerve has no effect on the cochlear microphonic (Gulick et al., 1989). It's also clear that the inner hair cells make little contribution to the cochlear microphonic (Chertoff et al., 2002). Moreover, the cochlear microphonic increases in intensity as an electrode is inserted nearer to the stereocilia of the outer hair cells (Yost, 2007).

After exposure to loud noises, the cochlear microphonic is diminished (Pedemonte et al., 2004). Thus, the cochlear microphonic may play a role in testing one's hearing. That is, an audiologist could diagnose a hearing problem when the cochlear microphonic is diminished or absent. However, even if the cochlear microphonic is *present*, if otoacoustic emissions are absent, it's likely that the outer hair cells have suffered damage (Withnell, 2001).

In summary, current research on the hair cells suggests that the inner hair cells transmit auditory information through the afferent fibers of the auditory nerve. The inner hair cells undergo graded potential changes (depolarizing or hyperpolarizing) as a result of displacement of their stereocilia in one direction or the other. The outer hair cells move independently as a result of stimulation, and thereby influence the movement of the basilar membrane. Outer-hair-cell motility serves as the cochlear amplifier that enhances our ability to make precise frequency discriminations.

Taken as a whole, the auditory system includes an effective distribution of bony structures and elastic structures to guarantee that the sound pressure (which the middle ear works so hard to maintain) is ultimately transmitted to the auditory transducers and then to the auditory nerve. At this point in your reading, jargon shock may have reached an advanced state. Keep in mind, however, that each of these tiny structures has an important function. In Chapter 10, we will explore the ways in which these structures work together to enable us to hear. For now, however, we will trace the path of the auditory information into the auditory cortex.

Higher Levels of Auditory Processing

Just as the optic nerve carries information from the retina to the cortex, the afferent fibers in the auditory nerve carry information from the cochlea to the cortex. As you might then imagine, researchers interested in the auditory system use many of the same methodologies that visual researchers use (e.g., microelectrode recording, electroencephalography, fMRI). In an effort to make the higher levels of auditory processing more comprehensible, we will simplify the descriptions of the components of the auditory system and ignore the efferent pathways entirely.

Researchers can record the activity of an individual fiber in the auditory nerve to determine the frequency to which the fiber is most sensitive. You may recall that we discussed single-cell recording from a simple cell in the visual cortex to determine a visual orientation tuning curve, a graph showing the relationship between the orientation of a line and the cell's response rate. (Look at a representative orientation tuning curve in Figure 3.20, on page 71.)

Similarly, an *auditory tuning curve* is a graph showing the relationship between the frequency of an auditory stimulus and an auditory nerve fiber's response rate. This information can be graphed in several ways. Figure 9.14 shows a typical auditory tuning curve, with stimulus frequency along the *x*-axis and the intensity of sound (in dB) required to produce neural firing along the *y*-axis. Lower decibel values indicate greater sensitivity, because those lower intensities would be sufficient to cause the neuron to fire. The nerve fiber in this diagram is particularly sensitive (has the lowest threshold) to a stimulus around 1000 Hz, a frequency often found in speech. You could cause the cell to fire with other frequencies, but you would have to increase the intensities of those frequencies. For example, for an 800-Hz tone, you would

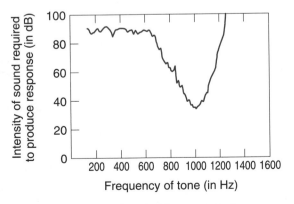

▶ **FIGURE 9.14** A typical frequency tuning curve. The neuron from which this curve was obtained is tuned to a frequency of 1000 Hz because the sound pressure at that frequency is the lowest needed to produce firing. Note the characteristic sharp rise to the right of the curve (for frequencies higher than the tuned frequency).

need to increase the amplitude to 60 dB. Other auditory nerve fibers have frequency tuning curves with sensitivities in other frequency ranges.

Now let's trace the pathway of auditory stimuli, from the inner ear to the auditory cortex. Then we'll see how stimuli are processed within the auditory cortex.

THE PATHWAY FROM THE INNER EAR TO THE AUDITORY CORTEX   After leaving the inner ear, the auditory nerve travels to the *cochlear nucleus*, which is at the bottom of the back part of the brain. (This route is shown schematically in Figure 9.15.) In the cochlear nucleus, the auditory nerve cells transmit their information to new cells. Researchers have not found inhibitory connections within the auditory nerve, but they do exist in the cochlear nucleus. The lateral inhibition found in the cochlear nucleus probably serves to enhance frequency resolution (Yost, 2007).

You may recall that the visual system has a complex mechanism for ensuring that the information from each eye goes to both sides of the brain. Similarly, in the auditory system, output from each of the two cochlear nuclei goes to the *superior olivary nucleus* on the same side of the brain as that cochlear nucleus, as well as to the superior olivary nucleus on the opposite side of the brain. Because the auditory nerve and the cochlear nucleus on either side of the head receive input only from the cochlea on that side of the head, the auditory information is *monaural* (*mono* means "one"). Beyond the cochlear nuclei, however, the auditory information is *binaural* (*bi* means "two"). As you can see in Figure 9.15, input from both ears is present at the superior olivary nucleus and beyond. The binaural auditory information at the superior olivary nucleus and beyond allows our auditory system to compare the information from the two ears. We will discuss the significance of this comparison in Chapter 10 when we focus on how we determine the direction from which a sound is coming.

Each superior olivary nucleus sends its information to an *inferior colliculus*, which is just below (or

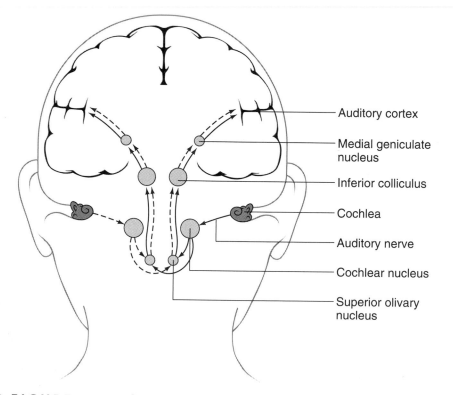

▶**FIGURE 9.15**   Schematic representation of the pathway from the ear to the brain. Only structures on the right side have been labeled; notice corresponding structures on the left side. Notice also that input from both ears is present from the superior olivary nucleus onward.

Labels in figure:
- Auditory cortex
- Medial geniculate nucleus
- Inferior colliculus
- Cochlea
- Auditory nerve
- Cochlear nucleus
- Superior olivary nucleus

inferior to) the superior colliculus discussed in the anatomy of the visual system (see Figure 3.16). Auditory information also travels to the superior colliculus, which contains an aligned spatial map from both the auditory and visual systems, as well as motor information (Carney, 2002). The inferior and superior colliculi play a role in many auditory reflexes, such as the startle response (muscles contracting in response to a loud noise) and turning your head toward a sound source.

The inferior colliculus also illustrates a principle for organizing auditory information. Remember that parts of the visual system demonstrated a retinotopic organization. That is, information from adjacent areas of the retina is represented in adjacent areas of the lateral geniculate nucleus, as well as in the visual cortex. Similarly, the auditory system is arranged in terms of frequency information. This arrangement is referred to as a **tonotopic** organization, meaning that neurons sensitive to similar frequencies are found near one another in the inferior colliculus.

As we mentioned previously, higher frequencies cause the greatest displacement along the basilar membrane near the stapes. Lower frequencies cause the greatest displacement along the basilar membrane near the helicotrema. Thus, the correspondence operates as if a map of the basilar membrane were laid out on the inferior colliculus. Spatial position on the retina is crucial for vision, which leads to retinotopic organization. Frequency information is crucial for audition, which leads to tonotopic organization. Given its importance, tonotopic organization continues into the auditory cortex (Hackett & Kaas, 2003). The highly organized cortical regions found in both the auditory and visual systems provide an example of the similarities of our senses (Theme 1 of this text).

From the inferior colliculus, information passes on to the **medial geniculate nucleus** of the thalamus, a structure near the lateral geniculate nucleus of the visual system. The medial geniculate nucleus also exhibits tonotopic organization (Hackett & Kaas, 2003). Moreover, most of the cells in the medial geniculate nucleus receive information from both ears. This arrangement allows the auditory system to compare both intensities and times of arrival—information vital for auditory localization.

Incidentally—and consistent with the tonotopic organization—we should mention that the auditory tuning curves discussed earlier are not unique to the auditory nerve. Afferent neurons in the medial genic-

ulate nuclei (as well as the cochlear nuclei, the superior olivary nuclei, and the inferior colliculi) also exhibit auditory tuning curves. In other words, at all these points between the cochlea and the cortex, each nerve fiber is particularly sensitive to a fairly narrow frequency range.

PROCESSING IN THE AUDITORY CORTEX   Information from the medial geniculate nucleus next travels to the **primary auditory cortex**, which is in a deep groove on the temporal lobe of the cortex (at the side of the brain). Its inaccessible location in primates makes it quite challenging to study, so much of this research has been conducted using cats (Yost, 2007). Nonetheless, researchers are making progress in studying human auditory cortex (using functional imaging) and macaque monkey auditory cortex, which is quite similar to humans (Recanzone & Sutter, 2008).

We have pointed out several similarities between auditory processing and visual processing—similarities that provide additional evidence for Theme 1 of this book. In the visual system, many areas of the brain that are not explicitly "visual" have an impact on visual perception. Thus, it should come as no surprise that areas outside of the auditory system have an impact on auditory perception (Zatorre, 2007).

Another similarity between the auditory and visual cortex is that both contain regions that play vital roles in processing complex stimuli. Recall that some cells in the visual cortex respond optimally to certain visual features, such as the orientation of a line or its movement pattern. Similarly, some cells in the auditory cortex respond to more complex characteristics of stimuli than simple frequency and intensity (Hackett & Kaas, 2003). For instance, in some species, specialized neurons respond to vocalizations such as the complex calls made by members of that species. As in the visual system, the nature of the effective stimulus becomes more complex as you record from cells higher in the auditory system.

How essential is the auditory cortex? People with disorders in this region have difficulty discriminating changes in the timing within a sequence of sounds. They usually have a major problem with speech perception. They also have difficulty localizing sounds in space. Thus, the auditory cortex is essential for more complex kinds of auditory tasks.

DEVELOPMENT AND PLASTICITY   We've already discussed the importance of experience, a topic to which we'll return in Chapter 14. For now, it's important to point out that neural organization in the auditory system is not entirely fixed at birth; rather, it is influenced by experience. For example, there are critical periods in which auditory experience is crucial. Birds that don't hear their species' song at the right time are incapable of producing that song properly (e.g., Heaton et al., 1999).

The connections in the auditory cortex are certainly malleable, depending on the organism's experience (Chang et al., 2005; de Villers-Sidani et al., 2007; Nakahara et al., 2004; Zhang et al., 2001). For example, ordinarily cells in the auditory cortex are not sensitive to visual orientation. However, suppose you route visual input into auditory cortex. Sharma and colleagues (2000) did this with ferrets, and they found that the cells will become orientation sensitive! Moreover, the auditory cortex can be used to process visual stimuli in a person whose hearing is severely damaged (Finney et al., 2001). Such plasticity certainly underlies the effectiveness of the cochlear implants we'll discuss in the next section.

Section Summary

The Auditory System

1. The outer ear consists of the pinna, the external auditory canal, and the tympanic membrane.

2. The middle ear contains three bones—the malleus, the incus, and the stapes—important in reducing the effects of the impedance mismatch between air pressure and the fluids of the inner ear.

3. The inner ear contains the cochlea, which houses the organ of Corti, a structure that contains the auditory receptors, or hair cells. The organ of Corti lies on the basilar membrane and is covered by the tectorial membrane.

4. The inner ear has relatively few inner hair cells, although they monopolize most of the afferent auditory nerve fibers. In contrast, the inner ear has relatively many outer hair cells; although they share a small number of the afferent auditory nerve fibers, they receive most of the efferent fibers. Outer hair cell motility is responsible for amplifying the traveling wave on the basilar membrane, though it may be modified by efferent input.

5. Transduction in the inner ear is due to displacement of the stereocilia of the inner hair cells. The tip links of the stereocilia are crucial to the rapid response of hair cells to displacement.

6. The graded potentials of the hair cells serve as input to the afferent fibers of the auditory nerve.

7. The auditory nerve has nerve fibers sensitive to particular frequencies; this nerve travels to the cochlear nucleus. The auditory pathway continues to the superior olivary nucleus, then to the inferior colliculus, then to the medial geniculate nucleus, and finally to the auditory cortex.

8. Parts of the inferior colliculus and the auditory cortex are organized tonotopically; furthermore, some cells in the auditory cortex respond to complex characteristics of sounds. The auditory cortex is essential for sound localization, speech perception, and other complex auditory tasks.

Hearing Impairments and Treatments

As we discussed the auditory system, many components (e.g., ossicles and hair cells) may have struck you as exceedingly fragile. That realization should remain with you when you attend a loud concert or crank up the volume of your iPod. Exposure to loud sounds can lead to severe hearing loss. Hearing problems can also emerge for a variety of other reasons (e.g., exposure to certain chemicals such as toluene, antibiotics such as streptomycin, or even aspirin). We'll discuss a number of different hearing impairments, but first let's explore how hearing deficits are assessed.

Assessing Auditory Sensitivity

Generally speaking, measurement of auditory sensitivity is called *audiometry*. We've already discussed how testing for otoacoustic emissions can assess whether the outer hair cells are functioning properly. The current test isn't capable of providing detailed information about the nature of hearing deficits. However, it has the advantage of requiring no response, making it a good test of outer hair cell damage in infants.

When testing adults, audiologists typically use the method of constant stimuli to determine the absolute threshold for a series of pure tones presented monaurally. They typically use a set of tones such as 250, 500, 1000, 2000, 3000, 4000, 6000, and 8000 Hz. Audiologists then measure the decibel difference at each frequency between a person's threshold and the average threshold of a normal population (Martin & Clark, 2005). A test that adheres more closely to real-world auditory experience is the Hearing in Noise Test, which tests the ability to hear sounds against background noises. Another technique, called *electric response audiometry*, involves recording electrical activity at locations in the auditory pathway in response to auditory stimulation. Other hearing tests measure the perception of speech sounds.

As a result of such testing, people's auditory sensitivity may be classified in a number of different ways. Generally speaking, a deficit of 90 dB or more is described as profound hearing loss. To consider this loss in terms of vision deficits, recall that 20/200 vision means that a person sees at 20 feet what a person with normal vision would see at 200 feet. A person with profound hearing loss would need to increase the intensity level of a sound by 90 dB above the level needed by a person with normal hearing. That's a huge intensity increase! Moderate to severe hearing loss is characterized as a deficit of about 60 dB. If you think of a normal conversation as occurring at roughly 60 dB, you'll note that with moderate to severe hearing loss, you would miss most of the content of typical conversations.

In the United States, over 28 million people are hearing impaired. About three-quarters of those people are over 55 years of age. Just as the visual system is affected by advancing age (presbyopia), so is the auditory system. *Presbycusis* (sometimes called *presbyacusis*) refers to the loss of hearing (typically higher frequencies) that often accompanies the aging process (Dubno & Mills, 2003; Yost, 2007). Such hearing loss is more common in men than women, with presbycusis the most common chronic condition among men over 65 years of age. Low folate levels are associated with a number of problems, including such age-related hearing loss, so taking folic acid may help (Dobie, 2007).

Before considering two broad categories of hearing loss, we'll first consider an interesting, but annoying, hearing disorder called *tinnitus*. As you'll note, tinnitus is often associated with many of the disorders that give rise to hearing loss.

Tinnitus

Tinnitus is a persistent noise, such as a ringing or hissing, in one's ears in the absence of any auditory stimulus (Andersson, 2007; Snow, 2008). Thus, one might well describe it as a phantom sound (Eggermont, 2005; Eggermont & Roberts, 2004). Most people have experienced a brief bout of tinnitus, but for some people the condition becomes chronic. The ringing or noise does not seem to be particularly loud for most sufferers. However, for a small subset (about 2% of the population), the disturbance is sufficiently severe as to affect their lives. For instance, Till Fellner, a concert pianist, could not perform or even teach music for several months due to the discomfort of tinnitus (Mermelstein, 2007). He also experienced a hypersensitivity to sounds that often accompany tinnitus.

Because tinnitus may be due to a number of different causes, it's difficult to tell you how to avoid it. However, it is often associated with some of the forms of hearing loss that we will next consider. As we better understand the neural underpinnings of tinnitus, we may also develop effective treatments for the disorder (Eggermont, 2005; Noreña & Eggermont, 2006). For now, however, there is no effective treatment for tinnitus beyond strategies to help the sufferer cope with the disorder.

Conductive Hearing Loss

As the name implies, *conductive hearing loss* involves problems in conducting the sound stimulus; the problem occurs in either the external ear or the middle ear. We have already mentioned one category of conduction deafness, which results from a puncture of the eardrum.

Ear infections are another common disorder, especially among young children. In an ear infection, the eustachian tube becomes swollen, cutting off the middle ear from the respiratory tract. Bacteria may multiply in the middle ear, resulting in a painful earache and the presence of fluid in the middle ear, which may impair sound conduction. You may hear this condition referred to as *otitis media with effusion*. The medical community was concerned that children who have frequent ear infections might have difficulties developing normal language. Two common treatments for this disorder were antibiotics and the insertion of small tubes into the eardrum. In fact, the insertion of those tubes was so common, it's quite likely that you underwent that operation yourself. In the recent past, it was the second most common pediatric surgical procedure (behind circumcision). Although the topic is somewhat controversial, current research suggests that inserting ear tubes is not an effective treatment (Paradise et al., 2005; Paradise et al., 2003; Smith et al., 2006).

A final source of conductive hearing loss that we'll discuss is otosclerosis. *Otosclerosis* is an inherited bone disease in which the ossicles (particularly the stapes) may calcify and become immobilized. As you might imagine, restriction of the lever action of the ossicles impairs conduction of the sound stimulus. Treatment of otosclerosis may involve replacing the calcified ossicles with artificial ones (Yost, 2007).

Sensorineural Hearing Loss

In contrast to conductive hearing loss, *sensorineural hearing loss* occurs due to problems in the cochlea or in the auditory nerve. For example, extremely loud noises may destroy the stereocilia of the hair cells in the organ of Corti. (Figure 9.11 showed intact hair cells.) Because the stereocilia of outer hair cells are embedded in the tectorial membrane, they are especially susceptible to damage. In fact, the entire hair cell may be damaged by even very brief exposure to loud sounds (Hu et al., 2006). The outer hair cells don't transduce the sound stimulus. However, if they are destroyed, then the cochlear amplifier doesn't work properly, which causes hearing loss as surely as damage to inner hair cells.

But you can take some comfort in the fact that inner and outer hair cells will regenerate—as long as you're a bird, a fish, or an amphibian. If you're a human, you're out of luck! There is some promising research suggesting some hope for regeneration of hair cells in the future (Kros, 2007; Shou et al., 2003; Tennesen, 2007). However, for now you'd be well advised to take great care with your precious auditory system.

Exposure to Loud Sounds

For ethical reasons, psychologists cannot present extremely loud sounds to humans. Therefore, one approach is to present loud, but safe, tones to humans for short periods and to observe the temporary changes that occur in hearing ability. A second approach is to present extremely loud sounds to other animals to observe the impact on their auditory systems.

Extended exposure to some sounds can make it more difficult to hear sounds that are presented afterwards. For example, *auditory adaptation* may occur when one tone is presented continuously; the perceived loudness of that tone decreases as time passes. In normal ears, a short exposure to a continuous tone produces loudness adaptation of 15 to 20 dB (Moore, 2004). Thus, a tone that was initially presented at 80 dB might appear to be only 60 dB after a 3-minute exposure. A number of factors (e.g., frequency, intensity, complexity) affect the extent of adaptation, but the auditory system exhibits the sort of adaptation seen in the visual system (consistent with Theme 1).

Some sounds result in a more long-lasting effect called *auditory fatigue*, such that when a sound is presented and then turned off, subsequently presented sounds are harder to hear. At the very least, auditory fatigue results in a *temporary threshold shift*, which is a temporary increase in a hearing threshold as a result of exposure to a loud sound (Moore, 2004). A number of factors (e.g., frequency, intensity, and duration) influence the extent of the temporary threshold shift. For low intensities (e.g., below 75 dB) people don't usually experience auditory fatigue. However, even moderate intensities (e.g., from 80 to 105 dB) can produce temporary threshold shifts, with the size of the shift growing with longer exposures (Yost, 2007).

A temporary threshold shift, as the name implies, may last for shorter or longer durations, but people eventually recover. Exposure to some sounds, however, can lead to severe anatomical damage that has more lasting effects (Nordmann et al., 2000). A *permanent threshold shift* is a permanent increase in a hearing threshold as a result of exposure to a loud sound. Sometimes a permanent threshold shift is produced by a single loud noise, such as an extremely loud firecracker explosion. More often, permanent threshold shifts result from repeated exposures to loud sounds.

In many cases, people are exposed to such loud sounds in their work or home environments. In other cases, people actually seek out such loud sounds, as at music concerts where sound intensities may exceed 120 dB (Moore, 2004). Because of sensory deficits that accompany aging, you would probably predict hearing loss in older people (presbycusis). However, many young people also experience hearing loss as a result of regular exposure to loud music through portable music players and loud concerts (Daniel, 2007; Maassen et al., 2001). The "safe" exposure to such loud sounds is extremely brief. So, to prevent permanent hearing loss, you should seriously consider reducing the volume of your iPod and using ear plugs at concerts or fireworks displays. In Switzerland, producers of concerts are required by law to provide such ear plugs (Mercier et al., 2003). You should learn to treat your auditory system as the extremely delicate instrument it is. Otherwise, you may be forced to consider one of the treatments for permanent hearing loss that we will discuss next.

Treatments: Hearing Aids and Cochlear Implants

Some forms of both conductive and sensorineural hearing loss may be treated with hearing aids. Hearing aids are becoming increasingly sophisticated (and expensive), as researchers work to make the devices more effective. In the past, many people with hearing deficits were unwilling to use hearing aids because their auditory experience was not sufficiently improved by the devices. As you consider the many types of hearing disorders, you can understand why it's difficult to develop effective hearing aids.

Conductive hearing loss often involves an equal loss of intensity across the range of frequencies, so hearing aids that amplify all frequencies may be effective. Some people who suffer from conductive hearing loss may also benefit from a hearing aid (Baha) that is implanted in the bone behind the pinna. This type of hearing aid conducts the sound through the bone surrounding the inner ear, thereby bypassing the outer and middle ear entirely.

Sensorineural hearing loss due to damage of hair cells in specific locations may also be corrected by hearing aids that amplify specific frequencies. For example, a person may not require amplification of the low-frequency tones but does require amplification of some high-frequency tones. However, many people with sensorineural hearing loss also show a disorder related to loudness perception, called *recruitment*. **Recruitment** is a condition in which a person with some sensorineural hearing loss perceives very loud sounds normally. This person's perception does not differ from the perception of an individual with normal hearing, if we consider only loud sounds.

However, this person may not hear low-intensity sounds of some frequencies. Thus, you can see how recruitment complicates the task of designing hearing aids. The hearing aid must deal with two problems: a differential sensitivity to the various pitches and a differential sensitivity to the various loudnesses.

People with more serious sensorineural hearing loss may consider receiving a cochlear implant. A cochlear implant consists of an external microphone, a signal processor, and then a number of microelectrodes dispersed throughout the cochlea. Those microelectrodes stimulate the afferent neurons appropriate to the frequencies present in the sound stimulus. Current cochlear implants are effective, as long as the auditory nerve is intact (Clark, 2004; Rubinstein, 2004; Zeng, 2004). In the future, devices may be able to bypass the auditory nerve and send information directly to the brain (Rauschecker & Shannon, 2002).

It's clear that the neural information provided by a cochlear implant is impoverished, relative to a normally functioning auditory system. Nonetheless, the device allows people to hear auditory stimuli as complex as speech (Shannon et al., 2004). One indicator of the effectiveness of cochlear implants is in the number of people who have chosen to undergo the operation to install the device. To date, over 60,000 people have received cochlear implants, with increasing numbers of people receiving the implants each year (Niparko, 2004). Evidence suggests that a combination of a hearing aid in one ear and a cochlear implant in the other ear may be even more effective than a cochlear implant alone (Ching et al., 2005).

Unfortunately, cochlear implants are not always completely successful in restoring hearing (Pisoni & Cleary, 2004). It's not yet clear why some people benefit more than others. However, with sustained research interest and increasing numbers of recipients of cochlear implants, it's clear that future refinements will lead to greater effectiveness of these devices.

Section Summary

Hearing Impairments

1. Tinnitus is a ringing in the ears that results from a variety of causes.

2. A person with conductive hearing loss shows a consistent loss of hearing at all frequencies. Because the sound stimulus is not properly con-

ducted, this person can be helped by a hearing aid. Conductive hearing loss results from outer-ear or middle-ear impairments, such as punctured eardrums, ear infections, or otosclerosis.

3. A person with sensorineural hearing loss shows a deficit at certain frequencies, although hearing may be normal for other frequencies; this person often shows recruitment. Thus, designing a hearing aid for people with sensorineural hearing loss is difficult because of their differential sensitivity to various pitches and loudnesses.

4. Auditory adaptation produces a decreased perceived loudness for a tone that is presented continuously.

5. Auditory fatigue occurs when a loud noise is presented and then turned off, making subsequent tones more difficult to hear. Auditory fatigue can lead to a temporary threshold shift or a permanent threshold shift.

6. Electronic devices, such as hearing aids and cochlear implants, can restore hearing to many people with hearing impairments.

Review Questions

1. Describe the auditory stimulus with respect to frequency, amplitude, phase, and complexity. Then turn back to Chapter 3 and compare the auditory stimulus with the visual stimulus. For instance, how do the perceivable auditory and visual stimuli differ in frequency?

2. Draw a rough sketch of the auditory system, identifying the parts of the outer ear, middle ear, inner ear, and the pathway from the inner ear to the auditory cortex. Point out the similarities between the higher levels of auditory processing and the higher levels of visual processing.

3. The organ of Corti should strike you as quite different from the retina, yet both structures perform similar transduction functions for audition and vision. Describe the similarities and differences between the two structures. To what extent do you think the differences are due to the nature of the differences between the auditory and the visual stimuli? What might be the source of the similarities between the organ of Corti and the retina?

4. You might think of the auditory system as a type of game. The goal of the game is to deliver the auditory stimulus to the receptors so that the dB level is as high as possible. You lose points because of some events, and you gain points because of other events. Describe this "game" with particular attention to the obstacles (e.g.,

impedance mismatch) and the means of overcoming them.

5. Discuss the two kinds of hair cells and the functions they serve in providing our auditory experience.

6. Inserting a microelectrode into the auditory nerve resembles the procedure used in studying the activity of ganglion cells in the optic nerve. Work through the similarities and differences between the activity in the auditory and optic nerves. Do you think that there is any equivalent of the cochlear microphonic in the visual system? Support your answer.

7. Compare the visual and auditory pathways in the brain, focusing on the nature of the information and its organization in each sensory system. Be sure to discuss the locations at which the visual system can compare information from the two eyes and the locations at which the auditory system can compare information from the two ears. Why might such comparisons may be important?

8. Tinnitus might be confused with otoacoustic emissions. Given the definition of tinnitus and the evidence on otoacoustic emissions, why would you argue that the two are different?

9. Suppose that you know two people who are deaf. One has conduction deafness and the other has sensorineural deafness. List various ways in

which the perceptual experiences of these two people would differ.

10. A cochlear implant operation may cost over $40,000 (and batteries can cost as much as $300/year). Costly as it is, the operation is not always completely successful. If you had a deaf child, would you want your child to undergo this operation? What arguments might you use to justify this costly procedure for your deaf child? Would your arguments change if you were talking about an older person who had recently become deaf? What do your arguments tell you about the importance of our auditory sense?

Key Terms

pure tone, p. 242
cycle, p. 242
sounds, p. 242
frequency, p. 243
Hz, p. 243
absolute thresholds, p. 243
difference threshold, p. 243
complex tones, p. 244
amplitude, p. 244
dyne, p. 245
sound-pressure level (SPL), p. 245
decibel (dB), p. 245
phase angle, p. 246
pinna, p. 247
external auditory canal, p. 247
eardrum, p. 247
tympanic membrane, p. 247
impedance, p. 247

impedance mismatch, p. 247
eustachian tube, p. 247
ossicles, p. 248
malleus, p. 248
incus, p. 248
stapes, p. 248
cochlea, p. 249
oval window, p. 249
vestibular canal, p. 249
helicotrema, p. 249
tympanic canal, p. 249
round window, p. 250
cochlear duct, p. 250
Reissner's membrane, p. 250
basilar membrane, p. 250
traveling wave, p. 250
organ of Corti, p. 251
tectorial membrane, p. 251
hair cells, p. 251
inner hair cells, p. 251
outer hair cells, p. 252

afferent fibers, p. 252
efferent fibers, p. 252
auditory nerve, p. 252
stereocilia, p. 252
tip links, p. 252
motility, p. 252
otoacoustic emissions, p. 256
evoked otoacoustic emissions, p. 256
spontaneous otoacoustic emissions, p. 256
cochlear microphonic, p. 256
auditory tuning curve, p. 257
cochlear nucleus, p. 258
superior olivary nucleus, p. 258
monaural, p. 258
binaural, p. 258
inferior colliculus, p. 258
tonotopic, p. 259

medial geniculate nucleus, p. 259
primary auditory cortex, p. 259
audiometry, p. 260
electric response audiometry, p. 261
presbycusis, p. 261
tinnitus, p. 261
conductive hearing loss, p. 261
ear infections, p. 261
otosclerosis, p. 262
sensorineural hearing loss, p. 262
auditory adaptation, p. 262
auditory fatigue, p. 262
temporary threshold shift, p. 262
permanent threshold shift, p. 263
recruitment, p. 263

Recommended Readings

Everest, F. A. (2001) *Master handbook of acoustics* (4th ed.). New York: McGraw-Hill.

If you have an applied interest in sound, you'll enjoy this text. It provides illustrations of sound wave propagation in various settings that are quite useful to recording engineers.

Martin, F. N., & Clark, J. G. (2005). *Introduction to audiology* (9th ed.). Boston: Allyn & Bacon.

This textbook has a clinical orientation, so it's helpful not only for providing a general perspective on the audi-

tory system but also for specific information about hearing impairments and hearing assessment. The enclosed CD is a useful ancillary for teaching about hearing.

Møller, A. R. (2006). *Hearing: Anatomy, physiology, and disorders of the auditory system* (2nd ed.). New York: Academic.

Although Møller's text is not pitched at the introductory level, the illustrations are quite nice and the chapters on anatomy are clearly written.

Rossing, T. D., Moore, F. R., & Wheeler, P. A. (2002). *The science of sound* (3rd ed.). San Francisco: Addison-Wesley.

If you want to learn more about sound waves, and how musical instruments, the human voice, and stereos produce them, this is the book for you. It's very interesting reading, and it provides coverage of a wealth of interesting topics.

Yost, W. A. (2007). *Fundamentals of hearing: An introduction* (5th ed.). New York: Academic.

This book provides a fairly detailed overview of the topics considered in this chapter. Yost does a particularly good job of explaining the complexities of the anatomy and physiology of audition.

Basic Auditory Functions

CHAPTER 10

THE NEXT TIME you watch a movie at a theater, close your eyes for a couple of minutes and consider all of the auditory information that is present. Some of the sounds will be high in pitch and others low. You'll likely be able to distinguish the actors' voices—even if they're roughly the same pitch. Some of the sounds will be louder and some softer. If the audio system is of sufficiently high quality, some of the sounds will seem to come from one direction and some from other directions. It's truly amazing, but all of these perceptual experiences emerge from sound waves causing a very tiny, thin, hairy piece of tissue on each side of your head to bounce wildly up and down in a complex fashion. In this chapter, we'll discuss how organisms extract these different perceptual qualities from the sound pressure changes in the environment. We begin by studying the perceptual experience of pitch.

Pitch Perception

Pitch is an attribute of a sound stimulus that can be ordered on a scale from low to high, such that it may be used to construct melodies (Plack & Oxenham, 2005). Both simple sine waves and complex waves can create the perceptual experience of pitch. However, to keep matters relatively simple, at the outset it may help to think of sound stimuli as pure sine waves. Thus, low-frequency sine waves give rise to a low pitch, and high-frequency sine waves give rise to a high pitch. You can revisit www Demonstration 9.2 to hear how the physical property of frequency is tied to your perceptual experience of pitch. Given the frequency-pitch relationship, we learn a lot about pitch perception by studying how frequency information is encoded in the inner ear. Keep in mind, however, that the relationship between frequency and pitch is not a simple one. After we look at the encoding of frequency information, we will shift our attention to the complexities of that relationship.

In Chapter 9, we examined how sound waves are transmitted into the inner ear. We also touched briefly on how sounds of particular frequencies create different traveling waves that move along the basilar membrane. We'll now explore two broad approaches to frequency encoding that emerged—place theory and temporal theory.

Background: Early Theories of Pitch Perception

A *place theory* proposes that particular frequencies are encoded at specific locations on the basilar membrane (see Figure 9.7). Such theories have existed since the 1600s, but their modern versions can be traced to Hermann von Helmholtz (1863), the nineteenth-century researcher whose work we've discussed throughout the book. Helmholtz knew that the width of the basilar membrane increases from the area near the stapes toward the area near the helicotrema. He proposed that the basilar membrane consists of a series of transverse fibers under tension, with each segment resonating to a tone of a particular frequency (Bell, 2004). Just as particular strings of a harp or a piano will vibrate in response to high-amplitude sound waves, so Helmholtz thought that the fibers in the basilar membrane vibrated in response to sound stimuli.

Helmholtz's theory was flawed in several ways. For example, the basilar membrane is *not* under tension. Furthermore, even if the basilar membrane fibers were under tension, the range of basilar membrane widths could not produce the wide range of frequencies to which humans are sensitive. Given the problems with early place theory, you shouldn't be surprised that a competing theory developed.

William Rutherford (1886) argued that the rate of vibration of the basilar membrane was crucial for pitch perception. He was very much influenced by advances in the communication technology of his era—specifically, the telephone. The vibrations of the diaphragm in the telephone produce electrical changes that encode complex auditory stimuli. Rutherford needed only a short conceptual leap to infer that the vibrations of the basilar membrane produced electrical changes in the neurons of the auditory nerve.

According to *temporal theory*, the basilar membrane vibrates at a frequency that matches the frequency of a tone. This part of the original theory is essentially correct. For example, the membrane vibrates 25 times each second for a 25-Hz tone and 1,600 times each second for a 1600-Hz tone. The vibration rate in turn causes nerve fibers in the auditory nerve to fire at a matching rate—for example, 25 times each second. Neurons can easily keep pace with a 25-Hz tone. But what about the 1600-Hz tone? As we mentioned when discussing the visual system, neurons take a rest after firing, called the **refractory period**. This refractory period restricts the maximum number of responses to 1,000 each second, still an impressive rate. If a neuron is limited to 1,000 responses a second, how can we hear frequencies of 1600 Hz, let alone 20,000 cycles per second? Thus, early temporal theory seems as flawed as early place theory.

Developments in Place Theory

The details of Helmholtz's place theory are not accurate, but Georg von Békésy further developed the spirit of his theory. As you might recall, a **traveling wave** describes the physical motion of the basilar membrane, as illustrated in Figure 9.9. The traveling wave would reach a peak of maximum displacement at some point, which would then create the greatest displacement of the stereocilia in that area.

The location of this maximum-displacement point depends on the frequency of the auditory stimulus. For example, a low-frequency tone of 25 Hz produces the greatest displacement in a region near the helicotrema. In contrast, a higher-frequency tone of 1600 Hz produces the greatest displacement in the middle of the basilar membrane. Thus, when a 1600-Hz tone is played, stereocilia in the inner hair cells of the organ of Corti will be bent the most at the point where the traveling wave peaks. These particular stereocilia will therefore produce the greatest change in electrical potential in the hair cells, which will ultimately be passed along through the auditory nerve.

The frequency of the sound determines not only the location of the peak along the basilar membrane but also the sharpness of that peak. To simplify the picture, researchers often just display the **envelope** of the traveling wave—a line connecting the peaks of the wave as it progresses. Figure 10.1a (page 270) shows a side view "snapshot" of a typical traveling wave moving along the basilar membrane, with the peaks of the waves connected to form the envelope. The traveling-wave envelopes shown in Figures 10.1b through 10.1d illustrate that low-frequency stimuli (e.g., Figure 10.1b) reach their peaks toward the helicotrema and have relatively wide peaks. In contrast, high-frequency stimuli (e.g., Figure 10.1d) reach their peaks near the stapes and have relatively sharp, narrow peaks. Békésy determined that the basilar membrane is stiffer near the stapes than at the helicotrema, which causes the traveling wave to die out more rapidly near the stapes (Yost, 2007).

The peak of the traveling wave is also apparent in studies of stimulation deafness. In a **stimulation deafness experiment**, animals are exposed to an extremely high-amplitude tone of a particular frequency. Although this technique is crude, it illustrates the differential effects of frequency on the basilar membrane. The delicate stereocilia are damaged by the loud tone. A loud low-frequency tone damages the stereocilia nearer the helicotrema, and the damage extends over a fairly wide area. A loud high-frequency tone damages the stereocilia nearer the stapes, and the range of damage is fairly narrow. Note that the nature of the damage to the stereocilia is consistent with the traveling-wave envelopes shown in Figure 10.1. (Keep these stimulation deafness experiments in mind the next time you're tempted to crank up the volume on your iPod!)

It would be unethical to conduct stimulation deafness experiments on humans, but naturalistic studies have produced similar data. People who work in environments with very loud noises often experience hearing losses for particular frequencies. Some terminally ill patients with such hearing losses allowed their inner ears to be examined postmortem. Hair-cell damage occurs at exactly the portions of the basilar membrane that one would have predicted from the hearing losses observed in the patients before death.

Auditory tuning curves, such as the one you saw in Figure 9.14, also confirm the importance of place information. Figure 10.2 (page 271) shows three auditory tuning curves, each illustrating the differential sensitivity of a different auditory neuron. Remember that the auditory tuning curve represents the activity of an auditory neuron when tones of particular frequencies and amplitudes are played. The x-axis represents the frequency of the tone presented, and the y-axis represents the amplitude of the tone necessary to produce firing in the neuron.

In Figure 10.2, the low point on the curve is the frequency to which the neuron is "tuned," because the neuron requires the least stimulation to fire at that frequency. Higher and lower frequencies might cause the neuron to fire, but these stimuli would require greater amplitude. The neuron from which the recording is being made is connected to hair cells

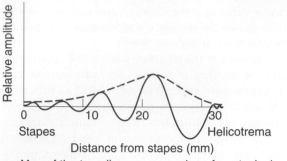

a. Map of the traveling wave envelope for a typical auditory stimulus

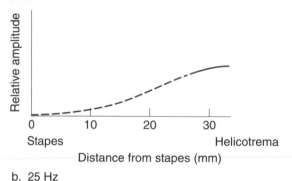

b. 25 Hz

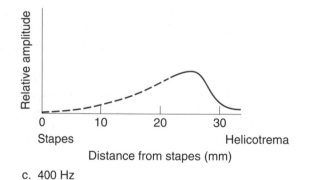

c. 400 Hz

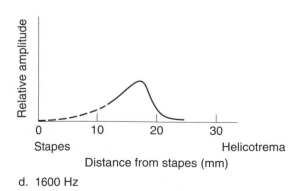

d. 1600 Hz

▶ **FIGURE 10.1** Traveling waves envelopes. Part *a* shows how the envelope is determined, by connecting the high points of the traveling wave. Parts *b* through *d* show the traveling wave envelopes for increasingly high-frequency sounds. Note that the peaks of the envelopes are wider and nearer the helicotrema for low-frequency sounds and narrower and nearer the stapes for high-frequency sounds. Note, also, that the relative amplitude of the waves reaches a maximum, then decreases rapidly. (From von Békésy, 1960)

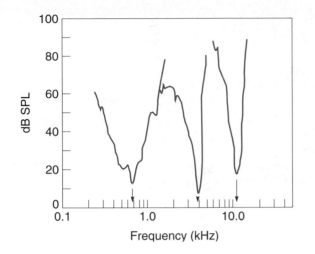

FIGURE 10.2 Representative tuning curves for three neurons in the auditory nerve. The low points for each of the curves is the frequency (*x*-axis) for which the smallest sound pressure (*y*-axis) can cause firing in the neuron. Note that this point is sharper for the high-frequency sounds. The curves are also steeper to the right than to the left of the low point in all cases. The steepness is due to two factors. First, the traveling wave of higher-frequency sounds dies out rapidly. Thus, increasing the amplitude of higher-frequency sounds is not sufficient to affect points further along the basilar membrane. Second, the axis is logarithmic, which places higher frequencies closer together. (From Kiang, 1975)

at a particular location along the basilar membrane. Thus, the place to which the neuron is connected is most sensitive to a particular frequency. Such place information is retained in the tonotopic organization found through portions of the brain devoted to auditory information.

In spite of all the evidence for place theory, some problems have lingered. For instance, human frequency-discrimination abilities are much more precise than one would expect, given the relatively wide peaks of the traveling waves studied by von Békésy. As we noted in Chapter 9, this paradox was partially resolved when it became clear that the discrepancy emerged because von Békésy depended on cadavers for his models. The outer hair cells play an active role in a living person because these hair cells sharpen the traveling wave. However, these cells cease to function when a person is dead.

More recent techniques allow researchers to observe inner-ear functioning in live animals. For instance, in one technique (the Mössbauer technique) a small radioactive source is placed on the basilar membrane. By measuring shifts in radiation frequency, a researcher can determine the velocity of the basilar membrane at the location of the radioactive source. In another technique, a laser beam is directed at a tiny gold mirror that has been placed on the basilar membrane. Using these techniques, researchers determined that the peak of the traveling wave is much sharper than Békésy had thought (Yost, 2007).

Nonetheless, it's clear that we can discriminate many low-frequency tones whose traveling waves have similar peaks. Place theories of pitch perception also face problems when researchers study complex waves, so we need to turn our attention to those stimuli.

COMPLEX WAVES AND TIMBRE If we dealt only with simple sine waves, we might be able to derive a simple theory of pitch perception. Alas, the world is not that simple. Remember that in our everyday experience, complex waves are far more common auditory phenomena than pure sine waves. Thus, we hear voices, musical instruments, and a variety of environmental noises—all of which produce complex waves. In fact, most people go for days without experiencing a sound that approximates a pure tone.

However, as you've learned about Fourier analysis (e.g., in Chapter 5), you've come to appreciate that any complex wave can be broken down into constituent pure sine waves. Using the tool of Fourier analysis, we can determine the components of a complex sound. Figure 10.3 (page 272) shows the graphic results of such an analysis.

The pure sine-wave components of the complex sound are called ***harmonics***. The component of a complex tone that has the lowest frequency is called the ***fundamental frequency***, or the *first harmonic*. Thus, 200 Hz is the fundamental frequency in a complex tone comprised of 200 Hz, 400 Hz, 600 Hz, and 800 Hz. The other harmonics of a complex tone may also be called ***overtones***. In this example, 400 Hz, 600 Hz, and 800 Hz could be considered the second, third, and fourth harmonics *or* the first, second, and third overtones. Using another example, if you play the A above middle C on the piano, the fundamental frequency of 440 Hz is produced. In addition, the vibrations of the multiple piano strings produce overtones of 880 Hz (2 × 440) and 1320 Hz (3 × 440), as well as higher-frequency overtones.

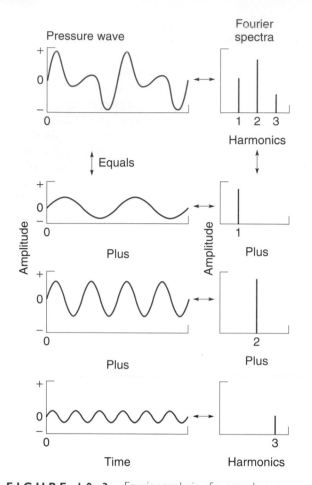

▶ **FIGURE 10.3** Fourier analysis of a complex wave. The complex wave is shown at the top of the figure, with a typical representation of a Fourier analysis shown to the right of the complex wave. The Fourier analysis indicates that the complex wave is composed of a fundamental frequency (1) with moderate amplitude, an overtone of twice the fundamental frequency (2) and high amplitude, and an overtone of three times the fundamental frequency (3) and very low amplitude. Each of these three waves is shown separately in the lower part of the figure. If you were to take each discrete point in time along the x-axis and add up the amplitudes of the three waves in the lower part of the figure, you would arrive at the complex wave seen at the top of the figure (Fourier synthesis). (From Handel, 1989)

The fundamental frequency typically contributes the greatest amplitude to the complex tone, but the harmonics also contribute substantially. Suppose that you play the A above middle C on a variety of instruments. The fundamental frequency of 440 Hz will be produced in each case, so the pitch will be identical for all instruments. One instrument, however, may emphasize the overtone of 880 Hz; this overtone may have a greater amplitude than other overtones. In contrast, a different instrument may emphasize the overtone of 1320 Hz.

You might think of our ears as Fourier analyzers—analyzing complex tones and detecting the energy present in the fundamental and harmonics. In doing so, we gain information that may allow us to distinguish among the sounds made by different instruments. Some instruments, such as the flute and piccolo, have very few overtones, and any overtones that do exist have relatively low amplitude. As a consequence, the tones produced by these instruments approximate pure tones. In contrast, other instruments, such as the guitar, have many high-amplitude overtones. As a consequence, the tones produced by the guitar sound thick and rich.

The psychological quality **timbre** (pronounced "tamber") corresponds to the physical quality of complexity. Timbre is a tone's sound quality. Two sounds may have the same pitch and the same loudness yet differ in timbre. A piece of chalk squeaking across a blackboard seems different in quality from the sound produced by a valuable violin. Furthermore, they both seem different from the voice of a soprano— even though all three sounds may be nearly identical in pitch and loudness. Furthermore, think about two males you know whose voices are similar in pitch and loudness but quite different in timbre. We'll have more to say about timbre in the next chapter. For now, you should know that differences in the particular mix of fundamentals and the harmonics contribute to a sound's timbre, but they don't determine it completely.

COMPLEX WAVES AND THE PROBLEM OF THE MISSING FUNDAMENTAL   Helmholtz and others thought that the fundamental frequency in a complex sound determined the pitch of the sound. However, it turns out that other harmonics are actually more important in determining the pitch of a sound (Plack, 2005). In fact, the fundamental frequency doesn't need to be present at all! The **missing fundamental** refers to a complex sound in which the upper harmonics are present but the fundamental frequency is absent.

Let's now consider an example of a complex tone with a missing fundamental. Suppose that an experimenter combines 400-Hz, 600-Hz, 800-Hz, and 1000-Hz tones to produce a complex tone. We'll have more to say about simultaneously presented tones later in the chapter, but for now you need to understand that you would not hear the separate pure tones. Instead, you would hear a complex sound. However, you would not hear it as a complex tone with a 400-Hz fundamental frequency. (Note that 600 Hz and 1000 Hz would not be overtones of a 400-Hz fundamental.) Instead, listeners report that they hear a pitch similar to the pitch produced by a 200-Hz tone. Even though no 200-Hz tone is present, all of the tones in the complex tone are overtones of a 200-Hz tone.

In a way, the case of the missing fundamental is similar to illusory contours. With sufficient context, the visual system can see an illusory contour that is not physically there. Similarly, with the overtones providing sufficient context, the auditory system can hear a tone that is not physically there. Try www Demonstration 10.1 to get a sense of the missing fundamental.

Can you see why the missing fundamental is a problem for place theory? With no 200-Hz component to the complex sound, no activity should exist at the 200-Hz location on the basilar membrane. Nonetheless, people typically report hearing a pitch consistent with a 200-Hz tone. Actually, instead of removing the fundamental, it's better to mask the fundamental with a lot of noise. J. C. R. Licklider (1915–1990) used that approach to demonstrate the missing fundamental. Licklider (1954) presented a scale of pure tones in alternation with the same scale made up of complex tones. Then he turned on noise that wiped out the pure tones and the fundamentals of the complex tones. People could no longer hear the scale produced by the pure tones, but they could still hear the scale produced by the complex tones. So the *place* on the basilar membrane where the scale information is presumably encoded could not be the source for the scale heard by the audience, because the noise was overriding any activity in that part of the basilar membrane.

Developments in Temporal Theory

We've just seen that place theory seems to have a major problem. Can the alternative—temporal theory—provide an adequate explanation of pitch perception? Remember that the problem with Rutherford's temporal theory was that neurons could not fire at a rate fast enough to encode the high frequencies that humans can clearly hear. E. Glen Wever (1902–1991) was a prominent advocate of temporal theory. He proposed a *volley principle*, whereby groups of neurons share in producing the required firing rate (Wever,

1949). Consider an analogy. Suppose that, for some obscure reason, you want to produce one scream each second for about a minute. This task would be impossible for you alone, but with the appropriate community effort, you and four friends could organize your screams so that you would take turns. Each of you would need to produce only one scream every 5 seconds—a manageable task. The net result, however, would be the required one scream per second. Similarly, a 1000-Hz tone could be registered if each of five neurons fired 200 times each second—again, a manageable task.

However, for the volley principle to encode frequency information, the auditory neurons would need to fire in an organized, systematic fashion. The reality is not so neat. Neurons don't take systematic turns, but for frequencies below 5 kHz they do tend to fire near the peak of a sound wave. Due to *phase locking*, neurons "lock onto" the peak of a wave and fire. As you see in the Figure 10.4, as long as each neuron

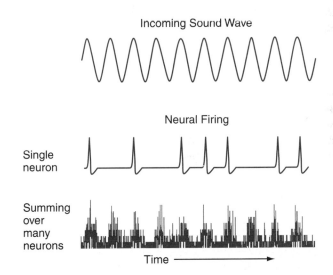

▶ **FIGURE 10.4** Phase locking. At the top of the figure is the incoming sound wave, with changes in sound pressure. In the middle of the figure is the activity of a single neuron, which tends to fire near the peak of the sound wave. However, note that this neuron does not fire at each peak, so it could not encode the frequency of the sound wave by itself. Another single neuron might fire for some of the same peaks as the neuron portrayed here, but it would also fire for other peaks. As a result, as seen at the bottom of the figure, the cumulative activity of a large number of neurons actually mimics the incoming sounds wave. Think of each vertical line as representing the number of neurons firing, so higher lines represent more neurons firing at that one time.

tends to fire at the peak of the wave, the collective firing over a number of neurons will be consistent with the frequency of the sound wave (Plack, 2005; Yost, 2007). Given that neurons fire for no reason at all (maintained activity), the pattern of neural firing doesn't precisely mirror the sound wave input. At higher frequencies (e.g., above 5000 Hz) phase locking appears to break down, so temporal theory would not work for very high frequencies. However, although we can hear such high frequencies, they don't have melodic characteristics, so they don't give rise to a sense of pitch. Thus, temporal information may be effective for the range of frequencies that give rise to pitch perception.

How Do We Perceive Pitch?

Thus far, we have briefly reviewed the historical development of theories of pitch perception. You might expect that by now researchers would have produced a definitive theory of pitch perception—but they have not. Pure tones occur with great regularity inside research laboratories and only rarely in the "real world." Both place and temporal information are likely useful for these pure tones. The pitch of low-frequency pure tones is probably encoded by temporal information. In contrast, the pitch of high-frequency pure tones is probably encoded by place information (Moore, 2004). For the fairly ubiquitous complex tones, theories of pitch perception have become quite complicated. However, place and temporal information continue to play important roles.

Many of the theories emphasize the role of temporal information in the perception of the pitch of complex tones (de Cheveigné, 2005; Moore, 2004; Plack, 2005). However, Andrew Oxenham and his colleagues (2004) constructed a clever experiment that illustrated the importance of place information. They shifted the temporal information for a low-frequency tone so that it excited hair cells that would normally encode high-frequency tones. Thus, the auditory system had all the temporal information needed to perceive a low-frequency tone. However, people who heard these tones did not hear the proper pitch, indicating that the places that complex tones excite along the basilar membrane are crucial for pitch perception (Shamma, 2004).

Researchers will continue to investigate the role of place and temporal information in pitch perception, but it seems likely that both play important roles. Furthermore—even though the inner ear and auditory

nerve play important roles in coding pitch information—the areas of the brain to which that information is sent are also crucial for pitch perception.

For example, in a classic study, Houtsma and Goldstein (1972) showed that pitch perception can emerge at stages of processing beyond the inner ear. They modified the typical missing fundamental experiment by presenting one overtone to the left ear and another overtone to the right ear. People reported hearing the fundamental frequency for which the two tones were overtones. Because neither ear alone had sufficient information to determine the missing fundamental, our perception of pitch must be due not only to inner ear activity but also to higher-level processing that includes input from both ears.

As we noted in Chapter 9, many areas of the auditory system exhibit tonotopic organization, with similar frequencies encoded in nearby areas of the auditory system. However, some of these neurons may be sensitive to pitch rather than frequency. That is, not only do these neurons respond to a particular tone (e.g., 200 Hz) but they also respond to its overtones (e.g., 400 Hz, 600 Hz, 800 Hz, etc.), even if the fundamental frequency is absent (Bendor & Wang, 2005; Zatorre, 2005).

In fact, it may well be that the area of the brain responsible for pitch perception lies outside of the primary auditory cortex as it is anatomically defined. A number of studies indicate that portions of Henschl's gyrus near the primary auditory cortex play a vital role in pitch perception (Bendor & Wang, 2006; Krumbholz et al., 2003; Penagos et al., 2004; Schneider et al., 2005). However, it's not yet clear where a pitch center might be located (Hall & Plack, 2007). Moreover, given neural plasticity, experience will have an impact on the areas of the brain that process pitch information (Pantev, Weisz et al., 2003; Schulte et al., 2002).

The Complex Relationship between Frequency and Pitch

Throughout this text, we've emphasized an important point: Although the physical stimulus drives a perceptual experience, it does not determine it completely. We'll now consider a number of examples to illustrate the complexity of the relationship between the frequency of a sound and your perception of its pitch.

As we've just noted, research indicates that experience affects our perception of pitch. Thus, some musicians may actually be more sensitive to pitch information than nonmusicians (Fujioka et al., 2004; Micheyl et al., 2006; Pantev, Ross et al., 2003; Seither-Preisler et al., 2007; Tervaniemi et al., 2005). Or people who have been blind from an early age may well hear pitch better than others who have not been as reliant on their auditory input (Gougoux et al., 2004). Thus, the same sound frequency input may lead to slightly different perceptions of pitch, depending on our experience.

Our discussion of the missing fundamental provides another indication of the complex relationship between sound frequency and pitch. You may recall that in metameric matching, the color of a particular wavelength could be matched by combining three other wavelengths. Thus, color perception is not tied to a particular wavelength. Similarly, with the missing fundamental, different combinations of overtones can give rise to the same perception of pitch.

There are other reasons that complicate the relationship between the physical stimulus of frequency and the perceptual experience of pitch. Some of the reasons are general psychophysical ones. For instance, some sound frequencies are too low or high to be audible to humans, so no sense of pitch will be created. Even among audible frequencies, if they are too high (e.g., above 5000 Hz), no clear sense of pitch will emerge (Plack, 2005).

Presenting tones for a very brief duration also disrupts pitch perception. With extremely short-duration tones, the abrupt onset and offset of the tone produces a broad distribution of frequency components that will cause it to be heard as a click.

Given our emphasis on the importance of context throughout the text, you won't be surprised to learn that pitch perception can be affected by context. As we'll discuss further in the next chapter, we organize sounds using some of the same Gestalt principles we discussed in connection with vision (Plack, 2005). Consider a complex sound with a fundamental frequency of 200 Hz and overtones of 400 Hz, 600 Hz, 800 Hz, and 1000 Hz. If you were to raise the third overtone from 800 Hz to 900 Hz, the perceived pitch of the complex tone would go up. However, if you first started playing the 900 Hz tone by itself and *then* played a complex tone comprised of 200, 400, 600, and 1000 Hz, its pitch would not go up. Instead, you'd hear it as a complex tone with a pitch of 200 Hz (with a 900-Hz tone playing simultaneously). In other words, the two complex tones (containing 200 Hz, 400 Hz, 600 Hz, 900 Hz, and 1000 Hz) are identical. However, your perception of their pitch would be quite different if the 900-Hz tone doesn't come on at the same time as the rest of the tones.

Is pitch related to the frequency of a tone? Yes, definitely! As we have seen, however, the relationship between frequency and pitch is not simple. The complex relationship between frequency (a physical quality) and pitch (a psychological quality) adds further evidence to the complexities in perceptual processes we've been addressing throughout the text. In the next section, we'll discuss the complex relationship between sound intensity and loudness. Before doing so, however, we should note that sound intensity also affects pitch. For instance, with pure sine waves, low-frequency tones appear to have a *lower* pitch as their intensity increases (Everest, 2001; Fastl & Zwicker, 2007). Contrarily, high-frequency tones appear to have a *higher* pitch as their intensity increases. Even with the complex waves produced by musical instruments such as the trumpet, as intensity increases, the high-frequency components become more pronounced. The Doppler Shift (e.g., changes in the pitch of a train's whistle as it rapidly approaches) is another example in which intensity changes can affect pitch perception (McBeath & Neuhoff, 2002).

Measuring Pitch

We talked about the units of measurement used to scale the physical attribute, frequency. We can determine the frequency of a sound with great precision. Unfortunately, no one can construct an equally accurate pitch meter. Because pitch is a psychological phenomenon, we cannot measure it directly. Pitch exists only in a listener's head.

Musicians and psychologists have both tackled the problem of a scale for pitch. Musicians have developed all sorts of terms to label pitch (Shepard, 1999a). For example, consider a keyboard instrument, where you'll note that there is a recurrent pattern of seven white keys. Each of these keys is given a different name (C, D, E, F, G, A, B), which is referred to as a **tone chroma**. Thus, within a set of keys, D would have a higher pitch than C, E would have a higher pitch than D, and so on. As illustrated in Figure 10.5, each tone chroma can appear at a different **tone height**. Each successive height is separated by an **octave**, which represents a doubling of frequency. Thus, from one A to either the next higher A or the next lower A is an octave difference. For instance, middle A has a fundamental frequency of 440 Hz, so its pitch is higher than middle C, which has a frequency of about 262 Hz. At the next

Tone height

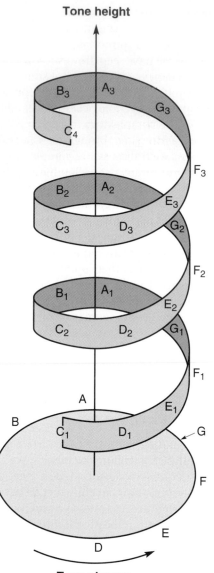

Tone chroma

▶ **FIGURE 10.5** Schematic diagram of pitch, showing tone chroma and tone height. This spiraling representation captures the nature of perceived pitch better than a linear representation (e.g., a piano keyboard) because it illustrates the basic similarity of tone chromas.

higher octave, A has a frequency of 880 Hz, and at the next lower octave, A has a frequency of 220 Hz.

In describing the pitch of pure tones, psychologists often use the mel scale, which was suggested by S. S. Stevens, John Volkman, and Edwin Newman (1937). You may recall Stevens's name from the discussion of Stevens's power law and magnitude estimation in Chapter 2. In the *mel scale*, a 1000-Hz pure tone is arbitrarily assigned a pitch of 1000 mels. Then listeners are asked to adjust a comparison tone until it seems to be half as high as this 1000-Hz tone; this tone is assigned a value of 500 mels. To complete the scale, listeners locate comparison tones that represent other fractions and multiples of the standard 1000-Hz tone.

Section Summary

Pitch Perception and Related Phenomena

1. Two major types of theory explain how the ear registers frequency information:

   a. Place theories propose that each sound-wave frequency causes a traveling wave, which makes a particular place on the basilar membrane vibrate to a greater extent than other places.

   b. Temporal theories propose that sound-wave frequency is matched by the vibration rate on the basilar membrane, which then causes nerve fibers in the auditory nerve to fire at a matching rate; the volley principle is added to explain higher frequencies.

2. Timbre, a tone's sound quality, corresponds to complexity, which involves the combination of sound waves. The auditory system performs a crude Fourier analysis to analyze a complex sound wave into its components. The nature of the overtones is one determinant of the timbre of musical instruments and the timbre of human voices.

3. For pure sine waves, place information may suffice to explain how we perceive the pitch of high-frequency tones, and temporal information may suffice to explain how we perceive the pitch of low-frequency tones. Both place and temporal information are likely crucial for perceiving the pitch of complex waves, but no model can yet fit all the data.

4. The psychological experience of pitch is largely driven by the physical stimulus of frequency. However, the relationship is not a simple one, because different combinations of frequencies give rise to the same pitch or the same combinations of frequencies give rise to different pitches.

5. Musicians measure pitch in a number of ways (e.g., tone chroma, tone height, octaves). Psychologists measure pitch with the mel scale.

Loudness Perception

How Do We Perceive Loudness?

Consistent with Theme 1, both our visual system and our auditory system have evolved to encode an enormous range of intensities. As you may recall from Chapter 9, we can accurately measure auditory intensities using the decibel scale. Because it is a logarithmic scale, the fact that we can hear intensities from about 0 dB to over 120 dB may not sound that impressive. However, this range of intensities is roughly 1,000,000,000,000 to 1 (Moore, 2004).

Sound intensity is the physical stimulus that gives rise to the perception of *loudness*. However, as we've seen over and over, the relationship between the physical stimulus and the psychological experience is not simple. For loudness, we can provide a simplistic and basically correct explanation for how intensity is coded as loudness. You should be able to make a simple bet about a more accurate explanation: It will be both more complex and more controversial.

To understand how loudness might be encoded, stretch a rubber band over an open box. The rubber band represents your basilar membrane. A low-intensity sound would cause little displacement of the basilar membrane, roughly equivalent to pressing down lightly on the rubber band. A high-intensity sound would cause much greater displacement of the basilar membrane, roughly equivalent to pressing harder on the rubber band. Instead of looking at the rubber band where you've placed your finger, look to the sides of your finger as you press down. You should note that when you press down harder on the rubber band, you've displaced more distant points along the rubber band.

If you now consider the afferent neurons attached to the inner hair cells all along the basilar membrane, you should have a sense of the explanation. For low-intensity sounds, it might be that only those neurons at the point of displacement would fire. Look back at the auditory tuning curves in Figure 10.2. Note that a 1000-Hz tone with little energy (or basilar membrane displacement) could cause a neuron to fire if that neuron is tuned to 1000 Hz. Recall that a neuron is particularly sensitive to a frequency because it is connected to the hair cells at a particular location along the basilar membrane.

However, you *could* get the neuron to fire with a different frequency so long as you increased the intensity. That is, a neuron tuned to 1000 Hz would also fire for an 800 Hz tone, but the 800-Hz tone would need to be more intense than the 1000-Hz tone. In general, as you increase the intensity of a sound, more and more of the hair cells along the basilar membrane would be displaced sufficiently to cause them to fire. Thus, the number of neurons firing along the basilar membrane encodes loudness. You could think of loudness as the sum of activity of neurons in the auditory nerve (Moore, 2004; Plack, 2005).

This theory of loudness perception has much to recommend it. On the other hand, loudness perception is too complex a process to arise from simply summing the neural firing in the auditory nerve. For instance, most of the neurons reach their maximum firing rate with intensities around 60 dB. How might they contribute to our perception of sounds as loud as 100 dB? As in the case of pitch perception, so many factors influence loudness perception that a complete explanation will require a fairly complex theory. We'll now discuss a number of factors that influence loudness perception, complicating the relationship between amplitude and loudness.

The Complex Relationship between Amplitude and Loudness

A more complete theory of loudness perception will need to address a number of different factors that influence loudness. One factor that affects loudness perception is the duration of a tone, with tones of longer duration appearing louder than tones of shorter duration but equal amplitude (Fastl & Zwicker, 2007). For example, using the magnitude estimation method, people reported that a 200-ms sound is louder than a 5-ms sound of equal amplitude (Epstein & Florentine, 2006).

As is often the case, the context in which a sound occurs also affects loudness. When our ears are "fresh," as when we've just awakened, a sound will appear to be louder than that same sound after we've been listening to some loud sounds. Similarly, when we listen to the same continuous tone, it seems to decrease in loudness over time. Such context effects are examples of adaptation, which we've discussed in the context of a number of visual stimuli. Try **www** Demonstration 10.2 to illustrate the influence of previous sounds on loudness perception.

Another type of context is produced by the other sounds that occur in proximity to the target sound. For example, observers listened to a sequence of low-frequency tones of low amplitude alternating with high-frequency tones of high amplitude. These observers judged the high-frequency tones to sound softer due to the immediate context in which they occurred (Marks, 1994). When people listened to low-frequency tones of high amplitude alternating with high-frequency tones of low amplitude, they heard the high-frequency tones as louder (Arieh & Marks, 2003).

A final factor may be the most important of all: Perceived loudness depends on the frequency of a tone. We noted earlier that pitch perception depends on the amplitude of a tone. Similarly, loudness perception depends on the frequency of a tone. The exact same amplitude of a sound (e.g., 40 dB) sounds louder if it is presented at 1000 Hz than if it is presented at 100 Hz. Try www Demonstration 10.3 to experience the impact of frequency on loudness.

The relationship between stimulus frequency and loudness perception is most often illustrated in *equal loudness contours* (also called *Fletcher-Munson curves*). The basic procedure for determining an equal loudness contour is simple: One tone (e.g., a 1000-Hz tone) is presented at a particular intensity level (e.g., 40 dB). This tone serves as a reference tone throughout the experiment. A comparison tone of a different frequency is then varied in amplitude until the listener judges its loudness to be equal to that of the reference tone; this amplitude is recorded. Then the procedure is repeated with tones of other frequencies. The relationship between tone frequency and the number of decibels required to produce a tone of equal loudness is called an **equal loudness contour**. As the name suggests, all the points along an equal loudness contour sound equally loud.

Figure 10.6 shows a set of seven different equal loudness contours in which the reference tone is presented at amplitudes up to 120 dB SPL. Let's first concentrate on the lowest curve, marked "hearing threshold." This curve represents the absolute threshold of audition for varying frequencies. For instance, the reference tone of 1000 Hz is just barely audible at about 5 dB. Suppose that observers are asked to match the reference tone with an equally loud (i.e., just detectable) tone of 5000 Hz. As you can see, they adjust the amplitude to about 0 dB. Likewise, if asked to match the reference tone with a tone of 20 Hz, they set the 20-Hz tone to about 75 dB. The rest of that "hearing threshold" line seen in the figure is obtained by presenting the range of frequencies to the observers, who match the loudness of each frequency to the reference loudness. The lowest line on the figure represents the absolute thresholds for the typical audible range of frequencies.

Before moving on, let's be sure that you are clear on the lowest equal loudness contour (for absolute thresholds). Because all of the points on that line are equally detectable, and just barely detectable, what would happen if you presented a frequency at an amplitude that would be below the line? For instance, suppose you presented a 20-Hz tone at 40 dB. What would an observer report? If you said "Nothing!" you're absolutely correct. A 20-Hz tone requires more sound pressure than 40 dB to be audible. To add more evidence to the points we've been making about distinctions between physical and perceptual dimensions, notice that an equal level of sound pressure (40 dB) for other frequencies (e.g., 1000 Hz) would be clearly audible (i.e., above the lowest curve).

Let's make two more points about equal loudness contours. First of all, notice that for each curve the smallest amplitude required to match the reference tone is at 3000 to 5000 Hz. This finding is entirely consistent with the sensitivity information presented in Chapter 9—we are most sensitive to frequencies in this range. Second, notice that the higher curves are also flatter. That is, the range of amplitudes on the contour becomes attenuated. For the lowest curve, the smallest amplitude needed to match the reference tone is below 0 dB and the highest amplitude is above 70 dB. The 100-dB reference contour is the highest curve that shows the full range of frequencies. Here, the smallest and largest amplitudes are about 90 and 130 dB, respectively. Therefore, at higher amplitudes, audible frequencies are perceived to be more similar in loudness than is the case at lower amplitudes.

If you have understood all this, you can now appreciate the function of the loudness (or loudness boost) button found on many stereos. If you never play your stereo at a low amplitude, you'll never need to touch your loudness button. The loudness button functions to boost the amplitude of low-frequency sounds while leaving higher-frequency sounds untouched. As we mentioned earlier, the difference between the low-frequency sounds and the higher-frequency sounds is more pronounced at lower amplitudes. Pushing in a loudness button selectively raises the amplitude of these lower frequencies, without affecting the other frequencies—essentially flattening the equal loudness contour. At low amplitudes, the bass guitar might be difficult to hear. With the loud-

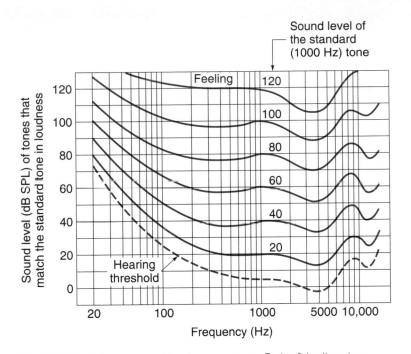

▶ **FIGURE 10.6**   Equal loudness contours. Each of the lines is an equal loudness contour, so any point along the line will sound equally loud. The figure illustrates the relationship between sound pressure and frequency in determining our perception of loudness. The low points on each curve indicate that for certain frequencies (roughly 1000 to 5000 Hz) less sound pressure is necessary for the sound to appear as loud as other frequencies outside of that range. The dashed curve (labeled "Hearing threshold") represents the minimal pressure necessary to hear a pure tone at each frequency level. Pressure-frequency combinations that fall below the dashed curve would not be audible. The area above the highest curve (labeled "Feeling") represents pressure-frequency combinations that are perceived as pressure or pain as much as sound. (Adapted from Fletcher & Munson, 1933)

ness button engaged, the bass guitar would become appropriately loud.

Now shift your attention to the curve in Figure 10.6 representing the points obtained in matching the 1000-Hz reference tone at 80 dB. Suppose you present a 1000-Hz tone, as well as a 20-Hz tone, both at an amplitude of 80 dB. Which would an observer say was louder? The observer should report that the 1000-Hz tone is louder (even though it has equal amplitude). How much sound energy would you have to put into the 20-Hz tone for the observer to say that it seemed as loud as the 1000-Hz tone? Roughly 110 dB. Suppose that you left your loudness button engaged but turned up your stereo so that it was pumping out 80 dB of sound pressure. Now the bass guitar will be far too loud!

Intensity Discrimination

Researchers are interested not only in the relationship between amplitude and loudness perception (and factors that might influence that relationship) but also in listeners' abilities to discriminate intensities. In terms of the discussion in Chapter 2, psychologists are also interested in discrimination of intensity differences, or just noticeable differences (jnd's)—that is, relative to a comparison stimulus, how large a change is needed for a new stimulus to appear different.

As we discussed in Chapter 2, a Weber fraction is roughly constant and represents the ratio of a jnd to a specific intensity. Sound intensity discrimination depends on the nature of the sound. For both white noise (a complex sound with components from a wide frequency range) and pure tones, the Weber fraction is quite high for low-intensity sounds (i.e., below 30 dB). For amplitudes between 30 and 80 dB, both white noise and pure tones yield a Weber fraction of about 0.10. However, at higher intensities the Weber fraction for pure tones decreases, whereas the Weber fraction for white noise remains roughly the same.

For complex sounds, the situation is also different. David M. Green (1987) has argued that people can detect changes in complex sounds by comparing the activity taking place all along the basilar membrane at one instant in time, a process he calls **profile analysis**. Intensity discrimination of complex sounds is much more difficult when the two sounds have substantially different component frequencies. Conversely, when the profiles created by complex sounds are more similar, observers can detect very small changes in the intensity of just one of the component frequencies. So the Weber fraction cannot be easily determined with complex stimuli, because the component frequencies of the complex sound have a strong influence on discriminability.

Measuring Loudness

In the discussion of pitch, we saw that musicians and psychologists have developed methods for measuring pitch. Likewise, musicians and psychologists have developed methods for measuring loudness. Musicians, for example, scale loudness in terms of an eight-level marking system that ranges from *ppp* for the very softest sound (about 30 dB) through *fff* for the very loudest sound (about 90 dB).

Psychologists measure loudness in a number of different ways. One of the most widely used systems is the sone scale (Stevens, 1955). The **sone scale** is a scale of loudness obtained by the magnitude estimation technique. In the sone scale, a 40-dB pure tone at 1000 Hz is arbitrarily assigned a loudness of 1 sone. Researchers asked listeners to judge the loudness of other tones in relationship to this standard tone. Thus, a tone that appears to be twice as loud would be judged as 2 sones, and a tone that appears to be half as loud would be judged as 0.5 sone.

In general, Stevens found that for sound pressures above 40 dB, the tone had to be increased by 10 dB for listeners to judge it to be twice as loud. Thus, a 50-dB tone appeared to be twice as loud as a 40-dB tone; the 50-dB tone would therefore equal 2 sones. We noted earlier that about 6 dB of sound pressure represents a doubling of physical intensity, so a doubling of physical intensity does not produce a doubling of *perceived* loudness for sounds above 40 dB. Below 40 dB, loudness grows more rapidly with changes in intensity.

The sone scale has been criticized because people's judgments are heavily influenced by the order in which stimuli are presented, the range of stimuli, and other biasing factors (Moore, 2004). Nevertheless, many researchers continue to use the sone scale.

Section Summary

Loudness Perception

1. Loudness depends mainly on amplitude, but it also depends on other factors—particularly frequency.

2. All the points along equal loudness contours are perceived as equally loud. In general, as seen in Figure 10.6, tones in the 1000- to 5000-Hz range sound louder to us than equal-amplitude tones outside that range.

3. The Weber fraction for intensity discrimination differs, depending on the nature of the sounds. The Weber fraction for pure tones decreases with increases in intensity, which is not the case for white noise. Intensity discrimination for complex tones depends on a profile analysis of the tone. When complex sounds have similar profiles, even small changes in the intensity of a component of the sound are detectable.

4. Loudness can be measured by an eight-level musical system devised by musicians and by the sone scale, a measurement system based on magnitude estimation.

Auditory Localization

You reach out in the darkness of early morning to turn off the ringing alarm clock, and your hand locates the source of that unpleasant noise. A button pops off your coat and rolls away, but you can trace it from its sound effects. You experience an installation by the artist Janet Cardiff and hear voices all around you (Schaub, 2005). The human auditory system allows us to identify with some accuracy where a sound is coming from. In other words, we show **auditory localization**—the ability to locate objects in space solely on the basis of sounds they make. There are actually three kinds of auditory localization we might consider. The first is localization along the horizontal plane (azimuth), which tells us whether the sound is coming from straight ahead or off to the side. The second is localization along the vertical plane, which tells us if the sound is coming from above us or below us. And finally, there is distance localization, which tells us that a sound is closer or farther away. Using only auditory cues, we're quite good at making judgments in the horizontal plane, we're less good in the vertical plane, and we tend to routinely underestimate distances (Plack, 2005).

Researchers have long been intrigued by the auditory localization ability of humans and other animals. One reason that sound localization is so mysterious is that auditory space is not represented directly on the basilar membrane. Frequency, amplitude, and complexity are all represented, so pitch, loudness, and timbre can all be perceived with monaural hearing. However, our auditory system relies heavily on binaural cues to determine spatial location.

Notice the differences in spatial encoding for the auditory and visual systems. We can determine both horizontal and vertical location from the information on either retina. And though binocular cues are helpful in determining depth, monocular cues are sufficient to give rise to a vivid sense of depth. Thus, our visual system needs only monocular input to determine spatial location. And we're quite good at making horizontal, vertical, and distance judgments in visual space.

In spite of the quality of visual spatial information, auditory spatial information is quite important. Of course it is the *only* spatial information available when we can't see. Even when we can see, however, it's helpful to look in one direction and determine that a wailing siren is coming toward you from a different direction. In this section, we look at the auditory localization abilities of humans and other creatures, the neural underpinnings of auditory localization, and interrelationships between spatial perception using vision and audition.

Sources of Information for Auditory Localization

It's easy enough to say that we localize sounds in space because of the input to our two ears. *How* our auditory system makes use of the binaural information is another matter.

Imagine that you are on the edge of a lake and a friend challenges you to play a game. The game is this: Your friend digs two narrow channels up from the side of the lake. Each is a few feet long and a few inches wide, and they are spaced a few feet apart. Halfway up each one, your friend stretches a handkerchief and fastens it to the sides of the channel. As waves reach the side of the lake they travel up the channels and cause the two handkerchiefs to go into motion. You are allowed to look only at the handkerchiefs and from their motions to answer series of questions: How many boats are there on the lake and where are they? Which is the most powerful one? Which one is closer? Is the wind blowing? Has any large object been dropped suddenly into the lake? Solving this problem seems impossible, but it is a strict analogy to the problem faced by our auditory systems. (Bregman, 1990, pp. 5–6)

To explain how we are able to localize sounds in space, we need to consider two different types of information that emerge due to the fact that our ears are located on either side of our head: time differences and intensity differences. As Figure 10.7 illustrates, a

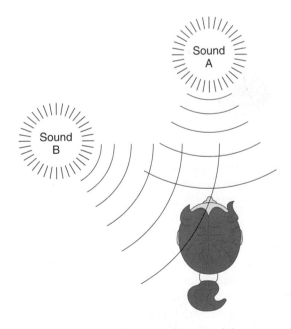

▶ **FIGURE 10.7** Diagram of interaural time difference. Sound A would appear to come from directly ahead of the observer, because it reaches the two ears at the same time. Sound B would appear to come from the left of the observer, because it reaches the listener's left ear before the right ear.

sound coming from the left travels different distances to the two ears. This difference in distance has two consequences with respect to temporal effects: (1) traveling at over 1000 feet/sec, the sound will arrive at one ear slightly before the other, producing an **onset difference**; and (2) typically the sound will be at a different phase of its cycle when it arrives at each ear—perhaps at the maximum point in its cycle for the right ear and at the minimum point for the left ear, producing the **phase difference** illustrated in Figure 10.8. These are the two components of the interaural time difference. The **interaural time difference**, therefore, is a cue to sound localization that is produced by the different arrival times at the two ears.

The onset difference is a useful source of information for sounds throughout the entire frequency range. Figure 10.9 (page 284) shows typical findings on the relationship between the direction from which the sound is coming and the size of the onset difference. As you can see, when the sound comes from directly ahead, there is no onset difference. However, when the sound comes directly from the side (e.g., straight out from the right ear), the sound reaches one ear about 0.6 millisecond before reaching the other ear. Obviously, this is not an enormous discrepancy, but the auditory system can use this minuscule time difference to figure out the location of sounds.

Sounds such as a waterfall or a noisy fan don't provide a distinct onset. Nonetheless, we can localize those sounds with timing information, using differences in the phase of the wave at each ear. Our auditory system can readily detect the phase difference of low-frequency pure tones, as well as complex tones with a low-frequency component. On the other hand, high-frequency pure tones would be difficult to localize using phase information because the peaks are very close together. As a result, it's difficult to compare the phase information from the two ears. Some high-frequency complex sounds may have sufficiently distinctive wave envelopes that we would localize the sounds by comparing phase differences.

Although high-frequency sounds may pose a problem for localization using timing information, another cue to location works particularly well for high-frequency waves. Sounds that are directly ahead of us (or behind us) will be equally loud at each ear. However, for a couple of reasons, when the sound originates off to one side or the other, the intensity of the sound will often be different at the two ears, cre-

ating an **interaural intensity difference**. One reason is that the intensity of a sound decreases over distance. Because the left ear is closer than the right ear to Sound B in Figure 10.7, the sound is slightly more intense in the left ear. A second reason is that for high-frequency sounds, the head produces a sound shadow, or a barrier that reduces the intensity of the sound. We are accustomed to a reduction in intensity when something large—such as a building—separates us from a sound source. However, it may surprise you to learn that your head may block some of the sound coming to one ear from sources on the opposite side of the head.

What is crucial to creating the intensity difference is the frequency of the sound waves *relative* to the size of the head. To give you an idea of the relationship between head size and frequency, think about ocean waves falling on rocks. Waves hitting against a large rock formation jutting out of the water create spray on the ocean side, as the rock breaks up the waves. Just behind the large rock, on the shore side, the water is typically calm. In this example, the frequency of the waves is high relative to the size of the rock.

When smaller rocks protrude out of the water, they create little or no spray, and the waves just roll right around the rock. In this example, the frequency of the waves is low, relative to the size of the rock. In these two examples, the frequency of the ocean waves is roughly constant and the obstruction varies in size. Thus, you might imagine a 500-Hz tone and three creatures: a mouse, a human, and an elephant. Such a tone produces only a modest sound shadow in humans. However, it would produce virtually no sound shadow in the mouse and a much greater sound shadow in the elephant.

Now, instead of imagining a sound of fixed frequency and different head sizes, consider different frequencies and a single head size—yours. The same principles operate. Sounds that come from straight ahead (or directly behind) will be equally loud at each ear. Low-frequency sounds off to the side will wrap around your head and create little intensity difference at the two ears. However, high-frequency sounds off to the side will easily enter the ear on the side of the head from which the sound originates, but won't be able to wrap around your head. Instead, the waves will bounce off your head, so that the waves that do make it to the ear on the opposite side of your head will be less intense.

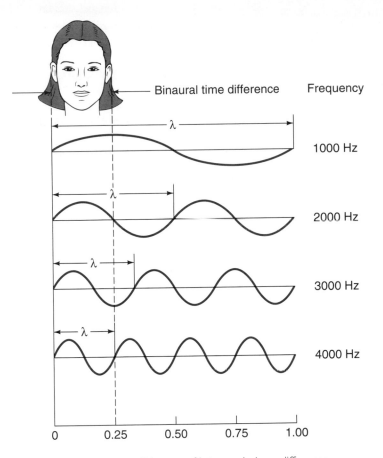

►FIGURE 10.8 Diagram of interaural phase difference. Given the width of the observer's head, a 1000-Hz sound directly to the right of the observer would reach the left ear 90° out of phase with the right ear. A 2000-Hz sound would be 180° out of phase, a 3000-Hz sound would be 270° out of phase, and a 4000-Hz sound would be in phase at both ears. Note that the localization information in the 4000-Hz sound is ambiguous, because a 4000-Hz tone directly ahead of the observer would also be in phase at both ears. (Adapted from Gulick et al., 1989. Used with permission.)

We have seen that auditory localization depends on both interaural time differences and interaural intensity differences. Time differences are helpful for localizing low-frequency sounds, and intensity differences are helpful for localizing high-frequency sounds (Macpherson & Middlebrooks, 2002; Møller, 2006). What about sounds in the mid-range? You may be surprised to learn that we have a difficult time localizing pure tones in the mid-range (1000 to 3000 Hz). It appears that neither cue works particularly well for these sounds. Note that these are the very frequencies that we can detect so readily.

Physiological Basis of Auditory Localization

We know that little spatial information is encoded at the inner ear. In fact, both cues to auditory localization require a comparison of information from the two ears. Information from the two ears remains segregated until it reaches the superior olivary nucleus. As a result, auditory localization cannot occur until this part of the auditory system. Research indicates that the superior olivary nucleus plays an important role in auditory localization, as

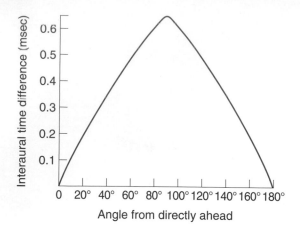

▶ **FIGURE 10.9** Interaural time differences as a function of sound location. The greatest disparity (about 0.6 msec) would occur for a sound directly to one side of the observer (90°). Sounds directly ahead of the observer (0°) or directly behind the observer (180°) would create no timing disparity.

do the inferior colliculus, the superior colliculus, and the auditory cortex.

Because of the extremely small interaural time differences that encode auditory location, the inner hair cells in each ear must fire with great precision (Moser et al., 2006). Long ago, Lloyd Jeffress (1900–1986) proposed a theory about how neurons might compare the firing information from the two ears. Jeffress (1948) thought that timing information could be encoded by neurons that needed simultaneous input from two other neurons in order to fire. Here's how it might work. As seen in the highly schematic illustration in Figure 10.10*a*, if a sound arrived at both ears simultaneously, neural input from each ear would reach Neuron C simultaneously. Thus, Neuron C would signal that a sound was directly ahead (or behind). Now let's consider Figure 10.10*b*, in which a sound arrived first at the right ear. When neural firing from that ear reached Neuron C, input from the left ear might just be at Neuron A. Thus, with only a single input to those two neurons, neither would fire. However, as the input from the right ear reached Neuron B, input from the left ear might also arrive. When such simultaneous input occurs, Neuron B fires, it signals a sound that is coming from the right.

Long after Jeffress proposed the existence of such "coincidence" neurons, researchers located neurons with these properties in the medial superior olivary nucleus (MSO) (Joris, 2006). Information is sent from the MSO to the inferior colliculus, which is also involved in coding interaural time information (Chase & Young, 2005; Hancock & Delgutte, 2004; Thompson et al., 2006). The timing information is probably not encoded in exactly the way that Jeffress proposed. However, his basic model remains useful in thinking about how the brain processes interaural time differences (Møller, 2006).

Interaural intensity differences are encoded in the lateral (side) portion of the superior olivary nucleus (LSO) (Park et al., 2004). Once again, information goes from the LSO to the inferior colliculus, so that portion of the mid-brain encodes both timing and intensity information. In fact, the timing and intensity information may be combined to aid in auditory localization (Peña & Konishi, 2001).

As we've already mentioned, the inferior colliculus has a tonotopic organization. That is, within layers of the inferior colliculus, the neurons are arranged tonotopically (i.e., according to pitch). In addition, the inferior colliculus also serves to map auditory space. Thus, the inferior colliculus processes important information about the sound stimulus (e.g., frequency), as well as its location in space. The inferior colliculus sends information to the superior colliculus, which integrates the auditory spatial information with visual spatial information. Your ability to look quickly toward a sound source likely originates in the superior colliculus.

The inferior colliculus also sends information to the auditory cortex. Many researchers believe that, much like the visual system, the auditory cortex has both a *What* and a *Where* pathway (Rauschecker & Tian, 2000). The *What* system processes the nature of the auditory object, and the *Where* system processes its location. However, some evidence doesn't entirely support this model (Middlebrooks, 2002).

Measuring Localization Abilities

One measure developed to assess these localizing abilities is the minimum audible angle. The ***minimum audible angle*** (***MAA***) is the smallest angle between two sound sources that a person can detect. To determine the MAA, researchers first present one tone, followed by a second tone. The observer reports whether

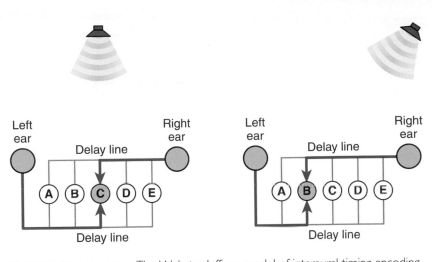

▶ **FIGURE 10.10** The Webster-Jeffress model of interaural timing encoding. They proposed that neurons (A–E) would fire only if stimulated simultaneously by input from each ear. For a sound directly ahead of the listener (*a*), the sound would arrive at both ears simultaneously. The neural firing would arrive at Neuron C, causing it to fire. Thus, activity in Neuron C means that a sound is directly ahead. For a sound to the right of the listener (*b*), the sound would arrive first at the right ear, initiating a neural signal. When the sound arrives at the left ear, it would also initiate a neural signal. However, because the signal from the right ear has a head start, it arrives at Neuron B at the same time as the later signal from the left ear. Thus, activity in Neuron B means that a sound is to the right.

the tones came from the same location or not. For instance, if the MAA is 10°, then you could not reliably discriminate the directions of two sound sources separated by less than 10°. However, sound sources separated by 10° or more would appear to come from different locations.

A classic study was conducted on the roof of a building at Harvard University. S. S. Stevens and Edwin Newman (1936) put a speaker at the end of a boom that could be rotated around the observer. By using the roof, Stevens and Newman did not have to worry about reflected sounds. Furthermore, by using the boom, they could rotate the sound source to many different locations in a horizontal plane (the elevation of the sound source was constant). On the basis of this and other studies, we have learned that humans are quite accurate in localizing sounds that are in front of them. Here, the MAA can be as small as 1°. We are not as good at localizing sounds that are off to the side. However, we can overcome this deficit by moving our heads.

For several reasons, much research has been done with headphones rather than speakers. For instance,

headphones allow researchers to exercise greater control over the stimuli presented to the two ears. When headphones are used, the stimuli typically give rise to the experience that the sound is located inside the observer's head rather than outside, as is the case when speakers are used. When the typical localization cues are manipulated over headphones, the sound seems to shift to the right or to the left *inside* the head. Thus, these studies using headphones are often called *lateralization* studies instead of localization studies (Yost, 2007). If you haven't already noticed this phenomenon, you can easily try it out for yourself.

When Interaural Differences Aren't Enough: Localization Difficulties

Given the binaural cues we've discussed, there are four types of localization that should be difficult for us. First, we should have difficulty localizing sounds if we hear out of only one ear (monaural hearing). Second, we should have difficulty localizing in the vertical dimension. Third, we should have difficulty determining if a sound is coming from in front of us or behind us. And fourth, we should have difficulty localizing any sounds that fall in the *cone of confusion*. As seen in Figure 10.11, every location on a circular slice through the cone is an equal distance from the near ear (e.g., 2 feet) and an equal distance from the far ear (e.g., 2 feet plus head width). Therefore, sound sources at any locations on that slice should theoretically send the same set of information about the source of the sound to each ear. In all four cases, interaural time differences and interaural intensity differences will not help us to localize the sounds.

Nonetheless, we are able to make reasonably good localization decisions in all four scenarios. How do we do so? Unless you wear glasses, your pinnae may strike you as largely useless. However, they play an important role in localization. Because of their location, those flaps of skin help you to make front/back discriminations. Moreover, the ridges and cavities of the pinnae cause incoming sound waves from above to differ slightly from sound waves coming from below us. As a result, in the vertical dimension, we have a MAA of about 4° for sounds coming from straight ahead. Were you to change the shape of your pinnae (using plastic inserts), your auditory localization abilities would initially decrease (Yost, 2007). However, over time your localization abilities

▶ **FIGURE 10.11** The cone of confusion. Sounds located on any circular slice through the cone of confusion would appear to come from the same location.

would improve, which is consistent with what we know about learning and brain plasticity.

Given that you have such accurate auditory localization abilities for sounds directly ahead of you, there is a simple way to resolve ambiguities—move your head toward the sound! We have evolved to be active perceivers of the world, so when we face an ambiguous sound source, we naturally move to resolve the ambiguity. When people are allowed to move their heads, even their monaural localization improves (Moore, 2004).

IN-DEPTH

Nonhuman Localizing Abilities

Most animals need to localize complex sounds that occur naturally in the environment in order to avoid predators or to seek prey or other members of their species. Humans and other animals make use of the same basic monaural and binaural cues. Therefore, you might expect auditory localization abilities to be similar, except for anatomical differences such as head size and pinnae shape. There are, in fact, some similarities. For instance, humans and other animals are better at localizing complex sounds than pure tones and better at horizontal localization than vertical localization (Brown & May, 2005).

Nonetheless, there *are* differences in auditory localization abilities, with humans better than most other animals. For instance, for sounds directly ahead, the MAA in humans is roughly the same as that found in elephants and bottlenose dolphins, and it's better

than that found in macaque monkeys, cats, rats, opossums, and horses (Brown & May, 2005; Moss & Carr, 2003). For vertical localization, humans are comparable to dolphins and cats, but better than opossums and chinchillas. However, using the same basic cues, humans don't navigate as well in the dark as the barn owl, so we'll spend some time discussing this nocturnal predator.

Auditory Localization in Barn Owls

There are few nocturnal birds, so barn owls evolved to hunt small rodents and other prey at night, when they don't face much competition. But how do they accomplish this task? Have they developed night vision or a particularly good sense of touch or smell? These possibilities were ruled out in a clever demonstration (Konishi, 1973). An owl was waiting in a completely dark room in which the floor was covered with a foam rubber pad to cut down on noises. Researchers used a short piece of string to tie a small ball of paper to a mouse's tail and then released the mouse into the room. Dinner time, right? In fact, the owl attacked the ball of paper that was rustling behind the quietly running mouse—even though the mouse was only a few inches away! So, in the absence of light, the barn owl will locate its "prey" using only auditory information. Of course, in its natural environment, in which some light is available, the owl uses both its excellent low-light vision and auditory localization to navigate.

Because of its perceptual abilities, and because rodents are not clever enough to think of the old ball-of-paper trick, the barn owl is fairly successful at catching them in the wild. However, while the barn owl was evolving to catch these nocturnal rodents, the rodents were evolving to avoid becoming prey. For instance, many rodents (e.g., voles and mice) will attempt to avoid notice by walking along soft surfaces in order to minimize noise. When these rodents detect that an owl is hunting them, largely due to the sound of the owl in flight, they engage in a variety of evasive maneuvers. For example, they may stop (quietly) and then run rapidly or else run in a series of random directions (Edut & Eilam, 2003, 2004).

The kangaroo rat appears to be particularly adept at detecting and avoiding the barn owl. That is, when examining barn owl excrement, researchers find kangaroo rat remains in disproportionately small amounts. (Who said science isn't exciting?) Apparently the kangaroo rat has evolved to hear the oncoming owl particularly well and then jumps up about a foot when it fears a barn-owl attack (Stangl et al., 2005). That evasive maneuver seems to work quite well.

The owl's skill at auditory localization can be traced to some important anatomical features. The barn owl is able to localize sounds in the vertical plane better than any other animal. This ability is due to an asymmetrical ear structure—the right ear is oriented upward and the left ear is oriented downward. In addition, the feathers on the owl's face serve as a parabolic reflector to enhance the perception of high-frequency sounds (6000 to 12,000 Hz). These two features are illustrated in Figure 10.12.

The barn owl uses the same binaural cues used by humans for localization—time and intensity differences. As is true for humans, the barn owl uses time differences to localize in the horizontal plane. How-

ever, because of its asymmetrical ear structure, the barn owl receives intensity differences that underlie its ability to localize sounds in the vertical plane (Konishi, 2003).

Because of the barn owl's amazing localizing abilities, researchers have been particularly interested in its auditory system (Konishi, 2000, 2003). For instance, we know that structures in the owl's brain have evolved to allow the precise detection of microsecond differences in time necessary for localization (Carr & Soares, 2007; Wagner et al., 2005). Maps of auditory space are found in both the inferior colliculus and the owl's equivalent of the superior colliculus. As is true of the superior colliculus in humans, the owl's equivalent also has a visual map of space that is aligned with the auditory map (DeBello & Knudsen, 2004). However, the auditory map isn't stationary; instead, it shifts as the owl tracks a moving sound source (Witten et al., 2006).

Consistent with Theme 4, experience plays a vital role in auditory localization in the barn owl (Knudsen, 2002). For example, when one of its ears is plugged, at first the owl will mistakenly localize a sound as coming from the direction of the open ear. However, the owl's localization abilities improve with additional experience in having only one functional ear. When the plug is removed, it then takes the owl a period of adjustment to regain its ordinary localization abilities.

Another example of the role of experience is found in the owl's inferior colliculus, which contains a map of auditory space. As it happens, visual spatial information (coming from the owl's equivalent of the superior colliculus) is essential for the formation of the auditory map in the inferior colliculus (Knudsen, 2002). As we stated in Theme 1, the senses share similarities and interact with one another. The impact of visual experience on the barn owl's auditory map is an exciting example of Theme 1.

Echolocation in Air and Water

Rather than relying on environmental sounds for localization, some animals navigate their worlds using *echolocation*, sending out an auditory signal and gathering information about the environment from the returning echoes. Although humans don't normally make use of such a strategy, we can learn to do so (Amedi et al., 2007; Waters & Abulula, 2007).

 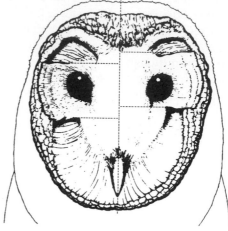

▶ **FIGURE 10.12** Facial structure of the barn owl. The barn owl is able to localize vertically because its facial feathers are asymmetrical. As you can see in the figure, the feathers around the owl's right eye are lower than those around the owl's left eye. Because the opening for the left ear is higher and tilted downward, the owl's left ear is more sensitive to sounds coming from below. Because the opening for the right ear is lower and tilted upward, the owl's right ear is more sensitive to sounds coming from above. (Photo from PGC/Hal Korber, figure from Knudsen, 1981)

For example, people with visual impairments have long used self-generated noises (e.g., tapping canes) to help them navigate. In this section, we'll focus our attention on animals that are natural masters at echolocation.

Bats. Most species of bats rely heavily on auditory information for survival. As is true of barn owls, most bats are nocturnal creatures, evolving in a niche of lessened competition. Few flying carnivores are about at night, so bats can concentrate on being predators without worrying about becoming prey themselves. Most bats hunt insects, although some eat fruit, and others eat fish or small amphibians. Despite our aversion to bats, they represent little potential harm to humans. In fact, some species of bats consume huge numbers of that dreaded predator of humans—the mosquito. The aversion to bats probably comes from several sources, such as the fact that bats are not especially cute creatures (see Figure 10.13).

In the late 1700s, Lazaro Spallanzani (1729–1799) became one of the first people to conduct research on bats. By blinding the bats and observing that they were still able to fly without hitting obstacles, he was able to determine that bats do not need visual information to navigate. However, Spallanzani couldn't figure out the precise means by which the bats were avoiding obstacles as they flew. No wonder Spallanzani could not figure out how the bats were navigating after being blinded—he couldn't hear them make any noise! There followed an embarrassingly long period during which prominent researchers ascribed the bat's navigation abilities to the sense of touch (Hughes, 1999).

The problem, of course, is that many species of bats emit sounds that are far above the frequencies humans can hear. In fact, researchers had to develop extremely sensitive sound-recording instruments, so that they could unravel the complexities of bat spatial perception. Researchers have learned that echolocating bats actually emit very high-intensity signals (i.e., above 100 dB). However, those signals have a fundamental frequency above 20,000 Hz, which is why we can't hear them in spite of all the energy. Various

▶ **FIGURE 10.13** California leaf-nosed bat. Note the unusual facial features, including the large pinnae and unusual nasal structure. Bats send out their echolocation signals through the nose and mouth.

species of bats emit different types of signals. Some use a single frequency, combined with a sweep of frequencies, and others use only the sweep of frequencies (Moss & Sinha, 2003; Schuller & Moss, 2004). When they approach a flying meal, bats emit a series of very short bursts of sound, referred to as a *feeding buzz*. Echoes of those brief signals allow the bat to home in on its prey, especially against background clutter, such as vegetation (Moss et al., 2006).

The bat is flying along as it emits sounds. Therefore, any returning echoes will be compressed, or Doppler-shifted, just as a train's whistle changes pitch as it comes toward you (Behrend & Schuller, 2004). Because many bats emit calls with very high fundamental frequencies (e.g., above 20,000 Hz), they must be sensitive to even higher returning frequencies (e.g., above 60,000 Hz). Because of those high frequencies, interaural intensity differences play a vital role in echolocation. Although bats have auditory systems that are basically the same as ours, differences in the outer ear, middle ear, inner ear, and brain produce these auditory capabilities (Vater, 2004; Vater & Kössl, 2004).

Although the bat's brain is roughly pea-sized, its auditory system is similar to that found in other mammals (Moss & Sinha, 2003). As you should predict, the inferior colliculus plays a vital role in echolocation. Moreover, the superior colliculus contains a three-dimensional map of auditory space.

Echolocation is a very sensitive navigational instrument. For instance, some bats can detect and avoid wires just a bit larger than 0.5 millimeter—about the width of a cotton thread. Bats are also quite good at discriminating among different kinds of prey (Houston & Jones, 2004). Nonetheless, they will occasionally attack a floating insect-sized leaf (Fenton, 2004). Bats even exhibit size constancy in their echolocation, recognizing objects as the same in spite of changes in actual size (Firzlaff et al., 2007).

Although bats rely heavily on echolocation, the saying "Blind as a bat" is not at all accurate. In fact, bats' visual abilities are equivalent to those of many nocturnal creatures (Eklöf, 2003). Under a number of different circumstances, bats will actually rely on vision rather than echolocation. For instance, as swarms of echolocating bats leave a cave at twilight, they fly toward the light at the cave's entrance rather than relying on potentially confusing auditory information. Similarly, if bats are loose in a house during daylight, they will often crash into a window as they seek to escape. Blinded bats are much less likely to do so.

As is true for owls, the relations between bats and their prey are interesting. For instance, many insects have evolved to detect the bat's signals (Denzinger et al., 2004; Masters & Harley, 2004). When they detect the bat's signal, some flying insects actually stop beating their wings, so that they drop rapidly. Others fly away from the signal in an erratic pattern. Still others (e.g., arctiid moths) actually emit a click that may interfere with the bat's echolocation (Tougaard et al., 2004). (Or, because they are not particularly tasty, the arctiid moth may be signaling, "It's me, the yucky moth!") But what's a male moth to do when he's attracted by a female moth's pheromone and at the same time detects a bat's signal? Balancing sex and survival, he'll try to get to the female moth, unless the bat's signal is really intense, indicating that the bat is nearby (Skals et al., 2005). In that case, he'll attempt to avoid the bat and seek out the female moth at a more propitious moment.

Dolphins. Denizens of the ocean are presented with a number of challenges. One problem is that the deeper underwater they travel, the less light is available. Thus, like owls and bats, these ocean-dwelling creatures cannot rely on vision to locate food sources. Fortunately, echolocation works well in the underwater environment, because water is a fine elastic medium, so it transmits sound waves well. However, given what you know about impedance to sound waves, you should recognize that underwater echolocation requires very high-intensity sound waves.

A number of aquatic animals have developed the ability to echolocate, but we'll focus on dolphins. Bats produce their signals through the larynx. In contrast, dolphins produce very high-intensity (as high as 200 dB) clicks by means of structures in their forehead (Cranford & Amundin, 2004; Hughes, 1999). These multi-frequency clicks are nearly ideal means of providing the dolphin with both time and frequency information.

Unlike bats and humans, dolphins don't have functional outer ears. Instead, the lower jaw of the dolphin actually transmits the sound waves to its middle and inner ear, which are not encased in its skull. Because the dolphin brain is so highly developed, ethical concerns limit the types of research conducted on dolphins (e.g., single-cell recording is avoided). As a result, we know much more about how

the bat's auditory system processes echolocation signals than we do about the dolphin's auditory system. Nonetheless, it's clear that the inferior colliculus plays an important role in echolocation in dolphins, as it does in bats (Glezer et al., 2004).

Because of the dolphin's intelligence, researchers have investigated a number of cognitive and perceptual abilities, typically using trained captive dolphins (Masters & Harley, 2004). For instance, using echolocation, dolphins are capable of discriminating between simple objects (e.g., cubes and cylinders), even when they are presented in different orientations.

Several studies suggest that dolphins perceive the same sort of unitary experience of an object as a human might (Pack et al., 2004). That is, when they can both see and bounce auditory signals off an object, they integrate both types of information into their "image" of the object. We'll now turn our attention to the integration of visual and auditory localization information in humans.

Integrating Visual and Auditory Localization

Theme 1 of this text focuses on multiple senses. However, until we introduced the auditory system in Chapter 9, we focused almost entirely on the visual system. In discussing the localization of objects in space, we can now make some fruitful comparisons of auditory and visual information.

The world around us is, of course, three-dimensional. We typically receive consistent spatial information about that world from both our auditory and visual systems. However, it's clear that the visual system provides more precise spatial location information than the auditory system. Thus, it should come as no surprise that we rely heavily on visual information to determine an object's location in space. This dependence becomes obvious when the visual and auditory information are discrepant.

For example, when you go to the movies or watch television, you will hear a voice coming from an actor's mouth, even though the speakers generating the auditory information are located elsewhere.

This "ventriloquism effect" emerges as a result of *visual capture*, in which we misperceive a sound as coming from a likely visual origin. Such visual capture can take place even when the visual object is moving (Vroomen & de Gelder, 2003).

Although we do rely heavily on visual information, it's best not to think of visual input as generally dominating auditory input. Instead, humans probably evolved to emphasize the input that provides us with better information (Witten & Knudsen, 2005). The auditory system is usually better than the visual system at processing temporal information. As a result, when auditory information about rate (e.g., a tapping sound) differs from visual information about rate (e.g., a light flashing), we trust the auditory information. However, when the auditory information is degraded, people will then weigh the visual input more heavily (Roach et al., 2006). Similarly, we usually rely heavily on visual localization information. However, when such information is degraded, we will weigh the auditory information more heavily in determining the spatial location (Recanzone & Sutter, 2008).

It's obvious that we do make use of both visual and auditory information, especially in localizing objects in space. However, it's less obvious where in the brain such integration might take place. Because of its closely related auditory and visual spatial maps, the superior colliculus probably plays a vital role in our unitary perception of space (Stein & Meredith, 1993). However, a number of cortical regions are also involved, including the temporal, frontal, and visual cortex (Zimmer et al., 2004).

Visual and auditory information about the location of a sound-emitting object are typically consistent. Therefore, the interaction of the senses (Theme 1) enhances our ability to localize objects in space. The richness of information about sound that is available in the stimulus (Theme 2) and the impressive capacity of auditory systems to make use of this information (Theme 3) combine to make the task of identifying the direction of a sound appear to be effortless.

processes interaural time differences. The lateral superior olivary nucleus processes interaural intensity differences.

5. Barn owls, bats, and dolphins all have capable visual systems. However, they rely on amazingly effective auditory localization abilities to maneuver in the dark. Barn owls are particularly effective in vertical localization due to their asymmetrical ear structure.

6. Both bats and dolphins use echolocation (listening to the echoes of their signals) to locate objects in their environment. However, their mechanisms differ because bats maneuver through air and dolphins through water.

7. Our "map" of space is a unified one, with strong interrelations between auditory and visual information. When there is a conflict between visual and auditory information, people tend to rely more heavily on the sense that provides better information.

Section Summary

Auditory Localization

1. Auditory localization involves identifying the direction and the distance of a sound. One cue to the direction of a sound comes from the fact that a sound has to travel different distances to the two ears, creating an interaural time difference with two components, an onset difference and a phase difference. The interaural time difference is particularly useful for low-frequency sounds.

2. A second cue to the direction of a sound comes from the fact that a sound reaches the two ears at different intensities, creating an interaural intensity difference. The interaural intensity difference is particularly useful for high-frequency sounds.

3. When the auditory system has information only about interaural time difference and interaural intensity difference, some ambiguities might emerge; information based on pinnae contours and head or body movements helps resolve these ambiguities.

4. The superior olivary nucleus is an important structure in auditory localization. Within that structure, the medial superior olivary nucleus

Perception of Simultaneous Sounds

Typically, we do not hear a single sound in isolation. The worker is hammering away at the newly installed door, birds chirp in the background, neighbors converse—and we hear it all at once. Researchers have been particularly interested in certain types of simultaneously occurring sounds. We will take a look at three such instances: combinations of pure tones, masking, and noise.

Perception of Pure Tone Combinations

If I were to play several pure tones simultaneously, what would you hear? The answer is not a simple one. For instance, the answer would depend in part on the location of the two pure tones. We've discussed complex tones in which the pure tones coming from one location are multiples of one another (e.g., 200 Hz, 400 Hz, 600 Hz, 800 Hz, etc.). In that case, you would not hear the separate components, but a single complex tone with a pitch similar to that of a 200-Hz pure tone presented by itself.

What would happen if the pure tones were not multiples of a fundamental? When two tones that are similar in frequency are sounded, we do not hear just one complex tone, nor do we hear two distinct tones. Instead, we hear a single strange tone! Depending on the difference in frequency between the two tones, we might hear either a single tone pulsing in loudness or an unpleasant roughness. The loudness pulses are called *beats*.

These beats occur by combining the two sounds outside the head, and they can be heard with one ear (monaural beats). Interestingly, beats can also occur if one low-frequency sound is played to the left ear, and another sound to the right ear (Moore, 2004). Such beats are called *binaural beats* to distinguish them from *monaural beats*. Binaural beats arise from some neural combination of the information from both ears, presumably due to the same phase comparison abilities that underlie our auditory localization. Although the auditory experience of both types of beats is similar, the binaural beats are typically less distinct than monaural beats. Try www Demonstration 10.4 to hear auditory beats.

What happens when we present a monaural combination of two tones that differ substantially? When two tones differ in frequency by more than 10%, we can hear two distinct tones. A *consonance* is a combination of two or more tones, played at the same time, judged to be pleasant. In general, tone combinations are consonant if the ratios of the frequencies of the two tones are simple fractions, such as 2/3 (Pierce, 1999). In contrast, a *dissonance* is a combination of two or more tones, played at the same time, judged to be unpleasant. In general, when the ratio of two tones is not a simple fraction, the combination sounds are dissonant. We'll have more to say about consonance and dissonance in our discussion of music in Chapter 11.

Masking

When we present two tones simultaneously, we sometimes don't hear two separate tones, nor do we hear a single tone that combines the two tones. Instead, one tone will make it more difficult to hear the other tone, a phenomenon called *masking* (Yost, 2007). The ability of one tone to mask another depends on the nature of the two tones (their frequency and intensity, whether they are pure tones or complex tones, etc.). Generally speaking, of course, the more intense tone will mask the less intense tone.

The range of frequencies that can be masked by a particular tone is referred to as the *critical band* of that tone (Moore, 2004). In general, a tone masks other tones that are equal to or higher in frequency than itself. A tone is less successful in masking other tones lower in frequency than itself (Plack, 2005; Yost, 2007). The width of the critical band is larger for higher-frequency tones and smaller for lower-frequency tones (Fastl & Zwicker, 2007). The concept of the critical band should remind you of auditory tuning curves, and for a good reason. The inner-ear anatomy and physiology that underlie the auditory tuning curves should help you understand the basis of critical bands. For instance, given what you know about auditory tuning curves and place theory, why should it be easier for a low-frequency tone to mask a higher-frequency tone?

Masking may arise when we present two tones simultaneously, but masking may also occur for tones that aren't presented simultaneously (Moore, 2004). You may recall that we discussed visual masking in Chapter 5. With shape perception, backward masking is easier to demonstrate than forward masking. In other words, a mask presented *after* the test stimulus is more effective in blocking perception than a mask presented *before* the test stimulus. In contrast, with auditory stimuli, forward masking tends to be more effective than backward masking (Moore, 2004). Thus, a tone can block you from hearing another tone presented later.

Noise

We can define *noise* simply as unwanted sounds, but particularly those sounds that have an adverse effect (Hygge, 2007). Of course, people differ with respect to their judgments about noise. A sound may be irrelevant, excessive, and unwanted to you, and yet it may be sweet music to a friend. Moreover, for people interested in auditory phenomena, many types of noise (e.g., white noise, band-pass noise) are crucial for research (Plack, 2005).

Psychologists, engineers, and audiologists have become increasingly concerned about the impact of noise on our health. The most obvious effect, as we discussed in the last chapter, is that exposure to loud noises may lead to permanent hearing loss (Daniel, 2007; Hygge, 2007; Rabinowitz, 2000). Permanent damage within the organ of Corti is especially likely if the noise is of short duration but explosive (e.g., the sharp crack of a gunshot or firecracker) or of longer duration but very high intensity (Price, 2007). Noise may also have a negative impact on processing at higher levels in the auditory system (Kujala et al., 2004; Salvi et al., 2007). Research suggests you might be able to offset some of the noise-induced hearing loss by ingesting magnesium, but before doing so you should consult your health-care provider (Attias et al., 2004; Nageris et al., 2004; Scheibe et al., 2001).

It may surprise you to learn that noise has negative effects on health beyond hearing impairment. For instance, chronic noise may produce stress and lead to cardiovascular problems (Hygge, 2007; Ising & Kruppa, 2004, 2007). Such effects are even found in children who live near airports and are exposed to loud aircraft noise (Matheson et al., 2003). Noise can also impair your ability to sleep soundly, which has a number of residual consequences (Griefahn, 2007).

Noise has an impact on your ability to complete relatively complex cognitive tasks (Evans & Hygge, 2007; Hygge, 2007). For example, people performed more poorly on a proofreading task (and were more annoyed) in the presence of low-frequency noise (Persson Waye et al., 2001). School children who live near airports also exhibit deficits on cognitive tasks (e.g., difficult reading assignments), as a result of airplane noise (Matheson et al., 2003; Stansfeld & Matheson, 2003).

Given all the negative consequences of noise, it's clear that noise abatement is a serious concern. In the workplace, current government regulations prohibit industries from exposing their workers to noise greater than 85 dB for an eight-hour day (Martin & Clark, 2005). Moreover, the louder the noise, the shorter the length of time the person can work under those conditions. For instance, a person can work for only two hours if the noise level is 96 dB. Although such workers are likely required to wear hearing protectors, the protectors have the negative effect of shutting off the worker from other sounds, such as shouted warnings (Starck et al., 2007).

People are also making efforts to reduce environmental noise. For example, people are designing quieter machinery for the workplace, or they may enclose the machinery to reduce the noise effects on workers (Bramer, 2007). Much of the noise we routinely experience is due to cars or planes, which is becoming increasingly problematic (Lercher, 2007). Engineers are making efforts to reduce the noise produced by cars and planes, but it's also helpful to design homes and communities to minimize the impact of transportation noise.

Section Summary

Perception of Simultaneous Sounds

1. When two tones are combined, the resulting sound depends on the frequencies of the two tones; we can hear a single complex tone, beats, roughness, or two distinct tones.

2. The combination of two distinct tones can sound consonant if the ratios of the frequencies of the two tones form a simple fraction; otherwise, the combination sounds dissonant.

3. One tone can mask another in a tone combination, depending on the relative amplitude and frequency of the two tones.

4. Noise, or unwanted sound, is an increasing problem in modern society, leading to a range of health problems beyond hearing impairment.

5. Noise pollution can be addressed by reducing the intensity of the noise or by minimizing its effects, such as limiting workers' exposure to loud noises and providing hearing protectors.

Review Questions

1. Discuss the place and temporal theories of pitch perception, reviewing the evidence in support of each theory. Point out the problems with both theories, and illustrate ways in which they both contribute to pitch perception.

2. In the auditory tuning curves shown in Figure 10.2, notice that the curves are sharper for high-frequency tones, and that the curves are steeper to the right than they are to the left. Can you use what you know (especially Figure 10.1) to explain these phenomena?

3. Discuss why pitch is not perfectly correlated with frequency. Consider the factors that influence pitch perception. Repeat this same process

with the relationship between loudness and intensity, including a discussion of the impact of frequency on loudness.

4. Using the equal loudness contours shown in Figure 10.6, answer the following questions (answers are given below):

   a. For a 1000-Hz tone at 40 dB, what sound pressure will be equally loud for a 300-Hz tone? A 50-Hz tone?

   b. For a 1000-Hz tone at 100 dB, what sound pressure will be equally loud for a 150-Hz tone? A 50-Hz tone?

5. Discuss the ways in which sound intensity and sound frequency might be measured, and contrast this with the ways in which pitch and loudness are measured.

6. Notice a sound in your present environment and list the cues that help you judge the direction of the sound source. What are the factors that could help you resolve potential ambiguities about the location of that sound? Using only intensity differences, what frequency range would best be localized by a mouse, a human, and an elephant?

7. Our perception of space is unitary—auditory and visual information provide us with consistent details about the world. Compare the informa-tion we discussed in Chapter 6 on visual space perception with the information in this chapter. How do you think the information might be integrated?

8. Consider the auditory systems of echolocating creatures such as bats and dolphins. How do they differ from humans? Try to describe what it would be like to perceive the world entirely through echolocation (cf. Nagel, 1974).

9. Discuss the difference between monaural and binaural beats. How might monaural beats be helpful to musicians tuning instruments?

10. Consider the combination of visual stimuli (e.g., additive color mixing) discussed in earlier chap-ters and the combination of auditory stimuli (e.g., combining pure tones, masking, noise) dis-cussed in this chapter. How does the visual sys-tem differ from the auditory system in encoding these combined stimuli? How might those differ-ences lead to perceptual differences?

For Question 4, above, the answers are:

a. 300-Hz tone at <u>40 dB</u> would be as loud as a 1000-Hz tone at 40 dB; 50-Hz tone at <u>65 dB</u> would be as loud as a 1000-Hz tone at 40 dB;

b. 150-Hz tone at <u>100 dB</u> would be as loud as a 1000-Hz tone at 100 dB; 50-Hz tone at <u>110 dB</u> would be as loud as a 1000-Hz tone at 100 dB.

Key Terms

pitch, p. 268
place theory, p. 268
temporal theory, p. 268
refractory period, p. 268
traveling wave, p. 269
envelope, p. 269
stimulation deafness
    experiment, p. 269
harmonics, p. 271
fundamental frequency,
    p. 271
overtones, p. 271

timbre, p. 272
missing fundamental,
    p. 272
volley principle, p. 273
phase locking, p. 273
tone chroma, p. 275
tone height, p. 275
octave, p. 275
mel scale, p. 276
loudness, p. 277
equal loudness contour,
    p. 278

profile analysis, p. 280
sone scale, p. 280
auditory localization,
    p. 280
onset difference, p. 281
phase difference, p. 281
interaural time difference,
    p. 281
interaural intensity
    difference, p. 282
minimum audible angle
    (MAA), p. 284

lateralization, p. 285
cone of confusion, p. 286
echolocation, p. 287
visual capture, p. 290
beats, p. 292
consonance, p. 292
dissonance, p. 292
masking, p. 292
critical band, p. 292
noise, p. 292

Recommended Readings

Hughes, H. C. (1999). *Sensory exotica: A world beyond human experience*. Cambridge, MA: MIT Press.

This book is quite interesting because of the range of topics considered (e.g., navigation in ants, bees, and birds, chemical communication). For this chapter, the discussion of echolocation in dolphins and bats is particularly relevant. Hughes has an engaging writing style, so the book is a pleasure to read.

Luxon, L. & Prasher, D. (Eds.). (2007). *Noise and its effects*. Chichester, England: Wiley.

This edited book contains numerous chapters by experts in the field of noise perception and noise abatement. Some of the chapters are basic (e.g., measuring noise, the impact of noise on the auditory system) and others have a very narrow focus (e.g., noise effects on military personnel, noise in medical environments).

Moore, B. C. J. (2004). *An introduction to the psychology of hearing* (5th ed.). Burlington, MA: Elsevier.

Moore is a prominent researcher in this area, so his text is an authoritative one. His discussions of pitch, loudness, auditory space, and especially masking phenomena are all quite helpful for the topics in this chapter.

Plack, C. J. (2005). *The sense of hearing*. Mahwah, NJ: Erlbaum.

Plack's book is as close to a "fun read" as you'll get in this complex field. Although he may not provide as much detail as you'll find in other texts, his readable account is quite broad in scope. Because of his own interests in pitch perception, his coverage of that topic makes for especially interesting reading.

Auditory Pattern Perception

BY THIS POINT in the text, you are certainly aware that our perceptual world is an extremely complex one. Objects around us vary in many ways, including size, shape, wavelength of reflected light, and distance—which our visual system has evolved to represent. Those objects also give rise to extremely complex sound waves—which our auditory system has evolved to represent.

In Chapters 9 and 10, we examined the structure and basic functions of the auditory system. Although much of the research employed pure sine waves, it's clear that our auditory system has evolved to process complex waves. Thus, this chapter addresses how we perceive those complex auditory stimuli. Stop for a minute and listen carefully to the sounds around you. In spite of your best efforts to find a quiet place to read, you might hear music playing, people talking, and the welter of sounds produced by machinery. Each of those sounds is itself a complex wave. Moreover, when they occur simultaneously, they create a complex wave along your basilar membrane.

However, the complex motion of the basilar membrane contains no signposts to the auditory system saying that one ripple in the wave is due to a guitar, another due to voices, and others due to the wind or a fan. Nonetheless, most often our auditory experience is effortlessly analytical. We do not hear a complex waveform—we simply hear guitars, voices, and fans. The puzzle of how we do so is endlessly intriguing to most people.

As we indicated in Chapter 10, researchers are using complex tones more frequently in the laboratory. The peripheral auditory apparatus (the inner ear) may be sufficient for analyzing simple tones. However, tones of greater complexity begin to overwhelm the analytical ability of the inner ear. Consistent with Theme 4 of this book, central processes (knowledge and expectations) become crucial for the perception of complex sounds.

The sound waves discussed in this chapter are extremely complex in that the multiplicity of frequencies is varied, or modulated, over time. After discussing some research on perceiving patterns in such complex auditory stimuli, we will turn our attention to two specific examples of complex auditory stimuli—music and speech.

Perception of Complex Auditory Patterns

Why did it take so long for psychologists to begin studying complex sounds? Perhaps you've heard the joke about the stranger who comes upon a drunk searching for his keys under a streetlight. The stranger joins in the unsuccessful search for a while, and then asks the drunk where he lost his keys. The drunk points further up the road, prompting the stranger to ask, "Then why are you searching here?" The drunk replies, "Because the light is better here."

The necessity for precise control in the laboratory often leads researchers to address questions that are limited by available technology—searching where the "lighting" is good, even though more crucial problems lie elsewhere. As we have seen in previous chapters, technological advances often pave the way for important empirical advances.

Similarly, interest in the perception of complex auditory patterns grew out of technological advances that allowed researchers to control several parameters of the sound stimulus simultaneously. When researchers studied these complex auditory stimuli, they soon realized that experience, memory, and attention play vital roles in auditory perception (Watson & Kidd, 2007). The important role of these higher-level processes is entirely consistent with Theme 4 of this text.

Because complex auditory stimuli present challenges similar to those of complex visual stimuli, our discussion will overlap substantially with the earlier discussion of visual pattern perception. As you will recall, our discussion focused on the central processes used by the visual system to make sense of complex visual stimuli—contributions of the Gestalt and cognitive psychologists. After first describing the complexities facing our auditory system, we will revisit the Gestalt approach and the cognitive approach, but now apply them to auditory stimuli.

The Nature of Complex Sound Stimuli

As Theme 2 of this text suggests, our perceptual world is rich with information. Whether we're processing the complex wave that emerges from a single source, such as a guitar, or the combination of complex waves from many sources, the auditory stimulus is laden with information.

That information creates a complex analytical problem for our auditory system. Have you ever had difficulty following the threads of conversations that swirl around you at a crowded party? If so, then you've experienced the "cocktail party" problem. For our purposes, we can refer to each person's voice as an auditory object (Griffiths & Warren, 2004; Kubovy & Van Valkenburg, 2001). How, then, do we extract auditory objects from the complex motion of our basilar membranes?

The nature of the problem is illustrated by the following visual example from Albert Bregman (1994):

AI CSAITT STIOTOS

What could this possibly mean?

The problem emerges because two different messages are mixed together. Such a mixture of information along our basilar membranes is quite typical. Our auditory system has evolved to enable us to segregate the various streams of information. To make the visual example easier to segregate, we can highlight some of the letters and offset them slightly:

Aɪ CₛAɪTT STₒoTₒS

Now the meaning becomes clear! How do we segregate the various auditory streams of information falling on our ears? What factors allow us to segregate one auditory message ("A cat sits") from another ("I sit too")?

In order to extract the auditory objects and determine separate streams of information, our auditory system appears to latch onto salient features of the sound stimuli (McAdams & Drake, 2002). Such features include frequency, timbre, spatial location, and timing. Thus, the more similar the auditory objects (e.g., two males with deep bass voices speaking from the same location), the more difficult it is to separate the two streams of information.

Bregman (e.g., 1994, 2008) refers to the auditory system's ability to analyze simultaneous complex sounds as auditory scene analysis. He argues that the complexities of such analysis suggest that several processes are probably involved. One way to think about how we organize the overlapping auditory information into separate streams is to invoke some of the Gestalt and cognitive principles discussed earlier in the context of visual stimuli.

Making Sense of Complex Sounds

Principles derived from both the Gestalt approach (e.g., similarity) and the cognitive approach (e.g., top-down processing) may play important roles in determining auditory objects and separating auditory streams. In the next two sections, we'll look at examples of how these principles apply to our perception of music and speech. However, people also need to distinguish many environmental sounds, such as animal calls, sounds of tools, and mechanical devices (Gygi et al., 2004, 2007). Thus, you should recognize the utility of any principle that allows you to separate the information coming from one sound source from the information coming from a different sound source.

The same grouping principles that might connect features into a visual object may also allow us to group features into an auditory object. Imagine that you're walking along a beach where you hear the splashing of the waves, the roar of a boat engine, the ringing of the bell on a buoy, and the screeching of a gull. Can you think of Gestalt principles that would allow you to distinguish the sounds? Consider, for instance, how the similarity of frequency or timbre would enable you to distinguish the bell from the waves. The proximity in time of the splashing sounds of the waves would create a good continuation that would identify that auditory object. And as you focus your attention on the ringing of the bell, the other noises become background—the auditory equivalent of the separation of figure and ground.

In this chapter, you have already seen several illustrations of the necessity to invoke higher-order processes to explain how we process complex auditory stimuli. One reason that cognitive processes play an important role is that complex auditory stimuli, such as music and speech, occur over fairly long periods of time. Memory is also apparent when we find evidence that a person's performance improves over time. Thus, memory plays a crucial role in processing complex auditory stimuli, with the processes of perception and memory tightly intertwined (Dowling, 2001).

Charles Watson and Gary Kidd have conducted many interesting experiments illustrating the importance of cognitive factors in auditory perception. To illustrate one area of their research, let's examine a pro-totypical experiment. People were asked to listen to many thousands of pairs of 10-tone sequences, with each pair separated by a brief interval. The listener then judged whether the tone sequences were the same or different. On half the trials, the pairs were in fact identical. When the pairs were different, a single tone in the sequence might differ in frequency, intensity, or duration. Figure 11.1 illustrates a pair of sequences in which the fourth tone differs in duration.

People are far worse at making such discriminations (compared to discriminating simple tones in isolation) when they have had little experience and when they have no idea where in the segment the difference might occur. However, after thousands of trials of practice, their performance improves, which suggests that central processes are important. Although there are notable individual differences, decades of research have demonstrated that people become much more competent at detecting subtle details of complex auditory sounds when they are familiar with the sounds (Watson & Kidd, 2007).

The effects of learning and memory found by Watson and Kidd parallel those found in David Green's work in profile analysis. As we discussed in Chapter 10, profile analysis requires people to discriminate complex auditory stimuli that are presented simultaneously. Identifying small changes in a single component of the multitone complex is a very difficult task. However, research on profile analysis also reveals that people become much more adept at such tasks when they have had a great deal of experience (Green, 1987).

In summary, whether we characterize them as Gestalt or cognitive, higher-level processes contribute to many aspects of auditory functioning. Such processes play a particularly prominent role in the processing of complex auditory stimuli. We now turn our attention to two extremely complex types of auditory stimuli—music and speech.

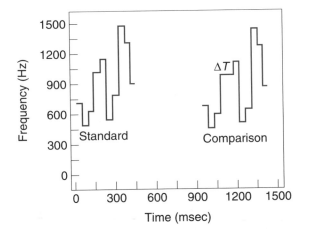

▶ **FIGURE 11.1** Typical complex stimuli used in studies by Watson, Kidd, and their colleagues. The 10-tone sequence is identical for both the standard and the comparison stimulus except for one change. In this case, the fourth tone in the sequence is slightly longer in the comparison sequence. On some trials the standard stimulus is repeated twice, and on other trials the standard is followed by the comparison stimulus. People listen to a series of trials and indicate whether they think the two sequences are the same (standard-standard) or different (standard-comparison). With practice, people improve their ability to discriminate between tone sequences, illustrating the importance of experience for perception of complex stimuli. (From Espinoza-Varas & Watson, 1989)

Section Summary

Perception of Complex Auditory Patterns

1. The growing trend toward the study of complex auditory patterns stems from technological advances and a belief that central processes are important in auditory perception.

2. Although complex sounds often occur simultaneously, we are able to separate the many different streams of information. We segregate the streams on the basis of many properties of the sound stimuli, such as frequency, timbre, location, and timing.

3. Gestalt principles of organization and the figure-ground relationship can be readily applied to the perception of complex auditory patterns.

4. The importance of cognitive processes is illustrated by research showing that memory helps us detect subtle differences between complex auditory patterns.

Music Perception

What role does music play in your life? In a typical week, how many hours do you spend listening to music? One might argue that music is a vital human activity because of its ubiquity across cultures and the early development of music perception in human infants (Justus & Bharucha, 2002; Patel, 2008; Radocy & Boyle, 2003). A good deal of controversy surrounds theories about the evolution of music. However, there is no doubt that at many levels music is a complex auditory phenomenon. As such, it is of great interest to psychologists such as Diana Deutsch, who has made many important contributions to our understanding of the psychology of music. You'll see her name throughout this section on music.

To understand the many complexities of the musical stimulus, consider a musical performance. Each sound that the instruments emit is a complex wave. At any given time in the musical piece, several different instruments are likely to be playing simultaneously. However, the sounds are rarely salient as isolated notes. Instead, they are woven into a melodic contour of pitch and rhythm. Because that melodic contour typically emerges during several minutes, memory and organization also play important roles in the integration of the music (McAdams & Drake, 2002).

Furthermore—and consistent with Theme 4—the listener is not a passive perceiver, but is actively engaged in processing the music. Your memories of prior experiences allow you to bring acoustic memories, aesthetic judgments, and expectations to bear as you listen to the piece. Think of a song that you know very well. Can you "hear" the song playing in your mind? Can you recognize the timbre of the singer's voice and the instruments? Do the words and the music seem to go together? Research indicates that we do remember many aspects of the auditory stimulus, such as pitch, timbre, and rhythm (Dowling, 2001).

Given this complexity, the organizing principles we have just been discussing certainly apply to music perception. In this section of the chapter, we will first review some of the perceptual qualities discussed in Chapter 10—pitch, tone combinations, timbre, and loudness. However, now we will emphasize how these qualities are important in music.

The Musical Stimulus

In this chapter, we are primarily concerned with music as an auditory pattern. However, we will begin by returning to some auditory features we've already discussed. These basic features are central to the music stimulus and play important roles in the emergence of auditory patterns. We will then turn our attention to other characteristics of the musical stimulus.

PITCH   In Chapter 10, we saw that humans can hear frequencies in the range of 20 to about 20,000 Hz, although sounds with fundamental frequencies above 5000 Hz do not appear to have a pitch. As a result, the fundamental frequencies essential to music form a subset of the range of perceivable frequencies. For example, as seen in Figure 11.2, the fundamental frequencies on the piano range from 27.5 to 4186 Hz. As you can also see, all the instruments in an orchestra—and also the human voice—have even more limited ranges. Their ranges are typically less than half the range of the piano. Given the narrow range of fundamental frequencies important to music, you might well wonder why stereo systems tout their ability to reproduce sounds over a wider range (often the full 20- to 20,000-Hz range). The answer is that the overtones produced by musical instruments can easily reach into the upper range of our auditory capabilities. The rich timbre of musical instruments can be reproduced only with the faithful rendition of the fundamental frequency *and* the overtones.

Figure 11.2 shows a piano keyboard with tones progressing from low to high, an arrangement that suggests that pitch is one-dimensional. However, organizing principles operate even for such basic qualities as pitch. These principles are evident on the keyboard in the repetitive arrangement of the keys. After every 12 keys, the pattern repeats itself. As you can see, the white keys are labeled C, D, E, F, G, A, and B. The tones produced by the intervening black keys are called sharps (or flats)—C#, D#, F#, G#, and A# (or, alternatively, D♭, E♭, G♭, A♭, and B♭).

As we discussed in Chapter 10, if one tone is twice the frequency of another tone, the two tones are an *octave* apart. Even people from many different Western and non-Western cultures tend to perceive the similarity of tones in this two-to-one frequency relationship (Patel, 2008; Sethares, 2005). Because of that similarity, these tones are given the same name. For example, all C's on the piano sound similar, even though they differ in frequency and are separated by many other tones. *Tone chroma* (or pitch class) refers to the similarity shared by all musical tones that have the same name.

The same tone chroma found at different octaves are said to differ in *tone height*. Thus, the highest C on the piano has greater tone height than all the

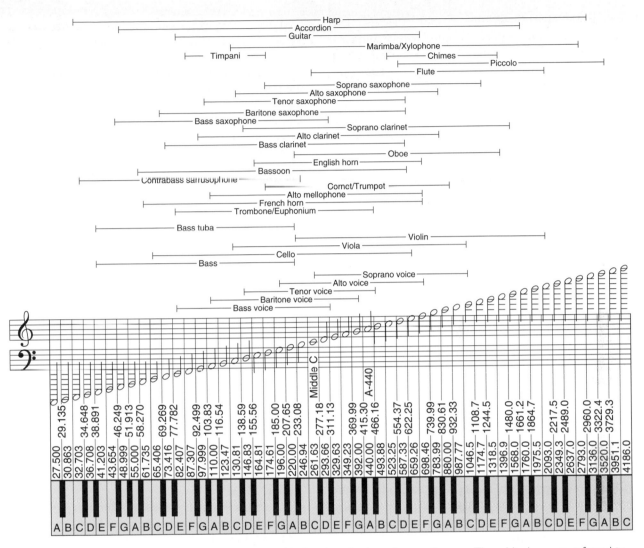

▶ **FIGURE 11.2**   Pitch of musical instruments, with the piano keyboard as a reference. The white keys are referred to as naturals, and the black keys are sharps or flats. As you go up the keyboard from one key to the next of the same name, you've gone up one octave. With each octave, the frequency is doubled. Notice that other instruments have an even narrower range of fundamental frequencies than the piano. (From Pierce, 1983)

other C's. Following the musical convention of using subscripts to represent a tone's position on the piano, C_1 is the lowest C, C_2 is the next higher C, and so forth, up to C_8. Because C_1 has a frequency of 32.7 Hz, C_2 has a frequency of 32.7×2, or 65.4 Hz. Conceptually, then, you should think of pitch organized as in Figure 10.5 (p. 276), rather than in the linear keyboard fashion shown in Figure 11.2. Figure 10.5 highlights the repetitive organization of pitch, with each tone chroma appearing at increasing tone heights.

Western musicians and composers further organize the 12-tone chroma into scales that are often com-prised of seven tones. For example, the C major scale is comprised of the notes C, D, E, F, G, A, B (which then repeats at the next tone height). The F major scale is comprised of the notes F, G, A, B♭, C, D, E. Whether a piece of music is played in the key of C or the key of F (and thus using different notes), you can readily identify the piece as the same. Thus, the relationships among the notes are crucial to perceiving music.

RELATIVE PITCH, ABSOLUTE PITCH, AND TONE DEAFNESS   Consistent with the importance of pitch relationships, many people have **relative pitch**

perception, which means they cannot judge the pitch of a note accurately unless presented with a comparison pitch. As Deutsch (2006) notes, an equivalent situation in the visual realm would arise if someone could not name a color (e.g., a wavelength called green) without first seeing another color (e.g., a wavelength called orange). Of course, most people don't need a comparison stimulus before naming a color.

A few people (approximately 1 in 10,000) *are* able to name the note of a tone presented in isolation, and they possess **absolute pitch** perception. Another way to assess absolute pitch perception is to have people produce tones (e.g., by singing them). That is, the researcher presents a tone (e.g., F#) and, after a delay, asks the person to sing that exact tone (or produce it on some instrument). Tone production allows researchers to study absolute pitch perception in animals or people who don't know the names of tones. Using this approach, many more people may approximate absolute pitch perception, singing popular songs in the same key as the original version or correctly recognizing the initial note (Levitin, 2006; Schellenberg & Trehub, 2003). Other species, including some species of songbirds, also exhibit absolute pitch perception (Weisman et al., 2006).

Although the ability to accurately name notes may be rare among humans, such absolute pitch perception is more prevalent among musicians than nonmusicians. However, the lack of absolute pitch perception is not a major impediment to producing or appreciating music. In fact, musical training typically focuses on relative pitch perception. Musicians have learned that, as long as the relationships between adjacent tones in the melody remain constant, you can identify a melody (Deutsch, 1999b). Changing the key of a piece of music from C major to F major, for example, would change the pitch of each note yet still preserve the relationships among the tones. Such a change is referred to as a **transposition**. Interestingly, people with absolute pitch perception are actually at a disadvantage in detecting whether or not a melody has been correctly transposed (Miyazaki, 2004).

Most people can readily identify the melody in spite of dramatic changes in the actual notes. Therefore, transposition illustrates a type of auditory constancy similar to visual constancies, such as size and shape constancy. However, the relationships in the melody are determined not only by tone chroma but also by tone height. Deutsch (1995) has demonstrated

that even a very common tune (e.g., "Yankee Doodle Dandy," "Three Blind Mice") becomes unrecognizable if the tone heights are varied in a random fashion (up or down by octaves), even though the tone chroma are transposed properly. We'll soon have more to say about perceptual organization in music. However, the Gestalt principles of similarity and proximity must surely play a role in organizing tones into a melody. Leaps of octaves make it difficult to organize the notes into a coherent melody. You can experience this effect in www Demonstration 11.1.

Absolute pitch perception is of great interest to auditory researchers, but particularly those interested in music perception. However, as is often true in psychology, in attempting to explain the origins of this ability, people disagree about the relative contribution of nature and nurture (Deutsch, 2006). Converging evidence suggests an underlying genetic component. For instance, members of the same family are more likely to have absolute pitch perception. Moreover, many very young infants display absolute pitch perception, though changing the experimental task may lead them to use relative pitch information instead (Saffran, 2003a; Saffran & Griepentrog, 2001; Saffran et al., 2005). However, in order for adults to develop absolute pitch, it also seems important that people with the proper genetic underpinnings undertake musical training at an early age (Deutsch, 2006; Levitin & Rogers, 2005; Levitin & Zatorre, 2003; Zatorre, 2003).

Another indication of the role of experience is that people with absolute pitch are particularly good at identifying the notes found in the key of C major (a common key), but they perform poorly on notes found in unusual keys (Takeuchi & Hulse, 1993). And lest you misinterpret the term, it's important to understand that people with absolute pitch actually make some errors in identifying tones (e.g., labeling the chroma correctly, but mislabeling the height).

Although learning music at an early age may be vital to the development of absolute pitch, other evidence suggests that a focus on pitch for nonmusical reasons may also lead to absolute pitch. For example, in some languages—such as Chinese—pitch carries crucial meaning. Many people who speak these languages also develop absolute pitch (Deutsch, 2006; Deutsch et al., 2004a).

At the opposite extreme from people with absolute pitch are those who suffer from **tone-deafness**. People with tone-deafness have difficulty accurately perceiving pitch (Hyde & Peretz, 2004). For example, Oliver Sacks (2007) describes the case of Jacob, for whom the distortion of pitch perception is localized to a small portion of the frequency spectrum. However, for a very small percentage of people (about 4%), the tone-deafness is more extensive. These people do not enjoy music, and they have difficulty perceiving and recognizing melodies (Ayotte et al., 2002; Cuddy et al., 2005; Foxton et al., 2004; Sloboda et al., 2005). Their difficulties are likely due to abnormal brain development in the right auditory cortex (Hyde et al., 2007).

A fair number of people report that they are tone-deaf, but they actually mean that they cannot produce melodies accurately (i.e., they cannot sing on key). These people may enjoy listening to music, and they may perceive music accurately, so they are not truly tone deaf.

PERCEPTION OF SIMULTANEOUS TONE COMBINATIONS   Why is it that some tone combinations sound pleasant? As you might anticipate, there is no simple answer to that question. From the discussion in Chapter 10, you know that two tones that are close in frequency will be dissonant if they are presented simultaneously. For example, if two instruments play the "same" note when they are out of tune, they will produce two slightly different fundamental frequencies. As you know from Chapter 10, you would then perceive beats or a dissonant roughness. Similarly, the same instrument playing two nearby chroma (e.g., C and C# or C and D) would sound dissonant. Try [www] Demonstration 11.2 to illustrate various consonant and dissonant tone combinations. This demonstration also lists the commonly used names for the musical intervals.

Why are nearby frequencies dissonant? The consonance of tone combinations largely depends on whether the frequencies of the two tones form a simple ratio. We've already noted that two frequencies separated by an octave (e.g., 880 Hz and 440 Hz, a 2:1 ratio) will sound similar and therefore consonant. On the other hand, if the ratio is not simple, you will hear two simultaneous sounds as dissonant, whether they are near one another (e.g., 440 Hz and 441 Hz) or separated from one other (e.g., 440 Hz and 700 Hz).

Musicians knew about these simple ratios even before the ancient Greeks. However, in the sixth century BC the Greek philosopher Pythagoras formalized theories about the ratios of the lengths of vibrating strings (Patel, 2008; Pierce, 1999). Over the years, other prominent thinkers such as Descartes, Galileo, and our old friend Helmholtz were also interested in the impact of ratios of frequencies on consonance.

However, as is often true in the area of perception and in psychology in general, explanations are rarely simple. Thus, consonance is not determined solely by simple ratios (Shepard, 1999b). For instance, in writing a song in the key of C major, a composer would be unlikely to use C#, because it would be heard as dissonant among the notes in that key (C, D, E, F, G, A, B). However, if the composer provided an appropriate preceding musical context, the C# would not sound dissonant.

The situation is made even more complex when one considers the music of other cultures (Sethares, 2005). For example, a North American who hears East Indian music for the first time may judge the combination of notes dissonant and unpleasant. Of course, a native East Indian listener would hear only consonance. Similarly, cultural preferences change as a function of exposure. The music of Stravinsky (e.g., *The Rite of Spring*) was condemned as unpleasant dissonance almost a century ago, yet it sounds consonant to most of us today. Consistent with Theme 4, experience plays a role in the perception of consonance and dissonance.

LOUDNESS   Loudness plays important roles in music, such as highlighting a particular instrument and its melody, signaling transitions in the music, and evoking emotional responses. As you listen to a song, note how parts of the song vary in loudness. Within a particular passage, you'll also note that different instruments are playing with varying loudness.

As we pointed out in the previous chapter, musicians indicate loudness with a system that goes from *ppp* (softest) to *fff* (loudest). The intensity of sound pressure level plays a vital role in the production of loudness. However, as illustrated by the Fletcher-Munson curves (Figure 10.6, p. 279), the frequency of sound also influences loudness. Loudness also affects pitch because increasing loudness (crescendo) allows us to hear higher frequencies that were not audible at lower loudness levels.

TIMBRE   Even when matched for pitch and loudness, sound sources are often distinctive. For example, a flute and an oboe may both play the same tone at the same loudness, but you can still distinguish between the nasal quality of the oboe and the pure quality of the flute. The distinctive "sound signature" of a source is its timbre.

Helmholtz's classical view of timbre proposed that differences in the sound quality of musical instruments could be traced entirely to the distribution of harmonics (Risset & Wessel, 1999). Figure 11.3a shows the fundamental frequency and harmonics resulting from Fourier analysis of one of the higher tones in the oboe's range. Notice that the harmonics have relatively high amplitude, in comparison to the fundamental frequency, and this particular tone contains eight harmonics. Contrast this distribution of harmonics with that of the flute, in Figure 11.3b, for one of the higher tones in the flute's range. Impressively, this tone has only a single harmonic, and its amplitude is so low that you might miss it on first inspection. An important characteristic of the flute's distribution of energy is that when a tone in the high range is played, the fundamental frequency carries almost all the energy output. The harmonics are practically nonexistent. As a result, the sound in this range is clear and pure (Rossing et al., 2002).

However, harmonics cannot fully explain timbre. For instance, playing a sound backwards preserves all the contributing frequencies, but it has a timbre that differs markedly from that of the original sound. More recent theories of timbre stress the importance of the shape of the sound envelope, particularly the attack. The **attack** is the beginning buildup of a tone, after which the sound decays to the sustained part of the note before the final release. The attack is critical when we try to recognize an instrument, because recognition accuracy drops when the

attack portion of a tone has been eliminated from a recording (Levitin, 2006; Patel, 2008; Sethares, 2005).

TEMPO AND RHYTHM   As you should recall, our auditory system is particularly sensitive to timing information. Perhaps as a result, many aspects of timing are important to music (Radocy & Boyle, 2003). Each song will have a basic **tempo**, or pace, measured in beats per minute and possibly indicated by a metronome. Within a given tempo, however, songs may organize the beats into different rhythmic structures (meters). Thus, a waltz will have a rhythmic structure that differs from a march.

Within limits, people are quite good at perceiving and remembering tempos (Levitin, 2006; Patel, 2008; Quinn & Watt, 2006). Although we have no difficulty maintaining a tempo of about 100 beats per minute, we do have difficulty keeping up with a very fast tempo of 300 beats per minute. We're also challenged by tempos slower than 50 beats per minute.

It's easy to understand the role of tempo and rhythm in aligning the performance of members of an ensemble of musicians or in aiding any accompanying dancing (Patel, 2008). However, were we to consider only a single performer and a person simply listening to the song, it's clear that tempo and rhythm play important roles in organizing the song. The similarity in pitch and timbre that allows us to link notes together into a melodic structure is aided by the temporal proximity of the notes in the rhythmic structure (Krumhansl, 2000; Palmer & Jungers, 2003).

We've just revisited a number of basic auditory processes first introduced in Chapter 10, but now in the context of music perception. We'll now turn our attention to the areas of the brain involved in

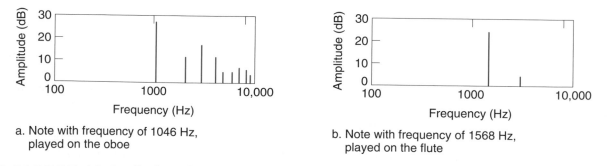

a. Note with frequency of 1046 Hz, played on the oboe

b. Note with frequency of 1568 Hz, played on the flute

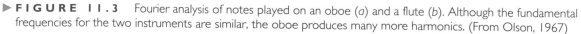

▶ **FIGURE 11.3**   Fourier analysis of notes played on an oboe (a) and a flute (b). Although the fundamental frequencies for the two instruments are similar, the oboe produces many more harmonics. (From Olson, 1967)

auditory perception, with the focus on their role in music perception.

Music and the Brain

Complex auditory phenomena such as music and speech must certainly be processed within the auditory system we've described in prior chapters. However, one controversial question that emerges is whether or not areas of the brain are specialized for processing music. (You'll see the question reprised in our discussion of speech.) Regardless of how this question is ultimately answered, there is no doubt that researchers will continue to investigate a host of questions related to brain activity while listening to music. In this section, we'll briefly examine a small number of studies conducted in this burgeoning area.

Both pitch and rhythm are central to music perception, although it's not clear whether they are processed separately or in an integrated fashion (Peretz & Zatorre, 2005). Brain-imaging research has identified an area of the frontal cortex that appears to be important for coding tone chroma (Janata et al., 2002; Zatorre & Krumhansl, 2002). As you may recall from Chapter 10, regions of the superior temporal cortex are also involved in pitch perception, so researchers must still map the linkage between the superior temporal cortex and the frontal cortex.

In discussing pitch perception, we focused some attention on absolute pitch perception. Researchers are quite interested in the neural underpinnings of that ability. In doing such research, it's crucial that researchers compare musicians with absolute and relative pitch perception, because their musical training causes the brains of musicians to differ from those of nonmusicians (Pascual-Leone, 2003; Schlaug, 2003). Nonetheless, it does appear that the brains of musicians with absolute pitch perception differ from those of musicians with relative pitch (Levitin & Rogers, 2005; Zatorre, 2003). For example, when identifying a single tone, musicians with absolute pitch show activation in an area of the frontal cortex responsible for associative learning. Those with relative pitch show similar activation only when making relative judgments of pairs of tones.

As you know, we can learn a lot about brain function by studying the impact of brain injury on performance. That's certainly true for music perception. Consider the case of Ian McDonald, who is a neurologist and an amateur musician (McDonald, 2006).

After experiencing a stroke that affected a small area of his right parietal cortex, Dr. McDonald lost his ability to play a piece by reading a musical score. Moreover, he could no longer appreciate the emotional content of music. The exact function of this area of the parietal cortex awaits further study. However, it may well serve to bind together specific pieces of information, such as the visual information about notes in a piece of music and the actions needed to produce them on an instrument (Janata, 2007).

Lest you think that brain trauma has only negative consequences, consider the amazing case of Dr. Tony Cicoria, a surgeon who was struck by lightning (Sacks, 2007). After a few weeks of recovery, Dr. Cicoria first began to crave listening to piano music, and then he began to hear novel music playing in his head. Those effects would be surprising in a musician, but Dr. Cicoria had little prior interest in music. However, he soon began to devote himself to music, learning to both play and compose music. Although the neural realignment that occurred is not clear, Dr. Cicoria's transformation illustrates that one's brain has the capacity for a deep appreciation of music.

The Role of Cognition in Music Perception

To create a piece of music, the composer organizes a sequence of notes that occur over time. When the song is played, listeners don't hear a series of disconnected tones. Instead, they hear the melodic phrases created by the composer. What are the factors that lead us to organize the individual notes into melodic structures? Given our earlier discussions, you should correctly surmise that the factors that enable us to analyze complex auditory scenes are also applied to music. Thus, the qualities of the notes (pitch, timbre, spatial location, loudness) and how they are spaced in time (rhythm) lead people to organize the notes into melodies (Deutsch, 1999a). When you listen to a guitar solo, you are able to follow the melody because the sounds are similar in quality (pitch and timbre) and occur fairly close together in time.

As we have mentioned earlier, Gestalt laws of grouping and the figure-ground relationship can be applied to music (Deutsch, 1999a; Radocy & Boyle, 2003). Consider the law of similarity, for example, which states that similar objects tend to be seen as a unit. Look at the music by Beethoven in Figure 11.4. This is a melody played by a single instrument. As you

▶ **FIGURE 11.4** Melody typically heard as two melodic streams on the basis of the law of similarity. (From Beethoven's *Six Variations on the Duet* "Nel cor piu non mi sento" from Paisiello's *Molinara*)

can see, the tones alternate between two different pitch ranges. In ordinary music, listeners tend to group a tone with immediately preceding or following tones because of the law of proximity. When the Beethoven passage is played fast enough, however, listeners prefer to group a tone together with tones from approximately similar pitch ranges. As a consequence, listeners report hearing two simultaneous melodic streams—one high and one low—rather than a single melody that flutters between high and low pitch. At slower speeds, listeners still tend to group in terms of similarity rather than proximity, although the grouping is not nearly so compelling.

Another important Gestalt principle involves the figure-ground relationship. As is the case for visual stimuli, only one melodic line can be heard as "figure" at any given time. We focus our attention on this line so that we can notice relationships within the melody and recognize it. In contrast, any other melodic lines form the background. We are aware of these other lines, but they merely add interest. As with the famous vase-faces illustration in Figure 5.9, we cannot concentrate on both the figure and the ground at the same time. However, we can usually force ground to become figure. You might want to turn on the radio and notice whether you can readily force a guitar melody to become the figure, making the singer's melody retreat into the ground.

In a classic experiment, Dowling (1973) examined listeners' ability to separate two melodies and perceive figure-ground relationships. He presented two familiar tunes: "Mary Had a Little Lamb" and "Three Blind Mice." In this unusual presentation, however, the tones in the two tunes were interwoven, so that "Three Blind Mice" was played for tones 1, 3, 5, and so on, and "Mary Had a Little Lamb" was played for tones 2, 4, 6, and so on. When the two tunes were presented in similar pitch ranges, observers were unable to perceive two different tunes. However, two separate melodies could be recognized

if the tunes were spaced about an octave apart, or if the two tunes were made to differ in timbre or loudness (Dowling, 2001). Once the melodies were recognized, however, listeners reported an interesting figure-ground relationship. When they attended to "Three Blind Mice," for example, "Mary Had a Little Lamb" became background. The two melodies could not be simultaneously perceived as figures. Similarly, attending to "Mary Had a Little Lamb" forced "Three Blind Mice" into the background.

Of course, this experiment would not have worked if people did not know the two songs. Consistent with Theme 4 of this book, our experience with music shapes our perception of the music we hear. Whether it's the anticipation of the next note of a familiar song or the more general expectation of chords that might occur in a particular genre of music, experience plays a vital role (Huron, 2006). Even nonmusicians can recognize when notes to familiar songs are misplayed or when an unfamiliar song has a discordant note. And some of the creativity of musicians resides in their ability to violate our expectations and surprise us. Levitin (2006) provides a number of such examples, such as the Beatles' use of a seven-measure melodic phrase in "Yesterday," when most pop music of that era used eight measures.

As we'll discuss in the context of speech perception, infants are fairly open to a wide range of sounds. However, as they gain greater experience with a language, they become more adept at perceiving the phonemes of that language. Similarly, infants are fairly open to a wide range of musical components (e.g., rhythm, consonance). However, through experience they become more adept at perceiving aspects of the music that surrounds them (Hannon & Trainor, 2007; Hannon & Trehub, 2005a, 2005b; Tillmann, 2005).

Throughout the text, we acknowledge the impact of experience (Theme 4) and the plasticity of the brain. Thus, you should expect that the auditory areas of infants' brains would differ substantially from the brains of musicians (Peretz & Zatorre, 2005; Rauschecker, 2001). By that same logic, adult nonmusicians should perceive music in ways that differ from musicians. In fact, a good deal of evidence supports such a claim (Fujioka et al., 2004; Granot & Donchin, 2002; Krumhansl, 2003; Schubert & Stevens, 2006). For example, even infants are sensitive to the melodic contour (pattern) of a song, so transposing the key of a song doesn't impair their ability to recognize the song (Justus & Bharucha, 2002). Because even neo-phyte nonmusicians recognize melodic contour, it is fairly basic to perceiving a piece of music. However, even for such a basic ability, musicians develop more sophisticated encoding strategies than nonmusicians, enabling them to become much more automatic than nonmusicians in processing melodic contour. As a result, musicians are more sensitive than nonmusicians to violations of expectations in the harmonic components of Bach chorales (Steinbeis et al., 2006).

Illusions in Music

One of the themes of this book is that the perceptual processes share similarities. Thus, organization and constancy play important roles in the perception of complex visual and auditory stimuli such as music. Similarly, music researchers have reported a number of musical illusions; illusions are not limited to visual processes. For instance, Roger Shepard (1964) used a computer to produce a series of complex tones that seem to increase endlessly in pitch. Each tone seems to be distinctly higher in pitch than the previous tone, yet after numerous tones you are back to the tone where you began! By carefully manipulating the harmonics, Shepard created the illusion of increasing pitch. You can hear examples of these Shepard tones in www Demonstration 11.3. Does this illusion remind you of the apparent spirals in the twisted cord illusion (Figure 5.27)?

Among Diana Deutsch's many contributions to music perception are a number of illusions. One of the most interesting is called the *octave illusion* (Deutsch, 2004, 2008). As illustrated in Figure 11.5, one tone is presented to one ear, and another tone an octave away is simultaneously presented to the other ear. For example, the first combination presented to the listener is G_4 (392 Hz) presented to the left ear and G_5 (784 Hz) presented to the right ear. In the next tone combination, however, the tone heights are shifted between the ears, so that G_4 is presented to the right ear and G_5 is presented to the left ear.

Try to predict what you'd hear if you were to listen to this simple auditory stimulus. You might think that you'd hear it just as presented (G_4 to the left side and then to the right side back and forth, while at the same time G_5 starts on the right side and then shifts to the left side and repeats). Surprisingly, that's not at

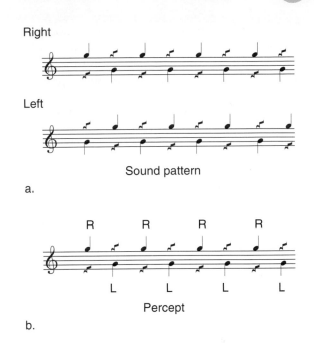

▶ **FIGURE 11.5**   The octave illusions as studied by Diana Deutsch. As illustrated in part *a*, alternating tones (H-L-H . . . in the right ear and L-H-L . . . in the left ear) are simultaneously presented to the right ear and the left ear. However, as illustrated in part *b*, people typically hear the high tone only in the right ear and the low tone only in the left ear. Note that people are hearing the low tone in the left ear when the high tone is actually presented to that ear! (From Deutsch, 1987)

all what you'd hear. In fact, you'd never hear the two tones simultaneously (even though the stimuli are entering each ear simultaneously). Instead, you'd hear a single tone, G_5, typically in your right ear, followed by a single tone, G_4, typically in your left ear, with a continuous alternation between the two. Note that such a perception means that even though a tone is presented to your left ear (e.g., G_5), you will mistakenly hear it in your right ear! Beyond that perplexing result, for most people the right ear hears only high tones and the left ear hears only low tones. This bias to hear the lower-frequency tone in the left ear appears to be due to an asymmetry between brain hemispheres in processing frequency information. Try this phenomenon for yourself in www Demonstration 11.4.

Deutsch has investigated another interesting auditory experience called the *tritone paradox*. (*Tritone* is a musical term for a half octave.) The ***tritone para-dox*** involves a misperception of pitch change, so it is related to the Shepard illusion mentioned earlier. In Figure 11.6, you see the tones of a scale portrayed in circular fashion. If you hear adjacent tones in a clockwise direction, you perceive the second tone to be higher than the first tone. If you hear adjacent tones in a counterclockwise direction, you perceive the second tone to be lower than the first one.

However, what would happen if the tones were not adjacent but far apart, such as E and A#? In the tritone paradox, pairs of complex tones on opposite sides of the pitch class circle are presented to listeners. The listeners judge simply whether the second tone is higher or lower in pitch than the initial tone.

Two interesting results emerge from judgments of these tone pairs. First, some people will hear the second tone as *higher* in pitch than the first, and other people will hear the second tone as *lower* in pitch than the first. As illustrated in Figure 11.7, one person (a) would hear an identical series of tones in a completely different way than would another person (b). Second,

a.

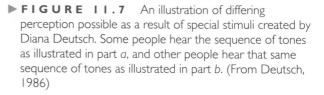

b.

▶ **FIGURE 11.7** An illustration of differing perception possible as a result of special stimuli created by Diana Deutsch. Some people hear the sequence of tones as illustrated in part *a*, and other people hear that same sequence of tones as illustrated in part *b*. (From Deutsch, 1986)

for the same person, an identical relative upward shift from one complex tone to another will appear to be upward with one starting tone and downward with a different starting tone!

What might form the basis for the individual differences in perception of the ordering of these complex tone pairs? In a series of studies, Deutsch and her colleagues have accumulated a good deal of evidence that experience underlies the tritone paradox (Deutsch, 1997, 2007, 2008; Deutsch et al., 2004b). Thus, people from southern England are more likely to hear G# as higher than D, but people from California are more likely to hear D as higher than G#. Moreover, people in the same family (e.g., mothers and children) tend to hear the tones as going up or down in a similar fashion. Deutsch hypothesizes that these differences arise from the pitch range that is typical of the speaking voices experienced in a particular geographical region, or more narrowly, within a family.

As in the case of visual illusions, you should find these auditory illusions to be very interesting. Our auditory system (peripheral and central components together) is extremely competent in perceiving complex stimuli. However, the auditory system will occasionally be led astray by particular stimuli—producing illusory experiences. Again, however, the illusions are important for their implications for perceptual processes. Investigations of these auditory illusions inform us about the role of neurophysiological and cognitive processes in the perception of complex auditory stimuli.

We have covered a lot of ground in our brief overview of music perception. At a very basic level, we can describe a musical passage in physical terms, with the two auditory canals receiving sound waves that

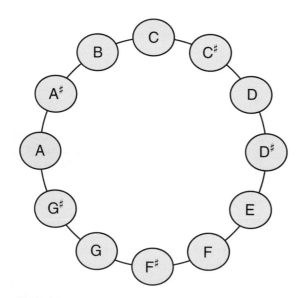

▶ **FIGURE 11.6** The pitch class circle. Complex tones that go around this circle in a clockwise fashion appear to rise. Complex tones that go around this circle in a counterclockwise fashion appear to fall. When pairs of tones that are not near one another (e.g., D and G#) are played after one another, some people hear the second tone as higher than the first tone and some people hear the second tone as lower than the first tone. (From Deutsch, 1991)

vary in frequency, amplitude, and complexity. Although humans may be predisposed to process musical stimuli, experience with musical stimuli is also quite important. To explore the relative contribution of these two components, researchers are paying close attention to the development of music perception in infants (Dowling, 2002; Ilari, 2002; Saffran, 2003b; Trainor, 2005; Trehub & Hannon, 2006). Consistent with Theme 4, cognitive processes are crucial to organizing the music, as they are for complex auditory patterns in general.

Section Summary:

Music Perception

1. Two aspects of pitch are tone chroma and tone height. Chromas at different heights are separated by octaves (doubling of frequency), and they are psychologically similar.

2. Most people have relative pitch perception and are quite good at remembering the pitch of the first notes in a familiar piece of music, even if they cannot name the note. A small number of people have either excellent pitch perception (absolute pitch) or terrible pitch perception (tone-deafness).

3. The frequency ratios of consonant tone combinations tend to be simple fractions. Perceptions of consonance and dissonance also depend on individual differences and cultural experience.

4. Musical instruments differ in their pattern of harmonics, which is an important component of timbre. However, the initial (attack) component of an instrument's sound wave is also important.

5. Because music is a complex auditory phenomenon, it activates areas of the brain that process such auditory stimuli. However, many other areas of the brain are also essential for music perception.

6. Music perception exhibits pattern and organization, based on the principles that seem to govern the organization of complex auditory stimuli, such as the Gestalt laws of grouping. For example, the law of similarity can be demonstrated when listeners perceive two simultaneous streams of music by grouping together tones that are similar in pitch. The figure-ground relationship can be observed in music; this effect can also be demonstrated when two tunes have been combined.

7. Along with the physical aspects of the stimuli (pitch, timbre, loudness, rhythm), cognitive processing is crucial for perceiving the patterns in music. Experience plays an important role in the development of music perception.

8. Researchers have devised several musical illusions (e.g., the octave illusion), indicating that our perception of music is not entirely consistent with the musical stimulus.

Speech Perception

Because we are social animals, communication among human beings is vitally important. We often communicate through the spoken word, although we obviously have other means of communicating. As is true of music, human speech is an extraordinarily complex auditory stimulus. However, we typically underestimate the complexity of both music and speech because we perceive them so effortlessly. To illustrate the complexity of speech and the operation of these central processes, think about a time when you overheard a conversation in a foreign language. The speakers seem to talk very rapidly, with no audible pauses between words. As we'll see shortly, even though you hear distinct words in your own language, those words are not easily identified within the speech stream.

Another indication that speech requires cognitive effort is the difficulty of talking while performing another task, such as driving a car. It's easy enough to carry on a conversation while driving—as long as nothing unusual happens. However, if we're devoting attention to talking, we cannot easily attend to all the other events around us when we're driving. For that reason, it's very dangerous to talk on a cell phone while driving (Horrey & Wickens, 2006). You may be surprised to learn that the root of the problem is not holding the cell phone, because it's equally dangerous to use a hand-free device. Instead, the problem seems to be that it's difficult to divide one's attention between speaking on the cell phone and looking around as you drive (Spence & Read, 2003; Strayer & Drews, 2008).

We will discuss a number of cognitive factors that influence speech perception. However, we'll begin with the physical stimulus—how speech is produced and what the sound waves look like when they reach our ears.

The Speech Stimulus

If we are concerned about speech *perception*, why should we discuss characteristics of speech *production*? First, when you learn more about the regularities of speech production and the resultant complex auditory stimulus, you'll better appreciate the problem confronting your auditory system. Second, as you will see later, some theorists think that speech production is crucial to speech perception.

PRODUCING SPEECH   A *phoneme* is the basic unit of speech—the smallest unit that makes an important difference between speech sounds (Cleary & Pisoni, 2001). Thus, /h/ and /r/ are both phonemes in Eng-

lish because it makes a difference whether you say you want to wear a "hat" or a "rat." (Notice, incidentally, that a phoneme is written with slashes on either side.) However, once you learn more about the complexity of the speech waveform (and coarticulation), you'll understand that identifying the segment of a wave as "the" phoneme /h/ or /r/ is a bit of a fiction (Greenberg, 2006).

A phoneme can also be defined as a group of sounds that are indistinguishable to native speakers of a language (Plomp, 2002). For example, try pronouncing the words *pie* and *top*, attending to the pronunciation of the phoneme /p/. When you pronounce the /p/ in *pie,* you release a small puff of air; no air puff is released for the /p/ in *top*. The two sounds are actually slightly different, and this difference could be important in other languages. Native speakers of English, however, classify both of these sounds as belonging to the same /p/ phoneme category.

Let us examine how the basic phonemes in English are produced. Figure 11.8 shows the major fea-

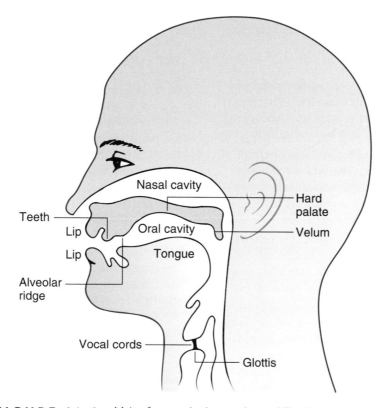

▶ **FIGURE 11.8**   Major features in the vocal tract. Vibration in the vocal cords produces voicing. The figure also illustrates various places of articulation.

tures in the *vocal tract*, the anatomical structures involved in speaking that are above the vocal cords. We speak by allowing air to pass through the vocal tract in a fashion that allows us to define the various phonemes. Table 11.1 shows how the tongue is important in producing vowels. For example, notice that when the front part of your tongue is raised high in your mouth, you can produce either the *ee* sound in *tree* or the *i* sound in *hid*.

The consonant sounds vary along three dimensions, as illustrated in www Demonstration 11.5: (1) *place of articulation*, which specifies where the airstream is blocked when the consonant is spoken (e.g., blockage by the two lips pressed together); (2) *manner of articulation*, which specifies how completely the air is blocked and where it passes (e.g., complete closure or blockage); and (3) *voicing*, which specifies whether the vocal cords vibrate. In www Demonstration 11.5, the top member of each pair of words is a *voiceless consonant*, which means that the vocal cords do not vibrate. Hold the palm of your hand on your throat as you pronounce the phoneme /p/; you should feel no vibration. In contrast, the bottom member of each pair of words in www Demonstration 11.5 is a *voiced consonant*, and the vocal cords *do* vibrate. With the palm of your hand on your throat, contrast the vibration for the phoneme /b/ as opposed to /p/.

When you speak, you also stress particular syllables in a word. You also have a rhythm to your speech, and you vary the tone of your voice. Collectively, these almost musical aspects of speech are referred to as *prosody*. Prosody is quite important for understanding speech, and it is related to the three dimensions of speech sounds discussed above (Greenberg, 2006).

PHYSICAL CHARACTERISTICS OF THE SPEECH STIMULUS   In the previous section you learned that researchers classify speech sounds by the way they are produced. If you watch a person speak, however, you will quickly see how difficult it is to determine exactly what the mouth, tongue, and vocal cords are doing at every instant. Imagine the problems you faced as an infant who wanted to communicate with those around you. Perhaps in addition to watching people speak, you focused on the speech sounds as you heard them and as you produced them yourself.

Researchers interested in studying the speech sounds developed the *speech spectrogram* or *sound spectrogram*, which is a diagram that shows the frequency components of speech (Plomp, 2002). Figure 11.9 (page 312) shows a speech spectrogram produced when a speaker said the word *dough*. As you can see, a spectrogram represents the passage of time along the *x*-axis, with the word *dough* requiring somewhat less than half a second to produce. The frequency of the sound waves is shown along the *y*-axis. The amount of energy at each frequency-time combination is indicated by the darkness of the region. White areas indicate that—at a particular time—virtually no energy was present at the corresponding frequency.

Notice that Figure 11.9 shows horizontal bands of concentrated sound energy called *formants*. In this figure, a first (lowest frequency) formant is located at about 500 Hz, and a second formant is initially located at about 1500 Hz, but it moves downward a mere 1/10 of a second later. You can also see a third formant at about 2500 Hz and a fourth formant at about 3800 Hz.

Analyses of speech spectrograms have revealed some interesting characteristics of human speech. For example, we might guess that the phonemes of a spoken word would appear as discrete units in time, rather like beads on a string. Thus, you might expect that the word *dog* would have a spectrogram with three segments, with /d/ first, then /o/, and finally /g/. Contrary to expectations, speech spectrograms typically reveal that the phonetic segments overlap considerably. Some acoustic energy from the final /g/ sound is present even before the energy from the initial /d/ sound has faded completely. As Hockett (1955) picturesquely described spoken language, the stimulus reaches the listener not in the form of beads on a

▶ **TABLE 11.1**   Producing Vowel Sounds

Part of Tongue Used	Height of Raised Portion of Tongue		
	High	**Medium**	**Low**
Front	tr<u>ee</u>	l<u>a</u>te	f<u>a</u>t
	h<u>i</u>d	l<u>e</u>t	
Middle	carr<u>y</u>	sof<u>a</u>	n<u>u</u>t
Back	r<u>oo</u>t	c<u>oa</u>t	t<u>o</u>p
	n<u>u</u>t	s<u>ough</u>t	

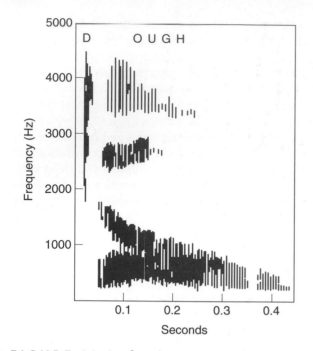

▶ **FIGURE II.9** Speech spectrogram of the word *dough*. Time is indicated on the *x*-axis and frequency on the *y*-axis. Darker areas of the figure illustrate increased amounts of sound energy at those particular frequency-time combinations. Thus, there is virtually no energy at 2000 Hz after 0.1 second (figure is all white across from 2000 Hz after 0.1 second). The four horizontal darkened areas are referred to as formants. The lowest formant (F1) shows a slight upward formant transition, and the second formant (F2) shows a downward formant transition (from 1500 Hz to about 1000 Hz). (Speech spectrogram courtesy of Speech Science Laboratory, Department of Speech Pathology and Audiology, State University of New York at Geneseo)

string but like a row of uncooked colored Easter eggs run through a wringer! This tendency for some of the sounds in a syllable to be transmitted at about the same time, rather than one at a time, is called **coarticulation** (Fowler & Galantucci, 2005; Plomp, 2002). Thus, although we can define a word as being comprised of phonemes, coarticulation makes it difficult to isolate individual phonemes within a speech spectrogram.

Phonemes are not normally pronounced in isolation. As a result, producing the surrounding phonemes actually modifies the sound of an individual phoneme. In other words, phonemes often do not have a single, constant pronunciation. The information in ▩ Demonstration 11.5 implied that a conso-

nant phoneme always has a consistent pronunciation—for example, that an /s/ always requires the same placement of tongue and lips, restriction of airflow, and vibration of vocal cords, no matter what word uses the /s/ phoneme. However, pay attention to the shape of your mouth for the /s/ sound when you say the words *seat* and *sorry*. The corners of your mouth are stretched far apart in *seat* but are close together in *sorry*. Your mouth anticipates the sounds that follow the /s/ sound, so that the resulting speech spectrograms would differ even though portraying the same phoneme.

The speech spectrogram is also a useful tool for studying a speech stream of many words. Given what you've just learned about the difficulty of identifying unique phonemes in the spectrogram of individual words, you can safely predict that it is also difficult to identify the boundaries between words in a speech spectrogram. In spite of the absence of clear boundaries in the speech stream of any language, speakers of that language hear distinct words (Jusczyk & Luce, 2002). Jusczyk (1986) provides us with a helpful visual analog of the problem confronting our auditory system. Read the following line:

THEREDONATEAKETTLEOFTENCHIPS.

Without spaces (the visual analog of pauses in speech), and with multiple potential interpretations, you'll struggle to read the line. Did you read the line as "There, Don ate a kettle of ten chips," or as "The red on a tea kettle often chips"? Did you have difficulty simply reading the line?

If there are no reliable markers to the beginnings and endings of words in a speech stream, how do we hear distinct words? Various approaches have been proposed, some drawing on physical information in the speech stimulus. Other approaches are more cognitive, using the meaning inherent in the stimulus or our expectations based on experience (Jusczyk & Luce, 2002). As you might imagine, many processes are likely involved.

These processes are not foolproof. Bond (1999, 2005) has catalogued several kinds of "slips of the ear," or cases in which we misperceive speech. Often these errors involve difficulties determining word boundaries in normal speech. For instance, "He works in an herb and spice shop," might be heard as "He works in an urban spice shop." In fact, such misperceptions are so common in hearing song lyrics that they are given the name *mondegreens*. Searching the Internet will provide you with many examples, such as hearing "Excuse me while I kiss this guy" instead of the actual Hendrix lyric "Excuse me while I kiss the sky."

Whether considering individual words or a speech stream of many words, it's clear that the stimulus is quite complex. Thus, any theory of speech perception must explain how we are able to understand speech in the face of such complexity. However, the difficulties are exacerbated when we consider the fact that people vary in their speech production (Luce & McLellan, 2005).

VARIABILITY IN SPEECH PRODUCTION   If you are a native speaker of American English, consider how different the language sounds when spoken in different regions of the country. Then consider listening to people speaking with British accents, or to people whose primary language affects their pronunciation of English words. The pronunciations of specific sounds vary tremendously, and yet we are able to understand the speech, albeit sometimes with difficulty.

Even within the same dialect of a language, we encounter variability in speech. Consider, for example, how physical differences in the vocal apparatus create variety. When a 6-year-old boy speaks the word *cat,* the physical characteristics of the sound waves may be entirely different in amplitude, frequency, and complexity from when that same word is spoken by his 60-year-old grandfather. Even among adults, the vocal tract—which is used to produce speech—is 15% longer in males than in females. As a consequence, female speakers have comparatively higher frequencies than males (Jusczyk & Luce, 2002).

We also encounter variability in the speech of the same person. For example, think how the pitch of your voice would change if you wanted to say the sentence "Isn't that just marvelous?" with sarcasm, as opposed to enthusiasm. Clearly, emotions affect the speech stimulus (Juslin & Scherer, 2005; Trainor et al., 2000). For example, when people smile, their vocal tracts shorten somewhat, which raises the pitch of their voices. Emotions affect a number of different aspects of speech prosody. Of course, pronunciation can also be influenced by what the speaker is doing while talking. Think of how different the speech stimulus would be if the person were speaking while eating a cookie or using a toothbrush.

Another source of variability in pronunciation is our own sloppiness. If people are asked to read a list of isolated words, their pronunciation is reasonably precise and standardized. However, almost all speech perception involves strings of words. In everyday language, our pronunciation of words is imprecise and variable. Cole and Jakimik (1980) point out how the word *what* can be pronounced numerous ways in the sentence "What are you doing?" They include the variants "Whacha doing?"; "Whadaya doing?"; and "Whaya doing?" You may be able to add other possibilities.

With normal speech, our pronunciation is often so sloppy that you can barely identify a word or phrase when it occurs out of context. For example, in a classic study Pollack and Pickett (1963) recorded the conversation of people waiting for an experiment to begin. Later, these people were asked to identify isolated words and phrases from their own conversations. People who heard a single word were only about 50% accurate, and recognition rose to only about 70% when two or three words were presented.

In short, any given word can be pronounced in a wide variety of ways because of differences in the age and gender of the speaker, other sources of individual differences, dialect, emotions, and sloppiness. And yet—miraculously—we generally manage to perceive speech accurately. In this respect, speech perception resembles two visual processes. Recall that our discussion of pattern recognition pointed out how we can identify the letter *M* even when it is written in a variety of sizes and styles. Furthermore, the discussion of constancy pointed out our ability to perceive qualities of an object even though the distance, angle of orientation, and brightness differ from one viewing to the next. An inherent property of perceptual systems is that they can extract important information out of potentially misleading clutter.

The enormous number of patterns it must be prepared to decipher further complicates the task facing our auditory system. Consider that the average American high-school graduate's vocabulary may be as large as 45,000 words (Comings et al., 2006). The mystery, then, is that we can perceive speech quickly and with a generally high degree of accuracy when so many potential words exist, when those words are pronounced with such variability, and when clear boundaries between individual words are nonexistent. Given the complexity of the problems involved in speech perception, several theorists have proposed that humans must have evolved specialized processors for speech. You'll see such a proposal in one of the theories of speech perception we'll now consider.

Theories of Speech Perception

At this point in the chapter, you should recognize the problems facing theories of speech perception. The speech stimulus is extraordinarily complex and seemingly ambiguous, yet we typically extract clear individual words and meaningful messages. How are we able to do so? Researchers have proposed a number of different theories of speech perception, but we'll focus our attention on two broad camps: Special Mechanism accounts and General Mechanism accounts of speech perception (Diehl et al., 2004).

Special Mechanism accounts propose that speech perception relies on special speech modules. A *module* is a separate, special-purpose neural mechanism designed for a specific task such as object recognition or color perception (Fodor, 1983). You should think of a module as a heuristic device or artificial construct. That is, scientists find it useful to propose a module in order to develop a theory, even though they may not have any evidence that such a neural mechanism actually exists.

People in favor of the Special Mechanism accounts feel that we have separate speech modules that confer distinct abilities on the listener, much like sound localization in the barn owl and echolocation in the bat. These proposed speech modules are thought to enable listeners to segment the blurred stream of auditory information exhibited in spectrograms into distinct phonemes and words. These theorists believe that a more generalized auditory perception module handles other acoustic information. Many of these theorists also believe that humans are born with an innate ability to represent speech at a phonetic level.

In contrast, proponents of *General Mechanism accounts* argue for a more parsimonious interpretation—no special speech modules exist. These theorists argue that our auditory systems have evolved in such a way that humans are able to process both speech and nonspeech stimuli by means of the same mechanisms. For example, Lori Holt (2005, 2006) has shown that preceding a speech segment with nonspeech stimuli (tones) will affect the perception of the speech segment. Such results support the notion that speech perception can be explained by the same perceptual

and cognitive mechanisms that support all auditory perception.

When we discussed speech production earlier in this chapter, we noted that some theories of speech perception were closely tied to speech production. We'll now explore the motor theory of speech perception, which closely links speech perception and speech production.

THE MOTOR THEORY OF SPEECH PERCEPTION
The motor theory proposes a special mechanism for speech perception. The original version of this theory appeared in the 1950s, and it has evolved over the intervening years in response to ongoing research (Galantucci et al., 2006; Plomp, 2002). According to the *motor theory of speech perception*, humans have a specialized device (phonetic module) that allows them to decode speech stimuli and permits them to connect the stimuli they hear with the way these sounds are produced by the speaker. One of the prime movers of the motor theory of speech perception was Alvin Liberman (1982, 1992, 1996), who died in 2000 at the age of 82.

For example, Liberman didn't think of coarticulation as a problem, but as an efficient way to convey phonetic information. However, with the evolution of coarticulation, humans also evolved methods of perceiving individual phonemes and words present in the complex speech stimulus. In its earliest version, the theory proposed that people could perceive speech by determining the motor commands involved in producing speech. For example, you can hear the phoneme /t/ in any word and immediately recognize that it was made by pressing the tongue against the alveolar ridge, thereby blocking air passage while not vibrating the vocal cords.

We should stress that this recognition occurs automatically and without cognitive analysis. This explanation is somewhat similar to the explanation for the ability of humans to immediately perceive biological motion, as described in Chapter 8 (Johansson, 1985). Our perceptual systems may be specially designed to process messages from other human beings, whether those messages represent body movement or speech.

Over the years, Liberman and his colleagues modified the motor theory in the face of research developments (Galantucci et al., 2006; Plomp, 2002). In the end, however, there is little support for the notion that speech processing is special. Nonetheless, other aspects of the motor theory may be worth retaining, including the important connections between speech production and speech perception.

For instance, Carol Fowler (2003; Fowler & Galantucci, 2005) has developed the direct realist theory, in the spirit of Gibson's "direct perception" approach (Cleary & Pisoni, 2001). Like the motor theory, this theory emphasizes the importance of speech production (e.g., vocal tract movements), but without postulating any special mechanisms (Diehl et al., 2004).

General Mechanism theorists acknowledge the correlation between speech production and speech perception, but argue that the relationship is not causal. That is, speech production yields a speech stimulus that contains a wealth of information. However, the essential part of speech perception is not the speech production itself, but the rich auditory product of speech. We will now survey two major battlegrounds—categorical speech perception and duplex perception—that developed in the controversy between the Special and General Mechanism theorists.

CATEGORICAL SPEECH PERCEPTION   In Chapter 7, we discussed how the smooth continuum represented by the color spectrum that runs between 400 and 700 nm does not produce a similarly smooth continuum in our perception. Instead, we tend to categorize the colors of the spectrum. For example, an abrupt boundary in the region of 490 nm separates the greens from the blues. On one side of the boundary, we call the colors green; on the other side, we call the colors blue.

We've already seen that both musicians and nonmusicians can categorize continuous auditory frequencies into segments called chroma. Even though they may not be able to name each note, people can distinguish one note from another. Such categorization of auditory stimuli is vital for speech perception.

In general, *categorical perception* occurs when we have difficulty discriminating between members of the *same* category, but we are readily able to discriminate between members of *different* categories (Diehl et al., 2004). When we consider speech sounds, for example, listeners can easily discriminate between sounds from two different categories, such as /p/ and /b/. If humans do have categorical perception, then discrimination between two different /p/ sounds from the same speaker should be poor.

What is the basis for the discrimination between /p/ and /b/? As we have already mentioned, /b/ is a voiced consonant and /p/ is an unvoiced consonant; otherwise they are similar sounds. Vowels, such as the /a/ in *pad*, are voiced. Therefore, when we say "pad," the voicing does not begin until the /a/ phoneme. However, /b/ is a voiced consonant, so voicing begins with the /b/ when we say "bad." The onset of voicing in *bad* comes slightly sooner than the voicing in *pad*, and in fact determines whether we will hear "bad" or "pad." The time from the beginning of an utterance until voicing begins is referred to as *voice onset time* (*VOT*).

Using artificially created "speech" stimuli, researchers can vary VOT systematically. Varying the onset of voicing before /a/ continuously from 0 to 60 milliseconds does *not* result in continuous perceptual changes. Instead, people report hearing either "ba" or "pa" (see Figure 11.10a). With very brief VOTs, people always report "ba," and with longer VOTs, people always report "pa." (Keep in mind that the basis for these discriminations is a difference of a small fraction of a second.)

At an intermediate voice onset time, around 25 milliseconds, people shift from reporting "ba" to reporting "pa." The *phonetic boundary* is the point at which people shift from reporting one phoneme to reporting the other phoneme. On either side of the phonetic boundary, people have difficulty discriminating between the sounds. For example, VOTs of 0 or 20 milliseconds would both be heard as "ba."

How did categorical speech perception become a battleground among speech perception theorists? The Special Mechanism theorists argued that categorical perception was due to the special speech module. They argued that continuous nonspeech sounds (e.g., a birdsong, the sound of a jackhammer) were perceived as a whole, and not categorized. As further evidence, they presented a particular speech sound (such as "ba") until people showed adaptation. In a fashion similar to that observed with visual stimuli, adaptation was thought to "fatigue" the speech module, leading to a shift in the phonetic boundary seen in Figure 11.10b. After people listened to "ba" for a long time, the phonetic boundary shifted so that a much shorter VOT was sufficient for them to report hearing "pa."

Such evidence seemed quite strong, but the General Mechanism theorists were able to provide even stronger counterevidence. Because nonhuman species

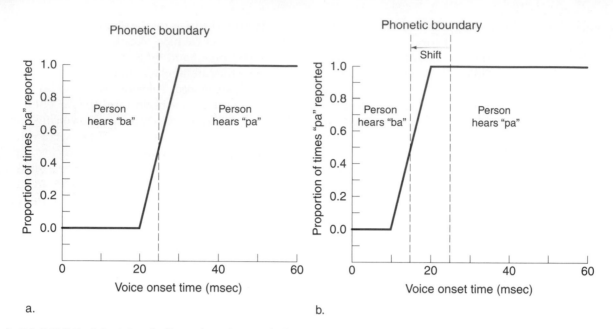

FIGURE 11.10 An illustration of categorical perception. Voise onset time is shown on the x-axis, and the proportion of times people report hearing "pa" is indicated on the y-axis. Part *a* illustrates that the phonetic boundary between "ba" and "pa" is at a voice onset time of about 25 milliseconds (msec). When voicing doesn't begin until after 25 msec, people are more likely to report hearing "pa." When voicing begins earlier, people report hearing "ba." Part *b* illustrates the impact of first adapting the listener to "ba"—a shift in the phonetic boundary that leads to the perception "pa" with a shorter voice onset time. (*Source:* Reprinted from *Cognitive Psychology, 4,* 1, Peter D. Eimas & John D. Corbit, "Selective Adaptation of Linguistic Feature Detectors," p. 11, copyright © 1973, with permission from Elseiver.)

do not have the speech abilities of humans, they should not have a speech module. Therefore, one would not expect nonhuman species to exhibit categorical perception. However, using methods adapted to the various species involved, researchers have demonstrated categorical perception among a veritable menagerie of animals, including budgerigars, chinchillas, Japanese quail, and macaques (Dooling et al., 1995; Kuhl, 1989).

An additional problem for Special Mechanism theorists is that humans exhibit categorical perception for complex *nonspeech* sounds (Diehl et al., 2004). These findings argue that categorical perception in humans is most likely a product of a more general auditory processor. Furthermore, researchers have found that—with extensive practice—people are able to make discriminations among speech sounds on the *same* side of the phonetic boundary (Cleary & Pisoni, 2001).

Thus, the evidence seems quite strong that a specialized speech module is not responsible for categor-

ical perception. However, proponents of the Special Mechanism account felt that they had another piece of evidence in support of the existence of a special speech module, and we address that issue now.

DUPLEX PERCEPTION   Another effect that could reflect the operation of a special speech module is referred to as *duplex perception*. **Duplex perception** arises when the same sound can have both speech and non-speech qualities (Cleary & Pisoni, 2001; Liberman & Mattingly, 1989). Ordinarily, as seen in Figure 11.11*a*, speech sounds are heard as a complex sound present at both ears (binaural). Duplex stimuli are created by cutting out a small portion of a speech sound—a formant transition—as illustrated in Figure 11.11*c*. When presented in isolation, this sound is heard as a chirp. In a typical experiment, the formant transition is presented to one ear, and the remaining speech sound segment (base) that would typically be heard as "da" is presented to the other ear (see Figure 11.11*b*). Interestingly, what people typically report hearing when these

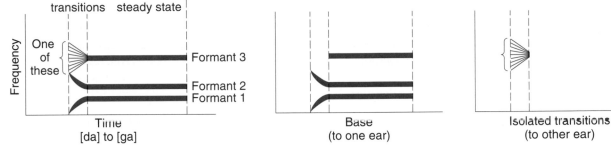

a.

Formant transitions | Vowel steady state

One of these {

Frequency

Formant 3

Formant 2
Formant 1

Time
[da] to [ga]

Normal (binaural) presentation

b.

Base
(to one ear)

c.

Isolated transitions
(to other ear)

Duplex-producing (dichotic) presentation

▶ **FIGURE 11.11**   A schematic figure of speech spectrograms to illustrate a typical duplex perception study. As in Figure 11.9, the x-axis indicates time and the y-axis indicates frequency, but the spectrogram is simplified to show the formants and formant transitions more clearly. The top of the figure shows the base sound and the nine possible formant transitions of the third formant (F3) leading to the perception of sounds from "da" to "ga." A person would typically report hearing "da" when hearing the base sound alone (part b). A person reports hearing an upward or downward chirp when hearing only the formant transitions presented to one ear (part c). The crucial test occurs when the formant transition is presented to one ear simultaneously with the base in the other ear. It probably comes as no surprise that a person hears a chirp in the ear to which the formant transition was presented. However, in the other ear a person hears a speech sound that combines the formant transition (from the opposite ear) and the base sound (presented in that ear). The fact that the same auditory information (formant transition) can take on both nonspeech and speech characteristics was seen as evidence that humans have both a general acoustic module and a specialized speech module. (From Liberman, 1982)

two sound stimuli are presented together is a chirp in one ear and "da" or "ga" in the other ear (depending on which of the nine formant transitions is presented). Similar results are obtained with 3- and 4-month-old infants (Eimas & Miller, 1992).

Thus, the same sound (the formant transition) is heard as a simple nonspeech sound (in one ear) *and* as part of a speech sound (in the other ear). This result appears to support the Special Mechanism account, because the same acoustical information is processed as both general auditory information and as a part of a speech sound.

As in the case of categorical perception, however, proponents of the General Mechanism account were able to offer evidence that argues against these interpretations of duplex perception (Mattingly & Studdert-Kennedy, 1991). For example, Ciocca and Bregman (1989) varied the duplex perception procedure very slightly. Earlier duplex perception studies presented only a single formant transition (chirp) in one ear, while simultaneously presenting the base to the other ear. Instead of presenting just one formant

transition (the chirp) to one ear, Ciocca and Bregman first repeated the formant transition over and over (a string of chirps). Then, after presenting the string of chirps to one ear, they presented the typical base to the other ear simultaneously with one of the formant transitions. Note that this final complex stimulus is *identical* to the one presented in a typical duplex perception study.

What would you predict that people hear in the Ciocca and Bregman study? (It may help to first think of Gestalt principles, such as good continuation and similarity.) With the slight contextual change of a series of formant transitions, people were much less likely to integrate the formant transition with the base. Consistent with the Gestalt principles of good continuation and similarity, the series of formant transitions (chirps) form an integrated stream. As a result, each chirp seems to go with the other chirps and *not* with the base. Thus, people heard the base as though no formant transition were present (i.e., as "da"). A special module for speech should *always* integrate the formant transition and the base. Ciocca and

Bregman interpret their results as arguing against a special speech module.

Eventually, even Liberman (1992) was forced to admit that the notion of a special speech module was not widely accepted. But, rather than completely dismiss all elements of the motor theory of speech perception, some theorists hope to salvage some components (Galantucci et al., 2006). Even though there may be no special speech module, it is surely the case that speech is a special human ability (Massaro, 2004). In fact, our ability to perceive speech without a special module may be even more impressive. If there is one area where some evidence might emerge that areas of the brain are specialized for speech processing, it is in studies of brain activity during speech perception.

Speech and the Brain

As is true of music, speech is a complex auditory stimulus, so it will be processed by the auditory system discussed in Chapter 10 (Adams, 2006; Greenberg & Ainsworth, 2004). Although one may make the case that speech is special, there is little evidence thus far that areas of the brain are specialized for speech perception (Meyer, 2006). For instance, even 3-month-old infants listening to speech show activity not only in the auditory areas but also in the prefrontal cortex (Dehaene-Lambertz et al., 2002; Dehaene-Lambertz et al., 2006).

As we'll demonstrate later in this chapter, both visual and auditory information play important roles in speech perception. Thus, areas of the brain that process visual information play important roles in speech perception (Bernstein, 2005). The auditory cortex is certainly vital for the processing of all complex auditory stimuli, including speech. However, so many other areas of the brain are involved in speech perception that it's difficult to specify which areas of the brain are specific to speech. Nonetheless, you have likely heard of two areas that are involved in speech.

In the late 1800s, Paul Broca identified an area of the (typically left) frontal cortex that is involved in language processing, though it isn't limited to spoken language (Horwitz et al., 2003). People with damage to Broca's area typically exhibit an aphasia that leads to difficulty in producing speech, but only moderate problems in comprehending speech. People with **Broca's aphasia** will produce a type of telegraphic speech that is comprised primarily of content words with few connecting words. They clearly struggle to produce coherent speech and may be well aware of the impoverished nature of their communications.

Carl Wernicke was a contemporary of Broca's, and he identified another part of the brain involved in speech. This area is called *Wernicke's area*, which is in the (typically left) temporal cortex near the auditory cortex. People with damage to this area exhibit **Wernicke's aphasia**, which is characterized by a deficit in language comprehension; their language production is typically wordy and confused, even though the rhythm and syntax seem roughly normal.

The contribution of areas of the brain outside of the auditory cortex is certainly consistent with the notion that cognitive processes play important roles in speech perception. We'll next investigate a number of different phenomena that illustrate how these cognitive processes operate.

The Role of Cognition in Speech Perception

Our discussion of auditory perception in Chapter 10 and in this chapter has focused primarily on physical characteristics of sound stimuli and how the auditory system transforms these stimuli. According to Theme 4 of this book, our prior knowledge, context, and expectations are critical in shaping our perceptions. Given that speech is a complex auditory phenomenon, these higher mental processes would certainly be expected to influence speech perception. Our perception of speech, for example, will be aided by top-down processing as well as bottom-up processing. That is, we perceive speech because of the combination of our cognitive processes and the information available in the auditory stimulus. Let's discuss several ways in which top-down processing affects speech perception.

PRIOR KNOWLEDGE INFLUENCES SPEECH PERCEPTION It's actually easier to perceive speech if you know that the auditory stimulus is speech. For example, Remez and his colleagues (1981) recorded a spoken sentence, "Where were you a year ago?" and then transformed the sentence by eliminating some of the acoustical information. One group of listeners was told nothing about the nature of the sounds; they were simply asked to report their impressions of the stimuli. Most did not realize that it was speech, and only 2 people out of 18 correctly identified the sentence. Another group of listeners was told that they would hear a sentence produced by a computer; half the people correctly identified the sentence in this condition. If we are oriented toward hearing speech, we are more likely to perceive it.

In fact, prior knowledge is so powerful that people will "hear" words when no words are present. When you play speech backwards, no real words are present. As a result, when people listen to backwards speech or music—without any special instructions— they rarely hear any words, let alone satanic messages. However, if people first hear a suggestion about the content of the passage, they are much more likely to hear the suggested message (Vokey & Read, 1985). To experience the impact of backwards speech for yourself, try www Demonstration 11.6.

CONTEXT INFLUENCES SPEECH PERCEPTION   By 1901, William Bagley (1874–1946) had completed the first empirical work on the influence of context on speech perception, using the newly invented Edison phonograph (Plomp, 2002). In fact, when researchers unearthed Bagley's work in the 1980s, they found that his conclusions were remarkably modern. For example, Bagley noted that degraded polysyllabic words are more easily recognized than degraded monosyllabic words. He also noted that "mutilated" words were correctly interpreted when presented in the middle of a complete sentence, but not when presented out of context. Note that his results foreshadowed the findings of Pollack and Pickett (1963) by 60 years. The important role of the surrounding context becomes especially evident when noise overwhelms a segment of speech.

Suppose that you join some friends for dinner. You make a screeching sound with your chair as one friend asks you to pass the salt. You still perceive her message as an intact utterance, with no missing phonemes. Every day, in every possible setting, portions of our utterances are concealed by both intentional and unintentional noises of short duration. Nevertheless, we perceive speech accurately, without lamenting the missing sounds. In everyday life—and also in the laboratory—we demonstrate **phonemic restoration**, which occurs when a speech sound is replaced or masked by an irrelevant sound, and the perceptual system restores or fills in the gap appropri-

ately. In most cases, phonemic restoration works so well that the listener cannot identify which speech sound was missing.

Richard Warren and Roslyn Warren (1970) reported the classic study on the phonemic restoration effect. They recorded the sentence "The state governors met with their respective legislatures convening in the capital city." Then they carefully cut one portion out of the recorded sentence, basically, the first /s/ in "legislatures." A coughing sound was inserted to fill the gap. (Thus, in the laboratory studies, a phoneme is actually replaced by a cough rather than covered by a cough.) When listeners heard this revised sentence, they experienced a compelling auditory illusion. They reported that the /s/ sound was just as clear as any of the phonemes that were actually present. Even when they listened to the sentence repeatedly, they judged the sentence to be intact. The cough seemed to supplement the sentence rather than replace any speech sounds. You can experience the phonemic restoration effect yourself in www Demonstration 11.7.

In the study in which the word *legislatures* was interrupted, the phonemes are so highly constrained that "s" is the only possible missing sound that would complete the word in a meaningful way. What happens when phonemes are not so highly constrained? In other research, Warren and Warren (1970) played four sentences that were identical except for a different word spliced on at the end of each sentence. In these sentences, the asterisk symbol (*) represents the position at which a loud cough replaced a phoneme.

1. "It was found that the *eel was on the axle."
2. "It was found that the *eel was on the shoe."
3. "It was found that the *eel was on the orange."
4. "It was found that the *eel was on the table."

What did the listeners report hearing? Warren and Warren found that the interpretation of the ambiguous word *eel depended on which final word they had heard. Listeners reported hearing "wheel" in the first sentence, "heel" in the second, "peel" in the third, and "meal" in the fourth. Context clearly influenced speech perception, and memory must be involved because the people did not hear the contextual cue until late in the sentence.

Phonemic restoration does require contextual information. Consider the Dutch language, in which the word for "of course" may be spoken in its complete form (*natuurlijk*) or in a reduced form (*n'tyk*) that is common in casual speech. When the reduced words are presented in isolation, they are difficult to identify. However, when the same words are presented in the context of a string of words found in casual speech, they are more easily identified (Ernestus et al., 2002). Listeners exhibit phonemic restoration in these reduced forms when they occurred in the context of a string of words, but not when they occurred in isolation (Kemps et al., 2004).

In summary, then, phonemic restoration illustrates that top-down processes are important in speech perception (Samuel, 1996, 2001). Because we do not need to hear every phoneme distinctly to perceive speech, any theory of speech perception must incorporate some elements of top-down processing. Consistent with Theme 4 of this book, such cognitive factors play important roles in speech perception. However, consistent with Bagley's findings, many different kinds of context affect speech perception.

One important type of context is visual: Listeners can perceive speech more clearly when they can see lip movements. In the final section of this chapter, we will review research that investigates the relationship between auditory and visual information, beginning with research on visual effects on speech perception.

Section Summary

Speech Perception

1. Speech perception is a complex process, requiring attentional resources. As a result, it's dangerous to talk on a cell phone while driving.

2. A phoneme is the smallest unit that makes a difference between speech sounds. We produce phonemes by a unique combination of characteristics such as place of articulation, manner of articulation, and voicing.

3. A speech spectrogram illustrates the frequency components of speech, including bands of sound energy called formants. Speech spectrograms reveal that sounds in a syllable exhibit coarticulation, so that a phoneme may not be readily apparent in the spectrogram. In addition, a phoneme's sound can change, depending on the surrounding sounds.

4. A speech spectrogram of a speech stream will rarely show separation between words. Nonetheless, people can recognize words and identify the boundaries between them.

5. Speech perception theorists have typically held one of two basic orientations: Special Mechanism or General Mechanism. The Special Mechanism theorists argue that humans have a specialized module for speech perception. The General Mechanism theorists argue that speech is processed by the same mechanisms that process all auditory stimuli.

6. Two pieces of evidence for the Special Mechanism account of speech perception are categorical speech perception and duplex perception. However, proponents of the General Mechanism account have provided more compelling evidence that neither categorical speech perception nor duplex perception requires a special speech module. As a consequence, the General Mechanism account is currently more widely held.

7. Many areas of the brain process speech and other complex sounds. However, at least two areas of the brain are important for speech. Damage to Broca's area primarily produces an aphasia that reduces the ability to produce speech. Damage to Wernicke's area primarily produces an aphasia that reduces the ability to comprehend speech.

8. Both experience and context aid in the perception of speech. Thus, we're better able to perceive speech if we know that the auditory stimulus is speech or if we know the topic of the speech. We're also better able to perceive speech if it occurs in the context of a phrase or a sentence.

9. Phonemic restoration occurs when the perceptual system fills in a missing phoneme that has been replaced by an irrelevant sound. Listeners are unable to locate the position of the missing phoneme, and phonemic restoration is influenced by the nature of the sentence. Context clearly influences speech perception, consistent with Theme 4 of this book.

Interactions between Auditory and Visual Stimuli

As Theme 1 suggests, interactions among the senses are very important. In our everyday experience, sounds and the objects that produce them tend to go together. When they do coincide, auditory information can affect visual perception, and visual information can affect auditory perception. First we'll review research on the interaction between lip movements and speech perception. Then we'll review some research on the interaction between music and film.

Interactions between Speech and Visual Information

If you recall the ventriloquism effect we discussed in Chapter 10, you know that visual stimuli may affect auditory perception. Moreover, as we have discussed in earlier chapters, the face is a particularly salient visual stimulus. Lawrence Rosenblum is an important researcher of audiovisual speech. He points out that speech is often accompanied by visual information from the face of the speaker. Therefore, we might actually consider speech to be multimodal, rather than simply auditory (Rosenblum, 2005). Even though we can perceive speech as a purely auditory phenomenon (e.g., cell phone conversations), speech certainly evolved with face-to-face conversations. And we've seen that some theories of speech perception rely on our ability to see the speaker's face to learn how to produce and perceive speech.

To illustrate the importance of such visual information for speech perception, try the following demonstration. When you're next watching a news program (having a talking head looking directly at you), turn down the sound so that it is barely audible. Turn away from the screen and try to hear what's being said. You should find it a difficult task. Now listen while watching the screen. You should find the task to be much simpler. In fact, we routinely rely on lip movements when trying to hear someone speak in a noisy environment (Bernstein et al., 2004; Schwartz et al., 2004).

For example, when listening to speech in a noisy environment, we are much better at perceiving the speech when we are familiar with the speaker's lip movements (Rosenblum, Miller et al., 2007). Experi-

ence with lip movements is very important. For example, consider the fact that we can identify close friends if we see point-light displays (as used in studies of biological motion) of their lip movements as they speak (Rosenblum, Niehus et al., 2007). It's interesting that, in spite of the importance of lip movements, in a quiet environment, we look more at the speaker's eyes than his or her mouth (Everdell et al., 2007).

Obviously, the facial movements and the speech information are typically consistent. However, what happens when facial information disagrees with auditory information? Have you ever watched a foreign film in which the English dialogue was dubbed? Or have you ever seen a movie in which the soundtrack was out of synch, so that the actors' lip movements did not match the dialogue? If so, then you know how disturbing such disparity between lip movements and dialogue can be. Even infants find the disparity disturbing (Summerfield, 1992).

In some cases, discrepancies between visual and auditory information have been more illuminating than disturbing. For example, Dominic Massaro (1998, 2004) and his colleagues have done extensive research using a computer-generated face (called "Baldi") to investigate the role of visual information in speech perception. In a typical study, Massaro presented "ba" and "da" sounds and three intermediate sounds. He also had Baldi's lips produce "ba" and "da" and three intermediate lip movements. Of course, when the auditory and visual information were entirely consistent, people reported hearing either "ba" or "da." However, when people saw Baldi say "ba," they reported hearing the intermediate sounds as "ba" much more frequently than when relying on auditory information alone. Even the intermediate lip movements could bias the perception of the auditory stimulus.

Another disparity between auditory and visual information is found in the **McGurk effect**, in which the discrepancy between lip movements and speech sounds leads to a perception that differs from both the auditory and the visual information. This effect was discovered accidentally by McGurk and McDonald (1976). They used a video of a woman speaking, and they then superimposed different audio information over the video. As illustrated in Figure 11.12, people saw the lips of a speaker form one sound, such as "ga," while they heard a different sound, such as "ba."

In this example, what do you think people hear? If vision dominates, they should hear "ga." If audition dominates, they should hear "ba." The results show that people hear neither "ba" nor "ga." Instead, they hear a completely different sound produced by fusing the auditory and visual input—in this case "da." These unexpected effects are quite powerful and have been replicated by a number of different researchers (Campbell, 2008). Try www Demonstration 11.8 to experience the McGurk effect.

As you might imagine, the McGurk effect is sensitive to changes in the visual information. For instance, the McGurk effect is reduced (but doesn't disappear) when the facial information is greatly degraded (MacDonald et al., 2000). If you remember our discussion of face perception in Chapter 5, you'll recall that it is very difficult to perceive faces accurately when seen upside down. Rosenblum and his colleagues (2000) demonstrated that the McGurk effect is disrupted when the face (or the mouth) is inverted. Although some visual distractors can minimize the McGurk effect, it remains strong even when the visual and auditory information differ in time or space (Campbell, 2008). The McGurk effect is also sensitive to changes in the auditory stimulus, though it may be found with nonspeech stimuli such as clicks (Brancazio et al., 2006).

Research highlighting the interaction between vision and audition is important because it supports Theme 1 of this text. Thus, although we can investigate the senses in isolation, most perception is likely multimodal, with people integrating input from many senses. In later chapters, we will return to this important theme when discussing interactions among other senses. For now, we'll explore another interaction between vision and audition.

▶ **FIGURE II.12** An illustration of the McGurk effect. The observer sees a person repeating "ga" over and over, but the voice the observer hears is repeating "ba" over and over (synchronized with the lips of the person speaking). Surprisingly, the observer typically hears neither "ga" nor "ba," but hears "da" being repeated. The McGurk effect illustrates the interaction of auditory and visual information in the perception of speech.

Interactions between Music and Visual Information

Just as visual information can affect speech perception, so too can it affect the perception of lyrics in music. You may recall that people often mistakenly interpret the lyrics of songs (mondegreens). Hidalgo-Barnes and Massaro (2007) have shown that people are more accurate in identifying lyrics when they can watch Baldi (the computer-animated face) correctly pronounce the words in the song.

But can music affect our perception of visual information? One place to examine that question is the effect of background music on perception of movies. We already know that music can arouse emotional responses (Sloboda, 2005; Watt & Quinn, 2007; Zatorre & McGill, 2005). Does the background music serve to heighten the suspense or excitement you feel in certain scenes? Marilyn Boltz (2001, 2004) has conducted a number of studies to investigate the role of background music on the perception of films. In one study, Boltz and her colleagues (1991) presented short clips from commercial films. Half of the clips portrayed positive emotions (a happy ending) and half portrayed negative emotions (a tragic ending). Music was also recorded from the films, half of which was judged to be positive and half to be negative in emotional content.

In one experiment, people watched 16 film clips. Half of the clips were paired with "appropriate" (mood congruent) music and half with "inappropriate" (mood incongruent) music. Thus, appropriately upbeat music accompanied half the clips with happy endings and inappropriately somber music accompanied the other half. Appropriately somber music accompanied half the clips with tragic endings and inappropriately upbeat music accompanied the other half. People were first asked to recall as much detail as possible about the clips. Memory was better for the scenes from the film clips with appropriate background music.

Next, people were asked to listen to 32 melodies (16 old and 16 new) and identify which melodies they had heard earlier in the session. Although the people had previously heard the background music, they could not readily recognize it when tested on memory for the music by itself. Thus, memory for the background music by itself was poor.

Next, Boltz and her colleagues tested whether people could accurately match music with scenes from the film clips. People were reasonably good at matching the background music with the appropriate clip—even for film clips they had not recalled on the initial test. Thus, the results demonstrate that background music can actually enhance memory for visual scenes.

Section Summary

Interactions between Auditory and Visual Stimuli

1. One might characterize all speech perception as audiovisual. Visual information aids in the perception of speech, particularly under noisy conditions.

2. With the McGurk effect, there is a disparity between the lip movements and the sound being heard. People report hearing a sound that is intermediate between the sound that ordinarily accompanies the lip movements and the sound they actually heard.

3. The McGurk effect is reduced when people see distracting visual stimuli or degraded facial information, but not by a spatial or temporal discrepancy between the visual and auditory information.

4. Background music influences people's processing of visual images in movies, enhancing their ability to recall the scenes.

Review Questions

1. Contrast complex auditory stimuli with the simple auditory stimuli we often discussed in Chapters 9 and 10. Perception of complex auditory stimuli shares many similarities with perception of complex visual stimuli. Illustrate as many similarities between auditory and visual pattern perception as you can. Pay particular attention to cognitive factors. Why do you think these similarities might have emerged?

2. We discussed pitch perception in this chapter and in Chapter 10. Why is pitch more complicated than a simple arrangement of notes from low to high? Be certain to mention the concepts of tone chroma and octave. Then discuss how notes with similar tone chromas from different octaves are similar to each other. How might you use pitch to contrast the physical stimulus and the psychological stimulus?

3. Imagine yourself at a concert of your favorite music. Discuss how the material in the music perception portion of the chapter might make you more aware of perceptual qualities of the

music. Be certain to mention pitch, tonality, loudness, timbre, and tone combinations.

4. Speech perception seems so easy and effortless. Nonetheless, theories of speech perception are complex. Why? Describe the distinctions among the Special Mechanism and the General Mechanism accounts of speech perception. In spite of the evidence against Special Mechanisms, why might one still believe that speech is special?

5. Illusions play important roles in helping us to understand the operation of perceptual systems. How might the musical and speech illusions (e.g., phonemic restoration) in this chapter help inform our understanding of the auditory system? Can you make any links to visual illusions?

6. Integrate the information from the previous two chapters with information from this chapter to describe what happens in the brain as you listen to music and to speech. How might the complexity of brain activity argue against areas of the brain being specialized for music or speech?

7. Imagine that you have just heard a reporter on television deliver a report. As you watched the reporter, you heard one sentence distinctly except for a part of one word. Use the information from this chapter to illustrate how you would be able to understand the utterance in spite of incomplete auditory information.

8. In earlier chapters, we often commented on the importance of context for visual perception. In this chapter, you have seen a number of examples in which context influences auditory perception. Use several examples from this chapter to clarify the role of context in perception. Does the role of context seem to differ when dealing with auditory stimuli?

9. Top-down (or conceptually driven) processing becomes especially important in the perception of complex stimuli. Describe how top-down processes operate when we perceive complex auditory stimuli. How do bottom-up (data-driven) processes operate when we perceive complex auditory stimuli? Which class of processes do you think is dominant in the perception of complex stimuli?

10. After learning about visual perception, you've now completed three chapters about auditory perception. Given what you know now, how would you characterize the relationship between vision and audition? Use information in this chapter (e.g., the McGurk effect) to support your position.

Key Terms

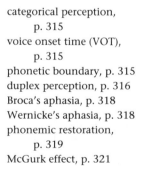

Recommended Readings

Bregman, A. S. (1994) *Auditory scene analysis: The perceptual organization of sound.* Cambridge, MA: MIT Press.

> Bregman has been a major contributor to the research on how we are able to isolate and understand portions of an ongoing complex "stream" of varying sound waves (such as music or speech). Don't be discouraged by this weighty tome (over 700 pages). If you follow Bregman's advice, you can get a clear picture of the research area by reading the first and last chapters. You'll find more recent articles about auditory scene analysis, but this book is a classic.

Diehl, R. L., Lotto, A. J., & Holt, L. L. (2004). Speech perception. *Annual Review of Psychology, 55,* 149–179.

> This review article provides a helpful overview of theoretical approaches to speech perception and the challenges that face the various approaches.

Levitin, D. J. (2006). *This is your brain on music.* New York: Dutton.

> Levitin has an interesting history. He first worked in the musical world as a musician and producer, and now he works in the academic world as a researcher interested in music. His well-written book bridges those worlds, illustrating a musician's sensibilities and a researcher's desire to understand (and explain) the world. It's a very approachable amalgam of autobiographical reflection and scientific exploration.

Patel, A. D. (2008). *Music, language, and the brain.* New York: Oxford.

> If you're interested in reading a text that integrates research on music and speech, you'll find Patel's book particularly useful. He provides an integrated exploration of the underlying basics (e.g., pitch, timbre, and rhythm) as well as more complex aspects (e.g., syntax and meaning) of both music and speech.

CHAPTER 12

The Skin Senses

The Skin
Receptors in the Skin
From the Skin to the Brain

Touch
Afferent Systems for Touch
Passive Touch
Active Touch
Interactions between Touch and Vision

Temperature
Afferent Systems for Temperature
Thresholds for Temperature
Adapting to Temperature

Pain
Afferent Systems for Pain and Gate-Control Theory
● IN DEPTH: Phantom Limbs and Pain
Measuring Pain
Adapting to Pain
Controlling Pain

Kinesthetic and Vestibular Senses
Kinesthetic Sense
Vestibular Sense

IN ELEMENTARY SCHOOL, your teacher might have told you about the five senses: vision, hearing, touch, smell, and taste. Aristotle used this classification system more than 2,300 years ago, and it is probably still the most common one. However, it's clear that we rely on more than five senses. In this chapter, we'll explore a set of senses embedded in our bodies, collectively called the **somatosensory system** (from the Latin and Greek *soma* meaning "body").

The somatosensory system has three separate systems that interact with one another (Pinel, 2006). We'll ignore one system, which monitors your body's internal states. We'll focus primarily on another system, which interprets the impact of the outside world on your body. This system provides you with touch, temperature perception, and pain perception. Finally, we'll consider the system that informs you about whether you are standing upright or tilted and where your body parts are in relation to each other. That somatosensory system is augmented by information from the vestibular system of the inner ear, which we first mentioned in Chapter 9.

The Skin

Your skin represents the largest sensory system you own, with a surface area of about 2 square yards in adults (Weisenberger, 2001). Contrast this size with the relatively minuscule receptive surfaces for vision and hearing. In spite of the size advantage of your skin senses, both vision and hearing may seem more important to you. However, have you ever contemplated what your skin and the skin senses can accomplish? First, consider the protective value of the skin. The skin senses inform you that an insect is crawling up your leg. The skin senses also detect changes in temperature and attempt to protect you from extremely hot or extremely cold temperatures. The pigmentation in your skin (melanin) protects you from some harmful effects of sunlight. Furthermore, the skin senses send you a pain signal to protect you from potential tissue damage. And, if you're careless—and you get a sunburn or a cut—your skin will usually repair itself.

Receptors in the Skin

Figure 12.1 shows a diagram of **hairy skin**, the kind that covers most of your body and contains either noticeable or almost invisible hairs. Another kind of skin, called **glabrous skin**, is found on the soles of your feet, the palms of your hands, and on the smooth surfaces of your toes and fingers. Glabrous skin is similar to hairy skin except that its outer layer is thicker and it has a more complex mixture of receptors. This complexity is probably related to the fact that these areas are sensitive to stimulation and that we use these areas of skin (especially our hands) to actively explore the physical qualities of objects (Carlson, 2007).

Notice that the skin in Figure 12.1 can be divided into two main layers. The **epidermis**, or outer layer, has many layers of dead skin cells. The **dermis** is the layer that makes new cells. These new cells move to the surface and replace the epidermis cells as they are rubbed off. Also notice that the skin contains an impressive array of veins, arteries, sweat glands, hairs, and receptors. The skin also contains melanocytes, which produce the melanin that causes the variety of skin colors (Jablonski, 2006). The skin varies greatly in thickness, ranging from about 0.2 mm thick (about as thick as 2 pages of this book pressed tightly together) to about 6 mm thick on the sole of the foot (Mountcastle, 2005).

Scattered throughout the skin are many kinds of receptors. With the variety of receptors present in the skin, you can easily understand why early theorists developed specificity theory. **Specificity theory** states that each of the different kinds of receptors responds exclusively to only one kind of physical stimulus (for example, pain), and each kind of receptor is therefore responsible for only one kind of sensation. Specificity theory emerged from the **doctrine of specific nerve energies**. Johannes Müller (1801–1858) initially proposed that different sensory nerves have their own characteristic type of activity and therefore produce different sensations. Maximilian von Frey (1852–1932) extended the doctrine of specific nerve energies by suggesting different types of receptors for touch, warmth, cold, and pain.

Another theory about our somatosensory system also focuses on the importance of the receptors. **Pattern theory** suggests that the *pattern* of activity from different types of receptors determines the sensation. According to pattern theory, each type of receptor responds to many different kinds of stimulation, but it responds more to some than to others. Advocates of both specificity and pattern theories contributed to our understanding of the skin senses.

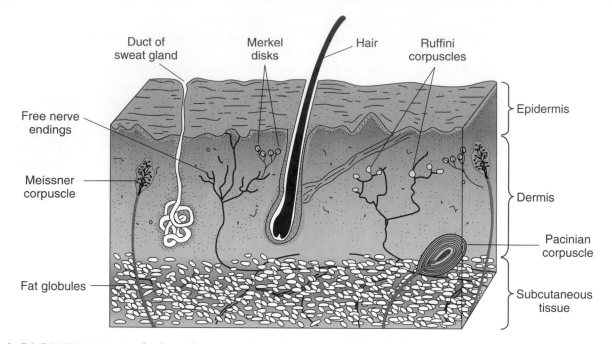

Duct of sweat gland · Merkel disks · Hair · Ruffini corpuscles · Free nerve endings · Meissner corpuscle · Fat globules · Epidermis · Dermis · Pacinian corpuscle · Subcutaneous tissue

▶ **FIGURE 12.1**   A schematic cross section of a segment of hairy skin. Notice the two layers of skin and the distribution of the receptors throughout the skin.

From a modern perspective, however, neither approach is completely correct.

As you know from reading about vision and audition, perception requires that we transduce a physical stimulus into neural energy. However, so much processing takes place beyond the receptors that a focus on receptors will likely produce an overly simplistic notion of perception. The same is true of our somatosensory system. The complexity of connections between neurons and receptors further complicates the situation. For example, a single neuron may innervate many receptors and a single receptor may be innervated by different neurons. Thus, it's very difficult to determine how each individual receptor contributes to activity in the afferent neurons. As a result, researchers have focused their attention on the function of the afferent neurons, rather than the specific types of receptors (Goodwin & Wheat, 2004; Weisenberger, 2001).

As we discuss receptors in subsequent sections, you'll see that neither a specificity theory nor a pattern theory is entirely adequate. In essence, most variants of these theories emphasize a bottom-up approach. However, consistent with Theme 4, cognition plays a vital role in the functioning of the somatosensory system. As we'll see later in the chapter, we must consider top-down processes to fully understand how our skin senses work.

From the Skin to the Brain

In previous chapters, we discussed the visual and auditory pathways from receptors to the brain. With the visual and auditory systems, the receptors occupied relatively small areas very near the brain. In contrast, the somatosensory receptors are distributed over the entire body. To gain a sense of the distances involved, consider that the afferent neurons from your toes are the longest neurons in your body (Pinel, 2006). Information from these widespread receptors then passes through the spinal cord on its way to the brain.

Within the spinal cord, we can identify two systems important for somatosensory information: the spinothalamic system and the lemniscal system (Weisenberger, 2001). The *spinothalamic system* has smaller nerve fibers and slower transmission. The spinothalamic system primarily conveys information about temperature and sharp pain, though it also conveys some crude touch information. In contrast, the *lemniscal system* has larger fibers and faster transmission; it primarily conveys fine touch and vibration

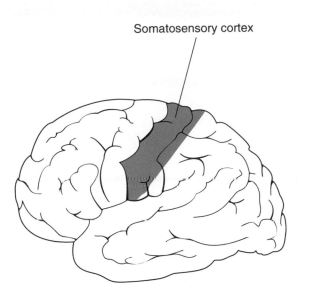

Somatosensory cortex

▶ **FIGURE 12.2** Location of the somatosensory cortex, the ultimate destination of the information from the skin receptors through the spinothalamic and lemniscal systems.

information. (It may be helpful to recall that the spinothalamic system is small and slow, whereas the lemniscal system is large.)

Both the spinothalamic and the lemniscal systems eventually pass on their information to the somatosensory cortex, shown in Figure 12.2. However, their routes differ slightly—consistent with their names. The spinothalamic system passes through the spinal cord and the thalamus in the midbrain. The lemniscal system passes through the spinal cord into the medial lemniscus on its way to the thalamus. Both systems pass their information from the thalamus to the *somatosensory cortex* and other nearby areas of the brain.

Section Summary

The Skin

1. Skin is the largest sensory system; many kinds of receptors are found in the skin. The diversity of receptors suggests that each kind may have a specific function. However, because many different receptors likely respond to a stimulus, the pattern of activity among the receptors may be more important.

2. Two systems convey information from receptors to the brain: the spinothalamic system and the lemniscal system. The spinothalamic system primarily conveys information about temperature and sharp pain. The lemniscal system primarily conveys information about touch.

3. Both the spinothalamic system and the lemniscal system pass their information on to the somatosensory cortex.

Touch

Touch includes the sensations produced by deformation of the skin. That is, your skin becomes slightly distorted when you touch an object or an object touches you. In this section, we'll focus on the sensory aspects of touch. However, you should keep in mind the many social and psychological implications of touch. Consider, for example, the work of Tiffany Field, of the Touch Research Institute. Field and her colleagues have demonstrated positive effects of touch and massage on infants and adults with an array of different problems (Field, 2007; Field, Diego et al., 2006; Field, Hernandez-Reif et al., 2006). For instance, they've found that massage enhances growth in preterm infants. It also elevates attentiveness, reduces pain, and enhances immune function. Touch also serves a number of important communicative functions, including communication within emotional and sexual situations (Hertenstein, Keltner et al., 2006; Hertenstein, Verkamp et al., 2006). For now, however, we'll turn our attention to the more basic topic of how we encode touch.

Afferent Systems for Touch

Of the many types of receptors lying within your skin, four convey touch information. In an elegant example of form following function, each of the receptors encodes different information. Each of the four types of receptor likely sends its information to a different type of afferent neuron, creating four afferent systems (Fain, 2003; Johnson, 2002). We'll discuss a number of ways in which these systems differ, but you can see a summary in Table 12.1.

One way in which these afferent systems differ is in the size of their receptive fields. Entirely consistent with Theme 1 of this text, touch neurons connect to skin receptors so as to produce receptive fields similar

▶ **TABLE12.1**   The Four Afferent Systems for Touch

Afferent Type	SA1	SA2	RA1	RA2
Receptor type	Merkel disk	Ruffini corpuscles	Meissner corpuscle	Pacinian corpuscle
Sensory function	Form and texture perception	Motion direction, hand shape	Motion detection, grip control	Perception of vibrations
Effective stimulus	Edges, points, corners, curvature	Skin stretch	Skin motion	Vibration
Response to sustained pressure	Sustained, with slow adaptation	Sustained, with slow adaptation	None	None
Receptive field area	Very small	Fairly large	Fairly small	Relatively large
Sensitivity	Moderate	Very low	High	Very high

to those found in the visual system. That is, stimulating one relatively small area of the skin excites these afferent touch neurons, whereas stimulating a surrounding area of the skin inhibits these neurons. Moreover, as was true for the visual system, some neurons have smaller receptive fields and other neurons have larger receptive fields. As seen in Figure 12.1, when receptors are located nearer the surface of the skin (Merkel disks and Meissner corpuscles), the afferent neurons will have smaller receptive fields. When their receptors are located deeper within the skin (Ruffini and Pacinian corpuscles), the afferent neurons will have larger receptive fields.

These afferent systems then send their information to the somatosensory cortex. Some cells in the somatosensory cortex also exhibit relatively simple receptive fields, but others are more complex. For example, some cells are sensitive to orientation, responding better to a small horizontal bar against the skin than to a small vertical bar (Haggard, 2006). We'll now say a bit about each of the four afferent touch systems.

There are two types of *slowly adapting (SA) neurons*. Sustained pressure on the skin causes neurons of both types to fire continuously, with little adaptation. However, the neurons differ in a number of ways. The SA1 system is important for form and texture perception because of its small receptive fields. The SA2 system is important for detecting skin stretching and changes in hand and finger shape, with fairly large receptive fields. The axons of SA1 neurons connect to Merkel disks, which are found in the dermis just below the epidermis. The axons of SA2 neurons con-

nect to Ruffini endings, which are found deeper within the dermis. Locate both the Merkel disks and Ruffini endings in Figure 12.1.

Table 12.1 also shows two types of *rapidly adapting (RA) neurons*. These neurons fire with the onset or removal of pressure on the skin, but they don't continue to fire with sustained pressure. The RA1 system is responsible for detecting low-frequency vibration, with fairly small receptive fields. RA1 neurons are connected to Meissner corpuscles, which—like Merkel disks—are found near the outer part of the dermis. Neurons in the RA2 system connect to Pacinian corpuscles. The Pacinian corpuscles are responsible for detecting rapid vibration on the skin, as well as the roughness of surfaces (Bensmaïa & Hollins, 2005). Compared to the other touch receptors, the Pacinian corpuscles are located deeper within the dermis, and they are relatively few in number. However, they are extremely sensitive. Because of that sensitivity, it's difficult to accurately map the receptive fields of RA2 neurons. However, they are certainly larger than the receptive fields of the other touch neurons.

The Pacinian corpuscles are the largest sensory end organs in the entire body. Of course, everything's relative—they're about the size of the period at the end of this sentence. Each Pacinian corpuscle consists of many layers assembled in an onion-like fashion on the end of an axon. The unusual layered structure permits the successive layers to slip over each other. It is this structure that makes the Pacinian corpuscle more sensitive to a change in touch than to sustained touch. Thus, a Pacinian corpuscle in the sole of your foot would not continue to send out signals after you have been standing at a party for 3 hours, deforming the structure continuously. This receptor would, however, be particularly sensitive to high-frequency *change* in stimulation. As a result, it would readily signal the vibrations in the platform caused by an approaching train.

THE CORRESPONDENCE BETWEEN SKIN AND CORTICAL LOCATIONS   We discussed organizational schemes (e.g., retinotopic, tonotopic, and spatial organization) in both the visual and auditory cortex. Thus, you shouldn't be surprised to learn that the somatosensory cortex has its own unique organization. In a classic paper, Penfield and Rasmussen (1950) report studying patients whose skulls were opened up for tumor removal. Penfield and Rasmussen electrically stimulated various points on the somatosensory cortex. Then they asked the patients, who were alert because they had only local anesthetics, to identify the part of their body that tingled.

Figure 12.3 (page 332) shows the correspondence they found. Notice that this distorted creature has its body parts scattered along the edge of the cortex in a pattern that bears little resemblance to your own body. For example, the area for the hand is located near the area for the face. Furthermore, some large body parts, such as the hip, receive much less cortex space than some much smaller body parts, such as the lip. In the next section, we will see that the amount of space occupied on the cortex is related to thresholds of the various body parts.

Figure 12.3 shows that the somatosensory cortex is organized by location on the body (albeit in an unusual fashion). In addition, there are strips along the somatosensory cortex that are sensitive to particular types of input, such as light touch (Pinel, 2006). Thus, in the area most sensitive to facial stimulation, you'd find a strip of neurons most sensitive to touch on the face, another strip most sensitive to temperature on the face, and so on. Moreover, as one moves from the front to the back of the somatosensory cortex, the receptive fields may become more complex.

Passive Touch

As we discussed in earlier chapters, James J. Gibson (1966) had an important influence on theories of vision. He also explored an important distinction in touch perception. In one study, people first saw six small metal cookie cutters shaped like a teardrop, a star, a triangle, and so forth (Gibson, 1962). Thus, they knew what the stimuli looked like. To study *passive touch*, the researcher presses an object against a person's skin. People closed their eyes, and then Gibson pressed one of the cookie cutters against the palm of one of their hands. Under these conditions, people's identification accuracy was only 29%, although it was still above chance performance (17%). Gibson next studied *active touch*, in which people closed their eyes, and the researcher allowed than to explore objects by holding and touching them. Under these conditions, identification accuracy soared to 95%. The comparison wasn't completely fair, because the fingertips are more sensitive than the palm of the hand. (In other words, both the type of touch and the area of the skin varied.) Nonetheless, the discrepancy in performance highlights the distinction between two different types of touch. Later on, we'll talk about active touch; let's first explore passive touch.

ABSOLUTE THRESHOLDS FOR TOUCH   In classic studies on passive touch, researchers measure thresholds for the detection of a single skin indentation. To illustrate how parts of your body differ in their sensitivity, take a small piece of cotton and lightly touch it (or have a friend touch it) to the following parts of your body: the thick part of the sole of your foot, your cheek, your back, your nose, and your thumb. The cotton was probably particularly noticeable when it touched your cheek, yet its impact on the sole of your foot was so minimal that you probably had to check visually to be certain that the cotton was really touching your sole.

As you may recall, an *absolute threshold* is the boundary point at which people report the presence of a stimulus half the time. Weinstein (1968) conducted extensive research on touch thresholds. He examined both men and women, touching them on 20 different body parts with a nylon hairlike strand for which the force could be precisely measured. Figure 12.4 (page 332) shows the sensitivity for females and males. Notice three features of this diagram: (1) Women are more sensitive to touch than men for several parts of the body (that is, their thresholds are lower); (2) the parts of the body vary in sensitivity—for example, people are more sensitive in the facial area than around the feet; and (3) women and men differ in their specific patterns of sensitivity—for example, women's bellies and backs are nearly as

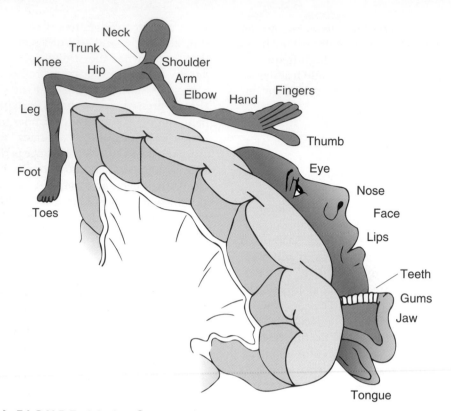

▶ **FIGURE 12.3** Correspondence between parts of the somatosensory cortex and body parts, as viewed from the front. The greater the size of the body part depicted, the larger the area of the cortex devoted to input from that part. (Based on Penfield & Rasmussen, 1950)

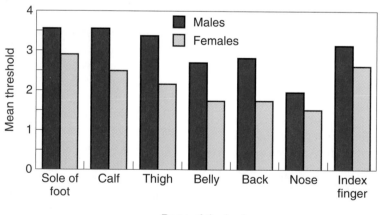

▶ **FIGURE 12.4** A comparison of detection thresholds for males and females. Note that a lower number indicates greater sensitivity. Females are typically more sensitive than males. Some body parts are more sensitive than others in both males and females. (Adapted from Weinstein, 1968)

sensitive as parts of their faces, but these body parts are relatively insensitive for men.

TWO-POINT THRESHOLDS FOR TOUCH   We have been discussing absolute thresholds. Another kind of threshold is a ***two-point discrimination threshold***, which measures the ability to detect that two stimuli are touching the skin, rather than a single point (Hollins, 2002). Typically, researchers assess two-point discrimination thresholds by selecting two blunt but narrow-diameter prongs and placing them some distance apart. Using the method of limits we discussed in Chapter 2, the observer reports whether he or she feels one or two stimuli. On descending trials, the distance between the two stimuli is systematically decreased until the observer consistently reports one stimulus. On ascending trials, the distance between the two stimuli is systematically increased until the observer consistently reports two stimuli.

Try WWW Demonstration 12.1 to illustrate two-point discrimination thresholds. We should mention that if you ever visit a neurologist for an extensive neurological examination, you are unlikely to escape without a test similar to this demonstration. We should also mention that people perform better on such discrimination tasks with practice, evidence consistent with Theme 4 of this text. WWW Demonstration 12.1 points out how two-point discrimination thresholds vary as a function of body location. When two toothpicks touch your calf, you feel one single touch rather than two. On your nose, however, you experience two distinctly separate touch sensations.

Weinstein (1968) measured two-point discrimination thresholds as well as the absolute thresholds discussed earlier. Again, the face was generally more sensitive than other regions. Weinstein also found that the fingers and toes are extremely sensitive in detecting two separate touch sensations.

Figure 12.3 illustrated that certain body parts correspond to large areas on the cortex, whereas other body parts correspond to smaller cortical areas. Weinstein discovered a consistent relationship between the size of the cortical area and the size of the two-point thresholds. For example, a large space on the cortex is devoted to the lip, and the lip is also very sensitive in its two-point discrimination threshold. In contrast, relatively little space on the cortex is devoted to the leg, and our discrimination is also poor in this area.

You may recall a similar relationship from Chapter 3. The largest space on the visual cortex is devoted to the fovea (cortical magnification), which also happens to be the area in which discrimination is best. Thus, the pattern is uniform across senses; when a large region of the cortex is devoted to information from a particular area of skin surface, we are quite sensitive to stimuli in that area of skin. This similarity between touch and vision is another illustration of Theme 1 of this textbook.

ADAPTATION TO TOUCH   As you know from our discussion of visual and auditory stimuli, change is important for perception. When stimuli don't change, we often adapt to them. In ***touch adaptation***, the perceived intensity of an unchanging tactile stimulus decreases over time. When you first put on the clothes you're wearing, you probably noticed the pressure of your pants, your shirt, and your socks. Very quickly, however, the sensations dissipated. In reading this paragraph, you probably directed your attention to your clothing, so you may have become aware of the pressures on your skin. Try WWW Demonstration 12.2 to illustrate touch adaptation.

Touch adaptation is not due solely to the receptors; it also involves neural factors (Hollins, 2002). As you recall (Table 12.1), there are two rapidly adapting afferent systems (RA1 and RA2), but there are also two slowly adapting afferent systems (SA1 and SA2). Given the diversity among these four systems and the nature of the stimuli they detect, touch adaptation has to be a complex process. Thus, adaptation to continuous pressure on the skin may well differ from adaptation to other types of tactile stimulation.

For example, our skin does adapt to vibrations on the skin. High-frequency vibrations (e.g., above 200 Hz) lead to adaptation to other high-frequency vibrations. Similarly, low-frequency vibrations (e.g., below 10 Hz) lead to adaptation to other low-frequency vibrations. However, high-frequency vibrations do not lead to adaptation to low-frequency vibrations. Nor do low-frequency vibrations lead to adaptation to high-frequency vibrations. Thus, humans seem to have two separate systems for detecting vibration (Hollins, 2002).

Our skin also allows us to determine the texture of a surface, such as fine or coarse sandpaper. Once again, however, there are differences in adaptation. For example, we do adapt to smooth, but not rough, surfaces (Hollins & Bensmaïa, 2007; Hollins et al., 2001). In fact, the adaptation for smoother surfaces probably emerges for the same reason that we adapt to vibrations. On the other hand, for rough surfaces, we may not adapt because we use spatial information (e.g., density of the grit on the rough sandpaper).

PASSIVE TOUCH AND PEOPLE WHO ARE VISUALLY IMPAIRED We've described research on passive touch using simple stimuli (one or two points) or vibrations of a small number of points. Devices that present more complex tactile stimuli have both theoretical and applied implications. For example, Sliman Bensmaïa (2006) conducts research using a device that has 400 unique vibrating points within an area as small as the pad of your index finger (1 cm^2).

It's possible that a version of Bensmaïa's device could one day be used as an assistive device for the blind. People have already developed devices that present a simpler pattern of stimulation to various parts of the body (e.g., back, tongue). One such device is the Optacon, which translates written letters and numbers into a 24 × 6 vibratory display (Johnson, 2002). The user points a camera at a written passage and the information is translated into the vibrotactile array, which stimulates the index finger. Essentially, blunt pins in the array vibrate where the camera detects darkness, creating a tactile image of the symbol being viewed by the camera. Using the Optacon, a person who is blind can learn to read a wide variety of texts.

Active Touch

So far, we have discussed situations in which a person sits patiently, waiting to be prodded, poked, and drawn upon. When we want to explore the world through touch, people are much more active. The perception of objects by touch is called *haptic perception*.

EXPLORING OBJECTS HAPTICALLY Roberta Klatzky, Susan Lederman, and their co-workers have had a tremendous impact on haptic perception research. They've identified a number of procedures people use when exploring different properties of objects (Klatzky & Lederman, 2008). For example, even if you could see an object, your hands would provide valuable information about its hardness and texture. To determine its hardness more precisely, you

would likely push against the object with a finger. In contrast, to determine its texture, you would likely rub your fingers laterally over the surface of the object. Try [www] Demonstration 12.3 to illustrate haptic perception and the various ways you explore objects by touch.

As you learned in the demonstration, you are able to determine properties of objects through a variety of haptic explorations. Moreover, haptic exploration allows you to identify objects. In fact, you would be able to identify a large number of relatively small common objects based solely on a few seconds of haptic exploration (Klatzky & Lederman, 2003a; Lederman & Klatzky, 2004a).

As you know, the human face is a very important stimulus. Ordinarily you are likely to use your visual system to learn about faces. However, if you were blindfolded, haptic information alone would allow you to identify faces and emotional expressions on faces with reasonable accuracy (Lederman, Kilgour et al., 2007; Lederman, Klatzky et al., 2007).

ACTIVE TOUCH AND PEOPLE WHO ARE VISUALLY IMPAIRED Consistent with Theme 4 of this text, people who are blind have a wealth of experience that makes them quite skilled at haptic exploration of objects. Some of their ability arises due to the plasticity of the brain (Merabet et al., 2008; Vanlierde et al., 2008). Even in people with normal vision, the visual cortex plays a role in haptic exploration (Sathian & Lacey, 2008). However, for people who are blind (including those blindfolded for only a couple of hours), the visual cortex plays an even greater role (Sathian & Lacey, 2007).

Morton Heller is a major contributor to touch research, with a special focus on haptic perception in people who are blind. Heller often compares active touch in people who became blind at an early age with people who became blind later in life and people who have normal vision (Heller, 2006; Heller et al., 2005). However, instead of actual objects, Heller typically uses raised line drawings in his research, which you should think of as "two-dimensional pictures." These complex "pictorial" representations are challenging haptic stimuli. In some studies, these raised-line drawings depict common objects, such as those seen in Figure 12.5a.

Based solely on haptic exploration of the raised line drawings, can you guess which group performed best at naming the stimuli? Because people who are

a. Raised line drawings of objects

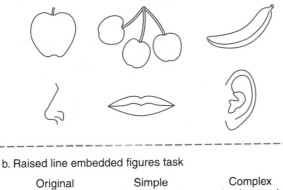

---

b. Raised line embedded figures task

| Original figure | Simple background | Complex background |

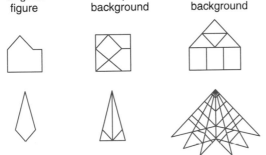

▶ **FIGURE 12.5** Examples of raised-line drawings used by Morton Heller in his research. Part *a* illustrates objects presented within categories (i.e., body parts, fruits). Part *b* illustrates the embedded figures test. The figure appears at the far left. People then had to determine where the figure occurred within either of the two types of background (simple or complex).

blind have more experience using only touch to learn about the world, you might expect both of the groups who are blind to perform best. However, Heller found that the late-blind group outperformed the other two groups (who didn't differ). Thus, the people best able to name the objects were those who had both prior experience with pictorial representation *and* substantial tactile experience.

Heller then made the task easier by first telling people the category (e.g., "fruit") for an object (e.g., "banana"). Once again, people who were blind from an early age performed poorly. However, the task still had an important semantic component. To make the task more purely perceptual, people were first given a raised line drawing and then asked to match it to one of four options. Under these conditions, all three groups performed extremely well.

Instead of raised line drawings of objects, Heller (2003) has also used the haptic equivalent of a visual task called the embedded figures task (Figure 12.5*b*). In essence, this task asks people to use only touch to detect a figure against backgrounds that are relatively simple or relatively complex. Simply looking at the stimuli should give you a clue as to the difficulty of this task. Once again, people who became blind later in life outperformed people who had been blind from an early age or blindfolded people with normal visual abilities. As is often the case in these tasks, people with normal visual abilities took longer to perform the task than those who had lost their sight (Postma et al., 2007).

An important application of active touch is the development of reading material for people who are blind. Louis Braille (1809–1852), a Frenchman who had been blind from the age of 3, developed the best-known system when he was only 15 years old. He was discouraged by the difficult task of trying to read the limited number of books specially prepared with raised versions of standard letters. After all, our visual system can readily distinguish a P from an R, but the task is much more challenging for our tactile system.

Figure 12.6 illustrates the letters in the **Braille** alphabet. Each black dot represents the raised portion of a 3 × 2 grid. As you might imagine after looking at the figure, reading Braille is a difficult skill to master. In fact, in spite of the proliferation of Braille resources, the vast majority of people who are blind

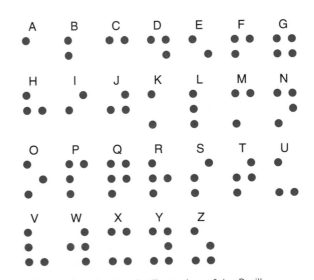

▶ **FIGURE 12.6** An illustration of the Braille alphabet.

never learn Braille. However, highly skilled readers process standard Braille at a rate of about 100 words per minute (Mountcastle, 2005). Some of that skill may be due to brain plasticity, because people who read Braille actually have larger areas of their cortex devoted to input from their index fingers (Melzer & Ebner, 2008).

People have developed many other tactile aids for people who are blind. For example, several systems have been developed to enable people who are blind to explore raised-line pictures. A number of systems, such as electronic touch tablets, provide tactile maps for navigation (Klatzky & Lederman, 2003b).

Touch can be useful for people who are deaf as well as people who are blind. For example, using the **Tadoma method**, a person who is deaf or deaf and blind places his or her hand on the lips and jaw of the speaker to pick up tactile sensations of speech such as airflow, lip and jaw movement, and vibration (Klatzky & Lederman, 2003b; Mountcastle, 2005).

Interactions between Touch and Vision

We have emphasized the relationships among the senses in Theme 1, and Chapters 10 and 11 have explored the interaction of vision and audition. The auditory system shares capabilities with the visual system (e.g., spatial perception). It also provides independent information (e.g., our ability to hear the approach of a train that we cannot see). Likewise, our sense of touch is capable of performing tasks that our visual system can also perform (e.g., raised-letter perception). However, the visual system also provides independent information (e.g., perception of hardness of objects or smoothness of fine-grained surfaces). In this section, we will continue to highlight relations among the senses by comparing touch and vision.

Earlier in the book, we noted that vision and audition typically provide consistent information. Vision and touch typically show the same consistency. For example, when you drive a car, the look and feel of the steering wheel will be quite consistent. Thus, it should make sense that as you perceive the world, you integrate information from various senses (Ernst & Newell, 2007; Lederman & Klatzky, 2004b). However, the information from different senses may be consistent but not identical. In fact, there may be an advantage to integrating the different information

weighted by the reliability of the source (Helbig & Ernst, 2007, 2008).

Farley Norman and his colleagues have conducted several studies suggesting that visual and haptic information about three-dimensional objects is similar, but not identical (Norman et al., 2008; Norman et al., 2004). They used stimuli that were molds of bell peppers, which have similar but discriminable shapes. With practice, people became quite good at feeling an unseen pepper and then picking the identical pepper from among 12 visible peppers. However, when people made same–different judgments between pairs of peppers, the visual information was more effective than the haptic information. The researchers used the signal detection method we discussed in Chapter 2. People experienced the peppers within the same modality (e.g., first looking at one pepper and then looking at a second pepper) or cross-modally (e.g., first feeling an unseen pepper and then looking at a second pepper). They then decided if the two pepper shapes were the same or different. People's sensitivity was best (measured with d') when looking at both peppers. Performance (measured by d' and by hit rate) suffered when people made cross-modal judgments (e.g., feeling the first pepper and seeing the second pepper).

Simple curves prove to be almost as tricky as bell peppers. In work similar to Norman's research, Ittyerah and Marks (2008) asked people to discriminate (same or different) between two curves carved into pieces of wood. To minimize the memory involved, people looked at both curves simultaneously, felt both curves simultaneously, or felt one curve while looking at the other. Consistent with Norman's results, they found that people performed best in the visual condition and worst in the cross-modal condition.

In touch research, there is a long history of creating a conflict between visual information and touch information. Which sense would you trust more? As in the case of visual and auditory information, you tend to trust the sense that is more capable at a particular task. Touch is particularly good at judging texture and hardness, and we will rely on touch rather than vision when making such judgments. In contrast, our visual system is very good at judging spatial location, size, and shape, and it will typically dominate the other senses in making such discriminations.

Here's an interesting demonstration of trusting vision over touch. Suppose, for instance, that you placed your hand inside a specially constructed wooden box. If you were to look into the box you would see a hand that you think is yours—but it's not. Instead it's a rubber hand located just to the side of your hidden hand. With such a set-up, Frank Durgin and his colleagues (2007) found that running a laser beam along the rubber hand led most people to feel the beam on their hand. Thus, seeing a laser beam on a hand that you think is yours is sufficient to lead you to feel the beam, even though there is actually no stimulation on your hand.

There are many circumstances under which we trust haptic information over visual information. Morton Heller (1992) provided an interesting situation in which people actually rely on touch more than vision. In our discussion of visual perception, we indicated that visual stimuli in unusual orientations are difficult to process—especially when the stimuli are upside down. Suppose that you were asked to discriminate between pairs of raised-line letters (*p* and *q*, *b* and *d*, and *W* and *M*) that you could only see upside down in a mirror. Not surprisingly, you would think that a *p* was a *b*, and so on. (Get a mirror and try this.) Heller found that, if you could also touch these raised-line letters, seen along with your hand in the mirror, you would often name the letter based on how the letter *felt* rather than on what you *saw*.

It's clear that touch plays important roles in our lives. Vision and audition provide us with information about stimuli that may be distant. However, touch specializes in telling us about very nearby stimuli, especially their texture (Heller & Clark, 2008). Under ordinary conditions, our perception of the world is a multisensory amalgam. When visual or auditory information is unavailable, touch information can enable us to navigate our complex world.

Section Summary

Touch

1. Researchers have identified four afferent systems that convey touch information. Two of the systems have rapidly adapting neurons and two have slowly adapting neurons. These afferent systems send their information to the somatosensory cortex.

2. Studies of passive touch show that females are often more sensitive than males and that some body parts (e.g., lips) are more sensitive than other body parts (e.g., back).

3. Two-point discrimination thresholds are also different for various body parts; these correspond to the amount of space occupied by that body part on the cortex.

4. Humans adapt to some touch stimuli, showing a gradual decrease in touch sensation as a result of prolonged stimulation.

5. Active touch is important when we explore objects and try to discover their properties; this is also called haptic perception. We use different haptic procedures depending on the quality of the object we are interested in investigating. Active touch is more precise and useful than passive touch.

6. Applications of active touch include Braille, designed to help people who are blind, and the Tadoma method, designed to help people who are either deaf or deaf and blind.

7. The senses are particularly dominant in their areas of specialization, and vision functions better than touch for the perception of structural features of stimuli, such as spatial location, shape, or size. Touch functions better than vision for the perception of hardness or roughness. Touch also provides more reliable information when the stimuli are in an unusual orientation for our visual systems (e.g., upside down).

Temperature

How hot or cold do you feel right now? Probably you feel reasonably comfortable. Your body has an impressive ability to regulate its own temperature and keep it at about 37° C (98.6° F). If you are in a snowstorm and your body temperature starts to drop, you shiver, a useful process for generating more heat. In addition, the blood vessels near the surface of the skin shrink in diameter so that less of the warmth from your blood will be lost on the surface. In contrast, if you are playing a fierce tennis game in the hot August sun, you sweat, and that cools your skin. Under these conditions, the blood vessels expand in diameter, so that more of the blood's warmth can be released.

Of course, in order to regulate temperature, your body must be able to perceive temperature (Jessen, 2001). Among the many receptors in your skin are some that encode temperature. In our brief discussion of temperature perception, we will examine the way your somatosensory system encodes temperature, detects temperature thresholds, and adapts to cool and warm temperatures.

Afferent Systems for Temperature

When discussing touch, we described four types of touch receptors that appear to connect to different types of somatosensory neurons. However, the temperature receptors are not so readily distinguished. Instead, the temperature receptors are the free nerve endings of somatosensory neurons. These free nerve endings are similar in appearance to one another, but they differ in function. Contrary to the predictions of specificity theory, these free nerve endings encode more than just temperature.

When you taste mint, would you describe the experience as "cool"? When you taste chili, would you describe the experience as "hot"? Have you experienced an object so cold or hot that it is painful to touch? If so, then you understand the complicated nature of the receptors for temperature, because of their linkages to taste and to pain.

A family of proteins called **transient receptor potential (TRP) channels** are responsible for the differences in sensitivity among the free nerve endings (Carlson, 2007; Story & Cruz-Orengo, 2007). Researchers have identified six types of temperature receptors, labeled by their TRP channels. Each of these TRP receptors signals a unique temperature range from extreme cold to extreme heat. The linkage to taste arises because, for example, the receptor that signals heat also responds to a chemical in chili and the receptor that signals coolness also responds to a chemical in menthol. The linkage to pain arises because some of the receptors also signal pain (Venkatachalam & Montell, 2007). We'll talk about taste perception in the next chapter and pain perception in more detail shortly.

Two types of neurons (called *A-* and *C-fibers*) carry temperature information from the skin to the brain. These neurons are also involved in pain perception. Thus, we'll have more to say about these neurons when we discuss pain perception. The information from temperature receptors is routed through the spinothalamic pathway to the somatosensory cortex and other brain areas (Gracely et al., 2002).

Given the different temperature receptors, you might think that you would feel extreme heat only by stimulating receptors for extreme heat. However, the situation is much more complicated. For example, most people can experience a phenomenon called *paradoxical heat*. A paradox emerges when an event has seemingly contradictory qualities, and **paradoxical heat** occurs when a combination of alternating warm and cold stimuli produces the sensation of painful heat (Bouhassira et al., 2005).

This demonstration can be found in museums such as the Ontario Science Center, and the experience is very powerful. Placing your hand solely on one set of tubes leads to a perception of cold, and placing your hand on the alternating set of tubes leads to a perception of warmth. However, placing your hand on both sets of tubes simultaneously leads to a sense of burning heat. If you are one of the people who feels the paradoxical heat, the experience is powerful, even though you know that the tubes cannot possibly be hot. Thus, you can perceive a painfully hot temperature by simultaneously stimulating both cold and warm receptors, as well as by stimulating just the extreme heat receptors.

Thresholds for Temperature

The temperature receptors are scattered throughout your body. As a result, some parts of your skin are sensitive to coolness (but not warmth) and other parts are sensitive to warmth (but not coolness). Try [www] Demonstration 12.4 to illustrate how temperature sensitivity varies greatly for different parts of your body.

We can often detect small changes in temperature on our skin, as minute as 0.003° C (0.006° F) (Weisenberger, 2001). No single value can be supplied as the absolute threshold for warmth and coolness sensations because the threshold depends on several factors. For example, the larger the portion of skin exposed to the warm or cool stimulus, the smaller the threshold. It makes sense that we can detect a modest change in temperature more readily on an entire arm than on a pinpoint-sized dot of skin.

People are remarkably poor at localizing temperature sensations for near-threshold stimuli. For example, radiant warmth applied to a person's chest might lead that person to report that her or his back was stimulated. However, we improve our localization ability for more extreme temperatures (Gracely et al., 2002). And under most circumstances, we can localize cold stimuli more accurately than warm stimuli.

Adapting to Temperature

When you first sit down in a hot bath, the temperature may seem unpleasantly hot. After a few minutes the temperature seems comfortable. If you then slide down further into the water so that your back is submerged, the temperature of the water surrounding your back is—once again—unpleasantly hot. The rest of your body had adapted to the hot temperature, but the newly immersed skin had not.

As you know, adaptation occurs when a stimulus is presented continuously; the perceived intensity of the stimulus decreases over time. ***Thermal adaptation*** is therefore a decrease in the perceived intensity of a hot or cold temperature as time passes. People seem to adapt to temperatures on the skin in the range of about 29° C to 37° C (84° F to 99° F). However, thermal adaptation is far less pronounced for extremely hot or cold stimuli. Outside this range, some adaptation will occur, but the temperature will seem persistently cold or warm (Gracely et al., 2002).

People are able to adapt fairly well to cool conditions and quite well to warm conditions. For example, Jessen (2001) describes Korean women divers who harvest abalones and seaweed from the ocean floor—even in winter. Even before they began wearing wetsuits in the 1970s, they would dive in water as cold as 10° C (50° F) for as long as 25 minutes, lowering their body temperature to 35° C (95° F). At the other extreme, endurance athletes can exercise for over an hour in warm environments, whether dry or humid. As a result, these athletes would raise their body temperature to 39.7° C (103.5° F).

To illustrate an adaptation effect that John Locke reported in the seventeenth century, try [www] Demonstration 12.5. As a result of the demonstration, you will note that people perceive relative, rather than absolute, temperature. A particular temperature can feel cold or hot, depending on the temperature to which we have become adapted. Once again, you should note the discrepancy between the physical world and the perceptual world.

Section Summary

Temperature

1. The body has several mechanisms for regulating its temperature.

2. Receptors with six different transient receptor potential (TRP) channels signal different temperature levels from extreme cold to extreme heat. These receptors are distributed throughout the body.

3. Thresholds for temperature are influenced by factors such as body part, or amount of skin exposed. People are poor at localizing temperature stimuli—especially when near threshold.

4. Thermal adaptation is a decrease in the perceived intensity of a cool or a warm temperature as a function of repeated exposure. People adapt fairly well to cool and better to warm conditions.

Pain

Pain researchers who are members of the International Association for the Study of Pain define ***pain*** as "an unpleasant sensory and emotional experience associated with actual or potential tissue damage" (Merskey, 2008, p. 13). Note the tight linkage of the sensory and emotional components of pain, which has not been the case in our discussion of other senses. Although some psychologists may ignore its contribution, emotion likely plays an important role in many areas of psychology—including perception. To acknowledge such complexity, David Krech (1909–1977) coined the term *perfink* to highlight the common interconnection of perception, feeling, and thinking (Aldous, 2001). Part of the reason that pain is such a complicated phenomenon is that numerous processes are involved.

As we've noted throughout this text, perceptual experience is subjective. That is, we can carefully measure and control physical stimuli, but the perceptual experience is much less easily measured. Nowhere is that disparity more obvious than in the study of pain. Suppose, for instance, that you see your friend suffer an injury. It's very difficult to know how much pain she is experiencing—even if she attempts to put the pain into words. Moreover, many people are in great pain without any sign of physical injury.

If you have an excruciating headache or have just hit your thumb with a hammer, you would gladly give up the experience of pain. That would be a rash decision, however. Some children are born with insensitivity to pain, yet they have otherwise normal sensory and cognitive abilities (Butler et al., 2006; Nagasako et al., 2003). Unfortunately, their lives are typically foreshortened because any damage they do to their bodies doesn't result in pain. Thus, their parents have to go to extreme lengths (e.g., requiring the children to wear goggles and helmets) to protect them from themselves. Pain protects your body from further damage, so it has important survival value.

Because this chapter deals with the skin senses, we'll focus primarily on pain that results from trauma to the skin. We'll first consider the physical systems that underlie pain perception. The second and third sections discuss how we measure pain and how we adapt to pain. The last section examines a variety of methods of relieving pain.

Afferent Systems for Pain and Gate-Control Theory

As was true for other aspects of the somatosensory system, researchers proposed both specificity and pattern theories of pain perception (Melzack & Katz, 2007a). One distinction between these theories of pain perception focused on the function of pain receptors in the skin, called *nociceptors*. The nociceptors are actually free nerve endings of different types of somatosensory neurons. These nociceptors initiate a warning signal about a potentially harmful stimulus, whether it's an extreme temperature, a high pressure, or a noxious chemical. We'll focus our attention on the types of afferent neurons that receive input from different free nerve endings. Given the important roles of emotion and cognition in pain perception, we must also consider the crucial top-down processes, with some discussion of efferent systems. The overall complexity of pain perception requires a theory that is broader than any of the specificity or pattern theories.

Ronald Melzack and Patrick Wall (1965) provided an appropriately complex theory that has been quite influential. Their *gate-control theory* proposes that pain perception is a complex process in which various neural fibers interact. This theory also pro-

poses that the brain has an important influence on pain perception.

We'll use gate-control theory as a model to explain pain perception. Figure 12.7 provides an overview of the theory. Admittedly, this diagram may look only slightly less complicated than a map of the New York City subway system; pain perception is not a simple process. For now, it's important that you note three important components of the theory: pain information ascending to the brain, brain processing of pain, and information descending from the brain. We'll return to this figure as we explore these three components of pain perception.

AFFERENT SYSTEMS   Let's begin with the actual nociceptors—the box labeled "Small fibers" on the left of Figure 12.7. These are the same small-diameter (A and C) fibers we mentioned earlier in our discussion of temperature perception. As we noted then, these small fibers are also pain receptors. Thus, the transient receptor potential (TRP) proteins that underlie temperature perception are also vital for pain perception (Story & Cruz-Orengo, 2007).

Beyond TRP proteins, researchers have also determined that sodium (Na) channels are crucial for pain perception (Wood, 2008). Sodium channels play an important role in the chemical process that generates an action potential in neurons. Their general role in pain perception was apparent because of the effectiveness of the local anesthetic lidocaine, which blocks sodium channels. Researchers have identified a number of different sodium channels (e.g., $Na_V1.7$) that affect pain perception. In fact, they have identified the gene (SCN9A) that leads to the congenital insensitivity to pain that we described earlier (Cox et al., 2006).

There are likely several types of these small A-fiber nociceptors (Caterina et al., 2005; Ringkamp & Meyer, 2008). Some of these thinly myelinated fibers respond best to heat, and others respond best to pressure on the skin or noxious chemicals. These nociceptors probably give rise to a sharp or pricking pain.

Unmyelinated C-fibers are relatively small neurons that signal pain from extreme heat as well as mechanical and chemical stimulation (Ringkamp & Meyer, 2008). These C-fibers respond relatively slowly to convey extreme heat or burning pain. When injured, we may feel first a sharp pain followed by dull pain, known as *double pain* (Caterina et al., 2005; Craig, 2003). Double pain can be traced to the quick

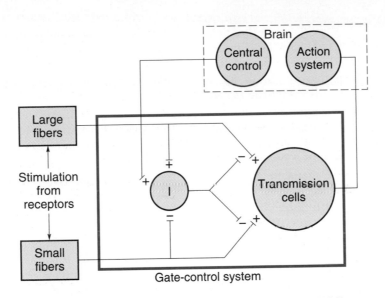

Gate-control system

▶ **F I G U R E   1 2 . 7**   Schematic depiction of Melzack's and Wall's gate-control theory of pain. The painful stimulus causes the receptors to fire, sending signals along both the large and small fibers. Input from the small fibers directly excites (+) the transmission cells to send along a message of pain to the brain. The action system then attempts to avoid the pain. In addition to affecting the transmission cells, the small fibers also inhibit inhibitory interneurons (I) fibers within the substantia gelatinosa of the spinal cord. The large fibers also stimulate inhibitory interneurons (I), leading to an inhibition (-) of the transmission cells. Note also that the brain can send a descending inhibitory signal to reduce the perception of pain by stimulating the inhibitory interneurons.

response of A-fibers and the more leisurely response of C-fibers.

If you look again at Figure 12.7, you'll notice the box on the left labeled "Large fibers." A larger type of A-fiber, called Aβ (A-beta), also plays a role in pain perception. However, Aβ fibers are not nociceptors. In fact, we'll soon describe how these fibers actually serve to *inhibit* the pain response.

All of these afferent fibers are part of the spinothalamic pathway, sending information through the dorsal (toward the back) horn of the spinal cord (High, 2008; Lima, 2008). They connect to neurons that convey pain information called **transmission cells**. These cells send pain information to the brain areas we'll discuss in the next section.

An area of the spinal cord called the **substantia gelatinosa** contains interneurons—and they often have an inhibitory effect on neural firing. That is, the stimulation of the inhibitory interneurons—which are connected to transmission cells—would send a message to decrease firing. Thus, the inhibitory interneurons serve as a gate for decreasing pain information. Let's return to Figure 12.7 to see how the gate works.

First, consider the effect of the nociceptors. Input from the small fibers inhibits (-) the inhibitory interneurons of the substantia gelatinosa, essentially opening the gate. The nociceptors also stimulate (+) the transmission cells, sending along pain information. Now, let's consider the effect of the large (Aβ) fibers. Input from these large fibers stimulates (+) the inhibitory interneurons of the substantia gelatinosa, which then inhibit (-) the transmission cells. The effect is to close the gate and decrease the perception of pain.

In Figure 12.7, you'll note that the transmission cells send pain information to the brain. You'll also note that the brain sends information that affects pain perception. We'll now consider the important role the brain plays in pain perception.

THE BRAIN AND PAIN   All along, we've argued that perception is more than just the processing of sensory information, so you should expect that pain perception is no different. To explain the complex interplay of factors that affect pain perception, Melzack proposes that each person's brain has a unique configuration of neurons called the **neuromatrix**. This neuromatrix is a "widespread network of neurons that generates patterns, processes information that flows through it, and ultimately produces the pattern that is felt as a whole body" (Melzack & Katz, 2007a, p. 6). Damage to the neuromatrix may well explain why one man kept throwing his own leg out of bed, thinking that it was someone else's leg (Sacks, 1985). Thus, the neuromatrix may be essential to your sense of self.

Just as many brain areas are involved in processing visual and auditory information, many brain areas are also involved in processing pain information (Apkarian, 2008; Treede & Apkarian, 2008). Melzack proposes three modules that are central to the neuromatrix: sensory, affective, and cognitive. The somatosensory cortex is likely the primary site of sensory processing of pain.

The affective (or emotional) module likely emerges from a number of different locations, including the anterior cingulate cortex, the limbic system, and the amygdala. The anterior cingulate cortex plays a role in a range of functions, including cognitive, empathetic, and emotional. As Pinel (2006) notes, the **limbic system** is composed of a number of structures surrounding the thalamus that are involved in motivation (fleeing, feeding, fighting, and sexual behavior). We've noted the role of the amygdala in perceiving emotion, and the pain signal is sent to this area (Flor & Bushnell, 2005).

The cognitive module represents the important contribution of attention, thinking, and memory—entirely consistent with Theme 4. The prefrontal cortex is the likely site of this aspect of pain perception.

Finally, let's return to Figure 12.7. Notice that the brain can influence pain perception. We have repeatedly emphasized the importance of cognitive processes in perception (Theme 4), and cognitive control is an important part of the gate-control theory. Signals from the brain (Central Control) excite the inhibitory interneurons, just like the large fibers. Thus the brain can inhibit the firing of the transmission cells, reducing the perception of pain. Keep this aspect of gate-control theory in mind when we discuss psychological approaches to controlling pain.

Not only can the brain decrease pain but it can also increase pain. If you've ever been anxious about an upcoming painful experience, you may have noted that your anxiety actually increases the pain. Fascinating research from Jeffrey Mogil's lab illustrates the important roles of affect and cognition in pain perception (Loggia et al., 2008). People watched a video of a person who acted in a way that either evoked high empathy (". . . and this is how my girlfriend died . . .") or low empathy (". . . and this is how I duped that blind man . . ."). People were then given a painful heat stimulus while they watched the actor in the video being given the same heat stimulus. Of course, everyone received the identical pain stimulus. However, those who had high empathy for the actor rated the pain they received as significantly greater than those who had low empathy for the actor.

To further emphasize the important role of the brain in pain perception, we'll turn our attention to phantom limb pain. The experience of a phantom limb is fascinating in itself, especially in the context of Melzack's neuromatrix. However, it's mind-boggling to consider that a person could actually feel pain in a nonexistent limb.

IN-DEPTH

Phantom Limbs and Pain

People who have had a limb amputated typically continue to feel that the limb is present (Brugger, 2006). The **phantom limb** cannot be due to input from receptors in the skin, because the receptors no longer exist. The exact cause of phantom limbs remains somewhat elusive, but Melzack's notion of the neuro-matrix may help to explain the phenomenon. That is, if neurons in your brain create a map of your body, then even after amputation, your brain will continue to represent the missing body part.

However, we must emphasize that phantom limbs are not due to learning to use a limb or to processing input from a limb. The evidence for this is quite strong—people who had been born without limbs experience phantom limbs (Brugger, 2006). One young woman who had been born without arms nonetheless "uses" her arms to gesticulate during a conversation (Ramachandran & Hirstein, 1998). Thus, some form of the neuromatrix may be innate.

We should be clear that the range of phantoms is quite extensive. Along with phantom arms and legs are phantom breasts and penises, as well as phantoms of removed internal organs (Melzack & Katz, 2007b; Ramachandran & Hirstein, 1998). For a moment, let's focus on the phantom penis. The majority of men who have their penis amputated (often due to cancer) report experiencing a phantom penis. However, what might you predict for transsexuals undergoing gender reassignment surgery? Transsexuals often report being trapped in the body of the other gender. One way to interpret such a statement is that the transsexual's neuromatrix is inconsistent with the person's body. Based on such reasoning, Ramachandran and McGeoch (2007) hypothesize that transsexuals should be less likely than men with cancer of the penis to report experiencing a phantom penis after male-to-female gender reassignment surgery. Provisional data support the hypothesis. Moreover, female-to-male transsexuals report having experienced a phantom penis *prior* to surgery.

What is it like to have a phantom limb? Typically it appears to be attached to the stump in a "normal" position, though over time it may appear to change position. For instance, over time, a phantom hand often appears to move closer to the remaining stump (Manchikanti et al., 2007). In some cases, however, the phantom limb seems to be located in an unusual position. One man felt that his phantom arm was stuck behind his back, so he was uncomfortable sleeping on his back (Melzack, 1992). Another man felt that his phantom arm was stuck out perpendicular to his side. He even walked through doors sideways, to be able to fit this phantom arm through the doorway. Some stroke victims actually experience extra phantom limbs, such as an arm extending from the middle of the chest or two legs attached to the same knee (Bakheit & Roundhill, 2005; Halligan et al., 1993). These cases don't involve amputation, but damage to brain cells—possibly affecting the neuromatrix.

The neuromatrix may be innate, but experience likely plays a role in phantom limbs. For instance, post-amputation experience may well explain why phantom limbs often disappear over time. To illustrate the extent to which the neuromatrix can be fooled by novel experience, see if you are susceptible to the Pinocchio Effect in www Demonstration 12.5.

Throughout the text we've noted that experience plays a major role in perception (Theme 4). As we've noted in earlier chapters, connections in our brains are quite malleable. Such brain plasticity appears to play an important role in the experience of phantom limbs. Researchers such as Michael Merzenich and Timothy Pons (1956–2005) have illustrated the extent of brain reorganization that takes place after amputation (Merzenich et al., 1984; Pons et al., 1991).

What brain reorganization might you expect for a person who has lost his arm from just above the elbow? Before answering, you should revisit Figure 12.3. Note that the arm, hand, and face send information to nearby areas of the somatosensory cortex. Vilayanur Ramachandran worked with a young man who had recently lost his left arm in an accident. Based on what he knew about organization in the somatosensory cortex, Ramachandran blindfolded the young man and then rubbed a cotton swab against parts of the man's face. Although the young man felt the pressure on his face, he also felt it on his missing hand (Ramachandran & Blakeslee, 1998). Rubbing the cotton swab on other parts of his body (e.g., his back) produced no sense of stimulation on his phantom hand. Of course, scientists are reluctant to consider the cotton swab a precise instrument. Ramachandran notes that subsequent brain imaging studies confirmed the brain reorganization.

However, for a number of reasons, Ramachandran believes that brain reorganization doesn't fully explain phantom limbs. Consider, for instance, the fact that phantom limbs emerge so soon after amputation. Surely there is not sufficient time for the new pattern of input to lead to brain reorganization. Instead, he believes that the "phantom connections" in the somatosensory cortex between the intact arm and the face areas are already present prior to amputation, but the stronger input determines our perception. That is, when we brush something against our face, we are also stimulating the area of the cortex that receives input from our arm. However, the absence of input from the arm is so strong that we perceive only the stimulation of our face. After the arm is amputated, it no longer sends the stronger "absent" signal, so brushing against the face is also perceived as stimulating the arm.

The phantom limb phenomenon currently defies complete explanation. Even more perplexing is the experience of phantom limb pain. Phantom limbs tend to disappear a few years after amputation, unless phantom limb pain develops (Manchikanti et al., 2007). Unfortunately, as many as 80% of amputees experience pain in their phantom limbs (Rosenquist & Haider, 2008). Physicians attempt to control phantom limb pain as they would other pain—typically with little success. Until we better understand the sources of phantom limb pain, treatments will likely remain ineffective (Flor, 2008).

Of course, the possibility that phantom limb pain emerges for a variety of reasons may make diagnosis and treatment complex. The impact of amputation on the peripheral nerves may well contribute to phantom limb in some people. In addition, the brain reorganization, which we've already discussed, likely plays an important role in producing phantom limb pain (Flor et al., 2006).

Lack of input to the neuromatrix may also explain phantom limb pain. It might be that in the absence of inhibitory input from the limb, portions of the neuromatrix begin to fire wildly. In fact, the person experiences these sensations as burning pain (Melzack & Katz, 2007b). How might one restore the inhibitory input? Try placing a mirror roughly perpendicular to your chest and facing to the right. If you move your right arm while looking in the mirror, you may be fooled into thinking that it's your left arm moving. Ramachandran suggested using such a mirror to fool the brain into thinking that the missing limb was present. Although researchers have yet to systematically test this approach, early results are not encouraging (Rosenquist & Haider, 2008).

The very perplexing experience of phantom limbs has a great deal to tell us about somatosensory experience—indeed, about perception in general. As Melzack (1992) writes, "The brain does more than detect and analyze inputs; it generates perceptual experience even when no external inputs occur. . . . Sensory inputs merely modulate that experience; they do not directly cause it. . . . We do not need a body to feel a body" (p. 126). These are, indeed, important lessons to learn.

Measuring Pain

Researchers have taken many different approaches to measuring pain. If researchers consider pain to be unidimensional, they can measure pain using the entire range of methods discussed in Chapter 2. Thus, some researchers have used the classical psychophysical methods to study pain (Gracely & Eliav, 2008). Other researchers have used signal detection methods to separate sensory abilities from criteria used to judge pain, though the use of signal detection is controversial (Craig & Rollman, 1999). Still other researchers have used category scale and magnitude estimation methods to judge the severity of pain. And, increasingly, researchers are employing various brain-imaging techniques to study pain perception (Moisset & Bouhassira, 2007; Wager et al., 2004). Clearly, the range of methods used to study pain is extremely wide.

The range of stimuli used to *produce* pain is equally wide, including pressure, temperature, and electrical stimulation. However, despite the value of research in pain perception, important ethical considerations make this research quite difficult to conduct (American Psychological Association, 2002). Just as auditory researchers limit the intensity of stimuli presented to human participants, researchers interested in human pain perception must exercise great care in their research.

Using the classical psychophysical methods, researchers attempt to determine the pain threshold (Gracely et al., 2002). The ***pain threshold*** is the intensity of stimulation at which an observer says, "It's painful" half the time and "It's not painful" half the time. Unlike thresholds for other sensory experiences (e.g., sound stimulus of a particular frequency), a pain threshold represents an almost qualitative change. Consider a sound stimulus, which would sometimes be inaudible (i.e., below threshold) and sometimes audible (i.e., above threshold). However, consider using a temperature probe to assess pain perception.

At lower temperatures, a person would report, "It's not painful." However, the person would feel a stimulus that is clearly warm. At higher temperatures, when a person would report, "It's painful," the stimulus will have shifted from temperature to pain.

Pain thresholds depend on many different factors. Consistent with what you know about touch sensitivity, some areas of your body (e.g., fingertips) have lower pain thresholds, and other areas (e.g., back) have higher pain thresholds. Given what you know about pain perception, you should expect that psychological factors play a large role in individual pain thresholds. These factors also play a role in determining *pain tolerance*, the maximum pain level at which people voluntarily accept pain. Due to the psychological factors, both pain threshold and pain tolerance show enormous variation from one individual to another.

Given the emotional component of pain, several pain measurement instruments have been developed that attempt to separate the sensory and emotional components of pain (Gracely & Eliav, 2008; Heapy & Kerns, 2008). One instrument, the McGill Pain Questionnaire, asks the respondent to choose descriptive terms that are thought to tap into either the sensory (e.g., sharp, hot, dull) or the affective (e.g., sickening, terrifying, punishing) components of pain (McDowell, 2006). Such distinctions might seem arbitrary to you—is *punishing* a purely affective term? If so, then you are sensitive to the difficulty of developing any instrument to measure the many dimensions of pain.

Adapting to Pain

Generally speaking, people adapt to sensory stimulation. That is, the same intensity of the stimulus is perceived as less intense over time. The same is true for mildly painful stimuli. If the pain isn't too intense (e.g., a mildly painful cold or hot stimulus), the pain will decrease over time without treatment. However, unlike most sensory stimuli, intensely painful stimuli do not decrease much in perceived intensity over time.

Of course, throughout our discussion of pain, we've described the pain experience as multidimensional. The many dimensions of pain make it difficult to determine whether or not a person adapts to pain. For instance, a pain may remain equally intense, but may no longer seem to be punishing or throbbing. Generally speaking, people with severe pain may not adapt to the pain, but they develop strategies to enable them to cope with the pain (Sofaer-Bennett et al., 2007; Turk & Okifuji, 2004). We'll now briefly review some of the strategies for controlling pain.

Controlling Pain

Although pain is an important signal about potential damage to our bodies, its survival value decreases once we've become aware of the problem. Because we don't adapt to severe pain, persistent pain can have a serious negative effect on our lives. Thus, it's no surprise that people have been attempting to control pain for millennia, with Egyptians writing about early pain control methods in 4000 BC (Gatchel, 1999). As we've learned more about the principles underlying pain perception, techniques for treating pain have improved. As continuing research more completely identifies pain mechanisms, increasingly effective treatments will become available (Basbaum & Julius, 2006; Stix, 2007).

One basic—yet important—consideration is the gender of the person experiencing pain. Growing evidence points to gender differences in pain perception (Fillingim, 2008; Greenspan et al., 2007). Differences in pain perception may well suggest differences in the underlying mechanisms, which would also indicate different treatments. Consider, for instance, the intense pain that women experience during childbirth (Wesselmann, 2008). How might one best control such pain? Drugs (e.g., an epidural) are quite effective at reducing labor pain. Some physical approaches (e.g., acupuncture, sterile water injections under the skin at the base of the spine) are moderately effective (Tournaire & Theau-Yonneau, 2007). Psychological approaches (e.g., prepared childbirth methods such as the Lamaze method) may not so much reduce the pain as allow the woman to tolerate the pain. Throughout the rest of this section, we'll briefly consider these three general approaches to controlling pain: pharmacological, physical, and psychological.

PHARMACOLOGICAL INTERVENTIONS The medical community has developed many types of *analgesic medication*—drugs that alleviate pain. Unfortunately, these drugs often have side effects, especially if people exceed the prescribed dosage. You need to be careful even with fairly benign over-the-counter analgesics such as aspirin, acetaminophen, and ibuprofen (Aronoff et al., 2002). Overdoses of these drugs can cause severe problems—especially in children.

Some analgesics, called *local* or *topical anesthetics*, work at the location where they are applied. These include drugs such as cocaine, novocaine, and lidocaine. Other analgesics are applied in one location (i.e., ingested or injected into the arm) but provide widespread relief from pain. These drugs include opium derivatives such as oxycodone, codeine, methadone, and morphine (Lipman & Jackson, 2004). Because of its effectiveness as an analgesic, morphine is the standard against which other analgesic drugs are compared (Cortazzo & Fishman, 2008).

Morphine may be as addictive as heroin when taken primarily for its euphoric effects. However, we now know that it is rarely addictive when taken to relieve pain. Of course, morphine use may *appear* to be addictive, because the person in pain continually seeks more morphine. However, it's vital to understand the person's motivation—to reduce the pain. Under such conditions, morphine and other opium derivatives appear to be effective means of preventing pain with little chance of addiction for psychologically healthy people (Lipman & Jackson, 2004).

Opium-based drugs such as morphine are effective because cells in the central nervous system have sites that are receptive to such drugs. These **opioid receptors** are specific locations on the surfaces of cells that respond to opiate drugs in a fashion similar to a lock and a key (Lipman & Jackson, 2004). Why should our brains have evolved to be sensitive to drugs that have only been recently developed? The logical conclusion is that our bodies must produce **endogenous opiates** similar to morphine. In fact, strenuous exercise can lead to the production of such endogenous opiates, resulting in a "runner's high." Some of these substances have analgesic effects that resemble morphine's ability to reduce pain (Yaksh, 2008).

PHYSICAL INTERVENTIONS   You may have discovered that you can reduce the intensity of pain from a wound by scratching the surrounding skin. Several methods of pain control involve **counterirritants**, which stimulate or irritate one area to diminish pain in another. These approaches may be effective on their own, or in conjunction with other pain-relieving approaches.

One kind of counterirritant is the classical Chinese technique called *acupuncture*. **Acupuncture** involves the insertion of thin needles into acupunc-

ture points on the body (Lin, 2008). The acupuncture points are parts of the body that are sensitive to pressure and they are often located at joints or the juncture of muscles (Garcia & Chiang, 2007). Adherents of this approach believe that stimulation of an acupuncture point relieves a particular symptom. Surprisingly, the stimulated location is often far away from the painful area. For example, an acupuncture point on the small toe may affect vision. An fMRI study appears to confirm that linkage because stimulating the acupuncture point activates the visual cortex (Audette, 2004).

Acupuncture has been widely used in China for centuries, but it was virtually unknown in the United States until the 1970s. Americans have been slow to accept acupuncture as an analgesic. However, increasing interest in alternative medicines may well lead to greater use of acupuncture—especially in combination with other methods of pain relief.

Another effective stimulation technique for reducing pain, called **transcutaneous electrical nerve stimulation (TENS)**, is produced by a stimulator placed on the surface of the skin (Waldman, 2007). Clinicians believe that TENS is effective for some types of pain. However, it's difficult to conduct good double-blind research with TENS because the patient can tell that the stimulator is on. Nonetheless, studies have shown that TENS and acupuncture were equally effective in treating lower back pain (Lin, 2008).

The counterirritant methods are likely to work through similar mechanisms. The gate-control theory seems useful for understanding the processes involved. Some of the analgesic effect is likely due to the stimulation of the large fibers (Aβ), which inhibit the pain signal. An additional analgesic effect can be traced to more central control processes, including a placebo effect, which we'll discuss next.

PSYCHOLOGICAL INTERVENTIONS   So far, we have seen that pain can be controlled by analgesics, by the release of endorphins, and by being prodded with sharp needles and electrical stimulation. However, given the cognitive and emotional components of pain, interventions based on psychological principles should be effective in controlling pain. We'll look at some procedures based on psychological principles: placebo effects, hypnosis, and cognitive-behavioral therapy.

A *placebo* is an inactive treatment or substance, such as a sugar pill, that the patient believes is an effective therapy. We've emphasized the important role of top-down processes in pain perception. Thus, it makes sense that what a person *believes* can affect that person's perception of pain (Price, Finniss et al., 2008; Price, Hirsh et al., 2008). It also follows that if you don't realize that you've been given a treatment, it will be less effective. For example, if a patient is given an analgesic medication surreptitiously, it is less effective than if the patient is told that an analgesic is being administered (Benedetti, 2008).

However, what if you'd been given a purely placebo treatment? Would knowing that you'd been "fooled" by a placebo treatment make you be less susceptible to a placebo effect? Chung and her colleagues (2007) found that people were not annoyed to learn that they received a placebo treatment, nor were they less susceptible to future placebo effects. Thus, knowing about placebo effects, or knowing that you've received a placebo treatment in the past, doesn't diminish the effectiveness of future placebo effects.

Why are placebos effective? Because pain arises in a complex psychosocial setting, a number of factors likely contribute to the effectiveness of placebos. Some of the effectiveness is probably psychological, with the placebo creating expectations of reduced pain consistent with the patient's desire for reduced pain (Price, Finniss et al., 2008). Placebos can also prompt the release of endorphins and other endogenous substances that reduce pain (Benedetti, 2008). Interestingly, brain scans show that a placebo results in activity in brain areas that are also activated by an opiate analgesic.

Another approach that relies on the power of the mind is hypnosis. *Hypnosis* is an altered state of consciousness in which a person becomes susceptible to suggestions made by the hypnotist (Turk & Swanson, 2008). Some research suggests that hypnosis may be effective in treating various types of pain, but it may be best used in conjunction with other analgesic methods (Hall, 2007).

Cognitive-behavioral approaches focus on helping the patient become actively involved in developing more adaptive cognitive, emotional, and behavioral responses to pain (Levin & Janata, 2007; Turk & Swanson, 2008). They include a wide variety of techniques. Some techniques that emphasize the cognitive aspect include teaching the patient to identify negative thoughts related to pain, substitute more adaptive thoughts, and use coping strategies such as distraction to minimize suffering. Cognitive-behav-

ioral approaches also borrow from behaviorism. Patients are frequently taught operant conditioning principles, in which people are reinforced for behavior not related to pain—such as increased physical activity. These approaches have been found to be effective in treating many different types of pain.

Section Summary

Pain

1. Pain involves sensory, affective, and cognitive components. It has survival value, alerting us to damage to our bodies. Children who are insensitive to pain often experience severe bodily harm.

2. Nociceptors (pain receptors) are free nerve endings in the skin that connect to different afferents (A- and C-fibers).

3. Melzack and Wall proposed a gate-control theory in which pain perception is hypothesized to be the result of complex interactions of large fibers and small fibers with inhibitory interneurons and the transmission cells. In addition, cognitive control from the brain has an important influence on pain perception.

4. Melzack's neuromatrix helps explain why we perceive our bodies as uniquely "ours." The three modules (sensory, affective, and cognitive) explain the complex interplay of brain areas involved in pain perception.

5. Phantom limbs and phantom limb pain are due to central processes, including the reorganization or neural connections after amputation. Phantom limb pain poses particular problems for some theories of pain perception.

6. The pain threshold is the lowest intensity of stimulation at which we perceive pain. Pain tolerance is the maximum pain level at which people accept pain; pain tolerance varies across individuals.

7. Humans adapt to mild pains but not to severe ones. Instead, they learn to cope with pain and control the pain.

8. Pain can be controlled by analgesics, including opiate drugs such as morphine. Naturally produced endogenous opiates have analgesic

Section Summary continued

properties and are released by strenuous exercise and other experiences.

9. Counterirritants diminish pain in one area by stimulating or irritating another area; they include acupuncture and transcutaneous electrical nerve stimulation.

10. Psychological techniques for controlling pain include placebo effects, hypnosis, and cognitive-behavioral approaches.

Kinesthetic and Vestibular Senses

Are you sitting down? Okay, try this. Close your eyes, grab your knees with your hands, and then rock forward and backward. Notice that even with your eyes closed you can tell when you're upright and when you're leaning forward. You can also feel your elbows bending and flexing as you rock back and forth. Your fingers are tightly (or loosely) grasping your knees. Information about your bodily orientation, movement, and position ordinarily comes through your kinesthetic and vestibular senses, though vision may also provide such information (Cole, 1991).

The kinesthetic sense is due to receptors within the skin, so it is part of the somatosensory system. However, the vestibular sense has little in common with the skin senses. Instead, the mechanisms underlying the vestibular sense have more in common with our auditory system than with the skin senses. First, we will examine the kinesthetic sense that gives us our sense of how our various body parts are positioned. Then, as we promised in Chapter 8, we will return to a discussion of the semicircular canals of the inner ear. These organs contribute to our vestibular sense. We will see how motion of the fluid in these canals gives rise to our sense of bodily orientation and movement.

Kinesthetic Sense

Kinesthesia is derived from a Greek word meaning "perception of movement." As it is usually employed today, the term *kinesthesia* refers to the sensation of movement or the sensation of static limb position. In

its broadest sense, kinesthesia includes sensations that come from the position and movement of body parts; this movement can be active or passive. A similar term often used interchangeably with kinesthesia is *proprioception*. To help increase your appreciation for kinesthesia, try 🌐 Demonstration 12.7.

MECHANISMS FOR KINESTHESIA The central nervous system has two methods for obtaining information about the position and the movement of body parts: (1) It can monitor the commands it sends to the muscles (outflow), on the assumption that the muscles carry them out, and (2) it can receive information from appropriate sensory receptors (inflow). Just as the visual system uses more than one source of information to determine the distance of an object, as you learned in Chapter 6, the kinesthetic system uses more than one source to determine the position of the body parts. If you stretch your arm out to the right in the direction of a pen, your central nervous system knows where your arm is because it sent that arm on this particular errand and because feedback from the arm tells your central nervous system where the arm is. These two kinds of kinesthetic information are supplemented by other senses. For example, your vision informs the central nervous system about the location of your arm, your touch senses let you know when your finger makes contact with the pen, and even your hearing may contribute information about the slight scrape that the pen makes on the desk surface as your hand reaches its destination.

Most of the time we are actively moving our bodies, as in reaching for a pen, when we make a kinesthetic judgment. Occasionally, however, we make a decision about limb position when we are stationary or when our limbs are being moved for us. In both cases it appears that receptors within our muscles play a major role in our sense of limb position. One kind of receptor that has been extensively researched is the Golgi tendon organ. The tendon is the tough, fibrous material that attaches the muscle to the bone. *Golgi tendon organs*, located in these tendons, respond when the muscle exerts tension on the tendon (Carlson, 2007). As a result, the Golgi tendon organs are effective in signaling the position of our limbs when we are actively moving.

For determining limb position with passive movement, it appears that muscle spindles are important. *Muscle spindles* are receptors that are located within the muscle itself, rather than in the tendon. Unlike the Golgi tendon organs, the muscle spindles don't respond to tension but instead respond to muscle length. The muscle spindles help us detect passive limb position. For example, if the muscles are vibrated at a rate that causes the muscle spindles to fire, people will experience an illusory sense of limb position. In some cases, people even report the limb to be in an anatomically impossible position, such as the hand bent back to the forearm.

KINESTHETIC PERCEPTION   Consider the simple task of walking down a flight of stairs. Note how important it is to know how your body is oriented in space. You may not even look at your feet as you navigate each step, but if you miscalculate the position of your feet, you'll likely fall down the stairs. Of course, kinesthetic perception contributes to your ability to descend the stairs without incident. Unfortunately, as you age, sensory input often declines, as we'll detail in Chapter 14. Your kinesthetic perception is also likely to decline with age, which contributes to the falls in elderly people (Lackner & DiZio, 2005).

One remedy for a decline in kinesthetic perception may be the use of vibrating insoles in a shoe (McCredie, 2007; Priplata et al., 2003). To remain standing upright, our bodies actually make small adjustments that lead us to sway slightly. James Collins and his colleagues have demonstrated that older people tend to sway to a greater extent than younger people. However, sway is reduced when older people place their feet on an insole that randomly vibrates so little as to be imperceptible. Stimulation of the receptors in the soles of their feet seems sufficient to improve their balance.

As important as our kinesthetic sense may be, it can be fooled fairly easily. For instance, stimulating an immobile limb with a vibrator leads people to think that the limb is moving (Collins et al., 2005). Perhaps more astounding are effects similar to one you read about when we discussed research using a rubber hand (Durgin et al., 2007). In that case, people felt warmth on their own (hidden) hand from a laser beam moving along a nearby rubber hand. Similar research on the rubber hand illusion shows that people will mistakenly think that their hand *is* the nearby rubber hand (Makin et al., 2008). For example, "stimulating" a nearby rubber hand while simultaneously stimulating their hidden hand led people

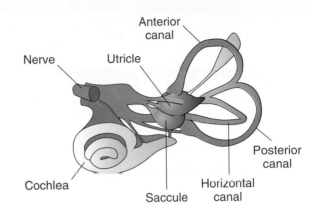

► **FIGURE 12.8**   The inner ear, showing the cochlea, the otolith organs (utricle and saccule), and the semicircular canals. The otolith organs and the semicircular canals are the organs of the vestibular sense.

to perceive the input as coming from the rubber hand (de Vignemont et al., 2006; Tsakiris & Haggard, 2005).

Vestibular Sense

Our *vestibular sense* provides us with information about changes in our body's orientation and whether or not we are in motion. We call it the vestibular sense because the receptors are located at the entrance (the vestibule) to the inner ear.

MECHANISMS OF THE VESTIBULAR SENSE   The vestibular system is comprised of the semicircular canals and the otolith organs. The three semicircular canals seen in Figure 12.8 are filled with fluids and lined with hair cells. Because the semicircular canals are part of the inner ear, the fluids and the hair cells within them are similar to those found in the cochlea. Therefore, much of what you learned regarding the receptors of the inner ear will apply to the vestibular sense as well.

It may be hard to tell from the two-dimensional figure, but the canals are arranged much like the x-, y-, and z-axes in a three-dimensional graph. As a result, the semicircular canals are remarkably well adapted to detect rotations forward or backward, left or right, and up or down. When our bodies move, we cause the fluid in the semicircular canals to move. The fluid then deflects the stereocilia of the hair cells (see Figure 9.12), whose firing tells us about the speed and direction of the movement. Try (www) Demonstration 12.8 to appreciate the vestibular sense more thoroughly.

As you can see in Figure 12.8, the **otolith organs** are the utricle ("little pouch") and the saccule ("little sack") at the base of the semicircular canals. Contrary to the pejorative comment, it's actually quite helpful to have rocks in your head. *Otolith* means "ear stones," because these organs contain small crystals of calcium carbonate. Movement of these "stones" produces changes in the hair cells at the base of the utricle and saccule. These changes inform you about linear acceleration, such as the pull of gravity (Angelaki & Cullen, 2008).

VESTIBULAR PERCEPTION   Although you are typically unaware of your vestibular sense, this perceptual system is quite important. In conjunction with kinesthetic information, the vestibular system is vital in maintaining your posture, detecting whether or not you're in motion, and determining how you're oriented in space (Cullen, 2004). For instance, if you rotate your head from side to side, notice how your eyes tend to rotate in the direction opposite to the direction of your head movement. This coordination of the vestibular information and eye-muscle function occurs because of the **vestibuloocular reflex (VOR)**, which serves to stabilize our view of the world (Lackner & DiZio, 2005).

You become consciously aware of input from the vestibular sense only under unusual circumstances. For example, you may experience an illusion of continued movement if you have been spinning around for an extended time—perhaps on a ride in an amusement park—and come to a sudden halt (McCredie, 2007). People who have Ménière's disease of the inner ear, or even simple inner-ear infections, may experience vertigo or a loss of balance (Harris & Salt, 2008). If you've ever experienced motion sickness, your vestibular sense was surely involved, because people without functional vestibular systems don't experience motion sickness. People develop motion sickness after riding a variety of vehicles from boats to camels to space ships. Although researchers don't yet fully understand motion sickness, the culprit may well be a conflict between input from your eyes and your vestibular sense (Zajonc & Roland, 2005).

Because our vestibular sense evolved for earth-bound conditions, spaceflight presents a particular challenge. When astronauts experience weightlessness, the fluids in their vestibular system float, lead-ing to atypical information, to say the least! Astronauts often experience space motion sickness, although the floating fluids are not solely responsible (Lackner & DiZio, 2006). In fact, space motion sickness is likely just motion sickness in space.

Given the unusual input from the vestibular system, weightless astronauts need to rely on other senses for determining orientation. Visual aids may be as simple as labeling the "top" and "bottom" of areas within the space shuttle—or placing a poster of an "upright" person on the bulkhead. Researchers have also developed tactile vests that use vibration to signal "down" (Clément et al., 2005; van Erp & van Veen, 2006).

We hope that you've now developed a greater appreciation of the important contributions of your skin senses. Even though you are dependent on visual and auditory input, it's quite clear that other senses contribute to your day-to-day existence. The skin senses are particularly useful for helping you orient yourself in space and in exploring nearby surfaces. Moreover, experiencing temperature and pain allows you to take measures to protect your body. Thus, your senses complement one another quite nicely.

Section Summary

Kinesthetic and Vestibular Senses

1. Kinesthesia (or proprioception) refers to the sensation of the position of limbs, whether moving or static. Sources of information about kinesthesia include monitoring of commands sent to muscles and information from sensory receptors, supplemented by visual, auditory, and tactile information.

2. Kinesthetic receptors include Golgi tendon organs and muscle spindles.

3. Older people experience a decline in kinesthetic perception, which contributes to falls. Research suggests that vibrating the soles of the feet of elderly people will enhance balance.

4. Although kinesthetic information is important, the rubber hand illusion illustrates the contribution of visual input to determining the location of one's limbs.

5. The vestibular senses are concerned with orientation, movement, and acceleration. The

vestibular receptors are the semicircular canals and otolith organs of the inner ear.

6. We are rarely aware of the functioning of our vestibular sense; however, it is crucial for the coordination of eye and head movement through the vestibuloocular reflex. We do become aware of the vestibular sense under unusual conditions such as inner ear infections, motion sickness, and weightlessness.

Review Questions

1. Refer to material in the chapter to explain each of the following observations about touch:

   a. Something touches your leg, and you have no idea what shape it is; then it touches your face, and its shape seems clear.

   b. The fabric on a chair seems rough against your arm when you first sit down, but you do not notice it after 5 minutes.

   c. You've placed your sleeping bag on a surface without noticing that a twig is underneath. In reality, the twig has two prominent points, yet when some parts of your body rest on the twig, it seems like a single point.

2. Heller's research suggests several advantages in touch perception for people who are not blind from birth. If you are now sighted, imagine that you found out that you were going blind. Describe specific tactics you could employ to take advantage of the advance notice that you're going blind. Once you were completely blind, how would your perceptual experience differ from that of sighted people?

3. In this chapter, we discussed thresholds for touch, temperature (both warmth and cold), and pain. We saw that each of these thresholds varied from one part of the body to another. Summarize the findings on these various kinds of thresholds and note the similarities and differences.

4. Adaptation has been a recurring theme throughout the text. Discuss adaptation to touch, temperature, and pain. Think of an example of each of these kinds of adaptation from your own recent experience. Can you think of an occasion when adaptation did not occur? Try to relate the experience of adaptation in these senses to adaptation in other senses.

5. What is pain, why does it differ from other perceptual experiences, and why are its thresholds different? What function does pain serve? What is phantom limb pain, and what does it tell us about theories of pain perception in particular and perception in general?

6. Discuss specificity theory and pattern theory, both in their application to the general skin senses and in their application to pain perception. Would the discovery of specific transient receptor potential (TRP) or sodium channel proteins support specificity theory? Describe the gate-control theory, considering the extent to which it supports a specificity or pattern approach to understanding pain.

7. Throughout the text, we've emphasized the importance of central processes in perception. Explain why each of the following topics documents the importance of central psychological processes in pain perception: (a) phantom limb pain, (b) placebo effect, (c) acupuncture, (d) cognitive-behavioral approaches, and (e) hypnosis. Then discuss other aspects of touch perception that indicate the operation of central processes.

8. Where are your hands right now? How do you know? Given research on the rubber hand illusion, people are easily confused about the location of their limbs. Why are we not constantly confused about the location of our limbs? How might you link research on kinesthesia to Melzack's notion of the neuromatrix?

9. People such as McCredie, Angelaki, and Cullen argue that our sense of balance should be considered a sixth sense. Explain the multisensory information that enables us to maintain a sense of balance. How might you argue that balance should be considered a separate sense?

10. Compare the senses discussed in this chapter with vision and hearing. Mention, for example, (a) the nature of the stimuli, (b) the size of the sensory systems, (c) the kind of receptors, and (d) the sensitivity of the systems. How do all of the senses work together to provide a "picture" of the world? What happens when the senses provide conflicting information?

Key Terms

somatosensory system, p. 327
hairy skin, p. 327
glabrous skin, p. 327
epidermis, p. 327
dermis, p. 327
specificity theory, p. 327
doctrine of specific nerve energies, p. 327
pattern theory, p. 327
spinothalamic system, p. 328
lemniscal system, p. 328
somatosensory cortex, p. 329
slowly adapting (SA) neurons, p. 329

rapidly adapting (RA) neurons, p. 330
passive touch, p. 331
active touch, p. 331
absolute threshold, p. 331
two-point discrimination threshold, p. 333
touch adaptation, p. 333
haptic perception, p. 334
Braille, p. 335
Tadoma method, p. 336
transient receptor potential (TRP) channels, p. 338
paradoxical heat, p. 338
thermal adaptation, p. 339
pain, p. 339

nociceptors, p. 340
gate-control theory, p. 340
double pain, p. 340
transmission cells, p. 341
substantia gelatinosa, p. 341
neuromatrix, p. 342
limbic system, p. 342
phantom limb, p. 342
pain threshold, p. 344
pain tolerance, p. 345
analgesic medication, p. 345
opioid receptors, p. 346
endogenous opiates, p. 346
counterirritants, p. 346
acupuncture, p. 346

transcutaneous electrical nerve stimulation (TENS), p. 346
placebo, p. 346
hypnosis, p. 347
cognitive-behavioral approaches, p. 347
kinesthesia, p. 348
proprioception, p. 348
Golgi tendon organs, p. 348
muscle spindles, p. 348
vestibular sense, p. 349
otolith organs, p. 350
vestibuloocular reflex (VOR), p. 350

Recommended Readings

Basbaum, A. I. et al. (Eds.). (2008). *The senses: A comprehensive reference*. New York: Academic Press.

This six-volume set is a wonderful reference for perception. However, it's particularly relevant to this chapter because one of the six volumes is devoted to somatosensory perception and one is devoted to pain perception.

Benzon, H. T., Rathmell, J. P., Wu, C. L., Turk, D. C., & Argoff, C. E. (Eds.). (2008). *Raj's practical management of pain* (4th ed.). Philadelphia: Mosby.

This book contains over 70 chapters covering a range of topics in pain mechanisms and treatments. Some of the chapters are likely to be too specific for the general reader (e.g., lumbosacral epiduroscopy), but many chapters about pain mechanisms and treatments are quite accessible.

McCredie, S. (2007). *Balance: In search of the lost sense*. New York: Little, Brown.

McCredie provides an intriguing survey of research findings in an effort to argue that our sense of balance is indeed a separate sense. He covers a number of topics from motion sickness to people with an extraordinary sense of balance. McCredie is also an advocate for working to improve one's sense of balance (e.g., balance exercises), including a description of the vibrating insoles developed by James Collins.

Rieser, J. J., Ashmead, D. H., Ebner, F. F., & Corn, A. L. (Eds.). (2008). *Blindness and brain plasticity in navigation and object perception*. New York: Erlbaum.

The editors have assembled 20 loosely related chapters, some of which address brain plasticity following disruption of visual input. However, other chapters provide general information about somatosensory perception and specific information about applications for the visually impaired.

CHAPTER 13

The Chemical Senses
Taste and Smell

YOU'VE NOW JOURNEYED through many chapters into which we've somewhat arbitrarily separated our discussion of many senses. However, throughout the text (consistent with Theme 1), we've pointed out the connections among your senses and the integrated nature of your perceptual experience. Nowhere is the multisensory nature of your experience more obvious than in taste and smell. These two senses are frequently grouped together under the name **chemical senses** because both are sensitive to chemical stimulation.

To illustrate the complexity of taste and smell, think of a particularly delicious meal you've enjoyed. Now ask yourself what made the food so delicious. One influential aspect of the meal was the flavor of the food. **Flavor** is a term that includes both taste and smell, as well as tactile experiences (Prescott, 2004; Taylor & Hort, 2004). When you say that something tastes good, you are really reflecting its flavor. Thus, you are reporting on stimulation to your nose as much as to your palate.

In addition to flavor, visual input (the presentation of the food) was surely important. The meal was also likely delicious for reasons beyond its sensory qualities. As rich as the information present in the food itself, the context in which you ate the meal had an influence (Theme 2). Were you particularly hungry? Was the setting especially beautiful? Did you share the meal with special friends? Beyond the context, your expectations likely had an impact as well (consistent with Theme 4). Do you see our point? The flavors of the meal were important, but several other factors helped make the meal delicious.

Let's focus solely on the flavors for now. Try to describe the flavors of that delicious meal without simply naming the food. Isn't that a difficult task? Humans have developed a rich language for describing visual and auditory experience, but our common language for describing tastes and smells is relatively impoverished (Wilson & Stevenson, 2006). You can immediately see the difficulty in communicating the concept of "redness" to a person who is blind, because that person lacks the visual experience that you would like to draw on to illustrate the concept. But try to tell a friend with a normal sense of taste and smell about broccoli sautéed in butter and garlic without using the words *butter, garlic,* or *broccoli.* The tastes and odors are certainly distinctive. However, we do not seem to have a sufficiently rich language for describing the experiences. Soon you will see that the lack of an extensive vocabulary for describing tastes and smells has had an impact on the research conducted in these areas.

Even though they are tightly linked, we'll first discuss taste and smell separately. As we have done for the other senses thus far, we will discuss the stimuli involved in taste and smell, along with the systems through which these stimuli are processed. We will also discuss some aspects of each sense separately. At the end of the chapter, we'll discuss flavor in a bit more detail, including the interactions among several senses.

Taste

As we noted, people often use the words *taste* and *flavor* interchangeably. Strictly speaking, however, **taste** (or gustation) refers only to the perceptions that result from the contact of substances with receptors in the mouth—primarily the tongue (Bailey, 2003). Thus, taste is similar to the skin senses, because the taste stimulus comes in direct contact with the receptors. In this section, we'll use this narrow definition of taste, though we'll discuss interactions between taste and other senses in the final section.

The location of the taste receptors in the mouth is a clue to their purpose. Taste perception tells us about qualities of substances we put in our mouth, so it is important for food consumption (Fain, 2003). We will first address the taste stimulus, then the sensory apparatus for processing taste information, and then various taste processes.

Sensory Aspects of Taste

Our sensory experience of taste arises from taste stimuli falling on our taste receptors, which process the information and relay it to the brain areas responsible for taste. In this section, we will discuss each aspect of the route along which taste information is encoded.

TASTE STIMULUS   The basic stimulus for taste (called a **tastant**) is a chemical compound dissolved in a solution such as saliva (DuBois et al., 2008). Thus, virtually every substance is a potential tastant. You may think that taste produces the rich range of flavors you've experienced while eating. However, when you remove vision and smell from the equation, you'll learn the limitations of taste perception. Try [www]

Demonstration 13.1 to experience taste in isolation. The reality is that the many taste stimuli give rise to a very limited number of qualities.

The search for the basic categories for taste dates back to the ancient Greeks. For example, Aristotle proposed this list of basic categories: sweet, bitter, salty, sour, astringent, pungent, and harsh. Hans Henning (1927) is generally credited with promoting the idea of four basic tastes: sweet, bitter, salty, and sour. Four representative substances that give rise to these tastes are sugar, quinine, table salt, and acids (such as vinegar), respectively. To those basic four tastes, many researchers add a fifth—umami or savory (DuBois et al., 2008). Foods that contain glutamate, such as monosodium glutamate (MSG), stimulate a umami taste (Bailey, 2003). Even if researchers expand the number of taste qualities (e.g., fat may have a unique taste), the number of taste qualities will remain quite small (Kinnamon & Margolskee, 2008).

It's not clear why there are so few taste qualities, but each of the qualities likely has survival value. For instance, people are inclined to eat substances that taste sweet or salty because they often provide energy or important nutrients. People tend to avoid substances that are sour or bitter because they are often "spoiled" (sour milk) or poisonous. Umami is harder to pin down, but it may signal a protein-rich food (Bailey, 2003).

TASTE RECEPTORS   Your tongue contains different types of small projections (little bumps) called **papillae**. Each papilla is small, but you can actually see your own papillae if you try www Demonstration 13.2. Figure 13.1 shows an enlarged picture of a papilla. The most common type of papillae does not contain taste buds, but other types of papillae contain taste buds (Breslin & Huang, 2006).

The basic receptor for taste stimuli is called the **taste bud**. Taste buds are visible only with a microscope. They are located throughout your mouth and throat, not just on the surface of your tongue (Witt et al., 2003). Most of the research and discussion, however, examines the taste buds on the upper surface of the tongue. As is true of the papillae, researchers have identified different types of taste buds (Kinnamon & Yang, 2008).

Figure 13.2 (page 356) shows an enlargement of a taste bud from Figure 13.1. This pear-shaped taste bud contains several **taste receptor cells** arranged like the segments of an orange. The tips of the taste recep-

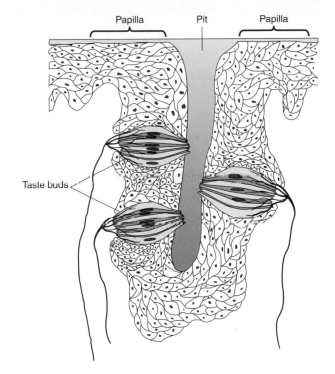

▶ **FIGURE 13.1**   Enlargement of the papilla on the surface of the tongue, containing many taste buds.

tor cells reach out into the opening and can touch any taste molecules in the saliva that flows into the pit. At the tips of the taste receptor cells are **microvilli**, which fill the opening of the taste bud, called the **taste pore**.

Although humans vary quite a bit, most of us probably have about 5,000 taste buds on our tongues (Halpern, 2002). Each taste bud contains about 60 or more receptor cells, so we have roughly 300,000 taste receptor cells on our tongues. Other species have far fewer taste buds. As you know, birds have highly developed visual systems, so they rely heavily on vision. Thus, chickens use their vision to determine food choice (e.g., preferring green feed to red). Chickens have only about 360 taste buds, with few located on the tongue itself (Ferket & Gernat, 2006). However, they do taste their feed. For instance, if fed low-energy food for a while, chickens will prefer sweet solutions. Other species of birds, which also have relatively few taste buds, will develop taste aversions (Werner et al., 2008).

Because of the way they eat, many birds have evolved so that their taste buds are not located on the tongue. In contrast, humans have evolved so that

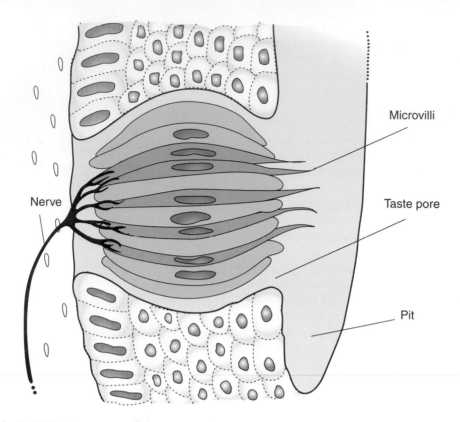

Microvilli

Taste pore

Nerve

Pit

▶ **FIGURE 13.2**   Enlargement of a taste bud. The taste stimuli in the saliva interact with molecules in the membranes of the microvilli.

most taste buds are located on the tongue. However, the central area of the human tongue lacks taste buds, so it could be considered a "blind spot." Like the blind spot on your retina, this location has no receptors.

You may well have learned that specific regions of the tongue are sensitive to different taste qualities (a tongue map). The misinterpretation of an early German article led to this widespread myth (Snyder et al., 2006). The reality is that any receptive area of the tongue will respond to all five taste qualities (Chandrashekar et al., 2006).

Our mouths are not particularly hospitable environments. Very hot and cold liquids pass over the taste buds, and the teeth and interior of the mouth wear down the taste buds. As a result, the cells within your taste buds are dying rapidly. In fact, the life span of the average taste cell is only about 10 days (Breslin & Huang, 2006). The fairly rapid turnover of cells within taste buds has important implications for taste. That is, at any given point, some of your taste cells will be immature and may not function well. Because the taste bud cells regenerate, some people

who lose their sense of taste due to trauma may eventually find that it is restored.

ENCODING TASTE QUALITIES   Within a taste bud, each taste receptor cell encodes a different taste quality (Chandrashekar et al., 2006). However, different mechanisms are involved in the encoding of the taste qualities. Various *G-proteins*—discussed in Chapter 3 in connection with vision—are responsible for our perception of sweet, bitter, and umami (Kinnamon & Margolskee, 2008; Zhang et al., 2003). When an appropriate molecule reaches the taste receptor cell, the interaction of the molecule with the G-proteins leads to a cascade of chemical changes that results in a neural impulse. Researchers have also identified the genes responsible for the differing sensitivities of the taste receptor cells (Max & Meyerhof, 2008).

The mechanisms for the perception of salty and sour tastes differ from those for sweet, bitter, and umami. An increase in the concentration of sodium ions in saliva likely gives rise to our perception of salty tastes (Fain, 2003). These ions flow directly through sodium ion channels in the cells (Beauchamp & Stein, 2008). Perception of salty taste may well involve other transduction mechanisms, so researchers are exploring those possibilities. The perception of sour tastes is also quite complex, though it likely involves the transient receptor potential (TRP) proteins we discussed in Chapter 12 (Kinnamon & Margolskee, 2008). Once again, genetic evidence has helped narrow the search for the way these taste receptor cells function.

Thus, the mechanisms differ for each of the taste receptor cells. Regardless of the mechanism involved, each taste receptor cell connects to a nerve fiber that signals the presence of that particular taste quality. Such evidence leads some researchers to propose that information about taste qualities flows along specific paths (called *labeled lines*) to the brain (Chandrashekar et al., 2006).

PATHWAY FROM RECEPTORS TO THE BRAIN

The nerves in the mouth and throat gather into three bundles, one from the front of the tongue, one from the back of the tongue, and one from the throat. These three nerves travel from the mouth area to an area of the medulla called the *nucleus of the solitary tract*. Information then travels to the thalamus and next to the primary taste cortex, located in the insular cortex and the adjacent part of the frontal cortex (Rolls, 2008). Information also flows to several other regions of the brain, including the secondary taste cortex, the amygdala, and hypothalamus.

Unlike other senses, the information from the right side of the tongue remains on the right side of the brain and information from the left side of the tongue remains on the left (Carlson, 2007). The five basic tastes seem to be represented neurally throughout the taste pathways, consistent with the notion of labeled lines. That is, within the primary and secondary taste cortex, one can find neurons that are particularly sensitive to each of the five tastes (Rolls, 2008).

Various brain-imaging techniques, such as fMRI and PET scans, have identified areas involved in taste perception in humans (Faurion et al., 2008). For instance, taste information goes to a region called the *orbitofrontal cortex* (a part of the frontal cortex above the eyes). This secondary taste cortex is part of the association cortex and may play an important role in making food pleasant or rewarding (Yamamoto & Shimura, 2008).

Modifying Taste Perception

After our brief review of the sensory aspects of taste perception, you are likely struck by the precision with which tastants are encoded (Theme 2). However, keep in mind that taste perception doesn't occur in isolation. That is, we should probably be more interested in flavor than taste, per se. We'll return to a discussion of flavor after discussing smell.

In this section, we want to point out some complexities in taste perception. For instance, because of adaptation, the same taste stimulus will not always produce the same intensity of a particular taste quality. In fact, as you'll soon learn, it's possible to completely change the taste quality we experience.

ADAPTATION   *Adaptation*, is a decrease in sensitivity following the continuous presentation of a stimulus, and it also occurs for taste (Breslin & Huang, 2006). When the same tastant leads to a loss of sensitivity to itself, the process is called *self-adaptation*. In other words, when a specific substance is placed on your tongue, your threshold for that substance increases—you require a stronger concentration of the substance to taste it. The threshold reaches its maximum in about 1 minute. This relationship is illustrated in Figure 13.3. Notice that, when the substance is removed, the threshold rapidly recovers to normal.

Try www Demonstration 13.3 to see one example of how taste adaptation works. When your tongue is adapted to the salt in your own saliva, your threshold for salt is relatively high. When you rinse your mouth out with distilled water or tap water, however, your tongue becomes adapted to a salt-free environment. Your receptors are now more sensitive to salt; in other words, your threshold is lower.

Cross-adaptation refers to the fact that adaptation to one substance *raises* the threshold for another substance; you will be less sensitive to the second substance. Think of situations in which you have experienced cross-adaptation. For example, if you have been drinking tea with lemon, the vinegar salad dressing will not taste so sour; you have experienced cross-adaptation.

In general, cross-adaptation is specific to a particular taste quality (Breslin & Huang, 2006). For example, if you are adapted to one sour taste, you are likely to be less sensitive to other sour tastes. Consistent with what you know about the encoding within taste

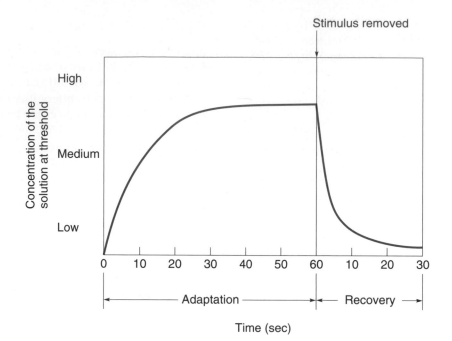

▶**FIGURE 13.3** Adaptation to a specific taste. As the stimulant remains in contact with the receptors, the threshold increases up to a maximum at about 30 seconds. When the stimulant is removed, the threshold begins to drop rapidly, so that about 30 seconds after removal of the stimulus, the threshold has returned to its original position.

receptor cells, adaptation to a sour taste will not decrease your sensitivity to other taste qualities. However, just because substances produce the same taste quality doesn't mean that they will cross-adapt. For example, some bitter taste stimuli (e.g., quinine) do not cross-adapt with other bitter taste stimuli (e.g., PTC).

WATER TASTE   What could be as tasteless as water? Actually, water can have a distinct taste when your tongue has been adapted to another taste; this phenomenon is called ***water taste*** (Lawless, 2001). Try Demonstration 13.4 to show how water can acquire a specific taste that depends on what you have previously eaten. Does plain water taste slightly bitter after you've been drinking a sweet soda? In general, sweet or salty substances produce a slightly sour or bitter water taste. Sour and bitter substances, such as vinegar, produce a slightly sweet water taste. Incidentally, urea (a component of human urine) is one of the few substances that produce a somewhat salty taste in plain water.

TASTE MODIFIERS   Many industries are interested in applications of taste research (Wenner, 2008). For instance, caffeine is widely used as an additive in beverages, but it has a bitter taste (Keast, 2008; Keast & Riddell, 2007). Many medications also have a bitter or a sour taste. You can imagine, then, that researchers are pursuing ways to make bitter and sour tastes more palatable (Reinberger, 2006). One approach is to mask the bitter taste with other tastes—especially sweet ones.

Another approach is to modify the taste experience itself. Some special substances—called ***taste modifiers***—actually change the taste of other substances. Miraculin is a taste modifier found in the ***miracle fruit***. Even though miraculin doesn't taste sweet, it makes sour substances taste sweet (Paladino et al., 2008). Keep in mind that the mechanisms for sweet (G-proteins) and sour (ions) are quite different. Thus, miraculin must transform the sour substance so that it can activate the G-protein cascade in sweet taste receptor cells (Danilova & Hellekant, 2006).

Brain-imaging research shows that—after eating miracle fruit—citric acid (ordinarily sour tasting) activates the sweet areas of the taste cortex (Yamamoto et al., 2006).

Another exotic taste modifier is *gymnema sylvestre*, a climbing plant found in India and Africa. A British officer stationed in India first reported its effects in Western literature. After chewing the leaves of this plant, he could not taste the sugar in his tea. After one tastes a tea brewed from gymnema sylvestre leaves, sugar crystals do not taste at all sweet (Schroeder & Flannery-Schroeder, 2005). In contrast, the tea has absolutely no effect on salt taste.

Measuring Taste Perception

As has been true of the other senses, researchers are interested in the smallest taste stimulus that people can detect. They are also interested in how people's taste experience changes with increases in concentration of the taste stimulus. Your own experience would lead you to predict that some stimuli are easier to detect than others. For instance, because taste helps protect us from ingesting harmful substances, we should easily detect bitter and sour tastes.

We can distinguish among several types of thresholds. As we discussed in Chapter 2, the *absolute threshold* tells us whether or not a person can detect the presence of a substance—even if he or she can't identify the taste. Of course, detecting the presence of some stimulus is very different from identifying that stimulus (e.g., "it's apple juice"). For taste, the *recognition threshold* is the concentration of a solution that can be identified by quality (Snyder et al., 2006). In other words, the recognition threshold specifies the amount of a substance that must be added to distilled water for tasters to recognize the taste as sweet, salty, and so on. Thus, recognition thresholds are generally higher than absolute thresholds because tasters require a relatively strong concentration of a substance to identify it as, for example, salty.

As you might expect, thresholds vary from one substance to another. The bitter taste of quinine sulphate is easy to detect in small quantities. In contrast, relatively large quantities of glucose are necessary for people to detect its sweet taste. When you tried the demonstrations in Chapter 2, you learned about your thresholds for table sugar.

As discussed before, the *difference threshold* is the difference between two stimuli that a person can just barely tell apart (a just noticeable difference). Thus, for taste perception, a difference threshold would be the smallest increase in concentration that would lead a person to report a difference. However, when working with above-threshold concentrations of a tastant, researchers often employ other methods, such as magnitude estimation (Fast et al., 2002).

Individual Differences in Taste Perception

So far, we've been describing taste perception in a typical person. However, people differ widely in their taste abilities. They differ in taste perception due to genetic differences, illnesses, the side effects of drugs, and the aging process. We'll consider each of these sources of variability in taste perception.

Most people perceive phenylthiocarbamide (*PTC*) and 6-n-propylthiouracil (*PROP*) as bitter (Snyder et al., 2006). We noted the role of G-proteins in taste for bitter substances. We also discussed how researchers have identified the genes responsible for the G-proteins. Therefore, it makes sense that the ability to taste these bitter substances may be genetically acquired, just like eye color or height.

For some people (*nontasters*), PTC and PROP do not taste at all bitter, except in very high concentrations (Snyder et al., 2008). Other people (medium tasters) do perceive PTC and PROP as increasingly bitter with increasing concentrations. However, some people (*supertasters*) taste even fairly low concentrations of PTC and PROP as bitter—and higher concentrations are *really* bitter. Supertasters are likely more sensitive to all tastes and flavors—not just bitter (Kamerud & Delwiche, 2007).

Ageusia means that a person has lost the ability to taste a substance. Total ageusia is a rare condition in which a person loses the ability to taste anything. Partial ageusia is more common. A wide array of medical conditions, such as head trauma or stroke, may lead to some level of ageusia (Kim et al., 2007). Medications for a variety of ailments have side effects that alter taste perception (Doty et al., 2008).

Consistent with evidence from the other senses, taste perception often declines with age. That is, both absolute and recognition thresholds are higher for older people compared to younger people (Schiffman, 2008). Of course, it's often true that older people are taking a variety of medications, which also affect taste perception. Therefore, researchers need to be alert for medication usage, which could be a confounding variable when researchers study changes in taste perception.

Finally, some people perceive a taste that isn't present—a disorder known as *dysgeusia*. Some medical conditions or medical treatments may lead to dysgeusia (Schiffman, 2008). People with dysgeusia may experience sweet, salty, metallic, or bitter tastes in their mouths even though no stimuli are present.

Section Summary

Taste

1. Taste refers only to perceptions resulting from substances in contact with special receptors in the mouth. Most psychologists believe that humans can taste five basic kinds of stimuli: sweet, bitter, salty, sour, and umami or savory.

2. Taste buds are located on the sides of some of the papillae of the tongue. Within the taste buds are taste receptor cells, which respond to the basic taste qualities. Typical taste receptor cells have a life span of about 10 days.

3. Each taste quality can be experienced wherever taste buds are located on the tongue. However, the central area of the tongue has no taste receptor cells.

4. Various G-proteins provide the mechanisms for taste receptor cells that encode sweet, bitter, and umami. On the other hand, ion channels provide the mechanisms for taste receptor cells that encode salty and sour.

5. The nerves from the mouth and throat travel to the thalamus, and taste information is then transmitted from the thalamus to the taste cortex.

6. Self-adaptation is a decrease in sensitivity when the same stimulus is presented continuously. Cross-adaptation occurs when adaptation to one substance decreases your sensitivity to another substance.

7. Various substances can modify the taste of water. For example, after you have tasted vinegar, water tastes sweet.

8. Applied research in taste perception includes studies on taste modifiers such as miracle fruit

(which makes sour substances taste sweet) and gymnema sylvestre (which makes sugar tasteless).

9. People differ in their taste perception. Due to genetic differences, nontasters are insensitive to certain substances, such as PTC and PROP. Supertasters are particularly sensitive to those same substances. A variety of medical conditions and drugs can affect taste perception, in some cases leading to the loss of taste perception (ageusia).

Smell

Patrick Süskind, in his novel *Perfume* (1987), illustrates the importance of smell:

> People could close their eyes to greatness, to horrors, to beauty, and their ears to melodies or deceiving words. But they could not escape scent. For scent was a brother of breath. Together with breath it entered human beings, who could not defend themselves against it, not if they wanted to live. And scent entered into their very core, went directly to their hearts, and decided for good and all between affection and contempt, disgust and lust, love and hate. He who ruled scent ruled the hearts of men. (p. 189)

Süskind's points should be amply illustrated in your everyday experience. For example, you meet someone at a party and dislike him instantly because his after-shave lotion reminds you of someone you loathe. You smell a piece of fish and decide to throw it out because of the spoiled odor. You pause in the doorway of a new Chinese restaurant and decide to enter because the aroma contains the appropriate mix of garlic, ginger, and sesame oil. You visit a friend's house, and one whiff immediately makes you think of your grandmother's attic, which you have not visited in 10 years.

Despite its importance, researchers know less about smell than vision or hearing. Mimi Teghtsoonian (1983) claimed that vision and hearing are like the two pampered daughters, whereas smell is the Cinderella of perception. As you've worked through this textbook, you certainly noted that six chapters were devoted to vision and three to audition. As you now approach the end of the text, you find that only a portion of one chapter is devoted to smell. This textbook certainly supports Teghtsoonian's claim!

Why should smell, also known as *olfaction*, suffer such neglect? As Teghtsoonian notes, it's difficult to classify the stimuli for smell, whereas specifying the dimensions of visual and auditory stimuli is far easier. As is true for taste research, it's also difficult to control the delivery of the smell stimulus, called an *odorant*. The result is a great deal of variability in research findings (Zelano & Sobel, 2005).

Sensory Aspects of Smell

Let's begin our discussion with an examination of the sensory aspects of smell. First, we will discuss the smell stimulus. Next, we will discuss the structure of the sensory receptors and the system that processes olfactory stimuli. Later sections will focus on other aspects of smell, such as cognitive influences.

THE SMELL STIMULUS   As you know, the basic stimulus for vision is electromagnetic radiation, and the stimulus for hearing is sound pressure changes. For smell, the stimulus is a molecule of a volatile substance that moves through the air to our receptors. There are hundreds of thousands of such molecules. However, many aromas are not the result of a single volatile substance, but an amalgam of volatiles. Consider the aroma of freshly brewed coffee. Over 600 different volatile components contribute to this aroma (Wilson & Stevenson, 2006). You may have visited a coffee shop in which the aroma of one type of coffee differs from that of another type of coffee. You could identify both aromas as coffee because of the commonality of some of their constituent volatiles. In contrast, your ability to distinguish between the two illustrates your ability to detect modest differences from among the hundreds of volatile components.

Going back at least as far as Aristotle, people have attempted to classify odorants into a smaller number of basic categories. In addition to his work on taste perception, Hans Henning (1916) proposed one commonly discussed system of odorant classification. Figure 13.4 illustrates the prism-shaped figure he constructed to show how smells could be defined in terms of six basic odors.

Amoore (1970) proposed a different classification system. Most systems emphasized perceivers' reactions to odors, whereas Amoore's system focuses on

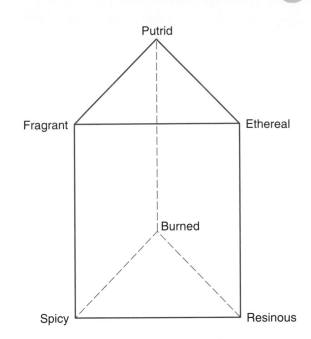

▶ **FIGURE 13.4**   Smell prism devised by Henning. According to Henning, simple odors must be located on the surfaces of the prism, not inside the prism.

the chemical structure of odors. According to Amoore's *stereochemical theory*, odorous molecules have definite shapes that determine the kind of odor we smell. Amoore initially suggested 7 primary odors, though he later added to that list. Table 13.1 shows one version of the list of primaries, together with examples.

▶ **TABLE 13.1**   Primary Odors Suggested by Amoore (1970)

Odor	Example
Camphoraceous	Mothballs
Pungent	Vinegar
Floral	Roses
Ethereal	Dry-cleaning fluid
Minty	Peppermint stick
Musty	Musk perfume
Putrid	Rotten egg

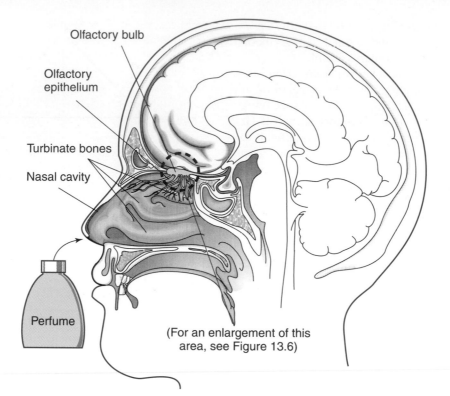

Olfactory bulb

Olfactory epithelium

Turbinate bones

Nasal cavity

Perfume

(For an enlargement of this area, see Figure 13.6)

▶ **FIGURE 13.5**   Anatomy of the olfactory system. Odors can enter the olfactory epithelium through the nose and through the mouth. The frontal cortex (near the eyes) is the location to which the receptors transmit much of the neural olfactory information.

It's certainly clear that—unlike the taste system—the olfactory system isn't based on a handful of basic odorants. For a variety of reasons, researchers have lost interest in identifying "primary" odorants (Wilson & Stevenson, 2006). Instead, recent attempts to understand the olfactory system have focused on the interaction between the chemical properties of the odorant and the receptor site. Let's turn our attention to the olfactory system, including some interesting developments in the study of olfactory receptor function.

SMELL RECEPTORS   Figure 13.5 illustrates the anatomy of the nasal (or nose) area. First, look at the region called the ***nasal cavity***, the hollow space behind each nostril. Air containing odorants reaches the nasal cavity through two routes. Most obviously, you sniff and inhale to bring in the outside air (Mainland & Sobel, 2006). Air can also come up from the back of the throat when you breathe through your mouth and when you chew or drink. This route allows

the food in your mouth to provide smell information to produce a wide range of flavors. [www] Demonstration 13.1 illustrated the importance of the olfactory information for flavor perception.

Notice the three bones lined up in the nasal cavity, called the ***turbinate bones***. (Think about how these bones would cause *turbulence* in the airstream, similar to rocks in a river.) Because of their position, these bones force most of the air you breathe in to go down your throat. Thus, only a little of the air will make its way up to the smell receptors at the top of the cavity (Hornung, 2006). As a side benefit, the air that does travel up to the top of the cavity has most of the dust cleaned away by the time it arrives.

At the top of the nasal cavity is the olfactory epithelium. The word *epithelium* refers to skin, so ***olfactory epithelium*** is the kind of skin you smell with! The size of the olfactory epithelium is about 2 cm^2 for each nostril, and it contains as many as 12 million receptors (Fain, 2003). (That number seems quite impressive until you learn that a German shep-

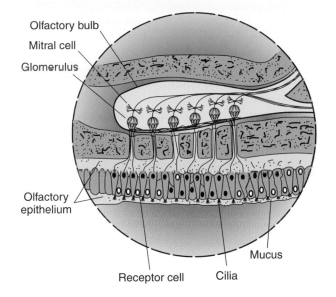

Olfactory bulb
Mitral cell
Glomerulus

Olfactory
epithelium

Mucus

Receptor cell   Cilia

▶ **FIGURE 13.6** An enlargement of part of the olfactory system. The olfactory bulb contains several layers of cells that process olfactory information. Some efferent nerves have their endings in the olfactory bulb as well.

herd has 4 billion!) These receptors are illustrated in Figure 13.6, which is an enlargement of a portion of Figure 13.5.

Note that tiny hair-like *cilia* protrude from each receptor. The cilia project into the mucus lining the nasal cavity. Not only does the mucus protect the cilia but it also affects the odorants we perceive. The cilia serve the important role of catching the odorant molecules that enter the olfactory epithelium. The interaction of a molecule with a cilium begins the process of olfaction (Takeuchi & Kurahashi, 2008). Like the receptors in your taste system, your olfactory receptors are continually renewed throughout your life (Cowart & Rawson, 2001). Most receptors are replaced about once a month.

ENCODING SMELL QUALITIES Taste has only a limited number of qualities, with receptors for each quality. Smell, on the other hand, has thousands of qualities. How are all those qualities encoded in the olfactory receptors? Linda Buck and Richard Axel (1991) provided a compelling answer to this question. They identified the genes responsible for differences in odor receptors. In recognition of their work, they received the 2004 Nobel Prize for Physiology or Medicine.

The starting point was the discovery of an olfactory G-protein (Buck, 2004). As you may recall, G-proteins play an important role in other sensory processing (e.g., vision and taste). However, given the range of odorants humans can perceive, the number of unique receptors must be relatively large. Buck (2005) managed to identify the family of about 1,000 olfactory genes that created the unique G-protein receptors. Not all of these genes are functional in humans, who have between 300 and 400 functional olfactory genes (Gilad et al., 2003; Malnic et al., 2004). The number is not rigidly defined, because humans vary fairly widely in the composition of the olfactory genes (Menashe et al., 2003). Differences in olfactory genes likely contribute to individual differences in perceptual abilities. For example, most of us find the smell of skunk unpleasant (to say the least), but some people actually like the odor (Herz, 2007).

We've already learned that dogs have many more olfactory receptors than humans. Thus, it should come as no surprise that dogs and other species (e.g., mice, lemurs) have many more functional olfactory genes than humans do (Olender et al., 2004).

The various G-proteins are found on the surface of the cilia of different olfactory receptors. Thus, each receptor is specialized, although it will respond to more than one type of odorant. Moreover, one odorant will stimulate receptors with different G-proteins. Thus, a particular pattern of activity among a combination of olfactory receptors likely encodes the various odorants (Buck, 2005). The chapter on color vision showed how the combinations of firing patterns from three types of cone receptors allow us to see a wide range of colors. Similarly, our perception of different odors probably arises from various combinations of firing patterns from the olfactory receptors.

The actual transduction process is complex, but it begins on the cilia of the receptors. Contact between an odorant molecule and a G-protein on the cilia initiates a series of chemical reactions, which results in an action potential (Takeuchi & Kurahashi, 2008). The pattern of firing among the olfactory receptors is sent to the olfactory bulb.

PATHWAY FROM RECEPTORS TO THE BRAIN Let's return to Figure 13.6. Notice that a structure located above the receptor cells is labeled the *olfactory bulb*. It performs the first processing on the signals from the smell receptors (Greer et al., 2008). Olfactory receptors send their information to the olfactory bulb in an organized fashion. Information leaves the olfactory bulb by means of the mitral cells. The olfactory bulb contains about 10,000 **olfactory glomeruli**, which are round bundles of axons from the olfactory receptors and dendrites from the mitral cells. In a tidy little bit of organization, each of the glomeruli receives input from olfactory receptors with the same G-protein (Carlson, 2007).

The mitral cells convey information from the olfactory bulb to a number of different destinations. Some of the information flows to the olfactory bulb on the other side of the head. Other information flows to parts of the amygdala and to parts of the limbic cortex: the piriform cortex and the entorhinal cortex. Most researchers consider the olfactory cortex to be any cortical area that receives direct input from the olfactory bulb. Thus, these three areas would comprise the olfactory cortex (Wilson, 2008).

Of course, these areas connect with other areas of the brain, including the orbitofrontal cortex. You may recall that this cortical area plays an important role in taste perception, as does the amygdala. The orbitofrontal cortex likely plays a role in whether or not you find an odor pleasant or unpleasant (Zelano & Sobel, 2005).

Cognitive Aspects of Smell

The sensory aspects of smell should strike you as more complex than those for taste. At the same time, consistent with Theme 2, you should be struck by the precision of the sensory apparatus. As a result, you may think that smell perception is primarily a bottom-up process. However, the picture changes when you consider that smell perception is dependent on the interplay of many brain areas (Doop et al., 2006; Petrulis & Eichenbaum, 2003). Thus, smell perception is quite complex, involving the same cognitive and emotional factors we mentioned in Chapter 12.

Researchers are well aware of the important research on sensory processes in smell. However, many of them argue for the importance of top-down processes. For instance, Donald Wilson and Richard Stevenson (2006) describe smells as "outcomes of highly synthetic, memory-dependent processing that is further modulated by expectation, context, and internal state" (p. 243). In other words, as we've noted throughout the text, perception involves much more than the physical stimulus.

A great deal of evidence supports the important role of memory and experience in smell perception

(Theme 4). Wilson and Stevenson (2006) review several studies showing that, compared to a control group, people who have experience smelling unfamiliar odors are better able to discriminate those odors. Consider the steroid androstenone, which some people have difficulty smelling. However, those people become better able to detect androstenone after sniffing it repeatedly over time (Johnson et al., 2008). Moreover, unless the odors are unpleasant, familiarity with odors leads people to prefer them. This result is entirely consistent with Robert Zajonc's (1974) mere exposure effect, which you may have learned about in a social psychology or cognition course.

People who have substantial experience with odors (e.g., perfumers) may well have better olfactory discrimination, in part, because they are better able to label odors (Stevenson et al., 2007). Semantic labels clearly have an impact on odor perception. For example, the names given to odors have an impact on perceived pleasantness (Djordjevic et al., 2008). Now you know why perfume companies are very careful when selecting a name for a new perfume!

Expectation also plays a role in your experience of odor (Gilbert, 2008). Telling people that you're releasing an odor will lead most of them to perceive an odor—even if no odor is present. Spraying water mist and telling people that it's pleasant leads them to like the smell of the room. People will perceive the same odor quite differently, depending on its label. For example, de Araujo and colleagues (2005) presented people with an odor that smelled a bit like cheddar cheese. Some people were told that the odor was cheddar cheese. Other people were told that the odor was body odor. Those people who thought that the odor was body odor rated it as less pleasant than those who thought it was cheddar cheese. As is often true of the other senses, your perceptual experience is only partially determined by the physical stimulus.

Modifying Olfactory Perception

You've just learned that your olfactory experience may be affected by a variety of cognitive factors. Even without such cognitive manipulations, the same odorant will not always smell the same. Given what you know about other senses, you would likely predict that the same odorant would begin to appear less intense over time. We'll first briefly review olfactory adaptation. Then, we'll examine how different concentrations of an odorant can affect your perception.

ADAPTATION   You have probably had this experience. You walk into a room in which onions have been frying, and the odor is overpowering. If you stay in the room for several minutes, however, the smell seems fainter and fainter. After a while, you notice only the faintest odor. You have experienced adaptation, the temporary loss of sensitivity as a result of continued stimulation (Johnson et al., 2008). Adaptation may occur when a single odorant is presented repeatedly, or when one repeated odorant is followed by a similar stimulus.

As we described for taste perception, self-adaptation occurs when the same odorant smells less intense over time. The power of self-adaptation is particularly impressive if you leave the room in which you have become adapted to an odor. When you return to this room, you can easily perceive the odor. Try www Demonstration 13.5 to illustrate the self-adaptation process.

What physiological explanations can account for self-adaptation? One nice, intuitive answer might be that the receptors simply become tired after high levels of stimulation. Olfactory receptors probably do play a role in adaptation. However, higher processing levels (e.g., olfactory bulb and cortex) also play important roles in olfactory adaptation (Johnson et al., 2008). Adaptation isn't a purely sensory process, because people don't adapt as rapidly to a substance if they direct their attention to the odor (Doty & Laing, 2003). For instance, if told that the odor is natural, people adapt normally. However, if told that it's hazardous, they don't adapt (Dalton, 2002). Consistent with our earlier observation about the role of cognitive processes, it's no surprise that attention has an impact on olfactory perception (Zelano et al., 2005).

We have been discussing self-adaptation, the temporary loss of sensitivity to an odor when that odor is presented for several minutes. With cross-adaptation—which we discussed in terms of taste— exposure to one odor reduces sensitivity to other odors. Cross-adaptation leads to a smaller reduction in sensitivity compared to self-adaptation (Doty & Laing, 2003). As a result, you might be less aware of cross-adaptation in your everyday experience of odors.

THE ROLE OF ODORANT INTENSITY   In our exploration of other senses, you've learned that increasing the intensity of a physical stimulus can lead to a change in perceptual experience. For instance, you can increase the intensity of an auditory stimulus to the point that it becomes painful. Your olfactory experience of an odorant may also change with increases in the concentration of the odorant.

Many, but not all, odorants become unpleasant at very high concentrations (Doty, 2006). For example, some substances that would be described as musky or floral will smell fecal or foul in high concentrations (Wilson & Stevenson, 2006). Even if they don't become unpleasant in high concentrations, many odorants change in quality at higher concentrations. For example, some substances that would be described as fragrant or earthy will smell oily or aromatic in high concentrations.

Measuring Olfactory Perception

As is true of the other senses, researchers are interested in determining how perception varies with stimulus intensity. At one end, researchers are interested in the smallest intensity that people can detect. At the other end, we've just seen that the quality of an odor may change at very high intensities. In between these two extremes, researchers are interested in the function that relates changes in intensity to changes in perceived intensity.

THRESHOLDS   As you'll recall from Chapter 2, researchers use several different methods to measure an absolute threshold (the boundary point at which something is reported half the time). Using these methods, the absolute threshold would be the concentration of a chemical for which a person says, "Yes, I smell it" half the time and "No, I don't smell it" half the time.

However, olfactory absolute thresholds are not easily measured. Part of the problem stems from the fact that it's quite difficult to control the concentration of the olfactory stimulus reaching the olfactory receptors. Researchers use a variety of methods to deliver the olfactory stimulus (Johnson et al., 2008). Some researchers use a machine to deliver a fixed concentration of an odorant to the perceiver. Other researchers place a concentration of the odorant in front of the perceiver and ask her or him to sniff.

In addition to methodological differences, it's an arduous process to precisely determine an absolute threshold. Table 13.2 lists thresholds for different odorants. However, you should consider each threshold a rough approximation. It's clear, however, that humans are impressively sensitive to some odors. To place some of these thresholds in perspective, imagine

▶**TABLE13.2** Human Odor Detection Thresholds (From Dalton, 2002)

Compound	Odor Threshold in Air (parts per million)
Methanol	141.0
Acetone (nail polish remover)	15.0
Isopropyl alcohol (rubbing alcohol)	10.0
Formaldehyde	0.87
Chlorine	0.50
Camphor (mothballs)	0.05
Menthol	0.04
Hydrogen sulfide (rotten eggs)	0.017
Vanillin	0.000035

a cube formed from 100 air molecules per side. That cube would contain a million air molecules. To detect isopropyl alcohol, you'd need to replace at least ten of those air molecules with alcohol molecules. In contrast, to detect hydrogen sulfide, you'd need to replace only a small portion (less than .2) of *one* air molecule with hydrogen sulfide. You're *really* sensitive to rotten egg smell, which allows you to avoid eating a potentially noxious substance.

Natural gas and propane are odorless but dangerous. To alert people to the presence of these gases, an odorant is added. For example, ethyl mercaptan is added to propane. Ethyl mercaptan can be detected at concentrations below one part per *trillion*. Imagine two Olympic-size swimming pools filled with plain water. Suppose that you add just *three drops* of ethyl mercaptan to one of the two pools. Amazingly, people could consistently smell which of the two pools contained the odorant (Johnson et al., 2008).

As we discussed earlier in this chapter, an absolute threshold differs from a recognition threshold. An absolute threshold task requires a person only to determine whether an odor is present, but not necessarily to say what the odor is. As is true for taste, recognition thresholds for odors are higher than detection thresholds. In a subsequent section, we will discuss people's abilities to identify odors that are well above threshold. For now, we'll turn our attention to measuring above-threshold odors.

SMELLING MORE INTENSE STIMULI People can detect impressively tiny concentrations of certain sub-

stances. Our difference thresholds may be less impressive. When researchers use variants of the classical psychophysical methods for discrimination, their estimates of difference thresholds for many odorants vary widely. Once again, methodological differences may well explain the variability. Consider how difficult it would be to determine a difference threshold using the method of constant stimuli. You'd need to deliver one concentration of the odorant, then another concentration of the odorant. The participant would then report "same" or "different." You'd repeat this process over and over until you'd arrived at a reliable difference threshold.

Using such procedures, researchers have often determined Weber fractions that are substantially higher than those found for other senses. In other words, we're not very sensitive to increases in the intensity of odorants. However, humans produce much lower Weber fractions for some odorants than they do for other odorants (Johnson et al., 2008).

Instead of the classical psychophysical methods, researchers often use other techniques, such as magnitude estimation. As you may recall, magnitude estimation requires a person to assign a number to indicate the intensity of a stimulus. Thus, the researcher would present a series of different concentrations of an odorant. On each trial, the participant would provide a number to indicate the intensity of the odor. Consistent with other senses, the relationship between judgments and odor intensity is well described by a power function with an exponent of less than one. Such fractional exponents mean that relatively large increases in odor concentration are needed to produce an increase in number estimates. (In contrast, electric shock has an exponent larger than one, so small increases in electric shock would lead to larger number estimates.)

Individual Differences in Olfactory Perception

One potential problem in measuring olfactory experience, such as thresholds, is that people can differ substantially. Avery Gilbert (2008) describes the range as *"American-Idol*-tryout bad to unbelievably excellent" (p. 48). What might produce such differences? To answer such a question, we round up the usual suspects—nature and nurture. People may have different olfactory genetic material and different olfactory experiences. As a result, you should expect that people differ in sensitivity to and preference for various odors (Hudson & Distel, 2002).

Let's begin with deficits in smell sensitivity. People with no sense of smell are said to suffer from *anosmia*. Anosmia may result from head trauma that breaks the connection between the olfactory bulb and the olfactory cortex (von Bothmer, 2006). As we mentioned at the beginning of this chapter, food flavors are vitally dependent on olfactory information, so all foods taste extremely bland to a person with anosmia.

People who have otherwise normal olfaction, but can't smell some odorants, suffer from specific anosmias. These specific anosmias may well be genetic. Earlier we mentioned the steroid androstenone, which a small percentage of people can't smell (Bremner et al., 2003). Although many factors may be involved, genetic differences may explain the specific androstenone anosmia.

Research suggests that women are more sensitive than men to androstenone (Good & Kopala, 2006). Those results are not particularly surprising, because a number of studies point to greater olfactory abilities in women (Gilbert, 2008). The explanation may be more cognitive, with women better than men at learning, remembering, and labeling odors. However, there are some sex differences in olfactory brain structures (Garcia-Falgueras et al., 2006). Moreover, some research suggests a link to female hormones, with postmenopausal women often exhibiting similar olfactory abilities to age-matched men (Gilbert, 2008).

Of course, you already know about the effects of age on taste and other senses, so you shouldn't be surprised to learn that olfactory abilities decline with age (Hummel et al., 2002; Johnson et al., 2008). In fact, olfactory sensitivity begins to decline in middle age. However, even much older people are as good as younger people at identifying unpleasant odors (Konstantinidis et al., 2006).

In earlier chapters, we've discussed the impact of the loss of a sense on brain plasticity. Thus, you might predict that a person who is blind might have better olfactory abilities. Research confirms that prediction, but not because of an improvement in sensory abilities. Instead, it appears that blindness leads to a compensatory cognitive ability—better ability to name an odor (Gilbert, 2008; Wakefield et al., 2004).

In our discussion of individual differences in taste, you learned about people who experienced phantom tastes. Do people also smell odors that aren't there? Yes, indeed! People experience a variety of olfactory hallucinations (Velakoulis, 2006). For example, individuals with schizophrenia often report smelling odors (e.g., gas, ammonia, perfume) that aren't present. Other people confuse odors, such that everything might smell like burnt toast. Or—worse yet—some people have cacosmia, in which everything smells like . . . well, fecal matter (Gilbert, 2008).

Recognizing and Identifying Odors

How accurate are humans at recognizing odors? Could you follow an odor trail like a bloodhound? If you were presented with a common odorant, such as vinegar or an orange, could you unfailingly supply its name? Finally, how accurate would you be in identifying other people based only on their odors? Let's first examine the identification of familiar odors and then move on to the recognition of humans on the basis of their odors.

RECOGNIZING ODORS   We've already noted that cognitive factors, including learning and memory, play important roles in odor perception. For instance, memory certainly underlies your ability to smell one odor and then later pick out that odor from among several alternatives (Wilson & Stevenson, 2003).

Humans are actually both quick and accurate at discriminating between two odors that have very similar molecular composition (Johnson et al., 2008).

However, keep in mind that familiarity and experience enhance such discrimination.

One task that involves odor discrimination is that faced by a bloodhound tracking a scent. A number of different odors assault the dog's nose, yet it seizes on one specific odor and follows it. Quite impressive! Knowing that dogs are comparatively well endowed with olfactory equipment, you might expect that a human couldn't perform such a task. However, you'd be wrong. Humans *are* able to track a scent using a strategy that mimics that of a bloodhound (Porter et al., 2007). First, researchers laid down a scent trail. Then, blindfolded people would get down on their hands and knees and follow the trail. To do so, they would sniff while moving their heads from side to side, just as a bloodhound does. When the scent grew weaker, the people would move in the opposite direction until the scent grew stronger. With such a strategy, they were quite good at tracking the odor trail.

IDENTIFYING FAMILIAR ODORS   Try [www] Demonstration 13.6 to illustrate an informal variation of experiments that assess the identification of familiar odors. It's much more difficult to identify odors than simply to determine that two odors are different (a discrimination task). Although humans are able to discriminate many thousands of odors, our identification abilities are much more limited.

One experimental approach presents familiar odors (e.g., popcorn, motor oil, coffee) and asks people to name them. Using this identification approach, untrained people get about half correct and experts do much better (Johnson et al., 2008). As we mentioned earlier, the problem seems to be an impoverished set of odor labels (Wilson & Stevenson, 2006).

To eliminate the naming problem, some researchers use a multiple-choice procedure. For example, the University of Pennsylvania Smell Identification Test presents 40 scratch-and-sniff odorants. People choose from among four labels for each odor. This test and its variants have been used in a number of different research settings (Doty, 2006). As you'd expect, people perform more accurately on this multiple-choice test than on odor-identification tests without labels.

BODY ODORS   Among the odor-producing stimuli in our environment are other people. Body odor arises due to the interactions of bacteria with sweat. Sweat is primarily water, but it also contains molecules of the *human leukocyte antigen (HLA)* system (Wilson & Stevenson, 2006). Especially for other species, you may also see this genetic material called the *major histocompatibility complex (MHC)*. Each human has a fairly unique body odor, which is largely produced by HLA. Thus, the more genetically related people are, the more similar their body odors. Identical twins, who share genetic material, smell so similar that even bloodhounds find it difficult to discriminate between them (Harvey et al., 2006).

Americans are obsessed with masking body odors. Thus, we spend enormous amounts of money each year on perfumes, deodorants, and mouthwashes. In 2007 alone, people spent about $20 billion on fragrances (Leffingwell, 2008). Given the common use of personal care products, how do researchers study unadulterated human odor?

In a prototypical body odor study, people don't wash or use deodorants for a day or two. For that period, they might wear a T-shirt or gauze pads under their arms. Researchers carefully collect the T-shirts or gauze pads, which serve as stimuli in the experiments. Researchers typically present the stimuli so that people don't know the source of the odor.

Given the difficulty of identifying odors, you may not be surprised to learn that people sniffing such stimuli can't identify the odor as human body odor (McClintock et al., 2005). However, even though they may not know what they're sniffing, people are good at discriminating body odors (Herz, 2007). For example, mothers are highly accurate at identifying the odor of their newborn children, even if they had experienced only minimal contact with the children. Moreover, mothers who don't know the source of the diapers think that soiled diapers from their own babies smell better than soiled diapers from other babies (Case et al., 2006). Of course, this preference may be due to a mere exposure effect.

Consistent with individual differences we reported earlier, women are better than men at identifying human odors (Platek et al., 2001). People sniffed five different gauze pads containing their own odor and odors of four other people. Most women (60%) were able to pick their own scent, but only about 6% of the men were able to do so. Women may perform better than men because they are better able to generate labels for odors.

Research on identification of body odors is quite intriguing, primarily because smelling such genetically determined odors may confer some adaptive advantage. That is, animals could potentially choose mates whose odor indicated that they were not closely related. In fact, many animals are sensitive to the genetic aspect of body odors of other members of their species. For example, squirrels develop unique odors that are used by other squirrels to determine relatedness (Mateo, 2006a, 2006b). The process even works across species. Based solely on odor, rats can determine genetic relatedness in humans and humans can determine genetic relatedness in mice (Ables et al., 2007; Gilbert, 2008).

Humans (especially women) are able to identify other humans based on body odor. Moreover, such information also leads to preferences. For instance, Claus Wedekind and his colleagues (e.g., Wedekind & Penn, 2000) found that women who were not taking contraceptive pills preferred the odor of men who were more genetically distant from themselves. Human mate choice is surely not determined solely by odor. However, odor may play some role. It is certainly the case that odor influences some behaviors in humans and other animals.

IN-DEPTH

Behavioral Influences of Odors

As you know, many factors influence human behavior. What role might olfactory stimuli play in determining your behavior? You are relatively adept at perceiving odors—especially if you're a woman. Your experiences thus far may suggest that odor has played little role in your day-to-day life. However, odors are sneaky. You may be unaware of their influence, but odors may be affecting your behavior.

Olfaction does have an important role in communication among members of a species. Researchers are especially intrigued by substances called **pheromones**, which act as chemical signals in communicating with other members of the same species (Wyatt, 2003). The name *pheromone* looks like *hormone*, which is a chemical used to send communications from one part of the body to another. Hormones are internal, though, and pheromones are external. Pheromones are excreted through the urine and various sweat glands.

One location that processes these chemical signals is the vomeronasal organ. The **vomeronasal organs (VNO)** are olfactory sense organs located on either side of the septum, which separates the two nostrils (Witt & Wozniak, 2006). These organs are found in many mammals, but they are likely vestigial in humans. However, some researchers believe that some humans have functioning vomeronasal organs (Meredith, 2001). In some sense, the controversy is irrelevant, because the same chemical signals are also processed within the main olfactory system (Kelliher, 2007; Liberles & Buck, 2006; Zufall & Leinders-Zufall, 2007). Thus, these chemical senses could influence

human behavior, even if no vomeronasal organ were present. We'll now briefly review some evidence for the functioning of chemical signals in lower animals and in humans.

Odor Effects on Behavior in Other Animals

Pheromones play a number of different roles, including the marking of territories. It's not completely clear why they do so, but many nonprimate males mark their territories with chemical signals (Wyatt, 2003). Rats, wolves, and dogs use urine to mark their territories. Deer and hartebeests have odor-producing glands in their foreheads that they use to mark their territories. They often mark trees by rubbing against them with their antlers and foreheads.

Some pheromones serve as alarms. For example, pronghorn antelopes release a strong odor when they encounter a predator (Wyatt, 2003). Both ants and honeybees release an alarm pheromone when an animal threatens their nest, attracting their mates to defend the nest.

Finally, let's consider pheromones that influence sexual behavior. For example, many female animals release pheromones when they are in heat. These odors attract the sexual interest of the males of her species. In fact, the effects are so powerful that a male tortoise will mount a head of lettuce over which a female tortoise in heat has just climbed. Bombykol, a sex pheromone secreted by female silkworm moths, will cause male moths to fly miles in search of the female (Gottfried, 2006).

Pheromones may also play a role in pregnancy in some species. Long ago, Hilda Bruce found that if an unfamiliar male mouse is placed near the cage of a newly pregnant female, she is likely to abort the fetuses (Herz, 2007). The Bruce effect has been replicated in a number of laboratory studies, but may not occur in the wild (Wolff, 2003). Moreover, factors other than pheromones may well explain the effect (Doty, 2003).

You should note the power of these pheromones in some species. Taking advantage of such compulsory behavior, scientists have designed pheromones to control pests. For example, scientists have duplicated the sex pheromone that the female gypsy moth emits to attract males. One strategy is to bait traps with the fake pheromone, luring the males into traps so they can't mate (Sharov et al., 2002).

Odor Effects on Behavior in Humans

The impact of odors on "lower" animals is interesting. However, odors can't control human behavior, right? Surely you wouldn't find yourself sexually attracted to another person, or find yourself trusting another person, simply because of an odor. Let's see what researchers have learned.

Martha McClintock is a prominent researcher in olfaction. However, she was a senior at Wellesley College when she produced an early demonstration of the behavioral effects of odor (McClintock, 1971). McClintock examined the folk belief that if women live together, their menstrual cycles become similar. At the beginning of the school year, close friends and roommates differed by 8 to 9 days in the date of menstrual cycle onset. Over the school year, the difference decreased to an average of 5 days apart.

The similarity in menstrual cycles might have been due to the fact that the women were undergoing similarly timed stresses, but McClintock hinted that pheromones might be involved. Subsequent research suggested that chemical signals between women may lead them unconsciously to synchronize their menstrual cycles. However, more recent research suggests that the apparent synchrony can be traced to an error in reseacrh methods (Schank, 2006; Ziomkiewicz, 2006).

If olfactory information doesn't lead to menstrual synchrony, you may find it even more difficult to believe that olfaction could lead to sexual attraction.

Nonetheless, you may well have seen advertisements for human sex pheromones. Some even claim to be supported by research. You should evaluate such claims with a healthy dose of skepticism (Jacob, Zelano et al., 2002). To date, you can't purchase a pheromone that will make you more sexually attractive.

However, various hormone-derived scents may have other effects on human behavior (Gilbert, 2008). For example, androstadienone is derived from the sex hormone testosterone. Sniffing this substance has a positive effect on mood in women (Bensafi et al., 2004; Jacob, Garcia et al., 2002). Women who sniff androstadienone show elevated levels of the hormone cortisol, which is often released in response to stress (Wyart et al., 2007). Sniffing another hormone, oxytocin, may lead people to become more trusting (Kosfeld et al., 2005).

Many retailers fill their stores with odors intended to influence shoppers' buying behavior. So far, these odors are not hormone-derived, but research has demonstrated that they can affect behavior. For instance, people are more helpful when they smell pleasant odors (e.g., cinnamon and coffee). A male-oriented odor leads to greater sales of menswear and a female-oriented odor leads to greater sales of womenswear (Gilbert, 2008).

Olfaction may also be linked to memory. For example, although you may not have smelled Play-Doh in a long time, you could probably recognize its distinctive odor right now. In a classic example of the link between odor and memory, the author Marcel Proust smelled the aroma of a French pastry, which then enhanced the memory of his youth. You may also find that particular odors, such as Play-Doh, evoke memories of events from your past. The emotional component of odors may make them effective cues to memory—especially over long time periods (Wyatt, 2003). However, such claims have been extremely difficult to support with research (Gilbert, 2008).

Odors may have a smaller influence on humans than they do on other species. However, they may have a greater influence on our lives than we realize. Following close on the heels of the scientists are the entrepreneurs who seek to turn the science into profit. Don't be surprised to see increasing numbers of advertisements for scents promising you control over other people. Can you imagine a future in which such products actually work as advertised?

Section Summary

Smell

1. As is true for taste, smell is considered a chemical sense. For taste perception, molecules dissolved in saliva come in contact with taste receptors. For smell perception, molecules suspended in air come in contact with smell receptors.

2. People have proposed many different classification systems for odorants. Henning's classification system defines smells in terms of six basic odors. Amoore proposed a classification system in which the shape of the odor molecule determines the odor. Modern researchers pay little attention to such classification schemes.

3. The nasal cavity is the hollow space inside the nose, and the olfactory epithelium—located at the top of the nasal cavity—contains the smell receptor cells. The cilia of the receptor cells make contact with the odorants. G-proteins, located on the surface of the cilia, determine the odorants to which that receptor is most sensitive.

4. The olfactory bulb processes information from the smell receptors, and information is then transmitted to many different brain areas.

5. Researchers have developed a deeper understanding about olfactory receptors. However, olfaction is a complex cognitive process, and it is influenced by many top-down processes.

6. Self-adaptation (a higher threshold with prolonged exposure to one specific odor) involves higher neural levels in addition to the receptors. In cross-adaptation, exposure to one odor raises the threshold for other, similar odors. Self-adaptation is typically more powerful than cross-adaptation.

7. Absolute thresholds can be extremely low for some odors. Increasing the concentration of most odorants has a relatively small impact on perceived intensity.

8. People differ in their olfactory abilities. Generally speaking, women have better olfactory abilities than men. Anosmia is a disorder in which a person is unable to smell. Some people have specific anosmias, so they can't smell particular odorants.

9. It's easier to discriminate between two different odors than to identify (name) an odor. Human odors (determined by human leukocyte antigen) enable people to determine genetic closeness based on the odor.

10. Pheromones are chemical signals that are important determinants of the behavior of nonhuman animals. Such chemical signals have an impact on some human behaviors (e.g., elevating cortisol levels in women), but to date there is no human sex pheromone.

Flavor: Interaction of Taste, Smell, and Other Senses

Think about eating a slice of pizza. Where would you locate the flavor of the pizza? If you're like most people, you'd say that it originates in your mouth (Taylor & Hort, 2004). However, your experience is much like the ventriloquism effect, where you think that the dummy is the source of the voice. As you now know, taste receptors in your mouth provide a limited number of qualities. The flavors emerge as a result of input from your nose—added to taste input. The odors of the crust, the tomato sauce, the oregano, and the mozzarella combine with the taste input to produce the familiar flavor. However, flavor involves more than taste and smell (Delwiche, 2004; Keast et al., 2004). We'll first examine the combined effects of taste and odor on flavor. Then, we'll examine other factors that influence flavor.

Contributions of Taste and Smell to Flavor

Smell and taste are major components of your perception of flavor, but how do they interact to create flavor? You may first sniff the food or drink on its way to your mouth. Once it's in your mouth, the taste receptors process the tastant. At the same time, the olfactory information flows up through the back of the mouth to the olfactory receptors. As you experienced in www Demonstration 13.1, your flavor experience is greatly reduced when you eliminate the olfactory component.

The taste and smell receptors send information to their respective areas of the brain. As you'll recall, information from the taste cortex and the smell cortex flows into the orbitofrontal cortex. It may well be in this area of the brain that taste and smell information are combined to give rise to flavor (Rolls, 2008; Small & Prescott, 2005). Moreover, this area contributes to the pleasure we derive from food (Small et al., 2007). Keep in mind, however, that flavor information involves a large number of brain areas, many of which likely contribute to your perception of flavor (Jones et al., 2006).

Contributions of Somatosensory Input to Flavor

Are you still thinking about that slice of pizza? If you're thinking of deep-dish pizza, you may well imagine a soft chewy crust. Otherwise, you may imagine a hard crunchy crust. Our point is that the texture of your food plays a role in the flavor you experience (Green, 2004; Taylor & Hort, 2004). Try to imagine a future in which all your foods are puréed (as in baby food)!

Researchers refer to the somatosensory qualities of foods and drinks as "mouth feel." Most of this information is processed in the trigeminal nerve. Thus, it is a sensory system entirely separate from the taste and smell systems. The *trigeminal nerve* has free nerve endings in the mouth and olfactory epithelium (Keast et al., 2004; Key, 1999). These nerve endings encode such somatosensory experiences as texture, shape, temperature, and even pain. The painful burn in your mouth or nose from eating a chili pepper or wasabi is certainly a part of the flavor experience.

Notice how your understanding of flavor perception has just become more complex. Now you must consider how input from the trigeminal nerve is combined with taste and smell information to provide your sense of flavor. Can you guess the brain location to which this somatosensory information would eventually go? Yes, indeed, it appears that the orbitofrontal cortex is where all the many aspects of flavor are combined (Rolls, 2005, 2008). Information about the temperature of the food may also be processed there. We'll now say a bit more about the role of temperature on flavor.

Contributions of Temperature to Flavor

Have you ever eaten a cold slice of pizza? Does it taste the same as a warm slice? All the components are the same, but the flavor is different. Thus, you should anticipate that temperature has an impact on flavor.

Heat makes molecules more volatile, so heating foods and drinks may generate stronger odors to enter your nose. However, it's also the case that simply changing the temperature of the tongue may generate a sense of taste (Delwiche, 2004). Researchers need to clarify the mechanisms by which temperature affects flavor. However, the temperature information from the mouth goes to the somatosensory cortex and other areas of the brain, including the orbitofrontal cortex (Guest et al., 2007).

Contributions of Vision to Flavor

Do you think that the flavor of the pizza would change if the crust were green, the sauce purple, and the cheese pink? If you've given careful consideration to Dr. Seuss's *Green Eggs and Ham*, you realize that visual information has an impact on flavor. Consistent with Theme 1, vision can influence flavor, just as it influences other senses.

We don't have to rely solely on Dr. Seuss's research—many people have studied the impact of color on flavor (Delwiche, 2004). Our experience with particular color-flavor combinations likely contributes to the impact of color. That is, researchers often find that flavor is altered when color information is removed or changed. In addition, flavor intensity increases when color intensity increases.

People ascribe very different flavor qualities to red and white wines. How much of the flavor experience is due to expectations driven by the color of the wine? The writer Calvin Trillin (2002) suggested that people couldn't correctly label red and white wines based solely on flavor. Several researchers have demonstrated the impact of wine color on wine flavor. For example, the same white wine will have different flavors if people see it as a white wine, a rosé, or a red wine (Delwiche, 2003; Morrot et al., 2001).

Of course, once we acknowledge the contribution of vision to flavor, visual areas of the brain become important. As is true of many other perceptual experiences, flavor perception involves a large number of brain areas. The evidence that vision may alter flavor is clear. However, it's equally clear that people still perceive flavor in the absence of visual input.

Contributions of Cognition to Flavor

If you haven't already stopped reading and gone in search of a slice of pizza, we have a couple of additional questions. Do you have a favorite pizzeria? Does knowing that you're about to enjoy a favorite slice of pizza contribute to the flavor? Cognitive processes, such as experience and expectations, play a role in flavor perception. Let's consider a study that shows the impact of such cognitive processes.

Leonard Lee and his colleagues (2006) asked bar patrons to choose between two different beers. Actually, the beers were identical except that Lee added a few drops of balsamic vinegar to one beer (labeled MIT Brew). Some people were first told about the composition of MIT Brew and others were not. When people knew nothing about the added vinegar, they actually preferred the MIT Brew. However, when people knew about the vinegar, they preferred the unadulterated brew. Lee argued that the information about vinegar actually changed flavor perception. That's because another group was told about the added vinegar *after* tasting the beers. Learning late about the vinegar didn't affect the flavor for this group—they preferred the MIT Brew about as much as the "blind" group. You can add this study to the list supporting the adage that ignorance is bliss.

Putting It All Together: Hedonics of Foods

Hedonic preferences, or *hedonics*, involve judgments of pleasantness and unpleasantness, which are central in our perceptual responses to food flavors. For example, suppose you have just lifted your spoon to your mouth to consume the first bite of maple-pecan-fudge-ripple ice cream. The issue of thresholds might be important if you contemplate whether you can detect the maple, which may be partly masked by the fudge sauce. Adaptation may be important because subsequent spoonfuls might be perceived as less sweet. For most people, however, the perceptual reaction that really matters most is, "Does this taste good?"

Given the wide range of foods that people in one culture think are delicious, but people in another culture would find unpalatable, hedonic preferences must be largely learned (Zellner, 1991). As we've noted, the mere exposure effect suggests that repeated exposure to a particular food can lead people to like that food more than they did prior to exposure. For example, most animals and human infants do not enjoy chili peppers. After all, they produce a painful, burning sensation! However, when your family meals repeatedly involve chili peppers, you'll probably come to enjoy chili peppers (Logue, 2004).

Cultures also differ in hedonic preferences for food temperatures. Americans vacationing in Greece often notice that the food they eat occasionally tastes less than ideal because it is served close to room temperature, rather than steaming hot. To a Greek, the moussaka might be best at 25° C, but a North American might prefer it at 45° C. North Americans prefer their beer cold, but other cultures prefer beer at room temperature.

Even within cultures, however, people's food preferences vary. For example, recall the supertasters, whose experience of flavors likely differs from those of us who aren't as sensitive (Logue, 2004). Genetics play a role, but people's experiences also play a role in hedonic preferences. Do you enjoy eating broccoli? If so, it surely has to do with early food experiences. Julie Mennella and her colleagues (2004, 2006) have studied the development of flavor preferences. She's found that feeding infants a bitter formula leads them to prefer that formula to a sweeter formula. Because the bitterness of the formula is similar to that found in broccoli, for example, such infants should also enjoy such vegetables. The flavor of breast milk is affected by the foods the mother consumes. Thus, breastfed infants should develop flavor preferences that reflect the mother's diet.

Experience can shape hedonic preference in another way. For example, most people have come to detest foods that others enjoy. In all likelihood, you too have a learned flavor aversion (Logue, 2004). As John Garcia (e.g., 1966, 1985) discovered many years ago, these food aversions can develop after a single pairing of nausea or sickness with a particular food. Even if you became nauseous for another reason (e.g., the flu), you may develop an aversion to a food (especially an unusual food) that you consumed before becoming ill. For example, people undergoing chemotherapy to treat cancer often develop aversions to foods eaten prior to their chemotherapy (Bernstein, 2008). The food aversions emerge even though these people fully understand that it's the chemotherapy causing the nausea. Logic and reasoning are competing with deep-seated principles that protect us from consuming foods that make us ill!

As you can now tell, our separate discussions of taste and smell were somewhat misleading because they treated the two senses as independent of one another. In the laboratory, we can separate the two senses. However, in real life they are greatly intertwined—providing vivid support for Theme 1 of the text. The other senses also have an impact on our sense of flavor, providing further support for our theme.

As functioning organisms, humans are surrounded by a wealth of sensory information—all of which is processed more or less simultaneously by our sensory systems. At any particular time, we might choose to emphasize one sense over another, and the evidence suggests a strong reliance on visual input. However, the input from *all* our sensory systems is continually being processed. We do not live in a visual world, or an auditory world, or a tactual world, but in a world rich with information of all kinds. To think of smell or taste information as somehow second-rate is to ignore the unitary experience we have of a vibrant, complex world filled with a wealth of information.

Section Summary

Flavor: Interaction of Taste, Smell, and Other Senses

1. Flavor is a multisensory experience, with contributions from taste, smell, and other senses. The orbitofrontal cortex seems to be the site at which flavor information is encoded.

2. The "mouth feel" of a substance includes texture, temperature, and even pain. These somatosensory qualities all contribute to flavor. Such information is carried through the trigeminal nerve.

3. Visual input, including color, has an impact on flavor. For example, changes in the typical color of foods and drinks have an effect on flavor. More intense colors often lead to more intense flavors.

4. Cognitive factors, such as your experience and expectations, affect flavor perception.

5. Hedonic taste judgments, or what people find pleasant, vary widely from culture to culture. Within a culture people vary considerably, with learned flavor aversions found in people who dislike foods that others in the culture enjoy.

Review Questions

1. Distinguish between taste and flavor. What are some of the components of flavor? Imagine a person with total ageusia and anosmia. Try to describe that person's experience of food.

2. Describe the five basic taste qualities that humans perceive. How are these qualities encoded in your mouth and then processed in your brain?

3. When attempting to understand human behavior, psychologists often look to the roles of nature (e.g., biology, genetics) and nurture (e.g., experience, memory). Examine the roles of nature and nurture in explaining taste, smell, and flavor.

4. Throughout the text, you've seen that the same person may perceive a stimulus as different depending on context. Furthermore, different people may perceive the identical stimulus as

different. Use the chemical senses to provide further examples of the disparity between the physical stimulus and perceptual experience.

5. What are the important characteristics of stimuli that determine whether they are odorous? Suppose you sniff an orange and a lemon, and they smell similar. How would Henning's and Amoore's systems explain the similarities?

6. In a laboratory at your college, suppose that a professor measures a student's threshold for a particular odor, and it is high. In a laboratory at another college, a different professor measures a different student's threshold for a second odor, and it is low. Identify as many factors as possible that might explain the different results.

7. Point out aspects of the following topics that might be relevant for a person who develops perfumes: absolute thresholds, difference thresh-

olds, adaptation, cross-adaptation, odor recognition, and odor constancy.

8. Two portions of this chapter discussed the importance of human body odors—the section on smell recognition and the section on pheromones. Summarize the results of these two sections. How might development of a human sex pheromone alter social interactions?

9. Researchers have made great strides in learning how the chemical sense receptors encode infor

mation. They have also learned a great deal about the areas of the brain responsible for encoding the information. Briefly describe these processes, but then illustrate how cognitive processes play an important role in your experience of flavor, taste, and smell.

10. Describe how flavor is a multisensory experience. You should emphasize the chemical senses, but also draw on other senses. Use examples from your own life to illustrate these principles where you can.

Key Terms

chemical senses, p. 354
flavor, p. 354
taste, p. 354
tastant, p. 354
papillae, p. 355
taste bud, p. 355
taste receptor cells, p. 355
microvilli, p. 355
taste pore, p. 355
G-proteins, p. 356
adaptation, p. 357
self-adaptation, p. 357

cross-adaptation, p. 357
water taste, p. 358
taste modifiers, p. 358
miracle fruit, p. 358
gymnema sylvestre, p. 359
absolute threshold, p. 359
recognition threshold,
     p. 359
difference threshold,
     p. 359
PTC, p. 359
PROP, p. 359

nontasters, p. 359
supertasters, p. 359
ageusia, p. 359
dysgeusia, p. 360
olfaction, p. 361
odorant, p. 361
stereochemical theory,
     p. 361
nasal cavity, p. 362
turbinate bones, p. 362
olfactory epithelium,
     p. 362

cilia, p. 363
olfactory bulb, p. 363
olfactory glomeruli, p. 364
anosmia, p. 367
human leukocyte antigen
     (HLA), p. 368
pheromones, p. 369
vomeronasal organ, p. 369
trigeminal nerve, p. 372
hedonics, p. 373

Recommended Readings

Gilbert, A. N. (2008). *What the nose knows: The science of scent in everyday life*. New York: Crown.

Gilbert is a prominent olfactory researcher. However, when you read this book, you get the impression that he would be a most pleasant traveling companion. Gilbert has stuffed his book with anecdotes and interesting research, all of which both engage and teach. The book may not make you laugh out loud, but you will surely smile on occasion. (Blast Master 3000, indeed!)

Logue, A. W. (2004). *The psychology of eating and drinking* (3rd ed.). New York: Routledge.

Logue's book addresses many of the topics in this chapter. In addition, it discusses related topics such as anorexia, obesity, and alcohol abuse. Her style is clear and interesting, so even people with little background in perception will enjoy the book.

Wilson, D. A., & Stevenson, R. J. (2006). *Learning to smell: Olfactory perception from neurobiology to behavior*. Baltimore: Johns Hopkins.

What do you get when you combine a zoologist from Norman, Oklahoma, with a psychologist from Sydney, Australia? Apparently, you get an extremely informative text on odor perception. This book is scholarly yet accessible to a general reader hoping to learn about odor perception. Taken as a whole, the book provides a very persuasive argument for the role of cognition in odor perception. This book will surely be required reading for students interested in olfaction.

Wyatt, T. D. (2003). *Pheromones and animal behaviour: Communication by smell and taste*. New York: Cambridge.

Wyatt provides a balanced summary of the fascinating role of pheromones in other animals and humans. He draws on a wealth of intriguing examples, but never sensationalizes a topic. You'll find the appendices helpful as a quick summary of the chemical aspects of pheromones.

Perceptual Development

THE PREVIOUS 13 chapters have examined how people perceive the world. In this final chapter we will focus on the development of vision and audition from birth to old age. This chapter will also allow you to review a variety of important concepts from earlier chapters.

A central controversy in human development is called *the nature–nurture question*: Are abilities due to inborn factors (nature), or are they the result of learning and experience (nurture)? This controversy may also be framed in terms of two philosophical positions: nativism and empiricism (Gordon & Slater, 1998; Lamb et al., 2002). Throughout the text, we've emphasized the exquisitely evolved nature of our perceptual systems (e.g., Theme 2). At the same time, we've emphasized the important role of experience (e.g., Theme 4). Thus, if you are interested in understanding perception and perceptual development, the evidence consistently leads to a middle ground in which it is crucial to consider both nature and nurture.

However, some psychologists have taken somewhat extreme positions. Consider William James, the nineteenth-century American psychologist, who proclaimed that the newborn's world is a "blooming, buzzing confusion" (James, 1890, p. 488). According to this empiricist perspective, newborn infants open their eyes and see an unstructured, random chaos. Given the newborn's limited motor and communication abilities, it's easy to see how James might have arrived at his conclusion. Clever developmental psychologists have found means to surmount these difficulties and learn about infants' perceptual abilities. In the next section, we'll review some of the research strategies used by developmental psychologists. Based on their findings, we now know that very young infants are quite competent. Those infants impose a structure on the world, unlike the chaos suggested by William James (Johnson et al., 2005; Newcombe & Sluzenski, 2004).

As you'll learn in this chapter, we are born with many innate abilities and with fairly capable sensory systems. However capable they may be, our sensory systems are not functioning optimally at birth. Instead, these systems develop over the course of our lifetimes. Some of those changes in perceptual abilities are due to natural development, some are due to experience, and some are due to a combination of natural development and experience. You'll note that our perceptual abilities continue to change as we age, with prior experience often playing a vital role in

allowing older people to compensate for some deterioration in sensory abilities that may occur. Thus, the interplay between nature and nurture is found throughout a person's life.

In earlier chapters, we've commented on the difficulty of fully understanding the private perceptual experience of an individual. That problem is compounded when researchers study infants, who lack verbal abilities and have limited movement abilities. In the next section, we'll examine how developmental psychologists have made great strides in spite of the complications involved in studying infants.

Studying Perceptual Development in Infancy

An infant cannot say to the researcher something like, "The left-hand figure is farther away." Nor can an infant walk over and grab the green ball rather than the blue ball. How, then, might we learn about an infant's depth or color perception? Psychologists have developed many clever methods for discovering infants' perceptual capacities.

At the heart of most of these methods is the reality that infants are actively engaged in exploring their worlds, even though their exploration is limited by their lack of motor ability. Nonetheless, we should not lose sight of the fact that in the words of Eleanor Gibson,

> Perception is active, exploratory, and motivated even in the neonate. Rather than being passive recipients of energy that falls willy-nilly on some receptor surface, very young infants can and do actively obtain information. (Gibson, 1987, p. 515)

Such active engagement is certainly at the heart of three basic methods we will discuss: preference, habituation, and conditioning. We'll first describe the basic procedures in this section, then we'll describe physiological methods that require no overt response from the infant.

Preference Method

The *preference method* is based on the idea that, if the infant spends consistently more time actively looking at one figure in preference to another, then the infant must be able to discriminate between the two figures (Bornstein et al., 2005; Cohen & Cashon, 2003). This procedure may strike you as so intuitively obvious that you might predict that it has a long history of use in developmental psychology. However, researchers first reported using the technique in 1958 (Berlyne, 1958; Fantz, 1958). Although to some of you that may seem like ancient history, in the grand scheme of things it's relatively recent.

Fantz (1961) describes placing infants in a small crib inside a special "looking chamber." He attached pairs of test objects—slightly separated from each other—onto the ceiling of the chamber. The researcher could look through a peephole between the two objects to see the infants' eyes. Mirrored in the center of the eye, just over the pupil, would be the tiny image of the test object on which the infant's eyes were focused (e.g., a striped patch or a gray patch). Fantz recorded the amount of time that the infant spent looking at the striped patch and the amount of time spent looking at the gray patch. For example, a particular infant might look at the striped patch 65% of the time and the gray patch 35% of the time. To ensure that any effects of position preference did not confound the study, the testing sessions were carefully controlled so that the striped patch would appear on the left side half the time and on the right side half the time.

What does the information about looking times tell us? Well, if the infants were *unable* to tell the difference between the two objects, then the two looking times should be roughly equivalent. For example, the baby might look at one figure 48% of the time and at the other figure 52% of the time. However, if the baby looks at one figure for a consistently longer time (such as 65% for a striped patch and 35% for a gray patch), then we can conclude that the baby can tell the difference between the two figures. You should be able to imagine how this technique could be used to study a wide range of perceptual abilities (e.g., acuity, color vision, and perception of objects such as faces).

Beyond the fact that the infant can tell a difference between the two stimuli, you should realize that it's very difficult to determine exactly how to interpret an infant's looking time (Aslin, 2007). Consider, for instance, two stimuli that are clearly detectable to the infant. Does no difference in preferential looking mean that both stimuli are interesting or that both are boring? Does a greater duration of looking at one stimulus mean that is more interesting, surprising,

confusing, frightening, or unfamiliar than the other stimulus?

Moreover, suppose one infant looked continuously at a stimulus for 80% of the time in a solid block and another infant looked at the stimulus in four blocks of 20% of the time, with four interspersed blocks of 5% looking away. Even though the total looking time would be identical, do you think that the two infants are performing in a similar fashion? As powerful as the preferential looking method is, it suffers from the same problems as most behavioral measures. That is, the observable behavior is easily measured, but the underlying psychological reasons for the behavior are not always obvious.

Habituation Method

Because the infant is actively engaged in the world, she or he will usually orient toward a novel stimulus (typically presented against a uniform background). However, if the stimulus is presented continuously or repeatedly, the infant will lose interest in the stimulus. The **habituation method** is based on this phenomenon, called **habituation**, which is a decrease in attending to a repeated stimulus (Bornstein et al., 2005). When a baby pays less attention to an object that has been presented several times, the baby is demonstrating that he or she remembers seeing the object.

What happens if we now present a completely different stimulus? If the infant can detect that the new stimulus is different, the infant should show **dishabituation**, or an increase in looking time. We can use the habituation technique to encourage infants to tell us, "Yes, I can tell the difference between this new stimulus and that tired old stimulus you kept showing me before." However, if the baby ignores this new stimulus, we conclude that the baby is basically saying, "Boring—this is the same stimulus you've shown me on the previous 20 trials."

Conditioning Method

As you probably learned in your introductory psychology course, there are two types of conditioning. Both classical and operant conditioning are used in developmental research (Rovee-Collier & Barr, 2001). With the **classical conditioning method**, the experimenter repeatedly pairs a conditioned stimulus of interest (e.g., a particular tone) with an unconditioned stimulus (e.g., a puff of air to the eye); the infant will exhibit an unconditioned response without training (e.g., blinking). When conditioned, the infant will blink (a conditioned response) to the tone in the absence of the puff of air, establishing that the infant can perceive the tone.

With the ***operant conditioning method***, researchers select a response that the baby can make, and they deliver a reward when the baby makes that particular response. Carolyn Rovee-Collier and her colleagues have made great use of the foot-kicking response in infants (Rovee-Collier & Barr, 2001). Infants naturally kick their feet, though not particularly often. But, if a ribbon is attached from one of the infant's feet to an overhead mobile (containing a number of brightly painted objects), the infant will kick a lot to make the mobile dance (the reward in this paradigm). When the ribbon is not attached to the mobile (as is the case when establishing a baseline for kicking or when testing), the conditioned baby will kick vigorously in an effort to move the mobile. Of course, the baby will be disappointed because the mobile doesn't move. However, as long as the test phase is relatively short, the baby's foot-kicking behavior won't extinguish. This conditioning paradigm has been applied to a number of areas of memory and perception.

Physiological Methods

The preference method, habituation method, and conditioning method rely on behavioral responses made by the infant. In the next section, we'll discuss eye movements, a topic first raised in Chapter 4. This behavioral response also provides an insight into an infant's perceptual abilities. However, as we discussed in Chapter 2, a number of different methods rely on physiological changes, rather than overt behavioral responses. These physiological methods are especially useful because they require no overt response from the infant.

Many of the physiological recording techniques used in studying adult perceptual experience have been applied to developmental research (Thomas & Casey, 2003). For example, changes in heart rate may give an indication of an infant's arousal or attention (Bornstein et al., 2005). Visual evoked potentials are electrical signals produced in the occipital cortex that allow researchers to make inferences about the processing of visual stimuli (Gwiazda & Birch, 2001). When researchers study such evoked potentials or

▶ **FIGURE 14.1** An infant wearing a HydroCel Geodesic Sensor Net for recording EEG/ERP. Photo courtesy of EGI.

other electrophysiological measures of brain activity, they place a cap on the child's head. As seen in Figure 14.1, the cap contains many electrodes. Other methods that have been applied to children involve generating images of neural function; one example is functional magnetic resonance imaging (fMRI) (Scerif et al., 2006; Spelke, 2002; Stiles et al., 2003).

Section Summary

Studying Perceptual Development in Infancy

1. Infants have limited communication and motor abilities, which may lead people to underestimate their perceptual abilities. Researchers have developed a number of methods—including preference, habituation, and conditioning—that allow us to overcome the communication barrier.

2. Infants actively explore their world, which leads them to look at stimuli that interest them. That fact lies at the heart of the preference method. If infants look longer at one stimulus than another, then they must be able to tell them apart.

3. The habituation method also relies on the active nature of infants. When a stimulus is presented repeatedly, infants become habituated to it, meaning that they look at it less often. When a novel stimulus is presented, infants will look at it if they can tell that it's different (dishabituation). If they can't distinguish it from the original stimulus, however, they will look at it less often.

4. Researchers have used both classical and operant conditioning techniques to study perceptual development.

5. Techniques that don't rely on behavioral responses, such as physiological recording, are useful in studying infant perceptual abilities.

Early Development of Visual Abilities

As we've noted, even young infants are actively engaged in their environment. Such active engagement is essential. Early research by Held and Hein (1963) illustrates that experience alone is not as valuable as active involvement with the environment. These researchers raised kittens in total darkness until they were several weeks old. After that time, the kittens were divided into two groups. Some of the kittens were allowed to actively explore the visual environment you see in Figure 14.2. These kittens could walk around freely. In contrast, the remaining kittens were passively engaged with their environment. These kittens were simply carried around in a little cart, propelled by the movement of the active kittens.

When the kittens were later tested, the active kittens showed normal depth perception, but the passive kittens did not. For instance, if you take a normal kitten and place it near a flat surface such as a table, it will extend its paws to meet the surface. The active kittens in Held and Hein's study extended their paws appropriately, but the passive kittens did not. Keep in mind that all kittens had identical visual experiences—they differed only in their degree of active engagement with the environment. Thus, not only must the developing organism have experience, but the particular kind of experience must also involve active engagement.

We'll next discuss the development of our visual system. However, keep in mind that much of the development of parts of the brain devoted to visual processing depends on visual experience. As we discussed in Chapter 4, people who have been deprived of visual input from an early age find it difficult to adapt to restored visual abilities. Much of their difficulty is presumed to arise due to the plasticity of the developing brain. That is, the wiring of the developing brain is not entirely fixed, but varies depending on the nature of the neural firing patterns. Without input from the visual pathways, the visual cortex creates a different pattern of connections than would have emerged in the presence of normal visual input. There is certainly mounting evidence for the negative impact of visual deprivation at an early age (Maurer, Ellemberg et al., 2006; Maurer et al., 2007). The situation may not be entirely bleak, however, as the case of S. R. D. illustrates (the young woman with congenital cataracts discussed in Chapter 4). That is, not only the developing brain but also the adult brain may be able to adapt to novel input (Maurer et al., 2005).

The Developing Visual System

The optical quality of the young infant's eye is good. However, there are a number of initial physical limitations to the infant's visual system. For instance, both the eye and lens are smaller than when fully developed. (The eye grows from about the size of a dime to about the size of a quarter.) As a result, the image formed on the retina is smaller. Moreover, the retina itself is not fully developed, particularly in the fovea (Hainline, 1998; Kellman & Arterberry, 1998; Oyster, 1999). For instance, the cones are not as densely packed in the infant fovea and their shape is not optimal for catching the incoming light. As a result, the infant's fovea sends less detailed visual information through the optic nerve. The retina is fully developed by about 6 years of age, but the eye continues to grow through adolescence.

The neural pathways between the eye and the cortex—as well as the visual cortex itself—are not fully developed at birth. However, a good deal of groundwork has been laid down prior to any visual experience (Finlay et al., 2003). Thus, for example, the optic chiasm is present, and the LGN already exhibits the layers separating input from the left and right eyes (Huberman et al., 2005). The infant's visual cortex exhibits the layered structures seen in the adult, but it

▶ **FIGURE 14.2** Two kittens, previously reared in the dark, being exposed to an environment of vertical stripes. The kitten on the right is active in its exploration of the environment. The kitten on the left is passively carried via the actions of the other kitten, although it has identical visual experience. The passive kitten has poorly developed perceptual abilities as a result of its diminished experience. (After Held & Hein, 1963)

is not fully organized (e.g., ocular dominance columns are not present).

The fact that parts of the visual system develop after birth means that early infant visual perception is far from optimal. However, it also means that there is ample opportunity for experience to shape some neural development (Maurer & Lewis, 2001b; Mrsic-Flogel et al., 2007; Westermann et al., 2007). Therefore, the visual system provides a microcosm of the nature–nurture controversy, with some of the development fixed and some dependent on experience.

We'll now examine a number of the visual abilities that we've already explored in earlier chapters (and roughly in that order). Given the complex interactions between experience and the development of the visual system, you shouldn't be surprised to learn that some abilities are more fully developed than others at a particular age.

Acuity

We discussed visual acuity in Chapter 4, with normal adult acuity described as 20/20. Using a variety of techniques, including the preference method and visual evoked potentials, a newborn infant's acuity can be described as 20/400, which is legally blind (Bornstein et al., 2005).

Not only does the newborn infant have poor acuity but the infant is also less sensitive to contrast than an adult (Kellman & Arterberry, 2006; Maurer & Lewis, 2001a). As we discussed earlier, acuity is typically tested under conditions of high contrast (e.g., black stimulus on a white background). Adult acuity typically decreases when the contrast is decreased (e.g., a dark gray stimulus on a light gray background). Newborn infants, then, would see a high-contrast stimulus as exhibiting much less contrast, which makes it even more difficult for them to discern the stimulus. In the end, what the newborn infant sees is quite a bit different from what an adult sees, as illustrated in Figure 14.3 (page 382).

Luckily, a newborn infant has a cushy life that largely involves input and output, neither of which requires peak visual abilities. The newborn infant can certainly see (and smell and hear) nearby objects, such as Mom and Dad. Moreover, infant acuity develops

▶ **FIGURE 14.3** These two images attempt to characterize the difference between adult and newborn infant visual perception. Note that not only is there less detail in the image on the right but it also has less contrast (restricted range of lightness).

rapidly. Using the preference method, researchers have learned that 1-month-old infants can discriminate between a gray patch and a stimulus of black-and-white stripes that are 1/16-inch wide. By the time infants are 6 months old, they can discriminate between a gray patch and black-and-white stripes that are only 1/64-inch wide. Although infants' contrast sensitivity develops more slowly than acuity, this sensitivity improves as well. By 5 or 6 years of age, both acuity and contrast sensitivity are at roughly adult levels. Of course, the normal course of visual development requires visual experience, consistent with Theme 4.

Eye Movements

In Chapter 4, we discussed several different types of eye movements. You may recall that **vergence eye movements** are necessary to align the foveas of both eyes with an object. Very young infants are not yet able to acquire depth from binocular vision, but their vergence movements are quite accurate (Gwiazda & Birch, 2001).

Researchers are interested in version eye movements, such as **saccadic eye movements**, because they contribute to clear vision. However, such eye move-

ments also provide an important methodology for learning about what an adult or an infant perceives. As is true for adults, infants actually shift their attention to an object before making an eye movement to the object. Thus, we can learn a lot about what in the world attracts their interest (Aslin & McMurray, 2004; Hayhoe, 2004). With recent advances in eye movement technology, this nonverbal response is an important addition to the tools used to study infant perception and cognition.

If you've ever played peek-a-boo with a young child, you know the child expresses great delight when the hidden object reappears. For very young infants, who have yet to achieve object permanence, the hidden object has disappeared! Researchers have made great use of hiding objects in studying infant development (Hespos & Baillargeon, 2006; Kaufman, Csibra et al., 2003; Kaufman et al., 2005). As a result, we've learned that children as young as 2.5 months have a form of object permanence (Baillargeon, 2004). Let's see how we can also use version eye movements to learn about young children's expectations regarding hidden objects.

Gredebäck and von Hofsten (2004) recorded the eye movements of infants as they watched a small smiley-face go around in circles on a computer screen. The smiley-face moved at different speeds and appeared to move behind a black square that occluded about 20% of the path of the face. The infants would track the smiley-face as it moved (a smooth pursuit movement), but what would they do when the face went "behind" the occluding square? Even when they first took part in the task (at 6 months of age), the infants would make a saccadic eye movement that fairly accurately predicted where and when the face would emerge. Infants also varied their eye movements, depending on the speed of the smiley-face. Thus, at age 6 months, eye movements are already fairly sophisticated and informative of what the infant knows about the world.

IN-DEPTH

Shape Perception

In Chapter 5 we discussed a number of cues that an adult uses to perceive an object. These cues include edge detection, Gestalt principles, shape-from-shading, and shape-from-motion. All of them are likely to play a role in infant shape perception (Kellman & Arterberry, 2006; Quinn, 1999). Does an infant need to learn all the cues in order to see shapes? If so, how does the infant pull off that feat? The question of infant shape perception is an intriguing one, which has inspired a multitude of studies.

Although a newborn infant has some notion of objects immediately after birth, it's clear that development of object perception takes place over months and even years (Mondloch et al., 2003). For example, before they are 4 months old, infants are sensitive to some properties of objects (e.g., solidity) and see objects as figures against a more distant background (Johnson, 1998). As we mentioned earlier, under some circumstances these infants realize that an object continues to exist even when they can no longer see it (object permanence). By the time they are 4 months old, infants have learned to see an object as whole, even when it is partly obscured by another object (Johnson, 2004). At that age they can also discriminate between possible and impossible objects, such as those seen in M. C. Escher prints (Shuwairi et al., 2007). However, it's not until they are about a year old that infants exhibit a clear sense of object identity (Carey & Xu, 2001). For instance, at that point, they can tell that two contiguous objects are, in fact, separate.

We'll now turn our attention to studies that focus on a very important kind of object for an infant. Given the crucial nature of social interactions, an infant needs to recognize and read faces as early as possible. How early are infants able to perceive faces?

In one of the early studies of infant face perception, Fantz (1961) used the preference method to demonstrate that 2- and 3-month-olds preferred to look at a cartoon-like face rather than other patterns or bright solid colors. However, those infants are relatively experienced. Would newborn infants prefer to look at faces? And, if so, would that finding provide support for the nature side of the nature–nurture controversy?

To see how early a face preference might emerge, Goren and her colleagues (1975) studied newborns who were roughly 9 minutes old and had never seen a face. In spite of a lack of experience, these newborns were more likely to follow the schematic face-like stimulus in Figure 14.4 (page 384) than either the scrambled-face stimulus or the blank-face stimulus. Using older newborns—in this case, about one hour old—Morton and Johnson (1991) also found that infants moved their eyes farther to follow the face-like stimulus, in contrast to the scrambled stimulus and the blank stimulus. Using different stimuli and methodologies, other studies have found that newborns perfer to look at faces (Farroni et al., 2005; Mondloch et al., 1999), although that is not always the case (Easterbrook, Kisilevsky, Hains et al., 1999; Easterbrook, Kisilevsky, Muir et al., 1999).

Given what we know about a newborn's visual abilities, it's not completely clear what the newborn actually sees when she or he looks at an adult face. As Figure 14.3 illustrates, both detail and contrast are surely reduced. Nonetheless, even newborns as young as 30 minutes old will often imitate adult facial expressions (Slater, 1998). Thus, infants must see

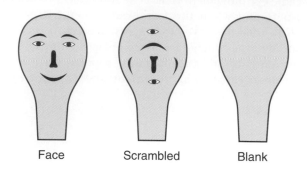

Face · Scrambled · Blank

▶ **FIGURE 14.4** In a study by Morton and Johnson (1991), newborns moved their eyes farther to track an intact, schematic face, in contrast to a scrambled face or a blank face.

sufficient detail to be able to detect specific face motions (e.g., sticking out the tongue). Even though they've never looked in a mirror, the infants must also understand that they share some equivalence with the adult they're watching (Meltzoff, 2002a, 2002b; Meltzoff & Moore, 1999). How these infants then mimic the behavior is an interesting question, given that they cannot see their own faces.

Why the infants will mimic an adult is also an interesting question. That answer may well lie in the fact that humans are social animals, so developing a relationship with other humans is very important—especially to the very dependent infant. The importance of social interactions may also explain why newborns are sensitive to some adult facial expressions, looking longer at a happy face than a fearful face (Farroni, Menon et al., 2007).

Research has also demonstrated that very young infants prefer to look at their own mother's face or a familiar face compared to a stranger's face. For example, Walton and her coauthors (1992) found that newborns around 24 hours old produced significantly more sucking responses to a video of their mother than to a video of a female stranger. Young infants also prefer to look at faces that gaze directly at them (Farroni et al., 2002; Farroni, Massaccesi et al., 2007; Farroni et al., 2006). For example, researchers first habituated the infant to a picture of an adult who appears to look directly at the infant. Later, when given the opportunity to look at that same face or a

novel face, the infant will look longer at a novel face. However, if the original picture showed an adult who appeared to be looking away from the infant, infants habituated more rapidly, which is consistent with a preference for faces that appear to gaze directly at the infant. When later given the choice of the original picture with averted gaze or a new picture of an adult with averted gaze, the infants in this condition showed no preference for the novel face.

In spite of their limited experience with faces, young infants prefer to look at faces that adults find attractive, rather than faces that adults find unattractive. That said, a child's perception of facial attractiveness continues to develop with experience (Cooper et al., 2006).

Perceived attractiveness is not the only area of face perception that illustrates the important role of experience. Generally speaking, younger children seem to focus more on facial features, whereas adults not only process features but also their holistic configuration. That is, adults are not only sensitive to a person's eyes but also to the spacing of the eyes relative to one another and to the whole face. It's not entirely clear when a child's face perception becomes adult-like, but it could be as young as age 4 or as old as adolescence (de Heering et al., 2007; Mondloch et al., 2004; Mondloch et al., 2002; Mondloch, Leis et al., 2006; Mondloch, Maurer et al., 2006).

Some of the changes in face perception could be due to the developing visual and cognitive abilities of the child, and not entirely due to experience. However, it is clear that experience is important when one looks at people who were deprived of visual input, such as children who are born with cataracts. Without the benefit of visual experience, especially via input to the right hemisphere, these people exhibit deficits in face perception (Geldart et al., 2002; Le Grand et al., 2003, 2004).

Thus, shape perception in general and face perception in particular demonstrate the important role of experience layered on a base of innate abilities. You'll see the interplay of nature and nurture throughout development, but pay particular attention to the controversy in the development of speech perception.

Depth and Distance Perception

Consider a 10-month-old infant who crawls down the hallway and pauses at the top of the stairs, looking back and forth between the floor and the first step down. Does that infant see depth? That question was of great interest to Eleanor J. Gibson (1910–2002), who was married to James J. Gibson (remember his direct perception approach). In classic studies, Eleanor Gibson and Richard Walk (1960) studied depth perception with a visual cliff.

As Figure 14.5 shows, a *visual cliff* is an apparatus in which infants must choose between a side that looks shallow and a side that looks deep. Babies are placed on a central board with a sheet of strong glass extending outward on both sides. On one side, a checkerboard pattern is placed directly under the glass. On the other side, the same checkerboard pattern is placed some distance beneath the glass. The apparatus is called a visual cliff because of the apparent drop-off on the "deep side" of the central board. To an adult, the pattern on the left side of Figure 14.5 looks farther away because the elements in the pattern are smaller. Gibson and Walk wondered whether infants' perceptions would be similar.

In one experiment, Gibson and Walk tested 36 babies between 6 and 14 months of age. They placed a baby on the central board and asked the baby's mother to call to the baby from both the shallow and the deep side. Gibson and Walk found that 27 babies moved off the central board at some time during the experiment, and all 27 crawled at least once onto the shallow side. In contrast, only 3 babies crawled onto the deep side. Thus, babies old enough to crawl are able to discriminate between deep and shallow. Their depth perception is well enough developed that most of them could avoid the potentially dangerous deep side.

Gibson's research is certainly consistent with the notion that—once infants are old enough to begin moving around their environment—they develop necessary perceptual abilities, such as depth perception (Campos et al., 2000). However, even before they begin to crawl, very young infants have depth- and distance-perception abilities. For instance, even 1-month-old infants can tell that an object is getting closer to them (Kellman & Arterberry, 2006). By about 2 months of age, infants begin to make use of motion as a cue to depth. As early as 3 months old, babies begin to use binocular depth information (Johnson et al., 2005). Several months later, babies begin to make use of pictorial depth information cues such as occlusion. By the time babies reach the ripe old age of 6 months, they are reasonably expert in knowing that their toes are farther away than their knees and that the mobile above their crib is closer than the ceiling.

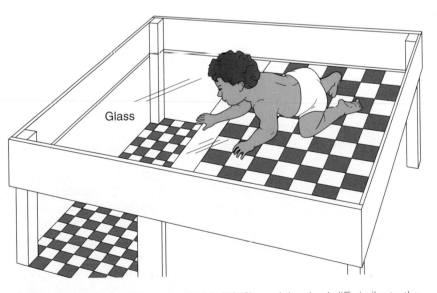

Glass

▶ **FIGURE 14.5** Gibson and Walk (1960) used the visual cliff, similar to the one depicted in this figure, to study infant depth perception.

That said, it's often difficult to understand the spatial relationship between your location and the location of another object. If you've tried to find a particular restaurant in an unfamiliar city, then you know exactly what we mean. Thus, there are many ways to conceive of spatial knowledge, and for some tasks a 6-month-old would be in trouble (Newcombe & Huttenlocher, 2000; Newcombe & Learmonth, 2005; Newcombe & Sluzenski, 2004). For example, suppose you hid a toy in a large sandbox in front of a child and then took the child away for a couple of minutes. On returning to the sandbox, a 2-year old would be able to retrieve the toy fairly easily. Younger children, however, would have difficulty. As competent as young infants may be, they continue to learn about depth and distance relationships for many years.

Color Perception

Can babies see color? You might think that it's a simple question, but it was not so easily addressed by research. Consider for a minute how adults with color-vision deficiencies maneuver through a world of wavelengths that they see quite differently from most people. They are able to use subtle lightness differences to make discriminations that other people could make based solely on wavelength. Thus, it's difficult to ensure that an infant is making a discrimination based on perceived color differences and not on perceived lightness differences.

In spite of the difficulties, careful research has now established that by around 8 weeks of age, infants have functional M- and L-cones (Orel-Bixler, 2002). Thus, at that young age, they are dichromats like many other mammals (Bowmaker & Hunt, 2006). The S-cones emerge later; by 4 months of age, infants exhibit color perception that is quite similar to adult color perception (Kellman & Arterberry, 2006).

Motion Perception

As we reach the end of this list of developing visual abilities, you can probably predict that assessing the development of motion perception is not a simple matter. Adding to the complexity is the nature of motion perception itself. As you know from Chapter 9, retinal information about motion is ambiguous.

Movement on the retina may or may not signal movement in the world.

Babies respond to some types of movement, such as a looming object, as soon as they are born. They will also track a nearby moving object with their eyes, which is one part of a test for healthy vision in a newborn (Ricci et al., 2007). However, they can't detect very slow or very fast motion that is detectable by adults. Sensitivity to the direction of motion isn't present in newborns, but it emerges after about 6 weeks.

At about 6 months of age, babies can make some relatively subtle motion discriminations. For instance, their directional sensitivity has improved (Mason et al., 2003). They are also better at tracking the movement of targets behind occluding objects (Bremner et al., 2005; Johnson et al., 2003), though an occluder still presents a challenge (Spelke & von Hofsten, 2001). Also at this age, infants have learned to perceive global biological motion (Pinto, 2005).

However, perception of some types of motion continues to develop over years. For instance, if you embed the point-light stimulus in visual noise, children as old as 6 years of age have more difficulty than adults in perceiving biological motion (Freire et al., 2006). And 5-year-old children have a more difficult time than adults in discriminating between two black-and-white gratings that moved at two different slow speeds (Ahmed et al., 2005).

The cumulative evidence suggests that babies immediately perceive some primitive motion. Furthermore, they understand more subtle kinds of movement by about the time they are 6 months old. However, children continue to develop perception of some types of complex motion for many years.

Section Summary

Early Development of Visual Abilities

1. Infant perception is active and exploratory, rather than a passive process. Such active engagement with the environment is crucial for perceptual development.

2. The fovea of the newborn is not mature at birth; the visual pathways and the visual cortex are also not fully developed. However, the visual systems develop rapidly.

3. Visual acuity can be measured in a number of ways, but converging evidence suggests that newborn infants are legally blind (20/400). Visual acuity develops rapidly and reaches adult levels by 5 to 6 years of age.

4. Even very young infants produce fairly accurate vergence eye movements. Researchers learn about an infant's cognitive and perceptual abilities by studying saccadic eye movements with eye-tracking devices.

5. Infants can perceive some objects at birth, but object perception continues to develop for years.

6. Within minutes of their birth, newborns prefer to look at faces. They especially prefer to look at their mother's face, faces that look directly at them, and faces that adults find attractive.

7. Face perception continues to develop for many years, from an emphasis on the features of faces to an emphasis on the holistic configuration of the features.

8. Studies suggest that 3-month-old babies use binocular depth information in perceiving distance. By age 6 months, they are able to use the kind of monocular cues found in pictures.

9. By 4 to 8 weeks of age, infants have functional M- and L-cones, so they are dichromats. By the age of 4 months, however, an infant's color vision is very adult-like.

10. Newborns appreciate simple motion, and 6-month-olds can perceive more complex motion stimuli, such as biological motion. Nonetheless, motion perception continues to develop for years.

Early Development of Auditory Abilities

We've seen that newborns' visual abilities are fairly limited at birth, although with the proper experience they develop substantially during infancy. In contrast, newborns' auditory skills are relatively sophisticated. Let's begin by examining the development of the auditory system and then focus on the development of speech perception.

The Developing Auditory System

The auditory system develops substantially between the 20th week of gestation and the infant's birth (Lasky & Williams, 2005). It's clear that by about the 25th week, a fetus will respond to a fairly loud external sound. If you recall the notion of an impedance mismatch, you'll realize that the fluid-filled fetal environment is not ideal for sound transmission. With the outer and middle ears filled with fluid, an external sound must be quite intense in order to cause the inner ear hair cells to fire.

Not all the sounds experienced by a fetus are external. Life in the uterus may be dark, but it certainly isn't quiet! For example, the sound level near the head of a fetus is about 80 dB, primarily due to the noise from the mother's pulse. Instead of habituating to the constant sound, a newborn actually exhibits a preference for the sound of a heartbeat. A near-birth fetus also shows a preference for mom's voice, exhibited through in an increase in heart rate compared to a stranger's voice (Kisilevsky et al., 2003).

Although newborns generally prefer their mother's voice over other voices, they actually prefer a fluid-transmitted version of her voice over an air-transmitted version (Lasky & Williams, 2005). The newborn even prefers to hear the language spoken by the mother rather than other languages (Werner & Bernstein, 2001). And the preferences can be fairly specific. For example, when the newborn's mother had repeatedly read Dr. Seuss's *The Cat in the Hat* out loud during the last 6 weeks of her pregnancy, her newborn prefers to hear *The Cat in the Hat* over a similar story (De Casper & Spencer, 1986). Clearly, the fetus is hearing a variety of sounds for weeks before birth.

To assess the auditory capabilities of newborn infants, audiologists typically conduct screening tests, including one for the otoacoustic emissions we discussed in Chapter 9 (Morton & Nance, 2006). It's clear that a newborn infant does not hear as well as an adult, with intensity thresholds elevated by about 40 dB and less sensitivity to particular frequencies (Werner & Bernstein, 2001). Auditory localization is only roughly accurate in newborns, allowing them to turn their heads reliably toward a sound source (Slater et al., 2002). By the age of 3 months, infants exhibit a minimum audible angle (MAA) of about 20 degrees. However, by about the age of 5 years, children have achieved the adult MAA of 1 degree (Werner & Bernstein, 2001).

The inner ear is relatively mature at birth, so neural development explains the development of auditory capabilities (Saffran et al., 2006). By 6 months of age, infants are much more sensitive to high-frequency sounds, but they still have difficulty discriminating between similar frequencies. At that age, auditory localization has improved to a MAA of 10 degrees. A variety of auditory capabilities continue to develop, with some not reaching maturity until the child is 6 years old or older.

Clearly, infants' developing auditory systems make them increasingly adept at perceiving a range of auditory stimuli. However, one could easily argue that the most important auditory stimulus an infant encounters is speech. We'll now turn our attention to this fascinating area of human development.

Speech Perception

To understand the crucial role of speech in development, consider that the word *infant* comes from the Latin for "without speech." How do children move so rapidly from being speechless to being able to understand and produce speech? As we discussed in Chapter 11, people have proposed many theories to explain this central human ability.

Consider that, by the age of 6, children have some mastery of about 14,000 words. To acquire a vocabulary this large, children must learn an average of about 8 new words each day from the time they are a year old until their sixth birthday. How can children master language so readily? Is it because the human brain is "hard-wired" for language?

The area of language development is certainly fertile ground for the nature–nurture controversy (Bates et al., 2002; Diehl et al., 2004; Lamb et al., 2002). Although we cannot describe the controversy in sufficient detail to do it justice, you should know that both sides have compelling evidence to support their positions. And if you are a betting person, you should put your money on a resolution that lies between the two poles of the controversy. That is, the brain is predisposed to support language development. However, experience plays a vital role in shaping brain development and in the acquisition of specific language skills.

Let's examine three areas that are important for the development of speech perception. As you know from Chapter 11, meaningful speech sounds (phonemes) vary only slightly in acoustical content. When do infants develop the ability to discriminate these phonemes? There is also a great variety in phonemes as produced by different speakers (or the same speaker at different times). When do infants learn that two phonemes are the same, even though they sound quite different? And finally, you know that in normal speech, the auditory information arrives in a stream with no clear demarcations between words. When does an infant learn to extract words from this auditory stream?

PHONEME DISCRIMINATION: LEARNING WHAT'S DIFFERENT Research shows that infants have a remarkable ability to discriminate between highly similar phonemes, the basic units of speech we discussed in Chapter 11. Peter Eimas (1934–2005) and his colleagues (1971) conducted the classic research on this topic by testing speech perception in infants between 1 and 4 months of age. Basically, they used the habituation method combined with the high-amplitude sucking procedure. In the **high-amplitude sucking procedure**, babies are conditioned to suck on a pacifier to produce a stimulus, such as a speech sound. For example, babies might suck to produce the sound "bah." At first, the babies would suck vigorously to produce the "bah" sound. However, after about 5 minutes the baby habituates, making fewer sucking responses. At that point, the researchers would pair a new sound with the infant's sucking, such as "pah." As you may recall from Chapter 11, these two utterances are identical except for minuscule differences in voice onset time.

Nonetheless, even the younger babies showed dishabituation; when the new speech sound was presented, their sucking returned to the previous vigorous level. In other words, even at 1 month of age, babies can distinguish "pah" from "bah." Subsequent research has established that these prelinguistic infants are capable of discriminating many different phonemes (Houston, 2005; Jusczyk et al., 1998; Jusczyk & Luce, 2002; Saffran et al., 2006). However, because they are not yet capable of speech, the phonemes cannot be linguistic units for the infants. Therefore, infants must distinguish the sounds on the basis of acoustic properties. And, as you may recall from the discussion of categorical perception in Chapter 11, even animals that are incapable of speech are able to make similar discriminations.

At this early age, infants all around the world make similar phonemic distinctions. However, by about the age of 7 months, infants have gained so much experience with their own language (or languages) that some distinctions disappear (Kuhl, 2004; Saffran et al., 2006). For example, two sounds that are distinct phonemes in Hindi but not in English are discriminable by 6-month-olds raised in an English-speaking home. However, these same children can no longer discriminate between the two phonemes when they are about 1 year of age. These phonemes are, of course, discriminable by 1-year-old Hindi-speaking children. Moreover, some phonemic distinctions within a child's native language actually become sharper with experience. These older children also prefer to hear words from their native language compared to words from other languages and to hear non-words that are more like words in their native language (Dehaene-Lambertz et al., 2001).

It appears, then, that newborn infants are well disposed to learn a language. They can make fine discriminations in speech sounds—even those that ultimately become irrelevant to the language they acquire. Because we are social animals, infants overhear all sorts of conversations and listen to speech directed specifically to them. As a result of this exposure, they become increasingly adept at perceiving the phonemes of a specific language.

SPEECH-SOUND CONSTANCY: LEARNING WHAT'S THE SAME   So far, our examination of speech perception during infancy has emphasized babies' skill in making discriminations, in determining whether two speech sounds are different. However, linguistic skill depends not simply on detecting *differences* but also on appreciating *similarities* (Kuhl, 1992). An infant needs to develop speech-sound constancy, such that when the sound /a/ is spoken by her 3-year-old sister, it matches the sound /a/ that is spoken by her uncle with a deep, bass voice. Language mastery depends on learning not only which differences you must pay attention to, but also which differences you must *ignore*.

For example, let's consider a study conducted in Patricia Kuhl's lab (Marean et al., 1992). The study used the conditioned head-turning method to reinforce a 2-month-old infant for identifying a change in a vowel sound. Let's imagine that 2-month-old Jason is sitting on his mother's lap. Both his mother and the researcher are wearing headphones, and they cannot hear the vowel sounds that Jason is hearing. The experimenter sits directly in front of Jason, jiggling some intriguing toys so that the infant will face

straight forward. Then a male voice speaks a stream of phonemes. On the no-change trials, the researcher presents a series of five /a/ sounds (like the vowel sound in *pop*). On the vowel-change trials, Jason hears one /a/ sound, then one /i/ sound (like the vowel sound in *peep*), then three more /a/ sounds. During the training portion of this study, Jason must learn that, if he turns his head to the side during one of the vowel-change trials, he will be rewarded by the activation of a truly fascinating mechanical toy. However, if Jason turns his head to the side on a no-change trial, nothing happens. Training continues until Jason turns his head only on trials when the second phoneme changes.

Next, Jason hears a male voice saying /a/ in the first, third, fourth, and fifth position, but a *female* voice saying /a/ in the second position in the five-vowel sequence. If Jason turns his head to the side, he's "telling" us that he regards the /a/—spoken by a female voice—to be a change. However, if Jason keeps looking straight ahead, he's "telling" us that he considers the five /a/ sounds to be the same, whether they are spoken by a male or a female. These infants looked straight ahead 80% of the time, whether they were 2, 3, or 6 months old, thus exhibiting speech–sound constancy. However, if the female voice said /i/ in the second position, the infants did turn their heads.

Thus, 2-month-olds are capable of identifying distinctive aspects of language. Meanwhile, they ignore other aspects of language that aren't as helpful in extracting meaning from speech.

SPEECH SEGMENTATION: CAPTURING WORDS FROM THE STREAM   Listening to a foreign language for the first time should give you immense respect for the problem confronting an infant. It may seem to you that the people are speaking very rapidly, and you should have difficulty determining specific words in the stream of language. What do you grab on to that will allow you to extract single words from the non-stop verbiage?

Peter Jusczyk (1948–2001) made a number of important contributions to this question (Gerken & Aslin, 2005). For instance, Jusczyk showed that 8-month-old infants remember words they've previously heard, even though they may not know what the words mean. When they later hear a story, the infants listen longer when the story contains the words they've previously heard (Houston & Jusczyk, 2000, 2003; Jusczyk & Aslin, 1995; Newman & Jusczyk, 1996). Thus, experience and memory play a role in isolating words that occur in fluent speech, a finding entirely consistent with Theme 4.

Jusczyk and others have learned that infants also use prosodic cues to extract words from the speech stream (Saffran et al., 2006). *Prosody* refers to acoustic properties of words, such as stress, intonation, and rhythm. For instance, many two-syllable words in English stress the first syllable. By about 9 months of age, infants have learned to use this stress as a means of segmenting speech, though how they learn to do so is not entirely clear. As you may infer from Jusczyk's other work, it's possible that infants learn about regularities of stress by hearing adults speak some single words in isolation. Younger infants don't make use of stress, but they appear to be sensitive to other regularities in transitions between words.

Section Summary

Early Development of Auditory Abilities

1. The auditory system develops early in the prenatal period, but higher levels of auditory processing are not mature at birth.

2. Infants have higher auditory thresholds than adults, but they become increasingly sensitive. By 6 years of age, the child has adult-like auditory capabilities.

3. Young infants can discriminate between highly similar phonemes, although this ability declines for phonemic contrasts not found in their language environment.

4. Even when people with very different voices speak the same phoneme, young infants recognize that it's the same phoneme.

5. Infants develop a number of different strategies for segmenting a speech stream into separate words, making great use of memory of earlier linguistic experiences.

Early Development of Intersensory Abilities

Objects in the world produce a variety of energies that may affect the developing infant's sensory systems. Thus, the infant may see, hear, touch, smell, or taste a parent, a pet, or a toy. However, an infant doesn't wake up one morning and think, "Today I'm going to work on improving my hearing." Instead, the infant interacts with multimodal stimuli in the world, affecting many senses simultaneously. Although an infant may not choose to focus on developing a particular sense, researchers often use unimodal stimuli in an effort to better control an experimental setting. Thus, they might study speech by presenting purely auditory stimuli, even though we often watch a person's face as he or she speaks.

Adults are quite adept at perceiving such multimodal stimuli, and we perceive them as unitary objects, integrating the information from various senses. An interesting question that has drawn the attention of a number of researchers is how adults develop the ability to do so (Bahrick, 2003, 2004; Bahrick et al., 2004).

Lorraine Bahrick and her colleagues have developed the Intersensory Redundancy Hypothesis, which states that very young infants' perceptual development is aided by common aspects of multimodal stimuli (Bahrick & Lickliter, 2002; Bahrick et al., 2004). Rhythm, for instance, is common to both vision and audition, as when you watch a person clapping hands or speaking. The redundancy of the multimodal information may aid the development of both senses, as well as the integration of the sensory information into a unitary experience. Let's examine just a few examples of multimodal stimuli.

Integrating Vision and Audition

We've already established the importance of faces for infants. Many researchers have also been interested in the infant's development of an association between face and voice. For example, children as young as 4 months old correctly expect a child's voice to come from a 9-year-old and an adult's voice to come from an adult (Bahrick et al., 1998). Thus, children are fairly sophisticated by 4 months. What about younger children?

Bahrick and her colleagues (2005) found that 2-month-old infants are sensitive to changes in a person's face *or* a person's voice. These researchers used the habituation technique with these unimodal stimuli. They showed that—after habituating to Anna's face (or voice)—the 2-month-olds exhibited dishabituation when presented with Sarah's face (or voice). The crucial study involved the multimodal stimuli of faces speaking. They first presented a video of two faces (e.g., Anna and Sarah) alternating in speaking a nursery rhyme in their own voices. The infants watched the alternating faces until they became habituated (looking time decreased to 50% of original looking time). Then the infants saw the same two faces reciting the same nursery rhyme, but now their voices were switched (Anna's face speaking with Sarah's voice and Sarah's face speaking with Anna's voice). All infants showed dishabituation, although the increased looking times were statistically significant for 4- and 6-month-olds and not for 2-month-olds. Thus, by 4 months of age (and possibly younger), infants link faces with voices.

By the time they are 2.5 to 3.5 years of age, children have fairly sophisticated notions of the visual and auditory properties of objects. Thus, they connect a small white bouncing ball with a high-pitched squeaking sound, whereas they connect a large dark bouncing ball with a lower-pitched sound (Mondloch & Maurer, 2004). They also exhibit the adult-like trait of naming objects based on the shape of the objects. For instance, look at Figure 14.6. Which figure is the *bouba* and which is the *kiki*? If you're like most adults, you associate the rounded shape with *bouba* and the angular shape with *kiki*. It's quite interesting that even though names are fairly arbitrary, even 2.5-year-old children are like adults in matching the shapes and names (Maurer, Pathman et al., 2006).

Integrating Vision and Touch

Young infants begin to reach for objects in their environment at about age 3 months. Now they have an opportunity to integrate visual and tactile information. Consistent with the importance of multimodal stimuli, they may process distant objects (that are purely visual stimuli) differently than objects that are within reach, and thus potentially multimodal (Kaufman, Mareschal et al., 2003).

Although they've had relatively little experience reaching out and grasping objects, 5-month-old infants anticipate the object that they're about to grasp (Barrett et al., 2007). They reach differently when given a small hard ball to grasp, as compared to a larger softer ball. (They are also more likely than older children to put the small hard balls in their mouths!) However, all of these infants were presented with real balls. What would happen if you presented infants with a realistic picture of a ball? They might well reach for the "fake" ball, because infants as old as 9 months attempt to grasp realistic pictures of objects (DeLoache et al., 2003; Pierroutsakos & DeLoache, 2003).

Section Summary

Early Development of Intersensory Abilities

1. Most objects in the world are multimodal—capable of stimulating a number of senses simultaneously. Infants develop intersensory integration, which allows them to perceive the object as the source of stimulation of multiple senses.

2. Infants as young as 4 months old, and possibly as young as 2 months old, have learned to match a person's face to that person's voice.

3. Infants as young as age 5 months reach differently for different objects.

Late Development of Perceptual Abilities

In this section, we will examine perceptual changes during aging. First, let's discuss some potential methodological problems in studies using elderly people. One problem is the difficulty of locating a group of young people that closely matches the group of elderly people in all important characteristics except

a.   b.

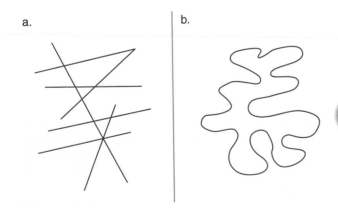

► **FIGURE 14.6** Which figure is the *bouba* and which is the *kiki*? Both adults and young children label the figures similarly.

age. Imagine, for example, that you want to determine whether hearing sensitivity declines during aging. You test a group of college students whose average age is 19 and a group of residents of a nursing home whose average age is 78. Suppose that you find that the college students have more sensitive hearing.

The problem is that the two groups differ not only with respect to age but also with respect to a number of confounding variables. A *confounding variable* is a factor—other than the factor being studied—that is present to different extents in the two groups and could influence the dependent variable. For example, the college students are probably much healthier, better educated, and more comfortable taking tests than the nursing home residents. Elderly people, particularly those living in nursing homes, are also more likely than younger people to be taking medications that may interfere with perceptual processes.

An additional problem arises if researchers measure the participants' response latency. Researchers often report that elderly individuals exhibit *cognitive slowing*, or a slower rate of responding on a variety of tasks (e.g., Bashore & Ridderinkhof, 2002; Rabbitt, 2002). In some cases, young adults and elderly people might have similar perceptual skills, but the elderly people may simply *respond* more slowly (Der & Deary, 2006). Moreover, although elderly adults may not learn some perceptual tasks as quickly as younger adults, with greater practice, they may become equally proficient (Richards et al., 2006).

Here is the dilemma. If researchers make no attempt to control for confounding variables, any differences between the younger and the elderly people could be due to these variables rather than changes in the perceptual processes that occur with aging. Thus, we must be cautious about interpreting age-comparison studies, particularly when other factors might be responsible for any differences in performance.

Even when we avoid the potential research problems, however, some sensory processes clearly decline during aging. If you are a younger student, try to imagine how these alterations in your perceptual experiences will affect your daily life as you age. How would you try to compensate for these changes? If you're nearer your authors' ages, then you already know how you've adapted to perceptual change over your lifespan.

Vision in Late Adulthood and Old Age

Let us first examine some changes that occur in vision during aging. We will begin with the visual system itself; then we will consider how aging affects some aspects of visual perception.

THE AGING VISUAL SYSTEM   A number of physical changes to the visual system have a negative impact on visual perception in elderly people. For example, the size of the pupil decreases and the lens becomes thicker as we age (Whitbourne, 2002, 2005). Due to these changes, the retina of a 60-year-old receives only about one-third as much light as the retina of a 20-year-old (Scialfa & Kline, 2007). Thus, older people have a more difficult time seeing in dim light. A related problem is that the enlarged lens leads elderly people to become more sensitive to glare. Thus, an older person may need a bright light to read clearly, but a glossy magazine may be difficult to read in that light, due to glare.

As you may recall from Chapter 3, *presbyopia* also arises due to the enlargement of the lens. This problem may emerge around the age of 40, and it leads to a decreased ability to accommodate. External lenses, such as bifocals, are used to treat presbyopia. Another lens problem mentioned earlier is *cataracts* (clouding of the lens), which is quite common in people over age 75 (Kline, 2006). Cataracts are particularly problematic for many everyday tasks, such as driving (Kline & Li, 2005). Replacing the cloudy lens with a synthetic lens is one approach to treating cataracts.

The retina itself shows signs of aging, with a great loss of rods (Scialfa & Kline, 2007). As a result, elderly people are at a disadvantage in dimly lit conditions. There may also be a loss of retinal ganglion cells in the eyes of elderly individuals.

In Chapter 3 we also discussed *glaucoma*, in which extra fluid inside the eyeball causes too much pressure, which may damage the optic nerve. Glaucoma is one of the leading causes of blindness, and it is particularly prevalent in people over the age of 60 (Whitbourne, 2005). However, as we saw earlier, glaucoma can strike at an early age, so it's imperative that even young adults have routine eye examinations that include a test for glaucoma.

CHANGES IN VISUAL PERCEPTION   We have discussed structural changes within the eye as people grow older. Let's see how these changes typically have a negative impact on basic visual abilities.

Acuity. Visual acuity decreases beyond age 40, and it is especially bad with low contrast and dim lighting (Haegerstrom-Portnoy, 2005). Acuity also decreases for objects that are presented to the periphery of an elderly person's visual field. Thus, elderly people have a smaller useful field of view (Kline & Dewar, 2004). Of course, typical tests of acuity, such as the Snellen test, use high-contrast targets that don't move. When the target moves (dynamic visual acuity), elderly individuals have a difficult time seeing details in the target.

Let's put these factors together. Acuity in elderly people is particularly bad when objects are moving, when lighting is dim and contrast is low, and when objects are in their peripheral field of view. As we noted earlier, older people also have a more difficult time seeing when glare is present. Taken together, these factors indicate that an elderly person may find driving a car challenging. The problem is particularly noticeable at night with the glare of streetlights and oncoming headlights, coupled with areas that are quite dimly lit. It's no wonder that many older people are hesitant to drive at night (Scialfa & Kline, 2007; Whitbourne, 2002). However, older men are more likely than older women to continue driving with vision deficits (Brabyn et al., 2005).

Face perception. Given our emphasis on the development of face perception, you may be interested in learning about face-perception research in elderly people. In Chapter 2, we noted that people are generally poor at eyewitness identification, but elderly people make even poorer eyewitnesses (Lott et al., 2005). People are generally worse at identifying a face after a delay. However, a long delay between seeing a face and being asked to pick it out of a lineup makes identification more difficult for older adults (Memon et al., 2003). Older eyewitnesses are also more likely to falsely identify a nontarget face, an error called a false positive (Memon et al., 2003; Memon et al., 2002).

Depth perception. Some evidence suggests that depth perception is diminished in elderly people (Whitbourne, 2002). For example, binocular disparity information is less effective for people over the age of 50. The decrease of depth perception and acuity certainly contribute to some of the falls that older people

experience (Lord & Dayhew, 2001; Lord et al., 2007). Moreover, the multifocal lenses that older people use to combat presbyopia lead to a decrement in peripheral depth perception, which can also contribute to falls (Lord et al., 2002).

Color vision. For a variety of reasons, including changes in the lens, color vision decreases in elderly people (Scialfa & Kline, 2007). The decrement appears to fall largely in the yellow-blue opponent system, but elderly people also experience general color vision deficits. Color coding is prevalent in our society (e.g., pills, labels, signs), so elderly people need to be particularly cautious.

Motion perception. Not only do older people have greater difficulty seeing detail in moving objects (dynamic visual acuity), but they also have difficulty detecting motion, particularly for low-contrast stimuli (Scialfa & Kline, 2007). Many of the studies of motion have very practical applications. For instance, older adults are less accurate than younger adults at judging the speed of moving targets (Norman et al., 2003). Older adults are also less accurate than younger adults at detecting impending collisions (Andersen & Enriquez, 2006).

Problems in detecting motion are particularly apparent in people over age 70. In a study using a signal detection approach, Patrick Bennett and his colleagues (2007) had younger and older people watch computer displays of black dots on a white background. For Noise trials, the dots moved around the screen in a random fashion, giving no sense of coherent motion. For Signal + Noise trials, all the dots moved in the same direction, such as to the right of the screen. Such coherent motion typically gives rise to a sense that the dots are moving in a particular direction, such as to the right. Observers over the age of 70 had difficulty detecting the motion with a very brief exposure to the stimuli. At longer exposures, these elderly participants could detect the motion. However, they were poorer than younger participants at determining the direction of the motion.

Hearing in Late Adulthood and Old Age

As you may recall from our discussion in Chapter 9, much of the auditory system is quite delicate. Thus, you should not be the least bit surprised to learn that people who have lived longer lives may well have suffered some damage to their auditory systems. After briefly reviewing such problems, we'll discuss some of the hearing problems encountered by many aging individuals.

THE AGING AUDITORY SYSTEM   The most common auditory problems associated with aging are conductive hearing loss (due to calcification of the ossicles) and *presbycusis*, which is a sensorineural hearing loss that occurs in both ears (Whitbourne, 2005). Conductive hearing loss will have a negative impact on a wider range of frequencies, and presbycusis will have a negative impact on sounds with frequencies above 500 Hz. Most elderly people use hearing aids if they experience these auditory deficits.

Keep in mind that presbycusis may be due in part to the accumulated exposure to loud sounds or chemicals that affect the auditory system, rather than aging itself. That said, the delicate hair cells of the inner ear may degenerate with age, as may the nerve fibers in the auditory nerve (Whitbourne, 2002). Moreover, the auditory brainstem and auditory cortex are likely to experience some deterioration over time, as indicated by the research on speech perception in elderly people. We will discuss this topic shortly.

CHANGES IN AUDITORY PERCEPTION   Hearing loss—particularly in the higher frequencies—has a number of effects on a person's life. For instance, music may become less enjoyable, and it may become more difficult to hear certain telephone ring tones. However, because of the importance of communication, we'll focus on the negative impact of aging on speech perception.

The loss of high-frequency hearing means that older people will have greater difficulty understanding people (often women) whose voices occupy the higher frequencies. They also have more difficulty hearing the English phonemes with high-frequency components. These include the underlined sounds in the following words: *plus, zebra, ship, azure, wrench,* and *drudge* (Whitbourne, 2002). A person with presbycusis will often confuse two acoustically similar words, such as *fifty* and *sixty*. Think of the implications of this confusion when discussing the cost of an item, a friend's address, or someone's age. Also, because the /s/ phoneme is especially difficult, English-speaking people with presbycusis will inevitably have trouble distinguishing between the singular and plural forms of a word.

There is mixed evidence about the role of hearing loss on speech perception. Some researchers argue that an elderly person's difficulty in speech perception is largely due to hearing loss (Schneider et al., 2005; Schneider et al., 2000; Schneider et al., 2002). In their research, they typically use speech stimuli that are loud enough to be equally audible to younger and older adults. When they do so, these researchers find no differences in speech perception. However, other researchers use a similar tactic, but they still find that elderly people perform worse on speech perception tasks (Sommers, 2005). Moreover, reducing the cognitive demands of the task (e.g., through contextual information) improves the speech perception of elderly individuals. Resolution of this controversy awaits further research, but it's clear that elderly people have particular difficulty following speech when more than one person is talking (Murphy et al., 2006; Sommers, 2005).

The Senses and Aging

In this section on older adults, we have described a number of perceptual abilities that decline with age. As you should expect, there are deficits in other senses such as taste and smell (Whitbourne, 2002). Most perceptual changes due to aging are quite gradual, so aging individuals are likely to detect a change only when comparing their current perceptual abilities with those in the more distant past. And, as challenging as the deficits may seem to you, the reality is that only a small proportion of elderly people experience disabling visual or hearing problems.

Although this text focused on perceptual abilities, age often brings a decline in attention and cognitive abilities as well (such as the cognitive slowing we discussed). Just as a decline in cognitive abilities may have an impact on assessing perceptual abilities, so too might a decline in perceptual abilities have an impact on assessing cognitive abilities (Glass, 2007; Scialfa, 2002). As you've seen illustrated throughout this book—and entirely consistent with Theme 4—perception and cognition are tightly intertwined.

Allow us to conclude this section with some words of optimism. As your aging authors can attest, the outlook for an aging individual is not at all grim. (And, as the quip goes, it beats the alternative.) Increasingly, we're learning about the resiliency of the aging brain, which uses the resources from novel brain areas to aid in the processing of perceptual stimuli (Bennett et al., 2007; Kemmer et al., 2004; Wingfield & Grossman, 2006). When we combine the natural plasticity of the brain with advances in medical procedures, hearing aid technology, and other assistive technologies, the future looks reasonably bright.

Section Summary

Vision and Hearing in Late Adulthood and Old Age

1. Some studies have confounding variables because they compare elderly people with college students, who differ not only in age but probably also in education level, intelligence, health, and medication status.

2. The lens of the eye thickens as we age. This thickening has several implications: reduced light to the retina, changes in color perception, presbyopia, and difficulty seeing under glare conditions.

3. Acuity decreases with old age, especially for moving objects and for objects in the periphery, which has implications for driving.

4. Speech perception decreases with increasing age, due to sensory changes, cognitive changes, or a combination.

5. As people age, some sensory and cognitive decrements are natural, but these are seldom disabling.

Review Questions

1. To what extent does the infant's visual world resemble the "blooming, buzzing confusion" that William James described? In what areas do infants have more perceptual ability than you might have imagined before reading this chapter?

2. The section on infancy introduced you to three experimental methods. Name them, describe how each was used to test perceptual skills, and discuss how you might use each to discover something about infants' capacities for smell.

3. Imagine that you have been asked to design toys that will be interesting for infants under the age of 6 months. What kinds of characteristics should these toys have?

4. A frequent issue in developmental psychology is the nature–nurture question. What would you conclude about the components of face and speech perception? What implications does your conclusion suggest for the development of language?

5. In what ways do young infants appreciate the relationship between sights and sounds? Spend a few minutes moving around your room, moving objects and making noises with them. What other aspect of intersensory perception would be interesting to test with infants? Be specific about which of the experimental methods you would use, and provide details about the study you would design to test your hypothesis.

6. Develop a time line of early perceptual development (i.e., what ability has developed by a given month). Be sure to include both vision and hearing. Given that various processes are interrelated and that they develop at different rates, what implications can you derive from differences in development of various perceptual abilities?

7. Studying perception in very young and very old individuals presents particular challenges to a researcher. Describe the problems these researchers face and the methodological solutions they have adopted.

8. How do the visual and auditory abilities of infants differ from those of elderly people? What similarities and differences do you notice? How well do infants and elderly people see objects closer than 6 inches, or objects that are very far away? How readily do infants and elderly people hear speech sounds?

9. Suppose that an elderly relative will be visiting you for the weekend. What kinds of information

from this chapter would be helpful in making the visit as successful as possible? Be sure to discuss both vision and hearing.

10. Throughout the text, you have seen instances of the importance of context for perception

(Theme 2). Compare examples of the role of context found in this chapter with examples from earlier chapters.

Key Terms

the nature–nurture question, p. 377
preference method, p. 377
habituation method, p. 378
habituation, p. 378
dishabituation, p. 378

classical conditioning method, p. 378
operant conditioning method, p. 379
vergence eye movements, p. 382

saccadic eye movements, p. 382
visual cliff, p. 385
high-amplitude sucking procedure, p. 388
prosody, p. 390

confounding variable, p. 392
cognitive slowing, p. 392
presbyopia, p. 392
cataract, p. 392
glaucoma, p. 392
presbycusis, p. 394

Recommended Readings

Kellman, P. J., & Arterberry, M. E. (2006). Infant visual perception. In D. Kuhn, R. S. Siegler, W. Damon, & R. M. Lerner (Eds.), *Handbook of child psychology: Vol. 2, Cognition, perception, and language* (6th ed., pp. 109–160). Hoboken, NJ: Wiley.

Kellman and Arterberry (1998) have also written a wonderful book on infant perceptual development. Although necessarily abbreviated, this chapter updates some of the findings in their earlier text and provides a highly readable discussion of many of the complexities of infant perceptual development.

Pascalis, O., & Slater, A. (Eds.). (2003). *The development of face processing in infancy and early childhood: Current perspectives.* Hauppauge, NY: Nova.

This edited book contains a number of interesting chapters by experts in the field of infant face perception. You should contrast the chapters that focus on innate aspects of face perception with those that focus on the role of experience.

Saffran, J. R., Werker, J. F., & Werner, L. A. (2006). The infant's auditory world: Hearing, speech, and the beginnings of language. In D. Kuhn, R. S. Siegler, W. Damon, & R. M. Lerner (Eds.), *Handbook of child psychology: Vol. 2, Cognition, perception, and language* (6th ed., pp. 58–108). Hoboken, NJ: Wiley.

Besides providing an excellent overview of infant auditory development, this chapter includes extensive detail about the development of speech—an area to which the three authors have made substantial contributions.

Whitbourne, S. K. (2002). *The aging individual: Physical and psychological perspectives* (2nd ed.). New York: Springer-Verlag.

Whitbourne has extensively studied the aging individual, and this text reflects her expertise. The chapter on sensory and perceptual processes is particularly helpful for topics in this chapter.

Glossary

A guide has been provided for words whose pronunciation may be ambiguous; the accented syllable is indicated by italics.

Absolute pitch People with absolute pitch are extremely accurate in identifying the pitch of an isolated tone or producing a requested tone.

Absolute threshold The smallest intensity required for a stimulus to be reported 50% of the time.

Accommodation Change in the shape of the lens of the eye, necessary to keep an image in proper focus on the retina; it occurs as the observer focuses on objects at different distances.

Achromatic (a-crow-*maa*-tick) Without color.

Achromatic afterimage Image that appears after the presentation of a stimulus; both the stimulus and the afterimage are uncolored, and one is the opposite of the other.

Achromatic colors Colors found along the middle axis of the color spindle—white, shades of gray, and black.

Achromatopsia A disorder of the visual cortex leading to an inability to see color.

Action potentials Short bursts of electrical activity such as those generated by the ganglion cells.

Active touch Touch perception in which a person actively explores objects and touches them.

Acuity Degree of precision with which fine details can be seen.

Acupuncture A procedure to relieve pain that involves inserting thin needles into various locations on the body.

Adaptation Change in sensitivity. (*See also* Dark adaptation and Light adaptation.)

Adaptation stimulus In dark adaptation studies, the intense light to which observers are exposed prior to the darkness.

Additive mixture In color mixing, the addition of beams of light from different parts of the spectrum.

Afferent fibers Nerve fibers carrying information from the receptors to the brain.

Affordances Actions one could perform with objects—a concept introduced by James J. Gibson.

Ageusia The inability to perceive taste.

Akinetopsia The inability to perceive motion, caused by damage to the cortex.

Albedo Proportion of light reflected by an object; the albedo remains constant despite changes in the amount of light falling on the object.

Allocentric distance How far two objects are from each other; this distance does not involve the observer. (*See also* Relative distance.)

Amacrine cells (*am*-ah-krihn) Cells in the retina that allow the ganglion cells to communicate with each other. They also allow the bipolar cells to communicate with each other.

Ambiguous figure–ground relationships Situations in which the figure and the ground reverse from time to time, with the figure becoming the ground and then becoming the figure again.

Ames room Room specially designed to produce distance and size illusions (see Figure 6.31).

Amodal completion Closely related to the Gestalt principle of closure; the notion that people complete the missing contours of an incomplete image.

Amplitude In vision, the height of the light wave; amplitude is related to the brightness or lightness of a visual stimulus. In audition, the change in pressure created by sound waves; amplitude is related to the loudness of an auditory stimulus.

Analgesic medication Class of drugs specifically designed to relieve pain.

Analytic sense Sense in which the observer can detect the separate parts. For example, in hearing, an observer can typically separate two notes played together.

Analytical orientation In contrast to a holistic orientation, an analytical orientation emphasizes the importance of the components that combine to form our perceptual experiences.

Anomalous trichromat The most common form of color deficiency. An anomalous trichromat has all three cone systems, but one of the systems has an abnormal absorption spectrum.

Anosmia Inability to perceive smells.

Antagonistic surrounds The surrounding or outer region of a receptive field that responds in an opposite manner to the inner region. For example, if the inner region is excited by a light stimulus, the outer or antagonistic surround will be inhibited by it.

Anterior chamber The area directly behind the cornea and in front of the iris—contains the aqueous humor.

Aqueous humor (*a*-kwee-us) Watery liquid found between the cornea and the lens.

Area 17 Area of the visual cortex where the neurons from the lateral geniculate nucleus terminate. Also called the striate cortex or the primary visual cortex.

Ascending series Series of trials in the method of limits in which the stimulus is systematically increased.

Astigmatism Visual disorder in which the cornea is not perfectly round. Therefore, if the eye is focused for some parts of the cornea, it is out of focus for others.

Atmospheric perspective Distance cue provided by the fact that distant objects often look blurry and bluish in contrast to nearby objects.

Attack In music perception, the beginning buildup of a tone.

Attention Focusing or concentration of mental activity.

Audiometry Measurement of the sensitivity of audition, typically by measuring thresholds for tones of differing frequency.

Auditory adaptation Decrease in the perceived loudness of a tone after it has been presented continuously.

Auditory fatigue Change in thresholds for other tones that occurs after a loud tone is presented and then turned off.

Auditory localization Ability to identify the location of sound sources in the environment.

Auditory nerve Bundle of nerve fibers that carries information from the inner ear to the auditory cortex.

Auditory tuning curve A graph showing the relationship between the frequency of an auditory stimulus and an auditory nerve fiber's response rate.

Autokinesis (ah-toe-kin-*nee*-siss) Illusion of movement in which a stationary object, with no clear background, appears to move.

Autostereogram Developed by Tyler, an autostereogram is a single image that contains binocular depth information when viewed appropriately.

Backward masking Phenomenon in which accuracy is reduced for reporting a stimulus because it was followed rapidly by a second stimulus. Backward masking is found in both vision and audition.

Basilar membrane Membrane on the base of the organ of Corti, in the inner ear.

Beats Changes in loudness produced by combinations of pure tones with similar frequencies.

Behaviorism Approach to psychology that stresses the objective description of an organism's behavior.

Bifocals Special eyeglasses that have two types of lenses, one for viewing distant objects and one for viewing close objects.

Binaural (buy-*nohr*-ul) Pertaining to both ears.

Binocular cue Depth cues that rely on two eyes (e.g. stereopsis).

Binocular disparity Source of distance information provided by the fact that the two eyes have slightly different views of the world.

Binocular rivalry Occurs when the images falling on each eye are too different to be fused into one unified percept.

Biological motion Pattern of movement of living things.

Bipolar cells (*buy*-pole-ur) Cells in the retina that receive information from the rods and cones and pass it on to ganglion cells.

Blind spot Region of the eye in which there is no vision because the optic disk contains no light receptors.

Blobs   "Blob"-shaped cells distributed throughout the column structure in the primary cortex; these cells are responsive to color.

Bottom-up processing   Approach that emphasizes how the sensory receptors register the stimuli, with information flowing from this low level upward to the higher (more cognitive) levels.

Boundary extension   A tendency to report seeing more of a scene than was actually visible.

Braille   Representation of letters in the alphabet by a system of raised dots, used in books for the blind.

Brightness   Psychological reaction corresponding to the intensity of light waves; the apparent intensity of a light source.

Broca's aphasia   A condition that leads to difficulty in producing speech, but only moderate problems in comprehending speech.

Cataract   Clouding of the lens of the eye, caused by injury or disease.

Categorical perception   Grouping perceptions into categories. People have difficulty discriminating between members of the same category, even though discriminations can be readily made between members of different categories.

Categorization   Process of treating objects as similar or equivalent, as in categorical perception.

Cerebral achromatopsia   A disorder of the visual cortex leading to an inability to see color.

Chemical senses   Smell and taste.

Choroid   (*kore*-oid) Layer on the back of the eye just inside the sclera. The choroid provides nutrients for the retina and absorbs extra light.

Chromatic adaptation   Decrease in response to a color after it is viewed continuously for a long time.

Cilia   (*sill*-ee-uh) Tiny hairlike protrusions from the receptor cells in the auditory and olfactory systems.

Ciliary muscle   (*sill*-ee-air-ee) Muscle that controls the shape of the lens.

Circadian rhythm   Roughly a 24-hour cycle of physiological changes that influences many behaviors, including sleeping and eating.

Classical conditioning method   A conditioning method whereby the experimenter repeatedly pairs a conditioned stimulus of interest with an unconditioned stimulus.

Coarticulation   The tendency for some of the sounds in a syllable to be transmitted at about the same time, rather than one at a time.

Cochlea   (*cock*-lee-ah) Bony, fluid-filled structure containing the receptors for auditory stimuli.

Cochlear duct   (*cock*-lee-er) One of the canals in the cochlea.

Cochlear microphonic   Phenomenon in which a waveform falling on the ear is replicated by graded potentials from the outer hair cells.

Cochlear nucleus   A structure in auditory processing to which the auditory nerve travels after leaving the inner ear.

Cognition   Acquisition, storage, retrieval, and use of knowledge.

Cognitive–behavioral approaches   In the treatment of pain, methods that help the patient develop more adaptive cognitive and behavioral reactions to a physical problem.

Cognitive slowing   A slower rate of responding to tasks often found in the elderly.

Color constancy   Tendency to see the hue of an object as staying the same despite changes in the color of the light falling on it.

Color solid   Three-dimensional figure, resembling two cones joined together, that represents the hue, saturation, and lightness of all colors; also called a color spindle.

Color spindle   A color solid.

Color stereopsis   Depth differences due to viewing color stimuli binocularly through some lenses (such as magnifying glasses).

Color vision deficiencies   Disorders or difficulties in discriminating different colors, commonly called color-blindness.

Color wheel   Circle with the different wavelengths arranged around the edge; used to represent the colors of the spectrum.

Column   In the visual cortex, a vertical series of cells that have the highest response rate to a line of one particular orientation.

Common region   An area determined by edges or shading, within which we tend to group stimuli together (see Figure 5.11).

Comparison stimulus   The stimulus in discrimination studies that varies throughout the experiment.

Complementary hues   Hues whose additive mixture makes gray, such as blue and yellow.

Complex cells   Cells in the primary visual cortex that respond most vigorously to moving stimuli.

Complex tones   Tones that cannot be represented by a simple sound wave and are more likely to be encountered in everyday life.

Computational approach   Approach to perception suggesting that although the stimuli themselves are rich in information, higher-level processes involving general physical principles are also necessary for perception to occur.

Conceptually driven processing   Approach that emphasizes the importance of the observers' concepts and cognitive processes in shaping perception.

Conditioning method   In testing infant perception, a method in which the experimenter selects a response that the baby can make and delivers a reward when the baby makes that particular response. Later, the experimenter tests for generalization to new stimuli.

Conductive hearing loss   A condition that involves problems in conducting the sound stimulus; the problem occurs in either the external ear or the middle ear.

Cone of confusion   Cone-shaped area around each ear in which the auditory system receives the same set of information about the location of the source of the sound.

Cones   Photoreceptors used for color vision under well-lit conditions.

Confounding variable   Factor in an experiment—other than the factor being studied—that may be responsible for the effects being observed.

Consonance   Combination of two or more tones, played at the same time, that is judged pleasant.

Constancy   Tendency for qualities of objects to seem to stay the same, despite changes in the way people view the objects.

Constrict   Refers to the action of the iris that makes the pupil become smaller.

Constructivist theory   Theory that proposes that the perceiver has an internal constructive (or problem-solving) process that transforms the incoming stimulus into the perception.

Contour   Location at which lightness, brightness, or color changes suddenly; also called an edge.

Contrast sensitivity function   Diagram that shows the relationship between spatial frequency and sensitivity.

Converge   When viewing nearby objects, each eye rotates in its socket, bringing the pupil toward the nose. (*See also* Diverge.)

Convergence   (of eyes) Type of vergence movement used when looking at nearby objects. (*See also* Converge.)

Convergence   (of photoreceptors) Refers to the number of photoreceptors that synapse onto each ganglion cell. For the rods, a great deal of convergence occurs (perhaps 100 rods per ganglion cell). For the cones, much less convergence occurs (a few cones per ganglion cell).

Cornea   (*kore*-nee-uh) Clear membrane just in front of the iris.

Corollary discharge theory   Theory of motion perception in which the visual system compares the movement registered on the retina with signals that the brain sends regarding eye movements.

Correct rejection   In signal detection theory, a correct rejection occurs when a signal is not presented and the observer does not report it.

Correspondence problem   The correspondence problem is the difficulty our visual system can face in linking the input from the two retinas. The difficulty occurs in both distance and motion perception when input at similar areas of the two retinas differs.

Cortical magnification   Overrepresentation of information from the fovea with respect to the cortex.

Counterirritants   Methods of pain control that stimulate or irritate one area so that pain is diminished in another.

Criterion   The measure in signal detection theory that assesses the observer's willingness to say, "I detect the stimulus."

Critical band   The range of frequencies that can be masked by a particular tone is referred to as the critical band of that tone.

Cross-adaptation   In odor perception, the change in threshold for one odor that occurs after exposure to another.

Cross-modality matching Technique in which observers are asked to judge stimuli in one mode of perception (such as hearing) by providing responses from another mode (such as sight).

Crossed disparity Objects nearer to the viewer than to the focal point create crossed disparity, with the image falling outside of the focal point on each retina.

Cue Any factor that lets an observer make a decision automatically, such as a distance cue; cues do not require elaborate thought.

Cycle For sound stimuli, a cycle is the full range of pressure changes from normal, to high, to normal, to low, and back to normal.

d′ (dee prime) In signal detection theory, an index of sensitivity; d′ depends upon the intensity of the stimulus and the sensitivity of the observer.

Dark adaptation Increase in sensitivity that occurs as the eyes remain in the dark.

Dark adaptation curve Graph showing the relationship between the time in the dark and the threshold for the test stimulus.

Data-driven processing Approach that emphasizes how sensory receptors register stimuli, with information flowing from this low level upward to the higher, more cognitive levels.

Decibel (dB) One measure of the amount of pressure created by a stimulus such as a sound wave.

Depolarization Process in which a neuron changes from its resting potential to a less negative potential.

Depth perception Perception of objects as three-dimensional, having depth in addition to height and width.

Dermis Middle layer of skin, which makes new skin cells.

Descending series Series of trials in the method of limits in which the stimulus is systematically decreased.

Detection In acuity measures, a task that requires the observer to judge whether a target is present or absent.

Deuteranopes (doo-tur-uh-nopes) People who are dichromats and are insensitive to red and green.

Dichromat (die-krow-mat) Person who requires only two primary colors to match his or her perception of all other colors due to a missing cone system.

Difference threshold The smallest change in a stimulus that is required to produce a difference noticeable 50% of the time.

Diffuse cone bipolar cells Diffuse cone bipolar cells make several connections with different photoreceptors, typically rods, initiating the convergence process. (See also Midget bipolar cells.)

Dilate Refers to the action of the iris that makes the pupil become larger.

Direct perception Approach to perception proposed by J. J. Gibson. It suggests that the stimuli themselves contain all the necessary information for perception to occur—learning and cognition are not needed.

Disc shedding Process of shedding old discs in the photoreceptors.

Discrimination In psychophysics, the smallest amount that a stimulus must be changed to be perceived as just noticeably different.

Dishabituation Increase in looking time that occurs when a new stimulus is presented following repeated presentation of another stimulus.

Disocclusion (dis-uh-clue-zyun) Process in which a moving object systematically uncovers the background.

Disparity-selective cells Disparity-selective cells are important for depth perception because they have high rates of electrical discharge when stimuli are registered on different (disparate) areas of the two retinas.

Dissonance Combination of two or more tones, played at the same time, that is judged unpleasant.

Distal stimulus Stimulus or object as it exists in the world, as opposed to the proximal stimulus.

Distance perception Distance perception refers to your ability to perceive the distance relationships within the visual scene. (See also Depth perception.)

Diverge Rotation of the eyes to bring the pupils to the center, for viewing distant objects. (See also Converge.)

Divergence Type of vergence movement of the eyes in which the eyes rotate away from each other. (See also Diverge.)

Divisionism A painting technique that is based on the interactive effects of larger patches of colors than pointillism. (See also Pointillism.)

Doctrine of specific nerve energies   Theory proposed by Müller that each different sensory nerve has its own characteristic type of activity and therefore produces different sensations.

Double pain   Experience of sharp pain followed by dull pain, presumably caused by A-delta and C-fibers.

Duplex perception   Kind of auditory perception in which the listener perceives both a speech and a nonspeech sound from the same auditory information—originally thought to provide support for a distinct speech module.

Duplex theory   A theory that highlights the fact that our retinas contain two very different types of photoreceptors (rods and cones).

Duplicity theory   Approach to vision that proposes two separate kinds of photoreceptors: rods and cones.

Dyne   Unit for measuring energy.

Dysgeusia   Damage to a taste nerve can lead to the perception of a taste that is not present.

Ear infection   Condition in which the eustachian tube becomes swollen, cutting off the middle ear from the respiratory tract.

Eardrum   Thin piece of membrane that vibrates in response to sound waves.

Echolocation   Sensory technique used by bats, in which the emission of a high-frequency sound is translated into a measure of distance based on the time elapsed before the sound returns.

Edge   Place where there is a sudden change in brightness, lightness, or color; an edge is necessary for vision.

Efferent fibers   Nerve fibers carrying information from the brain to the receptors.

Egocentric distance   Distance between the observer and an object, as used in depth perception.

Electric response audiometry (ERA)   Techniques that record varying electrical potentials on the scalp that arise in response to auditory stimulation.

Electroencephalograph   A machine that studies the massed activity of many neurons by attaching electrodes to the scalp; also called EEG.

Electromagnetic radiation   All forms of waves produced by electrically charged particles.

Emmert's law   Principle that an afterimage appears larger if it is projected on a more distant surface.

Empiricism   Approach to perception that states that basic sensory experiences are combined, through learning, to produce perception.

Endogenous opiates   Substances that have analgesic effects that resemble morphine's ability to reduce pain.

End-stopped cells   Some simple and complex cortical cells are referred to as end-stopped cells because they respond most vigorously if the stimulus ends within the cell's receptive field.

Energy model   A computational approach to motion detection that focuses on changes that take place over space and time.

Envelope   The shape of a traveling wave determined by connecting the maximum and minimum points of the wave.

Epidermis   Outer layer of skin, which has many layers of dead skin cells.

Epistemology   Branch of philosophy that concerns how we acquire knowledge.

Equal loudness contour   Graph showing the relationship between tone frequency and the number of decibels required to produce a tone of equal loudness.

Errors of anticipation   Errors in psychophysics testing in which observers provide a different answer from the one they provided on the last trial; they "jump the gun."

Errors of habituation   Errors in psychophysics testing in which observers keep giving the same answer as on the last trial.

Eustachian tube   (you-*stay*-she-un) Structure in the middle ear that connects the ear to the throat.

Evoked otoacoustic emissions   Phenomenon in which a sound presented to the ear is echoed back.

Excitation   Stimulation of neurons sufficient to generate an action potential.

External auditory canal   Tube that runs inward from the pinna to the eardrum.

Extrastriate cortex   (*ex*-tra-*strie*-ate) Region of the visual cortex that receives information already processed by the primary visual (or striate) cortex as well as from the superior colliculus.

Eye-movement explanation Explanation of illusions in terms of eye-movement patterns.

False alarm In signal detection theory, a false alarm occurs when the signal is not presented yet the observer reports it nevertheless.

Familiar size An object's customary or standardized size, used as a source of information in distance perception.

Far point The farthest point that the viewer can see clearly.

Farsighted Referring to people who cannot see nearby objects.

Feature-integration approach Approach suggesting that we use different levels of processing for different kinds of shape perception.

Fechner's law (feck-nurz) ($R = k \log I$) Fechner's law says that the magnitude of the psychological reaction (R) is equal to a constant (k) multiplied by the logarithm of the intensity (I) of the physical stimulus.

Figure In shape perception, a distinct shape with clearly defined edges.

Fixation pause The pause between two saccadic eye movements.

Flavor Experience of taste, smell, touch, pressure, and pain associated with substances in the mouth.

Floaters Solid matter suspended in the vitreous humor that will become visible under appropriate conditions.

Focused attention In Treisman's feature-integration theory, the identification of objects in the second stage of processing.

Form An area set off from the surrounding space by its edges.

Formants Horizontal bands of concentrated sound in a speech spectrogram.

Fourier analysis (foo-ryay) Process in which a stimulus is analyzed into its component sine waves.

Fourier synthesis Process of adding together a series of sine waves; the reverse of Fourier analysis.

Fovea (foe-vee-ah) Central region of the retina in which vision is sharpest.

Frequency Number of cycles a sound wave completes in 1 second.

Functional magnetic resonance imaging A non-invasive brain mapping technique that is precise in measuring maps within a few millimeters.

Fundamental frequency The component of a complex sound wave that has the lowest frequency.

G-proteins Short for GTP-binding proteins, this family of about 1,000 proteins is important in vision and the chemical senses.

Ganglion cells (gang-glee-un) Cells that run from the bipolar cells of the retina toward the brain.

Ganzfeld (gahnz-feldt) A visual field that has no contours, based on the German word for "whole field."

Gate-control theory Theory that proposes that pain perception is a complex process in which the neural fibers interact and the brain also has an influence.

General Mechanism account Theory of speech perception positing that speech and other kinds of auditory information are processed by the same mechanisms (no special speech module).

Geons (geometric icons) Basic shapes from which objects may be constructed.

Gestalt (geh-shstahlt) Configuration or pattern.

Gestalt approach Approach to perception that emphasizes that we perceive objects as well-organized, whole structures rather than as separated, isolated parts.

Gibsonian approach (gibb-sone-ee-un) Approach to perception that emphasizes that perceptions are rich and elaborate because the stimuli in the environment are rich with information rather than because thought processes provide that richness; the Gibsonian approach is named after psychologist J. J. Gibson. (See also Direct perception.)

Glabrous skin Kind of skin on the soles of the feet and the palms of the hands; does not contain hairs.

Glaucoma (glaw-koe-mah) Visual disorder in which excessive fluid inside the eye causes too much pressure, ultimately producing damage to the ganglion cells in the retina and to the optic nerve.

Golgi tendon organs (goal-jee) Receptors in tendons that respond when the muscle exerts tension on the tendon.

Ground In shape perception, the background that appears to be behind the figure.

Ground theory   Theory proposed by J. J. Gibson, in which distance perception depends upon information provided by surfaces in the environment.

Gymnema sylvestre   A taste modifier that reduces the intensity of sweet substances.

Habituation   A decrease in the perceived intensity of a stimulus after repeated exposure over time.

Habituation method   In testing infant perception, a method based on a decrease in attention to repeated stimulation.

Hair cells   Receptors for auditory stimuli, located in the organ of Corti.

Hairy skin   Type of skin that covers most of the human body and contains hairs.

Haptic perception   Perception of objects by touch.

Harmonics   Those multiples of the fundamental frequency that are present in a complex sound; also called overtones.

Hedonics   (hih-*donn*-icks) Area of perception that involves judgments of pleasantness and unpleasantness.

Height cues   Distance information provided by the fact that objects near the horizon are farther away than those far from the horizon.

Helicotrema   (*hell*-ih-koe-*treh*-ma) Tiny opening at the end of the vestibular canal in the inner ear.

High-amplitude sucking procedure   Technique used to assess infant perception, in which babies suck on a pacifier attached to a recording device; a sufficiently fast sucking rate produces a stimulus such as a speech sound.

Hit   In signal detection theory, a hit occurs when the signal is presented and the observer reports it.

Holistic orientation   Characterized by the Gestalt approach, a holistic orientation argues that the final percept that we experience is not simply the sum of its parts. (*See also* Analytical orientation.)

Horizontal cells   Cells in the retina that allow the photoreceptors to communicate with each other.

Horizontal–vertical illusion   An illusion shaped like an inverted T, in which the vertical line looks longer than the horizontal line.

Horopter   An imaginary curved line that can be drawn to represent all the points that are the same distance from the observer as the focal object.

Hue   Psychological reaction of color that corresponds to the length of light waves.

Human leukocyte antigen   The name of a gene family in humans; contains a large number of genes related to immune system function in humans.

Hypercolumn   A sequence of 18 to 20 adjacent columns in the visual cortex. A hypercolumn includes enough columns to complete a full cycle of stimulus-orientation preferences.

Hypermetropic   Refers to people who are farsighted and cannot see nearby objects.

Hyperpolarization   Process in which a neuron changes from its resting potential to a more negative potential.

Hypnosis   Altered state of consciousness in which a person is susceptible to suggestions from the hypnotist. Hypnosis is sometimes used to help people suffering from chronic pain.

Hz   (hurtz) Abbreviation for the name of Heinrich Hertz; Hz represents the number of cycles a sound wave completes in 1 second.

Illusion   An incorrect perception.

Illusory conjunction   In Treisman's feature-integration theory, an inappropriate combination of features from two stimuli.

Illusory contour   Phenomenon in which contours are seen even though they are not physically present.

Illusory movement   Perception that an object is moving even though it is really stationary.

Impedance   Resistance to the passage of sound waves.

Impedance mismatch   Condition in which the impedances for two media differ; sound waves cannot be readily transmitted when an impedance mismatch exists.

Incorrect comparison explanation   An explanation of illusions that states that observers base their judgments on the incorrect parts of the figure.

Incus   A small anvil-shaped bone in the middle ear.

Indirect perception   Approaches that assume that the information received by the senses is insufficient by itself to arrive at an accurate description of the world.

Induced movement   Illusion of movement that occurs when a visual frame of reference moves in one direction and produces the illusion that a stationary target is moving in the opposite direction.

Inferior colliculus (kole-*lick*-you-luss) Structure in auditory processing between the superior olivary nucleus and the medial geniculate nucleus.

Inferior temporal cortex The inferior temporal cortex is located on the lower part of the side of the cortex and is important for object perception.

Inferotemporal cortex (IT) Located on the lower part (inferior) of the side (temporal) of the cortex and considered the end of the What pathway.

Information-processing approach The approach that identifies psychological processes and connects them by specific patterns of information flow. (*See also* Cognition.)

Inhibition Stimulation of a neuron that results in a reduced rate of action potentials.

Inner hair cells Auditory receptors on the inner side of the organ of Corti, most likely sensitive to a tone's frequency.

Interaural intensity difference Cue to auditory localization based on small sound intensity differences between the two ears.

Interaural time difference Cue to auditory localization based on small differences between the time a sound arrives in each ear.

Interblobs Cells between blobs that are sensitive to orientation and not wavelength.

Interposition Distance cue in which one object partly covers another.

Intraocular lens Substitute lens inserted into the eye after surgical removal of a defective lens.

Invariants In the theory of J. J. Gibson, the aspects of perception that persist over time and space and are left unchanged by certain kinds of transformations.

Involuntary eye movements Unavoidable small eye movements that occur during fixation.

Iris Ring of muscles in the eye surrounding the pupil; the colored part of the visible eye.

Ishihara test (ih-she-*hah*-rah) Test for color deficiencies, in which the observer tries to detect a number hidden in a pattern of different-colored circles (see Color Plate 6).

Just noticeable difference (jnd) Smallest difference in sensation that can be noticed.

K pathway A pathway that gets input from the S-cone "on" bipolar cells that feed information to the small bistratified ganglion cells.

Kemp echoes Phenomenon in which a sound presented to the ear is echoed back.

Kinesthesia Sensation of movement or static limb position.

Kinesthetic information Nonvisual information (such as muscular information) that can be used to judge distance.

Kinetic depth effect Phenomenon in which a figure looks flat when it is stable but appears to have depth once it moves.

Lateral geniculate nucleus (LGN) (jen-*ick*-you-late) Part of the thalamus where most of the ganglion cells transfer their information to new neurons.

Lateral inhibition Inhibition of neural activity for points near the part of the retina that is stimulated by light.

Lateralization The perception that sounds move from side to side inside the listener's head, because the sounds are delivered through headphones. (*See also* Auditory localization.)

Law of closure Gestalt law that says that a figure is perceived as closed and complete rather than containing a blank portion.

Law of common fate Gestalt law that says that items perceived as moving in the same direction are seen as belonging together.

Law of good continuation Gestalt law that says that a line is perceived as continuing in the same direction it was going prior to intersection.

Law of Prägnanz (*Prahg*-nahntz) Gestalt law that says that when faced with several alternate perceptions, the one that will actually occur is the one with the best, simplest, and most stable shape.

Law of proximity Gestalt law that says that objects near each other are grouped as one unit.

Law of similarity Gestalt law that says that items that are similar are grouped together.

Laws of grouping Ideas that explain the way we organize or group information.

Left visual field Portion of the visual world on the left-hand side.

Lemniscal system (lemm-*niss*-kull) One of the two neuronal systems responsible for the skin senses.

It has larger nerve fibers and faster transmission than the spinothalamic system.

Lens Structure inside the eye whose shape changes to bring objects into focus.

Light Portion of the electromagnetic radiation spectrum made up of waves that range in length from about 400 nm to about 700 nm.

Light adaptation Decline in sensitivity that occurs as the eyes remain in the light.

Lightness Psychological reaction corresponding to the amount of light reflected by an object.

Lightness constancy Phenomenon in which an object seems to stay the same lightness despite changes in the amount of light falling on it.

Limbic system A portion of the brain that is involved in regulating behaviors such as fleeing, fighting, feeding, and sexual behavior.

Linear perspective Distance cue provided by the fact that parallel lines appear to meet in the distance.

Logarithm Type of numerical transformation; the logarithm of a number equals the exponent to which 10 must be raised to equal that number.

Looming A cue to time-to-contact.

Loudness Psychological reaction that corresponds roughly to a tone's amplitude.

M pathway A pathway that begins with diffuse bipolar cells, which feed parasol ganglion cells.

Mach band (mock) Phenomenon in which bright and dark regions are perceived within a single stripe, although there is no corresponding variation in the physical distribution of light.

Magnitude estimation Technique in which the observer is told that one particular stimulus is to be assigned a certain value, and this value is used as a "yardstick" to estimate the magnitude of all future stimuli.

Maintained activity In the absence of a visual stimulus, a ganglion cell fires at a relatively low rate, referred to as spontaneous or maintained activity.

Malleus (*mal*-lee-uss) A small hammer-shaped bone in the middle ear.

Manner of articulation One of the three dimensions in pronouncing consonants; it specifies how completely the air is blocked and where it passes.

Margin illusion We usually perceive the margins of a page as taking up little room, but in fact they can take up over a third of the page.

Masking A phenomenon in which one stimulus makes another stimulus difficult to perceive. The masking stimulus can precede the obscured stimulus (forward masking) or it can follow the obscured stimulus (backward masking).

McGurk effect Occurs when listeners are exposed to one phoneme and simultaneously observe a speaker saying a different one. Listeners report hearing a completely different phoneme that is actually a combination of the two.

Medial geniculate nucleus (jen-*ick*-you-late) Structure involved in auditory processing that lies between the inferior colliculus and the auditory cortex.

Mel scale In audition, a scale produced by magnitude estimation, in which a 1000-Hz tone with an intensity of 60 dB is assigned a pitch of 1000 mels, and comparison tones are assigned other, relative mel values.

Memory color Phenomenon in which an object's typical color influences the observer's perception of the object's actual color.

Mesopic Mesopic conditions exist when the light is sufficiently bright that cones are still functional, but sufficiently dim that rods can also function.

Mesopic vision Vision that uses both rods and cones.

Metameric matching Process in which a subject can match any hue of a single wavelength by combining various amounts of three different colored lights (usually red, green, and blue).

Metamers Pairs of lights that look exactly the same but are composed of physically different stimuli.

Method of adjustment Psychophysical technique in which observers adjust the intensity of the stimulus until it is just barely detectable.

Method of adjustment for measuring discrimination Psychophysical technique in which observers themselves adjust the comparison stimulus until it seems to match the standard stimulus.

Method of constant stimuli Psychophysical technique in which the stimuli are presented in random order.

Method of constant stimuli for measuring discrimination Psychophysical technique in which the experimenter presents the comparison stimuli in random order and asks observers to judge whether each comparison stimulus is greater than or less than the standard stimulus.

Method of limits Psychophysical technique in which the researcher begins with a stimulus that is clearly noticeable and then presents increasingly weaker stimuli until observers are unable to detect the stimulus; these trials alternate with trials in which increasingly stronger stimuli are presented.

Method of limits for measuring discrimination Psychophysical technique in which the standard stimulus remains the same, and the comparison stimulus varies from low to high on some series and from high to low on other series.

Mexican-hat filter A filter with characteristics similar to the receptive fields found in the visual system (see Figures 5.14 and 5.15c). Computational theorists have demonstrated that this filter is capable of extracting edges from visual input.

Microelectrode Very small electrode used in single cell recording.

Microsaccade An involuntary eye movement that is characterized by a fast-jerking motion.

Microspectrophotometry Procedure in which an extremely small beam of light from one part of the color spectrum is passed through individual receptors in dissected retinal tissue. The amount of light absorbed at each wavelength is then measured.

Microvilli (*my*-crow-*vill*-lie) Tips of the taste receptors.

Midget bipolar cells Cells that connect to a single cone or a small number of cones, initiating the parvo pathway. (*See also* Diffuse cone bipolar cells.)

Midget ganglion cells Cells that carry information away from the midget bipolar cells, continuing the parvo pathway. (*See also* Parasol ganglion cells.)

Minimum audible angle (MAA) The smallest difference (measured in degrees) between two sound sources such that a listener can perceive them as coming from two different sources.

Miracle fruit A taste modifier that sweetens the taste of sour substances.

Misapplied constancy explanation According to the misapplied constancy explanation, an illusion occurs because observers interpret portions of the illusion as cues for maintaining size constancy.

Miss In signal detection theory, a miss occurs when a signal is presented and the observer does not report it.

Missing fundamental An auditory illusion in which only the harmonics but not the fundamental frequency of a complex sound are present. Nonetheless, listeners do not perceive its absence.

Module A special-purpose neural mechanism used to process one kind of information.

Monaural (monn-*ahr* ul) Pertaining to only one ear.

Monochromat (*mah*-noe-crow-mat) Person who requires only one color to match his or her perception of all other colors; every hue looks the same to this person.

Monochromatic colors Colors produced by a single wavelength.

Monocular cues Depth cues that need only one eye (e.g., pictorial depth cues such as overlap).

Monocular factors Factors seen with one eye that can provide information about distance.

Moon illusion Illusion in which the moon at the horizon looks bigger than the moon at its highest position.

Motility The independent elongation and contraction of the outer hair cells that enhances our ability to make fine frequency discriminations.

Motion parallax Distance cue provided by the fact that as the observer moves the head sideways, objects at different distances appear to move in different directions and at different speeds.

Motion perspective Continuous change in the way objects look as the observer moves about in the world.

Motor theory of speech perception Theory in which humans possess a specialized device that allows them to decode speech stimuli and permits them to connect the stimuli they hear with the way these sounds are produced by the speaker.

Movement aftereffects Illusion of movement that occurs after looking at continuous movement. When looking at another surface, it will seem to move in a direction opposite that of the original movement.

Müller–Lyer illusion (*mew*-lur *lie*-ur) Famous illusion in which two lines of the same length appear to be different in length because of wings pointing outward on one line and inward on the other line (see Figure 6.25).

Muscle spindles   Muscle spindles are receptors that are located within the muscle itself, which are important for kinesthesia. (*See also* Kinesthesia.)

Myopic   Refers to people who are nearsighted and cannot see faraway objects.

Nanometer (nm)   One-billionth of a meter; measure used for wavelength.

Nasal cavity   Hollow space behind each nostril.

Nativism   A theory that stresses the importance of natural, innate abilities.

Nature–nurture question   Are abilities—such as perceptual abilities—due to inborn factors (nature), or are they the result of learning and experience (nurture)?

Near point   The nearest point that the viewer can see clearly.

Nearsighted   Refers to people who cannot see faraway objects.

Negative afterimage   Image that appears after the presentation of a stimulus. The afterimage is the opposite of the original stimulus. (*See also* Successive color contrast.)

Neuromatrix   Proposed by Ronald Melzack, the neuromatrix receives input from three brain systems to generate a unique pattern of impulses that serves to identify the self.

Neurons   (*new*-rons) Nerve cells.

Nociceptors   Pain receptors in the skin that initiate a warning signal about a potentially harmful stimulus whether it's an extreme temperature, a high pressure, or a noxious chemical.

Noise   In signal detection theory, the situation in which no signal occurs. In audition, irrelevant, excessive, or unwanted sound.

Nonspectral hues   Hues that cannot be described in terms of a single wavelength from a part of the spectrum.

Nontasters   In taste perception, people who are insensitive to some particular tastes.

Normal trichromat   (*try*-krow-mat) Person who requires three primary colors to match all other colors.

Occlusion   (uh-*clue*-zyun) Process in which a moving object systematically covers up the background.

Octave   A doubling of frequency; used by musicians to represent the distance between two notes that have the same name, such as two successive C notes on the piano.

Octave illusion   Musical illusion in which one tone is presented to one ear and another tone an octave away is simultaneously presented to the other ear. The tones shift from ear to ear, yet the listener reports one ear hearing only high notes and the other hearing only low notes.

Ocular dominance   Tendency for cells in the visual cortex to have a higher response rate for one of the two eyes.

Odor constancy   Odor constancy means that the perceived strength of an odor remains the same despite variations in sniff vigor.

Odorant   Smell stimulus.

Olfaction   Smell.

Olfactory bulb   Structure that receives the signals from the smell receptors.

Olfactory epithelium   Region at the top of the nasal cavity that contains the smell receptor cells.

Olfactory glomeruli   Round bundles of axons from the olfactory receptors and dendrites from the mitral cells.

Onset difference   An important cue in auditory localization, because a sound originating from one side will arrive at the ear on that side prior to arriving at the ear on the other side. (*See also* Interaural time difference.)

Operant conditioning method   Conditioning in which people are reinforced for behavior not related to pain—such as increased physical activity.

Ophthalmologists   Doctors specializing in eye diseases.

Ophthalmoscope   Special tool used to look inside the eye.

Opiate receptors   Specific locations on the surface of brain cells that respond to opiate drugs in a lock-and-key fashion.

Opioid receptors   Specific locations on the surfaces of cells that respond to opiate drugs in a fashion similar to a lock and a key.

Opponent-process theory   Theory of color vision that states that there are cells in the visual system that respond to stimulation by an increase in activity when one color is present and by a decrease in activity when another color is present.

Opsin   The large protein in photopigments.

Optacon II   The Optacon II translates written letters and numbers into a vibratory display, to allow people who are blind to read.

Optic chiasm   (*kie*-as-em) Area in which the two optic nerves come together and cross over.

Optic disc   Region of the retina in which the optic nerve leaves the eye.

Optic flow   The passing of images over the retina as the result of one's movement through the world.

Optic flow field   The complex pattern on our retinas where peripheral objects move more rapidly than central objects. The optic flow field is important for motion perception.

Optic nerve   Bundle of ends from the ganglion cells that passes out of the eye toward the optic chiasm.

Optic tract   Bundle of nerve fibers in the visual system that runs between the optic chiasm and the superior colliculus or the lateral geniculate nucleus.

Organ of Corti   (*court*-eye) Part of the cochlea that contains the auditory receptors.

Orientation tuning curve   Graph illustrating the relationship between the angular orientation of a line and a cell's response rate.

Ossicles   Three small bones in the middle ear: malleus, incus, and stapes.

Otoacoustic emissions   All emissions produced by the ear, whether in response to a stimulus or not.

Otolith organs   Organs comprised of the utricle ("little pouch") and the saccule ("little sack") at the base of the semicircular canals.

Otosclerosis   A bone disease that causes immobility of the stapes, ultimately making conduction of sound stimuli difficult.

Outer hair cells   Auditory receptors on the outer side of the organ of Corti, most likely responsible for tuning the traveling wave on the basilar membrane to allow fine frequency discrimination. (*See also* Motility.)

Oval window   Membrane that covers an opening in the cochlea.

Overtones   Harmonics, or the other components of a complex tone, excluding the fundamental frequency, that are multiples of that fundamental frequency.

Pain   Perception of actual or threatened tissue damage and the private experience of unpleasantness.

Pain threshold   Intensity of stimulation in which pain is reported on half the trials.

Pain tolerance   Maximum pain level at which people voluntarily accept pain.

Panum's area   An area on and near the horopter in which the images of the object on the two retinas can be fused. (*See also* Horopter.)

Papillae   (paa-*pill*-ee) Small bumps on the tongue that contain the taste buds.

Paradoxical cold   Phenomenon in which a very hot stimulus produces the sensation of cold by stimulating a cold spot.

Paradoxical heat   Something that occurs when a combination of alternating warm and cold stimuli produces the sensation of painful heat.

Parallel process   Process that allows several targets or tasks to be handled simultaneously, typically by different modules. (*See also* Module.)

Parasol ganglion cells   Ganglion cells with widely spread dendrites, which are primarily connected to rods. These cells receive input from diffuse bipolar cells, continuing the magno pathway. (*See also* Diffuse cone bipolar cells.)

Passive touch   Touch perception in which an object is placed on a person's skin.

Pathway   The pathway that carries information that is important for binocular disparity; crucial for binocular disparity information.

Pattern theory   Theory about the skin senses that proposes that the pattern of nerve impulses determines sensation.

Payoff   In signal detection theory, the rewards and punishments associated with a particular response.

Perception   Interpretation of sensations, involving meaning and organization.

Perceptual span   The vertical and horizontal span that allows the human eye to have sharp enough vision to read text.

Permanent threshold shift   Permanent increase in a hearing threshold as a result of exposure to noise.

Phantom limb   Perceived pain in an amputated arm or leg.

Phase angle   Phase angle is the position of the wave in degrees over one complete cycle (0 degrees, 90 degrees, etc.). It helps to describe the wave's pressure at each position. For example, at 90 degrees, pressure is at a maximum, and at 270 degrees a minimum.

Phase difference   The difference in phase angle of a sound at the two ears, which serves as a cue to the location of the sound source (see Figure 10.8).

Phase locking   When neurons "lock onto" the peak of a wave and fire.

Pheromones   (*fear*-uh-moans) Substances that act like chemical signals in communicating with other members of the same species.

Phi movement   Illusion of movement in which observers report that they see movement, yet they cannot perceive an actual object moving across a gap; phi movement can be produced by two light flashes about 100 milliseconds apart.

Phoneme   Basic unit of speech, such as an /h/ or an /r/ sound.

Phonemic restoration   Phenomenon that occurs when a speech sound is replaced or masked by an irrelevant sound and the perceptual system restores or fills in the gap appropriately.

Phonetic boundary   Refers to auditory perception; the point on a continuum where our perception of phonemes changes—to the left of the boundary we perceive one phoneme, and to the right we hear a different one.

Photopic vision   (foe-*top*-ick) Vision that uses cones.

Photopigments   Chemical substances that accomplish the transduction of light.

Photoreceptors   Light receptors; the rods and cones.

Pictorial cues   Cues used to convey depth in a picture.

Pinna   Flap of external tissue that aids in auditory localization, typically referred to as "the ear."

Pitch   Psychological reaction that corresponds to the frequency of a tone.

Place of articulation   One of the three dimensions for consonants; specifies where the airstream is blocked when the consonant is spoken.

Place theory   Theory of auditory processing that proposes that frequency information is encoded at different places along the basilar membrane.

Placebo   (pluh-*see*-bow) Inactive substance such as a sugar pill that the patient believes is a medication.

Point of subjective equality   The point at which a comparison stimulus is judged to be equal to the standard stimulus.

Pointillism   Artistic technique in which discrete dots of pigment are applied to a canvas; the dots blend into solid colors when viewed from a distance.

Point–light display   A display that shows only points of light at the joints of an organism. Such a minimal display is useful in studying biological motion.

Ponzo illusion   Illusion in which two parallel lines the same length appear to be different lengths because of the presence of depth cues.

Positron emission tomography   A procedure that involves injecting a radioactive chemical into the bloodstream to reach the brain, generating a computer image that illustrates brain activity.

Posterior chamber   A chamber that lies between the retina and the lens.

Preattentive processing   In Treisman's feature-integration theory, the automatic registration of stimulus features.

Preference method   In testing infant perception, a method based on the idea that if the infant spends consistently longer looking at one figure in preference to another figure, the infant must be able to discriminate between the two figures.

Presbycusis   (prez-bee-*koo*-siss) Progressive loss of hearing in both ears for high-frequency tones, occurring with aging.

Presbyopia   (prez-bee-*owe*-pee-ah) Type of farsightedness that occurs with aging, caused by inelasticity of the lens.

Primal sketch   A kind of map for shape perception produced by the visual system, which yields edges and intensity differences.

Primary auditory cortex   Located in the temporal lobe, it receives information from the medial geniculate nucleus.

Primary visual cortex   Area of the visual cortex where the neurons from the lateral geniculate nucleus terminate.

Profile analysis   Process in which subjects are able to detect differences in intensities of complex tones by comparing the activity that each produces on the basilar membrane.

PROP Bitter substance, 6-n-propylthiouracil, which some people cannot taste.

Proprioception Sensation of movement or static limb position; synonym for kinesthesia.

Prosody The musical aspects of speech: the stress on syllables, the rhythm to your speech, and the variation in tone of voice.

Prosopagnosia A disorder in which a person cannot organize facial features to recognize a face.

Protanopes (*proe*-tuh-nopes) People who are dichromats and insensitive to deep red.

Prototype Ideal figure proposed to serve as a basis of comparison in the prototype-matching approach to pattern recognition.

Prototype-matching approach Approach to shape perception suggesting that we have information regarding various abstract shapes and patterns stored in memory (the prototype) and recognition occurs when we match a newly presented stimulus to a prototype.

Proximal stimulus Representation of objects in contact with a sense organ, such as the representation on the retina, as opposed to the distal stimulus.

Psychophysics Study of the relationship between physical stimuli and psychological reactions to those stimuli.

PTC Bitter substance, phenylthiocarbamide, which some people cannot taste.

Pupil Opening in the center of the iris.

Pure tone Tone that can be represented by a simple sine wave.

Purity In the description of color, the lack of white light. Colors low in purity have large amounts of white light added to the monochromatic light.

Purkinje shift (purr-*kin*-gee) Phenomenon in which an observer's sensitivity to various wavelengths shifts toward the shorter wavelengths as he or she shifts from cone to rod conditions.

Pursuit movements Slow, smooth eye movements used in tracking an object moving against a stationary background.

Rapidly adapting (RA) fibers Kind of touch receptors that respond to a change in stimulation.

Ratio principle According to the ratio principle, the important factor that determines how light an object appears is the stimulus intensity of that object in comparison to other objects in the scene.

Receiver operating characteristic (ROC) curve In signal detection theory, a curve showing the relationship between the probability of a hit and the probability of a false alarm.

Receptive field For a given cell, the portion of the retina that, when stimulated, produces a change in the activity of that cell.

Recognition-by-components approach The approach suggesting that recognition of complex shapes occurs by analyzing the basic components from which they are constructed.

Recognition threshold In taste perception, the concentration of a solution that can be recognized by quality.

Recruitment Condition in which a person who is deaf perceives very loud sounds normally but does not hear weak sounds at all.

Refractory period Time immediately following an action potential, during which a nerve cell returns to its resting potential.

Reissner's membrane Membrane separating the cochlear duct from the vestibular canal.

Relative distance Distance between two objects, as used in depth perception.

Relative pitch The inability of some people to judge the pitch of a note accurately unless presented with a comparison pitch.

Relative size Object's size relative to other objects, used as a cue in distance perception.

Relativist A theorist who would argue that color naming is arbitrary.

Retina (*reh*-tin-nuh) Portion of the eye that absorbs light rays; contains the photoreceptors.

Retinal An organic molecule that is one of the two parts of photopigments (the other is a large protein called opsin) and forms the visual pigment found in the rods and cones.

Retinex theory Retinex theory seeks to explain color perception and color constancy based primarily on perception of the pattern of reflectances from the stimuli.

Retinotopic   Arrangement in which the spatial distribution is similar to that found on the retina. For example, in the lateral geniculate nucleus (LGN), ganglion cells that originated on neighboring parts of the retina also terminate on neighboring parts of the LGN.

Rhodopsin   (roe-*dopp*-sin) Photopigment found in rods.

Right visual field   Portion of the visual world on the right-hand side.

Rod bipolar cells   Cells that ultimately pass their information to the same ganglion cells that receive information from cones.

Rods   Photoreceptors used for black-and-white vision under poorly lit conditions.

Round window   Membrane that covers an opening in the tympanic canal.

Saccade   (suh-*kaad*) A single rapid eye movement in which the eye is moved from one location to the next.

Saccadic eye movements   (suh-*kaad*-dick) Very rapid eye movements in which the eye is moved from one fixation point to the next.

Saccadic suppression   The process by which the mind selectively blocks visual processing during saccades so that the motion of the eye, any subsequent blur of the image, or the gap in visual perception is noticeable to the viewer.

Sander parallelogram   Line-length illusion involving the diagonal lines in a parallelogram (see Figure 6.27).

Saturation   Psychological reaction to the purity of a light; a highly saturated light appears to have very little white light added to it.

Sclera   Shiny white part of the external eye.

Scotoma   (skuh-*toe*-muh) Blind area caused by damage to the visual cortex; plural is scotomata (skuh-*toe*-muh-tuh).

Scotopic vision   (skoe-*top*-ick) Vision that uses rods.

Secondary visual cortex   Region of the visual cortex that receives information that has already been processed by the primary visual cortex as well as from the superior colliculus.

Self-adaptation   When a particular odorant leads to a loss of sensitivity to that odorant, the process is called self-adaptation.

Self-motion illusion   Perception that you are moving, although you are really stationary.

Sensation   Immediate and basic experiences generated by isolated, simple stimuli.

Sensitivity   Ability to detect a change in the stimulus; sensitivity is inversely related to threshold level.

Sensorineural hearing loss   Hearing loss occurring due to problems in the cochlea or in the auditory nerve.

Serial process   Processing information that requires the targets or tasks to be handled one at a time.

Shading   Distance cue provided by the pattern of light and shadows.

Shape   Area set off from the rest of a visual stimulus because it has a contour.

Shape constancy   Phenomenon in which an object seems to stay the same shape despite changes in its orientation.

Shape from highlights   Cue to the three-dimensionality of a shape arising from light reflected from the surface of the object.

Shape from motion   Cue to the three-dimensionality of a shape arising from the motion of the object. (*See also* Kinetic depth effect.)

Shape from shading   Cue to the three-dimensionality of a shape from the shadows attached to the object.

Signal   Stimulus used in psychophysics studies, most often in signal detection theory.

Signal detection theory (SDT)   Psychophysical approach that assesses both the observer's sensitivity and his or her decision-making strategy (or criterion).

Signal + noise   In signal detection theory, the situations in which the appropriate signal occurs, in addition to the irrelevant "noise."

Simple cells   Cells in layer IVb of the primary visual cortex that respond most vigorously to lines.

Simultaneous color contrast   The changing of an object's perceived color, or hue, due to the surrounding color.

Sine wave   Smooth wave pattern resembling the pattern of light waves or pure tones.

Single-cell recording   Research technique in which small electrodes are placed in a precise location to record action potentials, such as those generated by a single ganglion cell.

Sinusoidal grating (sine-you-*soid*-ul) Set of blurry stripes that alternate between dark and light.

Size constancy Phenomenon in which an object seems to stay the same size despite changes in its distance.

Size cues Distance information conveyed by relative size.

Size-distance invariance hypothesis Theory of constancy in which the viewer calculates an object's perceived size by combining the object's retinal size and its perceived distance.

Slowly adapting (SA) receptors Kind of touch receptor that responds to steady continuous stimulation (pressure on skin).

Small bistratified ganglion cells Cells that serve the function of comparing S-cone input with input from M- and L-cones.

Soft palate Region in the upper part of the mouth above the back of the tongue.

Somatosensory cortex Region of the cortex that processes information about touch and taste.

Somatosensory system A set of senses embedded in our bodies.

Sone scale Scale of loudness obtained by the magnitude-estimation technique, in which a 40-dB tone at 1000 Hz is assigned a loudness of 1 sone.

Sound-pressure level (SPL) A logarithmic scale of sound pressure relative to threshold pressure. It is used to measure amplitude in decibels.

Sound spectrogram Diagram that shows the frequency components of speech.

Sounds Successive changes in atmospheric pressure.

Spatial frequency analysis approach Approach to shape perception suggesting that to process visual information, the visual system breaks the stimulus down into a series of light and dark stripes. (*See also* Fourier analysis.)

Spatial frequency channels Channels in the visual system that are sensitive to a narrow range of spatial frequencies.

Special Mechanism account Theory of speech perception positing that speech is processed by a distinct unit separate from that used for other auditory information. (*See also* Module.)

Specificity theory Theory based on the doctrine of specific nerve energies stating that each kind of skin receptor responds exclusively to only one kind of physical stimulus, and each kind of receptor is responsible for only one kind of sensation.

Spectral sensitivity Region of the spectrum in which light is absorbed, such as the region in which a particular kind of cone absorbs light.

Speech spectrogram Diagram that shows the frequency components of speech.

Spinothalamic system (spy-know-thuh-*laa*-mick) One of the two neuronal systems responsible for the skin senses. It has smaller nerve fibers and slower transmission than the lemniscal system.

Spontaneous otoacoustic emissions Emissions produced by the ear when no stimulus has been presented.

Stabilized retinal image An image that is kept on the same part of the retina through various means. A stabilized retinal image will ultimately disappear, showing the importance of change for perception.

Standard stimulus The stimulus in discrimination studies that remains constant throughout the experiment.

Stapes (*stay*-peas) Small stirrup-shaped bone in the middle ear.

Steady state In music perception, the middle portion of a tone.

Stereochemical theory Theory proposed by Amoore that odorous molecules have definite shapes that determine the kind of odor we smell.

Stereocilia Tiny hairs attached to the ends of the inner and outer hair cells. Displacement of the stereocilia causes action potentials to be produced, the first step in auditory perception.

Stereopsis Ability to judge depth with two eyes, as provided by binocular disparity.

Stereoscope Piece of equipment that presents two photographs of a scene taken from slightly different viewpoints; one picture is presented to each eye, creating the impression of depth.

Stereoscopic picture Two pictures, one presented to the right eye and one presented to the left eye, creating the impression of depth.

Stevens's power law ($R = kI^n$) Stevens's power law says that the magnitude of the psychological reaction (*R*) is equal to a constant (*k*) multiplied by the intensity (*I*) of the stimulus, which has been raised to the *n*th power.

Stimulation deafness experiment   An experiment in which an animal is exposed to an extremely high-amplitude tone, which causes damage to the stereocilia. The location of the damage depends on the frequency used.

Stress-induced analgesia   A reduction in pain perception caused by stress.

Striate cortex   (*strie*-ate) Area of the visual cortex where the neurons from the lateral geniculate nucleus terminate, called striate because of its microscopically visible stripes. This area is also called the primary visual cortex and Area 17.

Stroboscopic movement   (stroe-buh-*skope*-ick) Illusion of movement produced by a rapid pattern of stimulation on different parts of the retina.

Structuralists   A group of theorists who sought to explain perception by a focus on individual elements.

Subcutaneous tissue   Inner layer of skin, which contains connective tissue and fat globules.

Subjective colors   Impressions of color that are produced by a black-and-white stimulus (like Benham's top).

Subjective contour   Phenomenon in which contours are seen even though they are not physically present; also known as illusory contour.

Substantia gelatinosa   Proposed part of the gate-control theory, which produces stimulation with input from the large fibers and inhibition with input from the small fibers.

Subtractive mixture   In color mixing, combining dyes or pigments, or placing two or more colored filters together.

Successive color contrast   Situation in which the appearance of a color is changed because of another color presented beforehand. (*See also* Negative afterimage.)

Superior colliculus   (kole-*lick*-you-luss) Portion of the brain important for locating objects and their movement.

Superior olivary nucleus   A structure in auditory processing between the cochlear nucleus and the inferior colliculus.

Supertasters   People who are more sensitive to all tastes and flavors.

Synapse   The gap between neurons across which chemical messages are sent.

Synthetic sense   One of the senses in which an observer cannot detect the separate parts; for example, in vision an observer cannot detect the components of a color mixture.

Tadoma method   Method of communication in which a person who is deaf places his or her hands on the lips and jaw of the speaker to pick up tactile information about speech.

Tapetum   The equivalent of the human choroid in nocturnal animals. Unlike the choroid, though, the tapetum reflects light rather than absorbing it.

Tastant   The basic stimulus for taste.

Taste   Perceptions that result from the contact of substances with special receptors in the mouth.

Taste bud   Receptor for taste stimuli.

Taste modifiers   Special substances that change the flavor of other food by modifying the receptors on the tongue.

Taste pore   The opening in the taste bud.

Taste receptor cell   Contained in taste buds, arranged like the segments of an orange. The tips of the taste receptor cells reach out into the opening and can touch any taste molecules in the saliva that flows into the pit.

Taste tetrahedron   Four-sided figure representing one of the four basic tastes (sweet, salty, bitter, and sour) at each of the four corners.

Tectorial membrane   Membrane that rests at the top of the organ of Corti in the inner ear.

Template-matching approach   Approach to shape perception suggesting that we store specific patterns of information in memory and that recognition occurs when we match a newly presented stimulus to a template.

Tempo   The pace of a song, measured in beats per minute.

Temporal theory   A theory that states that the basilar membrane vibrates at a frequency that matches the frequency of a tone.

Temporary threshold shift   Temporary increase in a hearing threshold as a result of exposure to noise.

Test stimulus   In dark adaptation studies, the small spot of light for which the threshold is measured after the lights have been turned off.

Texture gradient   Distance cue provided by the fact that the texture of surfaces becomes denser as the distance increases.

Thermal adaptation   Decrease in the perceived intensity of a hot or cold temperature as time passes.

3-D sketch   Relating to Marr's theory of space perception, the third step in achieving a 3-D percept. Here the percept changes from viewer- to object-centered, providing a more accurate representation of depth than the 2.5-D sketch.

Timbre   (*tam*-burr) A tone's sound quality.

Tinnitus   High-pitched ringing in the ears, caused by a high fever, ear infection, or large doses of aspirin.

Tip links   The fine strands that link the stereocilia—tiny hairs you see extending from the hair cells—to one another.

Tonality   Organization of pitches around one particular tone.

Tone chroma   (*crow*-mah) Similarity shared by all musical tones that have the same name.

Tone height   Increase in pitch of a tone that accompanies an increase in frequency.

Tonic   One of the 12 pitches within an octave; serves as the tone around which all others in the octave are organized.

Tonometry   Technique in which a special instrument is used to measure the pressure inside the eye.

Tonotopic   Arrangement in which neurons sensitive to similar frequencies are near one another in the inferior colliculus.

Top-down processing   Approach that emphasizes the importance of the observers' concepts and cognitive processes in shaping perception.

Touch adaptation   Decrease in the perceived intensity of a repeated tactile stimulus.

Transcutaneous electrical nerve stimulation (TENS)   An effective technique for reducing pain produced by stimulating the surface of the skin.

Transduction   Process of converting a physical stimulus into a form that can be transmitted through the perceptual system.

Transformation theory   A theory by Wagner and Baird that involves two stages: The first stage is the creation of the proximal stimulus on the retina, which is a strictly physical process. The second stage is psychological, translating the retinal image into a spatial perception. It's in the second stage that there is room for error (e.g., in perceiving the visual angle of the stimulus).

Transient receptor potential (TRP) channels   A family of proteins responsible for the differences in sensitivity among the free nerve ending.

Transmission cells   Cells proposed by the gate-control theory that are in the spinal cord and receive input from two kinds of neural fibers.

Transposition   In a piece of music, changing the pitch of each note while retaining the same spatial relationships.

Transsaccadic integration   The collection and combination of information from the eye fixation at the beginning of a saccade with the information from the eye fixation at the end of a saccade.

Traveling wave   Pressure wave in auditory processing that travels from the base to the apex of the cochlea.

Trichromatic theory   Theory of color vision stating that there are three kinds of color receptors, each sensitive to light from a different part of the spectrum.

Trigeminal nerve   A nerve important in olfaction and taste; it has free nerve endings extending into the olfactory epithelium and also registers the spiciness of food such as chili peppers.

Tritanopes   (*try*-tuh-nopes) People who are dichromats and have difficulty with blue shades.

Tritone paradox   The tritone paradox involves a misperception of tone heights.

Trompe l'oeil   (tromp *ley*-yeh) Technique in painting that "fools the eye" by creating an impression of depth when the surface is really just two-dimensional.

Turbinate bones   Three bones located in the nasal cavity.

Two-alternative forced choice procedure   (2AFC) Psychophysical procedure with several variants. In one variant, a person is presented with a stimulus and then must decide which of two subsequent stimuli is identical to the original stimulus. This procedure eliminates consideration of a criterion, because the stimulus is always one of the two subsequently presented stimuli.

Two-point discrimination threshold   Point at which the perceiver can determine that two distinct stimuli—rather than one—are being presented. For touch perception, this is done by pricking the skin with two pinpoints.

2.5-D sketch   Relating to Marr's theory of space perception, the next step in achieving a 3-D percept after the primal sketch is achieved. It is viewer-centered and contains information about motion and the primal sketch.

Tympanic canal   Canal in the cochlea.

Tympanic membrane   Thin piece of membrane that vibrates in response to sound waves.

Unconscious inference   Proposed explanation for constancy in which the observer arrives at a perception via a reasoning-like process without conscious awareness.

Uncrossed disparity   Objects behind the horopter create uncrossed disparity, which is a cue that objects are far from us. (*See also* Horopter.)

Uniform connectedness   According to the principle of uniform connectedness, we organize input as a single unit when we perceive a connected region of uniform visual properties, such as lightness, color, and so on.

Universalists   People who believe that the color categories are common to all people, but that languages developed different names for those categories.

Vergence eye movements   Movements necessary to align the foveas of both eyes with an object.

Vergence movement   Eye movements in which the angle between the lines of sight changes and the eyes move toward or away from each other.

Version movement   Eye movement in which the angle between the lines of sight remains constant and the eyes move in the same direction.

Vestibular canal   (ves-*tih*-bue-lur) Canal in the cochlea on which the stapes rests.

Vestibular sense   System that provides information about orientation, movement, and acceleration.

Vestibuloocular reflex (VOR)   The vestibuloocular reflex (VOR) coordinates vestibular information with eye muscle function, which serves to stabilize our view of the world.

Virtual lines   Lines that are not actually present in a display, but are "created" by our perceptual system to organize the display into "objects." (*See also* Illusory contours.)

Visual acuity   Ability to see fine details in a scene.

Visual agnosia   Caused by temporal lobe damage, a person with visual agnosia has intact basic visual abilities but cannot identify a picture of an object.

Visual angle   Size of the angle formed by extending two lines from the observer's eye to the outside edges of the target.

Visual capture   When sound is misperceived as coming from a likely visual source.

Visual cliff   Kind of apparatus in which infants must choose between a side that looks shallow and a side that looks deep.

Visual cortex   Portion of the cerebral cortex that is concerned with vision.

Visual object agnosia   People with agnosia have basic visual abilities but cannot recognize objects.

Vitreous humor   (*vit*-ree-us) Thick, jellylike substance found within the eye, behind the lens.

Vocal tract   Anatomical structures involved in speaking, located above the vocal cords.

Voice onset time (VOT)   In speaking, the VOT is the time before the voiced part of the vowel begins.

Voiced consonant   Consonant that is spoken with vibration of the vocal cords.

Voiceless consonant   Consonant that is spoken without vibration of the vocal cords.

Voicing   One of the three dimensions for consonants; voicing specifies whether the vocal cords vibrate.

Volley principle   Proposal that was added to the frequency theory of auditory processing, which stated that clusters of neurons could "share" in producing a required firing rate.

Vomeronasal organs   Olfactory sense organs located on either side of the septum, which separates the two nostrils.

Water taste   Distinct taste for water following adaptation to another taste; for example, water tastes sweet after adaptation to a sour substance.

Wavelength   The distance light travels during one cycle.

Weber's fraction   (*k*) Number obtained in discrimination studies that represents the change in stimulus intensity divided by the original intensity.

Weber's law   (vay-burz) ($\Delta I / I = k$) Weber's law says that if we take the change in intensity (ΔI) and divide it by the original intensity (I), we obtain a constant number (k).

Wernicke's aphasia   A condition characterized by a deficit in language comprehension; people with this disorder experience language production that is typically wordy and confused, even though the rhythm and syntax seem roughly normal.

What pathway   A pathway important for object recognition; it runs from the primary visual cortex through the secondary visual cortex to the temporal lobe.

Where pathway   A pathway important for spatial location; it runs from the primary visual cortex through the secondary visual cortex to the parietal lobe.

Word-apprehension effect   Word-superiority effect.

Word-superiority effect   Phenomenon in which letters are perceived better when they appear in words than in strings of unrelated letters.

Zero-crossing   Related to edge perception; the point of a change in intensity within the visual field.

Zonules   Tiny fibers that connect the lens and the ciliary muscle.

References

Ables, E. M., Kay, L. M., & Mateo, J. M. (2007). Rats assess degree of relatedness from human odors. *Physiology & Behavior, 90*, 726–732.

Adams, J. C. (2006). Neuroanatomical considerations of speech processing. In S. Greenberg & W. A. Ainsworth (Eds.), *Listening to speech: An auditory perspective* (pp. 79–90). Mahwah, NJ: Erlbaum.

Adelson, E. H. (2000). Lightness perception and lightness illusions. In M. S. Gazzaniga (Ed.), *The new cognitive neurosciences* (2nd ed., pp. 339–351). Cambridge, MA: MIT Press.

Adolphs, R. (2007). Looking at other people: Mechanisms for social perception revealed in subjects with focal amygdala damage. *Novartis Foundation Symposium, 278*, 146–159; discussion 160–144, 216–121.

Agostini, T., & Proffitt, D. R. (1993). Perceptual organization evokes simultaneous lightness contrast. *Perception, 22*, 263–272.

Ahmed, I. J., Lewis, T. L., Ellemberg, D., & Maurer, D. (2005). Discrimination of speed in 5-year-olds and adults: Are children up to speed? *Vision Research, 45*, 2129–2135.

Albert, M. K. (2007). Mechanisms of modal and amodal interpolation. *Psychological Review, 114*, 455–469.

Albright, T. D., & Stoner, G. R. (2002). Contextual influences on visual processing. *Annual Review of Neuroscience, 25*, 339–379.

Aldous, C. R. (2001). Measuring cognitive and non-cognitive systems of reasoning: Some preliminary findings. *International Education Journal, 2*, 1–16.

Allman, J., & Brothers, L. (1994). Faces, fear and the amygdala. *Nature, 372*, 613–614.

Amedi, A., Stern, W. M., Camprodon, J. A., Bermpohl, F., Merabet, L. B., Rotman, S., et al. (2007). Shape conveyed by visual-to-auditory sensory substitution activates the lateral occipital complex. *Nature Neuroscience, 10*, 687–689.

American Psychological Association. (2002). Ethical principles of psychologists and code of conduct. *American Psychologist, 57*, 1060–1073.

Ames, A. (1952). *The Ames demonstrations in perception.* New York: Hafner.

Amoore, J. E. (1970). *Molecular basis of odor.* Springfield, IL: Thomas.

Anastasi, A. (1936). The estimation of areas. *Journal of General Psychology, 14*, 201–225.

Andersen, G. J., & Enriquez, A. (2006). Aging and the detection of observer and moving object collisions. *Psychology and Aging, 21*, 74–85.

Anderson, B. L. (2003). The role of occlusion in the perception of depth, lightness, and opacity. *Psychological Review, 110*, 785–801.

Anderson, B. L., Singh, M., & Meng, J. (2006). The perceived transmittance of inhomogeneous surfaces and media. *Vision Research, 46*, 1982–1995.

Anderson, B. L., & Winawer, J. (2005). Image segmentation and lightness perception. *Nature, 434*(7029), 79–83.

Andersson, G. (2007). Tinnitus. In S. Ayers, A. Baum, C. McManus, S. Newman, K. Wallston, J. Weinman, & R. West (Eds.), *The Cambridge handbook of psychology, health, and medicine* (pp. 906–907). New York: Cambridge.

Angelaki, D. E., & Cullen, K. E. (2008). Vestibular system: The many facets of a multimodal sense. *Annual Review of Neuroscience, 31*, 125–150.

Anstis, S. (2002). The Purkinje rod-cone shift as a function of luminance and retinal eccentricity. *Vision Research, 42*, 2485–2491.

Anstis, S. (2007). The flash-lag effect during illusory chopstick rotation. *Perception, 36*, 1043–1048.

Anstis, S., & Casco, C. (2006). Induced movement: The flying bluebottle illusion. *Journal of Vision, 6*, 1087–1092.

Apkarian, A. V. (2008). Pain and brain changes. In H. T. Benzon, J. P. Rathmell, C. L. Wu, D. C. Turk, & C. E. Argoff (Eds.), *Raj's practical management of pain* (pp. 151–170). Philadelphia: Mosby.

Arend, L. (1994). Surface colors, illumination, and surface geometry: Intrinsic-image models of human color perception. In A. Gilchrist (Ed.), *Lightness, brightness, and transparency* (pp. 159–213). Hillsdale, NJ: Erlbaum.

Arieh, Y., & Marks, L. E. (2003). Recalibrating the auditory system: A speed-accuracy analysis of intensity perception. *Journal of Experimental Psychology: Human Perception & Performance, 29*, 523–536.

Arkes, H. R., & Mellers, B. A. (2002). Do juries meet our expectations? *Law and Human Behavior, 26*, 625–639.

Aronoff, G. M., Gallagher, R. M., & Patel, J. G. (2002). Pharmacological management of chronic pain: A review. In C. D. Tollison, J. R. Satterthwaite, & J. W. Tollison (Eds.), *Practical pain management* (pp. 253–277). Philadelphia: Lippincott Williams & Wilkins.

Arrese, C. A., Beazley, L. D., & Neumeyer, C. (2006). Behavioural evidence for marsupial trichromacy. *Current Biology, 16*, R193–194.

Arrese, C. A., Hart, N. S., Thomas, N., Beazley, L. D., & Shand, J. (2002). Trichromacy in Australian marsupials. *Current Biology, 12*, 657–660.

Asbury, T., & Sanitato, J. J. (1992). Trauma. In D. Vaughn, T. Asbury, & P. Riordan-Eva (Eds.), *General ophthalmology* (13th ed., pp. 363–370). Norwalk, CT: Appleton & Lange.

Aslin, R. N. (2007). What's in a look? *Developmental Science, 10*, 48–53.

Aslin, R. N., & McMurray, B. (2004). Automated corneal-reflection eye tracking in infancy: Methodological developments and applications to cognition. *Infancy, 6*, 155–163.

Atkinson, R. C., & Schiffrin, R. M. (1968). Human memory: A proposed system and its control processes. In K. W. Spence & J. T. Spence (Eds.), *The psychology of learning and motivation: Advances in research and theory* (Vol. 2, pp. 89–195). New York: Academic Press.

Attias, J., Sapir, S., Bresloff, I., Reshef-Haran, I., & Ising, H. (2004). Reduction in noise-induced temporary threshold shift in humans following oral magnesium intake. *Clinical Otolaryngology and Allied Sciences, 29*, 635–641.

Audette, J. F. (2004). Acupuncture. In C. A. Warfield & Z. H. Bajwa (Eds.), *Principles and practice of pain medicine* (pp. 785–791). New York: McGraw-Hill.

Awater, H., Kerlin, J. R., Evans, K. K., & Tong, F. (2005). Cortical representation of space around the blind spot. *Journal of Neurophysiology, 94*, 3314–3324.

Ayotte, J., Peretz, I., & Hyde, K. (2002). Congenital amusia: A group study of adults afflicted with a music-specific disorder. *Brain, 125*, 238–251.

Bahill, A. T. (2005). Predicting a baseball's path. *American Scientist, 93*, 218–225.

Bahill, A. T., & Baldwin, D. G. (2004). The rising fastball and the perceptual illusions of batters. In G. Hung & J. Pallis (Eds.), *Biomedical engineering principles in sports* (pp. 257–287). New York: Kluwer.

Bahrick, L. E. (2003). Development of intermodal perception. In L. Nadel (Ed.), *Encyclopedia of cognitive science* (pp. 614–617). London: Nature.

Bahrick, L. E. (2004). The development of perception in a multimodal environment. In G. Bremner & A. Slater (Eds.), *Theories of infant development* (pp. 90–120). Malden, MA: Blackwell.

Bahrick, L. E., Hernandez-Reif, M., & Flom, R. (2005). The development of infant learning about specific face-voice relations. *Developmental Psychology, 41*, 541–552.

Bahrick, L. E., & Lickliter, R. (2002). Intersensory redundancy guides early perceptual and cognitive development. *Advances in Child Development and Behavior, 30*, 153–187.

Bahrick, L. E., Lickliter, R., & Flom, R. (2004). Intersensory redundancy guides the development of selective attention, perception, and cognition in infancy. *Current Directions in Psychological Science, 13*, 99–102.

Bahrick, L. E., Netto, D., & Hernandez-Reif, M. (1998). Intermodal perception of adult and child faces and voices by infants. *Child Development, 69*, 1263–1275.

Bailey, S. A. (2003). Taste. In S. F. Davis (Ed.), *Handbook of research methods in experimental psychology* (pp. 285–298). Malden, MA: Blackwell.

Baillargeon, R. (2004). Infants' reasoning about hidden objects: Evidence for event-general and event-specific expectations. *Developmental Science, 7*, 391–414.

Baird, J. C. (1997). *Sensation and judgment: Complementary theory of psychophysics*. Mahwah, NJ: Erlbaum.

Baird, J. C., & Noma, E. (1978). *Fundamentals of scaling and psychophysics*. New York: Wiley.

Baker, C. I., Peli, E., Knouf, N., & Kanwisher, N. G. (2005). Reorganization of visual processing in macular degeneration. *Journal of Neuroscience, 25*, 614–618.

Bakheit, A. M., & Roundhill, S. (2005). Supernumerary phantom limb after stroke. *Postgraduate Medical Journal, 81*(953), e2.

Bar, M., Kassam, K. S., Ghuman, A. S., Boshyan, J., Schmid, A. M., Dale, A. M., et al. (2006). Top-down facilitation of visual recognition. *Proceedings of the National Academy of Sciences of the USA, 103*, 449–454.

Barinaga, M. (2002). Circadian clock. How the brain's clock gets daily enlightenment. *Science, 295*(5557), 955–957.

Barlow, R. B., Jr. (1990). What the brain tells the eye. *Scientific American, 262*, 90–95.

Barlow, R. B., Jr., & Kaplan, E. (1993). Intensity coding and circadian rhythms in the *Limulus* lateral eye. In R. T. Verrillo (Ed.), *Sensory research: Multimodal perspectives* (pp. 55–73). Hillsdale, NJ: Erlbaum.

Barrett, H. C. (2005). Adaptations to predators and prey. In D. M. Buss (Ed.), *The handbook of evolutionary psychology* (pp. 200–223). New York: Wiley.

Barrett, T. M., Traupman, E., & Needham, A. (2007). Infants' visual anticipation of object structure in grasp planning. *Infant Behavior & Development, 31*, 1–9.

Bartlett, J. C., Searcy, J. H., & Abdi, H. (2003). What are the routes to face recognition? In M. A. Peterson & G. Rhodes (Eds.), *Perception of faces, objects, and scenes: Analytic and holistic processes* (pp. 21–47). New York: Oxford.

Basbaum, A. I., Bushnell, M. C., Smith, D. V., Beauchamp, G. K., Firestein, S. J., Dallos, P., et al. (Eds.). (2008). *The senses: A comprehensive reference*. New York: Academic Press.

Basbaum, A. I., & Julius, D. (2006). Toward better pain control. *Scientific American, 294*, 61–67.

Baseler, H. A., Brewer, A. A., Sharpe, L. T., Morland, A. B., Jagle, H., & Wandell, B. A. (2002). Reorganization of human cortical maps caused by inherited photoreceptor abnormalities. *Nature Neuroscience, 5*, 364–370.

Bashore, T. R., & Ridderinkhof, K. R. (2002). Older age, traumatic brain injury, and cognitive slowing: Some convergent and divergent findings. *Psychological Bulletin, 128*, 151–198.

Bates, E., Thal, D., Finlay, B. L., & Clancy, B. (2002). Early language development and its neural correlates. In S. J.

Segalowitz & I. Rapin (Eds.), *Handbook of neuropsychology* (2nd ed., pp. 109–176). Amsterdam: Elsevier.

Beason, R. C., & Loew, E. R. (2008). Visual pigment and oil droplet characteristics of the bobolink (Dolichonyx oryzivorus), a new world migratory bird. *Vision Research, 48*, 1–8.

Beauchamp, G. K., & Stein, L. J. (2008). Salt taste. In A. I. Basbaum, M. C. Bushnell, D. V. Smith, G. K. Beauchamp, S. J. Firestein, P. Dallos, D. Oertel, R. H. Masland, T. D. Albright, J. H. Kaas, & E. P. Gardner (Eds.), *The senses: A comprehensive reference* (Vol. 4, pp. 401–408). New York: Academic Press.

Beauchamp, M. S., Lee, K. E., Haxby, J. V., & Martin, A. (2003). FMRI responses to video and point-light displays of moving humans and manipulable objects. *Journal of Cognitive Neuroscience, 15*, 991–1001.

Beauchamp, M. S., Yasar, N. E., Frye, R. E., & Ro, T. (2008). Touch, sound and vision in human superior temporal sulcus. *Neuroimage, 41*, 1011–1020.

Becker, M. W., & Anstis, S. (2004). Metacontrast masking is specific to luminance polarity. *Vision Research, 44*, 2537–2543.

Becker, M. W., Pashler, H., & Lubin, J. (2007). Object-intrinsic oddities draw early saccades. *Journal of Experimental Psychology: Human Perception & Performance, 33*, 20–30.

Beckers, G., & Homberg, V. (1992). Cerebral visual motion blindness: Transitory akinetopsia induced by transcranial magnetic stimulation of human area V5. *Proceedings of The Royal Society B: Biological Sciences, 249*(1325), 173–178.

Behrend, O., & Schuller, G. (2004). New aspects of Doppler-shift compensation in the Horseshoe Bat, Rhinolophus rouxi. In J. A. Thomas, C. F. Moss, & M. Vater (Eds.), *Echolocation in bats and dolphins* (pp. 17–21). Chicago: University of Chicago.

Behrmann, M., & Avidan, G. (2005). Congenital prosopagnosia: Face-blind from birth. *Trends in Cognitive Sciences, 9*, 180–187.

Behrmann, M., & Kimchi, R. (2003a). Visual perceptual organization: Lessons from lesions. In R. Kimchi, M. Behrmann, & C. R. Olson (Eds.), *Perceptual organization in vision: Behavioral and neural perspectives* (pp. 337–376). Mahwah, NJ: Erlbaum.

Behrmann, M., & Kimchi, R. (2003b). What does visual agnosia tell us about perceptual organization and its relationship to object perception? *Journal of Experimental Psychology: Human Perception & Performance, 29*, 19–42.

Behrmann, M., Marotta, J., Gauthier, I., Tarr, M. J., & McKeeff, T. J. (2005). Behavioral change and its neural correlates in visual agnosia after expertise training. *Journal of Cognitive Neuroscience, 17*, 554–568.

Behrmann, M., Peterson, M. A., Moscovitch, M., & Suzuki, S. (2006). Independent representation of parts and the rela-tions between them: Evidence from integrative agnosia. *Journal of Experimental Psychology: Human Perception & Performance, 32*, 1169–1184.

Bell, A. (2004). Hearing: Traveling wave or resonance? *PLoS Biol, 2*(10), e337.

Bendor, D., & Wang, X. (2005). The neuronal representation of pitch in primate auditory cortex. *Nature, 436*(7054), 1161–1165.

Bendor, D., & Wang, X. (2006). Cortical representations of pitch in monkeys and humans. *Current Opinion in Neurobiology, 16*, 391–399.

Benedetti, F. (2008). The placebo effect. In A. I. Basbaum, M. C. Bushnell, D. V. Smith, G. K. Beauchamp, S. J. Firestein, P. Dallos, D. Oertel, R. H. Masland, T. D. Albright, J. H. Kaas, & E. P. Gardner (Eds.), *The senses: A comprehensive reference* (Vol. 5, pp. 1003–1008). New York: Academic Press.

Benham, C. E. (1894). The artificial spectrum top. *Nature, 51*, 200.

Benjamin, L. T., Jr. (2008). *A history of psychology: Original sources and contemporary research* (3rd ed.). Malden, MA: Blackwell.

Bennett, A. T. D., & Théry, M. (2007). Avian color vision and coloration: Multidisciplinary evolutionary biology. *The American Naturalist, 169*, S1–S6.

Bennett, P. J., Sekuler, R., & Sekuler, A. B. (2007). The effects of aging on motion detection and direction identification. *Vision Research, 47*, 799–809.

Bensafi, M., Tsutsui, T., Khan, R., Levenson, R. W., & Sobel, N. (2004). Sniffing a human sex-steroid derived compound affects mood and autonomic arousal in a dose-depend-ent manner. *Psychoneuroendocrinology, 29*, 1290–1299.

Bensmaïa, S. J., Craig, J. C., Yoshioka, T., & Johnson, K. O. (2006). SA1 and RA afferent responses to static and vibrat-ing gratings. *Journal of Neurophysiology, 95*, 1771–1782.

Bensmaïa, S. J., & Hollins, M. (2005). Pacinian representations of fine surface texture. *Perception & Psychophysics, 67*, 842–854.

Benzon, H. T., Rathmell, J. P., Wu, C. L., Turk, D. C., & Argoff, C. E. (Eds.). (2008). *Raj's practical management of pain*. Philadelphia: Mosby.

Berkeley, G. (1709/1957). *An essay towards a new theory of vision*. London: Dent.

Berlin, B., & Kay, P. (1969). *Basic color terms*. Berkeley, CA: University of California.

Berlyne, D. E. (1958). The influence of the albedo and com-plexity of stimuli on visual fixation in the human infant. *British Journal of Psychology, 49*, 315–318.

Bernstein, I. L. (2008). Flavor aversion learning. In A. I. Basbaum, M. C. Bushnell, D. V. Smith, G. K. Beauchamp, S. J. Firestein, P. Dallos, D. Oertel, R. H. Masland, T. D. Albright, J. H. Kaas, & E. P. Gardner (Eds.), *The senses: A comprehensive reference* (Vol. 4, pp. 429–435). New York: Academic Press.

Bernstein, L. E. (2005). Phonetic processing by the speech perceiving brain. In D. B. Pisoni & R. E. Remez (Eds.), *The handbook of speech perception* (pp. 79–98). Malden, MA: Blackwell.

Bernstein, L. E., Auer, E. T., & Moore, J. K. (2004). Audiovisual speech binding: Convergence or association? In G. A. Calvert, C. Spence, & B. E. Stein (Eds.), *The handbook of multisensory processes*. Cambridge, MA: MIT Press.

Berson, D. M. (2003). Strange vision: Ganglion cells as circadian photoreceptors. *Trends in Neurosciences, 26*, 314–320.

Bertamini, M., Latto, R., & Spooner, A. (2003). The Venus effect: People's understanding of mirror reflections in paintings. *Perception, 32*, 593–599.

Bertenthal, B. I., & Pinto, J. (1994). Global processing of biological motions. *Psychological Science, 5*, 221–225.

Berthoz, A. (2000). *The brain's sense of movement* (G. Weiss, Trans.). Cambridge, MA: Harvard University.

Best, P. J., White, A. M., & Minai, A. (2001). Spatial processing in the brain: The activity of hippocampal place cells. *Annual Review of Neuroscience, 24*, 459–486.

Bhadri, P. R., Rowley, A. P., Khurana, R. N., Deboer, C. M., Kerns, R. M., Chong, L. P., et al. (2007). Evaluation of a stereoscopic camera-based three-dimensional viewing workstation for ophthalmic surgery. *American Journal of Ophthalmology, 143*, 891–892.

Bhayani, S. B., & Andriole, G. L. (2005). Three-dimensional (3D) vision: Does it improve laparoscopic skills? An assessment of a 3D head-mounted visualization system. *Reviews in Urology, 7*, 211–214.

Bian, Z., Braunstein, M. L., & Andersen, G. J. (2006). The ground dominance effect in the perception of relative distance in 3-D scenes is mainly due to characteristics of the ground surface. *Perception & Psychophysics, 68*, 1297–1309.

Biederman, I. (1987). Recognition-by-components: A theory of human image understanding. *Psychological Review, 94*, 115–147.

Biederman, I. (2007). Recent psychophysical and neural research in shape recognition. In N. Osaka, I. Rentschler, & I. Biederman (Eds.), *Object recognition, attention, and action* (pp. 71–88). New York: Springer.

Biersdorfer, J. D. (2004, September 30). Headphones that make the world go away. *The New York Times*, p. G6.

Billino, J., Bremmer, F., & Gegenfurtner, K. R. (2008). Motion processing at low light levels: Differential effects on the perception of specific motion types. *Journal of Vision, 8*(3), 14, 1–10.

Birch, J. (2001). *Diagnosis of defective colour vision* (2nd ed.). New York: Elsevier.

Biswell, R. (2004). Cornea. In P. Riordan-Eva, T. Asbury, & J. P. Whitcher (Eds.), *Vaughn & Asbury's general ophthalmology* (16th ed., pp. 129–153). New York: McGraw-Hill Medical.

Blake, R. (1993). Cats perceive biological motion. *Psychological Science, 4*, 54–57.

Blake, R. (1994). Gibson's inspired but latent prelude to visual motion perception. *Psychological Review, 101*, 324–348.

Blake, R. (2003). Binocular rivalry. In L. M. Chalupa & J. S. Werner (Eds.), *The visual neurosciences* (Vol. 2, pp. 1313–1323). Cambridge, MA: MIT Press.

Blake, R., Rizzo, M., & McEvoy, S. (2008). Aging and perception of visual form from temporal structure. *Psychology and Aging, 23*, 181–189.

Blake, R., Sekuler, R., & Grossman, E. (2004). Motion processing in human visual cortex. In J. H. Kaas & C. E. Collins (Eds.), *The primate visual system* (pp. 311–344). Boca Raton, FL: CRC.

Blake, R., & Shiffrar, M. (2007). Perception of human motion. *Annual Review of Psychology, 58*, 47–73.

Blaser, E., Papathomas, T., & Vidnyanszky, Z. (2005). Binding of motion and colour is early and automatic. *The European Journal of Neuroscience, 21*, 2040–2044.

Bloom, W., & Fawcett, D. W. (1975). *A textbook of histology*. Philadelphia: W. B. Saunders.

Bochud, F. O., Abbey, C. K., & Eckstein, M. P. (2004). Search for lesions in mammograms: Statistical characterization of observer responses. *Medical Physics, 31*, 24–36.

Boltz, M. G. (2001). Musical soundtracks as a schematic influence on the cognitive processing of filmed events. *Music Perception, 18*, 427–454.

Boltz, M. G. (2004). The cognitive processing of film and musical soundtracks. *Memory & Cognition, 32*, 1194–1205.

Boltz, M. G., Schulkind, M., & Kantra, S. (1991). Effects of background music on the remembering of filmed events. *Memory & Cognition, 19*, 593–606.

Bonaiuto, P., Giannini, A. M., & Bonaiuto, M. (1991). Visual illusory productions with or without amodal completion. *Perception, 20*, 243–257.

Bond, Z. S. (1999). *Slips of the ear: Errors in the perception of casual conversation*. San Diego: Academic Press.

Bond, Z. S. (2005). Slips of the ear. In D. B. Pisoni & R. E. Remez (Eds.), *The handbook of speech perception* (pp. 290–310). Malden, MA: Blackwell.

Boothe, R. G. (2002). *Perception of the visual environment*. New York: Springer.

Boring, E. G. (1942). *Sensation and perception in the history of experimental psychology*. New York: Appleton-Century-Crofts.

Boring, E. G. (1961). Fechner: Inadvertent founder of psychophysics. *Psychometrika, 26*, 3–8.

Born, R. T., & Bradley, D. C. (2005). Structure and function of visual area MT. *Annual Review of Neuroscience, 28*, 157–189.

Bornstein, M. H., Arterberry, M. E., & Mash, C. (2005). Perceptual development. In M. H. Bornstein & M. E. Lamb (Eds.), *Developmental science: An advanced textbook* (5th ed., pp. 283–325). Mahwah, NJ: Erlbaum.

Bouhassira, D., Kern, D., Rouaud, J., Pelle-Lancien, E., & Morain, F. (2005). Investigation of the paradoxical painful sensation ("illusion of pain") produced by a thermal grill. *Pain, 114*, 160–167.

Bouvier, S. E., & Engel, S. A. (2006). Behavioral deficits and cortical damage loci in cerebral achromatopsia. *Cerebral Cortex, 16*, 183–191.

Bowmaker, J. K., & Hunt, D. M. (2006). Evolution of vertebrate visual pigments. *Current Biology, 16*, R484–489.

Brabyn, J. A., Schneck, M., Haegerstrom-Portnoy, G., & Lott, L. (2001). The Smith Kettlewell Institute (SKI) longitudinal study of vision function and its impact among the elderly: An overview. *Optometry & Vision Science, 78*, 264–269.

Brabyn, J. A., Schneck, M. E., Haegerstrom-Portnoy, G., & Lott, L. A. (2007). Dual sensory loss: Overview of problems, visual assessment, and rehabilitation. *Trends in Amplification, 11*, 219–226.

Brabyn, J. A., Schneck, M. E., Lott, L. A., & Haegerstrom-Portnoy, G. (2005). Night driving self-restriction: Vision function and gender differences. *Optometry & Vision Science, 82*, 755–764.

Brady, T. F., Konkle, T., Alvarez, G. A., & Oliva, A. (2008). Visual long-term memory has a massive storage capacity for object details. *Proceedings of the National Academy of Sciences of the USA, 105*(38), 14325–14329.

Bramer, T. P. C. (2007). Industrial noise control. In L. Luxon & D. Prasher (Eds.), *Noise and its effects* (pp. 650–666). Chichester, England: Wiley.

Brancazio, L., Best, C. T., & Fowler, C. A. (2006). Visual influences on perception of speech and nonspeech vocal-tract events. *Language and Speech, 49*, 21–53.

Bregman, A. S. (1990). *Auditory scene analysis: The perceptual organization of sound* (cloth). Cambridge, MA: MIT Press.

Bregman, A. S. (1994). *Auditory scene analysis: The perceptual organization of sound* (paper). Cambridge, MA: MIT Press.

Bregman, A. S. (2008). Auditory scene analysis. In A. I. Basbaum, M. C. Bushnell, D. V. Smith, G. K. Beauchamp, S. J. Firestein, P. Dallos, D. Oertel, R. H. Masland, T. D. Albright, J. H. Kaas, & E. P. Gardner (Eds.), *The senses: A comprehensive reference* (Vol. 3, pp. 861–870). New York: Academic Press.

Breitmeyer, B. (2007). Visual masking: Past accomplishments, present status, future developments. *Advances in Cognitive Psychology, 3*, 9–20.

Bremner, E. A., Mainland, J. D., Khan, R. M., & Sobel, N. (2003). The prevalence of androstenone anosmia. *Chemical Senses, 28*, 423–432.

Bremner, J. G., Johnson, S. P., Slater, A., Mason, U., Foster, K., Cheshire, A., et al. (2005). Conditions for young infants' perception of object trajectories. *Child Development, 76*, 1029–1043.

Brenner, E., & Cornelissen, F. W. (2005). A way of selectively degrading colour constancy demonstrates the experience dependence of colour vision. *Current Biology, 15*, R864–866.

Breslin, P. A., & Huang, L. (2006). Human taste: Peripheral anatomy, taste transduction, and coding. *Advances in Oto-Rhino-Laryngology, 63*, 152–190.

Bressan, P. (2001). Explaining lightness illusions. *Perception, 30*, 1031–1046.

Bressan, P. (2006). The place of white in a world of grays: A double-anchoring theory of lightness perception. *Psychological Review, 113*, 526–553.

Britten, K. H. (2008). Mechanisms of self-motion perception. *Annual Review of Neuroscience, 31*, 389–410.

Broadbent, N. J., Squire, L. R., & Clark, R. E. (2004). Spatial memory, recognition memory, and the hippocampus. *Proceedings of the National Academy of Sciences of the USA, 101*(40), 14515–14520.

Brockmole, J. R., & Henderson, J. M. (2005). Prioritization of new objects in real-world scenes: Evidence from eye movements. *Journal of Experimental Psychology: Human Perception & Performance, 31*, 857–868.

Brockmole, J. R., & Henderson, J. M. (2008). Prioritizing new objects for eye fixation in real-world scenes: Effects of object-scene consistency. *Visual Cognition, 16*, 375–390.

Bronstad, P. M., Langlois, J. H., & Russell, R. (2008). Computational models of facial attractiveness judgments. *Perception, 37*, 126–142.

Brown, C. H., & May, B. J. (2005). Comparative mammalian sound localization. In A. N. Popper & R. R. Fay (Eds.), *Sound source localization* (Vol. 25, pp. 124–178). New York: Springer.

Brown, R. J., & Thurmond, J. B. (1993). Preattentive and cognitive effects on perceptual completion at the blind spot. *Perception & Psychophysics, 53*, 200–209.

Brownell, W. E. (2006). The piezoelectric outer hair cell. In R. A. Eatock, R. R. Fay, & A. N. Popper (Eds.), *Vertebrate hair cells* (Vol. 27, pp. 313–347). New York: Springer.

Bruce, V., Green, P. R., & Georgeson, M. A. (2003). *Visual perception: Physiology, psychology, and ecology* (4th ed.). New York: Psychology Press.

Brugger, P. (2006). From phantom limb to phantom body: Varieties of extracorporeal awareness. In G. Knoblich, I. M. Thornton, M. Grosjean, & M. Shiffrar (Eds.), *Human body perception from the inside out* (pp. 171–209). New York: Oxford.

Buck, L. B. (2004). The search for odorant receptors. *Cell, 116*(Suppl), S117–119.

Buck, L. B. (2005). Unraveling the sense of smell (Nobel lecture). *Angewandte Chemie International Edition, 44*(38), 6128–6140.

Buck, L. B., & Axel, R. (1991). A novel multigene family may encode odorant receptors: A molecular basis for odor recognition. *Cell, 65*, 175–187.

Bullier, J. (2002). Neural basis of vision. In H. Pashler & S. Yantis (Eds.), *Stevens' handbook of experimental psychology* (3rd ed., pp. 1–40). Hoboken, NJ: Wiley.

Burke, M. R., & Barnes, G. R. (2006). Quantitative differences in smooth pursuit and saccadic eye movements. *Experimental Brain Research, 175*, 596–608.

Butler, J., Fleming, P., & Webb, D. (2006). Congenital insensitivity to pain—Review and report of a case with dental implications. *Oral Surgery, Oral Medicine, Oral Pathology, Oral Radiology, and Endodontics, 101*, 58–62.

Campana, G., Cowey, A., & Walsh, V. (2006). Visual area V5/MT remembers "what" but not "where." *Cerebral Cortex, 16*, 1766–1770.

Campbell, F. W., & Robson, J. G. (1964). Application of Fourier analysis of the modulation response of the eye. *Journal of the Optical Society of America, 54*, 518A.

Campbell, F. W., & Robson, J. G. (1968). Application of Fourier analysis to the visibility of gratings. *Journal of Physiology, 197*, 551–566.

Campbell, R. (2008). The processing of audio-visual speech: Empirical and neural bases. *Philosophical Transactions of The Royal Society of London B: Biologial Sciences, 363*, 1001–1010.

Campos, J. J., Anderson, D. I., Barbu-Roth, M. A., Hubbard, E. M., Hertenstein, M. J., & Witherington, D. (2000). Travel broadens the mind. *Infancy, 1*, 149–219.

Cao, A., & Schiller, P. H. (2002). Behavioral assessment of motion parallax and stereopsis as depth cues in rhesus monkeys. *Vision Research, 42*, 1953–1961.

Capaldi, E. J., & Proctor, R. W. (1994). Contextualism: Is the act in context the adequate metaphor for scientific psychology? *Psychonomic Bulletin & Review, 1*, 239–249.

Carbon, C. C., Gruter, T., Weber, J. E., & Lueschow, A. (2007). Faces as objects of non-expertise: Processing of Thatcherised faces in congenital prosopagnosia. *Perception, 36*, 1635–1645.

Carbon, C. C., & Leder, H. (2005). The wall inside the brain: Overestimation of distances crossing the former Iron Curtain. *Psychonomic Bulletin & Review, 12*, 746–750.

Carey, S., & Xu, F. (2001). Infants' knowledge of objects: Beyond object files and object tracking. *Cognition, 80*, 179–213.

Carlson, N. R. (2007). *Physiology of behavior* (9th ed.). Boston: Allyn & Bacon.

Carney, L. H. (2002). Neural basis of audition. In H. Pashler & S. Yantis (Eds.), *Stevens' handbook of experimental psychology* (3rd ed., Vol. 1, pp. 341–396). Hoboken, NJ: Wiley.

Carpenter, R. H. S. (2000). The neural control of looking. *Current Biology, 10*, R291–293.

Carpenter, R. H. S. (2005). Visual pursuit: An instructive area of cortex. *Current Biology, 15*, R638–640.

Carr, C. E., & Soares, D. (2007). Shared features of the auditory system of birds and mammals. In J. H. Kaas (Ed.), *Evolution of nervous systems: A comprehensive reference.* London: Elsevier.

Carroll, J., Choi, S. S., & Williams, D. R. (2008). In vivo imaging of the photoreceptor mosaic of a rod monochromat. *Vision Research.*

Carroll, J., Neitz, M., Hofer, H., Neitz, J., & Williams, D. R. (2004). Functional photoreceptor loss revealed with adaptive optics: An alternate cause of color blindness. *Proceedings of the National Academy of Sciences of the USA, 101*, 8461–8466.

Carson, W. G., Jr. (2004). Wakeboarding injuries. *The American Journal of Sports Medicine, 32*, 164–173.

Case, T. I., Repacholi, B. M., & Stevenson, R. J. (2006). My baby doesn't smell as bad as yours: The plasticity of disgust. *Evolution and Human Behavior, 27*, 357–365.

Castet, E., Jeanjean, S., & Masson, G. S. (2002). Motion perception of saccade-induced retinal translation. *Proceedings of the National Academy of Sciences of the USA, 99*, 15159–15163.

Castet, E., & Masson, G. S. (2000). Motion perception during saccadic eye movements. *Nature Neuroscience, 3*, 177–183.

Caterina, M. J., Gold, M. S., & Meyer, R. A. (2005). Molecular biology of nociceptors. In S. P. Hunt & M. Koltzenberg (Eds.), *The neurobiology of pain* (pp. 1–34). New York: Oxford.

Cattell, J. M. (1886). The time it takes to see and name objects. *Mind, 11*, 63–65.

Cavanagh, P. (2005). The artist as neuroscientist. *Nature, 434*(7031), 301–307.

Chandrashekar, J., Hoon, M. A., Ryba, N. J., & Zuker, C. S. (2006). The receptors and cells for mammalian taste. *Nature, 444*(7117), 288–294.

Chang, D. F. (2004). Ophthalmologic examination. In P. Riordan-Eva, T. Asbury, & J. P. Whitcher (Eds.), *Vaughn & Asbury's general ophthalmology* (16th ed., pp. 29–61). New York: McGraw-Hill Medical.

Chang, E. F., Bao, S., Imaizumi, K., Schreiner, C. E., & Merzenich, M. M. (2005). Development of spectral and temporal response selectivity in the auditory cortex. *Proceedings of the National Academy of Sciences of the USA, 102*(45), 16460–16465.

Chapanis, A. (1949). How we see: A summary of basic principles. In *Human factors in undersea warfare.* Washington, DC: National Research Council.

Chapman, C., Hoag, R., & Giaschi, D. (2004). The effect of disrupting the human magnocellular pathway on global motion perception. *Vision Research, 44*, 2551–2557.

Chase, S. M., & Young, E. D. (2005). Limited segregation of different types of sound localization information among classes of units in the inferior colliculus. *Journal of Neuroscience, 25*, 7575–7585.

Chen, J. C., Schmid, K. L., & Brown, B. (2003). The autonomic control of accommodation and implications for human myopia development: A review. *Ophthalmic and Physiological Optics, 23*, 401–422.

Chertoff, M. E., Amani-Taleshi, D., Guo, Y., & Burkard, R. (2002). The influence of inner hair cell loss on the instantaneous frequency of the cochlear microphonic. *Hearing Research, 174*, 93–100.

Ching, T. Y., Hill, M., Brew, J., Incerti, P., Priolo, S., Rushbrook, E., et al. (2005). The effect of auditory experience on speech perception, localization, and functional performance of children who use a cochlear implant and a hearing aid in opposite ears. *International Journal of Audiology, 44*, 677–690.

Chiu, C., & Moss, C. F. (2007). The role of the external ear in vertical sound localization in the free flying bat, Eptesicus fuscus. *Journal of the Acoustical Society of America, 121*, 2227–2235.

Chung, S. K., Price, D. D., Verne, G. N., & Robinson, M. E. (2007). Revelation of a personal placebo response: Its effects on mood, attitudes and future placebo responding. *Pain, 132*, 281–288.

Ciocca, V., & Bregman, A. S. (1989). The effects of auditory streaming on duplex perception. *Perception & Psychophysics, 46*, 39–48.

Clark, G. (2004). Cochlear implants. In S. Greenberg, W. A. Ainsworth, R. R. Fay & A. N. Popper (Eds.), *Speech processing in the auditory system* (Vol. 18, pp. 422–462). New York: Springer.

Clark, S. E. (2005). A re-examination of the effects of biased lineup instructions in eyewitness identification. *Law and Human Behavior, 29*, 395–424.

Cleary, M., & Pisoni, D. B. (2001). Speech perception and spoken word recognition: Research and theory. In E. B. Goldstein (Ed.), *Blackwell handbook of perception* (pp. 499–534). Malden, MA: Blackwell.

Clément, G., Reschke, M., & Wood, S. (2005). Neurovestibular and sensorimotor studies in space and Earth benefits. *Current Pharmaceutical Biotechnology, 6*, 267–283.

Cohen, L. B., & Cashon, C. H. (2003). Infant perception and cognition. In R. Lerner, A. Easterbrooks, & J. Mistry (Eds.), *Comprehensive handbook of psychology* (Vol. 6: Developmental psychology, pp. 65–89). New York: Wiley.

Coimbra, J. P., Marceliano, M. L., Andrade-da-Costa, B. L., & Yamada, E. S. (2006). The retina of tyrant flycatchers: Topographic organization of neuronal density and size in the ganglion cell layer of the great kiskadee Pitangus sulphuratus and the rusty margined flycatcher Myiozetetes cayanensis (Aves: Tyrannidae). *Brain, Behavior, and Evolution, 68*, 15–25.

Cole, G. G., Heywood, C., Kentridge, R., Fairholm, I., & Cowey, A. (2003). Attentional capture by colour and motion in cerebral achromatopsia. *Neuropsychologia, 41*, 1837–1846.

Cole, J. (1991). *Pride and a daily marathon.* Cambridge, MA: MIT Press.

Cole, R. A., & Jakimik, J. (1980). A model of speech perception. In R. A. Cole (Ed.), *Perception and production of fluent speech* (pp. 133–163). Hillsdale, NJ: Erlbaum.

Collins, D. F., Refshauge, K. M., Todd, G., & Gandevia, S. C. (2005). Cutaneous receptors contribute to kinesthesia at the index finger, elbow, and knee. *Journal of Neurophysiology, 94*, 1699–1706.

Comings, J., Garner, B., & Smith, C. (2006). *Review of adult learning and literacy: Connecting research, policy, and practice* (Vol. 6). Mahwah, NJ: Erlbaum.

Cook, N. D., Yutsudo, A., Fujimoto, N., & Murata, M. (2008). Factors contributing to depth perception: Behavioral studies on the reverse perspective illusion. *Spatial Vision, 21*, 397–405.

Cooper, N. P., & Guinan, J. J., Jr. (2006). Efferent-mediated control of basilar membrane motion. *Journal of Physiology, 576*, 49–54.

Cooper, P. A., Geldart, S. S., Mondloch, C. J., & Maurer, D. (2006). Developmental changes in perceptions of attractiveness: A role of experience? *Developmental Science, 9*, 530–543.

Cornelissen, F. W., Wade, A. R., Vladusich, T., Dougherty, R. F., & Wandell, B. A. (2006). No functional magnetic resonance imaging evidence for brightness and color filling-in in early human visual cortex. *Journal of Neuroscience, 26*, 3634–3641.

Cornish, E. E., Xiao, M., Yang, Z., Provis, J. M., & Hendrickson, A. E. (2004). The role of opsin expression and apoptosis in determination of cone types in human retina. *Experimental Eye Research, 78*, 1143–1154.

Cortazzo, M. H., & Fishman, S. M. (2008). Major opiods and chronic opioid therapy. In H. T. Benzon, J. P. Rathmell, C. L. Wu, D. C. Turk, & C. E. Argoff (Eds.), *Raj's practical management of pain* (pp. 597–611). Philadelphia: Mosby.

Cowart, B. J., & Rawson, N. E. (2001). Olfaction. In E. B. Goldstein (Ed.), *Blackwell handbook of perception* (pp. 567–600). Malden, MA: Blackwell.

Cox, J. J., Reimann, F., Nicholas, A. K., Thornton, G., Roberts, E., Springell, K., et al. (2006). An SCN9A channelopathy causes congenital inability to experience pain. *Nature, 444*(7121), 894–898.

Craig, A. D. (2003). Pain mechanisms: Labeled lines versus convergence in central processing. *Annual Review of Neuroscience, 26*, 1–30.

Craig, J. C., & Rollman, G. B. (1999). Somesthesis. *Annual Review of Psychology, 50*, 305–331.

Cranford, T. W., & Amundin, M. (2004). Biosonar pulse production in Odontocetes: The state of our knowledge. In J. A. Thomas, C. F. Moss, & M. Vater (Eds.), *Echolocation in bats and dolphins* (pp. 27–35). Chicago: University of Chicago.

Crano, W. D., & Brewer, M. B. (2001). *Principles and methods of social research* (2nd ed.). Mahwah, NJ: Erlbaum.

Crapse, T. B., & Sommer, M. A. (2008). Corollary discharge across the animal kingdom. *Nature Reviews Neuroscience, 9,* 587–600.

Crompton, A., & Brown, F. (2006). Distance estimation in a small-scale environment. *Environment and Behavior, 38,* 656–666.

Cropper, S. J., & Wuerger, S. M. (2005). The perception of motion in chromatic stimuli. *Behavioral and Cognitive Neuroscience Reviews, 4,* 192–217.

Cuddy, L. L., Balkwill, L.-L., Peretz, I., & Holden, R. R. (2005). Musical difficulties are rare: A study of "tone deafness" among university students. In G. Avanzini, L. Lopez, S. Koelsch, & M. Manjno (Eds.), *The neurosciences and music II: From perception to performance.* (pp. 311–324). New York: New York Academy of Sciences.

Cullen, K. E. (2004). Sensory signals during active versus passive movement. *Current Opinion in Neurobiology, 14,* 698–706.

Cumming, B. G., & DeAngelis, G. C. (2001). The physiology of stereopsis. *Annual Review of Neuroscience, 24,* 203–238.

Curcio, C. A., Sloan, K. R., Kalina, R. E., & Hendrickson, A. E. (1990). Human photoreceptor topography. *Journal of Comparative Neurology, 292,* 497–523.

Cutting, J. E. (1993). Perceptual artifacts and phenomena: Gibson's role in the 20th century. In S. C. Masin (Ed.), *Foundations of perceptual theory* (pp. 231–260). New York: Elsevier.

Cutting, J. E. (2007). Framing the rules of perception: Hochberg versus Galileo, Gestalts, Garner, and Gibson. In M. A. Peterson, B. Gillam, & H. A. Sedgwick (Eds.), *In the mind's eye: Julian Hochberg on the perception of pictures, films, and the world* (pp. 495–503). New York: Oxford.

Cutting, J. E., Moore, C., & Morrison, R. (1988). Masking the motions of human gait. *Perception & Psychophysics, 44,* 339–347.

Cutting, J. E., & Vishton, P. M. (1995). Perceiving layout and knowing distances: The integration, relative potency, and contextual use of different information about depth. In W. Epstein & S. J. Rogers (Eds.), *Perception of space and motion* (pp. 69–117). San Diego: Academic.

Dain, S. J. (2004). Clinical colour vision tests. *Clinical and Experimental Optometry, 87,* 276–293.

Dallos, P. (1996). Overview: Cochlear neurobiology. In P. Dallos, A. N. Popper, & R. R. Fay (Eds.), *The cochlea* (pp. 1–43). New York: Springer.

Dallos, P., Zheng, J., & Cheatham, M. A. (2006). Prestin and the cochlear amplifier. *Journal of Physiology, 576,* 37–42.

Dalton, J. (1798/1948). Extraordinary facts relating to the vision of colours: With observations. In W. Dennis (Ed.), *Readings in the history of psychology* (pp. 102–111). New York: Appleton-Century-Crofts.

Dalton, P. H. (2002). Olfaction. In H. Pashler & S. Yantis (Eds.), *Stevens' handbook of experimental psychology* (3rd ed., pp. 691–746). Hoboken, NJ: Wiley.

Daniel, E. (2007). Noise and hearing loss: A review. *The Journal of School Health, 77,* 225–231.

Danilova, V., & Hellekant, G. (2006). Elucidating coding of taste qualities with the taste modifier miraculin in the common marmoset. *Brain Research Bulletin, 68,* 315–321.

Davidoff, J., Davies, I., & Roberson, D. (1999). Colour categories in a stone-age tribe. *Nature, 398*(6724), 203–204.

Davies, W. L., Carvalho, L. S., Cowing, J. A., Beazley, L. D., Hunt, D. M., & Arrese, C. A. (2007). Visual pigments of the platypus: A novel route to mammalian colour vision. *Current Biology, 17,* R161–163.

Day, R. H. (1993). The Ames room from another viewpoint. *Perception, 22,* 1007–1011.

Day, R. H. (2006). Two principles of perception revealed by geometrical illusions. *Australian Journal of Psychology, 58,* 123–129.

de Araujo, I. E., Rolls, E. T., Velazco, M. I., Margot, C., & Cayeux, I. (2005). Cognitive modulation of olfactory processing. *Neuron, 46,* 671–679.

De Casper, A. J., & Spencer, M. J. (1986). Prenatal maternal speech influences newborns' perception of speech sounds. *Infant Behavior & Development, 9,* 133–150.

de Cheveigné, A. (2005). Pitch perception models. In C. J. Plack, A. J. Oxenham, R. R. Fay, & A. N. Popper (Eds.), *Pitch: Neural coding and perception* (pp. 169–233). New York: Springer.

de Fockert, J., Davidoff, J., Fagot, J., Parron, C., & Goldstein, J. (2007). More accurate size contrast judgments in the Ebbinghaus Illusion by a remote culture. *Journal of Experimental Psychology: Human Perception & Performance, 33,* 738–742.

De Haan, E. H. F. (1999). A familial factor in the development of face recognition deficits. *Journal of Clinical and Experimental Neuropsychology, 21,* 312–315.

de Heering, A., Houthuys, S., & Rossion, B. (2007). Holistic face processing is mature at 4 years of age: Evidence from the composite face effect. *Journal of Experimental Child Psychology, 96,* 57–70.

de Vignemont, F., Tsakiris, M., & Haggard, P. (2006). Body mereology. In G. Knoblich, I. M. Thornton, M. Grosjean, & M. Shiffrar (Eds.), *Human body perception from the inside out* (pp. 147–170). New York: Oxford.

de Villers-Sidani, E., Chang, E. F., Bao, S., & Merzenich, M. M. (2007). Critical period window for spectral tuning defined in the primary auditory cortex (A1) in the rat. *Journal of Neuroscience, 27,* 180–189.

de Wit, T. C. J., Bauer, M., Oostenveld, R., Fries, P., & van Lier, R. (2006). Cortical responses to contextual influences in amodal completion. *Neuroimage, 32,* 1815–1825.

DeBello, W. M., & Knudsen, E. I. (2004). Multiple sites of adaptive plasticity in the owl's auditory localization pathway. *Journal of Neuroscience, 24*, 6853–6861.

Dedrick, D. (2006). Explanation(s) and the petterning of basic colour words across languages and speakers. In N. J. Pitchford & C. P. Biggam (Eds.), *Progress in colour studies: Vol. 2, Psychological aspects* (Vol. 2, pp. 1–12). Philadelphia: John Benjamin.

Dehaene-Lambertz, G., Dehaene, S., & Hertz-Pannier, L. (2002). Functional neuroimaging of speech perception in infants. *Science, 298*(5600), 2013–2015.

Dehaene-Lambertz, G., Hertz-Pannier, L., & Dubois, J. (2006). Nature and nurture in language acquisition: anatomical and functional brain-imaging studies in infants. *Trends in Neurosciences, 29*, 367–373.

Dehaene-Lambertz, G., Mehler, J., & Pena, M. (2001). Cerebral bases of language aquisition. In A. F. Kalverboer & A. Gramsbergen (Eds.), *Handbook of brain and behaviour in human development* (pp. 939–966). Boston: Kluwer.

Delahunt, P. B., Webster, M. A., Ma, L., & Werner, J. S. (2004). Long-term renormalization of chromatic mechanisms following cataract surgery. *Visual Neuroscience, 21*, 301–307.

DeLoache, J. S., Pierroutsakos, S. L., & Uttal, D. H. (2003). The origins of pictorial competence. *Current Directions in Psychological Science, 12*, 114–118.

Delwiche, J. F. (2003). Impact of color on perceived wine flavor. *Foods and Food Ingredients Journal, 208*, 349–352.

Delwiche, J. F. (2004). The impact of perceptual interactions on perceived flavor. *Food Quality and Preference, 15*, 137–146.

Dennett, D. C. (1978). Where am I? In D. C. Dennett (Ed.), *Brainstorms* (pp. 310–323). Cambridge, MA: MIT Press.

Denzinger, A., Kalko, E. K. V., & Jones, G. (2004). Ecological and evolutionary aspects of echolocation in bats. In J. A. Thomas, C. F. Moss, & M. Vater (Eds.), *Echolocation in bats and dolphins* (pp. 311–326). Chicago: University of Chicago.

Der, G., & Deary, I. J. (2006). Age and sex differences in reaction time in adulthood: Results from the United Kingdom Health and Lifestyle Survey. *Psychology and Aging, 21*, 62–73.

Deutsch, D. (1986). A musical paradox. *Music Perception, 3*, 275–280.

Deutsch, D. (1987, March). Illusions for stereo headphones. *Audio, 71*, 36–48.

Deutsch, D. (1991). The tritone paradox: An influence of language on music perception. *Music Perception, 8*, 335–347.

Deutsch, D. (1995). Musical illusions and paradoxes [CD]. La Jolla, CA: Philomel Records.

Deutsch, D. (1997). The tritone paradox: A link between music and speech. *Current Directions in Psychological Science, 6*, 174–180.

Deutsch, D. (1999a). Grouping mechanisms in music. In D. Deutsch (Ed.), *The psychology of music* (2nd ed., pp. 99–134). New York: Academic.

Deutsch, D. (1999b). The processing of pitch combinations. In D. Deutsch (Ed.), *The psychology of music* (pp. 349–411). San Diego: Academic.

Deutsch, D. (2004). The octave illusion revisited again. *Journal of Experimental Psychology: Human Perception & Performance, 30*, 355–364.

Deutsch, D. (2006). The enigma of absolute pitch. *Acoustics Today, 2*, 11–19.

Deutsch, D. (2007). Mothers and their offspring perceive the tritone paradox in closely similar ways. *Archives of Acoustics, 32*, 3–14.

Deutsch, D. (2008). Musical illusions. In L. Squire (Ed.), *Encyclopedia of neuroscience*. New York: Elsevier.

Deutsch, D., Henthorn, T., & Dolson, M. (2004a). Absolute pitch, speech, and tone language: Some experiments and a proposed framework. *Music Perception, 21*, 339–356.

Deutsch, D., Henthorn, T., & Dolson, M. (2004b). Speech patterns heard early in life influence later perception of the tritone paradox. *Music Perception, 21*, 357–372.

Diehl, R. L., Lotto, A. J., & Holt, L. L. (2004). Speech perception. *Annual Review of Psychology, 55*, 149–179.

Djordjevic, J., Lundstrom, J. N., Clement, F., Boyle, J. A., Pouliot, S., & Jones-Gotman, M. (2008). A rose by any other name: Would it smell as sweet? *Journal of Neurophysiology, 99*, 386–393.

Dobie, R. A. (2007). Folate supplementation and age-related hearing loss. *Annals of Internal Medicine, 146*, 63–64.

Donderi, D. C. (2006). Visual complexity: A review. *Psychological Bulletin, 132*, 73–97.

Dooling, R. J., Best, C. T., & Brown, S. D. (1995). Discrimination of synthetic full-formant and sinewave/ra-la/continua by budgerigars (Melopsittacus undulatus) and zebra finches (Taeniopygia guttata). *Journal of the Acoustical Society of America, 97*, 1839–1846.

Doop, M., Mohr, C., Folley, B., Brewer, W. J., & Park, S. (2006). Olfaction and memory. In W. J. Brewer, D. Castle & C. Pantelis (Eds.), *Olfaction and the brain* (pp. 65–82). New York: Cambridge.

Doty, R. L. (2003). Mammalian pheromones: Fact or fantasy? In R. L. Doty (Ed.), *Handbook of olfaction and gustation* (pp. 345–383). New York: Marcel Dekket.

Doty, R. L. (2006). Assessment of olfaction. In W. J. Brewer, D. Castle, & C. Pantelis (Eds.), *Olfaction and the brain* (pp. 235–258). New York: Cambridge.

Doty, R. L., & Laing, D. G. (2003). Psychophysical measurement of human olfactory function, including odorant mixture assessment. In R. L. Doty (Ed.), *Handbook of olfaction and gustation* (pp. 203–228). New York: Marcel Dekker.

Doty, R. L., Saito, K., & Bromley, S. M. (2008). Disorders of taste and smell. In A. I. Basbaum, M. C. Bushnell, D. V. Smith, G. K. Beauchamp, S. J. Firestein, P. Dallos, D. Oertel, R. H. Masland, T. D. Albright, J. H. Kaas, & E. P.

Gardner (Eds.), *The senses: A comprehensive reference* (Vol. 4, pp. 859–887). New York: Academic Press.

Dowling, J. E., & Boycott, B. B. (1966). Organization of the primate retina: Electron microscopy. *Proceedings of the Royal Society of London, Series B, 166*, 80–111.

Dowling, W. J. (1973). The perception of interleaved melodies. *Cognitive Psychology, 5*, 372–377.

Dowling, W. J. (2001). Perception of music. In E. B. Goldstein (Ed.), *Blackwell handbook of perception* (pp. 469–498). Malden, MA: Blackwell.

Dowling, W. J. (2002). The development of music perception and cognition. In D. J. Levitin (Ed.), *Foundations of cognitive psychology: Core readings* (pp. 481–502). Cambridge, MA: MIT Press.

Drivonikou, G. V., Kay, P., Regier, T., Ivry, R. B., Gilbert, A. I., Franklin, A., et al. (2007). Further evidence that Whorfian effects are stronger in the right visual field than the left. *Proceedings of the National Academy of Sciences of the USA, 104*, 1097–1102.

Dubno, J. R., & Mills, J. H. (2003). Presbyacusis. In R. D. Kent (Ed.), *The MIT encyclopedia of communication disorders* (pp. 527–530). Cambridge, MA: MIT Press.

DuBois, G. E., DeSimone, J., & Lyall, V. (2008). Chemistry of gustatory stimuli. In A. I. Basbaum, M. C. Bushnell, D. V. Smith, G. K. Beauchamp, S. J. Firestein, P. Dallos, D. Oertel, R. H. Masland, T. D. Albright, J. H. Kaas, & E. P. Gardner (Eds.), *The senses: A comprehensive reference* (Vol. 4, pp. 27–74). New York: Academic Press.

Duchaine, B. C., & Nakayama, K. (2005). Dissociations of face and object recognition in developmental prosopagnosia. *Journal of Cognitive Neuroscience, 17*, 249–261.

Duchaine, B. C., & Nakayama, K. (2006). Developmental prosopagnosia: A window to content-specific face processing. *Current Opinion in Neurobiology, 16*, 166–173.

Duchaine, B. C., & Yovel, G. (2008). Face recognition. In A. I. Basbaum, M. C. Bushnell, D. V. Smith, G. K. Beauchamp, S. J. Firestein, P. Dallos, D. Oertel, R. H. Masland, T. D. Albright, J. H. Kaas, & E. P. Gardner (Eds.), *The senses: A comprehensive reference* (Vol. 2, pp. 330–352). New York: Academic Press.

Duncker, K. (1929). Uber induzierts Bewegung. *Psychologische Forschung, 12*, 180–259.

Durand, J. B., Celebrini, S., & Trotter, Y. (2007). Neural bases of stereopsis across visual field of the alert macaque monkey. *Cerebral Cortex, 17*, 1260–1273.

Durgin, F. H., Evans, L., Dunphy, N., Klostermann, S., & Simmons, K. (2007). Rubber hands feel the touch of light. *Psychological Science, 18*, 152–157.

Easterbrook, M. A., Kisilevsky, B. S., Hains, S. M. J., & Muir, D. W. (1999). Faceness or complexity: Evidence from newborn visual tracking of facelike stimuli. *Infant Behavior & Development, 22*, 17–35.

Easterbrook, M. A., Kisilevsky, B. S., Muir, D. W., & Laplante, D. P. (1999). Newborns discriminate schematic faces from scrambled faces. *Canadian Journal of Experimental Psychology, 53*, 231–241.

Ebert, J., & Westhoff, G. (2006). Behavioural examination of the infrared sensitivity of rattlesnakes (Crotalus atrox). *Journal of Comparative Physiology, 192*, 941–947.

Edut, S., & Eilam, D. (2003). Rodents in open space adjust their behavioral response to the different risk levels during barn-owl attack. *BMC Ecology, 3*, 10.

Edut, S., & Eilam, D. (2004). Protean behavior under barn-owl attack: Voles alternate between freezing and fleeing and spiny mice flee in alternating patterns. *Behavioural Brain Research, 155*, 207–216.

Eggermont, J. J. (2005). Tinnitus: Neurobiological substrates. *Drug Discovery Today, 10*, 1283–1290.

Eggermont, J. J., & Roberts, L. E. (2004). The neuroscience of tinnitus. *Trends in Neurosciences, 27*, 676–682.

Eimas, P. D., & Corbit, J. D. (1973). Selective adaptation of linguistic feature detectors. *Cognitive Psychology, 4*, 99–109.

Eimas, P. D., & Miller, J. L. (1992). Organization in the perception of speech by young infants. *Psychological Science, 3*, 340–345.

Eimas, P. D., Siqueland, E. R., Jusczyk, R., & Vigorito, J. (1971). Speech perception in infants. *Science, 171*, 303–306.

Eklöf, J. (2003). *Vision in echolocating bats.* Unpublished doctoral, Göteborg University.

Ekman, P., & O'Sullivan, M. (1991). Who can catch a liar? *American Psychologist, 46*, 913–920.

Ekman, P., O'Sullivan, M., & Frank, M. G. (1999). A few can catch a liar. *Psychological Science, 10*, 263–266.

Ekroll, V. (2005). *On the nature of simultaneous color contrast.* Christian-Albrechts-Universität zu Kiel, Kiel, Germany.

Ekroll, V., Faul, F., & Niederee, R. (2004). The peculiar nature of simultaneous colour contrast in uniform surrounds. *Vision Research, 44*, 1765–1786.

Ekroll, V., Faul, F., Niederee, R., & Richter, E. (2002). The natural center of chromaticity space is not always achromatic: A new look at color induction. *Proceedings of the National Academy of Sciences of the USA, 99*, 13352–13356.

Engbert, R., & Kliegl, R. (2004). Microsaccades keep the eyes' balance during fixation. *Psycholological Science, 15*, 431–436.

Enns, J. T., & Austen, E. (2007). Mental schemata and the limits of perception. In M. A. Peterson, B. Gillam, & H. A. Sedgwick (Eds.), *In the mind's eye: Julian Hochberg on the perception of pictures, films, and the world* (pp. 439–447). New York: Oxford.

Epstein, M., & Florentine, M. (2006). Loudness of brief tones measured by magnitude estimation and loudness matching. *Journal of the Acoustical Society of America, 119*, 1943–1945.

Ernestus, M., Baayen, H., & Schreuder, R. (2002). The recognition of reduced word forms. *Brain and Language, 81*, 162–173.

Ernst, M. O., & Newell, F. N. (2007). Multisensory recognition of actively explored objects. *Canadian Journal of Experimental Psychology, 61*, 242–253.

Espinoza-Varas, B., & Watson, C. S. (1989). Perception of complex auditory patterns by humans. In R. J. Dooling & S. H. Hulse (Eds.), *The comparative psychology of audition: Perceiving complex sounds* (pp. 67–94). Hillsdale, NJ: Erlbaum.

Esterman, M., Prinzmetal, W., & Robertson, L. (2004). Categorization influences illusory conjunctions. *Psychonomic Bulletin & Review, 11*, 681–686.

Esterman, M., Verstynen, T., & Robertson, L. C. (2007). Attenuating illusory binding with TMS of the right parietal cortex. *Neuroimage, 35*, 1247–1255.

Evans, G. W., & Hygge, S. (2007). Noise and cognitive performance in children and adults. In L. Luxon & D. Prasher (Eds.), *Noise and its effects* (pp. 549–566). Chichester, England: Wiley.

Everdell, I. T., Marsh, H., Yurick, M. D., Munhall, K. G., & Paré, M. (2007). Gaze behaviour in audiovisual speech perception: Asymmetrical distribution of face-directed fixations. *Perception, 36*, 1535–1545.

Everest, F. A. (2001). *Master handbook of acoustics*. New York: McGraw-Hill.

Fain, G. L. (2003). *Sensory transduction*. Sunderland, MA: Sinauer.

Fantz, R. L. (1958). Pattern vision in young infants. *The Psychological Record, 8*, 43–47.

Fantz, R. L. (1961). The origin of form perception. *Scientific American, 204*, 66–72.

Farah, M. J. (2004). *Visual agnosia: Disorders of object recognition and what they tell us about normal vision* (2nd ed.). Cambridge, MA: MIT Press.

Farroni, T., Csibra, G., Simion, F., & Johnson, M. H. (2002). Eye contact detection in humans from birth. *Proceedings of the National Academy of Sciences of the USA, 99*, 9602–9605.

Farroni, T., Johnson, M. H., Menon, E., Zulian, L., Faraguna, D., & Csibra, G. (2005). Newborns' preference for face-relevant stimuli: Effects of contrast polarity. *Proceedings of the National Academy of Sciences of the USA, 102*(47), 17245–17250.

Farroni, T., Massaccesi, S., Menon, E., & Johnson, M. H. (2007). Direct gaze modulates face recognition in young infants. *Cognition, 102*, 396–404.

Farroni, T., Menon, E., & Johnson, M. H. (2006). Factors influencing newborns' preference for faces with eye contact. *Journal of Experimental Child Psychology, 95*, 298–308.

Farroni, T., Menon, E., Rigato, S., & Johnson, M. H. (2007). The perception of facial expressions in newborns. *European Journal of Developmental Psychology, 4*, 2–13.

Fast, K., Duffy, V. B., & Bartoshuk, L. M. (2002). New psychophysical insights in evaluating genetic variation in taste. In C. Rouby, B. Schaal, D. Dubois, R. Gervais, & A. Holley (Eds.), *Olfaction, taste, and cognition* (pp. 391–407). New York: Cambridge.

Fastl, H., & Zwicker, E. (2007). *Psychoacoustics: Facts and models* (3rd ed.). New York: Springer.

Faurion, A., Kobayakawa, T., & Cerf-Ducastel, B. (2008). Functional magnetic resonance imaging study of taste. In A. I. Basbaum, M. C. Bushnell, D. V. Smith, G. K. Beauchamp, S. J. Firestein, P. Dallos, D. Oertel, R. H. Masland, T. D. Albright, J. H. Kaas, & E. P. Gardner (Eds.), *The senses: A comprehensive reference* (Vol. 4, pp. 271–279). New York: Academic Press.

Fechner, G. T. (1860). *Element der psychophysik*. Leipzig: Breitkopf & Harterl.

Fenske, M. J., Aminoff, E., Gronau, N., & Bar, M. (2006). Top-down facilitation of visual object recognition: Object-based and context-based contributions. *Progress in Brain Research, 155*, 3–21.

Fenton, M. B. (2004). Aerial-feeding bats: Getting the most out of echolocation. In J. A. Thomas, C. F. Moss, & M. Vater (Eds.), *Echolocation in bats and dolphins* (pp. 350–355). Chicago: University of Chicago.

Ferket, P. R., & Gernat, A. G. (2006). Factors that affect feed intake of meat birds: A review. *International Journal of Poultry Science, 5*, 905–911.

Fernandez, J. M., & Farell, B. (2005). Seeing motion in depth using inter-ocular velocity differences. *Vision Research, 45*, 2786–2798.

Fettiplace, R., & Ricci, A. J. (2006). Mechanoelectrical transduction in auditory hair cells. In R. A. Eatock, R. R. Fay, & A. N. Popper (Eds.), *Vertebrate hair cells* (Vol. 27, pp. 154–203). New York: Springer.

Field, T. (2007). Massage therapy research. *Developmental Review, 27*, 75–89.

Field, T., Diego, M. A., Hernandez-Reif, M., Deeds, O., & Figuereido, B. (2006). Moderate versus light pressure massage therapy leads to greater weight gain in preterm infants. *Infant Behavior & Development, 29*, 574–578.

Field, T., Hernandez-Reif, M., & Diego, M. (2006). Newborns of depressed mothers who received moderate versus light pressure massage during pregnancy. *Infant Behavior & Development, 29*, 54–58.

Fillingim, R. B. (2008). Sex, gender, and pain. In A. I. Basbaum, M. C. Bushnell, D. V. Smith, G. K. Beauchamp, S. J. Firestein, P. Dallos, D. Oertel, R. H. Masland, T. D. Albright, J. H. Kaas, & E. P. Gardner (Eds.), *The senses: A comprehensive reference* (Vol. 5, pp. 253–257). New York: Academic Press.

Findlay, J. M., & Gilchrist, I. D. (2003). *Active vision: The psychology of looking and seeing*. New York: Oxford.

Fine, I., Wade, A. R., Brewer, A. A., May, M. G., Goodman, D. F., Boynton, G. M., et al. (2003). Long-term deprivation affects visual perception and cortex. *Nature Neuroscience, 6*, 915–916.

Finlay, B. L., Clancy, B., & Kingsbury, M. A. (2003). The developmental neurobiology of early vision. In S. P. Johnson & B. Hopkins (Eds.), *Advances in infancy research* (pp. 1–42). Greenwich, CT: Ablex.

Finney, E. M., Fine, I., & Dobkins, K. R. (2001). Visual stimuli activate auditory cortex in the deaf. *Nature Neuroscience, 4*, 1171–1173.

Firzlaff, U., Schuchmann, M., Grunwald, J. E., Schuller, G., & Wiegrebe, L. (2007). Object-oriented echo perception and cortical representation in echolocating bats. *PLoS Biology, 5*, e100.

Fleming, R. W., Torralba, A., & Adelson, E. H. (2004). Specular reflections and the perception of shape. *Journal of Vision, 4*, 798–820.

Fletcher, H., & Munson, W. A. (1933). Loudness, its definition, measurement, and calculation. *Journal of the Acoustical Society of America, 5*, 82–108.

Flor, H. (2008). Phantom limb pain. In A. I. Basbaum, M. C. Bushnell, D. V. Smith, G. K. Beauchamp, S. J. Firestein, P. Dallos, D. Oertel, R. H. Masland, T. D. Albright, J. H. Kaas, & E. P. Gardner (Eds.), *The senses: A comprehensive reference* (Vol. 5, pp. 699–706). New York: Academic Press.

Flor, H., & Bushnell, M. C. (2005). Central imaging of pain. In S. P. Hunt & M. Koltzenberg (Eds.), *The neurobiology of pain (molecular and cellular neurobiology)* (pp. 311–331). New York: Oxford.

Flor, H., Nikolajsen, L., & Jensen, T. S. (2006). Phantom limb pain: A case of maladaptive CNS plasticity? *Nature Reviews Neuroscience, 7*, 873–881.

Fodor, J. A. (1983). *The modularity of mind.* Cambridge, MA: MIT Press.

Foley, J. M., Ribeiro-Filho, N. P., & Da Silva, J. A. (2004). Visual perception of extent and the geometry of visual space. *Vision Research, 44*, 147–156.

Foley, M. A., Foley, H. J., & Korenman, L. M. (2002). Adapting a memory framework (source monitoring) to the study of closure processes. *Memory & Cognition, 30*, 412–422.

Foley, M. A., Foley, H. J., Scheye, R., & Bonacci, A. M. (2007). Remembering more than meets the eye: A study of memory confusions about incomplete visual information. *Memory, 15*, 616–633.

Foster, D. H. (2003). Does colour constancy exist? *Trends in Cognitive Sciences, 7*, 439–443.

Foster, D. H. (2008). Color appearance. In A. I. Basbaum, M. C. Bushnell, D. V. Smith, G. K. Beauchamp, S. J. Firestein, P. Dallos, D. Oertel, R. H. Masland, T. D. Albright, J. H. Kaas, & E. P. Gardner (Eds.), *The senses: A comprehensive reference* (Vol. 2, pp. 119–132). New York: Academic.

Fowler, C. A. (2003). Speech production and perception. In A. F. Healy & R. W. Proctor (Eds.), *Handbook of psychology: Experimental psychology* (Vol. 4, pp. 237–266). Hoboken, NJ: Wiley.

Fowler, C. A., & Galantucci, B. (2005). The relation of speech perception and speech production. In D. B. Pisoni & R. E. Remez (Eds.), *The handbook of speech perception* (pp. 633–652). Malden, MA: Blackwell.

Foxton, J. M., Dean, J. L., Gee, R., Peretz, I., & Griffiths, T. D. (2004). Characterization of deficits in pitch perception underlying "tone deafness." *Brain, 127*, 801–810.

Francis, G., & Cho, Y. S. (2008). Effects of temporal integration on the shape of visual backward masking functions. *Journal of Experimental Psychology: Human Perception & Performance, 34*, 1116–1128.

Franklin, A., Clifford, A., Williamson, E., & Davies, I. R. L. (2005). Color term knowledge does not affect categorical perception of color in toddlers. *Journal of Experimental Child Psychology, 90*, 114–141.

Franklin, A., & Davies, I. R. L. (2004). New evidence for infant colour categories. *British Journal of Developmental Psychology, 22*, 349–377.

Franklin, A., & Davies, I. R. L. (2006). Converging evidence for pre-linguistic colour categorisation. In C. P. Biggam & N. J. Pitchford (Eds.), *Progress in colour studies: Vol. 2, Psychological aspects* (Vol. 2, pp. 101–120). Philadelphia: John Benjamins.

Franklin, A., Drivonikou, G. V., Bevis, L., Davies, I. R. L., Kay, P., & Regier, T. (2008). Categorical perception of color is lateralized to the right hemisphere in infants, but to the left hemisphere in adults. *Proceedings of the National Academy of Sciences of the USA, 105*, 3221–3225.

Freire, A., Lewis, T. L., Maurer, D., & Blake, R. (2006). The development of sensitivity to biological motion in noise. *Perception, 35*, 647–657.

Frishman, L. J. (2001). Basic visual processes. In E. B. Goldstein (Ed.), *Blackwell handbook of perception* (pp. 53–91). Malden, MA: Blackwell.

Fujioka, T., Trainor, L. J., Ross, B., Kakigi, R., & Pantev, C. (2004). Musical training enhances automatic encoding of melodic contour and interval structure. *Journal of Cognitive Neuroscience, 16*, 1010–1021.

Furness, D. N., & Hackney, C. M. (2006). The structure and composition of the stereociliary bundle of vertebrate hair cells. In R. A. Eatock, R. R. Fay, & A. N. Popper (Eds.), *Vertebrate hair cells* (Vol. 27, pp. 95–153). New York: Springer.

Galanter, E. (1962). Contemporary psychophysics. In R. Brown, E. Galanter, E. H. Hess, & G. Mandler (Eds.), *New directions in psychology* (pp. 87–156). New York: Holt, Rinehart and Winston.

Galantucci, B., Fowler, C. A., & Turvey, M. T. (2006). The motor theory of speech perception reviewed. *Psychonomic Bulletin & Review, 13*, 361–377.

Garcia, J., & Koelling, R. A. (1966). Relation of cue to consequence in avoidance learning. *Psychonomic Science, 4*, 123–124.

Garcia, J., Lasiter, P. S., Bermudez-Rattoni, F., & Deems, D. A. (1985). A general theory of aversion learning. *Annals of the New York Academy of Science, 443*, 8–21.

Garcia, M. K., & Chiang, J. S. (2007). Acupuncture. In S. D. Waldman (Ed.), *Pain management* (pp. 1093–1105). Phildelphia: Saunders.

Garcia-Falgueras, A., Junque, C., Gimenez, M., Caldu, X., Segovia, S., & Guillamon, A. (2006). Sex differences in the human olfactory system. *Brain Research, 1116*, 103–111.

Gardner, M. (1988). *Perplexing puzzles and tantalizing teasers.* New York: Dover.

Gaschler, K. (2006). One person, one neuron? *Scientific American Mind, 17*, 77–82.

Gatchel, R. J. (1999). Perspectives on pain: A historical overview. In R. J. Gatchel & D. C. Turk (Eds.), *Psychosocial factors in pain: Critical perspectives* (pp. 3–17). New York: Guilford.

Gauthier, I., & Bukach, C. (2007). Should we reject the expertise hypothesis? *Cognition, 103*, 322–330.

Gegenfurtner, K. R. (2003). Cortical mechanisms of colour vision. *Nature Reviews Neuroscience, 4*, 563–572.

Gegenfurtner, K. R., & Kiper, D. C. (2003). Color vision. *Annual Review of Neuroscience, 26*, 181–206.

Geisbauer, G., Griebel, U., Schmid, A., & Timney, B. (2004). Brightness discrimination and neutral point testing in the horse. *Canadian Journal of Zoology, 82*, 660–670.

Gelb, A. (1929). Die "Farbenkonstanz" der Sehding. *Handbuch der normalen and pathologischen Physiologie, 12*, 594–678.

Geldart, S., Mondloch, C. J., Maurer, D., de Schonen, S., & Brent, H. P. (2002). The effect of early visual deprivation on the development of face processing. *Developmental Science, 5*, 490–501.

Georgieva, S. S., Todd, J. T., Peeters, R., & Orban, G. A. (2008). The extraction of 3D shape from texture and shading in the human brain. *Cerebral Cortex, 18*, 2416–2438.

Gerardin, P., de Montalembert, M., & Mamassian, P. (2007). Shape from shading: New perspectives from the Polo Mint stimulus. *Journal of Vision, 7* (11), 13, 1–11.

Gerken, L., & Aslin, R. N. (2005). Thirty years of research on infant speech perception: The legacy of Peter W. Jusczyk. *Language Learning and Development, 1*, 5–21.

Gescheider, G. A. (1985). *Psychophysics: Method, theory, and application* (2nd ed.). Hillsdale, NJ: Erlbaum.

Gescheider, G. A. (1997). *Psychophysics: The fundamentals* (3rd ed.). Mahwah, NJ: Erlbaum.

Giaschi, D. (2006). The processing of motion-defined form. In M. R. M. Jenkin & L. R. Harris (Eds.), *Seeing spatial form* (pp. 101–119). New York: Oxford.

Gibson, B. S., & Peterson, M. A. (1994). Does orientation-independent object recognition precede orientation-dependent recognition? Evidence from a cuing paradigm. *Journal of Experimental Psychology: Human Perception & Performance, 20*, 299–316.

Gibson, E. J. (1987). Introductory essay: What does infant perception tell us about theories of perception? *Journal of Experimental Psychology: Human Perception & Performance, 13*, 515–523.

Gibson, E. J., & Walk, R. D. (1960). The "visual cliff." *Scientific American, 202*, 64–71.

Gibson, J. J. (1950). *The perception of the visual world.* Boston: Houghton Mifflin.

Gibson, J. J. (1959). Perception as a function of stimulation. In S. Koch (Ed.), *Psychology: A study of a science* (Vol. 1, pp. 456–501). New York: McGraw-Hill.

Gibson, J. J. (1962). Observations on active touch. *Psychological Review, 69*, 477–491.

Gibson, J. J. (1966). *The senses considered as perceptual systems.* Boston: Houghton Mifflin.

Gibson, J. J. (1979). *The ecological approach to visual perception.* Boston: Houghton Mifflin.

Gilad, Y., Bustamante, C. D., Lancet, D., & Paabo, S. (2003). Natural selection on the olfactory receptor gene family in humans and chimpanzees. *American Journal of Human Genetics, 73*, 489–501.

Gilbert, A. L., Regier, T., Kay, P., & Ivry, R. B. (2006). Whorf hypothesis is supported in the right visual field but not the left. *Proceedings of the National Academy of Sciences of the USA, 103*, 489–494.

Gilbert, A. N. (2008). *What the nose knows: The science of scent in everyday life.* New York: Crown.

Gilchrist, A. (1977). Perceived lightness depends on perceived spatial arrangement. *Science, 195*, 185–187.

Gilchrist, A. (1980). When does perceived lightness depend on perceived spatial arrangement? *Perception & Psychophysics, 28*, 527–538.

Gilchrist, A. (2005). Lightness perception: Seeing one color through another. *Current Biology, 15*, R330–332.

Gilchrist, A. (2006). *Seeing black and white.* New York: Oxford.

Gilchrist, A., Kossyfidis, C., Bonato, F., Agostini, T., Cataliotti, J., Li, X., et al. (1999). An anchoring theory of lightness perception. *Psychological Review, 106*, 795–834.

Gillam, B. (1998). Illusions at century's end. In J. Hochberg (Ed.), *Perception and cognition at century's end* (pp. 95–136). San Diego, CA: Academic.

Gillam, B. (2007). Stereopsis and motion parallax. *Perception, 36*, 953–954.

Gillam, B., & Nakayama, K. (2002). Subjective contours at line terminations depend on scene layout analysis, not image processing. *Journal of Experimental Psychology: Human Perception & Performance, 28*, 43–53.

Girard, B., & Berthoz, A. (2005). From brainstem to cortex: Computational models of saccade generation circuitry. *Progress in Neurobiology, 77*, 215–251.

Glass, J. M. (2007). Visual function and cognitive aging: Differential role of contrast sensitivity in verbal versus spatial tasks. *Psychology and Aging, 22*, 233–238.

Glasser, A. (2006). Accommodation: Mechanism and measurement. *Ophthalmology Clinics of North America, 19*, 1–12.

Glasser, A., Croft, M. A., & Kaufman, P. L. (2001). Aging of the human crystalline lens and presbyopia. *International Ophthalmology Clinics, 41*, 1–15.

Glezer, I. L., Hof, P., Morgane, P. J., Fridman, A., Isakova, T., Joseph, D., et al. (2004). Chemical neuroanatomy of the inferior colliculus in brains of echolocating and nonecholocating mammals: Immunocytochemical study. In J. A. Thomas, C. F. Moss, & M. Vater (Eds.), *Echolocation in bats and dolphins* (pp. 161–172). Chicago: University of Chicago.

Glickstein, M. (1988). The discovery of the visual cortex. *Scientific American, 259*, 118–127.

Goffaux, V., & Rossion, B. (2007). Face inversion disproportionately impairs the perception of vertical but not horizontal relations between features. *Journal of Experimental Psychology: Human Perception & Performance, 33*, 995–1002.

Gogel, W. C. (1993). The analysis of perceived space. In S. C. Masin (Ed.), *Foundations of perceptual theory* (pp. 113–182). New York: Elsevier.

Gold, J. M., Tadin, D., Cook, S. C., & Blake, R. (2008). The efficiency of biological motion perception. *Perception & Psychophysics, 70*, 88–95.

Gold, T. (1948). Hearing II. The physical basis of the action of the cochlea. *Proceedings of the Royal Society of London, Series B, 135*, 492–498.

Gold, T. (1989). Historical background to the proposal, 40 years ago, of an active model for cochlear frequency analysis. In J. P. Wilson & D. T. Kemp (Eds.), *Cochlear mechanisms: Structure, function, and models* (pp. 299–305). New York: Plenum.

Gold, T., & Pumphrey, R. J. (1948). Hearing I. The cochlea as a frequency analyzer. *Proceedings of the Royal Society of London, Series B, 135*, 462–491.

Goldsmith, T. H. (2006). What birds see. *Scientific American, 295*, 69–75.

Goldstein, E. B. (2001). Pictorial perception and art. In E. B. Goldstein (Ed.), *Blackwell handbook of perception* (pp. 344–378). Malden, MA: Blackwell.

Good, K. P., & Kopala, L. (2006). Sex differences and olfactory function. In W. J. Brewer, D. Castle, & C. Pantelis (Eds.), *Olfaction and the brain* (pp. 183–202). New York: Cambridge.

Goodwin, A. W., & Wheat, H. E. (2004). Sensory signals in neural populations underlying tactile perception and manipulation. *Annual Review of Neuroscience, 27*, 53–77.

Gordon, I. E. (2004). *Theories of visual perception* (3rd ed.). New York: Psychology Press.

Gordon, I. E., & Slater, A. (1998). Nativism and empiricism: The history of two ideas. In A. Slater (Ed.), *Perceptual development: Visual, auditory, and speech perception in infancy* (pp. 73–103). Hove, UK: Psychology Press.

Goren, C. C., Sarty, M., & Wu, P. Y. K. (1975). Visual following and pattern discrimination of face-like stimuli by newborn infants. *Pediatrics, 56*, 544–549.

Gottfried, J. A. (2006). Smell: Central nervous processing. *Advances in Oto-Rhino-Laryngology, 63*, 44–69.

Gougoux, F., Lepore, F., Lassonde, M., Voss, P., Zatorre, R. J., & Belin, P. (2004). Neuropsychology: Pitch discrimination in the early blind. *Nature, 430*(6997), 309.

Goutcher, R., & Mamassian, P. (2005). Selective biasing of stereo correspondence in an ambiguous stereogram. *Vision Research, 45*, 469–483.

Goutcher, R., & Mamassian, P. (2006). Temporal dynamics of stereo correspondence bi-stability. *Vision Research, 46*, 3575–3585.

Gracely, R. H., & Eliav, E. (2008). Psychophysics of pain. In A. I. Basbaum, M. C. Bushnell, D. V. Smith, G. K. Beauchamp, S. J. Firestein, P. Dallos, D. Oertel, R. H. Masland, T. D. Albright, J. H. Kaas, & E. P. Gardner (Eds.), *The senses: A comprehensive reference* (Vol. 5, pp. 927–959). New York: Academic Press.

Gracely, R. H., Farrell, M. J., & Grant, M. A. B. (2002). Temperature and pain perception. In H. Pashler & S. Yantis (Eds.), *Stevens' handbook of experimental psychology* (3rd ed., pp. 619–651). Hoboken, NJ: Wiley.

Graham, C. H., & Hsia, Y. (1958). Color defect and color theory. *Science, 127*, 675–682.

Grainger, J., Bouttevin, S., Truc, C., Bastien, M., & Ziegler, J. (2003). Word superiority, pseudoword superiority, and learning to read: A comparison of dyslexic and normal readers. *Brain and Language, 87*, 432–440.

Grainger, J., Rey, A., & Dufau, S. (2008). Letter perception: From pixels to pandemonium. *Trends in Cognitive Sciences, 12*, 381–387.

Grainger, J., & Whitney, C. (2004). Does the huamn mnid raed wrods as a wlohe? *Trends in Cognitive Sciences, 8*, 58–59.

Granot, R., & Donchin, E. (2002). Do Re Mi Fa Sol La Ti—Constraints, congruity, and musical training: An event-related brain potentials study of musical expectancies. *Music Perception, 19*, 487–528.

Gray, R., Geri, G. A., Akhtar, S. C., & Covas, C. M. (2008). The role of visual occlusion in altitude maintenance during simulated flight. *Journal of Experimental Psychology: Human Perception & Performance, 34*, 475–488.

Gray, R., & Sieffert, R. (2005). Different strategies for using motion-in-depth information in catching. *Journal of Experimental Psychology: Human Perception & Performance, 31*, 1004–1022.

Gredebäck, G., & von Hofsten, C. (2004). Infants' evolving representations of object motion during occlusion: A longitudinal study of 6- to 12-month-old infants. *Infancy, 6*, 165–184.

Green, B. G. (2004). Oral chemesthesis: An integral component of flavour. In A. J. Taylor & D. D. Roberts (Eds.), *Flavor perception* (pp. 151–171). Malden, MA: Blackwell.

Green, D. M. (1987). *Profile analysis: Auditory intensity discrimination*. New York: Oxford.

Green, D. M., & Swets, J. A. (1966). *Signal detection theory and psychophysics*. New York: Wiley.

Greenberg, S. (2006). A multi-tier framework for understanding spoken language. In S. Greenberg & W. A. Ainsworth (Eds.), *Listening to speech: An auditory perspective* (pp. 411–433). Mahwah, NJ: Erlbaum.

Greenberg, S., & Ainsworth, W. A. (2004). Speech processing in the auditory system: An overview. In S. Greenberg, W. A. Ainsworth, R. R. Fay, & A. N. Popper (Eds.), *Speech processing in the auditory system* (Vol. 18, pp. 1–62). New York: Springer.

Greene, M. R., & Oliva, A. (2008). Recognition of natural scenes from global properties: Seeing the forest without representing the trees. *Cognitive Psychology*.

Greeno, J. G. (1994). Gibson's affordances. *Psychological Review, 101*, 336–342.

Greenspan, J. D., Craft, R. M., LeResche, L., Arendt-Nielsen, L., Berkley, K. J., Fillingim, R. B., et al. (2007). Studying sex and gender differences in pain and analgesia: A consensus report. *Pain, 132 Suppl 1*, S26–45.

Greer, C. A., Whitman, M. C., Rela, L., Imamura, F., & Rodriguez Gil, D. (2008). Architecture of the olfactory bulb. In A. I. Basbaum, M. C. Bushnell, D. V. Smith, G. K. Beauchamp, S. J. Firestein, P. Dallos, D. Oertel, R. H. Masland, T. D. Albright, J. H. Kaas, & E. P. Gardner (Eds.), *The senses: A comprehensive reference* (Vol. 4, pp. 623–640). New York: Academic Press.

Gregory, R. L. (1974). *Concepts and mechanisms of perception*. New York: Scribner's.

Gregory, R. L. (1996). *Mirrors in mind*. New York: Oxford.

Gregory, R. L. (1997). *Eye and brain: The psychology of seeing* (5th ed.). Princeton, NJ: Princeton.

Griefahn, B. (2007). Noise and sleep. In L. Luxon & D. Prasher (Eds.), *Noise and its effects* (pp. 567–587). Chichester, England: Wiley.

Griffiths, T. D., & Warren, J. D. (2004). What is an auditory object? *Nature Reviews Neuroscience, 5*, 887–892.

Grill-Spector, K., & Malach, R. (2004). The human visual cortex. *Annual Review of Neuroscience, 27*, 649–677.

Gross, C. G. (2002). Genealogy of the "grandmother cell." *Neuroscientist, 8*, 512–518.

Grossberg, S. (2003). Filling-in the forms: Surface and boundary interactions in visual cortex. In L. Pessoa & P. De Weerd (Eds.), *Filling-in: From perceptual completion to cortical reorganization* (pp. 13–37). New York: Oxford.

Grossman, E. D. (2006). Evidence for a network of brain areas involved in perception of biological motion. In G. Knoblich, I. M. Thornton, M. Grosjean, & M. Shiffrar (Eds.), *Human body perception from the inside out* (pp. 361–384). New York: Oxford.

Guest, S., Grabenhorst, F., Essick, G., Chen, Y., Young, M., McGlone, F., et al. (2007). Human cortical representation of oral temperature. *Physiology & Behavior, 92*, 975–984.

Gulick, W. L., Gescheider, G. A., & Frisina, R. D. (1989). *Hearing: Physiological acoustics, neural coding, and psychoacoustics*. New York: Oxford.

Gutin, J. A. C. (1993). Good vibrations. *Discover, 14*, 44–54.

Gwiazda, J., & Birch, E. E. (2001). Perceptual development: Vision. In E. B. Goldstein (Ed.), *Blackwell handbook of perception* (pp. 636–668). Malden, MA: Blackwell.

Gygi, B., Kidd, G. R., & Watson, C. S. (2004). Spectral-temporal factors in the identification of environmental sounds. *Journal of the Acoustical Society of America, 115*, 1252–1265.

Gygi, B., Kidd, G. R., & Watson, C. S. (2007). Similarity and categorization of environmental sounds. *Perception & Psychophysics, 69*, 839–855.

Hackett, T. A., & Kaas, J. H. (2003). Auditory processing in the primate brain. In M. Gallagher & R. J. Nelson (Eds.), *Handbook of psychology: Biological psychology* (Vol. 3, pp. 187–210). Hoboken, NJ: Wiley.

Haegerstrom-Portnoy, G. (2005). The Glenn A. Fry Award Lecture 2003: Vision in elders—Summary of findings of the SKI study. *Optometry & Vision Science, 82*, 87–93.

Haggard, P. (2006). Sensory neuroscience: From skin to object in the somatosensory cortex. *Current Biology, 16*, R884–886.

Hainline, L. (1998). The development of basic visual abilities. In A. Slater (Ed.), *Perceptual development: Visual, auditory, and speech perception in infancy* (pp. 5-50). Hove, UK: Psychology Press.

Hall, D. A., & Plack, C. J. (2007). The human "pitch center" responds differently to iterated noise and Huggins pitch. *Neuroreport, 18*, 323–327.

Hall, H. (2007). Hypnosis. In S. D. Waldman (Ed.), *Pain management* (Vol. 2, pp. 1021–1024). Philadelphia: W. B. Saunders.

Hallett, P. E. (1986). Eye movements. In K. R. Boff, L. Kaufman, & J. P. Thomas (Eds.), *Handbook of perception and human performance* (pp. 10.11–10.112). New York: Wiley.

Halligan, P. W., Marshall, J. C., & Wade, D. T. (1993). Three arms: A case study of supernumerary phantom limb after right hemisphere stroke. *Journal of Neurology, Neurosurgery, and Psychiatry, 56*, 159–166.

Halpern, B. P. (2002). Taste. In H. Pashler & S. Yantis (Eds.), *Stevens' handbook of experimental psychology* (3rd ed., pp. 653–690). Hoboken, NJ: Wiley.

Hammond, C. J., Andrew, T., Mak, Y. T., & Spector, T. D. (2004). A susceptibility locus for myopia in the normal population is linked to the PAX6 gene region on chromosome 11: A genomewide scan of dizygotic twins. *American Journal of Human Genetics, 75*, 294–304.

Hancock, K. E., & Delgutte, B. (2004). A physiologically based model of interaural time difference discrimination. *Journal of Neuroscience, 24*, 7110–7117.

Handel, S. (1989). *Listening: An introduction to the perception of auditory events.* Cambridge, MA: MIT Press.

Hanke, F. D., Dehnhardt, G., Schaeffel, F., & Hanke, W. (2006). Corneal topography, refractive state, and accommodation in harbor seals (Phoca vitulina). *Vision Research, 46,* 837–847.

Hannon, E. E., & Trainor, L. J. (2007). Music acquisition: Effects of enculturation and formal training on development. *Trends in Cognitive Sciences, 11,* 466–472.

Hannon, E. E., & Trehub, S. E. (2005a). Metrical categories in infancy and adulthood. *Psychological Science, 16,* 48–55.

Hannon, E. E., & Trehub, S. E. (2005b). Tuning in to musical rhythms: Infants learn more readily than adults. *Proceedings of the National Academy of Sciences of the USA, 102,* 12639–12643.

Hansen, T., Olkkonen, M., Walter, S., & Gegenfurtner, K. R. (2006). Memory modulates color appearance. *Nature Neuroscience, 9,* 1367–1368.

Hardy, J. L., Frederick, C. M., Kay, P., & Werner, J. S. (2005). Color naming, lens aging, and grue: What the optics of the aging eye can teach us about color language. *Psychological Science, 16,* 321–327.

Harper, R. A., & Shock, J. P. (2004). Lens. In P. Riordan-Eva, T. Asbury, & J. P. Whitcher (Eds.), *Vaughn & Asbury's general ophthalmology* (16th ed., pp. 173–181). New York: McGraw-Hill Medical.

Harris, A. M., & Aguirre, G. K. (2007). Prosopagnosia. *Current Biology, 17,* R7–8.

Harris, J. M., & German, K. J. (2008). Comparing motion induction in lateral motion and motion in depth. *Vision Research, 48,* 695–702.

Harris, J. P., & Salt, A. N. (2008). Ménière's disease. In A. I. Basbaum, M. C. Bushnell, D. V. Smith, G. K. Beauchamp, S. J. Firestein, P. Dallos, D. Oertel, R. H. Masland, T. D. Albright, J. H. Kaas, & E. P. Gardner (Eds.), *The senses: A comprehensive reference* (Vol. 3, pp. 157–163). New York: Academic Press.

Hartline, H. K., Wagner, H. G., & Ratliff, F. (1956). Inhibition in the eye of Limulus. *Journal of General Physiology, 39,* 651–673.

Harvey, E. M., Dobson, V., Miller, J. M., & Clifford-Donaldson, C. E. (2007). Amblyopia in astigmatic children: Patterns of deficits. *Vision Research, 47,* 315–326.

Harvey, E. M., Dobson, V., Miller, J. M., & Clifford-Donaldson, C. E. (2008). Changes in visual function following optical treatment of astigmatism-related amblyopia. *Vision Research, 48,* 773–787.

Harvey, L. M., Harvey, S. J., Hom, M., Perna, A., & Salib, J. (2006). The use of bloodhounds in determining the impact of genetics and the environment on the expression of human odortype. *Journal of Forensic Sciences, 51,* 1109–1114.

Hayashi, T., Umeda, C., & Cook, N. D. (2007). An fMRI study of the reverse perspective illusion. *Brain Research, 1163,* 72–78.

Hayhoe, M. (2007). Integration of visual information across saccades. In M. A. Peterson, B. Gillam & H. A. Sedgwick (Eds.), *In the mind's eye: Julian Hochberg on the perception of pictures, films, and the world* (pp. 448–453). New York: Oxford.

Hayhoe, M., & Ballard, D. (2005). Eye movements in natural behavior. *Trends in Cognitive Sciences, 9,* 188–194.

Hayhoe, M. M. (2004). Advances in relating eye movements and cognition. *Infancy, 6,* 267–274.

He, D. Z., Jia, S., & Dallos, P. (2003). Prestin and the dynamic stiffness of cochlear outer hair cells. *Journal of Neuroscience, 23,* 9089–9096.

He, D. Z., Zheng, J., Kalinec, F., Kakehata, S., & Santos-Sacchi, J. (2006). Tuning in to the amazing outer hair cell: Membrane wizardry with a twist and shout. *Journal of Membrane Biology, 209,* 119–134.

He, Z. J., Wu, B., Ooi, T. L., Yarbrough, G., & Wu, J. (2004). Judging egocentric distance on the ground: Occlusion and surface integration. *Perception, 33,* 789–806.

Heapy, A., & Kerns, R. D. (2008). Psychological and behavioral assessment. In H. T. Benzon, J. P. Rathmell, C. L. Wu, D. C. Turk, & C. E. Argoff (Eds.), *Raj's practical management of pain* (pp. 279–295). Philadelphia: Mosby.

Heaton, J. T., Dooling, R. J., & Farabaugh, S. M. (1999). Effects of deafening on the calls and warble song of adult budgerigars (Melopsittacus undulatus). *Journal of the Acoustical Society of America, 105,* 2010–2019.

Hecht, H., Bertamini, M., & Gamer, M. (2005). Naive optics: Acting on mirror reflections. *Journal of Experimental Psychology: Human Perception & Performance, 31,* 1023–1038.

Hecht, S., Shlaer, S., & Pirenne, M. H. (1942). Energy, quanta, and vision. *Journal of General Physiology, 25,* 819–840.

Heft, H. (2003). Affordances, dynamic experience, and the challenge of reification. *Ecological Psychology, 15,* 149–180.

Helbig, H. B., & Ernst, M. O. (2007). Optimal integration of shape information from vision and touch. *Experimental Brain Research, 179,* 595–606.

Helbig, H. B., & Ernst, M. O. (2008). Visual-haptic cue weighting is independent of modality-specific attention. *Journal of Vision, 8(21),* 21–16.

Held, R. (1965). Plasticity in sensory-motor systems. *Scientific American, 213,* 84–94.

Held, R. (1980). The rediscovery of adaptability in the visual system: Effects of extrinsic and intrinsic chromatic dispersion. In C. S. Harris (Ed.), *Visual coding and adaptability* (pp. 69–94). Hillsdale, NJ: Erlbaum.

Held, R., & Hein, A. (1963). Movement-produced stimulation in the development of visually guided behavior. *Journal of Comparative and Physiological Psychology, 56,* 872–876.

Heller, M. A. (1992). Haptic dominance in form perception: Vision versus proprioception. *Perception, 21*, 655–660.

Heller, M. A. (2006). Picture perception and spatial cognition in visually impaired people. In M. A. Heller & S. Ballesteros (Eds.), *Touch and blindness: Psychology and neuroscience.* (pp. 49–71). Mahwah, NJ: Erlbaum.

Heller, M. A., & Clark, A. (2008). Touch as a "reality sense." In J. J. Rieser, D. H. Ashmead, F. Ebner, & A. L. Corn (Eds.), *Blindness and brain plasticity in navigation and object perception* (pp. 259–280). New York: Erlbaum.

Heller, M. A., McCarthy, M., & Clark, A. (2005). Pattern perception and pictures for the blind. *Psicológica, 26*, 161–171.

Heller, M. A., Wilson, K., Steffen, H., Yoneyama, K., & Brackett, D. D. (2003). Superior haptic perceptual selectivity in late-blind and very-low-vision subjects. *Perception, 32*, 499–511.

Henderson, J. M. (2006). Eye movements. In C. Senior, T. Russell, & M. S. Gazzaniga (Eds.), *Methods in mind* (pp. 171–191). Cambridge, MA: MIT Press.

Henderson, J. M., & Ferreira, F. (2004a). Scene perception for psycholinguists. In J. M. Henderson & F. Ferreira (Eds.), *The interface of language, vision, and action: Eye movements and the visual world* (pp. 1–58). New York: Psychology Press.

Henderson, J. M., & Ferreira, F. (Eds.). (2004b). *The interface of language, vision, and action: Eye movements and the visual world.* New York: Psychology Press.

Hendry, S. H. C., & Reid, R. C. (2000). The koniocellular pathway in primate vision. *Annual Review of Neuroscience, 23*, 127–153.

Henning, H. (1916). Die Qualitätsreibe des Geschmacks. *Zeitschrift für Psychologie, 74*, 203–219.

Henning, H. (1927). Psychologische Studien am Geschmacksinn. In E. Abderhalden (Ed.), *Handbuch der biologischen Arbeitsmethoden.* Berlin: Urban & Schwarzenberg.

Herbert, A. M., Beall, P. M., & Faubert, J. (2005). Last but not least: Ambiguous depth planes: Perceiving depth from motion. *Perception, 34*, 757–759.

Hertenstein, M. J., Keltner, D., App, B., Bulleit, B. A., & Jaskolka, A. R. (2006). Touch communicates distinct emotions. *Emotion, 6*, 528–533.

Hertenstein, M. J., Verkamp, J. M., Kerestes, A. M., & Holmes, R. M. (2006). The communicative functions of touch in humans, nonhuman primates, and rats: A review and synthesis of the empirical research. *Genetic, Social, & General Psychology Monographs, 132*, 5–94.

Herz, R. (2007). *The scent of desire: Discovering our enigmatic sense of smell.* New York: HarperCollins.

Hespos, S. J., & Baillargeon, R. (2006). Decalage in infants' knowledge about occlusion and containment events: converging evidence from action tasks. *Cognition, 99*, B31–41.

Hess, R. F., Hutchinson, C. V., Ledgeway, T., & Mansouri, B. (2007). Binocular influences on global motion processing in the human visual system. *Vision Research, 47*, 1682–1692.

Hesse, G. S., & Georgeson, M. A. (2005). Edges and bars: Where do people see features in 1-D images? *Vision Research, 45*, 507–525.

Heywood, C. A., & Cowey, A. (2003). Colour vision and its disturbances after cortical lesions. In M. Fahle & M. Greenlee (Eds.), *The neuropsychology of vision* (pp. 259–281). New York: Oxford.

Heywood, C. A., & Kentridge, R. W. (2003). Achromatopsia, color vision, and cortex. *Neurologic Clinics, 21*, 483–500.

Heywood, C. A., & Zihl, J. (1999). Motion blindness. In G. W. Humphreys (Ed.), *Case studies in the neuropsychology of vision* (pp. 1–16). Hove, UK: Psychology Press.

Hidalgo-Barnes, M., & Massaro, D. W. (2007). Read my lips: An animated face helps communicate musical lyrics. *Psychomusicology, 19*, 3–12.

Higashiyama, A., & Shimono, K. (1994). How accurate is size and distance perception for very far terrestrial objects? Function and causality. *Perception & Psychophysics, 55*, 429–442.

High, K. N. W. (2008). Pain pathways: Peripheral, spinal, ascending, and descending pathways. In H. T. Benzon, J. P. Rathmell, C. L. Wu, D. C. Turk, & C. E. Argoff (Eds.), *Raj's practical management of pain* (pp. 119–134). Philadelphia: Mosby.

Hill, H., & Johnston, A. (2007). The hollow-face illusion: Object-specific knowledge, general assumptions or properties of the stimulus? *Perception, 36*, 199–223.

Hiris, E. (2007). Detection of biological and nonbiological motion. *Journal of Vision, 7* (4), 1–16.

Hiris, E., Humphrey, D., & Stout, A. (2005). Temporal properties in masking biological motion. *Perception & Psychophysics, 67*, 435–443.

Hirt, B., & Wagner, H. J. (2005). The organization of the inner retina in a pure-rod deep-sea fish. *Brain, Behavior, and Evolution, 65*, 157–167.

Hochberg, J. (1971). Perception: II. Space and movement. In J. W. Kling & L. A. Riggs (Eds.), *Woodworth & Schlosberg's experimental psychology* (3rd ed., pp. 475–550). New York: Holt, Rinehart and Winston.

Hockett, C. F. (1955). A manual of phonology, memoir 11. *International Journal of American Linguistics, 21*.

Hofer, H., Carroll, J., Neitz, J., Neitz, M., & Williams, D. R. (2005). Organization of the human trichromatic cone mosaic. *Journal of Neuroscience, 25*(42), 9669–9679.

Hoffman, D. D. (1998). *Visual intelligence: How we create what we see.* New York: Norton.

Hoffman, D. D., & Richards, W. A. (1984). Parts of recognition. *Cognition, 18*, 65–96.

Hoffmann, J., & Sebald, A. (2007). Eye vergence is susceptible to the hollow-face illusion. *Perception, 36*, 461–470.

Hollingworth, A., & Henderson, J. M. (1998). Does consistent scene context facilitate object perception? *Journal of Experimental Psychology: General, 127*, 398–415.

Hollins, M. (2002). Touch and haptics. In H. Pashler & S. Yantis (Eds.), *Stevens' handbook of experimental psychology* (3rd ed., pp. 585–618). Hoboken, NJ: Wiley.

Hollins, M., & Bensmaïa, S. J. (2007). The coding of roughness. *Canadian Journal of Experimental Psychology, 61*, 184–195.

Hollins, M., Bensmaïa, S. J., & Washburn, S. (2001). Vibrotactile adaptation impairs discrimination of fine, but not coarse, textures. *Somatosens Mot Res, 18*, 253–262.

Holt, L. L. (2005). Temporally nonadjacent nonlinguistic sounds affect speech categorization. *Psychological Science, 16*, 305–312.

Holt, L. L. (2006). Speech categorization in context: Joint effects of nonspeech and speech precursors. *Journal of the Acoustical Society of America, 119*, 4016–4026.

Holway, A. F., & Boring, E. G. (1941). Determinants of apparent visual size with distance variant. *American Journal of Psychology, 54*, 21–37.

Hood, D. C., & Finkelstein, M. A. (1986). Sensitivity to light. In K. R. Boff, L. Kaufman & J. P. Thomas (Eds.), *Handbook of perception and human performance* (pp. 5.1–5.66). New York: Wiley.

Hornung, D. E. (2006). Nasal anatomy and the sense of smell. *Advances in Oto-Rhino-Laryngology, 63*, 1–22.

Horrey, W. J., & Wickens, C. D. (2006). Examining the impact of cell phone conversations on driving using meta-analytic techniques. *Human Factors, 48*, 196–205.

Horwitz, B., Amunts, K., Bhattacharyya, R., Patkin, D., Jeffries, K., Zilles, K., et al. (2003). Activation of Broca's area during the production of spoken and signed language: A combined cytoarchitectonic mapping and PET analysis. *Neuropsychologia, 41*, 1868–1876.

Hoss, R. A., & Langlois, J. H. (2003). Infants prefer attractive faces. In O. Pascalis & A. Slater (Eds.), *The development of face processing in infancy and early childhood: Current perspectives* (pp. 27–38). Happauge, NY: Nova.

Hou, C., Pettet, M. W., Vildavski, V. Y., & Norcia, A. M. (2006). Neural correlates of shape-from-shading. *Vision Research, 46*, 1080–1090.

Houston, D. M. (2005). Speech perception in infants. In D. B. Pisoni & R. E. Remez (Eds.), *The handbook of speech perception* (pp. 417–448). Malden, MA: Blackwell.

Houston, D. M., & Jusczyk, P. W. (2000). The role of talker-specific information in word segmentation by infants. *Journal of Experimental Psychology: Human Perception & Performance, 26*, 1570–1582.

Houston, D. M., & Jusczyk, P. W. (2003). Infants' long-term memory for the sound patterns of words and voices. *Journal of Experimental Psychology: Human Perception & Performance, 29*, 1143–1154.

Houston, R. D., & Jones, G. (2004). Discrimination of prey during trawling by the insectivorous bat, Myotis daubentonii. In J. A. Thomas, C. F. Moss, & M. Vater (Eds.), *Echolocation in bats and dolphins* (pp. 356–361). Chicago: University of Chicago.

Houtsma, A. J. M., & Goldstein, J. L. (1972). The central origin of the pitch of complex tones: Evidence from musical interval recognition. *Journal of the Acoustical Society of America, 51*, 520–529.

Howard, I. P. (2002). Depth perception. In H. Pashler & S. Yantis (Eds.), *Stevens' handbook of experimental psychology* (3rd ed., pp. 77–120). Hoboken, NJ: Wiley.

Howe, C. Q., & Purves, D. (2005a). *Perceiving geometry: Geometrical illusions explained by natural scene statistics.* New York: Springer Science & Business Media.

Howe, C. Q., & Purves, D. (2005b). The Müller-Lyer illusion explained by the statistics of image-source relationships. *Proceedings of the National Academy of Sciences of the USA, 102*, 1234–1239.

Howe, P. D., Thompson, P. G., Anstis, S. M., Sagreiya, H., & Livingstone, M. S. (2006). Explaining the footsteps, belly dancer, Wenceslas, and kickback illusions. *Journal of Vision, 6*, 1396–1405.

Hu, B. H., Henderson, D., & Nicotera, T. M. (2006). Extremely rapid induction of outer hair cell apoptosis in the chinchilla cochlea following exposure to impulse noise. *Hearing Research, 211*, 16–25.

Hubel, D. H. (1982). Explorations of the primary visual cortex, 1955–1978. *Nature, 299*, 515–524.

Hubel, D. H. (1990, February). Interview. *Omni, 12*, 74–110.

Hubel, D. H., & Wiesel, T. N. (1965). Receptive fields of single neurons in two nonstriate visual areas (18 and 19) of the cat. *Journal of Neurophysiology, 28*, 229–289.

Hubel, D. H., & Wiesel, T. N. (1979). Brain mechanisms and vision. *Scientific American, 241*, 150–162.

Hubel, D. H., & Wiesel, T. N. (2005). *Brain and visual perception: The story of a 25-year collaboration.* New York: Oxford.

Huberman, A. D., Dehay, C., Berland, M., Chalupa, L. M., & Kennedy, H. (2005). Early and rapid targeting of eye-specific axonal projections to the dorsal lateral geniculate nucleus in the fetal macaque. *Journal of Neuroscience, 25*, 4014–4023.

Hudson, R., & Distel, H. (2002). The individuality of odor perception. In C. Rouby, B. Schaal, D. Dubois, R. Gervais, & A. Holley (Eds.), *Olfaction, taste, and cognition* (pp. 408–420). New York: Cambridge.

Hudspeth, A. J. (1989). How the ear's works work. *Nature, 341*, 397–404.

Hughes, H. C. (1999). *Sensory exotica: A world beyond human experience.* Cambridge, MA: MIT Press.

Hummel, T., Heilmann, S., & Murphy, C. (2002). Age-related changes in chemosensory functions. In C. Rouby, B. Schaal, D. Dubois, R. Gervais, & A. Holley (Eds.),

Olfaction, taste, and cognition (pp. 441–456). New York: Cambridge.

Humphreys, G. W., & Riddoch, M. J. (2001). The neuropsychology of visual object and space perception. In E. B. Goldstein (Ed.), *Blackwell handbook of perception* (pp. 204–236). Malden, MA: Blackwell.

Hurlbert, A. C. (1999). Colour vision: Is colour constancy real? *Current Biology, 9,* R558–561.

Hurlbert, A. C. (2003). Colour vision: Primary visual cortex shows its influence. *Current Biology, 13,* R270–272.

Hurlbert, A. C., & Ling, Y. (2005). It it's a banana, It must be yellow: The role of memory colors in color constancy. *Journal of Vision, 5,* 787–787.

Hurlbert, A. C., & Wolf, K. (2004). Color contrast: A contributory mechanism to color constancy. *Progress in Brain Research, 144,* 147–160.

Huron, D. (2006). *Sweet anticipation: Music and the psychology of expectation.* Cambridge, MA: MIT Press.

Hurvich, L. M., & Jameson, D. (1957). An opponent-process theory of color vision. *Psychological Review, 64,* 384–404.

Hyde, K. L., Lerch, J. P., Zatorre, R. J., Griffiths, T. D., Evans, A. C., & Peretz, I. (2007). Cortical thickness in congenital amusia: When less is better than more. *Journal of Neuroscience, 27*(47), 13028–13032.

Hyde, K. L., & Peretz, I. (2004). Brains that are out of tune but in time. *Psychological Science, 15,* 356–360.

Hygge, S. (2007). Noise: Effects on health. In S. Ayers, A. Baum, C. McManus, S. Newman, K. Wallston, J. Weinman, & R. West (Eds.), *Cambridge handbook of psychology, health, and medicine* (2nd ed., pp. 137–140). New York: Cambridge.

Ichikawa, M., Saida, S., Osa, A., & Munechika, K. (2003). Integration of binocular disparity and monocular cues at near threshold level. *Vision Research, 43,* 2439–2449.

Ilari, B. S. (2002). Music perception and cognition in the first year of life. *Early Child Development and Care, 172,* 311–322.

Ilg, U. J., Churan, J., & Schumann, S. (2005). The physiological basis for visual motion perception and visually guided movements. In J. Kremers (Ed.), *The primate visual system* (pp. 285–310). New York: Wiley.

Inhoff, A. W., Weger, U. W., & Radach, R. (2005). Sources of information for the programming of short- and long-range regressions during reading. In G. Underwood (Ed.), *Cognitive processes in eye guidance* (pp. 33–52). New York: Oxford.

Intraub, H. (2007). Scene perception: The world through a window. In M. A. Peterson, B. Gillam, & H. A. Sedgwick (Eds.), *In the mind's eye: Julian Hochberg on the perception of pictures, films, and the world* (pp. 454–466). New York: Oxford.

Intraub, H., Hoffman, J. E., Wetherhold, C. J., & Stoehs, S. A. (2006). More than meets the eye: The effect of planned fixations on scene representation. *Perception & Psychophysics, 68,* 759–769.

Ising, H., & Kruppa, B. (2004). Health effects caused by noise: Evidence in the literature from the past 25 years. *Noise Health, 6,* 5–13.

Ising, H., & Kruppa, B. (2007). Stress effects of noise. In L. Luxon & D. Prasher (Eds.), *Noise and its effects* (pp. 516–533). Chichester, England: Wiley.

Ittelson, W. H., & Kilpatrick, F. P. (1951). Experiments in perception. *Scientific American, 185,* 50–55.

Ittyerah, M., & Marks, L. E. (2008). Intramodal and cross-modal discrimination of curvature: Haptic touch versus vision. *Current Psychology Letters, 24,* 1–11.

Jablonski, N. G. (2006). *Skin: A natural history.* Berkeley, CA: University of California Press.

Jacob, S., Garcia, S., Hayreh, D. J. S., & McClintock, M. K. (2002). Psychological effects of musky compounds: Comparison of androstadienone with androstenol and muscone. *Hormones and Behavior, 42,* 274–283.

Jacob, S., Zelano, B., Hayreh, D. J. S., & McClintock, M. K. (2002). Assessing putative human pheromones. In C. Rouby, B. Schaal, D. Dubois, R. Gervais, & A. Holley (Eds.), *Olfaction, taste, and cognition* (pp. 178–195). New York: Cambridge.

Jacobs, G. H. (2003). Comparative psychology of vision. In M. Gallagher & R. J. Nelson (Eds.), *Handbook of psychology: Biological psychology* (Vol. 3, pp. 47–70). Hoboken, NJ: Wiley.

Jacobs, G. H., & Rowe, M. P. (2004). Evolution of vertebrate colour vision. *Clinical and Experimental Optometry, 87,* 206–216.

Jacobs, G. H., Williams, G. A., Cahill, H., & Nathans, J. (2007). Emergence of novel color vision in mice engineered to express a human cone photopigment. *Science, 315*(5819), 1723–1725.

Jacobsen, A., & Gilchrist, A. (1988). The ratio principle holds over a million-to-one range of illumination. *Perception & Psychophysics, 43,* 1–6.

James, W. (1890). *The principles of psychology.* New York: Henry Holt.

Jameson, K. A. (2005a). Culture and cognition: What is universal about the representation of color experience? *The Journal of Cognition and Culture, 5,* 293–347.

Jameson, K. A. (2005b). On the role of culture in color naming: Remarks on the articles of Paramei, Kay, Roberson, and Hardin on the topic of cognition, culture, and color experience. *Cross-Cultural Research, 39,* 88–106.

Jameson, K. A., Bimler, D. L., & Wasserman, L. M. (2006). Reassessing perceptual diagnostics for observers with diverse retinal photopigment genotypes. In N. J. Pitchford & C. P. Biggam (Eds.), *Progress in colour studies: Vol. 2, Psychological aspects* (Vol. 2, pp. 13–33). Philadelphia: John Benjamin.

Jameson, K. A., Highnote, S. M., & Wasserman, L. M. (2001). Richer color experience in observers with multiple photopigment opsin genes. *Psychonomic Bulletin & Review, 8,* 244–261.

Janata, P. (2007). When music stops making sense: Lessons from an injured brain. [Electronic]. *Cerebrum.*

Janata, P., Birk, J. L., Van Horn, J. D., Leman, M., Tillmann, B., & Bharucha, J. J. (2002). The cortical topography of tonal structures underlying Western music. *Science, 298*(5601), 2167–2170.

Jankowiak, J., Kinsbourne, M., Shalev, R. S., & Bachman, D. L. (1992). Preserved visual imagery and categorization in a case of associative visual agnosia. *Journal of Cognitive Neuroscience, 4,* 119–131.

Jeffress, L. A. (1948). A place theory of sound localization. *Journal of Comparative and Physiological Psychology, 41,* 35–39.

Jessen, C. (2001). *Temperature regulation in humans and other mammals.* New York: Springer.

Jia, S., Dallos, P., & He, D. Z. (2007). Mechanoelectric transduction of adult inner hair cells. *Journal of Neuroscience, 27,* 1006–1014.

Jia, S., & He, D. Z. (2005). Motility-associated hair-bundle motion in mammalian outer hair cells. *Nature Neuroscience, 8,* 1028–1034.

Johansson, G. (1973). Visual perception of biological motion and a model for its analysis. *Perception & Psychophysics, 14,* 201–211.

Johansson, G. (1975). Visual motion perception. *Scientific American, 232,* 76–88.

Johansson, G. (1982). Visual space perception through motion. In A. H. Wertheim, W. A. Wagenaar, & H. W. Leibowitz (Eds.), *Tutorials on motion perception* (pp. 19–39). New York: Plenum.

Johansson, G. (1985). About visual event perception. In W. H. Warren, Jr. & R. W. Shaw (Eds.), *Persistence and change: Proceedings of the First International Conference on Event Perception* (pp. 29–54). Hillsdale, NJ: Erlbaum.

Johnson, B., Khan, R. M., & Sobel, N. (2008). Human olfactory psychophsyics. In A. I. Basbaum, M. C. Bushnell, D. V. Smith, G. K. Beauchamp, S. J. Firestein, P. Dallos, D. Oertel, R. H. Masland, T. D. Albright, J. H. Kaas, & E. P. Gardner (Eds.), *The senses: A comprehensive reference* (Vol. 4, pp. 823–857). New York: Academic Press.

Johnson, K. (2002). Neural basis of haptic perception. In H. Pashler & S. Yantis (Eds.), *Stevens' handbook of experimental psychology* (3rd ed., pp. 537–583). Hoboken, NJ: Wiley.

Johnson, R. L., Perea, M., & Rayner, K. (2007). Transposed-letter effects in reading: Evidence from eye movements and parafoveal preview. *Journal of Experimental Psychology: Human Perception & Performance, 33,* 209–229.

Johnson, S. P. (1998). Object perception and object knowledge in young infants: A view from studies of visual development. In A. Slater (Ed.), *Perceptual development: Visual, auditory, and speech perception in infancy* (pp. 211–239). Hove, UK: Psychology Press.

Johnson, S. P. (2004). Development of perceptual completion in infancy. *Psychological Science, 15,* 769–775.

Johnson, S. P., Bremner, J. G., Slater, A., Mason, U., Foster, K., & Cheshire, A. (2003). Infants' perception of object trajectories. *Child Development, 74,* 94–108.

Johnson, S. P., Hannon, E. E., & Amso, D. (2005). Perceptual development. In B. Hopkins (Ed.), *The Cambridge encyclopedia of child development* (pp. 210–216). New York: Cambridge.

Jones, B. C., DeBruine, L. M., & Little, A. C. (2007). The role of symmetry in attraction to average faces. *Perception & Psychophysics, 69,* 1273–1277.

Jones, B. C., DeBruine, L. M., Perrett, D. I., Little, A. C., Feinberg, D. R., & Law Smith, M. J. (2008). Effects of menstrual cycle phase on face preferences. *Archives of Sexual Behavior, 37,* 78–84.

Jones, K. S. (2003). What is an affordance? *Ecological Psychology, 15,* 107–114.

Jones, L. M., Fontanini, A., & Katz, D. B. (2006). Gustatory processing: A dynamic systems approach. *Current Opinion in Neurobiology, 16,* 420–428.

Joris, P. X. (2006). A dogged pursuit of coincidence. *Journal of Neurophysiology, 96,* 969–972.

Julesz, B. (2006). *Foundations of cyclopean perception.* Cambridge, MA: MIT Press.

Jusczyk, P. W. (1986). Speech perception. In K. R. Boff, L. Kaufman, & J. P. Thomas (Eds.), *Handbook of perception and human performance* (Vol. 2, pp. 27.21–27.57). Hillsdale, NJ: Erlbaum.

Jusczyk, P. W., & Aslin, R. N. (1995). Infants' detection of the sound patterns of words in fluent speech. *Cognitive Psychology, 29,* 1–23.

Jusczyk, P. W., Houston, D. M., & Goodman, M. (1998). Speech perception during the first year. In A. Slater (Ed.), *Perceptual development: Visual, auditory, and speech perception in infancy* (pp. 357–388). Hove, UK: Psychology Press.

Jusczyk, P. W., & Luce, P. A. (2002). Speech perception. In H. Pashler & S. Yantis (Eds.), *Stevens' handbook of experimental psychology* (3rd ed., pp. 493–536). Hoboken, NJ: Wiley.

Juslin, P. N., & Scherer, K. R. (2005). Vocal expression of affect. In K. R. Scherer & P. Ekman (Eds.), *The new handbook of methods in nonverbal behavior research* (pp. 65–135). New York: Oxford.

Justus, T. C., & Bharucha, J. J. (2002). Music perception and cognition. In H. Pashler & S. Yantis (Eds.), *Stevens' handbook of experimental psychology* (3rd ed., pp. 453–492). Hoboken, NJ: Wiley.

Kaas, J. H. (2000). The reorganization of sensory and motor maps after injury in adult mammals. In M. S. Gazzaniga (Ed.), *The new cognitive neurosciences* (2nd ed., pp. 223–236). Cambridge, MA: MIT Press.

Kamerud, J. K., & Delwiche, J. F. (2007). Individual differences in perceived bitterness predict liking of sweeteners. *Chemical Senses, 32*, 803–810.

Kanizsa, G. (1976). Subjective contours. *Scientific American, 234*, 48–52.

Kanwisher, N. (2003). The ventral visual object pathway in humans: Evidence from fMRI. In L. Chalupa & J. Werner (Eds.), *The visual neurosciences* (Vol. 2, pp. 1179–1189). Cambridge, MA: MIT Press.

Kanwisher, N. (2006). What's in a face? *Science, 311*(5761), 617–618.

Kanwisher, N., & Yovel, G. (2006). The fusiform face area: A cortical region specialized for the perception of faces. *Philosophical Transactions of the Royal Society of London, 361*(1476), 2109–2128.

Kaplan, E., Mukherjee, P., & Shapley, R. (1993). Information filtering in the lateral geniculate nucleus. In R. Shapley & D. M.-K. Lam (Eds.), *Contrast sensitivity: Proceedings of the Retina Research Foundation Symposia* (Vol. 5, pp. 183–200). Cambridge, MA: MIT Press.

Kasthurirangan, S., & Glasser, A. (2006). Age related changes in accommodative dynamics in humans. *Vision Research, 46*, 1507–1519.

Kaufman, J., Csibra, G., & Johnson, M. H. (2003). Representing occluded objects in the human infant brain. *Proceedings of The Royal Society B: Biological Sciences, 270 Suppl 2*, S140–143.

Kaufman, J., Csibra, G., & Johnson, M. H. (2005). Oscillatory activity in the infant brain reflects object maintenance. *Proceedings of the National Academy of Science, 102*(42), 15271–15274.

Kaufman, J., Mareschal, D., & Johnson, M. H. (2003). Graspability and object processing in infants. *Infant Behavior & Development, 26*, 516–528.

Kaufman, L., Vassiliades, V., Noble, R., Alexander, R., Kaufman, J., & Edlund, S. (2007). Perceptual distance and the moon illusion. *Spatial Vision, 20*, 155–175.

Kay, P., & Regier, T. (2006). Language, thought and color: Recent developments. *Trends in Cognitive Sciences, 10*, 51–54.

Kay, P., & Regier, T. (2007). Color naming universals: The case of Berinmo. *Cognition, 102*, 289–298.

Kayed, N. S., & van der Meer, A. L. (2007). Infants' timing strategies to optical collisions: A longitudinal study. *Infant Behavior & Development, 30*, 50–59.

Keast, R. S. J. (2008). Modification of the bitterness of caffeine. *Food Quality and Preference, 19*, 465–472.

Keast, R. S. J., Dalton, P. H., & Breslin, P. A. S. (2004). Flavor interactions at the sensory level. In A. J. Taylor & D. D. Roberts (Eds.), *Flavor perception* (pp. 228–255). Malden, MA: Blackwell.

Keast, R. S. J., & Riddell, L. J. (2007). Caffeine as a flavor additive in soft-drinks. *Appetite, 49*, 255–259.

Kelliher, K. R. (2007). The combined role of the main olfactory and vomeronasal systems in social communication in mammals. *Hormones and Behavior, 52*, 561–570.

Kellman, P. J., & Arterberry, M. E. (1998). *The cradle of knowledge: Development of perception in infancy*. Cambridge, MA: MIT Press.

Kellman, P. J., & Arterberry, M. E. (2006). Infant visual perception. In D. Kuhn, R. S. Siegler, W. Damon, & R. M. Lerner (Eds.), *Handbook of child psychology: Vol 2, Cognition, perception, and language* (6th ed., pp. 109–160). Hoboken, NJ: Wiley.

Kemmer, L., Coulson, S., De Ochoa, E., & Kutas, M. (2004). Syntactic processing with aging: An event-related potential study. *Psychophysiology, 41*, 372–384.

Kemp, D. T. (1978). Stimulated acoustic emissions from within the human auditory system. *Journal of the Acoustical Society of America, 64*, 1386–1391.

Kemps, R., Ernestus, M., Schreuder, R., & Baayen, H. (2004). Processing reduced word forms: the suffix restoration effect. *Brain and Language, 90*, 117–127.

Kentridge, R. W., Heywood, C. A., & Cowey, A. (2004). Chromatic edges, surfaces and constancies in cerebral achromatopsia. *Neuropsychologia, 42*, 821–830.

Kenyon, G. T., Hill, D., Theiler, J., George, J. S., & Marshak, D. W. (2004). A theory of the Benham Top based on center-surround interactions in the parvocellular pathway. *Neural Networks, 17*, 773–786.

Key, B. (1999). Anatomy of the peripheral chemosensory systems: How they grow and age in humans. In G. A. Bell & A. J. Watson (Eds.), *Tastes and aromas: The chemical senses in science and industry* (pp. 138–148). New York: Blackwell.

Khang, B. G., Koenderink, J. J., & Kappers, A. M. (2007). Shape from shading from images rendered with various surface types and light fields. *Perception, 36*, 1191–1213.

Kiang, N. Y.-S. (1975). Stimulus representation in the discharge patterns of auditory neurons. In E. L. Eagles (Ed.), *The nervous system* (Vol. 3, pp. 81–96). New York: Raven.

Kim, J. E., Song, H., Jeong, J. H., Choi, K.-G., & Na, D. L. (2007). Bilateral ageusia in a patient with a left ventroposteromedial thalamic infarct: Cortical localization of taste sensation by statistical parametric mapping analysis of PET images. *Journal of Clinical Neurology, 3*, 161–164.

Kim, N. G., & Grocki, M. J. (2006). Multiple sources of information and time-to-contact judgments. *Vision Research, 46*, 1946–1958.

Kimchi, R. (2003a). Relative dominance of holistic and component properties in the perceptual organization of visual objects. In M. A. Peterson & G. Rhodes (Eds.), *Perception of faces, objects, and scenes: Analytic and holistic processes* (pp. 235–263). New York: Oxford.

Kimchi, R. (2003b). Visual perceptual organization: A microgenetic analysis. In R. Kimchi, M. Behrmann, & C. R. Olson

(Eds.), *Perceptual organization in vision: Behavioral and neural perspectives* (pp. 117–153). Mahwah, NJ: Erlbaum.

Kimchi, R., Hadad, B., Behrmann, M., & Palmer, S. E. (2005). Microgenesis and ontogenesis of perceptual organization: Evidence from global and local processing of hierarchical patterns. *Psychological Science, 16,* 282–290.

Kingdom, F. A., & Kasrai, R. (2006). Colour unmasks dark targets in complex displays. *Vision Research, 46,* 814–822.

Kinnamon, J. C., & Yang, R. (2008). Ultrastructure of taste buds. In A. I. Basbaum, M. C. Bushnell, D. V. Smith, G. K. Beauchamp, S. J. Firestein, P. Dallos, D. Oertel, R. H. Masland, T. D. Albright, J. H. Kaas, & E. P. Gardner (Eds.), *The senses: A comprehensive reference* (Vol. 4, pp. 135–155). New York: Academic Press.

Kinnamon, S. C., & Margolskee, R. F. (2008). Taste transduction. In A. I. Basbaum, M. C. Bushnell, D. V. Smith, G. K. Beauchamp, S. J. Firestein, P. Dallos, D. Oertel, R. H. Masland, T. D. Albright, J. H. Kaas, & E. P. Gardner (Eds.), *The senses: A comprehensive reference* (Vol. 4, pp. 219–236). New York: Academic Press.

Kisilevsky, B. S., Hains, S. M., Lee, K., Xie, X., Huang, H., Ye, H. H., et al. (2003). Effects of experience on fetal voice recognition. *Psychological Science, 14,* 220–224.

Klatzky, R. L., & Lederman, S. (2008). Object recognition by touch. In J. J. Rieser, D. H. Ashmead, F. Ebner, & A. L. Corn (Eds.), *Blindness and brain plasticity in navigation and object perception* (pp. 185–207). New York: Erlbaum.

Klatzky, R. L., & Lederman, S. J. (2003a). The haptic identification of everyday life objects. In Y. Hatwell, A. Streri, & E. Gentaz (Eds.), *Touching for knowing: Cognitive psychology of haptic manual perception* (pp. 105–121). Amsterdam: John Benjamins.

Klatzky, R. L., & Lederman, S. J. (2003b). Touch. In A. F. Healy & R. W. Proctor (Eds.), *Handbook of psychology: Experimental psychology* (Vol. 4, pp. 147–176). Hoboken, NJ: Wiley.

Kline, D. W. (2006). Vision: System function and loss. In R. Schulz (Ed.), *The encyclopedia of aging* (pp. 1212–1215). New York: Springer.

Kline, D. W., & Dewar, R. (2004). The aging eye and transport signs. In C. Castro & T. Horberry (Eds.), *The human factors of transport signs* (pp. 115–134). Boca Raton, FL: CRC Press.

Kline, D. W., & Li, W. (2005). Cataracts and the aging driver. *Ageing International, 30,* 105–121.

Knoblauch, K. (2002). Color vision. In H. Pashler & S. Yantis (Eds.), *Stevens' handbook of experimental psychology* (3rd ed., pp. 41–75). Hoboken, NJ: Wiley.

Knoblich, G., Thornton, I. M., Grosjean, M., & Shiffrar, M. (Eds.). (2006). *Human body perception from the inside out.* New York: Oxford.

Knox, P. C., & Bruno, N. (2007). When does action resist visual illusion? The effect of Müller-Lyer stimuli on reflexive and voluntary saccades. *Experimental Brain Research, 181,* 277–287.

Knudsen, E. I. (1981). The hearing of the barn owl. *Scientific American, 245,* 112–125.

Knudsen, E. I. (2002). Instructed learning in the auditory localization pathway of the barn owl. *Nature, 417*(6886), 322–328.

Koenderink, J. J., & van Doorn, A. J. (2003). Shape and shading. In L. M. Chalupa & J. S. Werner (Eds.), *The visual neurosciences* (Vol. 2, pp. 1090–1105). Cambridge, MA: MIT Press.

Koenderink, J. J., van Doorn, A. J., & Kappers, A. M. L. (2006). Picotrial relief. In M. R. M. Jenkin & L. R. Harris (Eds.), *Seeing spatial form* (pp. 11–33). New York: Oxford.

Koffka, K. (1935). *Principles of Gestalt psychology.* New York: Harcourt Brace.

Kohl, S., Varsanyi, B., Antunes, G. A., Baumann, B., Hoyng, C. B., Jagle, H., et al. (2005). CNGB3 mutations account for 50% of all cases with autosomal recessive achromatopsia. *European Journal of Human Genetics, 13,* 302–308.

Köhler, W. (1947). *Gestalt psychology: An introduction to new concepts in modern psychology.* New York: Liveright.

Konishi, M. (1973). How the owl tracks its prey. *American Scientist, 61,* 414–424.

Konishi, M. (2000). Study of sound localization by owls and its relevance to humans. *Comp Biochem Physiol A Mol Integr Physiol, 126,* 459–469.

Konishi, M. (2003). Coding of auditory space. *Annual Review of Neuroscience, 26,* 31–55.

Konstantinidis, I., Hummel, T., & Larsson, M. (2006). Identification of unpleasant odors is independent of age. *Archives of Clinical Neuropsychology, 21,* 615–621.

Koretz, J. F., & Handelman, G. H. (1988). How the human eye focuses. *Scientific American, 259,* 92–99.

Kosfeld, M., Heinrichs, M., Zak, P. J., Fischbacher, U., & Fehr, E. (2005). Oxytocin increases trust in humans. *Nature, 435*(7042), 673–676.

Krauskopf, J. (1963). Effect of retinal image stabilization on the appearance of heterochromatic targets. *Journal of the Optical Society of America, 53,* 741–743.

Krauzlis, R. J. (2004). Recasting the smooth pursuit eye movement system. *Journal of Neurophysiology, 91,* 591–603.

Krauzlis, R. J. (2005). The control of voluntary eye movements: New perspectives. *Neuroscientist, 11,* 124–137.

Krekelberg, B. (2008). Motion detection mechanisms. In A. I. Basbaum, M. C. Bushnell, D. V. Smith, G. K. Beauchamp, S. J. Firestein, P. Dallos, D. Oertel, R. H. Masland, T. D. Albright, J. H. Kaas, & E. P. Gardner (Eds.), *The senses: A comprehensive reference* (Vol. 2, pp. 133–155). New York: Academic.

Kros, C. J. (2007). How to build an inner hair cell: Challenges for regeneration. *Hearing Research, 227,* 3–10.

Krueger, L. E. (1991). Toward a unified psychophysical law and beyond. In S. J. Bolanowski & G. A. Gescheider (Eds.), *Ratio scaling of psychological magnitude: In honor of the memory of S. S. Stevens* (pp. 101–114). Hillsdale, NJ: Erlbaum.

Krumbholz, K., Patterson, R. D., Seither-Preisler, A., Lammertmann, C., & Lutkenhoner, B. (2003). Neuro-magnetic evidence for a pitch processing center in Heschl's gyrus. *Cerebral Cortex, 13,* 765–772.

Krumhansl, C. L. (2000). Rhythm and pitch in music cognition. *Psychological Bulletin, 126,* 159–179.

Krumhansl, C. L. (2003). Experimental strategies for understanding the role of experience in music cognition. In G. Avanzini, C. Faienza, D. Minciacchi, L. Lopez, & M. Majno (Eds.), *The neurosciences and music* (Vol. 999, pp. 414–428). New York: NY Academy of Sciences.

Kubovy, M., Epstein, W., & Gepshtein, S. (2003). Foundations of visual perception. In A. F. Healy & R. W. Proctor (Eds.), *Handbook of psychology: Experimental psychology* (Vol. 4. pp. 87–119). Hoboken, NJ: Wiley & Sons.

Kubovy, M., & Van Valkenburg, D. (2001). Auditory and visual objects. *Cognition, 80,* 97–126.

Kuhl, P. K. (1989). On babies, birds, modules, and mechanisms: A comparative approach to the acquisition of vocal communication. In R. J. Dooling & S. H. Hulse (Eds.), *The comparative psychology of audition: Perceiving complex sounds* (pp. 379–419). Hillsdale, NJ: Erlbaum.

Kuhl, P. K. (1992). Psychoacoustics and speech perception: Internal standards, perceptual anchors, and prototypes. In L. A. Werner & E. W. Rubel (Eds.), *Developmental psychoacoustics* (pp. 293–332). Washington, DC: American Psychological Association.

Kuhl, P. K. (2004). Early language acquisition: Cracking the speech code. *Nature Reviews Neuroscience, 5,* 831–843.

Kujala, T., Shtyrov, Y., Winkler, I., Saher, M., Tervaniemi, M., Sallinen, M., et al. (2004). Long-term exposure to noise impairs cortical sound processing and attention control. *Psychophysiology, 41,* 875–881.

Kurson, R. (2007). *Crashing through: A true story of risk, adventure, and the man who dared to see.* New York: Random House.

Lackner, J. R., & DiZio, P. (2005). Vestibular, proprioceptive, and haptic contributions to spatial orientation. *Annual Review of Psychology, 56,* 115–147.

Lackner, J. R., & DiZio, P. (2006). Space motion sickness. *Experimental Brain Research, 175,* 377–399.

Lamb, M. E., Bornstein, M. H., & Teti, D. M. (2002). *Development in infancy: An introduction* (4th ed.). Mahwah, NJ: Erlbaum.

Lamb, T. D. (1990). The role of photoreceptors in light-adaptation and dark-adaptation of the visual system. In C. Blakemore (Ed.), *Vision: Coding and efficiency* (pp. 161–168). Cambridge: Cambridge University Press.

Lamb, T. D., & Pugh, E. N., Jr. (2004). Dark adaptation and the retinoid cycle of vision. *Progress in Retinal and Eye Research, 23,* 307–380.

Lamb, T. D., & Pugh, E. N., Jr. (2006). Phototransduction, dark adaptation, and rhodopsin regeneration the proctor lecture. *Investigative Ophthalmology & Visual Science, 47,* 5137–5152.

Land, E. H. (1977). The retinex theory of color vision. *Scientific American, 237,* 108–128.

Land, M. F. (2006). Visual optics: The shapes of pupils. *Current Biology, 16,* R167–168

Land, M. F., Furneaux, S. M., & Gilchrist, I. D. (2002). The organization of visually mediated actions in a subject without eye movements. *Neurocase, 8,* 80–87.

Land, M. F., & Hayhoe, M. (2001). In what ways do eye movements contribute to everyday activities? *Vision Research, 41*(2526), 3559–3565.

Land, M. F., Mennie, N., & Rusted, J. (1999). The roles of vision and eye movements in the control of activities of daily living. *Perception, 28,* 1311–1328.

Land, M. F., & Nilsson, D.-E. (2002). *Animal eyes.* New York: Oxford.

Lanthony, P. (1997). Seurat's pointillism: Optical mixture and color texture. In M. F. Marmor & J. G. Ravin (Eds.), *The eye of the artist* (pp. 118–129). St. Louis: Mosby.

Lappin, J. S., Shelton, A. L., & Rieser, J. J. (2006). Environmental context influences visually perceived distance. *Perception & Psychophysics, 68,* 571–581.

Lashley, K. S. (1941). Patterns of cerebral integration indicated by the scotomas of migraine. *Archives of Neurology and Psychiatry, 46,* 331–339.

Lasky, R. E., & Williams, A. L. (2005). The development of the auditory system from conception to term. *NeoReviews, 6,* 141–152.

Laszlo, S., & Federmeier, K. D. (2007). The acronym superiority effect. *Psychonomic Bulletin & Review, 14,* 1158–1163.

Lawless, H. T. (2001). Taste. In E. B. Goldstein (Ed.), *Blackwell handbook of perception* (pp. 601–635). Malden, MA: Blackwell.

Lawson, R., Bertamini, M., & Liu, D. (2007). Overestimation of the projected size of objects on the surface of mirrors and windows. *Journal of Experimental Psychology: Human Perception & Performance, 33,* 1027–1044.

Le Grand, R., Mondloch, C. J., Maurer, D., & Brent, H. P. (2003). Expert face processing requires visual input to the right hemisphere during infancy. *Nature Neuroscience, 6,* 1108–1112.

Le Grand, R., Mondloch, C. J., Maurer, D., & Brent, H. P. (2004). Impairment in holistic face processing following early visual deprivation. *Psychological Science, 15,* 762–768.

Lederman, S. J., Kilgour, A., Kitada, R., Klatzky, R. L., & Hamilton, C. (2007). Haptic face processing. *Canadian Journal of Experimental Psychology, 61,* 230–241.

Lederman, S. J., & Klatzky, R. L. (2004a). Haptic identification of common objects: Effects of constraining the manual exploration process. *Perception & Psychophysics, 66,* 618–628.

Lederman, S. J., & Klatzky, R. L. (2004b). Multisensory texture perception. In G. A. Calvert, C. Spence, & B. E. Stein (Eds.), *The handbook of multisensory processes.* Cambridge, MA: MIT Press.

Lederman, S. J., Klatzky, R. L., Abramowicz, A., Salsman, K., Kitada, R., & Hamilton, C. (2007). Haptic recognition of static and dynamic expressions of emotion in the live face. *Psychological Science, 18,* 158–164.

Lee, H., & Vecera, S. P. (2005). Visual cognition influences early vision: The role of visual short-term memory in amodal completion. *Psychological Science, 16,* 763–768.

Lee, L., Frederick, S., & Ariely, D. (2006). Try it, you'll like it: The influence of expectation, consumption, and revelation on preferences for beer. *Psychological Science, 17,* 1054–1058.

Leffingwell (2008). *Flavor & fragrance industry leaders.* Retrieved July 2008, from www.leffingwell.com/top_10.htm.

Lehrer, M. (1999). Shape perception in the Honeybee: Symmetry as a global framework. *International Journal of Plant Sciences, 160*(S6), S51–S65.

Lennie, P. (2000). Color vision: Putting it together. *Current Biology, 10,* R589–591.

Lennie, P., & Movshon, J. A. (2005). Coding of color and form in the geniculostriate visual pathway (invited review). *Journal of the Optical Society of America, 22,* 2013–2033.

Lercher, P. (2007). Environmental noise: A contextual public health perspective. In L. Luxon & D. Prasher (Eds.), *Noise and its effects* (pp. 345–377). Chichester, England: Wiley.

Lesher, G. W., & Mingolla, E. (1993). The role of edges and line-ends in illusory contour formation. *Vision Research, 33,* 2253–2270.

Levin, J. B., & Janata, J. W. (2007). Psychological interventions. In S. D. Waldman (Ed.), *Pain management* (pp. 1003–1009). Philadelphia: W. B. Saunders.

Levitin, D. J. (2006). *This is your brain on music.* New York: Dutton.

Levitin, D. J., & Rogers, S. E. (2005). Absolute pitch: Perception, coding, and controversies. *Trends in Cognitive Sciences, 9,* 26–33.

Levitin, D. J., & Zatorre, R. J. (2003). On the nature of early music training and absolute pitch: A reply to Brown, Sachs, Cammuso, and Folstein. *Music Perception, 21,* 105–110.

Li, X., & Gilchrist, A. L. (1999). Relative area and relative luminance combine to anchor surface lightness values. *Perception & Psychophysics, 61,* 771–785.

Li, Z., & Milgram, P. (2008). An empirical investigation of a dynamic brake light concept for reduction of rear-end collisions through manipulation of optical looming. *International Journal of Human-Computer Studies, 66,* 158–172.

Liberles, S. D., & Buck, L. B. (2006). A second class of chemosensory receptors in the olfactory epithelium. *Nature, 442*(7103), 645–650.

Liberman, A. M. (1982). On the finding that speech is special. *American Psychologist, 37,* 148–167.

Liberman, A. M. (1992). Plausibility, parsimony, and theories of speech. In J. Alegria, D. Holender, J. Junça de Morais, & M. Radeau (Eds.), *Analytic approaches to human cognition* (pp. 25–40). Amsterdam: North-Holland.

Liberman, A. M. (1996). *Speech: A special code.* Cambridge, MA: MIT Press.

Liberman, A. M., & Mattingly, I. G. (1989). A specialization for speech perception. *Science, 243,* 489–494.

Licklider, J. C. R. (1954). "Periodicity" pitch and "place" pitch. *Journal of the Acoustical Society of America, 26,* 945.

Lima, D. (2008). Ascending pathways: Anatomy and physiology. In A. I. Basbaum, M. C. Bushnell, D. V. Smith, G. K. Beauchamp, S. J. Firestein, P. Dallos, D. Oertel, R. H. Masland, T. D. Albright, J. H. Kaas, & E. P. Gardner (Eds.), *The senses: A comprehensive reference* (Vol. 5, pp. 477–526). New York: Academic Press.

Lin, Y.-C. (2008). Acupuncture. In H. T. Benzon, J. P. Rathmell, C. L. Wu, D. C. Turk, & C. E. Argoff (Eds.), *Raj's practical management of pain* (pp. 785–791). Philadelphia: Mosby.

Lindsay, P. H., & Norman, D. A. (1977). *Human information processing* (2nd ed.). New York: Academic Press.

Lindsay, R. C. L., Ross, D. F., Read, J. D., & Toglia, M. P. (Eds.). (2007). *The handbook of eyewitness psychology: Memory for people* (Vol. 2). Mahwah, NJ: Erlbaum.

Ling, Y., & Hurlbert, A. C. (2008). Role of color memory in successive color constancy. *Journal of the Optical Society of America, 25,* 1215–1226.

Link, S. W. (1994). Rediscovering the past: Gustav Fechner and signal detection theory. *Psychological Science, 5,* 335–340.

Lipman, A. G., & Jackson, K. C. (2004). Opioid pharmacotherapy. In C. A. Warfield & Z. H. Bajwa (Eds.), *Principles and practice of pain medicine* (pp. 583–600). New York: McGraw-Hill.

Little, A. C., Apicella, C. L., & Marlowe, F. W. (2007). Preferences for symmetry in human faces in two cultures: Data from the UK and the Hadza, an isolated group of hunter-gatherers. *Proceedings of The Royal Society B: Biological Sciences, 274*(1629), 3113–3117.

Little, A. C., Jones, B. C., Waitt, C., Tiddeman, B. P., Feinberg, D. R., Perrett, D. I., et al. (2008). Symmetry is related to sexual dimorphism in faces: Data across culture and species. *PLoS ONE, 3,* e2106.

Liu, B., & Todd, J. T. (2004). Perceptual biases in the interpretation of 3D shape from shading. *Vision Research, 44,* 2135–2145.

Loggia, M. L., Mogil, J. S., & Bushnell, M. C. (2008). Empathy hurts: Compassion for another increases both sensory and affective components of pain perception. *Pain, 136,* 168–176.

Logothetis, N. K. (1999). Vision: A window on consciousness. *Scientific American,* 69–75.

Logue, A. W. (2004). *The psychology of eating and drinking* (3rd ed.). New York: Routledge.

Logvinenko, A. D. (2002). The anchoring effect in lightness perception in humans. *Neuroscience Letters, 334,* 5–8.

Logvinenko, A. D., Epelboim, J., & Steinman, R. M. (2001). The role of vergence in the perception of distance: A fair test of Bishop Berkeley's claim. *Spatial Vision, 15,* 77–97.

Lonsbury-Martin, B. L. (2005). Otoacoustic emissions: Where are we today? *The ASHA Leader, 19,* 6–7.

Loomis, J. M., Beall, A. C., Macuga, K. L., Kelly, J. W., & Smith, R. S. (2006). Visual control of action without retinal optic flow. *Psychological Science, 17,* 214–221.

Lord, S. R., & Dayhew, J. (2001). Visual risk factors for falls in older people. *Journal of the American Geriatrics Society, 49,* 508–515.

Lord, S. R., Dayhew, J., & Howland, A. (2002). Multifocal glasses impair edge-contrast sensitivity and depth perception and increase the risk of falls in older people. *Journal of the American Geriatrics Society, 50,* 1760–1766.

Lord, S. R., Sherrington, C., Menz, H. T., & Close, J. C. T. (2007). *Falls in older people: Risk factors and strategies for prevention* (2nd ed.). New York: Cambridge.

Lott, L. A., Haegerstrom-Portnoy, G., Schneck, M. E., & Brabyn, J. A. (2005). Face recognition in the elderly. *Optometry & Vision Science, 82,* 874–881.

Lou, L. (2007). Apparent afterimage size, Emmert's law, and oculomotor adjustment. *Perception, 36,* 1214–1228.

Loula, F., Prasad, S., Harber, K., & Shiffrar, M. (2005). Recognizing people from their movement. *Journal of Experimental Psychology: Human Perception & Performance, 31,* 210–220.

Love, B. C., Medin, D. L., & Gureckis, T. M. (2004). SUSTAIN: A network model of category learning. *Psychological Review, 111,* 309–332.

Luce, P. A., & McLellan, C. T. (2005). Spoken word recognition: The challenge of variation. In D. B. Pisoni & R. E. Remez (Eds.), *The handbook of speech perception* (pp. 591–609). Malden, MA: Blackwell.

Luebke, A. E., & Foster, P. K. (2002). Variation in inter-animal susceptibility to noise damage is associated with alpha 9 acetylcholine receptor subunit expression level. *Journal of Neuroscience, 22,* 4241–4247.

Luebke, A. E., Foster, P. K., & Stagner, B. B. (2002). A multifrequency method for determining cochlear efferent activity. *Journal of the Association for Research in Otolaryngology, 3,* 16–25.

Luxon, L., & Prasher, D. (Eds.). (2007). *Noise and its effects.* Chichester, England: Wiley.

Maassen, M., Babisch, W., Bachmann, K. D., Ising, H., Lehnert, G., Plath, P., et al. (2001). Ear damage caused by leisure noise. *Noise Health, 4,* 1–16.

MacDonald, J., Andersen, S., & Bachmann, T. (2000). Hearing by eye: How much spatial degradation can be tolerated? *Perception, 29,* 1155–1168.

Mack, M. L., Gauthier, I., Sadr, J., & Palmeri, T. J. (2008). Object detection and basic-level categorization: Sometimes you know it is there before you know what it is. *Psychonomic Bulletin & Review, 15,* 28–35.

MacLaury, R. E., Paramei, G. V., & Dedrick, D. (Eds.). (2007). *Anthropology of color: Interdisciplinary multilevel modeling.* Philadelphia: John Benjamins.

MacLeod, D. I. A. (2003a). Colour discrimination, color constancy, and natural scene statistics. In J. D. Mollon, J. Pokorny, & K. Knoblauch (Eds.), *Normal and defective colour vision* (pp. 189–217). New York: Oxford.

MacLeod, D. I. A. (2003b). New dimensions in color perception. *Trends in Cognitive Sciences, 7,* 97–99.

MacLeod, D. I. A., Chen, B., & Stockman, A. (1990). Why do we see better in bright light? In C. Blakemore (Ed.), *Vision: Coding and efficiency* (pp. 169–174). Cambridge: Cambridge University Press.

Macmillan, N. A., & Creelman, C. D. (2005). *Detection theory: A user's guide* (2nd ed.). Mahwah, NJ: Erlbaum.

Macpherson, E. A., & Middlebrooks, J. C. (2002). Listener weighting of cues for lateral angle: The duplex theory of sound localization revisited. *Journal of the Acoustical Society of America, 111,* 2219–2236.

Macuga, K. L., Loomis, J. M., Beall, A. C., & Kelly, J. W. (2006). Perception of heading without retinal optic flow. *Perception & Psychophysics, 68,* 872–878.

Maertens, M., & Pollmann, S. (2005). fMRI reveals a common neural substrate of illusory and real contours in V1 after perceptual learning. *Journal of Cognitive Neuroscience, 17,* 1553–1564.

Maier, J. X., & Ghazanfar, A. A. (2007). Looming biases in monkey auditory cortex. *Journal of Neuroscience, 27,* 4093–4100.

Mainland, J., & Sobel, N. (2006). The sniff is part of the olfactory percept. *Chemical Senses, 31,* 181–196.

Maison, S. F., Luebke, A. E., Liberman, M. C., & Zuo, J. (2002). Efferent protection from acoustic injury is mediated via alpha9 nicotinic acetylcholine receptors on outer hair cells. *Journal of Neuroscience, 22,* 10838–10846.

Makin, T. R., Holmes, N. P., & Ehrsson, H. H. (2008). On the other hand: Dummy hands and peripersonal space. *Behavioural Brain Research, 191,* 1–10.

Malnic, B., Godfrey, P. A., & Buck, L. B. (2004). The human olfactory receptor gene family. *Proceedings of the National Academy of Sciences of the USA, 101,* 2584–2589.

Manchikanti, J., Singh, V., & Boswell, M. V. (2007). Phantom pain syndromes. In S. D. Waldman (Ed.), *Pain management* (pp. 304–315). Philadelphia: W. B. Saunders.

Mandler, G. (2007). *A history of modern experimental psychology: From James and Wundt to cognitive science.* Cambridge, MA: MIT Press.

Mar, R. A., Kelley, W. M., Heatherton, T. F., & Macrae, C. N. (2007). Detecting agency from the biological motion of veridical vs animated agents. [ElectronicElectronic;Print]. *Social Cognitive and Affective Neuroscience, 2,* 199–205.

Marean, G. C., Werner, L. A., & Kuhl, P. K. (1992). Vowel categorization by very young infants. *Developmental Psychology, 28,* 396–405.

Marks, L. E. (1994). "Recalibrating" the auditory system: The perception of loudness. *Journal of Experimental Psychology: Human Perception & Performance, 20,* 382–396.

Marks, L. E., & Gescheider, G. A. (2002). Psychophysical scaling. In H. Pashler (Ed.), *Stevens' handbook of experimental psychology* (3rd ed., Vol. 4, pp. 91–138). New York: Wiley.

Marr, D. (1982). *Vision: A computational investigation into the human representation and processing of visual information.* San Francisco: Freeman.

Marr, D., & Nishihara, H. K. (1978). Representation and recognition of the spatial organization of three-dimensional shapes. *Proceedings of the Royal Society of London B, 200,* 269–294.

Martin, F. N., & Clark, J. G. (2005). *Introduction to audiology* (9th ed.). Boston: Allyn & Bacon.

Martinez-Conde, S., Macknik, S. L., & Hubel, D. H. (2004). The role of fixational eye movements in visual perception. *Nature Reviews Neuroscience, 5,* 229–240.

Martinez-Conde, S., Macknik, S. L., Troncoso, X. G., & Dyar, T. A. (2006). Microsaccades counteract visual fading during fixation. *Neuron, 49,* 297–305.

Masland, R. H. (2001a). Neuronal diversity in the retina. *Current Opinion in Neurobiology, 11,* 431–436.

Masland, R. H. (2001b). The fundamental plan of the retina. *Nature Neuroscience, 4,* 877–886.

Masland, R. H. (2005). The many roles of starburst amacrine cells. *Trends in Neurosciences, 28,* 395–396.

Masland, R. H., & Raviola, E. (2000). Confronting complexity: Strategies for understanding the microcircuitry of the retina. *Annual Review of Neuroscience, 23,* 249–284.

Mason, A. J., Braddick, O. J., & Wattam-Bell, J. (2003). Motion coherence thresholds in infants—Different tasks identify at least two distinct motion systems. *Vision Research, 43,* 1149–1157.

Massaro, D. W. (1998). *Perceiving talking faces: From speech perception to a behavioral principle.* Cambridge, MA: MIT Press.

Massaro, D. W. (2004). From multisensory integration to talking heads and language learning. In G. A. Calvert, C. Spence, & B. E. Stein (Eds.), *The handbook of multisensory processes.* Cambridge, MA: MIT Press.

Masters, W. M., & Harley, H. E. (2004). Performance and cognition in echolocating mammals. In J. A. Thomas, C. F. Moss, & M. Vater (Eds.), *Echolocation in bats and dolphins* (pp. 249–259). Chicago: University of Chicago.

Mateo, J. M. (2006a). Development of individually distinct recognition cues. *Developmental Psychobiology, 48,* 508–519.

Mateo, J. M. (2006b). The nature and representation of individual recognition odours in Belding's ground squirrels. *Animal Behaviour, 71,* 141–154.

Matheson, M. P., Stansfeld, S. A., & Haines, M. M. (2003). The effects of chronic aircraft noise exposure on children's cognition and health: 3 field studies. *Noise Health, 5,* 31–40.

Matlin, M. W. (2009). *Cognition* (7th ed.). New York: Wiley.

Mattingly, I. G., & Studdert-Kennedy, M. (Eds.). (1991). *Modularity and the motor theory of speech perception: Proceedings of a conference to honor Alvin M. Liberman.* Hillsdale, NJ: Erlbaum.

Maurer, D., Ellemberg, D., & Lewis, T. L. (2006). Repeated measurements of contrast sensitivity reveal limits to visual plasticity after early binocular deprivation in humans. *Neuropsychologia, 44,* 2104–2112.

Maurer, D., & Lewis, T. L. (2001a). Visual acuity and spatial contrast sensitivity: Normal development and underlying mechanisms. In C. A. Nelson & M. Luciana (Eds.), *Handbook of developmental cognitive neuroscience* (pp. 237–250). Cambridge, MA: Bradford.

Maurer, D., & Lewis, T. L. (2001b). Visual acuity: The role of visual input in inducing postnatal change. *Clinical Neuroscience Research, 1,* 239–247.

Maurer, D., Lewis, T. L., & Mondloch, C. J. (2005). Missing sights: Consequences for visual cognitive development. *Trends in Cognitive Sciences, 9,* 144–151.

Maurer, D., Mondloch, C. J., & Lewis, T. L. (2007). Sleeper effects. *Developmental Science, 10,* 40–47.

Maurer, D., Pathman, T., & Mondloch, C. J. (2006). The shape of boubas: Sound-shape correspondences in toddlers and adults. *Developmental Science, 9,* 316–322.

Mausfeld, R., & Heyer, D. (Eds.). (2003). *Colour perception: Mind and the physical world.* New York: Oxford.

Max, M., & Meyerhof, W. (2008). Taste receptors. In A. I. Basbaum, M. C. Bushnell, D. V. Smith, G. K. Beauchamp, S. J. Firestein, P. Dallos, D. Oertel, R. H. Masland, T. D. Albright, J. H. Kaas, & E. P. Gardner (Eds.), *The senses: A comprehensive reference* (Vol. 4, pp. 197–217). New York: Academic Press.

May, P. J. (2006). The mammalian superior colliculus: Laminar structure and connections. *Progress in Brain Research, 151,* 321–378.

McAdams, S., & Drake, C. (2002). Auditory perception and cognition. In H. Pashler & S. Yantis (Eds.), *Stevens' hand-*

book of experimental psychology (3rd ed., pp. 397–452). Hoboken, NJ: Wiley.

McBeath, M. K., & Neuhoff, J. G. (2002). The Doppler effect is not what you think it is: Dramatic pitch change due to dynamic intensity change. *Psychonomic Bulletin & Review, 9*, 306–313.

McClintock, M. K. (1971). Menstrual synchrony and suppression. *Nature, 229*, 244–245.

McClintock, M. K., Bullivant, S., Jacob, S., Spencer, N., Zelano, B., & Ober, C. (2005). Human body scents: Conscious perceptions and biological effects. *Chemical Senses, 30 Suppl 1*, i135–137.

McCloskey, M. (2004). Spatial representations and multiple-visual systems hypotheses: Evidence from a developmental deficit in visual location and orientation processing. *Cortex, 40*, 677–694.

McCloskey, M., Rapp, B., Yantis, S., Rubin, G., Bacon, W. F., Dagnelie, G., et al. (1995). A developmental deficit in localizing objects from vision. *Psychological Science, 6*, 112–117.

McCredie, S. (2007). *Balance: In search of the lost sense.* New York: Little, Brown.

McCullough, C. (1965). Color adaptation of edge detectors in the human visual system. *Science, 149*, 1115–1116.

McDonald, I. (2006). Musical alexia with recovery: A personal account. *Brain, 129*, 2554–2561.

McDowell, I. (2006). *Measuring health: A guide to rating scales and questionnaires* (3rd ed.). New York: Oxford.

McGurk, H., & McDonald, J. (1976). Hearing lips and seeing voices. *Nature, 264*, 746–748.

McIntyre, S. E. (2008). Capturing attention to brake lamps. *Accident; Analysis and Prevention, 40*, 691–696.

McKee, S. P. (1993). Editorial: Psychophysics and perception. *Perception, 22*, 505–507.

McKone, E. (2008). Configural processing and face viewpoint. *Journal of Experimental Psychology: Human Perception & Performance, 34*, 310–327.

McKone, E., Kanwisher, N., & Duchaine, B. C. (2007). Can generic expertise explain special processing for faces? *Trends in Cognitive Sciences, 11*, 8–15.

McNeil, J. E., & Warrington, E. K. (1993). Prosopagnosia: A face-specific disorder. *The Quarterly Journal of Experimental Psychology, 46A*, 1–10.

McQuiston-Surrett, D., Malpass, R. S., & Tredoux, C. G. (2006). Sequential vs. simultaneous lineups: A review of methods, data, and theory. *Psychology, Public Policy, and Law, 12*, 137–169.

Meissner, C. A., & Brigham, J. C. (2001). Thirty years of investigating the own-race bias in memory for faces: A meta-analytic review. *Psychology, Public Policy, and Law, 7*, 3–35.

Meissner, C. A., & Kassin, S. M. (2002). "He's guilty!": Investigator bias in judgments of truth and deception. *Law and Human Behavior, 26*, 469–480.

Meissner, C. A., Tredoux, C. G., Parker, J. F., & MacLin, O. H. (2005). Eyewitness decisions in simultaneous and sequential lineups: A dual-process signal detection theory analysis. *Memory & Cognition, 33*, 783–792.

Meltzoff, A. N. (2002a). Elements of a developmental theory of imitation. In A. N. Meltzoff & W. Prinz (Eds.), *The imitative mind: Development, evolution, and brain bases* (pp. 19–41). Cambridge: Cambridge University Press.

Meltzoff, A. N. (2002b). Imitation as a mechanism of social cognition: Origins of empathy, theory of mind, and the representation of action. In U. Goswami (Ed.), *Handbook of childhood cognitive development* (pp. 6–25). Oxford: Blackwell.

Meltzoff, A. N., & Moore, M. K. (1999). Resolving the debate about early imitation. In A. Slater & D. Muir (Eds.), *The Blackwell reader in developmental psychology* (pp. 151–155). Malden, MA: Blackwell.

Melzack, R. (1992). Phantom limbs. *Scientific American, 266*, 120–126.

Melzack, R., & Katz, J. (2007a). A conceptual framework for understanding pain in the human. In S. D. Waldman (Ed.), *Pain management* (pp. 3–10). Philadelphia: W. B. Saunders.

Melzack, R., & Katz, J. (2007b). Amputation and phantom limb pain. In S. Ayers, A. Baum, C. McManus, S. Newman, K. Wallston, J. Weinman, & R. West (Eds.), *Cambridge handbook of psychology, health, and medicine* (2nd ed., pp. 548–550). New York: Cambridge.

Melzack, R., & Wall, P. D. (1965). Pain mechanisms: A new theory. *Science, 150*, 971–979.

Melzer, P., & Ebner, F. (2008). Braille, plasticity, and the mind. In J. J. Rieser, D. H. Ashmead, F. Ebner, & A. L. Corn (Eds.), *Blindness and brain plasticity in navigation and object perception* (pp. 85–112). New York: Erlbaum.

Memon, A., Bartlett, J., Rose, R., & Gray, C. (2003). The aging eyewitness: Effects of age on face, delay, and source-memory ability. *Journals of Gerontology: Series B: Psychological Sciences and Social Sciences, 58B*, P338–P345.

Memon, A., Hope, L., Bartlett, J., & Bull, R. (2002). Eyewitness recognition errors: The effects of mugshot viewing and choosing in young and old adults. *Memory & Cognition, 30*, 1219–1227.

Menashe, I., Man, O., Lancet, D., & Gilad, Y. (2003). Different noses for different people. *Nat Genet, 34*, 143–144.

Mendola, J. D., Conner, I. P., Sharma, S., Bahekar, A., & Lemieux, S. (2006). fMRI Measures of perceptual filling-in in the human visual cortex. *Journal of Cognitive Neuroscience, 18*, 363–375.

Mennella, J. A., Griffin, C. E., & Beauchamp, G. K. (2004). Flavor programming during infancy. *Pediatrics, 113*, 840–845.

Mennella, J. A., Kennedy, J. M., & Beauchamp, G. K. (2006). Vegetable acceptance by infants: Effects of formula flavors. *Early Human Development, 82*, 463–468.

Merabet, L. B., Pitskel, N. B., Amedi, A., & Pascual-Leone, A. (2008). The plastic human brain in blind individuals: The cause of disability and the opportunity for rehabilitation. In J. J. Rieser, D. H. Ashmead, F. Ebner, & A. L. Corn (Eds.), *Blindness and brain plasticity in navigation and object perception* (pp. 23–41). New York: Erlbaum.

Mercier, V., Luy, D., & Hohmann, B. W. (2003). The sound exposure of the audience at a music festival. *Noise Health, 5*, 51–58.

Meredith, M. (2001). Human vomeronasal organ function: A critical review of best and worst cases. *Chemical Senses, 26*, 433–445.

Mermelstein, D. (2007, January 28). Hearing things. The wrong kind of things. *The New York Times.*

Merskey, H. (2008). Taxonomy and classification of chronic pain syndromes. In H. T. Benzon, J. P. Rathmell, C. L. Wu, D. C. Turk, & C. E. Argoff (Eds.), *Raj's practical management of pain* (pp. 13–18). Philadelphia: Mosby.

Merzenich, M. M., Nelson, R. J., Stryker, M. P., Cyander, M. S., Schoppman, A., & Zook, J. M. (1984). Somatosensory cortical map changes following digit amputation in adult monkeys. *Journal of Comparative Neurology, 224*, 591–605.

Meyer, G. (2006). Anatomical and physiological bases of speech perception. In S. Greenberg & W. A. Ainsworth (Eds.), *Listening to speech: An auditory perspective* (pp. 143–156). Mahwah, NJ: Erlbaum.

Micheyl, C., Delhommeau, K., Perrot, X., & Oxenham, A. J. (2006). Influence of musical and psychoacoustical training on pitch discrimination. *Hearing Research, 219*, 36–47.

Middlebrooks, J. C. (2002). Auditory space processing: Here, there or everywhere? *Nature Neuroscience, 5*, 824–826.

Mitchell, J. F., Stoner, G. R., & Reynolds, J. H. (2004). Object-based attention determines dominance in binocular rivalry. *Nature, 429*(6990), 410–413.

Mitsudo, H., & Ono, H. (2007). Additivity of retinal and pursuit velocity in the perceptions of depth and rigidity from object-produced motion parallax. *Perception, 36*, 125–134.

Miyazaki, K. (2004). Recognition of transposed melodies by absolute-pitch possessors. *Japanese Psychological Research, 46*, 270–282.

Mohamed, F. B., Faro, S. H., Gordon, N. J., Platek, S. M., Ahmad, H., & Williams, J. M. (2006). Brain mapping of deception and truth telling about an ecologically valid situation: Functional MR imaging and polygraph investigation—Initial experience. *Radiology, 238*, 679–688.

Moisset, X., & Bouhassira, D. (2007). Brain imaging of neuropathic pain. *Neuroimage, 37 Suppl 1*, S80–88.

Møller, A. R. (2006). *Hearing: Anatomy, physiology, and disorders of the auditory system.* New York: Academic Press.

Mollon, J. D. (2003). The origins of modern color science. In S. K. Shevell (Ed.), *The science of color* (pp. 1–39). New York: Elsevier.

Mondloch, C. J., Dobson, K. S., Parsons, J., & Maurer, D. (2004). Why 8-year-olds cannot tell the difference between Steve Martin and Paul Newman: Factors contributing to the slow development of sensitivity to the spacing of facial features. *Journal of Experimental Child Psychology, 89*, 159–181.

Mondloch, C. J., Geldart, S., Maurer, D., & de Schonen, S. (2003). Developmental changes in the processing of hierarchical shapes continue into adolescence. *Journal of Experimental Child Psychology, 84*, 20–40.

Mondloch, C. J., Le Grand, R., & Maurer, D. (2002). Configural face processing develops more slowly than featural face processing. *Perception, 31*, 553–566.

Mondloch, C. J., Leis, A., & Maurer, D. (2006). Recognizing the face of Johnny, Suzy, and me: Insensitivity to the spacing among features at 4 years of age. *Child Development, 77*, 234–243.

Mondloch, C. J., Lewis, T. L., Budreau, D. R., Maurer, D., Dannemiller, J. L., Stephens, B. R., et al. (1999). Face perception during early infancy. *Psychological Science, 10*, 419–422.

Mondloch, C. J., & Maurer, D. (2004). Do small white balls squeak? Pitch-object correspondences in young children. *Cognitive, affective & behavioral neuroscience, 4*, 133–136.

Mondloch, C. J., & Maurer, D. (2008). The effect of face orientation on holistic processing. *Perception, 37*, 1175–1186.

Mondloch, C. J., Maurer, D., & Ahola, S. (2006). Becoming a face expert. *Psychological Science, 17*, 930–934.

Montaser-Kouhsari, L., Landy, M. S., Heeger, D. J., & Larsson, J. (2007). Orientation-selective adaptation to illusory contours in human visual cortex. *Journal of Neuroscience, 27*, 2186–2195.

Moore, B. C. J. (2001). Loudness, pitch and timbre. In E. B. Goldstein (Ed.), *Blackwell handbook of perception* (pp. 408–436). Malden, MA: Blackwell.

Moore, B. C. J. (2004). *An introduction to the psychology of hearing* (5th ed.). Burlington, MA: Academic.

Morgan, M. (2003). *The space between our ears: How the brain represents visual space.* New York: Oxford.

Morrot, G., Brochet, F., & Dubourdieu, D. (2001). The color of odors. *Brain and Language, 79*, 309–320.

Morton, C. C., & Nance, W. E. (2006). Newborn hearing screening—A silent revolution. *New England Journal of Medicine, 354*, 2151–2164.

Morton, J., & Johnson, M. H. (1991). CONSPEC and CONLERN: A two-process theory of infant face recognition. *Psychological Review, 98*, 164–181.

Moscovitch, M., Winocur, G., & Behrmann, M. (1997). What is special about face recognition? Nineteen experiments on a person with visual object agnosia and dyslexia but normal face recognition. *Journal of Cognitive Neuroscience, 9*, 555–604.

Moser, E. I., Kropff, E., & Moser, M. B. (2008). Place cells, grid cells, and the brain's spatial representation system. *Annual Review of Neuroscience, 31,* 69–89.

Moser, T., Neef, A., & Khimich, D. (2006). Mechanisms underlying the temporal precision of sound coding at the inner hair cell ribbon synapse. *Journal of Physiology, 576,* 55–62.

Moss, C. F., Bohn, K., Gilkenson, H., & Surlykke, A. (2006). Active listening for spatial orientation in a complex auditory scene. *PLoS Biology, 4,* e79.

Moss, C. F., & Carr, C. E. (2003). Comparative psychology of audition. In M. Gallagher & R. J. Nelson (Eds.), *Handbook of psychology: Biological psychology* (Vol. 3, pp. 71–107). Hoboken, NJ: Wiley.

Moss, C. F., & Sinha, S. R. (2003). Neurobiology of echolocation in bats. *Current Opinion in Neurobiology, 13,* 751–758.

Mountcastle, V. B. (2005). *The sensory hand: Neural mechanisms of somatic sensation.* Cambridge, MA: Harvard.

Mrsic-Flogel, T. D., Hofer, S. B., Ohki, K., Reid, R. C., Bonhoeffer, T., & Hubener, M. (2007). Homeostatic regulation of eye-specific responses in visual cortex during ocular dominance plasticity. *Neuron, 54,* 961–972.

Munoz, D. P. (2006). Stabilizing the visual world. *Nature Neuroscience, 9,* 1467–1468.

Murphy, D. R., Daneman, M., & Schneider, B. A. (2006). Why do older adults have difficulty following conversations? *Psychology and Aging, 21,* 49–61.

Murray, S. O., Boyaci, H., & Kersten, D. (2006). The representation of perceived angular size in human primary visual cortex. *Nature Neuroscience, 9,* 429–434.

Nadler, J. W., Angelaki, D. E., & DeAngelis, G. C. (2008). A neural representation of depth from motion parallax in macaque visual cortex. *Nature, 452,* 642–645.

Nagasako, E. M., Oaklander, A. L., & Dworkin, R. H. (2003). Congenital insensitivity to pain: An update. *Pain, 101,* 213–219.

Nagel, T. (1974). What is it like to be a bat? *The Philosophical Review, 83,* 435–450.

Nageris, B. I., Ulanovski, D., & Attias, J. (2004). Magnesium treatment for sudden hearing loss. *Annals of Otology, Rhinology, and Laryngology, 113,* 672–675.

Nakagama, H., Tani, T., & Tanaka, S. (2006). Theoretical and experimental studies of relationship between pinwheel centers and ocular dominance columns in the visual cortex. *Neuroscience Research, 55,* 370–382.

Nakahara, H., Zhang, L. I., & Merzenich, M. M. (2004). Specialization of primary auditory cortex processing by sound exposure in the "critical period." *Proceedings of the National Academy of Sciences of the USA, 101,* 7170–7174.

Nassi, J. J., Lyon, D. C., & Callaway, E. M. (2006). The parvocellular LGN provides a robust disynaptic input to the visual motion area MT. *Neuron, 50,* 319–327.

Nathans, J. (1989). The genes for color vision. *Scientific American, 260,* 42–49.

Nathans, J. (1999). The evolution and physiology of human color vision: Insights from molecular genetic studies of visual pigments. *Neuron, 24,* 299–312.

Nathans, J., Thomas, D., & Hogness, D. S. (1986). Molecular genetics of human color vision: The genes encoding blue, green, and red pigments. *Science, 232,* 193–202.

Nawrot, M., Frankl, M., & Joyce, L. (2008). Concordant eye movement and motion parallax asymmetries in esotropia. *Vision Research, 48,* 799–808.

Nawrot, M., & Joyce, L. (2006). The pursuit theory of motion parallax. *Vision Research, 46,* 4709–4725.

Neisser, U. (1981). Obituary: James J. Gibson (1904–1979). *American Psychologist, 36,* 214–215.

Neitz, J., Carroll, J., Yamauchi, Y., Neitz, M., & Williams, D. R. (2002). Color perception is mediated by a plastic neural mechanism that is adjustable in adults. *Neuron, 35,* 783–792.

Neitz, J., Neitz, M., & Jacobs, G. H. (1993). More than three different cone pigments among people with normal color vision. *Vision Research, 33,* 117–122.

Neitz, M., & Neitz, J. (1998). Molecular genetics and the biological basis of color vision. In W. G. K. Backhaus, R. Kleigl, & J. S. Werner (Eds.), *Color vision: Perspectives from different disciplines* (pp. 101–119). Berlin: de Gruyter.

Neppi-Mòdona, M., Auclair, D., Sirigu, A., & Duhamel, J.-R. (2004). Spatial coding of the predicted impact location of a looming object. *Current Biology, 14,* 1174–1180.

Newcombe, N. S., & Huttenlocher, J. (2000). *Making space: The development of spatial representation and reasoning.* Cambridge, MA: MIT Press.

Newcombe, N. S., & Learmonth, A. E. (2005). Development of spatial competence. In P. Shah & A. Miyake (Eds.), *The Cambridge handbook of visuospatial thinking* (pp. 213–256). New York: Cambridge University Press.

Newcombe, N. S., & Sluzenski, J. (2004). Starting points and change in early spatial development. In G. L. Allen (Ed.), *Human spatial memory: Remembering where* (pp. 25–40). Mahwah, NJ: Erlbaum.

Newman, R. S., & Jusczyk, P. W. (1996). The cocktail party effect in infants. *Perception & Psychophysics, 58,* 1145–1156.

Ni, R., Braunstein, M. L., & Andersen, G. J. (2005). Distance perception from motion parallax and ground contact. *Visual Cognition, 12,* 1235–1254.

Ninio, J. (2007). The science and craft of autostereograms. *Spatial Vision, 21,* 185–200.

Niparko, J. K. (2004). Cochlear implants: Clinical applications. In F.-G. Zeng, A. N. Popper, & R. R. Fay (Eds.), *Cochlear implants: Auditory prostheses and electric hearing* (Vol. 20, pp. 53–100). New York: Springer.

Nordmann, A. S., Bohne, B. A., & Harding, G. W. (2000). Histopathological differences between temporary and permanent threshold shift. *Hearing Research, 139,* 13–30.

Noreña, A. J., & Eggermont, J. J. (2006). Enriched acoustic environment after noise trauma abolishes neural signs of tinnitus. *Neuroreport, 17*, 559–563.

Norman, J. F., Bartholomew, A. N., & Burton, C. L. (2008). Aging preserves the ability to perceive 3D object shape from static but not deforming boundary contours. *Acta Psychologica, 129*, 198–207.

Norman, J. F., Clayton, A. M., Norman, H. F., & Crabtree, C. E. (2008). Learning to perceive differences in solid shape through vision and touch. *Perception, 37*, 185–196.

Norman, J. F., Clayton, A. M., Shular, C. F., & Thompson, S. R. (2004). Aging and the perception of depth and 3-D shape from motion parallax. *Psychology and Aging, 19*, 506–514.

Norman, J. F., Norman, H. F., Clayton, A. M., Lianekhammy, J., & Zielke, G. (2004). The visual and haptic perception of natural object shape. *Perception & Psychophysics, 66*, 342–351.

Norman, J. F., Norman, H. F., Pattison, K., Taylor, M. J., & Goforth, K. E. (2007). Aging and the depth of binocular rivalry suppression. *Psychology and Aging, 22*, 625–631.

Norman, J. F., Ross, H. E., Hawkes, L. M., & Long, J. R. (2003). Aging and the perception of speed. *Perception, 32*, 85–96.

Norman, J. F., Todd, J. T., & Orban, G. A. (2004). Perception of three-dimensional shape from specular highlights, deformations of shading, and other types of visual information. *Psychological Science, 15*, 565–570.

Norton, T. T., & Corliss, D. A. (2002). Adaptation to light and dark. In T. T. Norton, D. A. Corliss & J. E. Bailey (Eds.), *The psychophysical measurement of visual function* (pp. 75–103). Boston: Butterworth-Heinemann.

Nutter, F. W., & Esker, P. D. (2006). The role of psychophysics in phytopathology: The Weber-Fechner law revisited. *European Journal of Plant Pathology, 114*, 199–213.

O'Toole, A. J. (2004). Psychological and neural perspectives on human face recognition. In S. Z. Li & A. Jain (Eds.), *Handbook of face recognition*. New York: Springer-Verlag.

O'Toole, A. J., Bartlett, J. C., & Abdi, H. (2000). A signal detection model applied to the stimulus: Understanding covariances in face recognition experiments in the context of face sampling distributions. *Visual Cognition, 7*, 437–463.

O'Toole, A. J., & Kersten, D. J. (1992). Learning to see random-dot stereograms. *Perception, 21*, 227–243.

Olender, T., Fuchs, T., Linhart, C., Shamir, R., Adams, M., Kalush, F., et al. (2004). The canine olfactory subgenome. *Genomics, 83*, 361–372.

Oliva, A. (2005). Gist of the scene. In L. Itti, G. Rees, & J. K. Tsotsos (Eds.), *Encyclopedia of neurobiology of attention* (pp. 251–256). San Diego, CA: Elsevier.

Oliva, A., & Torralba, A. (2006). Building the gist of a scene: The role of global image features in recognition. *Progress in Brain Research, 155*, 23–36.

Oliva, A., Torralba, A., & Schyns, P. G. (2006). Hybrid images. *ACM Transactions on Graphics (Siggraph), 25*, 527–532.

Olson, H. F. (1967). *Music, physics, and engineering* (2nd ed.). New York: Dover.

Ölveczky, B. P., Baccus, S. A., & Meister, M. (2003). Segregation of object and background motion in the retina. *Nature, 423*(6938), 401–408.

Ono, H., & Wade, N. J. (2005). Depth and motion in historical descriptions of motion parallax. *Perception, 34*, 1263–1273.

Orban, G. A., Janssen, P., & Vogels, R. (2006). Extracting 3D structure from disparity. *Trends in Neurosciences, 29*, 466–473.

Orban, G. A., Van Essen, D. C., & Vanduffel, W. (2004). Comparative mapping of higher visual areas in monkeys and humans. *Trends in Cognitive Sciences, 8*, 315–324.

Orel-Bixler, D. (2002). Postnatal human vision development. In T. T. Norton, D. A. Corliss, & J. E. Bailey (Eds.), *The psychophysical measurement of visual function* (pp. 289–308). Boston: Butterworth-Heinemann.

Ostrovsky, Y., Andalman, A., & Sinha, P. (2006). Vision following extended congenital blindness. *Psychological Science, 17*, 1009–1014.

Ostrovsky, Y., Cavanagh, P., & Sinha, P. (2005). Perceiving illumination inconsistencies in scenes. *Perception, 34*, 1301–1314.

Owens, D. A., Antonoff, R. J., & Francis, E. L. (1994). Biological motion and nighttime pedestrian conspicuity. *Human Factors, 36*, 718–732.

Oxenham, A. J., Bernstein, J. G., & Penagos, H. (2004). Correct tonotopic representation is necessary for complex pitch perception. *Proceedings of the National Academy of Sciences of the USA, 101*, 1421–1425.

Oyster, C. W. (1999). *The human eye: Structure and function*. Sunderland, MA: Sinauer.

Pack, A. A., Herman, L. M., & Hoffmann-Kuhnt, M. (2004). Dolphin echolocation shape perception: From sound to object. In J. A. Thomas, C. F. Moss, & M. Vater (Eds.), *Echolocation in bats and dolphins* (pp. 288–298). Chicago: University of Chicago.

Pack, C. C., & Born, R. T. (2008). Cortical mechanisms for the integration of visual motion. In A. I. Basbaum, M. C. Bushnell, D. V. Smith, G. K. Beauchamp, S. J. Firestein, P. Dallos, D. Oertel, R. H. Masland, T. D. Albright, J. H. Kaas, & E. P. Gardner (Eds.), *The senses: A comprehensive reference* (Vol. 2, pp. 189–218). New York: Academic.

Paffen, C. L. E., Naber, M., & Verstraten, F. A. (2008). The spatial origin of a perceptual transition in binocular rivalry. *PLoS ONE, 3*, e2311.

Paladino, A., Costantini, S., Colonna, G., & Facchiano, A. M. (2008). Molecular modelling of miraculin: Structural analyses and functional hypotheses. *Biochemical and Biophysical Research Communications, 367*, 26–32.

Palanca, B. J., & DeAngelis, G. C. (2005). Does neuronal synchrony underlie visual feature grouping? *Neuron, 46*, 333–346.

Palczewski, K., Hofmann, K. P., & Baehr, W. (2006). Rhodopsin—Advances and perspectives. *Vision Research, 46*, 4425–4426.

Palmer, C., & Jungers, M. K. (2003). Music cognition. In L. Nadel (Ed.), *Encyclopedia of cognitive science* (Vol. 3, pp. 155–158). New York: Nature Publishing Group.

Palmer, S. E. (1975). Visual perception and world knowledge: Notes on a model of sensory-cognitive interaction. In D. A. Norman & D. E. Rumelhart (Eds.), *Explorations in cognition* (pp. 279–307). San Francisco: Freeman.

Palmer, S. E. (1992). Common region: A new principle of perceptual grouping. *Cognitive Psychology, 24*, 436–447.

Palmer, S. E. (1999). *Vision science: Photons to phenomenology.* Cambridge, MA: MIT Press.

Palmer, S. E. (2002). Perceptual organization in vision. In H. Pashler & S. Yantis (Eds.), *Stevens' handbook of experimental psychology* (3rd ed., pp. 177–234). Hoboken, NJ: Wiley.

Palmer, S. E. (2003a). Perceptual organization and grouping. In R. Kimchi, M. Behrmann, & C. R. Olson (Eds.), *Perceptual organization in vision: Behavioral and neural perspectives* (pp. 3–43). Mahwah, NJ: Erlbaum.

Palmer, S. E. (2003b). Visual perception of objects. In A. F. Healy & R. W. Proctor (Eds.), *Handbook of psychology: Experimental psychology* (Vol. 4, pp. 179–211). Hoboken, NJ: Wiley.

Palmer, S. E., & Rock, I. (1994). Rethinking perceptual organization: The role of uniform connectedness. *Psychonomic Bulletin & Review, 1*, 29–55.

Pantev, C., Ross, B., Fujioka, T., Trainor, L. J., Schulte, M., & Schulz, M. (2003). Music and learning-induced cortical plasticity. *Annals of the New York Academy of Science, 999*, 438–450.

Pantev, C., Weisz, N., Schulte, M., & Elbert, T. (2003). Plasticity of the human auditory cortex. In L. Pessoa & P. De Weerd (Eds.), *Filling-in: From perceptual completion to cortical reorganization* (pp. 231–251). New York: Oxford.

Papathomas, T. V. (2007). Art pieces that "move" in our minds—An explanation of illusory motion based on depth reversal. *Spatial Vision, 21*, 79–95.

Paradise, J. L., Campbell, T. F., Dollaghan, C. A., Feldman, H. M., Bernard, B. S., Colborn, D. K., et al. (2005). Developmental outcomes after early or delayed insertion of tympanostomy tubes. *New England Journal of Medicine, 353*, 576–586.

Paradise, J. L., Dollaghan, C. A., Campbell, T. F., Feldman, H. M., Bernard, B. S., Colborn, D. K., et al. (2003). Otitis media and tympanostomy tube insertion during the first three years of life: Developmental outcomes at the age of four years. *Pediatrics, 112*, 265–277.

Paramei, G. V. (2007). Russian "blues": Controversies of basicness. In R. E. MacLaury, G. V. Paramei, & D. Dedrick (Eds.), *Anthropology of color: Interdisciplinary multilevel modeling* (pp. 75–106). Philadelphia: John Benjamins.

Park, T. J., Klug, A., Holinstat, M., & Grothe, B. (2004). Interaural level difference processing in the lateral superior olive and the inferior colliculus. *Journal of Neurophysiology, 92*, 289–301.

Pascalis, O., & Slater, A. (Eds.). (2003). *The development of face processing in infancy and early childhood: Current perspectives.* Hauppauge, NY: Nova.

Pascual-Leone, A. (2003). The brain that plays music is changed by it. In R. J. Zatorre & I. Peretz (Eds.), *The cognitive neuroscience of music* (pp. 396–409). New York: Oxford.

Pasternak, T., Bisley, J. W., & Calkins, D. (2003). Visual processing in the primate brain. In M. Gallagher & R. J. Nelson (Eds.), *Handbook of psychology: Biological psychology* (Vol. 3, pp. 139–185). Hoboken, NJ: Wiley & Sons.

Patel, A. D. (2008). *Music, language, and the brain.* New York: Oxford.

Pearson, J., Clifford, C. W., & Tong, F. (2008). The functional impact of mental imagery on conscious perception. *Current Biology, 18*, 982–986.

Pedemonte, M., Drexler, D. G., & Velluti, R. A. (2004). Cochlear microphonic changes after noise exposure and gantamicin administration during sleep and waking. *Hearing Research, 194*, 25–30.

Peirce, J. W., Solomon, S. G., Forte, J. D., & Lennie, P. (2008). Cortical representation of color is binocular. *Journal of Vision, 8*(6), 1–10.

Peissig, J. J., & Tarr, M. J. (2007). Visual object recognition: Do we know more now than we did 20 years ago? *Annual Review of Psychology, 58*, 75–96.

Pellicano, E., Rhodes, G., & Peters, M. (2006). Are preschoolers sensitive to configural information in faces? *Developmental Science, 9*, 270–277.

Pelphrey, K. A., & Morris, J. P. (2006). Brain mechanisms for interpreting the actions of others from biological-motion cues. *Current Directions in Psychological Science, 15*, 136–140.

Peña, J. L., & Konishi, M. (2001). Auditory spatial receptive fields created by multiplication. *Science, 292*(5515), 249–252.

Penagos, H., Melcher, J. R., & Oxenham, A. J. (2004). A neural representation of pitch salience in nonprimary human auditory cortex revealed with functional magnetic resonance imaging. *Journal of Neuroscience, 24*, 6810–6815.

Penfield, W., & Rasmussen, T. (1950). *The cerebral cortex of man.* New York: Macmillan.

Pepperberg, I. M., Vicinay, J., & Cavanagh, P. (2008). Processing of the Müller-Lyer illusion by a Grey parrot (Psittacus erithacus). *Perception, 37*, 765–781.

Peretz, I., & Zatorre, R. J. (2005). Brain organization for music processing. *Annual Review of Psychology, 56*, 89–114.

Persson Waye, K., Bengtsson, J., Kjellberg, A., & Benton, S. (2001). Low frequency noise "pollution" interferes with performance. *Noise Health, 4*, 33–49.

Pessoa, I., & De Weerd, P. (Eds.). (2003). *Filling-in: From perceptual completion to cortical reorganization*. New York: Oxford.

Peterson, M. A. (2001). Object perception. In E. B. Goldstein (Ed.), *Blackwell handbook of perception* (pp. 168–203). Malden, MA: Blackwell.

Peterson, M. A. (2003). Overlapping partial configurations in object memory: An alternative solution to classic problems in perception and recognition. In M. A. Peterson & G. Rhodes (Eds.), *Perception of faces, objects, and scenes: Analytic and holistic processes* (pp. 269–291). New York: Oxford.

Peterson, M. A. (2007). The piecemeal, constructive, and schematic nature of perception. In M. A. Peterson, B. Gillam, & H. A. Sedgwick (Eds.), *In the mind's eye: Julian Hochberg on the perception of pictures, films, and the world* (pp. 419–428). New York: Oxford.

Peterson, M. A., & Enns, J. T. (2005). The edge complex: Implicit memory for figure assignment in shape perception. *Perception & Psychophysics, 67*, 727–740.

Peterson, M. A., & Gibson, B. S. (1994). Must figure-ground organization precede object recognition? An assumption in peril. *Psychological Science, 5*, 253–259.

Peterson, M. A., Gillam, B., & Sedgwick, H. A. (Eds.). (2007). *In the mind's eye: Julian Hochberg on the perception of pictures, films, and the world*. New York: Oxford.

Peterson, M. A., & Grant, E. S. (2003). Memory and learning in figure-ground perception. In B. Ross & D. E. Irwin (Eds.), *Cognitive vision* (Vol. 42, pp. 1–34). New York: Elsevier.

Peterson, M. A., Harvey, E. M., & Weidenbacher, H. J. (1991). Shape recognition contributions to figure-ground reversal: Which route counts? *Journal of Experimental Psychology: Human Perception & Performance, 17*, 1075–1089.

Peterson, M. A., & Rhodes, G. (2003). *Perception of faces, objects, and scenes: Analytic and holistic processes*. New York: Oxford.

Peterson, M. A., & Skow, E. (2008). Inhibitory competition between shape properties in figure-ground perception. *Journal of Experimental Psychology: Human Perception & Performance, 34*, 251–267.

Petrulis, A., & Eichenbaum, H. (2003). Olfactory memory. In R. L. Doty (Ed.), *Handbook of olfaction and gustation* (pp. 409–438). New York: Marcel Dekker.

Peuskens, H., Claeys, K. G., Todd, J. T., Norman, J. F., Van Hecke, P., & Orban, G. A. (2004). Attention to 3-D shape, 3-D motion, and texture in 3-D structure from motion displays. *Journal of Cognitive Neuroscience, 16*, 665–682.

Pezdek, K., Blandon-Gitlin, I., & Moore, C. (2003). Children's face recognition memory: More evidence for the cross-race effect. *Journal of Applied Psychology, 88*, 760–763.

Phillips, V. L., Saks, M. J., & Peterson, J. L. (2001). The application of signal detection theory to decision-making in forensic science. *Journal of Forensic Sciences, 46*, 294–308.

Pianta, M. J., & Gillam, B. J. (2003). Paired and unpaired features can be equally effective in human depth perception. *Vision Research, 43*, 1–6.

Pickles, J. O. (1988). *An introduction to the physiology of hearing* (2nd ed.). London: Academic Press.

Pierce, J. R. (1983). *The science of musical sound*. New York: Freeman.

Pierce, J. R. (1999). Consonance and scales. In P. R. Cook (Ed.), *Music, cognition, and computerized sound: An introduction to psychoacoustics* (pp. 167–185). Cambridge, MA: MIT Press.

Pierroutsakos, S. L., & DeLoache, J. S. (2003). Infants' manual exploration of pictorial objects varying in realism. *Infancy, 4*, 141–156.

Pinel, J. P. J. (2006). *Biopsychology* (6th ed.). Boston: Allyn & Bacon.

Pinna, B., & Brelstaff, G. J. (2000). A new visual illusion of relative motion. *Vision Research, 40*, 2091–2096.

Pinto, J. (2005). Developing body representations: A review of infants' responses to biological motion displays. In G. Knoblich, I. M. Thornton, M. Grosjean, & M. Shiffrar (Eds.), *Human body perception from the inside out* (pp. 305–322). New York: Oxford.

Pisoni, D. B., & Cleary, M. (2004). Learning, memory, and cognitive processes in deaf children following cochlear implantation. In F.-G. Zeng, A. N. Popper, & R. R. Fay (Eds.), *Cochlear implants: Auditory prostheses and electric hearing* (Vol. 20, pp. 377–426). New York: Springer.

Pizlo, Z. (2008). *3D shape: Its unique place in visual perception*. Cambridge, MA: MIT Press.

Plack, C. J. (2005). *The sense of hearing*. Mahwah, NJ: Erlbaum.

Plack, C. J., & Oxenham, A. J. (2005). Overview: The present and future of pitch. In C. J. Plack, A. J. Oxenham, R. R. Fay, & A. N. Popper (Eds.), *Pitch: Neural coding and perception* (pp. 1–6). New York: Springer.

Platek, S. M., Burch, R. L., & Gallup, G. G., Jr. (2001). Sex differences in olfactory self-recognition. *Physiology & Behavior, 73*, 635–640.

Plomp, R. (2002). *The intelligent ear: On the nature of sound perception*. Mahwah, NJ: Erlbaum.

Pokorny, J. (2004). The evolution of knowledge: Trichromacy as theory and in nature. *Clinical and Experimental Optometry, 87*, 203–205.

Pollack, I., & Pickett, J. M. (1963). The intelligibility of excerpts from conversational speech. *Language & Speech, 6*, 165–171.

Pons, T. P., Preston, E., Garraghty, A. K., Kaas, J., Taub, E., & Mishkin, M. (1991). Massive cortical reorganization after sensory deafferentation in adult macaques. *Science, 252*, 1857–1860.

Porter, J., Craven, B., Khan, R. M., Chang, S. J., Kang, I., Judkewitz, B., et al. (2007). Mechanisms of scent-tracking in humans. *Nature Neuroscience, 10*, 27–29.

Post, D. L., & Task, H. L. (2006). Visual display technology. In W. Karwowski (Ed.), *International encyclopedia of ergonomics and human factors* (pp. 850–855). Boca Raton, FL: CRC Press.

Postma, A., Kessels, R. P. C., & van Asselen, M. (2004). The neuropsychology of object-location memory. In G. L. Allen (Ed.), *Human spatial memory: Remembering where* (pp. 143–160). Mahwah, NJ: Erlbaum.

Postma, A., Zuidhoek, S., Noordzij, M. L., & Kappers, A. M. (2007). Differences between early-blind, late-blind, and blindfolded-sighted people in haptic spatial-configuration learning and resulting memory traces. *Perception, 36*, 1253–1265.

Potter, T., Corneille, O., Ruys, K. I., & Rhodes, G. (2007) "Just another pretty face": A multidimensional scaling approach to face attractiveness and variability. *Psychonomic Bulletin & Review, 14*, 368–372.

Poulet, J. F. A., & Hedwig, B. (2007). New insights into corollary discharges mediated by identified neural pathways. *Trends in Neurosciences, 30*, 14–21.

Poulton, E. C. (1989). *Bias in quantifying judgments*. Hove, UK: Erlbaum.

Prescott, J. (2004). Psychological processes in flavour perception. In A. J. Taylor & D. D. Roberts (Eds.), *Flavor perception* (pp. 256–277). Malden, MA: Blackwell.

Pressey, A. W., & Epp, D. (1992). Spatial attention in Ponzo-like patterns. *Perception & Psychophysics, 52*, 211–221.

Price, D. D., Finniss, D. G., & Benedetti, F. (2008). A comprehensive review of the placebo effect: Recent advances and current thought. *Annual Review of Psychology, 59*, 565–590.

Price, D. D., Hirsh, A., & Robinson, M. E. (2008). Psychological modulation of pain. In A. I. Basbaum, M. C. Bushnell, D. V. Smith, G. K. Beauchamp, S. J. Firestein, P. Dallos, D. Oertel, R. H. Masland, T. D. Albright, J. H. Kaas, & E. P. Gardner (Eds.), *The senses: A comprehensive reference* (Vol. 5, pp. 975–1002). New York: Academic Press.

Price, G. R. (2007). Predicting mechanical damage to the organ of Corti. *Hearing Research, 226*, 5–13.

Prinzmetal, W., & Beck, D. M. (2001). The tilt-constancy theory of visual illusions. *Journal of Experimental Psychology: Human Perception & Performance, 27*, 206–217.

Prinzmetal, W., Shimamura, A. P., & Mikolinski, M. (2001). The Ponzo illusion and the perception of orientation. *Perception & Psychophysics, 63*, 99–114.

Priplata, A. A., Niemi, J. B., Harry, J. D., Lipsitz, L. A., & Collins, J. J. (2003). Vibrating insoles and balance control in elderly people. *Lancet, 362*(9390), 1123–1124.

Proffitt, D. R. (2006a). Distance perception. *Current Directions in Psychological Science, 15*, 131–135.

Proffitt, D. R. (2006b). Embodied perception and the economy of action. *Perspectives on Psychological Science, 1*, 110–122.

Proffitt, D. R., Stefanucci, J., Banton, T., & Epstein, W. (2003). The role of effort in perceiving distance. *Psychological Science, 14*, 106–112.

Pugh, E. N., Jr. (1988). Vision: Physics and retinal physiology. In R. C. Atkinson, R. J. Herrnstein, G. Lindzey, & R. D. Luce (Eds.), *Stevens' handbook of experimental psychology* (2nd ed., Vol. 1, pp. 75–163). New York: Wiley.

Pullum, G. K. (1991). *The great Eskimo vocabulary hoax and other irreverent essays on the study of language*. Chicago: University of Chicago.

Puria, S., & Steele, C. R. (2008). Mechano-acoustical transformations. In A. I. Basbaum, M. C. Bushnell, D. V. Smith, G. K. Beauchamp, S. J. Firestein, P. Dallos, D. Oertel, R. H. Masland, T. D. Albright, J. H. Kaas, & E. P. Gardner (Eds.), *The senses: A comprehensive reference* (Vol. 3, pp. 166–201). New York: Academic.

Purves, D., & Lotto, R. B. (2003). *Why we see what we do: An empirical theory of vision*. Sunderland, MA: Sinauer.

Purves, D., Williams, S. M., Nundy, S., & Lotto, R. B. (2004). Perceiving the intensity of light. *Psychological Review, 111*, 142–158.

Putnam, N. M., Hofer, H. J., Doble, N., Chen, L., Carroll, J., & Williams, D. R. (2005). The locus of fixation and the foveal cone mosaic. *Journal of Vision, 5*, 632–639.

Qiu, F. T., & von der Heydt, R. (2005). Figure and ground in the visual cortex: V2 combines stereoscopic cues with Gestalt rules. *Neuron, 47*, 155–166.

Qiu, J., Li, H., Zhang, Q., Liu, Q., & Zhang, F. (2008). The Müller-Lyer illusion seen by the brain: An event-related brain potentials study. *Biological Psychology, 77*(2), 150–158.

Quinn, P. C. (1999). Development of recognition and categorization of objects and their spatial relations in young infants. In L. Balter & C. S. Tamis-LeMonda (Eds.), *Child psychology: A handbook of contemporary issues*. (pp. 85–115). New York: Psychology Press.

Quinn, P. C., Kelly, D. J., Lee, K., Pascalis, O., & Slater, A. M. (2008). Preference for attractive faces in human infants extends beyond conspecifics. *Developmental Science, 11*, 76–83.

Quinn, S., & Watt, R. (2006). The perception of tempo in music. *Perception, 35*, 267–280.

Quiroga, R. Q., Mukamel, R., Isham, E. A., Malach, R., & Fried, I. (2008). Human single-neuron responses at the threshold of conscious recognition. *Proceedings of the National Academy of Sciences of the USA, 105*, 3599–3604.

Quiroga, R. Q., Reddy, L., Kreiman, G., Koch, C., & Fried, I. (2005). Invariant visual representation by single neurons in the human brain. *Nature, 435*(7045), 1102–1107.

Rabbitt, P. (2002). Aging and cognition. In H. Pashler & J. T. Wixted (Eds.), *Stevens' handbook of experimental psychology* (3rd ed., pp. 793–860). Hoboken, NJ: Wiley.

Rabinowitz, P. M. (2000). Noise-induced hearing loss. *American Family Physician, 61*, 2749–2756, 2759–2760.

Radocy, R. E., & Boyle, J. D. (2003). *Psychological foundations of musical behavior* (4th ed.). Springfield, IL: Thomas.

Ramachandran, V. S. (2003). Foreword. In L. Pessoa & P. De Weerd (Eds.), *Filling-in: From perceptual completion to cortical reorganization* (pp. xi–xxii). New York: Oxford.

Ramachandran, V. S., & Blakeslee, S. (1998). *Phantoms in the brain: Probing the mysteries of the human mind.* New York: William Morrow.

Ramachandran, V. S., & Gregory, R. L. (1991). Perceptual filling in of artificially induced scotomas in human vision. *Nature, 350*, 699–702.

Ramachandran, V. S., & Hirstein, W. (1998). The perception of phantom limbs. The D. O. Hebb lecture. *Brain, 121*, 1603–1630.

Ramachandran, V. S., & McGeoch, P. D. (2007). Occurrence of phantom genitalia after gender reassignment surgery. *Medical Hypotheses, 69*, 1001–1003.

Ramachandran, V. S., & Rogers-Ramachandran, D. (2008). Illusions: Sizing things up. *Scientific American Mind, 19*(1), 18–20.

Ratliff, F. (1984). Why Mach bands are not seen at the edges of a step. *Vision Research, 24*, 163–165.

Rauschecker, J. P. (2001). Cortical plasticity and music. In R. J. Zatorre & I. Peretz (Eds.), *Biological foundations of music* (Vol. 930, pp. 330–336). New York: NY Academy of Sciences.

Rauschecker, J. P., & Shannon, R. V. (2002). Sending sound to the brain. *Science, 295*(5557), 1025–1029.

Rauschecker, J. P., & Tian, B. (2000). Mechanisms and streams for processing of "what" and "where" in auditory cortex. *Proceedings of the National Academy of Sciences of the USA, 97*, 11800–11806.

Ray, N. J., Fowler, S., & Stein, J. F. (2005). Yellow filters can improve magnocellular function: Motion sensitivity, convergence, accommodation, and reading. *Annals of the New York Academy of Science, 1039*, 283–293.

Rayner, K. (1998). Eye movements in reading and information processing: 20 years of research. *Psychological Bulletin, 124*, 372–422.

Rayner, K., & Johnson, R. L. (2005). Letter-by-letter acquired dyslexia is due to the serial encoding of letters. *Psychological Science, 16*, 530–534.

Rayner, K., & Liversedge, S. P. (2004). Visual and linguistic processing during eye fixations in reading. In J. M. Henderson & F. Ferreira (Eds.), *The interface of language, vision, and action: Eye movements and the visual world* (pp. 59–104). New York: Psychology Press.

Rayner, K., Reichle, E. D., & Pollatsek, A. (2005). Eye movement control in reading and the E-Z Reader model. In G. Underwood (Ed.), *Cognitive processes in eye guidance* (pp. 131–162). New York: Oxford.

Rayner, K., White, S. J., Johnson, R. L., & Liversedge, S. P. (2006). Raeding wrods with jumbled lettres: There is a cost. *Psychological Science, 17*, 192–193.

Read, J. C. A. (2005). Early computational processing in binocular vision and depth perception. *Progress in Biophysics and Molecular Biology, 87*, 77–108.

Read, J. C. A., & Cumming, B. G. (2004). Understanding the cortical specialization for horizontal disparity. *Neural Computation, 16*, 1983–2020.

Read, J. C. A., & Cumming, B. G. (2005). All Pulfrich-like illusions can be explained without joint encoding of motion and disparity. *Journal of Vision, 5*, 901–927.

Read, J. C. A., & Cumming, B. G. (2006). Does depth perception require vertical-disparity detectors? *Journal of Vision, 6*, 1323–1355.

Read, J. C. A., & Cumming, B. G. (2007). Sensors for impossible stimuli may solve the stereo correspondence problem. *Nature Neuroscience, 10*, 1322–1328.

Recanzone, G. H., & Sutter, M. L. (2008). The biological basis of audition. *Annual Review of Psychology, 59*, 119–142.

Reed, C. L., Stone, V. E., Bozova, S., & Tanaka, J. (2003). The body-inversion effect. *Psychological Science, 14*, 302–308.

Regan, D. (2000). *Human perception of objects: Early visual processing of spatial form defined by luminance, color, texture, motion, and binocular disparity.* Sunderland, MA: Sinauer.

Regier, T., Kay, P., & Khetarpal, N. (2007). Color naming reflects optimal partitions of color space. *Proceedings of the National Academy of Sciences of the USA, 104*, 1436–1441.

Reicher, G. M. (1969). Perceptual recognition as a function of meaningfulness of stimulus materials. *Journal of Experimental Psychology, 81*, 275–280.

Reichle, E. D., & Laurent, P. A. (2006). Using reinforcement learning to understand the emergence of "intelligent" eye-movement behavior during reading. *Psychological Review, 113*, 390–408.

Reinberger, S. (2006, June/July). Bitter could be better. *Scientific American Mind, 17*, 56–61.

Reinhardt-Rutland, A. H. (2003). Induced rotational motion with nonabutting inducing and induced stimuli: Implications regarding two forms of induced motion. *Journal of General Psychology, 130*, 260–274.

Remez, R. E., Rubin, P. E., Pisoni, D. B., & Carrell, T. D. (1981). Speech perception without traditional speech cues. *Science, 212*, 947–950.

Renouf, D. (1989). Sensory function in the harbor seal. *Scientific American, 260*, 90–95.

Revonsuo, A. (1999). Binding and the phenomenal unity of consciousness. *Consciousness and Cognition, 8*, 173–185.

Rhodes, G. (2006). The evolutionary psychology of facial beauty. *Annual Review of Psychology, 57*, 199–226.

Rhodes, G., Peters, M., & Ewing, L. A. (2007). Specialised higher-level mechanisms for facial-symmetry perception: Evidence from orientation-tuning functions. *Perception, 36*, 1804–1812.

Rhodes, G., Sumich, A., & Byatt, G. (1999). Are average facial configurations attractive only because of their symmetry? *Psychological Science, 10*, 52–58.

Ricci, D., Cesarini, L., Groppo, M., De Carli, A., Gallini, F., Serrao, F., et al. (2007). Early assessment of visual function in full term newborns. *Early Human Development, 84*, 107–113.

Ricci, F., Cedrone, C., & Cerulli, L. (1998). Standardized measurement of visual acuity. *Ophthalmic Epidemiology, 5*, 41–53.

Rich, A. N., Williams, M. A., Puce, A., Syngeniotis, A., Howard, M. A., McGlone, F., et al. (2006). Neural correlates of imagined and synaesthetic colours. *Neuropsychologia, 44*, 2918–2925.

Richards, E., Bennett, P. J., & Sekuler, A. B. (2006). Age related differences in learning with the useful field of view. *Vision Research, 46*, 1217–1231.

Richards, W., Nishihara, H. K., & Dawson, B. (1988). CARTOON: A biologically motivated edge detection algorithm. In W. Richards (Ed.), *Natural computation* (pp. 55–69). Cambridge, MA: MIT Press.

Riedel, E., Stephan, T., Deutschlander, A., Kalla, R., Wiesmann, M., Dieterich, M., et al. (2005). Imaging the visual autokinetic illusion with fMRI. *Neuroimage, 27*, 163–166.

Rieser, J. J., Ashmead, D. H., Ebner, F., & Corn, A. L. (Eds.). (2008). *Blindness and brain plasticity in navigation and object perception*. New York: Erlbaum.

Riggs, L. A. (1971). Vision. In J. W. Kling & L. A. Riggs (Eds.), *Woodworth & Schlosberg's experimental psychology* (3rd ed., pp. 273–314). New York: Holt, Rinehart and Winston.

Ringkamp, M., & Meyer, R. A. (2008). Physiology of nociceptors. In A. I. Basbaum, M. C. Bushnell, D. V. Smith, G. K. Beauchamp, S. J. Firestein, P. Dallos, D. Oertel, R. H. Masland, T. D. Albright, J. H. Kaas, & E. P. Gardner (Eds.), *The senses: A comprehensive reference* (Vol. 5, pp. 97–114). New York: Academic Press.

Riordan-Eva, P. (2004). Glaucoma. In P. Riordan-Eva, T. Asbury & J. P. Whitcher (Eds.), *Vaughn & Asbury's general ophthalmology* (16th ed., pp. 212–229). New York: McGraw-Hill Medical.

Riordan-Eva, P., & Whitcher, J. P. (Eds.). (2007). *Vaughn & Asbury's general ophthalmology* (17th ed.). New York: McGraw Hill Medical.

Risset, J.-C., & Wessel, D. L. (1999). Exploration of timbre by analysis and synthesis. In D. Deutsch (Ed.), *The psychology of music* (2nd ed., pp. 113–169). San Diego: Academic.

Rizzo, M., Nawrot, M., & Zihl, J. (1995). Motion and shape perception in cerebral akinetopsia. *Brain, 118 (Pt 5)*, 1105–1127.

Roach, N. W., Heron, J., & McGraw, P. V. (2006). Resolving multisensory conflict: A strategy for balancing the costs and benefits of audio-visual integration. *Proceedings of The Royal Society B: Biological Sciences, 273*(1598), 2159–2168.

Robbins, R., & McKone, E. (2003). Can holistic processing be learned for inverted faces? *Cognition, 88*, 79–107.

Robbins, R., & McKone, E. (2007). No face-like processing for objects-of-expertise in three behavioural tasks. *Cognition, 103*, 34–79.

Roberson, D., Davidoff, J., Davies, I. R. L., & Shapiro, L. R. (2005). Color categories: Evidence for the cultural relativity hypothesis. *Cognitive Psychology, 50*, 378–411.

Roberson, D., Davies, I. R. L., & Davidoff, J. (2000). Color categories are not universal: Replications and new evidence from a stone-age culture. *Journal of Experimental Psychology: General, 129*, 369–398.

Roberson, D., & Hanley, J. R. (2007). Color vision: Color categories vary with language after all. *Current Biology, 17*, R605–607.

Roberts, B., Harris, M. G., & Yates, T. A. (2005). The roles of inducer size and distance in the Ebbinghaus illusion (Titchener circles). *Perception, 34*, 847–856.

Robertson, L. C. (2003). Binding, spatial attention and perceptual awareness. *Nature Reviews Neuroscience, 4*, 93–102.

Robertson, L. C. (2004). *Space, objects, minds, and brains*. New York: Psychology Press.

Robinson, F. R., & Fuchs, A. F. (2001). The role of the cerebellum in voluntary eye movements. *Annual Review of Neuroscience, 24*, 981–1004.

Rock, I. (1997). *Indirect perception*. Cambridge, MA: MIT Press.

Rock, I., Nijhawan, R., & Palmer, S. E. (1992). Grouping based on phenomenal similarity of achromatic color. *Perception, 21*, 779–789.

Rock, P. B., Harris, M. G., & Yates, T. (2006). A test of the tau-dot hypothesis of braking control in the real world. *Journal of Experimental Psychology: Human Perception & Performance, 32*, 1479–1484.

Rodieck, R. W. (1998). *The first steps in seeing*. Sunderland, MA: Sinauer.

Rogers, T. B., Kuiper, N. A., & Kirker, W. S. (1977). Self-reference and the encoding of personal information. *Journal of Personality and Social Psychology, 35*, 677–688.

Rollag, M. D., Berson, D. M., & Provencio, I. (2003). Melanopsin, ganglion-cell photoreceptors, and mammalian photoentrainment. *Journal of Biological Rhythms, 18*, 227–234.

Rolls, E. T. (2005). Taste, olfactory, and food texture processing in the brain, and the control of food intake. *Physiology & Behavior, 85*, 45–56.

Rolls, E. T. (2008). The representation of flavor in the brain. In A. I. Basbaum, M. C. Bushnell, D. V. Smith, G. K. Beauchamp, S. J. Firestein, P. Dallos, D. Oertel, R. H. Masland, T. D. Albright, J. H. Kaas, & E. P. Gardner (Eds.), *The senses: A comprehensive reference* (Vol. 4, pp. 469–478). New York: Academic Press.

Rolls, E. T., & Deco, G. (2002). *Computational neuroscience of vision*. New York: Oxford.

Rose, D. (2000). Psychophysical methods. In G. M. Breakwell, S. Hammond, & C. Fife-Schaw (Eds.), *Research methods in psychology* (2nd ed., pp. 194–210). Thousand Oaks, CA: Sage Publications.

Rose, D., & Bressan, P. (2002). Going round in circles: Shape effects in the Ebbinghaus illusion. *Spatial Vision, 15,* 191–203.

Rosenbaum, R. S., Gao, F., Richards, B., Black, S. E., & Moscovitch, M. (2005). "Where to?" remote memory for spatial relations and landmark identity in former taxi drivers with Alzheimer's disease and encephalitis. *Journal of Cognitive Neuroscience, 17,* 446–462.

Rosenblum, L. D. (2005). Primacy of multimodal speech perception. In D. B. Pisoni & R. E. Remez (Eds.), *The handbook of speech perception* (pp. 51–78). Malden, MA: Blackwell.

Rosenblum, L. D., Miller, R. M., & Sanchez, K. (2007). Lip-read me now, hear me better later: Cross-modal transfer of talker-familiarity effects. *Psychological Science, 18,* 392–396.

Rosenblum, L. D., Niehus, R. P., & Smith, N. M. (2007). Look who's talking: Recognizing friends from visible articulation. *Perception, 36,* 157–159.

Rosenblum, L. D., Yakel, D. A., & Green, K. P. (2000). Face and mouth inversion effects on visual and audiovisual speech perception. *Journal of Experimental Psychology: Human Perception & Performance, 26,* 806–819.

Rosenquist, R. W., & Haider, N. (2008). Phantom limb pain. In H. T. Benzon, J. P. Rathmell, C. L. Wu, D. C. Turk, & C. E. Argoff (Eds.), *Raj's practical management of pain* (pp. 445–453). Philadelphia: Mosby.

Rosenzweig, S. (1987). The final tribute of E. G. Boring to G. T. Fechner: Concerning the date October 22, 1850. *American Psychologist, 42,* 787–790.

Ross, H., & Plug, C. (2002). *The mystery of the moon illusion: Exploring size perception.* New York: Oxford.

Rossing, T. D., Moore, F. R., & Wheeler, P. A. (2002). *The science of sound* (3rd ed.). San Francisco: Addison-Wesley.

Rossion, B. (2008). Picture-plane inversion leads to qualitative changes of face perception. *Acta Psychologica, 128,* 274–289.

Rotello, C. M., Macmillan, N. A., & Reeder, J. A. (2004). Sum-difference theory of remembering and knowing: A two-dimensional signal-detection model. *Psychological Review, 111,* 588–616.

Roumes, C., Meehan, J. W., Plantier, J., & Menu, J.-P. (2001). Distance estimation in a 3-D imaging display. *International Journal of Aviation Psychology, 11,* 381–396.

Rovee-Collier, C., & Barr, R. (2001). Infant cognition. In H. Pashler (Ed.), *Stevens' handbook of experimental psychology* (3rd ed., Vol. 4, pp. 693–791). New York: Wiley.

Rowe, M. H. (2002). Trichromatic color vision in primates. *News in Physiological Sciences, 17,* 93–98.

Rubin, E. (1915/1958). Synoplevede figurer (Figure and ground) (M. Wertheimer, Trans.). In D. C. Beardslee & M. Wertheimer (Eds.), *Readings in perception* (pp. 194–203). Princeton, NJ: Van Nostrand.

Rubinstein, J. T. (2004). How cochlear implants encode speech. *Current Opinion in Otolaryngology & Head and Neck Surgery, 12,* 444–448.

Ruppertsberg, A. I., Wuerger, S. M., & Bertamini, M. (2003). The chromatic input to global motion perception. *Visual Neuroscience, 20,* 421–428.

Ruppertsberg, A. I., Wuerger, S. M., & Bertamini, M. (2007). When S-cones contribute to chromatic global motion processing. *Visual Neuroscience, 24,* 1–8.

Rushton, W. A. H. (1958). Kinetics of cone pigments measured objectively in the living human fovea. *Annals of the New York Academy of Sciences, 74,* 291–304.

Rutherford, M. D., & Brainard, D. H. (2002). Lightness constancy: A direct test of the illumination-estimation hypothesis. *Psychological Science, 13,* 142–149.

Rutherford, W. (1886). A new theory of hearing. *Journal of Anatomy and Physiology, 21,* 166–168.

Sachtler, W. L., & Gillam, B. (2007). The stereoscopic sliver: A comparison of duration thresholds for fully stereoscopic and unmatched versions. *Perception, 36,* 135–144.

Sacks, O. (1985). *The man who mistook his wife for a hat, and other clinical tales.* New York: Summit Books.

Sacks, O. (1995). *An anthropologist on Mars: Seven paradoxical tales.* New York: Knopf.

Sacks, O. (2007). *Musicophilia: Tales of music and the brain.* New York: Knopf.

Saffran, J. R. (2003a). Absolute pitch in infancy and adulthood: The role of tonal structure. *Developmental Science, 6,* 37–49.

Saffran, J. R. (2003b). Musical learning and language development. In G. Avanzini, C. Faienza, D. Minciacchi, L. Lopez, & M. Majno (Eds.), *The neurosciences and music* (Vol. 999, pp. 397–401). New York: NY Academy of Sciences.

Saffran, J. R., & Griepentrog, G. J. (2001). Absolute pitch in infant auditory learning: Evidence for developmental reorganization. *Developmental Psychology, 37,* 74–85.

Saffran, J. R., Reeck, K., Niebuhr, A., & Wilson, D. (2005). Changing the tune: The structure of the input affects infants' use of absolute and relative pitch. *Developmental Science, 8,* 1–7.

Saffran, J. R., Werker, J. F., & Werner, L. A. (2006). The infant's auditory world: Hearing, speech, and the beginnings of language. In D. Kuhn, R. S. Siegler, W. Damon, & R. M. Lerner (Eds.), *Handbook of child psychology: Vol 2, Cognition, perception, and language* (6th ed., pp. 58–108). Hoboken, NJ: Wiley.

Salvi, R. J., Wang, J., & Caspary, D. M. (2007). Functional changes in the central auditory system after noise-induced cochlear damage. In L. Luxon & D. Prasher (Eds.), *Noise and its effects* (pp. 110–126). Chichester, England: Wiley.

Samuel, A. G. (1996). Does lexical information influence the perceptual restoration of phonemes? *Journal of Experimental Psychology: General, 125*, 28–51.

Samuel, A. G. (2001). Knowing a word affects the fundamental perception of the sounds within it. *Psychological Science, 12*, 348–351.

Sasaki, Y., Vanduffel, W., Knutsen, T., Tyler, C., & Tootell, R. (2005). Symmetry activates extrastriate visual cortex in human and nonhuman primates. *Proceedings of the National Academy of Sciences of the USA, 102*, 3159–3163.

Sathian, K., & Lacey, S. (2007). Journeying beyond classical somatosensory cortex. *Canadian Journal of Experimental Psychology, 61*, 254–264.

Sathian, K., & Laccy, S. (2008). Visual cortical involvement during tactile perception in blind and sighted individuals. In J. J. Rieser, D. H. Ashmead, F. Ebner, & A. L. Corn (Eds.), *Blindness and brain plasticity in navigation and object perception* (pp. 113–125). New York: Erlbaum.

Saygin, A. P. (2007). Superior temporal and premotor brain areas necessary for biological motion perception. *Brain, 130*, 2452–2461.

Scerif, G., Kotsoni, E., & Casey, B. J. (2006). The functional neuroimaging of development. In R. Cabeza & A. Kingstone (Eds.), *Functional neuroimaging of cognition* (pp. 351–378). Cambridge, MA: MIT Press.

Schank, J. C. (2006). Do human mesntrual-cycle hormones exist? *Human Nature, 17*, 448–470.

Schaub, M. (2005). *Janet Cardiff: The walk book*. New York: Walther Konig.

Scheibe, F., Haupt, H., Mazurek, B., & Konig, O. (2001). Therapeutic effect of magnesium on noise-induced hearing loss. *Noise Health, 3*, 79–84.

Schellenberg, E. G., & Trehub, S. E. (2003). Good pitch memory is widespread. *Psychological Science, 14*, 262–266.

Schenk, T., Ellison, A., Rice, N., & Milner, A. D. (2005). The role of V5/MT+ in the control of catching movements: An rTMS study. *Neuropsychologia, 43*, 189–198.

Schenk, T., Mai, N., Ditterich, J., & Zihl, J. (2000). Can a motion-blind patient reach for moving objects? *The European Journal of Neuroscience, 12*, 3351–3360.

Schermer, M. (2008). The brain is not modular: What fMRI really tells us. *Scientific American.*

Schieber, F. (2006). Vision and aging. In J. E. Birren & K. W. Schaie (Eds.), *Handbook of the psychology of aging* (6th ed., pp. 129–162). New York: Academic.

Schiffman, H. R. (2003). Psychophysics. In S. F. Davis (Ed.), *Handbook of research methods in experimental psychology* (pp. 441–469). Malden, MA: Blackwell.

Schiffman, S. S. (2008). The aging gustatory system. In A. I. Basbaum, M. C. Bushnell, D. V. Smith, G. K. Beauchamp, S. J. Firestein, P. Dallos, D. Oertel, R. H. Masland, T. D. Albright, J. H. Kaas, & E. P. Gardner (Eds.), *The senses: A comprehensive reference* (Vol. 4, pp. 479–498). New York: Academic Press.

Schiller, P. H. (1986). The central visual system. *Vision Research, 26*, 1351–1386.

Schiller, P. H., Slocum, W. M., & Weiner, V. S. (2007). How the parallel channels of the retina contribute to depth processing. *The European Journal of Neuroscience, 26*, 1307–1321.

Schiltz, C., & Rossion, B. (2006). Faces are represented holistically in the human occipito-temporal cortex. *Neuroimage, 32*, 1385–1394.

Schlaug, G. (2003). The brain of musicians. In I. Peretz & R. J. Zatorre (Eds.), *The cognitive neuroscience of music* (pp. 366–381). New York: Oxford.

Schmuckler, M. A., Collimore, L. M., & Dannemiller, J. L. (2007). Infants' reactions to object collision on hit and miss trajectories. *Infancy, 12*, 105–118.

Schneider, B. A., Daneman, M., & Murphy, D. R. (2005). Speech comprehension difficulties in older adults: Cognitive slowing or age-related changes in hearing? *Psychology and Aging, 20*, 261–271.

Schneider, B. A., Daneman, M., Murphy, D. R., & See, S. K. (2000). Listening to discourse in distracting settings: The effects of aging. *Psychology and Aging, 15*, 110–125.

Schneider, B. A., Daneman, M., & Pichora-Fuller, M. K. (2002). Listening in aging adults: From discourse comprehension to psychoacoustics. *Canadian Journal of Experimental Psychology, 56*, 139–152.

Schneider, P., Sluming, V., Roberts, N., Scherg, M., Goebel, R., Specht, H. J., et al. (2005). Structural and functional asymmetry of lateral Heschl's gyrus reflects pitch perception preference. *Nature Neuroscience, 8*, 1241–1247.

Schor, C. M. (2003). Stereopsis. In L. M. Chalupa & J. S. Werner (Eds.), *The visual neurosciences* (Vol. 2, pp. 1300–1312). Cambridge, MA: MIT Press.

Schroeder, J. A., & Flannery-Schroeder, E. (2005, June). Use of the herb Gymnema sylvestre to illustrate the principles of gustatory sensation: An undergraduate neuroscience laboratory exercise. *The Journal of Undergraduate Neuroscience Education, 3*, A59–A62.

Schubert, E., & Stevens, C. (2006). The effect of implied harmony, contour and musical expertise on judgments of similarity in familiar melodies. *Journal of New Music Research, 35*, 161–174.

Schuller, G., & Moss, C. F. (2004). Vocal control and acoustically guided behavior in bats. In J. A. Thomas, C. F. Moss, & M. Vater (Eds.), *Echolocation in bats and dolphins* (pp. 3–16). Chicago: University of Chicago.

Schulte, M., Knief, A., Seither-Preisler, A., & Pantev, C. (2002). Different modes of pitch perception and learning-induced neuronal plasticity of the human auditory cortex. *Neural Plast, 9*, 161–175.

Schwartz, J.-L., Berthommier, F., & Savariaux, C. (2004). Seeing to hear better: Evidence for early audio-visual interactions in speech identification. *Cognition, 93*, B69–B78.

Schwartz, S. H. (2004). *Visual perception: A clinical orientation.* New York: McGraw-Hill.

Schwarzschild, B. (2006, September). Neural-network model may explain the surprisingly good infrared vision of snakes. *Physics Today,* 18–20.

Schyns, P. G., & Oliva, A. (1999). Dr. Angry and Mr. Smile: When categorization flexibly modifies the perception of faces in rapid visual presentations. *Cognition, 69,* 243–265.

Scialfa, C. T. (2002). The role of sensory factors in cognitive aging research. *Canadian Journal of Experimental Psychology, 56,* 153–163.

Scialfa, C. T., & Kline, D. W. (2007). Vision. In J. E. Birren (Ed.), *Encyclopedia of gerontology* (pp. 653–660). San Diego: Elsevier.

Sedgwick, H. A. (2001). Visual space perception. In E. B. Goldstein (Ed.), *Blackwell handbook of perception* (pp. 128–167). Malden, MA: Blackwell.

Seghier, M. L., & Vuilleumier, P. (2006). Functional neuroimaging findings on the human perception of illusory contours. *Neuroscience and Biobehavioral Reviews, 30,* 595–612.

Seither-Preisler, A., Johnson, L., Krumbholz, K., Nobbe, A., Patterson, R., Seither, S., et al. (2007). Tone sequences with conflicting fundamental pitch and timbre changes are heard differently by musicians and nonmusicians. *Journal of Experimental Psychology: Human Perception & Performance, 33,* 743–751.

Sekuler, A. B., Gaspar, C. M., Gold, J. M., & Bennett, P. J. (2004). Inversion leads to quantitative, not qualitative, changes in face processing. *Current Biology, 14,* 391–396.

Sekuler, R., Watamaniuk, S. N. J., & Blake, R. (2002). Perception of visual motion. In H. Pashler & S. Yantis (Eds.), *Stevens' handbook of experimental psychology* (3rd ed., pp. 121–176). Hoboken, NJ: Wiley.

Sekunova, A., & Barton, J. J. (2008). The effects of face inversion on the perception of long-range and local spatial relations in eye and mouth configuration. *Journal of Experimental Psychology: Human Perception & Performance, 34,* 1129–1135.

Sereno, M. I., & Tootell, R. B. (2005). From monkeys to humans: What do we now know about brain homologies? *Current Opinion in Neurobiology, 15,* 135–144.

Sethares, W. A. (2005). *Tuning, timbre, spectrum, scale* (2nd ed.). New York: Springer.

Shaffer, D. M., Krauchunas, S. M., Eddy, M., & McBeath, M. K. (2004). How dogs navigate to catch frisbees. *Psychological Science, 15,* 437–441.

Shaffer, D. M., & McBeath, M. K. (2002). Baseball outfielders maintain a linear optical trajectory when tracking uncatchable fly balls. *Journal of Experimental Psychology: Human Perception & Performance, 28,* 335–348.

Shaffer, D. M., & McBeath, M. K. (2005). Naive beliefs in baseball: Systematic distortion in perceived time of apex for fly balls. *Journal of Experimental Psychology: Learning, Memory, & Cognition, 31,* 1492–1501.

Shaffer, D. M., McBeath, M. K., Krauchunas, S. M., & Sugar, T. G. (2008). Evidence for a generic interceptive strategy. *Perception & Psychophysics, 70,* 145–157.

Shaffer, D. M., McBeath, M. K., Roy, W. L., & Krauchunas, S. M. (2003). A linear optical trajectory informs the fielder where to run to the side to catch fly balls. *Journal of Experimental Psychology: Human Perception & Performance, 29,* 1244–1250.

Shamma, S. A. (2004). Topographic organization is essential for pitch perception. *Proceedings of the National Academy of Sciences of the USA, 101,* 1114–1115.

Shannon, R. V., Fu, Q.-J., Galvin, J., & Friesen, L. (2004). Speech perception with cochlear implants. In F.-G. Zeng, A. N. Popper, & R. R. Fay (Eds.), *Cochlear implants: Auditory prostheses and electric hearing* (Vol. 20, pp. 334–376). New York: Springer.

Shapiro, P. N., & Penrod, S. (1986). Meta-analysis of facial identification studies. *Psychological Bulletin, 100,* 139–156.

Shapley, R., Kaplan, E., & Purpura, K. (1993). Contrast sensitivity and light adaptation in photoreceptors or in the retinal network. In R. Shapley & D. M.-K. Lam (Eds.), *Contrast sensitivity: Proceedings of the Retina Research Foundation Symposia* (Vol. 5, pp. 103–116). Cambridge, MA: MIT Press.

Sharma, J., Angelucci, A., & Sur, M. (2000). Induction of visual orientation modules in auditory cortex. *Nature, 404,* 841–847.

Sharov, A. A., Leonard, D., Liebhold, A. M., & Clemens, N. S. (2002). Evaluation of preventive treatments in low-density gypsy moth populations using pheromone traps. *Journal of Economic Entomology, 95,* 1205–1215.

Sharpe, L. T., de Luca, E., Hansen, T., Jagle, H., & Gegenfurtner, K. R. (2006). Advantages and disadvantages of human dichromacy. *Journal of Vision, 6,* 213–223.

Sharpe, L. T., Stockman, A., Jägle, H., & Nathans, J. (1999). Opsin genes, cone photopigments, color vision, and color blindness. In K. Gegenfurtner & L. T. Sharpe (Eds.), *Color vision: From genes to perception* (pp. 3–51). New York: Cambridge.

Shepard, R. N. (1964). Circularity in judgments of relative pitch. *Journal of the Acoustical Society of America, 36,* 2346–2353.

Shepard, R. N. (1999a). Pitch perception and measurement. In P. R. Cook (Ed.), *Music, cognition, and computerized sound: An introduction to psychoacoustics* (pp. 149–165). Cambridge, MA: MIT Press.

Shepard, R. N. (1999b). Tonal structure and scales. In P. R. Cook (Ed.), *Music, cognition, and computerized sound: An introduction to psychoacoustics* (pp. 187–194). Cambridge, MA: MIT Press.

Shera, C. A. (2003). Mammalian spontaneous otoacoustic emissions are amplitude-stabilized cochlear standing waves. *Journal of the Acoustical Society of America, 114,* 244–262.

Shera, C. A. (2004). Mechanisms of mammalian otoacoustic emission and their implications for the clinical utility of otoacoustic emissions. *Ear and Hearing, 25*, 86–97.

Shevell, S. K. (2003a). Color appearance. In S. K. Shevell (Ed.), *The science of color* (pp. 149–190). New York: Elsevier.

Shevell, S. K. (Ed.). (2003b). *The science of color* (2nd ed.). New York: Elsevier.

Shevell, S. K., & Kingdom, F. A. (2008). Color in complex scenes. *Annual Review of Psychology, 59*, 143–166.

Shiffrar, M. (1994). When what meets where. *Current Directions in Psychological Science, 3*, 96–100.

Shiffrar, M. (2001). Movement and event perception. In E. B. Goldstein (Ed.), *Blackwell handbook of perception* (pp. 237–271). Malden, MA: Blackwell.

Shinoda, H., Hayhoe, M. M., & Shrivastava, A. (2001). What controls attention in natural environments? *Vision Research, 41*(2526), 3535–3545.

Shou, J., Zheng, J. L., & Gao, W. Q. (2003). Robust generation of new hair cells in the mature mammalian inner ear by adenoviral expression of Hath1. *Molecular and Cellular Neurosciences, 23*, 169–179.

Shrager, Y., Bayley, P. J., Bontempi, B., Hopkins, R. O., & Squire, L. R. (2007). Spatial memory and the human hippocampus. *Proceedings of the National Academy of Sciences of the USA, 104*, 2961–2966.

Shrager, Y., Kirwan, C. B., & Squire, L. R. (2008). Neural basis of the cognitive map: Path integration does not require hippocampus or entorhinal cortex. *Proceedings of the National Academy of Sciences of the USA, 105*, 12034–12038.

Shuwairi, S. M., Albert, M. K., & Johnson, S. P. (2007). Discrimination of possible and impossible objects in infancy. *Psychological Science, 18*, 303–307.

Sidaway, I. (2002). *Color mixing bible: All you'll ever need to know about mixing pigments in oil, acrylic, watercolor, gouache, soft pastel, pencil, and ink*. New York: Watson-Guptill.

Siegel, J. (2008). Otoacoustic emissions. In A. I. Basbaum, M. C. Bushnell, D. V. Smith, G. K. Beauchamp, S. J. Firestein, P. Dallos, D. Oertel, R. H. Masland, T. D. Albright, J. H. Kaas, & E. P. Gardner (Eds.), *The senses: A comprehensive reference* (Vol. 3, pp. 237–261). New York: Academic.

Silvanto, J., Cowey, A., Lavie, N., & Walsh, V. (2005). Striate cortex (V1) activity gates awareness of motion. *Nature Neuroscience, 8*, 143–144.

Simion, F., Regolin, L., & Bulf, H. (2008). A predisposition for biological motion in the newborn baby. *Proceedings of the National Academy of Sciences of the USA, 105*, 809–813.

Sincich, L. C., & Horton, J. C. (2005). The circuitry of V1 and V2: Integration of color, form, and motion. *Annual Review of Neuroscience, 28*, 303–326.

Sincich, L. C., Park, K. F., Wohlgemuth, M. J., & Horton, J. C. (2004). Bypassing V1: A direct geniculate input to area MT. *Nature Neuroscience, 7*, 1123–1128.

Singh, M., & Anderson, B. L. (2006). Photometric determinants of perceived transparency. *Vision Research, 46*, 879–894.

Sinha, P., Balas, B. J., Ostrovsky, Y., & Russell, R. (2006). Face recognition by humans: Nineteen results all computer vision researchers should know about. *Proceedings of the IEEE, 94*, 1948–1962.

Skals, N., Anderson, P., Kanneworff, M., Lofstedt, C., & Surlykke, A. (2005). Her odours make him deaf: Crossmodal modulation of olfaction and hearing in a male moth. *The Journal of Experimental Biology, 208*, 595–601.

Slater, A. (1998). The competent infant: Innate organisation and early learning in infant visual perception. In A. Slater (Ed.), *Perceptual development: Visual, auditory, and speech perception in infancy* (pp. 105–130). Hove, UK: Psychology Press.

Slater, A., Field, T., & Hernandez-Reif, M. (2002). The development of the senses. In A. Slater & M. Lewis (Eds.), *Introduction to infant development* (pp. 83–98). New York: Oxford.

Sloboda, J. A. (2005). *Exploring the musical mind: Cognition, emotion, ability, function*. New York: Oxford.

Sloboda, J. A., Wise, K. J., & Peretz, I. (2005). Quantifying tone deafness in the general population. In G. Avanzini, L. Lopez, S. Koelsch, & M. Manjno (Eds.), *The neurosciences and music II: From perception to performance*. (pp. 255–261). New York: New York Academy of Sciences.

Small, D. M., Bender, G., Veldhuizen, M. G., Rudenga, K., Nachtigal, D., & Felsted, J. (2007). The role of the human orbitofrontal cortex in taste and flavor processing. *Annals of the New York Academy of Science, 1121*, 136–151.

Small, D. M., & Prescott, J. (2005). Odor/taste integration and the perception of flavor. *Experimental Brain Research, 166*, 345–357.

Smith, C. G., Paradise, J. L., Sabo, D. L., Rockette, H. E., Kurs-Lasky, M., Bernard, B. S., et al. (2006). Tympanometric findings and the probability of middle-ear effusion in 3686 infants and young children. *Pediatrics, 118*, 1–13.

Smith, G., & Atchison, D. A. (1997). *The eye and visual optical instruments*. New York: Cambridge.

Smith, J. D., Redford, J. S., & Haas, S. M. (2008). Prototype abstraction by monkeys (Macaca mulatta). *Journal of Experimental Psychology: General, 137*, 390–401.

Smith, V. C., & Pokorny, J. (2003). Color matching and color discrimination. In S. K. Shevell (Ed.), *The science of color* (pp. 103–148). New York: Elsevier.

Snow, J. B., Jr. (2008). Tinnitus. In A. I. Basbaum, M. C. Bushnell, D. V. Smith, G. K. Beauchamp, S. J. Firestein, P. Dallos, D. Oertel, R. H. Masland, T. D. Albright, J. H. Kaas, & E. P. Gardner (Eds.), *The senses: A comprehensive reference* (Vol. 3, pp. 301–308). New York: Academic Press.

Snowden, R. J., & Freeman, T. C. (2004). The visual perception of motion. *Current Biology, 14*, R828–831.

Snyder, D. J., Duffy, V. B., Hayes, J. E., & Bartoshuk, L. M. (2008). Propylthiouracil (PROP) taste. In A. I. Basbaum, M. C. Bushnell, D. V. Smith, G. K. Beauchamp, S. J. Firestein, P. Dallos, D. Oertel, R. H. Masland, T. D. Albright, J. H. Kaas, & E. P. Gardner (Eds.), *The senses: A comprehensive reference* (Vol. 4, pp. 391–399). New York: Academic Press.

Snyder, D. J., Prescott, J., & Bartoshuk, L. M. (2006). Modern psychophysics and the assessment of human oral sensation. *Advances in Oto-Rhino-Laryngology, 63*, 221–241.

Soderquist, D. R. (2002). *Sensory processes*. Thousand Oaks, CA: Sage.

Sofaer-Bennett, B., Holloway, I., Moore, A., Lamberty, J., Thorp, T., & O'Dwyer, J. (2007). Perseverance by older people in their management of chronic pain: A qualitative study. *Pain Medicine, 8*, 271–280.

Solomon, S. G., & Lennie, P. (2007). The machinery of colour vision. *Nature Reviews Neuroscience, 8*, 276–286.

Solso, R. L., MacLin, O. H., & MacLin, M. K. (2008). *Cognitive psychology* (8th ed.). Boston: Allyn & Bacon.

Sommer, M. A., & Wurtz, R. H. (2008a). Brain circuits for the internal monitoring of movements. *Annual Review of Neuroscience, 31*, 317–338.

Sommer, M. A., & Wurtz, R. H. (2008b). Visual perception and corollary discharge. *Perception, 37*, 408–418.

Sommers, M. S. (2005). Age-related changes in spoken word recognition. In D. B. Pisoni & R. E. Remez (Eds.), *The handbook of speech perception* (pp. 469–493). Malden, MA: Blackwell.

Spelke, E. S. (2002). Developmental neuroimaging: A developmental psychologist looks ahead. *Developmental Science, 5*, 392–396.

Spelke, E. S., & von Hofsten, C. (2001). Predictive reaching for occluded objects by 6-month-old infants. *Journal of Cognition and Development, 2*, 261–281.

Spence, C., & Read, L. (2003). Speech shadowing while driving: On the difficulty of splitting attention between eye and ear. *Psychological Science, 14*, 251–256.

Stangl, F. B., Shipley, M. M., Goetze, J. R., & Jones, C. (2005). Comments on the predator-prey relationship of the Texas kangaroo rat (Dipodomys elator) and barn owl (Tyto alba). *American Midland Naturalist, 153*, 135–141.

Stansfeld, S. A., & Matheson, M. P. (2003). Noise pollution: Non-auditory effects on health. *British Medical Bulletin, 68*, 243–257.

Starck, J., Toppila, E., & Pyykkö, I. (2007). Hearing protectors. In L. Luxon & D. Prasher (Eds.), *Noise and its effects* (pp. 667–680). Chichester, England: Wiley.

Stefanucci, J. K., Proffitt, D. R., Banton, T., & Epstein, W. (2005). Distances appear different on hills. *Perception & Psychophysics, 67*, 1052–1060.

Stefanucci, J. K., Proffitt, D. R., Clore, G. L., & Parekh, N. (2008). Skating down a steeper slope: Fear influences the perception of geographical slant. *Perception, 37*, 321–323.

Stein, B. E., & Meredith, M. A. (1993). *The merging of the senses*. Cambridge, MA: MIT Press.

Steinbeis, N., Koelsch, S., & Sloboda, J. A. (2006). The role of harmonic expectancy violations in musical emotions: Evidence from subjective, physiological, and neural responses. *Journal of Cognitive Neuroscience, 18*, 1380–1393.

Sterzer, P., & Rees, G. (2006). Perceived size matters. *Nature Neuroscience, 9*, 302–304.

Stevens, J. K., Emerson, R. C., Gerstein, G. L., Kallos, T., Neufeld, G. R., Nichols, C. W., et al. (1976). Paralysis of the awake human. Vision perceptions. *Vision Research, 16*, 93–98.

Stevens, S. S. (1955). The measurement of loudness. *Journal of the Acoustical Society of America, 27*, 815–829.

Stevens, S. S. (1962). The surprising simplicity of sensory metrics. *American Psychologist, 17*, 29–39.

Stevens, S. S. (1986). *Psychophysics: Introduction to its perceptual, neural and social prospects*. New Brunswick: Transaction.

Stevens, S. S., & Newman, E. B. (1936). The localization of actual sources of sound. *American Journal of Psychology, 48*, 297–306.

Stevens, S. S., Volkman, J., & Newman, E. B. (1937). A scale for the measurement of the psychological magnitude of pitch. *Journal of the Acoustical Society of America, 8*, 185–190.

Stevenson, R. J., Case, T. I., & Mahmut, M. (2007). Difficulty in evoking odor images: The role of odor naming. *Memory & Cognition, 35*, 578–589.

Stiles, J., Moses, P., Passarotti, A., Dick, F. K., & Buxton, R. (2003). Exploring developmental change in the neural bases of higher cognitive functions: The promise of functional magnetic resonance imaging. *Developmental Neuropsychology, 24*, 641–668.

Stix, G. (2007). Better ways to target pain. *Scientific American, 296*, 84–88.

Story, G. M., & Cruz-Orengo, L. (2007). Feel the burn. *American Scientist, 95*, 326–333.

Strayer, D. L., & Drews, F. A. (2008). Cell-phone-induced driver distraction. *Current Directions in Psychological Science, 16*, 128–135.

Stryker, M. P. (1992). Elements of visual perception. *Nature, 360*, 301.

Sugita, Y. (2004). Experience in early infancy is indispensable for color perception. *Current Biology, 14*, 1267–1271.

Summerfield, Q. (1992). Lipreading and audio-visual speech perception. In V. Bruce, A. Cowey, A. W. Ellis, & D. I. Perrett (Eds.), *Processing the facial image* (pp. 71–78). Oxford: Clarendon.

Sumner, P., & Mollon, J. D. (2003). Did primate trichromacy evolve for frugivory or folivory? In J. D. Mollon, J. Pokorny, & K. Knoblauch (Eds.), *Normal and defective colour vision* (pp. 21–30). New York: Oxford.

Sundin, O. H., Yang, J. M., Li, Y., Zhu, D., Hurd, J. N., Mitchell, T. N., et al. (2000). Genetic basis of total colourblindness among the Pingelapese islanders. *Nature Genetics, 25*, 289–293.

Süskind, P. (1987). *Perfume: The story of a murderer* (J. E. Woods, Trans.). New York: Pocket Books.

Suzuki, T., Yi, Q., Sakuragawa, A., Tamura, H., & Okajima, K. (2005). Comparing the visibility of low-contrast color Landolt-Cs: Effect of aging human lens. *Color Research and Application, 30*, 5–12.

Takeuchi, A. H., & Hulse, S. H. (1993). Absolute pitch. *Psychological Bulletin, 113*, 345–361.

Takeuchi, H., & Kurahashi, T. (2008). Signal transduction in the olfactory receptor cell. In A. I. Basbaum, M. C. Bushnell, D. V. Smith, G. K. Beauchamp, S. J. Firestein, P. Dallos, D. Oertel, R. H. Masland, T. D. Albright, J. H. Kaas, & E. P. Gardner (Eds.), *The senses: A comprehensive reference* (Vol. 4, pp. 499–509). New York: Academic Press.

Tan, L. H., Chan, A. H., Kay, P., Khong, P. L., Yip, L. K., & Luke, K. K. (2008). Language affects patterns of brain activation associated with perceptual decision. *Proceedings of the National Academy of Sciences of the USA, 105*, 4004–4009.

Tanaka, J. W., & Farah, M. J. (2003). The holistic representation of faces. In M. A. Peterson & G. Rhodes (Eds.), *Perception of faces, objects, and scenes: Analytic and holistic processes* (pp. 53–71). New York: Oxford.

Tarr, M. J., & Gauthier, I. (2000). FFA: A flexible fusiform area for subordinate-level visual processing automatized by expertise. *Nature Neuroscience, 3*, 764–769.

Tarr, M. J., & Vuong, Q. C. (2002). Visual object recognition. In H. Pashler & S. Yantis (Eds.), *Stevens' handbook of experimental psychology* (3rd ed., pp. 287–314). Hoboken, NJ: Wiley.

Tayama, T. (2000). The minimum temporal thresholds for motion detection of grating patterns. *Perception, 29*, 761–769.

Taylor, A. J., & Hort, J. (2004). Measuring proximal stimuli involved in flavour perception. In A. J. Taylor & D. D. Roberts (Eds.), *Flavor perception* (pp. 1–38). Malden, MA: Blackwell.

Taylor, M. J., Arsalidou, M., Bayless, S. J., Morris, D., Evans, J. W., & Barbeau, E. J. (2008). Neural correlates of personally familiar faces: Parents, partner and own faces. *Human Brain Mapping*.

Technical Working Group for Eyewitness Evidence. (2003). *Eyewitness evidence: A trainer's manual for law enforcement.* Retrieved from www.ncjrs.org/nij/eyewitness.

Teghtsoonian, M. (1983). Olfaction: Perception's Cinderella. *Contemporary Psychology, 28*, 763–764.

Teghtsoonian, R. (1973). Range effects in psychophysical scaling and a revision of Stevens' law. *American Journal of Psychology, 86*, 3–29.

Tennesen, M. (2007). Gone today, ear tomorrow. *New Scientist, 193*, 42–45.

Terry, H. R., Charlton, S. G., & Perrone, J. A. (2008). The role of looming and attention capture in drivers' braking responses. *Accident; Analysis and Prevention, 40*, 1375–1382.

Tervaniemi, M., Just, V., Koelsch, S., Widmann, A., & Schroger, E. (2005). Pitch discrimination accuracy in musicians vs. nonmusicians: An event-related potential and behavioral study. *Experimental Brain Research, 161*, 1–10.

Thiele, A., & Stoner, G. (2003). Neuronal synchrony does not correlate with motion coherence in cortical area MT. *Nature, 421*(6921), 366–370.

Thomas, K. M., & Casey, B. J. (2003). Methods for imaging the developing brain. In M. de Haan & M. H. Johnson (Eds.), *The cognitive neuroscience of development* (pp. 19–41). New York: Psychology Press.

Thompson, P. (1980). Margaret Thatcher—A new illusion. *Perception, 9*, 483–484.

Thompson, R. F. (1985). *The brain: An introduction to neuroscience.* New York: Freeman.

Thompson, S. K., von Kriegstein, K., Deane-Pratt, A., Marquardt, T., Deichmann, R., Griffiths, T. D., et al. (2006). Representation of interaural time delay in the human auditory midbrain. *Nature Neuroscience, 9*, 1096–1098.

Thompson, W. B., Dilda, V., & Creem-Regehr, S. H. (2007). Absolute distance perception to locations off the ground plane. *Perception, 36*, 1559–1571.

Thornton, A. R., Lineton, B., Baker, V. J., & Slaven, A. (2006). Nonlinear properties of otoacoustic emissions in normal and impaired hearing. *Hearing Research, 219*, 56–65.

Thornton, I. M. (2006). Biological motion: Point-light walkers and beyond. In G. Knoblich, I. M. Thornton, M. Grosjean, & M. Shiffrar (Eds.), *Human body perception from the inside out* (pp. 271–303). New York: Oxford.

Tiddeman, B. P., Perrett, D. I., & Burt, D. M. (2001). Prototyping and transforming facial textures for perception research. *IEEE Computer Graphics and Applications, 21*, 42–50.

Tillmann, B. (2005). Implicit investigations of tonal knowledge in nonmusician listeners. In G. Avanzini, S. Koelsch, L. Lopez, & M. Majno (Eds.), *The neurosciences and music II: From perception to performance* (Vol. 1060, pp. 100–110). New York: NY Academy of Sciences.

Todd, J. T. (2004). The visual perception of 3D shape. *Trends in Cognitive Sciences, 8*, 115–121.

Todd, J. T., & Akerstrom, R. A. (1987). Perception of three-dimensional form from patterns of optical texture. *Journal of Experimental Psychology: Human Perception & Performance, 13*, 242–255.

Todd, J. T., & Norman, J. F. (2003). The visual perception of 3-D shape from multiple cues: Are observers capable of perceiving metric structure? *Perception & Psychophysics, 65*, 31–47.

Todd, J. T., & Reichel, F. D. (1990). The visual perception of smoothly curved surfaces from double-projected contour patterns. *Journal of Experimental Psychology: Human Perception & Performance, 16,* 665–674.

Toglia, M. P., Read, J. D., Ross, D. F., & Lindsay, R. C. L. (Eds.). (2006). *The handbook of eyewitness psychology: Memory for events* (Vol. 1). Mahwah, NJ: Erlbaum.

Tolman, E. C. (1948). Cognitive maps in rats and men. *Psychological Review, 55,* 189–208.

Tomchik, S. M., & Lu, Z. (2006). Modulation of auditory signal-to-noise ratios by efferent stimulation. *Journal of Neurophysiology, 95,* 3562–3570.

Tootell, R. B., & Hadjikhani, N. (2001). Where is "dorsal V4" in human visual cortex? Retinotopic, topographic and functional evidence. *Cerebral Cortex, 11,* 298–311.

Tosini, G. (2000). Melatonin circadian rhythm in the retina of mammals. *Chronobiology International, 17,* 599–612.

Tougaard, J., Miller, L. A., & Simmons, J. A. (2004). The role of arctiid moth clicks in defense against echolocating bats: Interference with temporal processing. In J. A. Thomas, C. F. Moss, & M. Vater (Eds.), *Echolocation in bats and dolphins* (pp. 365–372). Chicago: University of Chicago.

Tournaire, M., & Theau-Yonneau, A. (2007). Complementary and alternative approaches to pain relief during labor. *Evidence-Based Complementary & Alternative Medicine, 4,* 409–417.

Tozawa, J., & Oyama, T. (2006). Effects of motion parallax and perspective cues on perceived size and distance. *Perception, 35,* 1007–1023.

Trainor, L. J. (2005). Are there critical periods for musical development? *Developmental Psychobiology, 46,* 262–278.

Trainor, L. J., Austin, C. M., & Desjardins, R. N. (2000). Is infant-directed speech prosody a result of the vocal expression of emotion? *Psychological Science, 11,* 188–195.

Treede, R. D., & Apkarian, A. V. (2008). Nociceptive processing in the cerebral cortex. In A. I. Basbaum, M. C. Bushnell, D. V. Smith, G. K. Beauchamp, S. J. Firestein, P. Dallos, D. Oertel, R. H. Masland, T. D. Albright, J. H. Kaas, & E. P. Gardner (Eds.), *The senses: A comprehensive reference* (Vol. 5, pp. 669–697). New York: Academic Press.

Trehub, S. E., & Hannon, E. E. (2006). Infant music perception: Domain-general or domain-specific mechanisms? *Cognition, 100,* 73–99.

Treisman, A. M. (2006a). How the deployment of attention determines what we see. *Visual Cognition, 14,* 411–443.

Treisman, A. M. (2006b). Object tokens, binding, and visual memory. In H. D. Zimmer, A. Mecklinger, & U. Lindenberger (Eds.), *Handbook of binding and memory: Perspectives from cognitive neuroscience* (pp. 315–338). New York: Oxford.

Treisman, A. M., & Gelade, G. (1980). A feature-integration theory of attention. *Cognitive Psychology, 12,* 97–136.

Treisman, A. M., & Souther, J. (1985). Search asymmetry: A diagnostic for preattentive processing of separable features. *Journal of Experimental Psychology: General, 114,* 285–310.

Trillin, C. (2002, August 19 & 26). Annals of taste: The red and the white. *The New Yorker.*

Troje, N. F. (2008). Biological motion perception. In A. I. Basbaum, M. C. Bushnell, D. V. Smith, G. K. Beauchamp, S. J. Firestein, P. Dallos, D. Oertel, R. H. Masland, T. D. Albright, J. H. Kaas, & E. P. Gardner (Eds.), *The senses: A comprehensive reference* (Vol. 2, pp. 231–238). New York: Academic.

Troje, N. F., & Westhoff, C. (2006). The inversion effect in biological motion perception: Evidence for a "life detector"? *Current Biology, 16,* 821–824.

Troje, N. F., Westhoff, C., & Lavrov, M. (2005). Person identification from biological motion: Effects of structural and kinematic cues. *Perception & Psychophysics, 67,* 667–675.

Trotter, Y., Celebrini, S., & Durand, J. B. (2004). Evidence for implication of primate area V1 in neural 3-D spatial localization processing. *Journal of Physiology, 98,* 125–134.

Tsakiris, M., & Haggard, P. (2005). The rubber hand illusion revisited: Visuotactile integration and self-attribution. *Journal of Experimental Psychology: Human Perception & Performance, 31,* 80–91.

Tsao, D. Y., & Livingstone, M. S. (2008). Mechanisms of face perception. *Annual Review of Neuroscience, 31,* 411–437.

Turk, D. C., & Okifuji, A. (2004). Psychological aspects of pain. In C. A. Warfield & Z. H. Bajwa (Eds.), *Principles and practice of pain medicine* (pp. 139–147). New York: McGraw-Hill.

Turk, D. C., & Swanson, K. S. (2008). Psychological interventions. In H. T. Benzon, J. P. Rathmell, C. L. Wu, D. C. Turk, & C. E. Argoff (Eds.), *Raj's practical management of pain* (pp. 739–755). Philadelphia: Mosby.

Tyler, C. W. (2006). Spatial form as inherently three dimensional. In M. R. M. Jenkin & L. R. Harris (Eds.), *Seeing spatial form* (pp. 67–88). New York: Oxford.

Tyler, C. W., & Clarke, M. B. (Eds.). (1990). *The autostereogram* (Vol. 1256). Bellingham, WA: SPIE.

Ullman, S. (1996). *High-level vision: Object recognition and visual cognition.* Cambridge, MA: MIT Press.

Underwood, G. (2005). Eye fixations on pictures of natural scenes: Getting the gist and identifying the components. In G. Underwood (Ed.), *Cognitive processes in eye guidance* (pp. 163–187). New York: Oxford.

Valberg, A. (2005). *Light vision color.* Chichester: Wiley.

Vallortigara, G., Regolin, L., & Marconato, F. (2005). Visually inexperienced chicks exhibit spontaneous preference for biological motion patterns. *PLoS Biology, 3,* e208.

van Erp, J. B., & van Veen, H. A. (2006). Touch down: The effect of artificial touch cues on orientation in microgravity. *Neuroscience Letters, 404,* 78–82.

Van Essen, D. C., Anderson, C. H., & Felleman, D. J. (1992). Information procession in the primate visual system: An integrated systems perspective. *Science, 255,* 419–422.

Van Essen, D. C., Lewis, J. W., Drury, H. A., Hadjikhani, N., Tootell, R. B., Bakircioglu, M., et al. (2001). Mapping visual cortex in monkeys and humans using surface-based atlases. *Vision Research, 41,* 1359–1378.

Vanlierde, A., Renier, L., & De Volder, A. G. (2008). Brain plasticity and multisensory experience in early blind individuals. In J. J. Rieser, D. H. Ashmead, F. Ebner, & A. L. Corn (Eds.), *Blindness and brain plasticity in navigation and object perception* (pp. 67–83). New York: Erlbaum.

Vasilyev, N. V., Novotny, P. M., Martinez, J. F., Loyola, H., Salgo, I. S., Howe, R. D., et al. (2008). Stereoscopic vision display technology in real-time three-dimensional echocardiography-guided intracardiac beating-heart surgery. *The Journal of Thoracic and Cardiovascular Surgery, 135,* 1334–1341.

Vater, M. (2004). Cochlear anatomy related to bat echolocation. In J. A. Thomas, C. F. Moss, & M. Vater (Eds.), *Echolocation in bats and dolphins* (pp. 99–103). Chicago: University of Chicago.

Vater, M., & Kössl, M. (2004). The ears of whales and bats. In J. A. Thomas, C. F. Moss, & M. Vater (Eds.), *Echolocation in bats and dolphins* (pp. 89–89). Chicago: University of Chicago.

Velakoulis, D. (2006). Olfactory hallucinations. In W. J. Brewer, D. Castle & C. Pantelis (Eds.), *Olfaction and the brain* (pp. 322–333). New York: Cambridge.

Venkatachalam, K., & Montell, C. (2007). TRP channels. *Annual Review of Biochemistry, 76,* 387–417.

Verde, M. E., MacMillan, N. A., & Rotello, C. M. (2006). Measures of sensitivity based on a single hit rate and false alarm rate: The accuracy, precision, and robustness of d', Az, and A'. *Perception & Psychophysics, 68,* 643–654.

Verdon, W. A., & Adams, A. J. (2002). Color vision. In T. T. Norton, D. A. Corliss, & J. E. Bailey (Eds.), *The psychophysical measurement of visual function* (pp. 217–287). Boston: Butterworth-Heinemann.

Viguier, A., Clement, G., & Trotter, Y. (2001). Distance perception within near visual space. *Perception, 30,* 115–124.

Vitu, F. (2005). Visual extraction processes and regressive saccades in reading. In G. Underwood (Ed.), *Cognitive processes in eye guidance* (pp. 1–32). New York: Oxford.

Vokey, J. R., & Read, J. D. (1985). Subliminal messages: Between the Devil and the media. *American Psychologist, 40,* 1231–1239.

von Békésy, G. (1960). *Experiments in hearing.* New York: McGraw-Hill.

von Bothmer, E. (2006). When the nose doesn't know. *Scientific American Mind, 17,* 62–67.

von der Heydt, R. (2003). Image parsing mechanisms of the visual cortex. In L. M. Chalupa & J. S. Werner (Eds.), *The visual neurosciences* (Vol. 2, pp. 1139–1150). Cambridge, MA: MIT Press.

von Helmholtz, H. (1863). *Die Lehre von den Tonempfindungen als physiologische Grundlege für die Theorie der Musik. (The sensations of tone).* (A. J. Ellis, Trans.). New York: Longmans, Green.

von Helmholtz, H. (1866). *Handbuch der physiolgischen optik.* Hamburg & Leipzig: Voss.

Vroomen, J., & de Gelder, B. (2003). Visual motion influences the contingent auditory motion aftereffect. *Psychological Science, 14,* 357–361.

Wachtler, T., Dohrmann, U., & Hertel, R. (2004). Modeling color percepts of dichromats. *Vision Research, 44,* 2843–2855.

Wade, N. J. (2008). The Thatcherisation of faces. *Perception, 37,* 807–810.

Wager, T. D., Rilling, J. K., Smith, E. E., Sokolik, A., Casey, K. L., Davidson, R. J., et al. (2004). Placebo-induced changes in fMRI in the anticipation and experience of pain. *Science, 303*(5661), 1162–1167.

Wagner, H., Brill, S., Kempter, R., & Carr, C. E. (2005). Microsecond precision of phase delay in the auditory system of the barn owl. *Journal of Neurophysiology, 94,* 1655–1658.

Wagner, M. (2006). *The geometries of visual space.* Mahwah, NJ: Erlbaum.

Wakefield, C. E., Homewood, J., & Taylor, A. J. (2004). Cognitive compensations for blindness in children: An investigation using odour naming. *Perception, 33,* 429–442.

Waldman, S. D. (2007). Transcutaneous electrical nerve stimulation. In S. D. Waldman (Ed.), *Pain management* (pp. 1052–1054). Philadelphia: Saunders.

Wallach, H. (1948). Brightness constancy and the nature of achromatic colors. *Journal of Experimental Psychology, 38,* 310–324.

Wallach, H. (1959). Perception of motion. *Scientific American, 201,* 56–60.

Wallach, H., & O'Connell, D. N. (1953). The kinetic depth effect. *Journal of Experimental Psychology, 45,* 205–217.

Walton, G. E., Bower, N. J. A., & Bower, T. G. R. (1992). Recognition of familiar faces by newborns. *Infant Behavior & Development, 15,* 265–269.

Wandell, B. A. (1995). *Foundations of vision.* Sunderland, MA: Sinauer.

Wang, R., & Spelke, E. S. (2002). Human spatial representation: Insights from animals. *Trends in Cognitive Sciences, 6,* 376.

Warren, R. M., & Warren, R. P. (1970). Auditory illusions and confusions. *Scientific American, 223,* 30–36.

Warren, W. H. (2008). Optic flow. In A. I. Basbaum, M. C. Bushnell, D. V. Smith, G. K. Beauchamp, S. J. Firestein, P. Dallos, D. Oertel, R. H. Masland, T. D. Albright, J. H. Kaas, & E. P. Gardner (Eds.), *The senses: A comprehensive reference* (Vol. 2, pp. 219–230). New York: Academic.

Warrington, E. K., & Taylor, A. M. (1978). Two categorical stages of object recognition. *Perception, 7,* 695–705.

Waters, D. A., & Abulula, H. H. (2007). Using bat-modelled sonar as a navigation tool in virtual environments. *International Journal of Human-Computer Studies, 65,* 873–886.

Watson, C. S., & Kidd, G. R. (2007). Studies of tone sequence perception: Effects of uncertainty, familiarity, and selective attention. *Frontiers in Bioscience, 12*, 3355–3366.

Watt, R., & Quinn, S. (2007). Some robust higher-level percepts for music. *Perception, 36*, 1834–1848.

Wedekind, C., & Penn, D. (2000). MHC genes, body odours, and odour preferences. *Nephrology Dialysis Transplantation, 15*, 1269–1271.

Weinstein, S. (1968). Intensive and extensive aspects of tactile sensitivity as a function of body part, sex, and laterality. In D. R. Kenshalo (Ed.), *The skin senses* (pp. 195–218). Springfield, IL: Thomas.

Weisberg, D. S., Keil, F. C., Goodstein, J., Rawson, E., & Gray, J. R. (2008). The seductive allure of neuroscience explanations. *Journal of Cognitive Neuroscience, 20*, 470–477.

Weisenberger, J. M. (2001). Cutaneous perception. In E. B. Goldstein (Ed.), *Blackwell handbook of perception* (pp. 535–566). Malden, MA: Blackwell.

Weisman, R. G., Williams, M. T., Cohen, J. S., Njegovan, M. G., & Sturdy, C. B. (2006). The comparative psychology of absolute pitch. In E. A. Wasserman & T. R. Zentall (Eds.), *Comparative cognition: Experimental explorations of animal intelligence* (pp. 71–86). New York: Oxford.

Welchman, A. E., Deubelius, A., Conrad, V., Bulthoff, H. H., & Kourtzi, Z. (2005). 3D shape perception from combined depth cues in human visual cortex. *Nature Neuroscience, 8*, 820–827.

Welling, L. L., Jones, B. C., DeBruine, L. M., Smith, F. G., Feinberg, D. R., Little, A. C., et al. (2008). Men report stronger attraction to femininity in women's faces when their testosterone levels are high. *Hormones and Behavior, 54*, 703–708.

Wells, G. L., Malpass, R. S., Lindsay, R. C. L., Fisher, R. P., Turtle, J. W., & Fulero, S. M. (2000). From the lab to the police station: A successful application of eyewitness research. *American Psychologist, 55*, 581–598.

Wells, G. L., Memon, A., & Penrod, S. D. (2006). Eyewitness evidence: Improving its probative value. *Psychological Science in the Public Interest, 7*, 45–75.

Wells, G. L., & Olson, E. A. (2003). Eyewitness testimony. *Annual Review of Psychology, 54*, 277–295.

Wenner, M. (2008). Magnifying taste. *Scientific American, 299*, 96–99.

Werner, H. (1935). Studies on contour. *American Journal of Psychology, 37*, 40–64.

Werner, L. A., & Bernstein, I. L. (2001). Development of the auditory, gustatory, olfactory, and somatosensory systems. In E. B. Goldstein (Ed.), *Blackwell handbook of perception* (pp. 669–708). Malden, MA: Blackwell.

Werner, S. J., Kimball, B. A., & Provenza, F. D. (2008). Food color, flavor, and conditioned avoidance among red-winged blackbirds. *Physiology & Behavior, 93*, 110–117.

Wertheimer, M. (1923). Untersuchungen zür Lehre von der Gestalt, II. (Translated as Laws of organization in percep-

tual forms.). In W. D. Ellis (Ed.), *A source book of Gestalt psychology* (pp. 71–88). London: Routledge & Kegan Paul.

Wesselmann, U. (2008). Pain in childbirth. In A. I. Basbaum, M. C. Bushnell, D. V. Smith, G. K. Beauchamp, S. J. Firestein, P. Dallos, D. Oertel, R. H. Masland, T. D. Albright, J. H. Kaas, & E. P. Gardner (Eds.), *The senses: A comprehensive reference* (Vol. 5, pp. 579–583). New York: Academic Press.

Westermann, G., Mareschal, D., Johnson, M. H., Sirois, S., Spratling, M. W., & Thomas, M. S. (2007). Neuroconstructivism. *Developmental Science, 10*, 75–83.

Westheimer, G. (2008). Illusions in the spatial sense of the eye: Geometrical-optical illusions and the neural representation of space. *Vision Research, 48*, 2128–2142.

Westhoff, C., & Troje, N. F. (2007). Kinematic cues for person identification from biological motion. *Perception & Psychophysics, 69*, 241–253.

Wever, E. G. (1949). *Theory of hearing*. New York: Wiley.

Wever, E. G., & Bray, C. W. (1930). Action currents in the auditory nerve in response to acoustical stimulation. *Proceedings of the National Academy of Sciences of the USA, 16*, 344–350.

Wheeler, D. D. (1970). Processes in word recognition. *Cognitive Psychology, 1*, 59–85.

Wheeler, M. E., & Treisman, A. M. (2002). Binding in short-term visual memory. *Journal of Experimental Psychology: General, 131*, 48–64.

Whitbourne, S. K. (2002). *The aging individual: Physical and psychological perspectives* (2nd ed.). New York: Springer.

Whitbourne, S. K. (2005). *Adult development and aging: Biopsychosocial perspective* (2nd ed.). New York: Wiley.

Whitcher, J. P. (2004). Blindness. In P. Riordan-Eva & J. P. Whitcher (Eds.), *Vaughn & Asbury's general ophthalmology* (pp. 413–418). New York: McGraw-Hill Medical.

Whitney, D. (2006). Contribution of bottom-up and top-down motion processes to perceived position. *Journal of Experimental Psychology: Human Perception & Performance, 32*, 1380–1397.

Wickens, T. D. (2001). *Elementary signal detection theory*. New York: Oxford.

Wiechmann, A. F., Vrieze, M. J., Dighe, R., & Hu, Y. (2003). Direct modulation of rod photoreceptor responsiveness through a Mel(1c) melatonin receptor in transgenic Xenopus laevis retina. *Investigative Ophthalmology & Visual Science, 44*, 4522–4531.

Wilcox, M. (2002). *Blue and yellow don't make green* (2nd ed.). Tampa. FL: School of Color.

Wilkie, R. M., & Wann, J. P. (2005). The role of visual and non-visual information in the control of locomotion. *Journal of Experimental Psychology: Human Perception & Performance, 31*, 901–911.

Wilmer, J. B., & Backus, B. T. (2008). Self-reported Magic Eye stereogram skill predicts stereoacuity. *Perception, 37*, 1297–1300.

Wilson, D. A. (2008). Olfactory cortex. In A. I. Basbaum, M. C. Bushnell, D. V. Smith, G. K. Beauchamp, S. J. Firestein, P. Dallos, D. Oertel, R. H. Masland, T. D. Albright, J. H. Kaas, & E. P. Gardner (Eds.), *The senses: A comprehensive reference* (Vol. 4, pp. 687–706). New York: Academic Press.

Wilson, D. A., & Stevenson, R. J. (2003). Olfactory perceptual learning: The critical role of memory in odor discrimination. *Neuroscience and Biobehavioral Reviews, 27*, 307–328.

Wilson, D. A., & Stevenson, R. J. (2006). *Learning to smell: Olfactory perception from neurobiology to behavior.* Baltimore: Johns Hopkins.

Winawer, J., Witthoft, N., Frank, M. C., Wu, L., Wade, A. R., & Boroditsky, L. (2007). Russian blues reveal effects of language on color discrimination. *Proceedings of the National Academy of Sciences of the USA, 104*, 7780–7785.

Wingfield, A., & Grossman, M. (2006). Language and the aging brain: Patterns of neural compensation revealed by functional brain imaging. *Journal of Neurophysiology, 96*, 2830–2839.

Winter, Y., Lopez, J., & von Helversen, O. (2003). Ultraviolet vision in a bat. *Nature, 425*(6958), 612–614.

Withnell, R. H. (2001). Brief report: The cochlear microphonic as an indication of outer hair cell function. *Ear and Hearing, 22*, 75–77.

Witt, J. K., Linkenauger, S. A., Bakdash, J. Z., & Proffitt, D. R. (2008). Putting to a bigger hole: Golf performance relates to perceived size. *Psychonomic Bulletin & Review, 15*, 581–585.

Witt, J. K., & Proffitt, D. R. (2005). See the ball, hit the ball. *Psychological Science, 16*, 937–938.

Witt, J. K., & Proffitt, D. R. (2008). Action-specific influences on distance perception: A role for motor simulation. *Journal of Experimental Psychology: Human Perception & Performance, 34*, 1479–1492.

Witt, J. K., Proffitt, D. R., & Epstein, W. (2005). Tool use affects perceived distance, but only when you intend to use it. *Journal of Experimental Psychology: Human Perception & Performance, 31*, 880–888.

Witt, M., Reutter, K., & Miller, I. J., Jr. (2003). Morphology of the peripheral taste system. In R. L. Doty (Ed.), *Handbook of olfaction and gustation* (pp. 651–677). New York: Marcel Dekker.

Witt, M., & Wozniak, W. (2006). Structure and function of the vomeronasal organ. *Advances in Oto-Rhino-Laryngology, 63*, 70–83.

Witten, I. B., Bergan, J. F., & Knudsen, E. I. (2006). Dynamic shifts in the owl's auditory space map predict moving sound location. *Nature Neuroscience, 9*, 1439–1445.

Witten, I. B., & Knudsen, E. I. (2005). Why seeing is believing: Merging auditory and visual worlds. *Neuron, 48*, 489–496.

Wixted, J. T., & Stretch, V. (2004). In defense of the signal detection interpretation of remember/know judgments. *Psychonomic Bulletin & Review, 11*, 616–641.

Wolff, J. O. (2003). Laboratory studies with rodents: Facts or artifacts? *Bioscience, 53*, 421–427.

Wong, K. Y., Dunn, F. A., & Berson, D. M. (2005). Photoreceptor adaptation in intrinsically photosensitive retinal ganglion cells. *Neuron, 48*, 1001–1010.

Wood, J. N. (2008). Sodium channels. In A. I. Basbaum, M. C. Bushnell, D. V. Smith, G. K. Beauchamp, S. J. Firestein, P. Dallos, D. Oertel, R. H. Masland, T. D. Albright, J. H. Kaas, & E. P. Gardner (Eds.), *The senses: A comprehensive reference* (pp. 89–95). New York: Academic Press.

Wu, B., He, Z. J., & Ooi, T. L. (2007). The linear perspective information in ground surface representation and distance judgment. *Perception & Psychophysics, 69*, 654–672.

Wu, B., Ooi, T. L., & He, Z. J. (2004). Perceiving distance accurately by a directional process of integrating ground information. *Nature, 428*, 73–77.

Wurtz, R. H. (2008). Neuronal mechanisms of visual stability. *Vision Research, 48*, 2070–2089.

Wyart, C., Webster, W. W., Chen, J. H., Wilson, S. R., McClary, A., Khan, R. M., et al. (2007). Smelling a single component of male sweat alters levels of cortisol in women. *Journal of Neuroscience, 27*, 1261–1265.

Wyatt, T. D. (2003). *Pheromones and animal behaviour: Communication by smell and taste.* New York: Cambridge.

Xu, X., Bonds, A. B., & Casagrande, V. A. (2002). Modeling receptive-field structure of koniocellular, magnocellular, and parvocellular LGN cells in the owl monkey (Aotus trivigatus). *Visual Neuroscience, 19*, 703–711.

Yaksh, T. L. (2008). A review of pain-processing pharmacology. In H. T. Benzon, J. P. Rathmell, C. L. Wu, D. C. Turk, & C. E. Argoff (Eds.), *Raj's practical management of pain* (pp. 135–149). Philadelphia: Mosby.

Yamamoto, C., Nagai, H., Takahashi, K., Nakagawa, S., Yamaguchi, M., Tonoike, M., et al. (2006). Cortical representation of taste-modifying action of miracle fruit in humans. *Neuroimage, 33*, 1145–1151.

Yamamoto, T., & Shimura, T. (2008). Roles of taste in feeding and reward. In A. I. Basbaum, M. C. Bushnell, D. V. Smith, G. K. Beauchamp, S. J. Firestein, P. Dallos, D. Oertel, R. H. Masland, T. D. Albright, J. H. Kaas, & E. P. Gardner (Eds.), *The senses: A comprehensive reference* (Vol. 4, pp. 437–458). New York: Academic Press.

Yost, W. A. (2007). *Fundamentals of hearing: An introduction* (5th ed.). New York: Academic Press.

Young, F. A. (1981). Primate myopia. *American Journal of Optometry & Physiological Optics, 58*, 560–566.

Yovel, G., & Kanwisher, N. (2005). The neural basis of the behavioral face-inversion effect. *Current Biology, 15*, 2256–2262.

Zajonc, R. B., Crandall, R., & Kail, R. V., Jr. (1974). Effect of extreme exposure frequencies on different affective ratings of stimuli. *Perceptual and Motor Skills, 38*, 667–678.

Zajonc, T. P., & Roland, P. S. (2005). Vertigo and motion sickness. Part I: Vestibular anatomy and physiology. *Ear, Nose, & Throat Journal, 84,* 581–584.

Zatorre, R. J. (2003). Absolute pitch: A model for understanding the influence of genes and development on neural and cognitive function. *Nature Neuroscience, 6,* 692–695.

Zatorre, R. J. (2005). Neuroscience: Finding the missing fundamental. *Nature, 436*(7054), 1093–1094.

Zatorre, R. J. (2007). There's more to auditory cortex than meets the ear. *Hearing Research, 229,* 24–30.

Zatorre, R. J., & Krumhansl, C. L. (2002). Neuroscience. Mental models and musical minds. *Science, 298*(5601), 2138–2139.

Zatorre, R. J., & McGill, J. (2005). Music, the food of neuroscience? *Nature, 434*(7031), 312–315.

Zeki, S. (1993). *A vision of the brain.* Oxford: Blackwell Scientific Publications.

Zeki, S. (2001). Localization and globalization in conscious vision. *Annual Review of Neuroscience, 24,* 57–86.

Zelano, C., Bensafi, M., Porter, J., Mainland, J., Johnson, B., Bremner, E., et al. (2005). Attentional modulation in human primary olfactory cortex. *Nature Neuroscience, 8,* 114–120.

Zelano, C., & Sobel, N. (2005). Humans as an animal model for systems-level organization of olfaction. *Neuron, 48,* 431–454.

Zellner, D. A. (1991). How foods get to be liked: Some general mechanisms and some special cases. In R. C. Bolles (Ed.), *The hedonics of taste* (pp. 199–217). Hillsdale, NJ: Erlbaum.

Zeng, F.-G. (2004). Auditory prostheses: Past, present, and future. In F.-G. Zeng, A. N. Popper & R. R. Fay (Eds.), *Cochlear implants: Auditory prostheses and electric hearing* (Vol. 20, pp. 1–13). New York: Springer.

Zhang, L. I., Bao, S., & Merzenich, M. M. (2001). Persistent and specific influences of early acoustic environments on primary auditory cortex. *Nature Neuroscience, 4,* 1123–1130.

Zhang, Y., Hoon, M. A., Chandrashekar, J., Mueller, K. L., Cook, B., Wu, D., et al. (2003). Coding of sweet, bitter, and umami tastes: Different receptor cells sharing similar signaling pathways. *Cell, 112,* 293–301.

Zhang, Y., Weiner, V. S., Slocum, W. M., & Schiller, P. H. (2007). Depth from shading and disparity in humans and monkeys. *Visual Neuroscience, 24,* 207–215.

Zihl, J., von Cramon, D. Y., & Mai, N. (1983). Selective disturbance of movement vision after bilateral brain damage. *Brain, 106,* 313–340.

Zihl, J., von Cramon, D. Y., Mai, N., & Schmid, C. (1991). Disturbance of movement vision after bilateral posterior brain damage. Further evidence and follow up observations. *Brain, 114,* 2235–2252.

Zimmer, U., Lewald, J., Erb, M., Grodd, W., & Karnath, H. O. (2004). Is there a role of visual cortex in spatial hearing? *The European Journal of Neuroscience, 20,* 3148–3156.

Ziomkiewicz, A. (2006). Menstrual synchrony: Fact or artifact? *Human Nature, 17,* 419–432.

Zone, R. (2007). *Stereoscopic cinema and the origins of 3-D film, 1838–1952.* Lexington: University Press of Kentucky.

Zufall, F., & Leinders-Zufall, T. (2007). Mammalian pheromone sensing. *Current Opinion in Neurobiology, 17,* 483–489.

Zur, D., & Ullman, S. (2003). Filling-in of retinal scotomas. *Vision Research, 43,* 971–982.

Name Index

Subject Index

COLOR PLATE 4
An Example of Colors Arranged in a Color Solid
Courtesy of Inmont Corporation.

COLOR PLATE 5
An Example of Pointillism by Georges Seurat
George Seurat, French, 1859–1891, *A Sunday on La Grande Jatte—1884*, 1884–1886, Oil on canvas, 81-3/4 × 121-1/4 inc.
(207.5 × 308.1 cm), Helen Birch Bartlett Memorial Collection, 1926.224. Reproduction, The Art Institute of Chicago. Detail
(right) from George Seurat, French, *A Sunday on La Grande Jatte—1884*, 1884–1886, Oil on canvas, 81-3/4 × 121-1/4 inc.
(207.5 × 308.1 cm), Helen Birch Bartlett Memorial Collection, 1926.224. Reproduction, The Art Institute of Chicago.